THE MIDDLE EAST

U.S. POLICY, ISRAEL, OIL AND THE ARABS

FOURTH EDITION

Timely Reports to Keep
Journalists, Scholars and the Public
Abreast of Developing Issues, Events and Trends

July 1979

CONGRESSIONAL QUARTERLY
1414 22ND STREET, N.W., WASHINGTON, D.C. 20037

Congressional Quarterly, Inc.

Congressional Quarterly Inc., an editorial research service and publishing company, serves clients in the fields of news, education, business and government. It combines specific coverage of Congress, government and politics by Congressional Quarterly with the more general subject range of an affiliated service, Editorial Research Reports.

Congressional Quarterly was founded in 1945 by Henrietta and Nelson Poynter. Its basic periodical publication was and still is the CQ *Weekly Report,* mailed to clients every Saturday. A cumulative index is published quarterly.

The CQ *Almanac,* a compendium of legislation for one session of Congress, is published every spring. *Congress and the Nation* is published every four years as a record of government for one presidential term.

Congressional Quarterly also publishes books on public affairs. These include the twice-yearly *Guide to Current American Government* and such recent titles as *Energy Policy* and *Politics in America.*

CQ Direct Research is a consulting service which performs contract research and maintains a reference library and query desk for the convenience of clients.

Editorial Research Reports covers subjects beyond the specialized scope of Congressional Quarterly. It publishes reference material on foreign affairs, business, education, cultural affairs, national security, science and other topics of news interest. Service to clients includes a 6,000-word report four times a month bound and indexed semi-annually. Editorial Research Reports publishes paperback books in its fields of coverage. Founded in 1923, the service merged with Congressional Quarterly in 1956.

Editor: Patricia Ann O'Connor.
Major Contributor: Margaret Thompson. **Contributors:** Howard Fields, Robert E. Healy, Sari Horwitz, Lynda McNeil, Mary M. Neumann, Sandra Spelliscy, Andrea J. Yank.
Index: Lynda McNeil.
Art Director: Richard Pottern. **Staff Artist:** Gwendolyn Hammond.
Production Manager: I.D. Fuller. **Assistant Production Manager:** Maceo Mayo.

Library of Congress Cataloging in Publication Data

Congressional Quarterly, inc.
The Middle East.

Bibliography: p.
Includes index.
1. Near East — Politics and government — 1945-
2. Jewish-Arab relations — 1973-   I. Title.

DS63.1.C63 1979   320.9′56′04   79-9112
ISBN 0-87187-176-9

Table of Contents

Summaries, Tables, Maps

Editor's Note

The Middle East: U.S. Policy, Israel, Oil and the Arabs (Fourth Edition) provides an up-to-date, in-depth analysis of the issues and disputes involving the countries of the Middle East. Emphasis is upon United States involvement in the entire region, historically and at present.

This fourth edition reflects the significant changes that have occurred in the Middle East during the years 1977-1979. Foremost among them was the U.S.-sponsored Egyptian-Israeli peace treaty, signed March 26, 1979. This book contains chapters detailing the negotiations leading up to the treaty and the Arab reaction to it, as well as the impact of the treaty on the Soviet role in the Middle East. Also included are updated chapters and background information contained in the previous three editions, published in 1974, 1975 and 1977.

The Middle East (Fourth Edition) is divided into three parts:

Part I provides analyses of the major issues affecting Middle East political and economic life: the evolution of U.S. Middle East policy; issues surrounding Middle East oil; the problems facing negotiations over the future of the West Bank and Gaza Strip and the Palestinian problem in general; chapters on the Arab and Israeli lobbies in Washington; and a background chapter on the Arab-Israeli wars during the past three decades.

Part II contains updated country-by-country profiles and a chapter on Arab history.

Part III is an appendix containing biographies of leading figures from Middle East history during the 20th century; a detailed chronology covering major Middle East events from 1945 through June 1979; texts of the Camp David accords and the Egyptian-Israeli treaty; and a selected bibliography.

Introduction

Between 1974, when the first edition of this book was published, and 1979, as the fourth edition went to press, the political, diplomatic, military and economic landscape of the Middle East had undergone a dramatic change — one that thrust the United States into the forefront of efforts to achieve peace in the region. From the years 1973-74 — which witnessed the October 1973 war between Israel and the Arabs; the first Arab-Israeli peace talks in Geneva; and an oil embargo imposed by the Arab members of the Organization of Petroleum Exporting Countries (OPEC) — to 1979 which saw the signing of a U.S.-sponsored Egyptian-Israeli peace treaty; the start of difficult negotiations over the future of Palestinians living on the Israeli-occupied West Bank and Gaza Strip; the growing isolation of Egypt from the rest of the Arab world; the overthrow of the shah of Iran and installation of a new regime under the Islamic religious leader, the Ayatollah Khomeini; and a steep hike in the price of oil exported by OPEC — the Middle East had increasingly become a lynchpin on which the economic fate and political stability of the rest of the world depended.

Yet, in addition to significant changes, there were some parallels in the situations existing in 1973-74 and 1978-79. In contrast to the 1967 Six Day War in which the Israelis achieved a lightning — and, for the Arabs, demoralizing — victory, the October 1973 war had challenged the widespread belief in Israel's invincibility and had led to an unprecedented display of Arab solidarity. At the same time, several Arab nations — particularly Egypt — began to turn away from heretofore close relations with the Soviet Union and toward developing more cordial relations with the non-communist West. The 1973-74 Arab oil embargo and the quadrupling of oil export prices vividly demonstrated the economic dependence of the rest of the world on the oil-producing nations of the region; while, at the same time, efforts at modernization using new-found wealth from petrodollars increased Arab reliance on imported goods and technical know-how from the West. Diplomatically, the period also was characterized by the increasing centrality of the United States as mediator in the search for a Middle East peace settlement. U.S. negotiation played a key role in ending the 1973 war and arranging the first Arab-Israeli peace conference in Geneva in December 1973. Throughout 1974 and 1975, Secretary of State Henry A. Kissinger shuttled back and forth from country to country to arrange Israeli-Egyptian and Syrian-Israeli military disengagement agreements in the Sinai which, it was hoped, would provide a stepping stone toward a more comprehensive Middle East peace.

The American role in the Middle East had become more pronounced by the late 1970s. When the Carter administration assumed office, it decided to abandon the Kissinger type of "shuttle diplomacy" that relied on a step-by-step negotiating process in favor of attempting to achieve a "comprehensive" settlement involving all nations in the region and addressing the fundamental and difficult issues of the future of the Palestinians and the security and inviolability of all borders. To carry out this objective, and in recognition of the fact that any lasting agreement would have to involve the Soviet Union, the United States issued a joint declaration with the Soviets in October 1977, calling for a reconvocation of the Geneva conference. The declaration was received unfavorably by both Arabs and Israelis, although their reasons were varied. At this juncture, Egyptian President Anwar al-Sadat made his now-famous journey to Jerusalem in November 1977.

Israeli-Egyptian Peace Treaty

Despite Sadat's initiative, efforts to negotiate a comprehensive settlement had reached an impasse by the fall of 1978. It was at this point that Carter took a major gamble, inviting Sadat and Israeli Prime Minister Menachem Begin to meet with him at the presidential retreat in Camp David, Md. After 13 days of arduous negotiations, the three agreed on two accords: "a framework for peace in the Middle East," and a "framework for the conclusion of a peace treaty between Egypt and Israel."

As had occurred after the 1973 war, however, Arab solidarity came to the forefront, this time in opposition to the accords. Meeting in Baghdad in November 1978, leaders of 20 Arab states and the Palestine Liberation Organization (PLO) issued a statement strongly condemning the Camp David accords and agreeing that, on the conclusion of a bilateral peace treaty, Egypt's membership in the Arab League would be suspended. Following the signing of the treaty in Washington in March 1979 — only after Carter had engaged in his own version of "shuttle diplomacy" to overcome snags that had developed following Camp David — the other Arab nations quickly broke off diplomatic relations with Egypt and reduced economic relations with and assistance to that country. Unlike 1973-74, when Sadat had emerged as a principal leader and spokesman for the

Carter on Peace Treaty

"During the past 30 years, Israel and Egypt have waged war. But for the past 16 months, these same two great nations have waged peace. Today we celebrate a victory — not of a bloody military campaign but of an inspiring peace campaign. . . .

"We have won at last the first step of peace, a first step on a long and difficult road. We must not minimize the obstacles which still lie ahead. Differences still separate the signatories to this treaty from one another, and also from some of their neighbors who fear what they have just done. To overcome these differences, to dispel these fears, we must rededicate ourselves to the goal of a broader peace with justice for all who have lived in a state of conflict in the Middle East.

"We have no illusions — we have hopes, dreams, and prayers, yes, but no illusions.

"There now remains the rest of the Arab world, whose support and whose cooperation in the peace process is needed and honestly sought. I am convinced that other Arab people need and want peace. But some of their leaders are not yet willing to honor these needs and desires for peace. We must now demonstrate the advantages of peace and expand its benefits to encompass all those who have suffered so much in the Middle East.

"Obviously, time and understanding will be necessary for people, hitherto enemies, to become neighbors in the best sense of the word.

"Just because a paper is signed, all the problems will not automatically go away. Future days will require the best from us to give reality to these lofty aspirations.

"Let those who would shatter peace, who would callously spill more blood, be aware that we three and all others who may join us will vigorously wage peace.

"So let history record that deep and ancient antagonism can be settled without bloodshed and without staggering waste of precious lives, without rapacious destruction of the land. . . ."

President Jimmy Carter
March 26, 1979

Arab world, Egypt by 1979 had become isolated from its Arab neighbors and was facing an uncertain economic and political future.

Although most observers in 1979 concluded that the peace treaty would make another Arab-Israeli war highly unlikely — without Egypt, the Arabs' military might was still no match for Israel's — the Arab reaction to the pact, and its limited nature (the only firm major agreements concerned Israeli return of the Sinai to Egypt and mutual diplomatic recognition) raised troubling questions as to whether the Camp David formula could in fact become the basis for a lasting peace. To some, it appeared that Carter had abandoned his search for a comprehensive settlement and his emphasis on an "evenhanded" approach in dealing with Arabs and Israelis (which was apparent in the administration's 1978 package sale of jet fighters to Saudi Arabia, Egypt and Israel) and had returned to the previous administration's "piecemeal" diplomacy.

Whether the United States could have secured a more stable and comprehensive agreement than the one achieved at Camp David was debatable. And whether the risks that Sadat faced in 1979 — isolation in the Arab world, a reduction in subsidies from the oil-rich Arab states and an economic peace dividend that did not meet Egyptian expectations — were worth the settlement he agreed to might not be apparent for some time. Perhaps the only certainty was that Washington would be increasingly involved, not only in keeping the peace process going but in providing considerably more economic and military assistance to Egypt and Israel. In the first increase in post-treaty U.S. economic aid, Congress in late June 1979 cleared the administration's fiscal 1979 $4.8 billion package of special aid to the two countries.

Obstacles to Comprehensive Settlement

In mid-1979, the major obstacle to a conclusion of a comprehensive settlement continued to be a resolution of the Palestinian question and agreement on the future of the West Bank, Gaza Strip and Golan Heights, in addition to the city of Jerusalem, holy to Jews, Christians and Moslems alike. Although Egypt and Israel opened negotiations on the future of the West Bank and Gaza in the spring of 1979, their positions were far apart. And, too, any lasting agreement would have to involve negotiations with Jordan's King Hussein as well as some representation by the PLO and possibly Syria. Hussein had been under considerable pressure from his Arab neighbors not to participate in the talks, Syria adamantly refused to join and Israel continued to oppose PLO representation.

Beyond the limitations of the U.S.-sponsored peace treaty, there were numerous other potentially destabilizing elements in the Middle East of 1979. The 1978-79 upheaval in Iran that deposed the autocratic but pro-Western and U.S.-supported shah, who was replaced by an anti-American, anti-Israeli Islamic government, raised apprehensions among some conservative Arab governments (particularly Saudi Arabia and the Persian Gulf states) and led them to question whether they could rely on effective U.S. support. Moreover, the March 1979 peace treaty led to an increase in the violence in Lebanon, which in 1975-76 had been torn by civil war among Christians, Moslems and Palestinians, with outside intervention by Syria and Israel. During 1979, guerrilla activities in the country notably stepped up.

The Egyptian-Israeli peace treaty not only did not resolve the Palestinian issue nor end the chaos in Lebanon; it — and the Iranian revolution — put considerable pressure on the moderate governments of Saudi Arabia and Jordan to join the Arab "hard-liners." Moreover, it placed severe strains on relations between the two nations and the United States. The United States has considered Saudi Arabia to be a particularly strategic ally economically, politically and militarily.

As in 1973-74, in 1978-79, the threat of the Arabs' use of the "oil weapon" hung over the rest of the world. Indeed, the global energy crisis and economic recession were caused in large part by the steadily growing demand for oil coupled with steep OPEC price hikes and some reduction in output. A big, and as yet unanswered question was what steps the Arab oil producers might take to increase pressure on Israel to meet Arab demands for a full peace settlement.

Another unanswered question was the role the Soviet Union would play in the search for stability in the Middle East.

Writing in the summer 1979 issue of *Foreign Affairs,* American University Professor Amos Perlmutter offered this cautiously optimistic assessment:

"The peace treaty ratified by Egypt and Israel on March 26, 1979 is neither an end to a problem nor a fresh point of departure in the efforts to resolve it. Rather, it represents a stage in a protracted series of negotiations. misunderstandings, cajoleries, and tacit agreements extending back for years. All these will continue — but the situation has changed, for Egypt and Israel now have a document with which they can map out their future haggling. . . . In spite of the many problems that still lie ahead, however, the successful achievement of this first accommodation between Egypt and Israel creates a momentum of negotiation that will be of considerable importance in the years to come.

"Besides that momentum, another important influence on the talks that lie ahead is the role of the United States. Without American intervention there would be no glimmer of peace in the Middle East, and without continued American guidance and pressure there will be no hope for a satisfactory agreement on elections in the West Bank, or for any lasting peace in the region. American pressure has been crucial ever since Henry Kissinger wrung from Egypt and Israel the Sinai troop disengagement agreement of 1975. Now the United States will have a vital role to play in attempting to bring the Palestinians to the bargaining table and in defusing the threat of the Baghdad front of Arab rejectionist states. . . .

"The stakes are high and the risks are evident. But the success of the process so far, and the creation of that momentum of negotiation which helps to establish a presumption of success, may yet prevail."

As of mid-1979, it appeared that the momentum was continuing, although the drama had faded somewhat. Meeting in Alexandria, Egypt, in July, Sadat and Begin agreed on several modest steps to improve their economic relations. The two governments were also continuing negotiations on the future of the West Bank and Gaza, but little progress had been made. It was expected that the pace of the talks might pick up in the fall under the mediation of Robert S. Strauss, former U.S. special trade representative, who had been named by the Carter administration as its special Middle East envoy.

THE MIDDLE EAST

ISSUES AND POLICIES

SEARCHING FOR A MIDEAST PEACE SETTLEMENT

The Carter administration entered office aware that a historic opportunity had presented itself for reversing the bitter course of Arab-Israeli relations through seeking a comprehensive political settlement. Quick to grasp the fundamentals of the Middle East stalemate, Carter by March 1977 had begun to outline a three-point Middle East settlement plan involving:

• Israeli withdrawal to approximately the 1967 borders;
• Creation of a "Palestinian homeland" probably in the West Bank and Gaza Strip areas;
• Establishment of permanent peace between Israel and her Arab neighbors.

By 1977 it was widely recognized, in fact, that the United States had become, in the wake of the Yom Kippur War and through the initiatives of Secretary of State Henry A. Kissinger, the key outside participant in the conflict. Indeed, it was often said that the Arab-Israeli war had been partially transformed into a political war for support in Washington. But the Soviet Union remained actively involved, and it was feared the Soviets could pick up the pieces if U.S. efforts collapsed and America found itself in the middle of another Arab-Israeli war.

"The search for a just and lasting peace in the Middle East is one of the highest priority items on the foreign policy agenda of our country," said Cyrus R. Vance soon after becoming secretary of state. Said Carter: "To let this opportunity [for a settlement] pass could mean disaster not only for the Middle East, but perhaps for the international political and economic order as well."

Carter was the first American president to discuss the concept of a "Palestinian homeland." It first came as a shock, for just two years earlier when asked if he had plans for dealing with the Palestinian problem, Kissinger had responded to a questioning journalist, "Do you want to start a revolution in the United States?" But within a short time there was general recognition that some form of Palestinian self-determination must be granted if there was to be a chance of achieving any comprehensive settlement.

However, Carter refused to specify what he had in mind even after completing, by May 1977, a first round of personal meetings with all the important leaders of Middle East countries. And Menachem Begin's victory in Israel confused the picture even further. Not only had Begin's Likud party refused to contemplate the idea of a Palestinian homeland, but it was elected on a platform of never returning the West Bank and Gaza Strip areas to Arab sovereignty.

Prime Minister Begin came to the United States on July 19, 1977, for two days of talks with Carter and members of his unofficial Middle East team which included Zbigniew Brzezinski and William Quandt of the National Security Council, Secretary of State Vance, Intelligence and Research Director Harold Saunders and Assistant Secretary for Near Eastern Affairs Alfred Atherton at the State Department.

Although the atmosphere was cordial, it was clear during Begin's visit that the new American administration and the new Israeli government were far apart on many important issues.

By mid-1977 Carter appeared to be very much aware of the criticism of his policies and of the possibility of a major battle with Congress and Israel's supporters should he continue to pursue them. Ford and Kissinger had faced a similar situation in the spring of 1975, but the Middle East pressures on the American government to find some way to defuse the time-bomb in the Middle East were much greater two years later.

Though President Carter and Secretary of State Vance had repeatedly stressed that the United States would not and could not impose a settlement on both the Arabs and the Israelis, the possibility continued to be discussed in 1977. Former Under Secretary of State George Ball wrote in the April 1977 issue of the Council on Foreign Relation's journal, *Foreign Affairs,* that what Carter did about the Middle East would be the "acid test of political courage and decisiveness. If America should permit Israel to continue to reject inflexibly any suggestion of a return to earlier boundaries and the creation of a Palestinian state, and to refuse even to negotiate about Jerusalem, we should be acquiescing in a policy hazardous not only to Israel but for America and the rest of the world. That would not be responsible conduct for a great power."[1]

Having discarded the Kissinger approach of step-by-step shuttle diplomacy in favor of a comprehensive settlement, the Carter administration first focused on a reconvening of the Geneva Conference. (That conference was first convened in December 1973 but recessed after only two days of ceremonial and propagandistic exchanges.) This resulted in a U.S.-Soviet Joint Statement on the Middle East, issued on Oct. 1, 1977, calling for a Geneva Conference "not later than December 1977" to work out a full resolution of the Arab-Israeli conflict "incorporating all parties concerned and all questions." *(Text, p. 55)*

The Israeli and Egyptian reaction to the prospect of bringing the Soviet Union into the forefront of the peace negotiations was negative. In addition, the radical Arab governments in Algeria, Iraq and Libya opposed any direct negotiations with Israel. For its part, the reaction of Israel and the American Jewish lobby to the Soviet-American statement was swift and visceral. Fearing that it would allow the Palestine Liberation Organization (PLO) to participate in the conference, Israeli officials and their American supporters put sufficient pressure on the Carter administration to scuttle the guidelines for Geneva.

The Egyptian reaction to the guidelines was also negative. Since 1972, when President Anwar Sadat expelled 20,000 Russian military advisers from Egypt, Soviet-Egyptian relations had turned increasingly sour. A Geneva Conference, with the Soviet Union as co-chairman, was no more appealing to Sadat than it was to the Israelis, and the unpleasant prospect that the conference might be recon-

---

[1] George W. Ball, "How To Save Israel in Spite of Herself," *Foreign Affairs,* April 1977, p. 471.

vened has been pointed to as an underlying impetus behind Sadat's decision to visit Jerusalem and ask for peace.

Sadat's Jerusalem Visit

The reasons most frequently cited for Sadat's dramatic visit to Jerusalem on Nov. 19, 1977, were the Egyptian president's conviction that in another war the Arabs would suffer a 1967-type defeat; his anger and frustration about involving the Soviet Union in a settlement, as outlined in the joint American-Soviet statement of Oct. 1; his fears of radical upheaval in Egypt; and, finally, his belief that a face-to-face encounter between Arabs and Israelis would do much to remove the psychological barriers that separated them. *Time* magazine in mid-1978 revealed yet another factor.

Time reported in its Aug. 14 issue that "Israel has always maintained secret contacts with its Arab enemies, largely through Mossad," the Israeli intelligence service. Early in 1977, Mossad learned that "leftist Arab extremists, trained in Libya," were plotting to overthrow the moderate governments in Egypt, Saudi Arabia and the Sudan. In July, the magazine account continued, Prime Minister Begin decided to warn Egyptian, Saudi and Sudanese leaders of the danger and dispatched Foreign Minister Moshe Dayan "on a round of visits to Middle Eastern capitals." According to *Time,* "Dayan met at least twice with Jordan's King Hussein and Egyptian officials and three times with King Hassan II of Morocco." The center of "this diplomatic activity was Morocco, which has had close but secret relations with Israel since 1962."

> Dayan [*Time* continued] assured his Arab hosts that the Begin government was prepared to make more 'generous compromises than previous Israeli governments'.... Coming as they did on the heels of Israel's much-appreciated tip to Egypt, Dayan's proposals may well have persuaded Sadat that a dramatic trip to Jerusalem could bring a quick end to the 30-year Mideast impasse.[2]

Knesset Address

Addressing the Israeli parliament Nov. 20, 1977, Sadat laid down five "principles" that he said must govern any peace settlement:

● "Ending the Israeli occupation of the Arab territories occupied in 1967;

● "Achievement of the fundamental rights of the Palestinian people and their right to self-determination, including their right to establish their own state;

● "The right of all states in the area to live in peace, within their boundaries, their secure boundaries, which will be secured and guaranteed through procedures to be agreed upon....

● "Commitment of all states in the area to administer the relations among them in accordance with the objectives and principles of the UN Charter, particularly the principles concerning the nonresort to force and the solutions to differences among them by peaceful means;

● "Ending the state of belligerence in the region."

Hard-line Arab reaction to the Jerusalem visit, despite Sadat's demand in the Israeli Knesset for full Israeli withdrawal from all occupied territories and his refusal to consider a separate peace, was loud and negative. Moderate Arabs tried to straddle the fence without alienating either

2 "Israel's Secret Contacts," *Time,* Aug. 14, 1978, pp. 21-22.

Sadat or the hard-liners. Washington seemed initially surprised and confused and only later gave its full support to the peace effort, in effect abandoning the comprehensive approach and supporting direct Egyptian-Israeli discussions that led to the non-comprehensive and separate Egypt-Israel agreement.

Stalemate in Negotiations

Sadat's Jerusalem visit was followed by meetings between Israeli and Egyptian officials in Cairo. Sadat had invited the United States, Soviet Union and other Arab nations to attend, but only the United States accepted. Prior to the conference, Secretary of State Vance journeyed to Israel, where he conferred with Prime Minister Begin Dec. 10-11. Subsequently, Begin visited Washington, where he met with President Carter on Dec. 16 to present his plan for relinquishing control of the Sinai in return for normal relations and limited self-rule to Palestinians on the West Bank and Gaza Strip. While neither endorsing nor rejecting the Israeli 26-point program, Carter termed the proposal "constructive."

Begin and Sadat met on Dec. 25 in Ismailia, Egypt, where the Israeli prime minister presented his West Bank proposal pinned to local "autonomy" for the Palestinians there during a five-year period. Israeli troops and settlements would remain; the plan contained nothing on the issue of eventual sovereignty for the territory, a critical point for Sadat.

These talks ended in disagreement, and lower-level discussions over the next few months failed to produce any progress. Indeed, although the two governments agreed to form a political committee to continue discussions concerning the future of the West Bank and a military committee to negotiate on Sinai, Sadat Jan. 18, 1978, recalled Egyptian delegates to the political committee, stating that there was "absolutely no hope" of reaching an agreement.

U.S. Peace Efforts

Meeting with Carter at Camp David in early February, Sadat commented that the United States was no longer a "go between" but a "full partner in the establishment of peace." He also denounced Israel's policy of going ahead with new settlements in the occupied territories — a move that the United States also condemned as an "obstacle to peace." U.S.-Israeli relations became even cooler with the announcement of the Carter adminstration's plan to sell sophisticated jet fighters to Egypt and Saudi Arabia, as well as to Israel (significantly, the number of planes proposed for Israel fell considerably short of the request.) *(Middle East plane sales, p. 47)*

A low point in U.S.-Israeli relations was reached in March 1978, when Begin met with Carter in Washington. The two leaders differed sharply over territorial issues. Although the U.S. administration repeated assurances of support for Israel, the latter's settlements policy was sharply criticized.

As negotiations became increasingly frozen, the United States undertook a series of emergency attempts to rescue the situation, among them sponsoring a foreign ministers' conference at Leeds Castle outside London on July 18. Although the meeting — between Secretary of State Vance, Israeli Foreign Minister Dayan and Egyptian Foreign Minister Mohammed Ibrahim Kamel — produced no concrete results (previous proposals of both sides were simply restated), Vance noted some flexibility in the discussions.

But in August the atmosphere deteriorated, with Egypt and Israel renewing strong criticism of one another. At this point, President Carter became concerned that the impasse could jeopardize the fragile relations between the two nations and wreck any chance for peace in the Middle East. He then invited the two leaders to Camp David for informal face-to-face talks aimed at breaking the stalemate. No advance agenda was planned. Vance had personally delivered the handwritten letter from Carter to Begin and Sadat in August. Both accepted the invitation unconditionally and immediately.

Camp David Summit Conference

Carter's decision to call the Camp David summit was widely seen as a brash gamble that paid off beyond all expectations. The announcement of the summit came in August, just as the president's popularity was at its lowest point and there was increasing speculation that Carter would be a one-term president.

In 13 days of arduous negotiations, initiated in an atmosphere of gloom and mutual criticism, Carter, with the aid of Vice President Walter F. Mondale, convinced Sadat and Begin to accept two agreements that broke new ground. Both Sadat and Begin later said Carter's firmness was the key to the breakthrough.

The accords reached at Camp David, the presidential retreat in western Maryland, essentially represented agreements to agree, rather than an actual settlement of the difficult issues dividing the two nations, or the even broader disputes between Israel and all Arab nations.

"This is one of those rare, bright moments of history," Carter declared as the historic accords drafted at Camp David were signed Sept. 17 by Prime Minister Begin and President Sadat. *(Texts, p. 220)*

But by the end of 1978, that success was threatened by a renewal of the discord that had made the Middle East a volatile region for thousands of years. As negotiations continued and the euphoria of Camp David dissipated, both Israeli and Egyptian leaders found that agreeing to the specifics of a treaty under political pressures at home was more difficult than agreeing to a "framework" in the seclusion of the presidential retreat in the Maryland mountains.

President Carter repeatedly expressed puzzlement that Israel and Egypt would quibble over what he saw as minor issues. But to both sides, none of the issues were minor. Israeli and Egyptian leaders were being asked to resolve longstanding hostilities and to give up positions they considered essential to their national interests.

The negotiations were especially difficult for Israel. In return for a peace treaty, Israel was asked to give up territory that for more than 11 years had served as a buffer against neighboring enemies. Egypt was pressured by other Arab nations not to sign a separate peace treaty with Israel.

Two Agreements

There were two agreements at Camp David, one dealing with the Sinai Peninsula and a future peace treaty

Egypt's President Sadat, President Carter and Israeli Prime Minister Begin Sign One of Camp David Documents

Chronology of Camp David Summit

Following is a chronology of events which took place during the 13 days of peace negotiations Sept. 5-17, 1978, at the Camp David, Md., presidential retreat:

Sept. 5-6. After Begin and Sadat arrived at Camp David — Carter had made the trip the day before — exploratory meetings were held. The president met with Begin alone on Sept. 5, with Sadat the following morning.

Those initial meetings, an administration official said, gave Carter a chance "to set forth at length his views on the unique opportunity the three leaders had to advance the cause of peace, the consequences that we foresaw if there should be no progress, and the key issues, as we understood them and reviewed them."

The meetings also gave the president the opportunity to discuss in a preliminary way the objectives of the talks and how they might be structured.

Camp David, the official commented, lent itself ideally to the discussions: It was a chance for easy informality — meetings at different levels, during meals and in cabins with different members of the other delegations.

During the afternoon of Sept. 6, Carter, Sadat and Begin met for the first time at Aspen Lodge. Sadat introduced a new proposal for a comprehensive peace settlement, but the plan, which called for Palestinian sovereignty in the West Bank and the Gaza was tabled at this meeting.

Sept. 7-8. Bilateral talks between the United States and Egypt and the United States and Israel — conducted at various levels — were held "to clarify the proposals that had been put forward" by each delegation. The three leaders were to meet on Sept. 7 for the last time as a group until the summit ended, because, according to one report, it had become clear to Carter that for progress to be made, the two leaders would have to be separated.

Sept. 9-10. By Saturday, Sept. 9, the parties had a clear picture of the major features of the Egyptian and Israeli proposals. "By this time, it became clear that both sides would welcome an effort by the United States to break the deadlock," said a senior administration official.

The Israelis, according to another report, became intransigent over the issue of removing their settlements from the Sinai.

The United States delegation, after receiving directions from Carter, worked during the weekend to produce a draft negotiating text, drawing on the proposals offered by Egypt and Israel but also introducing new language where the positions were far apart, recalled a U.S. official.

It was at this time that separate work began on the Sinai framework separating the differences between Egypt and Israel on Sinai from those involved in the West Bank. The draft texts were discussed separately with the Egyptians and the Israelis by Carter, Mondale, Vance and Zbigniew Brzezinski, Carter's national security adviser.

Sept. 11. On Monday morning, the Israelis gave their reactions to the U.S. text and offered suggestions; the Egyptians went through the same process later in the day.

Revised drafts based on the reactions from each side then were prepared. This shuttle process continued through Sept. 12.

Sept. 13. By Wednesday of the second week, it had become clear to the United States negotiators that there were too many participants in the talks and "that it was necessary to try to reduce the size of the meetings and get down to a small negotiating drafting group," according to a participant.

Carter then asked Sadat and Begin to delegate one person each to meet with him and to meet for trilateral drafting sessions "in an effort to narrow the differences, identify agreed language and draft alternatives for items in disagreement."

On key issues — Sinai settlements, Jerusalem, West Bank settlements and Palestinian rights — the sides remained far apart. "We had to reach a judgment as to what formulations we felt to be fair and reasonable and would protect the vital interests of both sides," said a senior official.

Over an eight-hour period, Sept. 13, Israeli and Egyptian officials met with Carter, adjourned for supper and returned for another two-hour session. Bilateral meetings were conducted later and the decisions sent to the drafting team, which worked into the early morning hours.

This process continued on Thursday, Sept. 14, with Carter, Mondale and others reviewing the latest drafts in the morning before planning the next round of talks.

Sept. 15. Without explaining why, Sadat told reporters after the summit ended that he had threatened to walk out of talks on Friday, but was persuaded to remain by Carter.

Also on this day, Mondale persuaded the two parties to set Sunday as the deadline for ending the negotiations and discussed with the two leaders, according to one report, how they all would look to the world if the summit ended in failure.

Sept. 16. Three issues remained — Jerusalem, Sinai settlements and language relating to the West Bank transition period — at the day's outset. During a meeting Saturday night, Begin agreed to take the future of Sinai settlements up with the Knesset and seemed ready to reach agreement on the West Bank Palestinian issue. The decision to exchange letters on Jerusalem came earlier.

Sept. 17. The controversy over Jerusalem surfaced again, but was resolved when the United States agreed to drop the word "occupied" from its draft letter. The final item — the question of Palestinian rights on the West Bank — was resolved about 4:30 or 5 p.m. "I am really not quite sure when it was," said a senior official. "We had all gotten so groggy by that time that we lost track of the time."

between Israel and Egypt; and the other a "framework" for settling the future of the West Bank of the Jordan River and the Gaza Strip.

The Sinai agreement contained these major elements:

● Israel would return all the Sinai to Egypt, including three airbases, oil fields and 13 settlements established since the Israeli occupation in 1967. Abandonment of the settlements was left up to the Israeli Knesset, which agreed Sept. 28.

● Israel and Egypt would conclude a peace treaty by Dec. 17. Israel would begin its military withdrawal from Sinai within three to nine months, with final withdrawal to occur within three years. When withdrawal from the Sinai began, Egypt and Israel would "normalize" diplomatic relations. The Dec. 17 deadline was not met.

The West Bank-Gaza Strip framework included these elements:

● Negotiations between Egypt, Jordan, Israel and Palestinian representatives would be held over a five-year period to determine the future of the West Bank and the Gaza Strip. The Palestinians would have a veto over the final arrangement for those areas. Israel was given a veto over Palestinian representatives if they came from outside the West Bank or Gaza. During the negotiating period, residents of the areas would govern themselves. Most Palestinian leaders in those areas denounced the Camp David accords and said they wouldn't participate in negotiations.

● Israel would maintain troops in the two regions, but the numbers would be sharply reduced and they would be stationed in outposts away from cities.

● The Israeli military government would be withdrawn as soon as an Arab self-governing unit was established to administer the areas and to begin the five-year talks.

Many Issues Untouched

Because they were agreements, not formal treaties, the Camp David accords left untouched several sensitive issues, such as the future of East Jerusalem (occupied by Israel but claimed by Jordan), the eventual date for pullout of Israeli troops from occupied territory, the eventual legal status of the occupied territory, and the fate of Palestinian refugees scattered throughout the Middle East.

Shortly after the Camp David accords were signed, Secretary of State Cyrus Vance optimistically predicted that a treaty could be signed by Nov. 19. That date was the anniversary of Sadat's historic visit to Jerusalem, when he and Begin pledged that there would be "no more war" between Egypt and Israel.

But it soon became obvious that negotiating the treaty would be a time-consuming process. Predictions of a treaty-signing were pushed back to Dec. 10, the date Sadat and Begin were to receive the Nobel Peace Prize, and then to Dec. 17, the date specified in the Camp David agreement. As the end of the year came, officials stopped predicting when the treaty would be agreed on.

In mid-November Carter expressed frustration that the negotiations had taken so long, and complained that both Israel and Egypt were spending too much time picking over "little, tiny technicalities."

Disagreements

Even before negotiations got underway, disagreements broke out over what had actually been said and agreed on

at Camp David; within weeks Egypt and Israel were conducting negotiations through the news media.

While Begin was still in the United States after Camp David, he and Carter were disputing the terms of an agreement on Israeli settlements on the West Bank and Gaza. Begin said Israel could establish new settlements after a three-month moratorium, but Carter said Begin had agreed at Camp David not to establish any new settlements during the five-year negotiating period.

Twice, on Oct. 25 and Nov. 21, the Israeli cabinet approved draft treaties, each time adding reservations that made the drafts unacceptable to Egypt. President Carter had to personally intervene in the talks at two early points to prevent major breakdowns.

Sadat had more freedom than Begin in accepting or rejecting proposals on behalf of his own country, but the Egyptian president was pressured by other Arab nations not to make a separate peace with Israel.

While they were being pressured by the United States to reach agreement, both Sadat and Begin were under intense pressure at home not to make concessions.

Other Arab nations, including such moderates as Jordan and Saudi Arabia, warned Sadat not to relinquish the rights of Palestinians in the rush toward a peace treaty. And Begin, who led a minority party in a coalition government, was sharply criticized at home for his apparent willingness to abandon Israeli claims to territories occupied in the 1967 war.

On Dec. 10 Secretary Vance started his first effort at shuttle diplomacy in the Middle East to break the deadlock. He got Sadat to agree to a plan to deal with the remaining major problems in side letters to the treaty, rather than in the text of the treaty itself. But when Vance presented that plan in Jerusalem Dec. 13, Begin objected strongly, saying he could not make substantial changes beyond the draft treaty his cabinet had already accepted. Vance returned to Washington with no agreement Dec. 16. American officials publicly rebuked Israel for refusing to accept the latest draft; Israeli officials responded by accusing the United States of taking Egypt's side.

Vance met with the Egyptian and Israeli foreign ministers in Brussels Dec. 24 in an unsuccessful attempt to set up new negotiations.

West Bank and Gaza Strip

Throughout the negotiations, the so-called "Palestinian question" was the key stumbling block.

Egypt wanted Israel to completely abandon all territories occupied in the 1967 war, including the West Bank of the Jordan River and the Gaza Strip and the Sinai peninsula.

Begin agreed at Camp David to returning the Sinai to Egypt, and agreed to self-rule by residents of the West Bank and Gaza Strip during negotiations on the future of those regions. Palestinians vastly outnumber Israeli settlers in both areas.

Linkage

As negotiations proceeded, the main question became whether, and to what extent, the peace treaty between Egypt and Israel would be linked to the West Bank and Gaza issues. The United States and Egypt insisted that the treaty be linked to the resolution of the occupied territories issue. Israel wanted the treaty, but did not want provisions dealing with the occupied territories.

Sadat continually raised the stakes, first insisting only that the treaty be linked to the future of the occupied territories, then eventually demanding a specific timetable for Palestinian self-rule in those territories. Sadat made those demands largely to soften criticism from fellow Arab leaders, who had accused him of deserting the Palestinians.

At a summit meeting in Baghdad Nov. 2-5, the hard-line Arabs charged Sadat with treason, then offered Egypt $5 billion if Sadat would cut off negotiations with Israel. Sadat refused the offer, making it clear he expected assistance from the United States instead. American officials were distressed that Saudi Arabia and Jordan, two moderate Arab nations, joined in the hard-line attacks on Egypt.

The Israeli Cabinet on Nov. 21 finally accepted a vaguely-worded link between the peace treaty and the West Bank-Gaza issues, but flatly rejected any timetable for elections.

Begin contributed to the feud early in the negotiations by announcing plans to expand Israeli settlements on the West Bank. Those plans were bitterly protested by Carter and Sadat, then put on the back burner where they simmered throughout the negotiations.

That issue broke out in the open again Dec. 6 when Israeli sources said the government planned seven new settlements on the West Bank. The government denied that report, and Carter repeated his assertion that the establishment of new settlements would violate the Camp David accords.

As the disagreement over a West Bank-Gaza timetable continued, the United States early in December offered a compromise that would have put the issues in a "side letter" rather than in the treaty itself. Under that compromise, the two sides would have agreed to begin negotiations on the West Bank and Gaza within a month of ratification of the peace treaty. A target date of Dec. 31, 1979, would have been set for elections in those areas.

In the background, the Palestinian Liberation Organization (PLO) rejected all the timetables and self-rule proposals. PLO leader Yasir Arafat said his group was the only true representative of the one million-plus Palestinians on the West Bank and Gaza, and rejected Sadat's claim that he was negotiating on behalf of the Palestinians and other Arab states.

Just as important as the PLO objection was the refusal of Jordan's King Hussein to participate in the negotiations. The West Bank was administered by Jordan prior to the 1967 war, and the Camp David accords were based on the assumption that Hussein's involvement in the negotiation was crucial.

Egypt's Commitments

A second sticking point developed over Sadat's refusal to accept a section of the U.S.-sponsored draft treaty that pledged Egypt to give the peace treaty precedence over its agreements with other Arab states.

Israel insisted on that section, but Sadat demanded that it be eliminated or watered-down so that his country would not be giving preference to Israel, an enemy, over its fellow Arab countries.

Trade-Off

Vance and Sadat agreed Dec. 13 to a new proposal to settle the issues by forcing each side to make a concession in explanatory letters attached to the treaty.

That compromise would have required Israel to agree to a target date for elections on the West Bank and Gaza Strip. Egypt would have accepted the Article Six provision for precedence of the peace treaty, while setting out its position on the issue in a side letter.

But Begin, backed by the Israeli parliament, rejected that proposal as being too favorable to Egypt. At the end of the year Begin said he would be willing to reopen negotiations on the side letters.

American Aid

Implicit in the negotiations was the assumption that the United States would provide substantial aid to both Egypt and Israel once a peace treaty was signed. Although peace in the Middle East generally was seen as being in the long run interest of all parties concerned, the short-term cost would be heavy for both Israel and Egypt.

Beyond short-term aid to help the two countries recover the immediate costs of peace, the Middle East peace initiative clearly would deepen American military and economic commitments for years to come.

Israeli officials estimated that moving its military forces from the Sinai Peninsula to the Negev desert region in southern Israel would cost approximately $3 billion over three years, a huge sum for that nation. To help pay for that move, and for other costs of peace, the Israelis asked the United States for an additional $3.3 billion over three years. At Camp David, Carter committed the United States to building two replacement military bases for Israel in the Negev.

For his part, Sadat quietly spread the word that he expected the United States to pay a major share of the cost of economic development in Egypt, possibly as much as $10 billion to $15 billion over five years. The United States had been providing Egypt $1 billion a year.

In December, President Carter said any special aid for Egypt and Israel would have to be legislated separately from the annual foreign aid bill. *(Middle East aid request, p. 52)*

Major Points

The frameworks negotiated at Camp David centered on four categories of issues: "the nature of peace," security factors, territorial decisions and the Palestinian role.

Both documents carried commitments for the Arab recognition of Israel as well as the establishment of normal relations between Israel and the Arab nations to advance peace in the Middle East.

The Sinai accord between Israel and Egypt outlined security provisions for the Sinai, including the size and location of Egyptian forces, the introduction of United Nations troops and new early-warning stations. In the Gaza-West Bank accord, Israel's military presence was defined for the interim period and reduced from the existing 11,000 level.

The Sinai accord required Israel to return Sinai territory to Egypt and to withdraw from the airfields on the peninsula, while the West Bank framework called for negotiation of the "final status" of the territories of Gaza and the West Bank and their relationship to neighboring countries.

The fourth issue, that of the Palestinians, was treated in two ways: elected representatives from the West Bank and Gaza would participate in negotiations on the final status of the areas and related talks for a peace treaty between Jordan and Israel. And any final agreement on the two areas would be submitted to representatives of the residents of the areas for their approval.

West Bank Framework

To conclude a Middle East peace treaty, the Camp David negotiators recommended that negotiations over the future of the West Bank and the Gaza follow these steps:

● The governments of Egypt and Israel ("Jordan will be invited") would plan a five-year, transitional "self-governing authority" for the two areas. These negotiations over its powers and responsibilities were expected to take three months. The Arab delegations could include any Palestinians "as mutually agreed" by all the parties.

● As soon as the self-governing authority, called the administrative council, had been "freely elected" by the inhabitants of the West Bank and the Gaza "to provide full autonomy to the inhabitants" of these areas, the present Israeli military government and its civilian administration would be withdrawn.

● Withdrawal of Israeli armed forces to an estimated 6,000 level would then take place and these troops would be stationed in areas away from cities on the West Bank.

● The agreement also would make provision for assuring internal and external security of the areas; a "strong local police force" would be established, and Israeli and Jordanian forces would jointly man control posts at border points.

● Not later than the third year after the transition government took control, negotiations would be held to determine "the final status" of the West Bank and Gaza and its relationship with its neighbors, and to conclude a peace treaty between Israel and Jordan by the end of the transitional period. Two separate but related committees would be convened to handle these talks.

"The general theory for this," said a senior administration official, "is that the negotiation of the final status of Gaza and the West Bank is intertwined with issues which will come up in the negotiation of a final peace treaty. Therefore, they can't be treated in two separate and independent tracts. They have to be treated together."

● The negotiations would be based on all the provisions and principles in United Nations Security Council Resolution 242, which contained the basic formula that Israel would relinquish occupied territories in return for Arab recognition, peace and security.

● The negotiations would resolve, among other matters, the location of boundaries and the nature of the security arrangements and recognize the "legitimate rights of the Palestinian people."

Egypt-Israeli Peace Plan

Compared to the long list of issues purposely ignored or vaguely addressed in the framework relating to the West Bank and Gaza, only one problem divided Israel and Egypt under the accord returning the Sinai to Egypt and establishing "normal relations" between the two countries.

But it was a major one. The question of whether all the Jewish settlements in the Sinai should be dismantled as Sadat insisted nearly wrecked the Camp David talks in the final days, when Begin refused to concede the matter.

The summit impasse was broken when Begin eventually consented to turn the controversy over to the Israeli Knesset for its decision. The Knesset agreed to the dismantling Sept. 28.

"Egypt states that the agreement to remove Israeli settlements from Egyptian territory is a prerequisite to a peace treaty," said a high administration official. "Israel states that the issues of Israeli settlements should be resolved during the peace negotiations."

On other issues that would be incorporated in a peace treaty, Israel and Egypt agreed to these points:

● Israel would return all the Sinai to Egypt, including the three air bases it operated on the territory as well as oil fields, and, if the Knesset agreed, the territory occupied by the 13 settlements. If this controversy were not resolved to Sadat's satisfaction, the framework for the peace treaty would be in serious jeopardy.

● All Israeli forces would be withdrawn from the Sinai.

● The airfields abandoned by the Israelis would be used only for civilian purposes in the future, possibly for commercial international flights by all nations.

● The Israeli withdrawal would be accomplished in two steps, with the first major part taking place within three to nine months after the peace treaty was signed. In that period, Israeli forces would withdraw east of a line extending from El Arish on the Mediterranean coast to Ras Muhammed at the tip of the Sinai Peninsula.

● After the interim withdrawal was completed, normal relations would be established between the two countries including full recognition — diplomatic, economic and cultural — termination of economic boycotts and other barriers blocking the movement of people and goods, and protection of citizens of each nation by due process of law.

● The final withdrawal and implementation of the treaty between Israel and Egypt would take place between two and three years from the date of signing of the peace treaty.

● United Nations forces would be stationed in the Sinai west of the Israeli border and Egyptian forces would be limited along the Gulf of Suez and the Suez Canal.

● Israeli ships would be allowed to pass through the canal.

From Impasse to Treaty

Following preliminary discussions between Vance, Israeli Foreign Minister Dayan and Egyptian Premier Mustafa Khalil, in February 1979, Carter suggested that Begin and Sadat meet with him in a second round of summit talks at Camp David. The two leaders declined. Faced with the possible collapse of the talks, Carter then invited Begin to meet with him alone in Washington. Begin accepted, and the talks opened March 1.

Before leaving for the United States, Begin said that Israel and Egypt remained far apart and accused the Carter administration of supporting Egyptian proposals that were "totally unacceptable to us." Among the points at issue were Egypt's insistence on Israeli agreement to establish Palestinian autonomy within a year in the West Bank and Gaza Strip; Egyptian demands for deletion of a clause in the Camp David accords giving an Israeli-Egyptian peace treaty priority over Egyptian treaties with other nations; and Egyptian insistence that the question of supplying Israel with oil be discussed only after other treaty issues had been resolved. On Feb. 17, Sadat had said that Egypt would make no further concessions in the peace treaty negotiations and that it was "now up to the Israelis."

On March 5, Carter announced that he would press his personal mediation efforts by visiting Cairo and Jerusalem. A White House statement on the trip said: "There is

Impact of the Egyptian-Israeli Peace Treaty . . .

The Camp David agreements and subsequent peace treaty would alter several components of the Middle East military balance between Israel and its Arab neighbors.

West Bank

Some Israeli troops would be withdrawn from the occupied portion of Jordan on the West Bank of the Jordan River. Those remaining would be withdrawn into "specified security locations" during a five-year period for transition to West Bank autonomy. (Israeli Prime Minister Begin insisted after the Camp David agreements were signed that there was no commitment to withdraw all Israeli forces from the West Bank at the end of the five-year period.)

A high administration official told reporters the Israeli garrisons would be located away from the cities on the West Bank. Israel claimed that it had 10,000 to 11,000 troops in the region, according to this official, and although agreement had not been reached at Camp David on the number that would remain, a figure of 6,000 had been discussed.

A strong local police force — which may include Jordanian citizens — would be established, and Israeli and Jordanian forces would participate in joint patrols of the area and in the manning of border control posts.

This aspect of the agreement appears to greatly complicate the Israeli defense problem: A buffer zone more than 30 miles deep (the West Bank) is given up, the border that has to be protected is quadrupled in length and the portion of Israel between the West Bank and the Mediterranean Sea is less than 15 miles wide for much of its length.

Mitigating this ominous appearance are the continued presence of the Israeli garrisons and the Israeli-manned border posts and the feeble state of the Jordanian armed forces. The Jordanian army numbers about 61,000, with 520 tanks and 60 modern attack planes.

Sinai Peninsula

Within three years after Egypt and Israel signed the peace treaty — which occurred six months after the Camp David agreements were negotiated — all Israeli forces will have withdrawn from the Sinai. As a first step, they would be withdrawn east of El Arish within nine months from the signing of the treaty. This represents a withdrawal of more than 50 miles.

Troop Limits. Within a 30-mile-wide strip of the east bank of the Suez Canal and the Gulf of Suez, Egypt may station up to one infantry or mechanized division. Cur-

rently, Egypt is allowed to station only about half that many men (8,000) on the east bank of the canal within a strip 12 miles wide.

In the central part of the Sinai — an area averaging 60 miles in width — only Egyptian civil police and not more than three battalions of border patrol units will be allowed.

In a strip of the Sinai along the Israeli border and the Gulf of Aqaba, which will vary in width from 12 to 24 miles, only civil police units and United Nations forces will be allowed.

On the Israeli side of the border along a strip of 1.8 miles wide only U.N. forces and not more than four battalions of Israeli troops will be permitted.

U.N. forces will be stationed along the Egyptian-Israeli border for a distance of about 12.5 miles inland from the Mediterranean and at Sharm el Sheikh to ensure free movement of ships between the Strait of Tiran and Eilat, the port through which Israel imports most of its oil.

Israeli forces no longer will physically block the eastern ends of the Gidi and Mitla passes, the bottlenecks through which any Egyptian attack would have to pass. And they would lose a buffer zone about 80 miles wide in which any attack currently could be stopped short of Israeli territory.

But any large Egyptian force still would have to move onto the east bank of the canal and then through the two passes. In those narrow quarters, the Israeli Air Force would have a field day. Its planes carry very large bomb loads; it has large stocks of guided bombs that can home in on tanks and trucks; and its U.S.-supplied electronic gear intended to blind enemy radar is assumed by U.S. officials to be more than a match for Egyptian anti-aircraft weapons.

Air Bases. Egypt could operate only civilian flights from four Sinai air bases that Israel will be abandoning: El Arish, on the Mediterranean coast about 25 miles west of the border; Rafan (also called Refidim), in the central Sinai near the eastern end of the passes; Ras en Naqb (also called Etzion), just west of Eilat; and Sharm el Sheikh.

To replace the lost Israeli facilities, the United States is committed to construct two new bases in the Negev Desert just east of the Sinai. Included in the Carter $4.8 billion economic aid package was an $800 million grant to Israel to pay for construction of the bases.

Israeli fighter planes no longer will be based well out in front of such vital targets as Eilat and the urban concentration northeast of Gaza. And, setting aside the

certainly no guarantee of success, but . . . without a major effort such as this, the prospects for failure are almost overwhelming."

Carter's visits bore fruit. After agreeing to most aspects of the compromise proposals put forward by the American president, the Israeli Cabinet March 14 approved by 15-0 the two remaining points that had blocked an agreement. The Egyptian Cabinet followed suit the next day.

Under the terms of the agreement, Israel accepted an arrangement whereby Egypt would sell it 2.5 million tons of oil a year for an "extended period." For its part, Israel agreed to submit a detailed timetable for withdrawing its forces from the Sinai.

The Israeli Knesset (parliament) gave its overwhelming approval to the treaty March 22 (the vote was 95-18). Both Carter and Sadat hailed the Knesset's action. The

... on the Middle East Military Balance

prohibition on military use, Egypt will control bases from which the Strait of Tiran could be closed and Eilat and other Israeli cities theoretically could be subjected to a much heavier bombardment than the Egyptian Air Force currently could manage. For instance, El Arish is within 140 miles of Jerusalem, Tel Aviv and Haifa. Over that distance, each of the 50 F-5Es that the United States is selling Egypt can carry 5,000 pounds of bombs. *(F-5E sale, p. 47)*

Offsetting these threats are the men and equipment of the Israeli Air Force, which most U.S. officials assume are far superior to their Egyptian counterparts on a one-to-one comparison. Its planes are faster, carry more ammunition and have greater endurance. Its pilots have far more combat experience and its mechanics routinely have a far higher proportion of their planes ready to fly and take much less time to service their planes between missions than Egyptian ground crews.

Moreover, any Egyptian buildup of combat aircraft in the Sinai would be readily detected by Israeli reconnaissance units. Filling a key role in this mission would be four U.S.-built Hawkeye radar planes. An ungainly looking aircraft with two propellers and four tail fins, the Hawkeye can detect aircraft more than 150 miles away with its 24-foot diameter, saucer-shaped radar antenna balanced on its back. Elaborate computers on the plane could direct Israeli fighters against 30 such targets while keeping track of hundreds of others.

U.S. Arms Sales

One result of the Camp David agreements and peace treaty was that they increased the pressure for large U.S. arms transfers to Egypt and Israel as well as increased economic aid.

When Congress refused to block the fighter plane sales to Egypt and Saudi Arabia in May 1978, a key administration argument was that Sadat had shown his good faith and flexibility with his dramatic peace moves of November 1977. He needed concrete evidence to show his generals and other Arab moderates that Egyptian security had not suffered because of Sadat's dealings with Jimmy Carter.

With Sadat's surrender of some highly publicized demands about the West Bank, that line of argument became even more compelling to the administration and Congress in 1979 than it had been previously.

Supporters of new arms grants to Israel pointed to the concrete military advantages Begin yielded by withdrawing from the Sinai. And as Egypt and other Arab states

West Bank and Gaza Strip Israeli Occupation Since 1967

Mediterranean Sea · Haifa · Sea of Galilee · ISRAEL · Jordan River · JORDAN · WEST BANK · Tel Aviv · Jerusalem · Dead Sea · Gaza · GAZA STRIP

Miles
0   25

get more modern military equipment — including some from the United States — it becomes more difficult for executive branch officials to make the case that Israel retains a military superiority.

According to executive branch officials, that superiority rests not only on Israeli equipment but on factors that are much harder to quantify: superior training, more combat experience and more widespread familiarity with modern technology.

But supporters of additional grants to Israel argued that it would be difficult for Israel — or the United States — to detect improvements in these intangible dimensions of Arab military capability. To offset its undeniable numerical inferiority, they insist, Israel must have the most advanced equipment available. *(Arms aid, p. 45)*

Israeli parliament, said Carter March 22, "spoke with a voice heard around the world today — a voice for peace."

On March 26, Israel and Egypt formally ended the state of war that had existed between them ever since Israel's creation in 1948. The signing of the peace treaty took place at the White House, where about 1,600 guests attended the 45-minute ceremony. After signing three versions of the treaty — in Arabic, Hebrew and English — the

three leaders delivered speeches hailing the accord.

Calling the agreement a celebration of "a victory, not of a bloody military campaign, but of an inspiring peace campaign," Carter praised Begin and Sadat for having "conducted this campaign with all the courage, tenacity, brilliance and inspiration of any general leading men into combat." In turn, the Israeli and Egyptian leaders had high praise for the American president. Carter, said Sadat, "performed the greatest miracle," adding, "without exaggeration, what he did constituted one of the greatest achievements of our time."

Treaty Highlights

The treaty itself provides for the normalization of relations between Egypt and Israel for the first time since Israel became an independent nation in 1948. It implements the "framework" for a treaty agreed on at Camp David in September 1978. Specific details for further negotiations on trade, cultural, transportation and other agreements between the two countries are spelled out in Annex III. *(Text of treaty, annexes, p. 223)*

Details of a phased Israeli withdrawal from the Sinai Peninsula are contained in Annex I. Israel has occupied the Sinai, which is part of Egypt, since the 1967 war between the two countries. The 1975 Sinai agreement restored Egyptian control to the western edge of the peninsula.

Basically, Israel will withdraw eastward in stages. The most important steps will occur in the ninth month of the withdrawal, when Israel will give up two-thirds of the Sinai, and after three years, when Israel will completely withdraw all forces and settlements.

At the same time, Egypt and Israel will undertake negotiations on the future of the West Bank and the Gaza Strip — Israeli-occupied areas predominantly populated by Palestinian Arabs. Egypt has demanded that Israel turn those areas over to the Palestinians, but Israel has agreed only to limited local autonomy.

The negotiations on Palestinian self-rule, to be supervised by the United States, will begin one month after the formal exchange of treaty ratification documents, and are to be completed within one year. The treaty does not mention East Jerusalem, occupied by Israel since 1967 and claimed by both Israel and Jordan. Egypt has insisted that East Jerusalem is part of the West Bank, and thus subject to negotiation. Israel rejects that view.

Following is the timetable for implementing the peace treaty. The clock started running when the two nations officially exchanged the ratification documents on April 25.

● **Within one month.** Egypt and Israel open negotiations on implementing the Camp David provisions for future Palestinian self-rule on the West Bank and the Gaza Strip. The negotiations would focus first on Gaza, then proceed to the West Bank issue. The United States would be actively involved, and Jordan would be asked to participate. Egypt may include Palestinian representatives in the negotiations.

● **Within two months.** Israeli forces begin a phased withdrawal from the Sinai, by leaving El Arish, the largest city in the Sinai, located on the Mediterranean coast. In intervals of two months, Israeli forces would withdraw from other designated areas in the southwest portion of the Sinai. As Israeli forces leave, United Nations forces would establish buffer zones, and then Egyptian forces would take over. The United States would continue aerial surveillance of the Sinai throughout the transition period. Egypt and Israel have agreed informally to open their borders at this time.

● **Within seven months.** Israel is to turn over the oil fields in the Sinai to Egypt. Israel then may bid for Egyptian oil through commercial channels.

● **Within nine months.** Israel withdraws all its forces in the Sinai behind an imaginary line stretching from El Arish in the north to Ras Muhammed in the south. The withdrawal would be supervised by a joint commission. At the nine-month point, normal relations would be established between Egypt and Israel, including the termination of economic boycotts, and the opening of shipping, transportation, commercial and communications links.

● **Within 10 months.** Israel and Egypt would exchange ambassadors and open embassies in each other's capital.

● **Within one year.** Negotiations on self-rule in the West Bank and Gaza Srip are to be completed. Once elections for the self-governing authorities would be held, Israel would withdraw its military and civil government, and a five-year transition period would begin. Israeli military forces would be deployed into specified locations.

● **No later than 15 months.** The two nations would open negotiations on trade, cultural exchanges and civil aviation agreements.

● **Within three years.** Israel was to complete the withdrawal of all its military forces and civilian settlements from the Sinai.

U.S.-Israeli Security Agreement

Two hours after the peace treaty was signed, Secretary of State Vance and Israeli Foreign Minister Dayan signed a "memorandum of agreement" providing specific American assurances to Israel in the event the treaty fell apart. The memorandum reaffirmed, and broadened, U.S. assurances

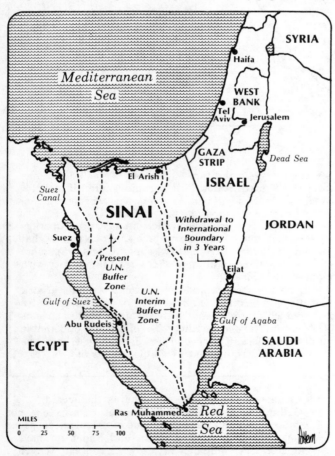

Israel was to withdraw east of the interim U.N. buffer zone within nine months and completely pull out of the Sinai and the Gaza Strip by April 1982, according to the treaty.

given Israel at the time of the 1975 Sinai disengagement agreement. *(p. 41)*

If the treaty were violated, the memorandum stated, the United States "will consult with the parties with regard to measures to halt or prevent the violation. . . ." And the United States "will take such remedial measures as it deems appropriate, which may include diplomatic, economic and military measures. . . ."

Among the actions the United States pledged to carry out were:

● If Israel is attacked or its ports blockaded, the United States will consider "such measures as strengthening the United States presence in the area, the providing of emergency supplies to Israel and the exercise of maritime rights" by the United States.

● The United States will support Israel's right to navigation and airspace through and over the Strait of Tiran and the Gulf of Aqaba.

● The United States will oppose any move in the United Nations that "adversely affects" the treaty.

● With congressional approval, the United States "will endeavor to be responsive to military and economic assistance requirements of Israel."

Administration officials emphasized that those specific pledges would be carried out only in response to a violation of the treaty by either Israel or Egypt. Those officials refused to speculate on an American response to hostile actions against Israel by any other nation.

The administration also insisted the agreement did not constitute an alliance or a mutual defense treaty with Israel.

"These are basically political-type assurances" to Israel, said a high State Department official.

The agreement brought a sharp protest from Egypt. In a letter to Vance, Egyptian Prime Minister Khalil said Egypt was "deeply disappointed to find the United States accepting to enter into an agreement we consider directed against Egypt."

The agreement "assumes that Egypt is the side liable to violate the treaty," Khalil said. He charged that Egypt was "never consulted on the substance" of the agreement. Khalil also took issue with the United States' right "to impose a military presence in the region for reasons agreed between Israel and the U.S., a matter which we cannot accept." In a second letter to Vance, Khalil said Egypt "will not recognize the legality of the memorandum and considers it null and void."

In a March 28 statement, Sadat said the memorandum violated the Israeli-Egyptian accord and that it "could be construed as an eventual alliance against Egypt.

The State Department issued a response saying Khalil's complaints were "based on a misreading of the document." The agreement "does not assume that Egypt is likely to violate the pact," the response said.

Egypt was informed of the agreement before the treaty was signed, and "in fact, frequently indicated that it would have no objections to security assurances or guarantees in the context of peace," the statement said.

The United States offered Egypt a similar security agreement, but the offer was refused, officials said.

Begin called the security agreement "a beautiful document" because "the United States gave us a commitment it will not accept a violation of the peace treaty."

Noting the contrasting reactions of Egypt and Israel, a State Department official said: "Obviously, the reactions of the parties are tailored to their constituencies."

Oil Guarantee

Potentially one of the most controversial assurances given by Carter to Israel was the guarantee to supply oil. At the time of the September 1975 Sinai agreement, President Ford agreed to guarantee Israel an adequate oil supply for a five-year period if that nation's normal supply was cut off. As an incentive to sign the peace treaty, Carter agreed to expand the guarantee to 15 years. Although Congress was not asked to approve the 1975 agreement, Carter said he would ask Congress for legislation to enact the 15-year guarantee.

A *New York Times*-CBS poll, published March 29, showed that the public opposed the Israel oil guarantee by nearly a two-to-one margin.

Under the agreement, the United States would supply Israel with enough oil "to meet all its normal requirements for domestic consumption." The promise was contingent on the United States being able to obtain enough oil "to meet its normal requirements." The United States also pledged to transport the oil to Israel, if necessary. Israel would pay the United States "world market prices" for any oil supplied under the emergency agreement.

Even if the United States were called on to supply all of Israel's oil requirements, the result would be "hardly noticeable to us," said Vance in congressional testimony April 11. Total Israeli oil consumption is only 165,000 barrels a day — less than 1 percent of daily U.S. consumption of 19 million barrels.

The Obstacles Ahead

All sides have admitted that the treaty was only a beginning, rather than an end, to the Middle East peace efforts and that numerous pitfalls lay ahead in the second, more difficult, stage of negotiations.

"We have won, at least, the first step of peace — a first step on a long and difficult road," Carter said at the treaty signing ceremony. "We must not minimize the obstacles that lie ahead. We have no illusions — we have hopes, dreams, prayers, yes — but no illusions."

Among the obstacles left unresolved by the treaty were the thorniest Arab-Israeli issues — the future of East Jerusalem, the West Bank and the Gaza Strip. The treaty postponed a decision on the future of Jerusalem, a city which is sacred not only to Jews and Christians, but also to Muslims. For Saudi Arabia, which had been Egypt's major financial backer, this issue is particularly important because the Saudis view themselves as protectors of the holy sites of Islam. *(West Bank-Gaza negotiations, p. 26)*

Negotiations on the Palestinian problem began in April 1979, with the two sides remaining far apart on the issue. Under the terms of the treaty, Egypt and Israel are to agree within a year on a plan for Palestinian self-rule. Sadat said that the negotiations would be "a good test" of Israel's willingness to live up to the treaty.

The Israelis have demanded the right to continue Israeli settlements on the West Bank, to keep Israeli control of land and water rights in the occupied territories, and to maintain security there. In essence, the Israeli position has been that Palestinian autonomy would mean only the right for Palestinians to elect an administrative council with limited authority. The controversy was further exacerbated by the continued establishment of new settlements by Israel, despite the Carter administration's often repeated view that the settlements "in occupied territories [were] illegal and obstacles" to achieving peace in the Middle East.

The treaty further split Sadat from his Arab neighbors, thus crippling the chance for a comprehensive Middle East peace. The treaty, and militant Arab reaction to it, placed intense pressures on moderate Arab nations, particularly Saudi Arabia, to join in the diplomatic and economic isolation of Egypt. Strains also appeared in the U.S.-Saudi relationship.

As of mid-1979, the prospects of Camp David and the peace treaty evolving into the comprehensive settlement that President Carter has long advocated did not look particularly promising. Soon after the Camp David agreements, former U.N. Ambassador Charles W. Yost, writing in the Oct. 6, 1978, *Christian Science Monitor,* warned, "There can be no stable peace" until the Palestinian problem and Israel's relations with Jordan, Syria and Lebanon are resolved. "With the Palestinians and Syrians frustrated and bitterly angry, and with radical Arabs and the Soviet Union ready to fuel their anger and Jordan and Saudi Arabia unwilling for sound reasons to disavow them, neither Israel nor Egypt would be secure.

The U.S. [Yost continued] would be foolish merely to press King Hussein [of Jordan] and the Saudis to do what

they cannot do — deliver Palestinian support of the Camp David agreement as written and as interpreted by Mr. Begin. If he will not deal with Palestinians in the liberal fashion which has any chance of producing a settlement, we shall have to do so. And to do so, we shall have to deal with various sorts of Palestinians, including the PLO.

Another impediment to a comprehensive settlement based on the Camp David accords was the strong opposition of the Soviet Union. Marshall Shulman, special adviser to Secretary of State Cyrus R. Vance on Soviet affairs, told the House International Relations Subcommittee on Europe and the Middle East on Sept. 26, 1978: "The Soviet Union has sought to become an active participant in Middle East negotiations through the convening of a Geneva conference, and it has bitterly expressed its frustrations at the course of events that followed President Sadat's trip to Jerusalem, leading to the Camp David summit meeting."

Indeed, many observers concluded that without Soviet-U.S. cooperation in finding a comprehensive solution to the Arab-Israeli conflict, the outlook for the future was at best a fragile and unstable Egyptian-Israeli peace and at worst an intensification of the chaos and upheavals that have wracked the area for more than three decades.

ARABS UNITE AGAINST EGYPTIAN-ISRAELI TREATY

When the Egyptian-Israeli treaty was signed in Washington on March 26, 1979, few observers expected the Arab reaction to be so harsh, so immediate and especially so unified. There was little doubt that the so-called Arab "radicals" — Algeria, Iraq, Libya, South Yemen, Syria and the Palestine Liberation Organization — would indulge in virulent condemnation of the treaty between the "traitor" Sadat and the "terrorist" Begin. As the prime mover behind the treaty, the United States would be subjected to at least verbal attack as "the tool of Zionism and imperialism."

Both Egypt and the United States anticipated some criticism from traditionally pro-Western, pro-Sadat Arab nations like Saudi Arabia, Jordan, Morocco and the Persian Gulf states. The so-called "moderates" might not like the treaty, but, it was thought, they would seek to minimize any anti-Sadat — or any anti-American — measures demanded by the "radicals." Treaty supporters seemed convinced that conservative Arab unhappiness over Egypt's new relationship with its longtime enemy was less important than fear of radical upheaval and Soviet influence in the area.

The Egyptian-American scenario soon proved false. A day after the Washington signing on March 26, 19 members of the Arab League — Algeria, Bahrain, Djibouti, Iraq, Jordan, Kuwait, Lebanon, Libya, Mauritania, Morocco, the Palestine Liberation Organization, Qatar, Saudi Arabia, Somalia, Syria, Tunisia, the United Arab Emirates, the Yemen Arab Republic (North Yemen) and the Yemen People's Democratic Republic (South Yemen) — met in Baghdad, Iraq, and adopted a package of political and economic sanctions against Egypt. Of the 22 Arab League members, only Oman and the Sudan, close allies of Sadat, boycotted the meeting in Baghdad. Egypt was not invited.

On March 31, the 19 Arab ministers for foreign affairs, economy and finance announced in Baghdad that as a result of the Egyptian-Israeli treaty, "the Egyptian Government has violated the rights of the Arab Nation and exposed the Nation to dangers and challenges which threaten it. It has also excommunicated itself from its national role to liberate the occupied Arab land, especially Jerusalem, as well as the restoration of full national rights of the Arab people of Palestine, including their return to their homeland and their right to self-determination and the setting up of the Palestinian state on their national soil."

Baghdad Conference Resolutions

Resolutions adopted unanimously at Baghdad called for:

- Withdrawal of Arab ambassadors from Egypt immediately;
- Severance of political and diplomatic relations with the government of Egypt;
- Suspension of membership of the Egypt Arab Republic from the Arab League, valid from the date of the signing of the peace treaty by Egypt with the Zionist enemy . . . Tunis shall be the temporary headquarters of the Arab League.
- Efforts to suspend Egypt's membership in the Non-Aligned Movement, Islamic Conference Organization and Organization of African Unity since it has violated the resolutions of these organizations concerning the Arab-Zionist conflict;
- Continued dealing with the Arab people of Egypt, except those directly or indirectly collaborating with the Zionist enemy;
- Member countries shall undertake to notify all foreign countries about their stand vis-à-vis the Egyptian-Zionist treaty and to call on these countries to refrain from supporting this treaty since it constitutes an aggression on the rights of the Palestinian people and the Arab Nation, and is a threat to peace and security in the world;
- Condemnation of the policy pursued by the United States of America for its role in the Camp David accords and the Egyptian-Zionist treaty;
- Halt in granting any loans, deposits, banking facilities and financial or technical aid by Arab governments and their establishments to the Egyptian government and its establishments as from the date of the signing of the treaty;
- Refrain from offering economic aid from Arab banks' funds and financial establishments within the Arab League to the Egyptian government and its establishments;
- Arab governments and their establishments shall refrain from obtaining shares and bonds issued by the Egyptian government and its financial establishments;
- Consequent to the suspension of Egypt's membership from the Arab League, its membership in the establishment funds and organizations shall also be suspended, and all the benefits Egypt may enjoy from these sources shall also be terminated. In case any of these bodies are based in Egypt, they should be transferred to other Arab countries temporarily;
- As the Egyptian-Zionist treaty and the annexes attached to it commit Egypt to sell oil to Israel, Arab countries shall refrain from supplying Egypt with oil and its derivatives;
- Ban on trade exchanges with public and private Egyptian establishments that engage in transactions with the Zionist enemy;
- Application of the Arab boycott laws, principles and provisions on Egyptian companies, establishments and individuals who deal directly or indirectly with the Zionist enemy. The Boycott Bureau shall implement and follow up this resolution;
- The Arab countries stress the importance of continuing to deal with the national institutions of Egypt that refrain from dealing with the Zionist enemy and encourage them to work in the Arab countries within the framework of their field of interest. The Arab

countries stress the importance of respecting the feelings of Egyptians working and living in the Arab countries;

• Ask the United Nations to transfer its regional offices which cover the Arab Region from Egypt to any other Arab capital;

• These measures taken by the Arab Foreign and Economy Ministers are considered the minimum necessary to face the dangers of the treaty and that the governments shall have the option to take whatever steps they deem necessary in addition to these resolutions.

Baghdad Conference Aftermath

Relations between the radical Arab states and Egypt had been severed before the Baghdad resolutions were announced. In early April, the rest of the Baghdad participants began recalling their ambassadors from Cairo. And on April 30, Iran became the first non-Arab country to break relations with Egypt. Since the ouster of Shah Mohammed Reza Pahlavi in mid-January and the establishment of a new Islamic government under the de facto leadership of Ayatollah Ruhollah Khomeini, Iran had severed all connections with Israel. And in February, the Iranians had given PLO Chairman Yasir Arafat an enthusiastic welcome and promises of material support.

By early May, all the Arab countries except Oman and the Sudan had cut diplomatic ties with Egypt. Oman and the Sudan argued that isolating Egypt would not advance the Arab cause. Under pressure, Sultan Qabus bin Said of Oman and President Gaafer Nimeiry of the Sudan pointedly refused to endorse the Egyptian-Israeli treaty.

In addition to the severance of bilateral diplomatic relations, Egypt was also suspended from the 22-member Arab League and the 43-member Islamic Conference and their affiliates. The 43 foreign ministers of Moslem countries refused to allow Egypt to participate in the conference and, on May 9, in Fez Morocco, excluded Egypt from all the group's activities and financial assistance.

Egypt was also expelled from several Arab financial institutions, including the Federation of Arab Banks, the Arab Investment Company, the Arab Bank for Economic Development in Africa and the Arab Fund for Economic and Social Development. The Arab Civil Aviation Organization asked its members to close their airspace to Egyptian planes and to close down their offices in Cairo.

Among the most serious of the multilateral Arab measures taken against Egyptian President Anwar Sadat was the disbanding of the Cairo-based Arab Organization for Industrialization. Saudi Defense Minister Prince Sulton ibn Abdel Aziz announced on May 14, that the arms industry would go out of existence because "the signing of a peace treaty between Egypt and Israel clashes with the purpose of establishing the company." The organization had been established in 1975 by Saudi Arabia, Qatar, the United Arab Emirates and Egypt to lessen Arab dependence on imported weapons, acquire military technology and spur employment and aid the economy in Egypt. As a result of the shutdown, Egypt stood to lose some 15,000 jobs as well as a source of technology and weapons. Egypt was also expelled from the Organization of Arab Petroleum Exporting Countries (OAPEC) in mid-April. In addition to the expulsion, oil ministers from Saudi Arabia, Kuwait, Bahrain, the United Arab Emirates, Qatar, Iraq, Syria, Libya and Algeria banned the sale of oil to Egypt.

A number of Arab countries have taken unilateral measures against Egypt. Several have barred Egyptian newspapers, broadcasts and films. Kuwait announced that it would withdraw more than $1 billion it had deposited in the Central Bank of Egypt. There was concern in Cairo that Saudi Arabia would also seek to withdraw almost $1 billion that it had deposited in Egyptian banks.

As Egypt's isolation in the Arab world increased after the signing of the treaty, Sadat lashed back at his critics. Since his visit to Jerusalem in November 1977 and the Camp David agreement in September 1978, Sadat had condemned and ridiculed his "radical" opponents — Syria, Libya, Iraq and, to a lesser extent, the PLO. The Libyan, Iraqi and Syrian leaders were customarily referred to as "dwarfs" and "buzzards." Sadat was particularly vituperative toward his Libyan counterpart, Muammar Qaddafi, who was referred to as the "Libyan lunatic" or the "Libyan madman."

As the Baghdad sanctions against Egypt took effect, Sadat began attacking his friends and financial supporters, particularly Jordan and Saudi Arabia. Jordan's King Hussein was accused of groveling before the oil-rich Arabs and of cowardice in refusing to participate in the negotiations for Palestinian autonomy on the Israeli-occupied West Bank and Gaza Strip. The Jordanian press, in turn, stepped up its attacks on Sadat and the "separate" peace treaty he had signed.

The most surprising — and, for the United States, the most disconcerting — of Sadat's attacks was directed against Saudi Arabia. The first public criticism of the Saudis came on May 1, in a long speech at the Red Sea town of Safaga. Before that, both Sadat and the Saudis had muted their attacks on each other and the Saudis had continued subsidizing Egypt. In his May Day speech, Sadat alleged that "the recent operation of severing the Arab relations [with Egypt] was arranged. The majority of the Arabs who severed their relations did so out of courtesy to Saudi Arabia. Saudi Arabia paid a price to the minority to sever these relations. Some of those who acted out of courtesy and who got paid wrote to me."

While at American urging Sadat toned down his attacks on the Saudis, the criticism continued. In an interview with French journalists on May 22 in Cairo, Sadat repeated his May Day allegations. In reply to a question on the Arab rejection of the peace treaty, he stated that "the rest of the Arab states severed their relations with us and rejected what they rejected out of courtesy toward Saudi Arabia. . . . Some of these states have been paid by Saudi Arabia; some others did it out of courtesy."

Sadat and other Egyptian officials have characterized many of the Arab sanctions against Egypt as "illegal" and "null and void." They have refused to permit Arab League headquarters to be transferred from Cairo to Tunis and have threatened to freeze Arab funds in Egyptian banks if attempts are made to withdraw them.

While Sadat has reacted to Arab criticism of him and measures against Egypt with scorn, insults and derision, he has offered a few carrots to placate his opponents. He announced that he would attend the Geneva Conference if the other Arabs, Israel and the two co-chairmen, the United States and the Soviet Union, thought that forum would be more acceptable or more effective. Egypt also called for a summit conference of all Islamic leaders to "consider ways of liberating" Arab Jerusalem from Israeli occupation. Sadat's Arab foes have shown little enthusiasm for either proposal.

Sadat's major argument has been that his was the only practical way to resolve the 30-year-old Arab-Israeli war, recover occupied Arab territory and resolve the Palestinian issue. The mass-circulation Egyptian daily newspaper *Al Akhbar* reflected Sadat's impatience with his Arab opponents when it editorialized on April 1, a day after the Baghdad resolutions were announced: "We were hoping that instead of these sanctions against Egypt they would tell us how they plan to liberate the occupied territory. . . . They didn't offer one thing for the Palestinian cause, as if the utmost they can offer to the liberation of Palestine is to cut diplomatic relations with Egypt."

Sadat has also tried to convince the Egyptian people and the outside world that the unity achieved at Baghdad after the treaty was signed will be short-lived. At a meeting with American businessmen in Cairo on May 8, for example, Sadat assured them that "You may hear, see and read about some shouts around us from the Arab world. This will never materialize into anything. It will not hinder progress either economically or politically." And referring to past Arab criticism of him for his disengagement agreements with Israel after the 1973 war and his trip to Jerusalem in November 1977, he told the businessmen: "I am accustomed to this. It happened before. . . . By next year, this will be history."

Background

The criticism that Sadat encountered after the 1973 war for the U.S.-sponsored Sinai accord of September 1975 and, to a lesser extent, for the January 1974 separation of forces agreement along the Suez Canal was muted and far from unanimous. In May 1974, Syria too agreed to a disengagement of forces with Israel along the Golan Heights. While Syria denounced the 1975 Sinai accord as "a setback to the march of the Arab struggle," that agreement was inconsequential compared to the Egyptian-Israeli peace treaty of March 1979. The Sinai pact required Israeli withdrawal from the Gidi and Mitla passes and the setting up of a United Nations demilitarized zone in the area. The accord, however, dealt with relatively trivial issues and did not touch upon such vital problems as recognition of Israel, the future of the Palestinians, permanent boundaries, the status of Jerusalem and peace guarantees.

Visit to Jerusalem

The reasons for, as well as the Arab reaction to, Sadat's visit to Jerusalem in November 1977 were many and mixed. The unprecedented trip by an Arab ruler to Israel has been explained by the Egyptian president's conviction that in another war the Arabs would suffer a 1967-type defeat; his anger and frustration about involving the Soviet Union in a peace settlement at Geneva, as outlined in the joint American-Soviet statement of Oct. 1, 1977; his fears of radical upheaval in Egypt; and his belief that a face-to-face encounter between Arabs and Israelis would do much to remove the psychological barriers that separated them. *(See also p. 4)*

Sadat's visit to Jerusalem underlined the split between Arab moderates and radicals. Despite Sadat's demand in his speech to the Israeli Knesset for full Israeli withdrawal from all occupied territories and self-determination for the Palestinians and his refusal to consider a separate peace, the reaction of Arab hard-liners was strong and negative.

Moderate Arabs tried to avoid alienating either Sadat or the hard-liners. The major criticism from Sadat's conservative allies was that Egypt had failed to consult them before visiting Israel.

Libyan President Muammar Qaddafi failed to persuade even hard-line Arabs to adopt strong anti-Sadat measures and disavow a negotiated settlement with Israel at a conference in Tripoli, Libya, in early December 1977. And at a press conference in Amman, Jordan, on Dec. 12, 1977, King Hussein admitted that Sadat had "taken a very courageous step on behalf of all of us. . . . This is a moment not to be lost and I hope that our friends in the United States will do all they can to insure that this opportunity is not lost."

Camp David Reaction

The Arab reaction to the Camp David accords was, on the surface at least, far less ambiguous. President Carter had invited Egyptian President Sadat and Israeli Prime Minister Menachem Begin to the presidential retreat in the Maryland mountains to revive the stalled peace negotiations. Talks continued from Sept. 5 until Sept. 17, 1978. The agreement reached at Camp David consisted of two parts: a framework for settling the Palestinian question on the Israeli-occupied West Bank and Gaza Strip and a framework for an Egyptian-Israeli peace treaty. *(Details, p. 5)*

Soon after the results of the Camp David summit were announced, two moderate Arab nations whose support was considered essential voiced grave reservations about the agreement. Oil-rich Saudi Arabia complained that "what has been reached at Camp David cannot be considered a final acceptable formula for peace." Jordan's King Hussein, whom the Camp David participants had given a major role in negotiations for autonomy on the West Bank and Gaza, expressed his unhappiness over the frameworks and disavowed any Jordanian "legal or ethical commitment" to the accords.

Sadat's hard-line Arab critics reacted more in anger than in sadness. They complained that the Camp David agreement was merely the culmination of what Sadat had been aiming at for years and particularly since his visit to Jerusalem: a separate Egyptian-Israeli peace. They saw the framework for a comprehensive peace involving the Palestinians, Jordan and perhaps Syria as meaningless and intended only to mask the selling out of the Arab cause for what PLO leader Yasir Arafat called "a handful of Sinai sand."

In addition to criticism from the moderates and condemnation from the hard-liners, the Arab world sought to unite its ranks against the agreement. The first step was the reconciliation between Syria and Iraq in late October. The two countries, which had been feuding for more than a decade, agreed to work toward a "full military union" against Israel and to overcome "the great dangers looming over the Arab nation" after Camp David. Both Iraq and Jordan moved to improve their relations with the PLO.

More alarming to Egyptian and American officials than the bilateral fence-mending of former Arab antagonists was the degree of pan-Arab unity exhibited by 20 Arab countries and the Palestine Liberation Organization at an Arab summit conference in Baghdad, Iraq, in early November 1978. While the moderates, notably Saudi Arabia, successfully resisted demands for strong and immediate sanctions against Egypt and the United States, the conference was widely viewed as a victory for the hard-liners.

The measures adopted at the first Baghdad conference included condemnation of the Camp David accords; the approval of a $3.5 billion-a-year war chest to help subsidize Syria, Jordan and the PLO; and, if an Egyptian-Israeli peace treaty were signed, the suspension of Egypt's membership in the Arab League, the removal of Arab League headquarters from Cairo and a boycott against Egyptian firms dealing with Israel.

Before the summit conference ended on Nov. 5, a delegation led by Lebanese Premier Salim Hoss was dispatched to Cairo to try to dissuade Sadat from signing a treaty with Israel. The delegation had been instructed to offer Sadat $5 billion a year for the next decade if he disavowed the Camp David accords. Sadat refused to see the delegation and told the Egyptian parliament that "my message . . . is that billions of dollars will not buy the will of Egypt." Egyptian officials and media referred to the Baghdad conference as a "comic farce."

There was some indication, however, that Sadat found the Baghdad resolutions neither comical nor farcical. Observers speculated that the Arab stand against the Camp David agreements had some influence on the tougher Egyptian position on the linkage between an Egyptian-Israeli treaty and autonomy for the Palestinians on the occupied West Bank and Gaza Strip after the Baghdad conference.

During the next few months, Sadat and his hard-line Arab critics traded threats and insults. By and large, the moderates, particularly Jordan and Saudi Arabia, continued to criticize the Camp David agreements but refrained from denouncing Sadat himself. American officials tried — unsuccessfully — to convince the Arab moderates to endorse the accords or at least to resist public criticism of them.

By late February 1979, negotiations on the Egyptian-Israeli peace treaty had stalled and the prospects that a treaty would be signed appeared increasingly dim. In a final effort to save the treaty, President Carter flew to Egypt and Israel; shortly thereafter, the treaty was signed in Washington on March 26. The Arabs then met again in Baghdad and implemented the resolutions that had been adopted four months earlier as well as a few others that had not been expected. The Arab world — minus Egypt and to a lesser extent Sudan and Oman — seemed more united than it had for many years.

Prime Minister Begin's assurances to the Israeli people after the Camp David agreements were reached in September 1978 that sooner or later the other Arab states would follow Egypt's example and make peace with Israel show little sign of being fulfilled in the near future. Israel itself bears a major responsibility for the failure of U.S. efforts to convince moderate Arabs, particularly Jordan and Saudi Arabia, to support the Camp David accords and, later, the Egyptian-Israeli peace treaty. Official Israeli statements on the West Bank and Gaza, on Syria's Golan Heights and on Israel's right to continue building Jewish settlements on occupied Arab lands have not encouraged the other Arab states to negotiate with Israel.

There was some question, however, as to whether the Arabs could have foiled the Egyptian-Israeli peace treaty had they supported Sadat — even minimally — after his visit to Jerusalem in November 1977. Almost all the Arabs would agree to peace with Israel in exchange for what Sadat demanded in his speech to the Knesset — Israeli withdrawal from all occupied Arab territories, including East Jerusalem, and self-determination for the Palestinians.

Had they joined Sadat, on the basis of his demands in the Knesset, and agreed to negotiations, would Egypt have been willing, in the face of strong objections from its Arab negotiating partners, to agree to the Camp David accords and to sign a peace treaty that did not fulfill the demands that Sadat himself had insisted upon in late 1977?

Revolution in Iran

For the United States, the strategic equation in the Middle East was seriously upset by events in Iran. On Jan. 16, 1979, Shah Mohammed Reza Pahlavi, long viewed in Washington as a guardian of stability in the turbulent area, left Iran for an indefinite "vacation." The United States attached so much importance to Iran, the world's second largest exporter of oil after Saudi Arabia, that it had given the shah wholehearted support, sold him vast quantities of the most advanced weapons, encouraged his ambitions for regional dominance and overlooked a reputation for violation of human rights considered among the worst in the world.

Since the shah's departure and particularly since the return of exiled religious leader Ayatollah Ruhollah Khomeini from Paris, anti-American and anti-Israeli sentiment has been evident throughout Iran. The United States had supported the shah, while Israel had formed a tacit, de facto alliance with him, thereby assuring Israel of needed oil supplies and at least some political cooperation. The establishment of an Islamic government in Iran, inspired and led by Ayatollah Khomeini, brought a swift halt to all political and material cooperation between Iran, a predominantly Moslem but non-Arab nation, and the Jewish state.

After the Islamic revolution, Iran lost little time in denouncing the Camp David agreements and, later, the Egyptian-Israeli peace treaty, severing all de facto relations with Israel and warmly supporting the PLO and the Arab countries which rejected Sadat's actions. In February, PLO Chairman Yasir Arafat received a tumultuous reception in Iran and was promised material support and friendship by the new Islamic government.

While publicly welcoming the new regime in Iran and pledging good and neighborly relations with it, most of the other Arab opponents of Camp David and the Egyptian-Israeli peace treaty showed considerable and increasing uneasiness about the Islamic government. On the one hand, there was relief that Iran seemed willing to replace Egypt in confronting the Zionist enemy. On the other hand, there was fear that the Iranian Islamic revolution could spread to their own countries and endanger their own governments.

Saudi Arabia, a moderate Arab country, and Iraq, a radical Arab nation, were illustrative of Arab uneasiness about the revolutionary government in Iran. In recent years, the Saudi royal family had been upset and unhappy about the shah of Iran's insistence on higher and higher oil prices and about his increasingly obvious cooperation with Israel. Balancing this, however, was gratitude to the shah for making Iran the guardian of stability and enemy of radicalism in the turbulent Persian Gulf. Like the Americans, the Saudis feared that the Islamic government would be unable to rule the country very long and would be replaced by a leftist, pro-Soviet regime.

Despite the strong tradition of Moslem orthodoxy in Saudi Arabia, the new Islamic government in Iran has voiced occasional criticism of the Saudi system. In an article in *The New York Times* on Feb. 25, 1979, Youssef

M. Ibrahim wrote from Teheran that "the new Islamic government of Iran feels closest to the governments in Algeria and Libya . . . and to the Palestinians." There was little warmth for Saudi Arabia, despite the fact that the Saudis used Islamic law as the basis of government. Ibrahim quoted Hossein Bani-Assadi, the son-in-law of Iranian Prime Minister Medhi Bazargan, as saying: "Ideologically, this revolution cannot support systems like Saudi Arabia. Islam has no kings."

Similar problems have unsettled the far more radical government in Iraq. Ideologically and politically, the new Islamic leadership was hailed and supported by Iraq which welcomed Khomeini's adherence to the Arab rejectionist front and Iran's denunciation of the Camp David accords and the Egyptian-Israeli peace treaty. Since that time, however, Baghdad has shown concern and irritation over possible Iranian aid to Iraqi Kurds, Shiite Moslems and communists, all of whom are viewed as seriously destabilizing factors by the government in Iraq.

The Kurds are currently the most serious problem in Iranian-Iraqi relations. A 14-year revolt by the Kurdish minority against Iraq's central government collapsed in March 1975 when the shah met Iraqi Vice President Saddam Hussein in Algiers and pledged to end all of Iran's military, material and psychological support for the Kurdish rebellion. The shah immediately closed the border and the Kurd's hopes for an autonomous Kurdistan seemed doomed.

But on June 4, 1979, Iraqi planes bombed several Kurdish villages in northwest Iran while pursuing Kurdish guerrillas who had fled across the border into Iran. Iraq was said to have apologized for the raid and called it a mistake. Iran also protested against the arrest of Iraqi Shiite leader Ayatollah Mohammad Bagher Sadr by the government in Baghdad. Ayatollah Sadr had been openly supportive of the Islamic revolution in Iran and of Ayatollah Khomeini. Iran further accused Iraq of promoting unrest among Iranian Arabs and other groups and of carrying out continuing attacks against border villages.

Despite Iran's difficulties with certain Arab countries opposing the Egyptian-Israeli peace treaty, the Islamic government's strongest criticism as of mid-1979 had been leveled at Arab Egypt. Ayatollah Khomeini and top Iranian officials hailed Egypt's Moslem Brotherhood, one of Sadat's strongest critics, and suggested that Egypt's turn toward the West and toward Israel could well provoke an Islamic uprising similar to the one that occurred in Iran. The Iranian news media compared Sadat to the ousted shah and warned the Egyptian president that if he continued to play the shah-like role of "policeman" in the area, he too would be overthrown by Islamic forces.

Sadat has been alternately critical and contemptuous of the Khomeini revolution and Iran's Islamic government. In an interview with Joseph Finklestone, published in London's *Jewish Chronicle* on May 25, 1979, Sadat described the situation in Iran as "very tragic. Muslim revolutions never used blood as a means of power. It is against Islam." He added that the Iranian leaders "have severed their relations with me, and I shall be asking my new parliament whenever it convenes — this is news for you — to give the shah asylum here in my country — officially. I shall be giving him asylum because this is the moral of Egypt. I am very deeply sad for those who are scared to give the man asylum."

Iran condemned Sadat's offer and pledged again to bring the shah to justice.

Chaos in Lebanon

The Egyptian-Israeli peace treaty has increased the bloodshed and chaos that have ravaged Lebanon since the 1975-76 civil war. Since the treaty was signed, there have been continuous Israeli raids into Lebanon, bombings of villages, particularly in the south, and shelling of coastal areas.

Thousands, primarily civilians, have died, been wounded or forced to flee their homes. Some of the Israeli incursions have been justified as reprisals for Palestinian raids into Israel from Lebanon or attacks by Palestinians living in Israel or the occupied territories. Others were undertaken to prevent or discourage future Palestinian attacks in Israel.

Israeli Defense Minister Ezer Weizman stated publicly that his country would strike at "terrorists" whenever, wherever and however it could. As a result of this policy, the Lebanese people and the 350,000 Palestinians who live in Lebanon have been the primary victims of the Israeli attacks and, according to some observers, of the Egyptian-Israeli peace treaty.

Salah Khalaf, a leader of the PLO, told a group of Palestinian students at the Arab University of Beirut on June 1, 1979:

> With all my heart and faith, I say to the Lebanese people that it was not the Palestinian people or their fighters who strangled them and made Israel play havoc. The cause of the sufferings of the Lebanese people, and of our sufferings, is this criminal and traitor Sadat who has plotted against the people of Egypt and the entire Arab nation. He has plotted against the people of Palestine and the people of Lebanon. This Sadat has told the world that he has brought peace. What peace is this? The Israeli planes are confirming each day that this is a false peace, a peace of blood that flows out of the people of the south and of our people in their camps."

In addition to increased Palestinian attacks in Israel and the occupied territories and incessant Israeli bombardment of Lebanon, there have been several other developments in Lebanon since the signing of the Egyptian-Israeli treaty. These include the declaration by Major Saad Haddad, a right-wing Christian with very close ties to Israel, of a state of Free Lebanon in the southern section of the country.

Haddad and his followers, who have vigorously opposed the presence of the Syrian army and the Palestinians in Lebanon, have been advised, armed and trained by Israel. Haddad has been opposed not only by the Syrians, Palestinians and Lebanese Moslems but by the Christian-dominated central government of President Elias Sarkis, which has a warrant out for his arrest as a traitor.

In an interview with French journalists in Alexandria, Egypt, on May 22, 1979, President Sadat likewise condemned Haddad and his alleged collaborator, former right-wing Christian President Camille Chamoun. Sadat told the French reporters that "we consider Haddad's operation in southern Lebanon as treason and that anybody who supports Haddad, particularly Camille Chamoun, is a traitor. Moreover, I requested Begin at Camp David, in the presence of the U.S. President, to stop the aid for Haddad and Chamoun. I also told him: Chamoun is a traitor and . . . he will not be allowed to enter Egypt. This is our position on southern Lebanon. The entity of Lebanon must not be harmed in any way, and I will stand against anyone who might try this."

In the same interview, Sadat was not content to attack only Haddad and Chamoun. He also lashed out at Syrian President Hafez Assad, a Moslem from the minority Alawite sect. While denouncing Haddad and Chamoun, Sadat said: "We condemn the Alawites in Syria who caused this situation. It is indeed comic that what Assad of Greater Syria has done should result in Israel's interference and its occupation of southern Lebanon. Israel is striking and Assad of Greater Syria is watching and doing nothing." In the interview, Sadat also accused the Syrian Alawites, primarily President Assad, of favoring "the partition of Lebanon."

In a report on June 4, 1979, the right-wing Christian radio station, Voice of Lebanon, broadcast the following dispatch: "Former President Camille Chamoun said today that he has in his possession a U.S.-CIA report — which he will publish later — that confirms some Beirut newspaper reports on the existence of a U.S.-Soviet plan to settle the Palestinians in Lebanon. The report is also confirmed by a past speech by President Hafez Assad in which he said that the plot against Lebanon aims at turning it into an alternative homeland for the Palestinians."

There has been no evidence that Syria supports either a permanent settlement of the Palestinians in Lebanon or, as Sadat claimed, the partition of Lebanon. Syria intervened in Lebanon in 1975 to prevent a takeover by leftist and Palestinian forces. Such a takeover could have provoked a war with Israel, a war that Syria neither wanted nor was ready for. A continuing Palestinian presence in Lebanon, allied with Lebanese nationalist factions, might produce the same result.

Adeed I. Dawisha, formerly a senior research fellow at the London-based International Institute for Strategic Studies, summed up Syria's longstanding fear of partition of Lebanon. In an article in the winter 1978-79 issue of *Foreign Policy* magazine, Dawisha argued that "at the very basis of Syria's decision to intervene in Lebanon [in 1975] was the Syrian conviction that Israel is innately expansionist. The Damascus regime was convinced that a partition of Lebanon would give Israel the pretext to move into southern Lebanon and occupy the area up to the Litani River. . . . Israel's occupation of southern Lebanon would, of course, increase Syria's strategic vulnerability considerably by providing Israel with a new front in any future confrontation." Since Major Haddad's declaration of a Free Lebanon, allied with Israel, Syria's "strategic" concern about partition is likely to have increased enormously.

With neither the Lebanese army nor the 6,000 U.N. troops in southern Lebanon able to maintain order in the country, the Sarkis government has been dependent, to a large extent, on Syria and the Syrian forces in Lebanon. This was apparent when Israeli Prime Minister Begin proposed a "comprehensive" Israeli-Lebanese peace treaty after the signing of the Egyptian-Israeli agreement. Such a treaty between Lebanon and Israel would have curtailed Syrian influence in the country and would have deprived the Palestinians of their last relatively free Arab base of operations. The Lebanese government quickly rejected the offer from Begin and pledged support for the Palestinians and the opponents of the Egyptian-Israeli treaty.

In order to help the Lebanese authorities and prevent repeated Israeli incursions into southern Lebanon, the PLO in early June 1979 ordered all its forces to move north of the Litani River. The organization also pledged support for the central government's efforts to regain control over the country and for the United Nations' peacekeeping role in southern Lebanon. Both PLO Chairman Yasir Arafat and the Lebanese government have sent urgent appeals to the United Nations Security Council to help restore order in Lebanon.

Most observers were convinced, however, that without a truly comprehensive peace in the Middle East and particularly without a just settlement of the Palestinian question, the situation in Lebanon would continue to deteriorate. As of mid-1979 there seemed scant hope that such a settlement could be reached in the foreseeable future. Perhaps the most that could be achieved in the short term, at least, would be a series of limited measures, including American pressure on Israel to halt its attacks in Lebanon, Arab pressure on the various factions in Lebanon to reach some sort of modus vivendi and a continuance of or increase in U.N. forces to maintain some semblance of order and security.

Wolf Blitzer, Washington correspondent of the *Jerusalem Post*, discussing the U.S. position on the increasing Israeli strikes into Lebanon, noted in an article in the June 28, 1979 issue of *The Jewish Week*, "the White House and the State Department are upset over Israel's continuous policy of using U.S.-supplied weapons and fighter aircraft against Palestinian targets in Lebanon." As a result, the United States on June 14, "joined with a majority in the United Nations Security Council to rebuke Israel's policies toward southern Lebanon. In a resolution extending the U.N. peacekeeping mandate in southern Lebanon for another six months, the Council condemned Israel's support for the Christian militia headed by Maj. Sa'ad Haddad. On several recent occasions [Blitzer continued]

> the U.S. has privately protested to Israel over the use of U.S.-supplied weaponry in southern Lebanon. The Americans have accused Israel of violating the terms of the sales contracts for those arms, charging 'illegal' use against Lebanon's 'territorial integrity'. . . . They believe that Israel's use of U.S. military equipment during recent retaliatory actions in Lebanon goes beyond the legitimate 'self-defense' clause in the contracts. They have forcefully asked Israel immediately to cease all such military operations.

American concern over Israeli raids into Lebanon was particularly apparent after Israeli warplanes shot down several Syrian planes over southern Lebanon on June 27. That was the first time that the American F15s were used in combat anywhere in the world. The United States had sold the sophisticated warplanes to Israel in 1976 with the stipulation that they be used only in self-defense.

In a statement following the battle, State Department spokesman Tom Reston refrained from formally blaming either Israel or Syria for the clash. Nevertheless, he noted that "the Israelis have been conducting a preemptive bombing strategy against Palestinian bases and concentrations in Lebanon" and that Israel's use of U.S. aircraft in Lebanon "has been of serious concern to us and to members of Congress." Reston strongly urged Israel and Syria to show restraint.

U.S. Dilemma

Since American sponsorship of the Camp David conference in September 1978, the United States has suffered a number of setbacks in the Arab world, excluding Egypt.

The first occurred in Lebanon. Immediately after Camp David, President Carter called for an international conference, attended by "those who live there," including the Palestinians; Syria; Israel; interested foreign countries like France and the United States; and the United Nations. The generally adverse Arab reaction to the Camp David accords helped put an end to U.S. proposals for a conference on Lebanon.

A month later, the United States received another, more serious setback when Arab moderates, particularly Jordan and Saudi Arabia, joined with Arab hard-liners in Baghdad in denouncing the Camp David accords. Despite strong U.S. pressure on the Arab moderates, criticism of the American-sponsored agreement continued and intensified. As of mid-1979, the virtually unanimous pan-Arab stand against the Egyptian-Israeli treaty had shown little sign of faltering — and the split between Arab moderates and hard-liners that American officials had forecast soon after the treaty was concluded had shown little sign of materializing.

U.S. prestige among the moderate Arab states was further harmed by the Islamic revolution in Iran and the ouster of Washington's erstwhile protegé and ally, the shah. Officials in Saudi Arabia and the other conservative Persian Gulf states complained that if the United States would not protect its closest ally in the region, what help could they expect from Washington if they faced radical upheaval or foreign intervention.

As the Jordanian and Saudi press became increasingly critical of American efforts to achieve a "comprehensive peace" through the Camp David formula, hard-line Arab countries sought to bolster their ties with the Soviet Union. The Syrian reaction to the U.S.-sponsored Egyptian-Israeli peace talks was notable in this regard. After the 1973 Middle East war, Syria had been moving closer to the United States and away from the Russians. The Camp David agreement and the Egyptian-Israeli peace treaty reduced the still nascent cooperation between Washington and Damascus and increased Syrian reliance on the Soviet Union.

If, as has been frequently mentioned, one of the major aims of the United States in encouraging negotiations between Egypt and Israel had been to prevent Soviet inroads in the area, the treaty may have, in the short-term at least, the exact opposite effect. By and large, the Arabs, particularly the Moslem Arabs, have been traditionally opposed to Marxist or communist influence. Even radical Arab states like Iraq have cracked down on their own communist sympathizers. By insisting on the Camp David formula for peace, a formula which few Arabs could accept, the United States may have encouraged a greatly expanded Soviet role in the region.

Israeli Role

For Egypt and the United States, the policies of the Israeli government and particularly the provocative statements of Prime Minister Begin have succeeded so far in discouraging moderate Arabs from accepting the Egyptian-Israeli peace treaty and supporting the negotiations for autonomy on the West Bank and Gaza Strip. Since the treaty was signed, Egyptian officials and the Egyptian media had tried to refrain from criticizing Israel or its leadership.

Such restraint came to an abrupt end on June 11, when Moussa Sabri, the chief editor of Egypt's largest daily paper, *Al Akhbar*, and a staunch supporter of President Sadat, editorially advised the United States to intervene against Israel and "lop off the head of the snake" — specifically "Begin and the other snakes in Tel Aviv" — "before it spews out its venom."

The editorial, which was written as talks on Palestinian autonomy resumed in Alexandria, also complained that "Begin deliberately raised a dust storm in the path of negotiations before they even started. Begin is making statements day and night to the effect that the West Bank is Israeli territory, that Israel will not withdraw, that Jerusalem will never be anything but Israel's capital, that the territories will continue to exist, that self-rule is intended for human beings and not for territories, and other slogans he never tires of repeating day and night." Begin imagines, the editorial continued,

> that such deliberate and demonstrative actions can widen the rift between Egypt and the moderate Arab countries that sided with the rejectionists, because Begin wants to give new pretexts to those countries to the effect that Israel does not want a comprehensive peace and that it will not fulfill the Palestinian peoples' requests and rights. Begin also imagines that he can continue these provocations as long as there are differences among the Arabs and as long as contradictory stands continue to exist among the rejectionist states. Therefore, Begin is starting a fire so that the negotiations will stumble at the outset, and so that time will be wasted. Thus, he will have concluded a separate peace with Egypt.

There were almost certain to be similar outbursts as negotiations for Palestinian autonomy on the Israeli occupied West Bank and Gaza Strip continued. Sadat, now virtually isolated in the Arab world, must convince the Arab rejectionists that he has no intention of selling out the Arab cause for what Yasir Arafat called "a handful of Sinai sand." but the comprehensive peace that Sadat and President Carter grandly proclaimed seemed remote and almost impossible a year later.

According to Egyptian and, less vocally at least, American officials, Israel was responsible for the deadlock in mid-1979. The chief problem was Israeli policies, actions and statements on the most intractible of the Camp David issues: autonomy on the West Bank and Gaza. Among other things, the Israeli government's autonomy plan, its insistence on establishing Jewish settlements in occupied areas and a series of statements by government officials have made it all but impossible for other Arabs or the Palestinians to participate in the autonomy negotiations. These provocations have led Sadat to characterize Begin as the staunch ally of his rejectionist foes.

Draft Autonomy Plan

The final version of Israel's autonomy plan, submitted on May 21, 1979, and entitled "Draft Principles for Full Autonomy for the Arab Inhabitants of Judea, Samaria and Gaza and for the Existence of the Jewish Settlements in These Territories," provided:

● The military government would be withdrawn once the self-administration authority was established;

● The powers accorded to the self-administration authority would be delegated by the military government;

• Negotiations would be conducted regarding the number of members on the administrative council and its departments, which would be elected;

• Internal security and the combating of terrorism, subversion and violence would be in the hands of the Israeli security elements;

• The Jewish settlements and/or Jewish population would be governed by Israeli administration and jurisdiction. The right to settle in the autonomous regions would be maintained;

• The Israeli Defense Force (IDF) would withdraw and redeploy within specified zones in the autonomous territories;

• Israel would be responsible for water resource planning, in consultation with the administrative council;

• State land and scrub land would be under Israeli control;

• There would be freedom of movement between Israel and the autonomous areas;

• The residents of Judea, Samaria and Gaza would be able to choose between Israeli and Jordanian citizenship;

• Israeli citizens would be able to purchase land in the autonomous area. Residents of Judea, Samaria and Gaza would be able to purchase land in Israel after they had taken Israeli citizenship;

• Negotiations would be held regarding the method of electing an administrative council;

• Declaration: Israel would at no time permit the establishment of a Palestinian state in Judea, Samaria and Gaza since this would constitute a danger to its survival and security;

• Declaration: after the five years of autonomy, Israel would lay claim to its right to extend its sovereignty over the territories of Judea, Samaria and Gaza.

Criticism of the hard-line Israeli plan for autonomy was by no means confined to the Arab rejectionists, Egypt or the United States. Israeli Defense Minister Ezer Weizman and Foreign Minister Moshe Dayan, the two most liberal members of Begin's Cabinet, voiced grave misgivings about the plan. And Daniyel Bloch wrote in the mass-circulation Israeli newspaper *Davar* on May 21, 1979: "If the Prime Minster's autonomy program includes the continuation of complete Israeli control over the land and water in the territories and the unrestricted right to settle and if to this is added an Israeli declaration that at the end of five years Israel will demand sovereignty over all of the territories, then this is a well-tried recipe for failure. Can any informed Israeli imagine that President Sadat will agree to such a document, even as a basis for bargaining, without being called, justifiably so in this case, a traitor to the Arab cause?"

Faced with strong objections by Defense Minister Weizman and Foreign Minister Dayan, Begin agreed that Israel's plan for autonomy would not be submitted to the Americans and the Egyptians but would serve as a set of guidelines for the seven-member Israeli negotiating team. With the possible exceptions of Weizman and Dayan, that team was generally rated as exceptionally hard-line. It was led by conservative Interior Minister Yosef Burg and included, besides Weizman and Dayan, Agriculture Minister and vocal advocate of large-scale Jewish settlements Ariel Sharon, Justice Minister Shmuel Tamir and Minister Without Portfolio Moshe Mishim.

Weizman's unhappiness about the Israeli negotiating position led him to request that he be dropped from the autonomy talks. After that request was made, there were reports of serious quarrels between Prime Minister Begin and his Defense Minister and rumors that Weizman would resign from the Cabinet. The Cabinet, on June 24, granted Weizman's request that he be dropped from the negotiating team. He was not replaced.

Meanwhile Dayan, the Israeli newspaper *Yediot Aharonct* reported on June 19, "is using a form of sanctions against the [negotiating] committee and is demonstrating complete indifference to it. . . . This means that, in substance, Dayan expresses his reservations by demonstrative indifference" rather than resigning.

In addition to the autonomy plan, or guidelines, Israel made it clear that if the autonomy council tried to declare independence, its members would be arrested and the military government would be fully restored. The council, elected by more than 1.1 million Palestinians on the West Bank and Gaza, would have authority only to manage local schools, hospitals and municipal and social services but would have no legislative or judicial functions.

Palestinians would also be barred from operating radio or television stations or controlling the balance of trade, and the council would have no jurisdictions over Jewish settlers or visitors. No member of or sympathizer with the Palestine Liberation Organization could serve on the autonomy council.

It was hardly surprising that no West Bank or Gaza Palestinian agreed to join the negotiations on autonomy, despite strong American pressure on them to give the autonomy framework a chance. Palestinians argued that the Camp David agreement promised "full autonomy" for them but that Israel insisted on full control over land and water resources, gave the elected council only meaningless responsibilities, encouraged further Jewish acquisition of their lands, deprived them of any hope of eventual independence and, worst of all, legitimized Israeli sovereignty over them.

On May 22, 1979, the day after the Israeli autonomy plan was announced, the usually pro-Israeli *Washington Post* editorialized that:

> Mr. Begin conveys the impression that he has even more in mind than discouraging Palestinian participation in the autonomy talks. He seems to want to press Mr. Sadat to the very limits of his political tolerance, to defy him to break off the talks. Mr. Begin is not making it easy for supporters of the Camp David process to argue to responsible Palestinians that there is something of value in it for them. In the circumstances, perhaps the best one can hope for is that the Israeli debate on autonomy will continue, under the surface, if not in public view.

American and Egyptian officials voiced little public criticism of the Israeli autonomy plan. Whatever pressure they have exerted on Israel for a more conciliatory approach has been made in private discussions inside or outside the meetings on autonomy. No such official restraint has been shown toward Israeli insistence on establishing new Jewish settlements in occupied Arab territory. Egypt has denounced Israeli plans for new settlements and made it known that it will concentrate on this issue during negotiations on autonomy. The United States has continued to refer to the settlements as "illegal" and "harmful to the peace process."

New Settlements

Prime Minister Begin and other Israeli officials have defended the establishment of new settlements as an "absolute right" of the Jewish people to live in all parts of "Eretz Israel" or as essential for the security and the defense of Israel. "Eretz Israel," a term continually used by Begin, refers to the biblical name for the Promised Land that stretches from the Nile River in Egypt to the Tigris and Euphrates rivers in Iraq.

The argument that Israeli settlements are necessary for security and defense and therefore do not constitute a violation of the Geneva Convention has been challenged, not only by Americans and Egyptians but by Israelis as well. In April 1979, the Israeli Supreme Court ruled that settlements in the West Bank did not violate the Geneva Convention because such settlements were established for security reasons. That decision was based on an Israeli defense report.

Shortly after the decision, *The New York Times* editorialized on April 25 that:

New civilian settlements in the West Bank will serve no conceivable security requirement; the Israeli Army has long since carved out the strategic high ground. Nor is there at this point any diplomatic justification for taunting the Arab world with demonstrations of Israel's power to settle into more contested land. To promote negotiation with its other neighbors, Israel should be demonstrating that it seeks only security, not more territory.

An article in the Israeli newspaper *Ha'olam Haze* on May 9, seemed to confirm the *Times'* editorial. The article described a symposium at Tel Aviv University. One of the participants was Moshe Arens, a member of Prime Minister Begin's Cabinet and chairman of the Knesset Foreign Affairs and Security Committee. In reply to a question on Israeli settlements, Arens replied: "The settlements have no security value. It has political value only. Anyone who supports the existence of Israeli control over the West Bank and Gaza Strip should also support settlement there, even though it does not have any defensive value."

In response to intense prodding by Agriculture Minister Ariel Sharon and occasionally violent demands from the ultranationalist Gush Emunim or Faith Bloc, the Israeli government approved a new settlement near Nablus on the occupied West Bank on June 3. This was the first new settlement authorized by the government since the signing of the Egyptian-Israeli peace treaty. The settlement was named Elon Moreh after the first settlement that Abraham built after he led the children of Israel to the Promised Land.

Egypt and the United States immediately protested the settlement decision but pledged to continue the negotiations on autonomy. The State Department described the Israeli Cabinet's action as "harmful to the peace process and particularly regrettable at this time" in a statement on June 4. That statement also alleged that the confiscation of privately owned Arab land for the settlement "would add another distressing dimension" to the Cabinet's action.

"The United States is in something of a box in protesting against the Israeli Cabinet's troublesome and wrongheaded decision to set up a new West Bank settlement," the *Washington Post* editorialized on June 6. "If the administration protests too little, it invites the accusation that it privately winks at new settlements. If it protests too much, it risks confirming the accusation that Israel has no

intention of going beyond a Sinai deal: hence others would not be wise to join Camp David. So it was that the State Department termed the Cabinet decision 'harmful' to the peace process and 'regrettable' in coming just as Egyptian-Israeli talks on Palestinian autonomy opened, but indicated it would not press the matter further. It wants those talks to move." The *Post* advised the Israeli government not to surrender "its authority on the West Bank to Israeli thugs, those religious fanatics who abuse — and sometimes even kill — Arab residents."

Relations with Syria

Israeli action in establishing new settlements and insistence that more and more settlements will be set up, that Jerusalem will remain forever the "eternal capital" of Israel and that the Palestinians will never be accorded meaningful autonomy much less independence on the West Bank and Gaza confirmed to some observers that the Begin government was seeking only a separate peace with Egypt and rejected the comprehensive peace outlined in the Camp David agreements. Toward Syria, the most hard-line and uncompromising of the Arab confrontation states, however, Israeli statements have implied a certain amount of flexibility and a great deal of confusion.

In a statement after the Egyptian-Israeli peace treaty was signed on March 26, Foreign Minister Dayan suggested that in return for peace with Syria, Israel might be forced to give up the Golan Heights and the settlements it has established there, just as it surrendered the Sinai and the Jewish settlements there for peace with Egypt. Dayan was severely criticized for these remarks by Israeli government officials and the press.

It was reported later that Dayan, at a meeting of the Knesset financial committee on May 15, completely reversed himself. At that meeting, Dayan was alleged to have said that as far as he is concerned, there is no prospect whatever of Israel's withdrawal from the Golan Heights and that he himself prefers Israel to retain control over the Golan rather than have peace with Syria.

An article by Jacob Erez in the May 25 issue of the Israeli daily *Ma'ariv* revealed that "a new, original idea involving the future debates about autonomy for Judea and Samaria was recently put forward by the defense establishment. According to this idea, it would be desirable for Israel to come to an agreement about the autonomy in Judea and Samaria not with Jordan but with Syria. Those who conceived the idea claim that the possibility should not be discounted that, in the future, there may be a Syrian willingness regarding this and, therefore, Israel should put forward such a proposal as a trial balloon." The idea, Erez continued, is based on the supposition that

Syria is the main component of the eastern front. The regime there supports the PLO and permits it to act. That country sees itself as being linked with the Palestinian matter more than any other Arab country and the hostility between Syria and Israel — according to this evaluation — is based on the Israeli-Palestinian conflict. Thus, there is a direct Syrian commitment to issues connected with Judea and Samaria. On the other hand, Syria has not lost these areas in war, as Jordan has, and so its approach to them would possibly be less sharp. Those making this evaluation say further that Egypt believes that if Syria finally joins the peace process, at any stage of the debates over the autonomy, then the Arab opposition will be undermined. The Arab world cannot stand against Egypt and Syria.

Today, Egypt is prepared to reach a settlement separately, but not a separate settlement, while Syria represents the extremist anti-Israeli line. Despite all this, authoritative elements continue to believe that Israel must not avoid checking on the situation in this sphere so that options are not closed to us in the future.

Syria's involvement in any conceivable negotiations on autonomy on the West Bank and Gaza Strip would be impossible without some indication that Israel would be willing to withdraw from the Golan Heights in exchange for peace. Thus, the Israeli defense establishment's proposal for talks with Syria on autonomy would require a virtually total reversal of Israel's hard-line attitude on the Golan. Indicative of this hard line was an article in the *Jerusalem Post* on June 10. That article cited reports that "Defense Minister Ezer Weizman and Agriculture Minister Ariel Sharon have signed a petition calling for the annexation of the Golan area to Israel."

Problems Ahead

The peace process that Anwar Sadat began with his visit to Jerusalem in November 1977 has placed Israel in a rather unenviable dilemma. True, the Jewish state has signed a peace treaty with its largest and strongest Arab enemy. As of mid-1979 Israel was considered militarily strong enough to defeat any combination of Arab armies.

And if history is any guide in this volatile region, Israelis could take comfort in the supposition that the Arab unity evident after the peace treaty was signed was unlikely to continue and that coups and countercoups, short-term alliances and short-term enmities and general instability would probably characterize the Arab Middle East for some time.

On the other side of the equation, however, is Israel's long-term existence as a Jewish state surrounded by Arab enemies. The population projections alone are disconcerting to any Israeli Jew. According to the United Nations Fund for Population Activities, the current Arab population of 150 million may double to 300 million by the year 2000. In contrast, only about three million Jews now live in Israel and the occupied territories. Even an influx of Jewish immigrants and a significant increase in the low Jewish birthrate is not likely to affect the population imbalance by the end of the century.

Israel's military superiority will probably diminish in the future as well. The Arab countries now have the financial ability to purchase a plethora of advanced weapons from other countries. Training and educational programs have improved enormously throughout the Arab world and this training and education is bound to have an impact on Arab military capabilities. As is already evident, Arab leverage in oil and financial circles and increased Arab contact with the West will probably bring about a change in the international climate. Support for Israel, even in the United States, may diminish further and empathy for the Arab may increase.

Another problem for Israel in the years to come is the impact of its current hard-line policies toward the Palestinians on the West Bank and Gaza and in Israel itself. In the occupied territories, Israeli military authorities have reacted to demonstrations and other forms of non-cooperative behavior in increasingly harsh fashion. The closing of schools and the imposition of all-day curfews and heavy fines and jail sentences had become commonplace by mid-1979.

Not all Israelis were happy about these measures against Palestinians in the West Bank, Gaza Strip and East Jerusalem. In an article in the Israeli daily newspaper *Davar* on June 8, 1979, Dani Rubenstein complained:

The trap into which the Israeli government's policy in the territories is falling has no exit. The closure of schools and colleges is not making the Palestinian youths less faithful, nor is it breaking their spirit. . . . The Israeli government and its means of punishment are only strengthening Palestinian national solidarity and increasing hostility toward Israel; then the Israeli government has to resort to more stringent measures and the vicious circle tightens. . . . We appear to be strong, forcefully imposing ourselves on the hostile population to restrain it. The truth of the matter is that the counteraction is very much stronger. The territories are taking their revenge upon us, weakening us and spoiling the society and government that is ruling them. This weakened Israeli government is being forced to get used to soldiers chasing stone-throwing children and to come to terms with the closing of schools, denying education and other measures of punishment and control. . . . The Palestinian national challenge, which the Israeli government posed with the aid of a demand for annexation, settlement and non-recognition of the Palestinian people has gradually covered over all the tensions and problems in the territories. Palestinian solidarity has become stronger and national unity for an independent West Bank and a Palestinian state has conquered all. The Arab public in the territories is taking its revenge on us because it has become stronger through its moral demand for self-determination while we are becoming tired victors who are weakening as a result of our demand to continue to rule over a million people from another nation.

While Palestinian nationalism on the West Bank and Gaza has been growing since Israel captured these territories in the 1967 war, the Arabs who had remained in Israel proper after the state came into being in 1948 were widely believed to be quiescent and relatively assimilated, if not happy, as citizens of the Jewish state. A recent poll, conducted by the Institute of Research and Development of Arab Education and financed by the Ford Foundation, revealed that the majority of Palestinians were dissatisfied about Israeli sovereignty.

Seventy-five percent of those questioned supported the establishment of a Palestinian state, 60 percent did not recognize Israel's right to exist and 64 percent believed that Zionism is a racist movement. Israeli Arabs, largely through their contact with Palestinians on the occupied West Bank since the 1967 war, have grown increasingly nationalistic and increasingly unhappy about discrimination in employment, housing and education and the expropriation of Arab-owned land for Jewish housing and shopping centers. As a result of growing Palestinian nationalism within the 1948 borders, the number of Arabs arrested on security charges has spiraled in the past year.

The discontent over Israeli rule that has been evident on the West Bank and Gaza and, increasingly, in Israel itself has resulted in a sharp crackdown on Palestinian dissidents. The crackdown in turn has fueled Palestinian nationalism. As of mid-1979 it was doubtful whether this Palestinian consciousness could be allayed by a more lenient or an even harsher Israeli policy. Without some more fundamental change in Israeli attitudes in the next few years, Palestinian nationalism, coupled with a much higher Arab birthrate, was likely to compound the problems facing the Jewish state.

Similar problems were likely to affect Israel's relations with Syria and Jordan. The central question confronting this and future Israeli governments was whether the Arabs were willing to conclude a true and lasting peace with the Jewish state in exchange for an Israeli return to the pre-1967 borders and meaningful self-determination — with the possibility of statehood — for the Palestinians. Virtually all of the Arabs profess that under these conditions, they would be willing to live in peace with Israel.

In mid-1979, few Israelis seemed willing to take the chance. Trust between Arabs and Israelis was likely to be a slow and painful process. Even Egyptian President Sadat's

favorite Israeli official, Ezer Weizman, has warned that if Egypt violates the treaty, Israel will not hesitate to reoccupy the Sinai. Until there is at least a modicum of trust between the warring parties, turmoil and instability will become increasingly obvious in Israel, among the Arab treaty rejectionists and in Egypt as well.

Turmoil and instability in the Middle East will almost certainly involve the superpowers, the United States and the Soviet Union, to a greater extent than they have been involved to date. The American-sponsored Egyptian-Israeli peace treaty excluded the Russians from any role in Middle East peacekeeping. As a result, the Soviets have been forced to move closer to the radical Arab rejectionists and to improve relations with such traditionally pro-Western Arab countries as Jordan and Saudi Arabia. *(See chapter on Soviet role in the Middle East.)*

WEST BANK TALKS AND THE PALESTINIAN QUESTION

The Arab-Israeli conflict was transformed by two historic events in 1979: an Egyptian-Israeli peace treaty and a revolution in Iran. The treaty focused attention on the next item on the agenda for Middle East negotiations: autonomy for the Palestinians in territories occupied by Israel. The Iranian revolution, which replaced the monarchy of Shah Mohammed Reza Pahlavi with an "Islamic Republic," brought to the surface cultural forces of immense power.[1] The interaction of such intangible cultural forces with concrete details of boundaries, administration and security measures in the occupied territories was both explosive and difficult to comprehend. And yet much depended on understanding, and peacefully resolving, the clash of civilizations represented in the 2,305 square miles of the West Bank and Gaza — an area less than half the size of Connecticut.

Egypt and Israel began negotiations on Palestinian autonomy May 25, 1979, in Beersheba, two months after the March 26 signing of the Egyptian-Israeli peace treaty in Washington. The treaty fulfilled one of the two agreements reached by Egyptian President Anwar Sadat and Israeli Prime Minister Menachem Begin at a secluded summit meeting sponsored by President Carter at Camp David, Md., Sept. 5-17, 1979. The treaty provided for a phased Israeli withdrawal from the occupied Sinai and establishment of normal diplomatic, economic and cultural relations between the two countries. The other agreement, "A Framework for Peace in the Middle East," outlined a process for determining the future of the West Bank and Gaza. (Box, p. 27)

Between the Camp David agreement and the signing of the Egyptian-Israeli treaty, negotiations were several times threatened with complete breakdown. Finally, in a dramatic gamble, President Carter went to Cairo and Jerusalem, March 8-13, and persuaded Begin and Sadat to accept a compromise.

A key issue in dispute was Israeli rejection of an Egyptian demand that implementation of the Egyptian-Israeli treaty be "linked" to progress in establishing Palestinian autonomy. When the treaty was finally signed it was accompanied by a joint letter to Carter in which Begin and Sadat promised to start, within a month after ratification, negotiations on the West Bank and Gaza "in order to provide full autonomy to the inhabitants."

The framework provided for U.S. participation in the autonomy talks, and on July 5, 1979, Robert S. Strauss, Carter's special ambassador for Middle East negotiations, joined the talks, promising to bring to them "a bit of impatience." On July 10 Begin met with Sadat for three days of talks in Alexandria, his fourth official visit to Egypt

since the epoch-making journey Sadat made to Jerusalem, where he told the Israeli Knesset (parliament) Nov. 17, 1977, "If you want to live with us in this part of the world, in sincerity I tell you that we welcome you among us with security and safety." He warned, however, "that there can be no peace without the Palestinians."[2]

Origins of the Controversy

The West Bank and Gaza were all that remained under Arab control after Israel's war of independence in 1948. A narrow strip of territory, only 140 square miles in all, Gaza was administered by Egypt after that war. Jordan annexed territory west of the Jordan River, the so-called West Bank (see map, p. 11). This area, far bigger and more populous than Gaza, included the eastern sector of Jerusalem, which was divided by the 1949 armistice line in such a way as to place the walled Old City and its Jewish, Christian and Moslem shrines in the area under Arab control. Israel's lightning victory in the Six Day War of June 1967 brought these territories, plus Egypt's Sinai Peninsula and Syria's Golan Heights, under Israeli occupation. Israel incorporated East Jerusalem and surrounding land in its own territory, an annexation not recognized by the United States or most other countries.[3]

"A land without a people for a people without a land," was the way one of the early Zionist leaders described Palestine. But the territory the Jews had left nearly 2,000 years earlier was not vacant when their descendants returned; for centuries it had been inhabited by Arabs. Now the Arabs of Palestine are "a people without a land."[4]

Some of them (about a half million) live in the state of Israel, created when the United Nations voted to partition Palestine in 1947. (A civil war ensued in which the nascent Jewish state held off the Palestinian Arabs and the armies of the surrounding Arab states.) Others (more than one million) live in the West Bank and Gaza Strip, parts of Palestine occupied by Israel since the 1967 war. The rest are scattered among neighboring Arab states. About 1.6 million Palestinian Arabs were registered as refugees in 1977; many of them were made refugees for the second time in 1967. The victims of repeated Arab defeats, living in bitterness and often in poverty, lacking a territory they can call their own and a state to represent them among nations, this hapless people nonetheless has seized the attention of the entire world. One hundred five governments voted, against precedent, to let the Palestinians' leader address the United Nations General Assembly in November 1974, and the great powers of the world worry about the threat

1. See chapter on Iran, p. 112.

2. During the July 10-12 talks in Alexandria, Sadat announced he would visit the Israeli port of Haifa late in August. The Egyptian-Israeli negotiations were meanwhile scheduled to resume Aug. 5 in Hertzlia, a Tel Aviv suburb.

3. The United States, for instance, continued to maintain its embassy in Tel Aviv rather than Jerusalem.

4. The history of the past century is well presented in the following two books:

Abaron Cohen, Israel and the Arab World (Beacon Press, abridged edition, 1976); and J. C. Hurewitz, The Struggle for Palestine (Schocken: 1976). For background information on the Arabs of Palestine see the following: Quandt, Jabber and Lesch, The Politics of Palestinian Nationalism (University of California Press, 1973); Michael Curtis (ed.), The Palestinians (Transaction: 1975); Fawaz Turki, The Disinherited, Journal of a Palestinian Exile (Monthly Review: 1974); Thomas Kiernan, Yasir Arafat (1976); Frank H. Epp, The Palestinians (Herald Press: 1976); Moshe Ma'oz (ed.) Palestinian Arab Politics (Jerusalem Academic Press: 1975); Sabri Jiryis, The Arabs in Israel (Montly Review: 1976), and Jureidini and Hazen, The Palestinian Movement in Politics (Lexington: 1976).

the Palestinians pose to international peace. How has such a small and unfortunate people gained such attention?

Palestinian organizations trace their growing influence to their reliance on violence, and many observers would agree. "It is sadly true," an American diplomat in the Middle East observed, "that you seem to have to hurt someone to get any attention, and the Palestinians didn't get any attention for 20 years."[5]

But the record of terrorism by which the Palestinian organizations forced the world to consider their demands could exclude them from negotiations to deal with those demands. The Israelis have refused to talk with this "coalition of murderers,"[6] and the Egyptians have feared that Palestinian intransigence could prevent a peace they need to regain their own occupied territory and to rebuild their economy.

Recognition of the PLO

The United Nations General Assembly voted Oct. 14, 1974, to recognize the Palestine Liberation Organization (PLO), a federation of Palestinian groups, as "the representative of the Palestinian people." The vote was 105 to 4, with 20 abstentions; only Israel, the United States, the Dominican Republic and Bolivia voted against the resolution. On Nov. 13, 1974, Yasir Arafat, leader of the PLO and head of its largest guerrilla group, Al Fatah, addressed the assembly. It was the first occasion when a nongovernmental organization participated in one of the assembly debates. "I have come bearing an olive branch and a freedom fighter's gun," Arafat said. "Do not let the olive branch fall from my hand."

Arafat's speech followed a unanimous agreement by 20 Arab heads of state, meeting in Rabat, Morocco, Oct. 26-28, 1974, to recognize the PLO as "the sole legitimate representative of the Palestinian people on any liberated Palestinian territory." Jordan's King Hussein, whose government had ruled the West Bank territory from the 1948 partition of Palestine until it was occupied by Israel in the 1967 war, abandoned his bitter opposition to the PLO claims and accepted the agreement "without any reservations." Since then Hussein has maintained considerable contact with Arab leaders on the West Bank.

The removal of the moderate Hussein from negotiations regarding the West Bank dismayed Western countries hoping for a compromise peace in which Israel would yield territories occupied in 1967. Because Israel refused to deal with the PLO, the prospects for peace talks appeared grim after the Rabat conference. Israeli Premier Yitzhak Rabin, in an interview with *U.S. News & World Report* after talks with President Ford in Washington June 11 and 12, 1975, reiterated the Israeli refusal to negotiate with the PLO, let alone accept its rule of the West Bank, because its goal, he said, is "the elimination of Israel." Rabin said that a "Jordanian-Palestinian state" is the solution of the Palestine issue."[7]

When Menachem Begin became Israeli prime minister in June 1977, he not only ruled out any thought of a Palestinian state, he also indicated that Israel would permanently retain the West Bank and Gaza Strip areas in which such a state could be created. "Such a state can

---

5. Quoted by Al McConogha, *Minneapolis Tribune*, June 1, 1975.
6. The phrase used by Israeli Ambassador to the U.S., Simcha Dinitz, in an interview with *Worldview* magazine, July-August 1977.
7. *U.S. News & World Report*, June 23, 1975, p. 30.

> ## 'Framework for Peace'
>
> Following are key provisions of the "Framework for Peace in the Middle East" agreed to by Egyptian President Anwar Sadat and Israeli Prime Minister Menachem Begin, Sept. 17, 1978, at Camp David, Md.:
>
> • The final status of the West Bank and Gaza, the location of boundaries, and the nature of security arrangements will be determined by Egypt, Israel, Jordan and elected representatives from these territories after a five-year transition period.
>
> • During the transition period, an elected self-governing authority will replace the existing Israeli military government.
>
> • Israeli armed forces will be withdrawn to specified security locations as soon as the self-governing authority is elected.
>
> • Jordan will be invited to join in negotiating the details of the transitional agreement.
>
> • The "modalities" for admitting Palestinians displaced from the West Bank and Gaza by the 1967 war will be decided by a committee of representatives of Egypt, Israel, Jordan and the self-governing authority.
>
> • Arrangements for internal and external security will include a strong local police force which may include Jordanians.
>
> • The United States is invited to participate in negotiating the implementation of the agreement.

never come into being" Begin said on his July 15 arrival in New York, prior to his meeting with President Carter.

Post-Rabat developments indicated that the setback to Hussein might have been temporary. The PLO failed to form a government in exile and to prepare for negotiations with Israel, as intended by the conference. Although its official position toward Israel softened somewhat since it achieved its new status, the PLO still refused to publicly acknowledge a goal of coexistence and permanent peace with Israel. To do so would probably split the organization and give extremist groups an opportunity to win the support of the many rank-and-file Palestinians unwilling to abandon their dream of eventually returning to all of Palestine as their homeland.

However, in May 1977, just before the Israeli election that brought Begin to power, Arafat told syndicated columnist Georgie Anne Geyer that recognition of Israel was possible and Arafat was prepared to discuss guaranteeing Israel's security. The PLO was "embarking on a new program of international legitimacy," Arafat told Geyer.[8]

Arafat's goal of a "secular democratic state" for all of Palestine by definition excluded a distinctly Jewish state and raised deep fears in Israelis about their future status and even their presence amidst an Arab majority. But in his United Nations speech, Arafat repeatedly referred to this goal as a "dream," and he has indicated PLO readiness to accept a Palestinian state in the occupied territories as an interim arrangement.

Struggle Over Homeland

The Palestinians were the chief victims of Zionist insistence on the establishment of a Jewish state in part of Palestine and Arab insistence on destroying the new state.

---

8. Georgie Anne Geyer, *The Washington Post*, 28 May 1977, p. A13.

Defining Palestine, Palestinians

The word "Palestine" is of Roman origin, referring to the biblical land of the Philistines. The name fell into disuse for centuries and was revived by the British as an official title for an area mandated to their control by the League of Nations in 1920 after the breakup of the Turkish Ottoman Empire in World War I.

The British mandate also applied to Transjordan (now Jordan), although it did not lie within the area designation "Palestine." Transjordan lay entirely east of the River Jordan, and Palestine lay entirely to the west.

However, because the mandate applied to both regions, there is the argument that "Palestinian" applied to persons east as well as west of the River Jordan. There is a further argument that it applies not just to Arabs—as is common practice today—but also to Jews and Christians in the former mandated area.

Palestine as a legal entity ceased to exist in 1948, when Britain, unable to keep control, relinquished its mandate and Israel declared its independence. The previous year, Palestine had been partitioned by the United Nations into Arab and Jewish sectors. Israel enlarged its partitioned areas in a war of independence in 1948-49. Other parts of Palestine fell under the control of Jordan and Egypt.

Who shoulders the major blame for the Palestinian plight—the Zionists, the Arab countries of Egypt, Jordan, Lebanon, Syria and Iraq, or the Palestinians themselves—depends to a large extent on the allegiance of those affixing blame.

Thus, the pro-Zionist publication *Near East Report* argued on July 17, 1974, that "those familiar with the history of 1948 [the year Israel declared its statehood] know that the Palestinians could have had their national homeland and that the Israelis accepted the establishment of a Palestinian state and at that time were ready to live in peace with it. But the neighboring Arab states invaded Palestine in order to crush the Jewish state and divide it up. The Palestinians were the victims of the Arab war against Israel."

A totally different account came from Sami Hadawi, a Palestinian refugee. Hadawi wrote that as soon as the United Nations adopted its resolution of Nov. 29, 1947, calling for the partition of Palestine into Jewish and Arab states, "Zionist underground forces came out into the open and began to attack Arab towns and villages, driving out all the non-Jewish inhabitants and massacring those who stood by their homes...."[9]

Similarly, Zionists and Palestinians blame each other for the massacres that followed partitioning and for an Arab exodus then and also after the establishment of the Jewish state on May 14, 1948.[10] Israel contends that Arab governments broadcast appeals to the Palestinians to leave until Arab armies liberated their homelands—a contention that Arabs label a "myth."[11] Regardless of the truth or falsity of the matter, it is generally acknowledged that Israelis razed property abandoned by Palestinian Arabs to discourage their return.

Whatever the basic reasons for the departure, some 525,000 to 900,000 Palestinians—there is no agreement as to exactly how many—had fled their homeland by the end of 1948. Most of them left with no material possessions and were dependent on the goodwill of Arab countries where they sought refuge—or on the United Nations—for food, clothing and shelter.

Soon after independence, the Knesset (Parliament) passed the "law of return," which provided that "every Jew has a right to immigrate to Israel." Don Peretz noted in his famous study, *Israel and the Palestine Arabs* (1958), that the abandoned property of the refugees "was one of the greatest contributions toward making Israel a viable state." He reported that of the 370 new Jewish settlements established between 1948 and the beginning of 1953, 350 were on absentee [owned] property, and nearly a third of the new immigrants (250,000) settled in urban areas abandoned by the Arabs."

West Bank Economy

Israeli occupation unquestionably has improved economic conditions. "Wherever one goes on the West Bank," John M. Goshko wrote June 1, 1975, in *The Washington Post,* "the eye constantly is struck by those symbols—late model cars on the roads, forests of TV antennas sprouting over every town, running water in remote villages—that are the physical evidence of growing affluence. From what was essentially an area on relief only a decade ago, the West Bank today stands on the threshold of becoming a consumer society."[12]

The territory has no natural resources, and half its population is under age 14—conditions which make its economic prospects bleak. But West Bank agriculture has benefited from expanded markets and Israeli technical assistance. A tenfold increase in the number of tractors in the area since 1967—from 120 to 1,200—is one indicator of the change under occupation. Agricultural production has increased 12 per cent annually in real terms, and the West Bank's gross national product has risen by an average of 18 per cent annually since 1967.[13]

About one-third of the West Bank labor force (40,000 out of 120,000 total) worked in Israel. "Palestinian workers in Israel have become a vital element in Israel's economy," according to John Richardson, former president of the American Near East Refugee Aid. "They are 45 per cent cheaper to employ than Israelis, and they are available in large numbers to do the menial work that Israelis are learning to disdain." Richardson viewed the integration of the West Bank and Gaza into the Israeli economy as deliberate policy and cited an Israeli Defense Ministry document:

> The areas are a supplementary market for Israeli goods and service on the one hand and a source of factors of production, especially unskilled labor, for the Israeli economy on the other.[14]

In 1977, the Carnegie Endowment for International Peace released a major study discussing what happened to the West Bank and Gaza Strip economies since 1967. In the

9. Sami Hadawi, *Palestine: Loss of a Heritage* (1963), p. 2.
10. See David Pryce-Jones' *The Fact of Defeat: Palestinian Refugees and Guerrillas* (1972), p. 15. See also "Arab Guerrillas," *Editorial Research Reports,* 1969 Vol. I, pp. 316-23.
11. Fawaz Turki, for example, wrote in *The Disinherited: Journal of a Palestinian Exile* (1972): "An examination of the monitoring records in the West revealed no such appeals to the population of Palestine from neighboring states; rather it was revealed that the Palestinians were exhorted *not to leave.*" (His emphasis.)
12. John M. Goshko, "The West Bank: Going It Alone," *The Washington Post,* June 1, 1975, p. C1.
13. Ibid., p. C5.
14. John Richardson, "Special Issue on the West Bank and Gaza," *The Link,* published by Americans for Middle East Understanding, Spring 1975, pp. 2, 5.

book's preface, the President of Carnegie, Thomas L. Hughes, noted that the author, Brian Van Arkadie, "has framed his appraisal in terms that could be meaningful as a baseline for thinking about the future of the West Bank and the Gaza Strip." Van Arkadie, in summary, found that "In 1967, the Israeli government did not conceive or attempt to implement any systematic, large-scale plan to alter the economic structure of the West Bank and the Gaza Strip. Nor was there an Israeli master-plan for changing the external economic relationships of the two occupied territories. For the West Bank and the Gaza Strip economies, however, what happened after 1967 was more complex and no less profound than if such a master-plan had actually existed."[15]

Rise of the PLO

Israel's refusal to repatriate more than a handful of Palestinian refugees and the Arab countries' hesitation about resettling them[16] led to the establishment of the United Nations Relief and Works Agency (UNRWA) to care for the refugees. Describing the plight of those in the refugee camps in the mid-1950s, Don Peretz wrote: "Many living in leaky, torn tents were middle-class urbanites who had owned modest but adequate houses in their native land.... The self-reliance and individual initiative of former tradesmen and farmers were drowned in the boredom and frustration which the camps bred...."

This resentment and frustration contributed to the growth of terrorist groups and the eventual formation of the Palestine Liberation Organization. In the early 1950s, some of the Arab governments trained and subsidized groups of Palestinian guerrillas. Egypt, for example, set up battalions of "Palestinian Fedayeen" under the direct command of Egyptian officers in the Gaza Strip. But according to Fawaz Turki, "the first clandestine organization that was a truly Palestinian expression" was Al Fatah ("conquest"), formed in the early 1950s by Palestinian students at Stuttgart University in West Germany.

One of these students was Yasir Arafat, alias Abu Ammur, who left Jerusalem with his family during the 1948 war and settled in Gaza. Arafat had become convinced that the Palestinians must look to themselves, not the Arab governments, for the recovery of their homeland. Within a few years, Al Fatah and other Palestinian groups were established in Europe and the Middle East to coordinate Palestinian liberation strategy. Members of the groups received military training in Algeria and by the early 1960s were conducting terrorist raids in Israel.

The Palestine Liberation Organization was established by Arab heads of state at the first National Palestinian Congress—held in the Jordanian sector of Jerusalem in May 1964—before the sector was seized by Israel in the 1967 war. The delegates declared that "the Palestinian problem will never be resolved except in Palestine and by the force of arms."

The PLO did not actually emerge as an autonomous faction in the Arab world, however, until Israel's victory in the Six Day War. Yehoshafat Harkabi maintained that the defeat of Arab armies raised the stature of the Palestinians, because only they were carrying on the fight. The Palestinians, he wrote, "were transformed from an inferior factor into standard-bearers of Arab nationalism and a

source of pride."[17] The PLO became more militant. The incident which more than any other gave the PLO stature in the Arab world was an Israeli attack on an Al Fatah camp in the Jordanian village of Karameh on March 21, 1968. In a 12-hour battle, about 300 guerrillas held off Israeli attackers, inflicted heavy losses and forced them to retreat. Young Palestinians rushed to join the movement.

The increased confidence and militance of the PLO were evident in the Palestine National Covenant, revised by the National Congress in Cairo in July 1968. It holds, among other things, that "armed struggle is the only way to liberate Palestine" (Article 9) and that "the partitioning of Palestine in 1947 and the establishment of the state of Israel are entirely illegal" (Article 19). In the new state the PLO proposed to create, only "The Jews who had normally resided in Palestine until the beginning of the Zionist invasion will be considered Palestinians" (Article 6).

Although the first Zionist immigrants arrived in the 1880s, Palestinians have used various dates at different times as the cutoff point in determining which Jews could remain in a Palestinian state. Sometimes 1917, the date of Britain's Balfour Declaration supporting a Jewish "national home" in Palestine, is used; at other times 1947, the date of partition, has been invoked. Palestinians now state that all Jews presently in Israel could remain, but past inconsistency on this point does not reassure Israelis, who in any case have no intention of living in a non-Jewish Palestinian state.

Guerrilla-National Uneasiness

One of the ironies of the Palestinian predicament has been that PLO sympathizers have often displayed as much animosity toward their supposed benefactors and friends, the Arab states, as they have toward the Zionist enemy. And the Arab states directly involved — Egypt, Syria, Jordan and Lebanon — have, while paying lip service to the Palestinian cause, tried to restrain the commandos. Jordan

---

17. Yehoshafat Harkabi, "The Position of the Palestinians in the Israeli-Arab Conflict and Their National Covenant," *New York University Journal of International Law & Politics,* spring 1970, p. 218.

Estimates of Palestinian Population, January 1978	
Area	**Population**
West Bank (including East Jerusalem)	825,000
Gaza	450,000
Israel*	500,000
Jordan (East Bank)	1,100,000
Lebanon	350,000
Syria	250,000
Kuwait	250,000
Saudi Arabia	50,000
Other Gulf States	75,000
Americas and Europe	175,000
Total	4,025,000

*Israel refers to its Arabs as "non-Jewish minorities" and considers them Israeli citizens. A majority of Israel's Arabs live in Galilee.

Source: Data compiled by Emile A. Nakhleh in *The West Bank and Gaza,* published by the American Enterprise Institute for Public Policy Research, Washington, D.C., 1979.

---

15. Brian Van Arkadie, *Benefits and Burdens: A Report on the West Bank and Gaza Strip Economies Since 1967* (Carnegie Endowment for International Peace, 1977).
16. The one exception was Jordan, the poorest of the Arab countries, which accorded the Palestinians citizenship.

and Lebanon and most recently and devastatingly, Syria, have event used their armed forces against them.

Arab Dilemma

The Palestinian presence has created a dilemma for Arab governments. A complete assimilation of the refugees would probably have destroyed the delicate political and religious balance in Lebanon and caused a dislocation of the Egyptian and Syrian economies. To allow the guerrillas to use their territory as a base from which to attack Israel invites quick and strong retaliation on and around the refugee camps. And to permit PLO terrorist attacks would make Israel even more reluctant to return the territories occupied in 1967. Moreover, most of the Palestinians have not desired assimilation in the countries in which they found themselves.

The concept of "the return" to Palestine is deep and widespread among the Palestinians. Palestinian children are taught that their homeland is this or that village in Palestine — a homeland which most have never even seen.

The strongest action against the guerrillas until the civil war in Lebanon was taken by King Hussein of Jordan in 1970 after years of seeing their raids from Jordan bring Israeli reprisals against his country. In trying to stop the raids, he incurred the wrath of extreme leftist guerrillas, who threatened his life and promised to "revolutionize" his kingdom. Hussein's troops clashed with the guerrillas in September 1970 and succeeded in closing all but a few of their bases.[18] The next July, the Jordanian army attacked the remaining outposts. Some of the guerrillas were captured and imprisoned, while others fled to Israel or Syria. Under pressure from the other Arab governments, Hussein later declared an amnesty for all terrorists except those who had been convicted of murder or espionage. This did little to lessen PLO demands for his overthrow and the destruction of the "reactionary" Hashemite kingdom.

Lebanon, too, even before the civil war in 1975, took military action against the guerrillas. After armed clashes in 1969, the PLO was restricted to bases in southern Lebanon under the supervision of the Lebanese army. This arrangement came to be known as the Cairo Agreement. Then, in May 1973, after Israeli retaliation in Lebanon for commando attacks in Israel, the army again fought with the PLO. The fighting lasted two weeks and resulted in more than 350 deaths and 700 injuries. As was the case with Jordan, Syria threatened to send military aid to the Palestinians while Israel was ready to assist Lebanon. Syrian troops did cross the border, but their quick withdrawal prevented a widening of the conflict. Further armed skirmishes between Lebanese rightists and Palestinians broke out in 1974 and 1975—and helped precipitate the civil war. The rightists began demanding that the government take control of the refugee camps. The PLO was equally insistent that the Palestinians retain control. By mid-June 1975, a series of efforts to form a new government had failed, and though PLO leader Arafat was said to want to avoid bringing on another civil war, he failed. *(See chapter on Lebanon, p. 137)*

The PLO fears that the Arab governments might make deals with Israel at the Palestinians' expense were exacerbated when the U.N. Security Council adopted Resolution 242 on Nov. 22, 1967. The resolution called for, among other things, "the withdrawal of Israel from territories occupied" in exchange for recognition of Israel by the Arab countries. Jordan and Egypt endorsed 242, provided that it was interpreted to mean all, not part, of the territories Israel seized. Syria did not accept the resolution until after the October 1973 war. The PLO has repeatedly denounced the resolution on the ground that it refers to refugees, not Palestinians, and puts forth no specific plan for a "just settlement."

Changing PLO Diplomacy

But after the 1973 war, the PLO gained considerable esteem. Gradually the "refugee" problem became recognized as one involving peoplehood and a national identity. In October 1974 the leaders of the Arab states clearly took the leadership of the Palestinian Arabs from King Hussein and Jordan and gave it to Yasir Arafat and the PLO. By 1976 the PLO had become the twenty-first full member of the Arab League. By 1977, more than 100 countries had granted the PLO some form of recognition.

The PLO, some analysts indicated, had offered the United States two specific signs in the first half of 1977—in addition to various ambiguous statements—of willingness to consider entering a process that could lead to coexistence with Israel. First, in clause 15 of the political declaration passed at the Palestine National Council meeting in March, the PLO indicated a willingness "to participate in all international conferences...dealing with the problem of Palestine and the Arab-Zionist conflict." In short, the PLO was willing to go to Geneva, where it would find itself negotiating with Israel, and consider a peaceful solution. Second, the new executive committee which emerged from the March PNC meeting excluded members of the so-called "rejection front" who refused to consider peaceful coexistence with Israel under any conditions. "This was the most significant political decision of the National Council meeting," the PLO's London representative, Said Hammami, noted, "That's the Palestinians' message, the signal."[19]

Throughout the first half of 1977, the PLO continued in its attempt to reach some kind of agreement with the United States that would bring the PLO into the diplomatic process. Beginning in November 1976, when two PLO officials visited the United States to talk with American Jewish representatives and indirectly with U.S. government officials, the PLO sought to open a Washington information office staffed by an official of the organization. The office was opened in 1978.

The PLO has had for some years important relations with the Soviet Union, where it has had considerable support. On April 7, 1977, Communist Party Secretary Leonid Brezhnev publicly met Yasir Arafat for the first time. Brezhnev confirmed at that time Soviet support for creation of an independent Palestinian state.

Following the signing of the Egyptian-Israeli peace treaty, relations between Hussein and the PLO, long complex and uncertain, showed signs of improvement. Moreover, the PLO found new stature within the Arab League, as its members joined in unanimous denunciation of the treaty and expelled Egypt from its ranks. *(See Arab reaction chapter, p. 15)*

---

18. During the fighting, a secret terrorist arm, Black September, was set up. It claimed responsibility for, among other things, the murder of Jordanian Prime Minister Wasfi al-Tal in Cairo Nov. 29, 1971, and the massacre of Israeli athletes at the Olympic Games in Munich in September 1972. For the story of Hussein's expulsion of the PLO and the growth of Black September see John K. Cooley, *Green March Black September* (Frank Cass, London: 1973).

19. See "PLO Awaits U.S. Reaction to New Stance on Peace," *The Washington Post*, 27 March 1977.

Barriers to a Palestinian Solution

When victorious Israeli forces captured the West Bank and Gaza in the Six Day War of June 1967, more than one million Palestinian Arabs came under Israeli occupational control. According to one recent estimate, about 825,000 live in the West Bank (including East Jerusalem) and 450,000 in Gaza *(see table, p. 29)*. But the triumph contained the seeds of tragedy. If Israel were to retain the West Bank and Gaza, the higher birthrate of the Arab population might eventually challenge the Jewish character of Israel. The Jews, whose numbers in Israel reached three million by the 1970s, had suffered too much as minorities in foreign lands ever to tolerate minority status in the land of their origins, where they had at terrible cost created a new state of their own.

In addition to the demographic threat, the occupation produced a less tangible, but no less sinister, challenge to the kind of national identity for which Israel had been created. The refugees who had suffered so terribly at the hands of hostile governments suddenly found themselves ruling a defeated people. After generations of feeling powerless, victory was inevitably sweet — and troubling. "Occupation corrupts," Uri Avneri, a leading Israeli dove, has written, "and lengthy occupation corrupts absolutely." A professor at Hebrew University in Jerusalem expressed a similar anxiety. "I am not concerned about our young kids who do [military] duty on the West Bank and come back to the kibbutz agonizing over having beaten up Palestinian youngsters," he said. "What worries me is the growing number who come back and actually say they liked it."[20]

The dilemma of occupying a land they wanted and a people they did not want has divided the Israelis. Former Israeli Defense Minister Moshe Dayan, "who more than anyone else set the character of the Israeli occupation,"[21] sought to integrate the life of the West Bank and Gaza with that of Israel. "For him," wrote Larry L. Fabian, director of the Carnegie Peace Endowment's Middle East Program, "this meant an intermixing of populations and activities across newly porous borders, including establishment of Israeli settlements in populated as well as unpopulated areas of the territories." Dayan's hope "was to create such a network of functional ties that issues of future sovereignty and precise political boundaries would become secondary."

Dayan's policy of maximum integration was never fully implemented. It met opposition from some leaders of the ruling Labor Party who feared the consequences of incorporation of so large an Arab population in Israel. In fact, the Labor Party government accepted the United Nations Security Council Resolution 242 of Nov. 22, 1967, which called for Israeli withdrawal from occupied territories as part of a general peace that would guarantee Israel's recognition, boundaries and security.[22]

But with the 1977 election victory of the Likud Party led by Menachem Begin, Israeli policy shifted sharply to the right. His government pressed ahead vigorously with Israeli settlements in the West Bank and Gaza, justifying them on the ground that Israel had "liberated" rather than occupied its biblical land. Begin has repeatedly insisted that Israel would never yield sovereignty over Judea, Samaria and East Jerusalem.

---

20. Quoted in *The Christian Science Monitor*, June 11, 1979.
21. So described by Larry L. Fabin in a prologue to a 1977 report published by the Carnegie Endowment for International Peace, entitled "Benefits and Burdens: A Report on the West Bank and Gaza Strip Economies Since 1967," p. 8.
22. The phrase "withdrawal of Israeli armed forces from territories occupied in the recent conflict" was deliberately vague as to whether they were to withdraw from all or only part of the territories.

How the Territories Are Ruled

In Gaza, the Israeli military administration established in 1967 assumed the authority of the previous Egyptian military governor; in the West Bank, the area's military commander was explicitly granted the legal authority of the pre-1967 Jordanian regime. The result was that Israeli policy was carried out on the West Bank through the forms of Jordanian law.

Twenty-five municipal governments on the West Bank plus that of the city of Gaza constitute the highest level of Palestinian political institutions in the occupied territories. Although Jordanian municipal law gives these local governments authority to act in 40 different areas, in practice their actions must have prior approval of the military government.

As a result, a 1979 study of the territories by Emile A. Nakhleh observed: "A wide gap exists between the theoretical or legal authority of West Bank local governments and the way they actually function."

The hostility this gap generates is aggravated by financial difficulties which force the municipalities to seek grants or loans from other Arab countries or from the military authorities, with political conditions often attached by the latter. "Often the municipalities are left frustrated and helpless, with their people angry and their towns barely operating," Nakhleh wrote.

Emile A. Nakhleh, The West Bank and Gaza: Toward the Making of a Palestinian State, American Enterprise Institute for Public Policy Research, Washington, 1979, pp. 10, 11.

Jordan's or PLO Role in West Bank's Future

In spite of its commitment to retain these occupied territories, the Israeli government might be forced to yield at least part of them by a combination of factors: pressure from the United States, demands for compromise from moderate Israelis, and fear that Egypt might rejoin Israel's Arab enemies unless the Palestinians gained substantial satisfaction. Israelis were profoundly apprehensive that any yielded territory would serve the Palestinians as a base for terrorism and be viewed by them as only the first step toward the recovery of the rest of Palestine from a retreating Israel.

That is one reason why the Israeli Labor government had insisted that any territory given up on the West Bank be closely linked with Jordan. The government of King Hussein, which controlled the West Bank from 1948 to 1967, was more moderate than the Palestine Liberation Organization and had largely repressed Palestinian commandoes operating from its territory in order to avoid Israeli retaliation.

Perhaps more important, the Jordanian government was centered east of the Jordan River and its regime was dependent on the loyalties of its East Bank subjects, especially the bedouins who formed the backbone of the Jordanian army. Israelis believed, therefore, that a West Bank under Jordanian control would be a safer neighbor than an independent Palestinian state with irredentist claims on Israeli territory.

Another advantage of a Jordanian rather than Palestinian West Bank, from the Israeli point of view, was that Jordan's capital is Amman. If the Palestinians secured a state of their own, they would insist on East Jerusalem as its capital.

Although Begin himself had commanded a Zionist terrorist group, the Irgun Zwai Leumi, during the British mandate, he has continued the Israeli government's refusal to negotiate with PLO "murderers."

Former Israeli Foreign Minister Abba Eban, however, has said that an Arab destiny in the West Bank was inevitable and that he would offer the region not only to Jordan, but to any regime that would not be hostile to Israeli security. "We ought to be considering how Israel should rescue its basic interests, which are modest but crucial territorial change, demilitarization, military balance, mutual accessibility — those things which would make an Arab West Bank feasible for Israel."[23]

Israelis who have expressed a willingness to negotiate with the PLO have usually attached as a prior condition its renunciation of all claims to the territory of Israel proper. Palestinians have complained that such a disclaimer is their "last card," and to give it up in advance of negotiations would rob them of bargaining leverage. Such a renunciation would also deeply divide the Palestinians. Those whose homes were within Israel's pre-1967 borders have been especially reluctant to give up their dream of recovering more than the West Bank and Gaza. Moreover, those among the estimated two million Palestinians living in other Arab countries who would return to Palestine if that were possible would not find ample room in the West Bank and Gaza.

The Israeli fear that a Palestinian state would, sooner or later, revive claims to all of Palestine has been accompanied by another anxiety. One of Israel's leading intellectuals, Saul Friedlander, explained that even among the Israelis "who are not in favor of annexing the West Bank and Gaza Strip, and among those who know that the security problems may eventually be resolved, there is profound resistance to granting sovereign rights to the Palestinians in part of Palestine." Such resistance, Friedlander wrote, "derives partly from the latent fear that recognition of the rights of Palestinians means, in itself, some measure of recognition of the justice of their arguments . . . and may, therefore, eventually imply a questioning of the very basis of Zionism."[24]

Begin made no apologies for basing Israel's claim to sovereignty in East Jerusalem and in Judea and Samaria — as he referred to the occupied territories of the West Bank — on the Bible. But many Israelis, whether motivated by a more secular spirit, a willingness to recognize rival Palestinian claims, a sense of a need for compromise, or recognition that biblical claims to territory have scant legitimacy among non-Jews, have sought to downplay religious motives in negotiating the future of the occupied territories. They focused instead on the danger that a hostile and independent Palestinian state could emerge on Israel's eastern border.

"I tell you we shall keep it," one young Israeli said of the West Bank. "We shall never give it up. I don't care that King David came from Bethlehem. That's for tourists. What I care about is this: from Bethlehem a sniper could put a bullet right through the window of my apartment."[25]

It is misleading to separate religion and security as motives for Israeli claims to the occupied territories. Even many of the most avowedly secular Israelis feel an attachment to the biblical lands that is religious in intensity if not in doctrine. Moreover, an Israeli analyst has observed, "The ideological commitment often determines the strategic arguments.

"Usually," he continued "people who are ideologically committed to retaining the whole of the land in Israeli hands also evolve strategic considerations which go with this position. . . .It rarely works the other way around, with strategic arguments shaping ideological ones."[26]

In any case, the love of the land of Israel itself has military value. Without that passionate Zionist attachment to the land, which motivated secular as well as religious Jews to great risks and sacrifices, Israel would not have been created or preserved in the midst of enemies. The driving force behind Israel's existence is so attached to territory that a loss of territory would challenge its spiritual as well its material well-being.

Problems Ahead

While both Israelis and Arabs naturally looked to the ultimate outcome of the negotiations that were just beginning in mid-1979, the Camp David accords provided only a transitional "framework" in which the contending parties could resolve their conflicts.

Participation by the Palestinians in the elected transitional authority in the occupied territories and in the later negotiations to determine the final status of the West Bank and Gaza has been considered crucial by the United States to the fulfillment of the Camp David accord. That accord had been greeted with anger and dismay by the Palestinians. Mayors, members of municipal councils, and leaders in education, religion, the professions and labor unions in the occupied territories issued a declaration Oct. 1, 1978, stating: "The so-called 'self-government' proposals for the occupied West Bank and Gaza only legitimize and strengthen the Israeli occupation."[27]

Even the mayor of Gaza, Rashad al-Shawa, a moderate who did not sign the declaration and who was once prepared to support autonomy if the United States would secure a freeze on new Israeli settlements and publicly commit itself to Palestinian self-determination, has said that the current Israeli version of autonomy would only "legalize Israeli occupation under a different image." He added: "We would rather continue as we are because we would always have the right to claim that Israel is occupying our land by force."[28]

The Jerusalem Question

At one time, the settlements on the West Bank were viewed by many Israelis as "bargaining chips" to be given up in return for concessions from the Arabs on other issues. While Begin's public statements suggested that nothing could be further from his mind, if he eventually concluded that pressure from the United States left him no choice but to give up most of Judea and Samaria, the sacrifice would seem all the greater because of the number of Israeli settlers and the passionate attachment to the land expressed in the settlement. After such a sacrifice, it would be extremely

23. Quoted in a *New York Times* editorial, June 10, 1979.

24. Quoted in "Benefits and Burdens: A Report on the West Bank and Gaza Strip Economies Since 1967," Carnegie Endowment for International Peace, 1977, p. 9.

25. Quoted by Martin Woolacott in the *Manchester Guardian Weekly*, June 17, 1979.

26. *Israelis Speak,* edited by Larry L. Fabian and Ze'ez Schiff, the Carnegie Endowment for International Peace, 1977, p. 23. This book records talks among 13 leading Israeli intellectuals of diverse professional and political positions who were assembled for a week of discussions.

27. Distributed by the Palestine Human Rights Campaign, Washington, D.C.

28. Statement in a Beirut press conference, quoted by Trudy Rubin in *The Nation,* June 20, 1979, p. 787.

difficult to urge that Israelis also make concessions on the holy city of Jerusalem.

"The conventional wisdom seems indisputable," wrote an American living in Israel. "Gaza will be harder to make a deal for than the Sinai, the West Bank will be many times more difficult than Gaza, and the hardest of all will be Jerusalem."[29] The sources of the Jewish attachment to Jerusalem are deep. The dream of a return to the City of David, expressed in countless rites and symbols of Jewish life, has kept alive a sense of identity and of hope through generations of dispersal and persecution.

With the capture in 1967 of the walled Old City in the Jordanian-controlled eastern sector of Jerusalem, the improbable dream came true. To yield political sovereignty over that sector, as the Arabs have demanded, would seem to most Jews, secular no less than religious, a betrayal of their history and their sacrifices.

Though it is less sacred in Moslem eyes than Mecca or Medina, Jerusalem is also holy to Islam, the site from which Mohammed is said to have ascended to heaven. The passion and crucifixion of Jesus in Jerusalem makes the city sacred also to Christians. There is agreement on all

sides that, whatever the political future of East Jerusalem, followers of all three religions should have free access to their shrines, though Jews fear a return to the pre-1967 situation when Jordan denied them access to the Old City.

The question of sovereignty in Jerusalem seems insoluble, but it may contain a hidden opportunity. The religions that contend for its soil and buildings have all summoned their believers to a loyalty that transcends soil and buildings. And among Jews and Moslems in recent times, as among Christians in the Middle Ages, a competing spiritual identity tempered the nationalism that now demands absolute sovereignty.

If something of the spirit of those traditions can be revived, it might lead in Jerusalem to imaginative departures from Western ideas of sovereignty that now prevail throughout the world. In an age when global dependence on resources such as oil and proliferation of nuclear weapons have made absolute sovereignty a dangerous anachronism, Jerusalem might supply what the Camp David "framework" declared as a goal of Arab-Israeli peace: "a model for coexistence and cooperation among nations." On the other hand, Jerusalem may supply a model of what Bernard Lewis and Bernhard Anderson called the idolatry of nationalism, the holy city serving as an idol that demands human sacrifices.

---

29. Edward Grossman, "Jerusalem of 'Peace,'" *Commentary*, June 1979, p. 66.

A DEEPENING ROLE AS MIDDLE EAST CONCILIATOR

In its withdrawal from Vietnam, the United States dramatically reduced its presence in the Far East; in the Middle East, however, the 1973 Arab-Israeli war and subsequent developments have propelled American diplomacy into a decisive role.

The Nixon, Ford and Carter administrations have all been deeply active in attempting to defuse the explosive conflict. First it was Secretary of State Henry A. Kissinger's "shuttle diplomacy" which aimed to bring about small agreements which might improve the climate and lead to discussions on the major issues at a later date. Then President Jimmy Carter took over and began discussing a com-

---

"To let this opportunity [for peace] pass could mean disaster not only for the Middle East, but perhaps for the international political and economic order as well."

President Jimmy Carter
May 1977

---

prehensive settlement to be implemented over a period of years once agreed upon. Within a month of coming into office, Carter emphasized that 1977 "may be the most propitious time for a genuine settlement since the beginning of the Arab-Israeli conflict almost 30 years ago. To let this opportunity pass could mean disaster not only for the Middle East, but perhaps for the international political and economic order as well."

The impact of the oil embargo at the time of the 1973 war and of rising oil prices ever since has demonstrated that the daily lives of Americans could be affected profoundly by events thousands of miles away. Because another war almost certainly would bring another embargo, and because the United States is attempting to protect its friendships with Israel and with many of the Arab states, vital American interests spur the Middle East peacemaking efforts of the U.S. government. One of the most serious consequences of renewed Arab use of the oil weapon would be the danger of a split between the United States and its European allies, who depend on Arab sources for two-thirds of their petroleum and are not willing to see their economic lifeline cut because of what they consider at times excessive American support of Israel.

America's commitment to Israel, dating from decisive U.S. support for the United Nations plan that led to the creation of the Jewish state, is fundamental to American Middle East policy. This commitment originated in concern for the terrible plight of Jewish refugees from Hitler's genocide and has been sustained by considerable public

support for a special friendship with Israel and by the politically active and influential Jewish minority in the United States.

Support for Israel, however, created strong anti-American feelings in Arab countries, opening many of them to Soviet influence. The arms with which Egypt and Syria attacked in 1973 had been supplied by the Soviet Union, and during the war shipments of Russian arms were countered by a massive airlift of U.S. weapons to Israel.

Paradoxically, however, Egyptian President Anwar Sadat regards the United States as the only country that can pressure Israel into returning Arab territory—because Israel depends on U.S. support. Anxious to reduce his own country's dependence on the Soviet Union, whose military advisers he had expelled in 1972, Sadat has staked his peace efforts on U.S. diplomacy. Kissinger was the first to see the diplomatic opening immediately when the 1973 war broke out. Before leaving office he created a diplomatic axis running from Cairo and Riyadh to Washington. Relations with Syria were greatly improved as well while ties with King Hussein's Jordan remained close.

Fearful of both a new oil embargo and a revival of Russian influence in the Middle East if peace talks failed, the Ford administration pressured the Israeli government to agree to a compromise troop withdrawal from the Sinai Peninsula. The amount of pressure any administration can bring to bear, however, has been limited by the strength of pro-Israeli pressures on Congress and by concern for the impact of Jewish votes and campaign funds. This concern became prevalent as the 1976 election approached and both President Ford and candidate Carter competed for Jewish support.

Still, President Ford told Sadat "with emphasis" on June 1, 1975, that "the United States will not tolerate stagnation in our efforts for a negotiated settlement—stagnation and a stalemate will not be tolerated."[1] Two years later, Jimmy Carter was telling a patiently waiting but increasingly anxious Sadat much the same thing.

U.S. Commitment to Israel

The United States—Israel's chief arms supplier and protector in international forums, target of a Middle East oil embargo and Arab hostility, and major barrier to Soviet influence in that region of the world—has made no formal treaty commitment to the defense of Israel. And the omission has been calculated.

The United States originally assumed the role of Israel's chief supporter with reluctance. Throughout the 1950s and early 1960s, Washington had shunned Israeli arms requests so as not to jeopardize either its friendships with Arab countries during the cold war or its oil interests in

---

1 Luncheon toast at meeting with Sadat in Salzburg, Austria, June 1, 1975. *The Department of State Bulletin,* June 30, 1975, p. 899.

the Middle East. But with the French decision in 1967 to cut off arms to Israel, U.S. policymakers felt they had no alternative but to step into the arms supplier role in order to counter Soviet assistance to Israel's enemies.

No formal agreement was concluded, however. The signing of a defense treaty would have provided a rallying point for Arab hostility, thus placing U.S. friends in the Arab world in a very awkward position. An unwritten commitment was much easier to live with. Moreover, it was thought that a treaty might have encouraged intransigence on the part of Israel in any future negotiations over land acquired in the 1967 war.

Also, the Israelis generally have reacted negatively to suggestions of a mutual security treaty with the United States. The proposed security guarantees, Foreign Minister Moshe Dayan has said, implied that the United States envisioned borders that were "not worth anything." Guarantees could supplement defensible borders, he said, but not substitute for them.

In testimony before the House International Relations Committee on June 10, 1975, Secretary of State Kissinger replied in these words to a question about proposals for U.S. guarantees to Israel: "I believe that a final peace settlement in the area will require some sort of American—I don't know whether I want to use the word 'guarantee'—but some sort of American assurance as to the viability of the state of Israel." The presence of Americans at Sinai monitoring stations, a feature of the second Sinai disengagement agreement in September 1975, has sometimes been viewed as something that could be expanded into the Golan Heights and West Bank, for instance.

Past U.S. Policy

In 1967, when the United States stood on the brink of becoming Israel's chief benefactor, Senate Foreign Relations Committee Chairman J. W. Fulbright (D Ark. 1945-75) asked the State Department whether the United States had a national commitment to provide military or economic aid to Israel or any of the Arab states in the event of armed attack or internal subversion.

The State Department reply, written in early August 1967, two months after Israel had decisively defeated the Arabs and had occupied the Sinai Peninsula and the West Bank of the Jordan River, stated: "President Johnson and his three predecessors have stated the United States interest and concern in supporting the political independence and territorial integrity of the countries of the Near East. *This is a statement of policy and not a commitment to take particular actions in particular circumstances....* The use of armed force in the Middle East can have especially serious consequences for international peace extending far beyond that area. We have bent our efforts to avoid a renewal of conflict there. Thus, we have stated our position in an effort to use our influence in the cause of peace." [Emphasis supplied.]

Such references to U.S. support of "territorial integrity of the countries of the Near East" typify the expression of the U.S. commitment to Israel. By 1977, some analysts noted, the basic commitment also extended to Saudi Arabia and maybe even to Egypt, which had developed a very close relationship with the United States since 1974. The commitment to Israel, however, while not in the form of a treaty, has been reiterated by all recent administrations. The following statements are characteristic:

● A tripartite declaration by Great Britain, France and the United States May 25, 1950, providing that the three governments would act, within the United Nations armistice lines resulting from the 1948-1949 war between Israel and the Arabs.

● A reply by President Kennedy at a press conference May 8, 1963: "In the event of aggression or preparation of aggression [in the Near East], we would support appropriate measures in the United Nations, adopt other courses of action on our own to prevent or to put a stop to such aggression.... [This] has been the policy which the United States has followed for some time."

● An address by President Johnson June 19, 1967, at a foreign policy conference sponsored by the State Department: "Our country is committed—and we here reiterate that commitment today—to a peace [in the Middle East] that is based on five principles: first, the recognized right of national life; second, justice for the refugees; third, innocent maritime passage; fourth, limits on the wasteful and destructive arms race; and fifth, *political independence and territorial integrity for all.*" [Emphasis supplied.]

● A statement by Secretary of State Henry A. Kissinger to reporters in Peking Nov. 12, 1973: "It has been a constant American policy, supported in every administration and carrying wide bipartisan support, that the existence of Israel will be supported by the United States. This has been our policy in the absence of any formal arrangement, and it has never been challenged, no matter which administration was in office." Again, on June 23, 1975, Kissinger stressed "our historical and moral commitment to the survival and well-being of Israel."

● At a press conference on May 13, 1977, President Carter restated the traditional pledge of uniquely close ties with the Jewish state. "We have a special relationship with Israel. It's absolutely crucial that no one in our country or around the world ever doubt that our No. 1 commitment in the Middle East is to protect the right of Israel to exist, to exist permanently, and to exist in peace. It's a special relationship."

Origins of Involvement

Vast oil reserves—and Britain's attempt to monopolize them at the end of World War I—first attracted the United States to the Middle East. Britain moved into the oil-rich region by securing a mandate from the League of Nations to Palestine and Mesopotamia (later to become Iraq). British companies, which produced less than 5 per cent of the world's oil, managed to corner more than half of the world's known reserves by 1919.

The United States, having fueled the Allied victory with large quantities of oil from U.S. reserves, protested British tactics and insisted on a share of the Middle East oil. The protests eventually paid off and, in 1928, several American companies joined with a European group to operate the Turkish (later the Iraq) Petroleum Company.

In addition to these early economic interests, the United States also had an influence on postwar peace settlements in the Middle East and Palestine policies. But a truly strong strategic interest did not emerge until the end of World War II, when the United States gradually began to fill the political role which the British and French were forced to relinquish in the Middle East. *(See box, p. 39)*

Soviet Challenge

America's first commitments to the Middle East were prompted by postwar Soviet expansionism. Greece, Turkey and Iran were the first states beyond the control of the Soviet army to come under this expansionist pressure.

The pressure on Iran began in early 1946 when the Russians refused to withdraw troops that had been stationed in northern Iran since 1941 under a wartime agreement with Great Britain whereby both powers acted to prevent Nazi influence in Iran. Under the agreement, both powers were supposed to withdraw their forces within six months of the end of hostilities. British and American troops—which had arrived after the U.S. entry into the war to help move supplies to the Soviet Union—were withdrawn, but Soviet troops remained after March 2, 1946, the final date set for evacuation. In addition, the Russians demanded that Soviet experts help administer the Iranian government.

When Iran rejected this demand, the Russians engineered a revolt in the north by a Communist-controlled Tudeh Party and used their own forces to prevent the Iranian government's efforts to put down the revolt. A "puppet" Soviet regime was set up in the northern Iranian province of Azerbaijan with the objective of forcing the Iranian government in Tehran to recognize the new regime. Only after a protest by President Truman March 6 that the continued Soviet occupation violated wartime agreements did the Soviets begin their withdrawal from Iran, completing it on May 4, 1946.

Turkey came under Soviet pressure in the summer of 1945, when Moscow demanded cession of several Turkish districts on the Turkish-Russian frontier and revision of the 1936 Montreux Convention, which provided for exclusive Turkish supervision of the Dardanelles Straits between the Black Sea and the Mediterranean. The Soviets demanded joint Russian-Turkish administration of the straits, and the conclusion of a treaty with the Soviet Union similar to those between Russia and its East European satellites, and above all, the lease to the Soviet Union of naval and land bases in the straits for the "joint defense" of Turkey and the Soviet Union. These demands were renewed in a Soviet note to the United States and Britain in August 1946. President Truman replied by sending a naval force into the Mediterranean immediately upon receipt of the note. Twelve days later Britain and the United States replied to the Soviet Union in a joint note rejecting Moscow's demands. This was followed by an easing of Soviet pressure on Turkey.

In Greece, Communist guerrilla warfare, aided from Albania, Bulgaria and Yugoslavia, threatened to take over the country by early 1947. British troops and military assistance in 1945 had averted an earlier attempt by the Communists to gain control of Athens. By 1947, however, Britain was no longer able—as a result of wartime exhaustion—to continue to fulfill its traditional role, dating from the 19th century, of resisting Russian pressure in the eastern Mediterranean. The United States moved into the breach, as it had in Iran and Turkey, thereby initiating what became the pattern in the postwar era—namely, the United States replacing Britain as the protector of weaker states bordering on the Russian (or Soviet) empire.

Truman Doctrine

Faced with the threatened Communist takeover in Greece and the probability that the collapse of Greece would lead to further Soviet pressure on Turkey, President Truman went before a joint session of Congress March 12, 1947, and spelled out the Truman Doctrine. The President

---

Truman's Constituents

Israel has been intimately involved in American domestic politics ever since President Truman decided to work for its creation after World War II. Truman's decision ran counter to the advice of U.S. diplomats who served in the Middle East. When they warned that support for Israel would jeopardize American relations with the Arabs and damage wider American interests in the Middle East, Truman reportedly replied: "I'm sorry, gentlemen, but I have to answer to hundreds of thousands who are anxious for the success of Zionism; I do not have hundreds of thousands of Arabs among my constituents."

Israel is a major political issue among the estimated 5.9 million American Jews—who far outweigh Arab-Americans both in numbers and in financial resources—but how much impact the so-called "Jewish lobby" has had on American Middle East policy is a matter of conjecture. "U.S. Middle Eastern policy is not now and never has been, in spite of the Arab belief to the contrary, formulated by 'Zionists,'" foreign policy analyst James E. Griffiths wrote in 1969. "Yet the votes and financial resources of the American Jewish community exercise influence on it in favor of Israel for which there is no pro-Arab equivalent."

Internally divided and overwhelmed by pro-Israeli sentiment, supporters of the Arab cause in the United States concede that in the past they have been ineffective in turning public and congressional support to their side. But a pro-Arab lobby, dedicated to persuading Congress to reverse its "overcommitment to Israel," has begun to emerge from political obscurity. *(Israel lobby, p. 89; Arab lobby, p. 96)*

---

asserted that the United States could only be secure in a world where freedom flourished. He said: "Totalitarian regimes imposed on free people, by direct or indirect aggression, undermine the foundations of international peace and hence the security of the United States."

President Truman stressed that it must be U.S. policy "to support free people who are resisting attempted subjugations by armed minorities or by outside pressure." To bolster the sagging Greek government and that of Turkey (again under Soviet pressure), the President urged Congress to authorize military as well as economic aid to the two countries, on a bilateral rather than a multilateral basis through the United Nations. Opponents argued that the Truman Doctrine undercut the U.N. and might provoke a clash with Russia, but a majority sided with the President. Along with the $400-million provided for Greece and Turkey went American civilian and military advisers.

(In an Oct. 17, 1951, protocol, the North Atlantic Treaty Organization extended mutual security guarantees to Greece, Turkey and the eastern Mediterranean Sea.)

Arab Reaction

The Arab states—which felt little threat from the Soviet Union and were still embittered by U.S. support for the 1917 Balfour Declaration calling for the establishment in Palestine of a national home for the Jewish people—did not like the Truman Doctrine. Arab hostility increased when, on Nov. 2, 1947, the United States, as well as the Soviet Union, voted with a two-thirds majority in the United Nations General Assembly to partition Palestine into Arab and Jewish states.

The United States and the Soviet Union were the first countries to extend diplomatic recognition to Israel when it declared independence minutes after British authority—mandated by the League of Nations and extended by the United Nations—expired at midnight May 14, 1948. Arabs saw U.S. actions as a betrayal of President Franklin D. Roosevelt's promise to King Ibn Saud of Saudi Arabia in 1945 that "no decision [will] be taken with respect to the basic situation in that country [Palestine] without full consultation with both Arabs and Jews."

The Arabs rejected the partition and went to war against Israel. The first Arab-Israeli war lasted from 1948 to 1949.

Arms Race

In an effort to bring stability to the Middle East, the United States joined with Britain and France in issuing the Tripartite Declaration May 25, 1950, in which the three powers attempted to reassure both Israel and the Arabs by declaring their opposition to the use of force throughout the Middle East.

The Tripartite Declaration notwithstanding, the United States had found itself drawn into a Middle East arms race of varying intensity since the mid-1950s. *(p. 45)*

Baghdad Pact

In an effort to block Soviet pressure on the Middle East, the United States promoted the formation of a mutual defense treaty in February 1955 among Britain, Iran, Iraq, Pakistan and Turkey. U.S. officials participated in the defense and anti-subversion committees of the Baghdad Pact, and U.S. military and economic aid was provided to the members of the organization; but the United States did

---

"All the cards in this game are in the hands of the United States...because they provide Israel with everything and they are the only [one] who can exert pressure on Israel."

Egyptian President Anwar Sadat,
June 1975

---

not formally become a member. The main reason for this ambivalence was that Iraq and Egypt were rivals for leadership of the Arab world; and the United States, in the hope that Egypt could eventually be persuaded to join the pact, did not want to alienate Egypt by formally allying itself with Iraq. An alliance with Iraq would also create problems for U.S. relations with Israel.

The hope that Egypt could be induced into joining the pact was not achieved. Egyptian President Gamal Abdel Nasser denounced Iraq for allying with the Western powers, and he turned to the Soviet Union in the fall of 1955 for military equipment in an effort to gain a decisive military lead over Israel.

Moscow, which had reacted sharply to the formation of the Baghdad Pact, responded quickly to Nasser's request and became Egypt's major arms supplier. The Soviet Union thereby began to build a reputation throughout the Arab world as the main support the Arabs had among the great powers in their struggle with Israel.

Suez Crisis

Soviet arms shipments to Egypt in 1955 and 1956 convinced Israel to prepare for a preventive war against Egypt, before the military balance shifted in Cairo's favor. Israel's request for U.S. arms was rejected by President Eisenhower, who said March 7, 1956, he opposed U.S. arms for Israel because this would lead to an "Arab-Israeli arms race." When Nasser announced July 26 nationalization of the British-run Suez Canal and refused to guarantee the safety of Israeli shipping, the threat to Israeli, as well as to British and French, interests made the situation explosive.

Nasser's decision followed U.S. refusal July 19 to provide Egypt financing for the Aswan Dam project, a high dam on the upper Nile intended to furnish cheap electricity and increased irrigation. The United States had initially expressed interest in the project but turned it down as a result of Nasser's deepening ties with the Soviet Union. In nationalizing the Suez Canal, Nasser claimed that revenues would pay for the Aswan project.

The British government held 44 per cent of all shares in the Suez Canal Company; private French investors held 78 per cent of the remainder. Apart from these direct interests, both nations were heavily dependent on the canal as the shortest waterway to their oil supplies on the Persian Gulf. Nationalization of the canal was intolerable in their view, because it meant that Nasser could bar their vessels at any time. The two governments immediately froze all Egyptian assets available and began talks on joint military action.

Israeli armed forces attacked Egypt Oct. 29, 1956, and completed occupation of the Sinai Peninsula to within 10 miles of the Suez Canal by Nov. 5. British and French aircraft attacked Egypt Oct. 31-Nov. 5, and an Anglo-French paratrooper force was dropped at the northern end of the Suez Canal Nov. 5. By Nov. 7, British and French forces had secured control of the canal.

Strong U.S. pressure in the United Nations and behind the scenes on Israel, Britain and France was instrumental in bringing the fighting to a quick halt and in forcing the three nations to withdraw their forces from Egypt by the end of the year. Although Americans sympathized with the invaders, they supported President Eisenhower's declaration Oct. 31 that the invasion "can scarcely be reconciled with the principles" of the United Nations. The U.S. condemnation of the invasion helped save Nasser from a disastrous defeat. The outcome of the conflict was a severe political and moral setback for Britain and France in the Middle East from which Nasser and the Soviet Union reaped the major benefits. The Suez crisis led to a major "power vacuum" in the Middle East, making the area prone to renewed Soviet penetration.

Eisenhower Doctrine

Following the Suez crisis, the Eisenhower administration feared that the Soviet Union might move into the Middle East vacuum resulting from the British and French diplomatic defeat. It was decided that the U.S. commitment to resist communism in the area had to be fortified.

On Jan. 5, 1957, President Eisenhower went before a joint session of Congress to urge support for a declaration which was promptly dubbed the Eisenhower Doctrine. H J Res 117 (Joint Resolution to Promote Peace and Stability in the Middle East) declared that "if the President determines the necessity...[the United States] is prepared to use armed forces to assist...any nation or groups of nations requesting assistance against armed aggression *from any country controlled by international communism."* [Emphasis supplied.]

The resolution did not draw a precise geographical line around the area to which it was intended to apply. The Senate and House reports on the resolution accepted the administration's view and defined the Middle East as the area bounded by Libya on the west, Pakistan on the east, Turkey in the north and the Sudan in the south. The Senate report said that no precise listing of nations was included in the resolution because this "would restrict the freedom of action of the United States in carrying out the purposes of the resolution."

The first test of the Eisenhower Doctrine and resolution came in 1958 following a coup in Iraq, which overthrew the pro-Western government, replacing it with a regime favorable to the Soviet Union and the United Arab Republic (UAR). The new Iraqi government immediately withdrew from the Baghdad Pact.

"The search for a just and lasting peace in the Middle East is one of the highest priority items on the foreign policy agenda of our country."

Secretary of State Cyrus R. Vance
May 1977

When the government of Lebanon came under similar pressure and its president requested U.S. assistance, Eisenhower ordered U.S. Marines from the 6th Fleet in the Mediterranean to land in Lebanon to protect the government. Citing the Eisenhower Doctrine, the President said July 15, 1958, that Lebanon's territorial integrity and independence were "vital to United States national interests and world peace." The UAR and the Soviet Union, Eisenhower charged, were trying to overthrow the constitutional government of Lebanon and "install by violence a government which subordinates the independence of Lebanon to...the United Arab Republic."

CENTO

Iraq's withdrawal from the Baghdad Pact convinced the Eisenhower administration that the three remaining "northern tier" members of the organization needed an additional pledge of U.S. support in resisting communism. With the Middle East resolution as a basis, the United States initiated negotiations with Turkey, Iran and Pakistan on defense arrangements, bringing the United States into closer cooperation with the Baghdad Pact, which was renamed the Central Treaty Organization (CENTO).

Three identically worded executive agreements were signed in March 1959 between the United States and each of the three nations. Washington pledged in the agreements to come to the defense of the three countries in the event of Communist aggression or subversion.

The executive agreements with Iran, Pakistan and Turkey completed the United States' formal commitment to resist communism in the Middle East. Throughout the 1960s, the Kennedy and Johnson administrations repeatedly pledged to uphold the territorial integrity of Israel and the Arab nations. U.S. military assistance and arms sales delivered weapons to pro-Western governments in the area, and limited arms sales to Israel were initiated in 1962.

1967 War

The perpetual Middle East tension flared June 5, 1967, into a third major Arab-Israeli war. During the Israeli-initiated, but Arab caused, Six-day War, Israel destroyed a substantial part of the armed forces of Egypt, Jordan and Syria. In addition, large amounts of Arab territory were captured — land which Israel continued to occupy.

U.S. Role

A few hours after war broke out early June 5, Robert J. McCloskey, deputy assistant secretary of state for public affairs, declared that the U.S. position was "neutral in thought, word and deed." The McCloskey statement was criticized by members of Congress and others who pointed to U.S. ties with Israel. Later June 5, George Christian, presidential press secretary, said the McCloskey statement was "not a formal declaration of neutrality." And, at a late afternoon news conference at the White House, Secretary of State Dean Rusk June 5 said the term "neutral" in international law expressed the fact that the United States was not a belligerent. He said it was not "an expression of indifference."

Israeli planes and naval vessels June 8 attacked the U.S. Navy communications ship *Liberty* about 15 miles off the Gaza Strip.[2] American carrier-based aircraft went to the assistance of the military moves in the Mediterranean. The White House immediately notified Moscow of the developments on the first teletype communications system between Washington and Moscow. The system, which was installed in 1963 and was known as the "hot line," never before had been used in a crisis.

The U.S. Security Council June 6 unanimously adopted a resolution calling for a cease-fire. The truce went into effect June 10, although periodic clashes continued.

Peace Proposal

In his first major statement on U.S. Middle East policy following the outbreak of the war, President Johnson June 19 laid down a five-point formula for peace in the Middle East. *(See p. 35)*

Johnson said the victorious Israeli troops "must be withdrawn." But he made it clear he would not press for a withdrawal to prewar lines in every respect.

---

2. This attack was officially termed an accident, and Israel's apology was accepted by the United States government. Yet many questions have remained unanswered about the attack. A two-part article by Anthony Pearson in the May and June 1976 issues of *Penthouse* magazine suggests the attack was deliberate and speculates on possible Israeli motivations.

Partition of Palestine: U.S. Policy Developments

With the breakup of the Ottoman Empire during World War I, Palestine's fate was left up to Great Britain, France and Russia. Britain had pledged to support the independence of the Arab areas, in correspondence during 1915 between Sir Henry McMahon, high commissioner of Egypt, and Hussein ibn Ali, sherif of Mecca.

But, according to a secret agreement reached in 1916 by the British, French and Russian governments (known as the Sykes-Picot Agreement), the Arab areas were to be divided into British and French spheres of influence and Palestine was to be internationalized. Arabs later cited this agreement in charging they had been deceived by European imperialists.

Balfour Declaration. On Nov. 2, 1917, British Foreign Secretary Arthur Balfour pledged in a letter to Lord Rothschild, leader of the British Zionists, that Britain would support the establishment in Palestine of a "national home" for the Jewish people, on the clear understanding that "nothing shall be done which may prejudice the civil and religious rights of existing non-Jewish communities in Palestine...."

Reaction to the Balfour Declaration in the United States was positive. President Woodrow Wilson endorsed the statement before its publication, and Congress adopted a resolution approving the declaration in September 1922.

U.S. Role. The United States never declared war on the Ottoman Empire, an ally of Germany in World War I, but President Wilson strongly influenced the final peace settlement which set forth the basic boundaries of the Middle East states. His major contribution was the concept of interim League of Nations mandates which would eventually lead to independent states.

The United States sent a commission (King-Crane Commission) to the former Arab areas of the Ottoman Empire to determine their views on postwar settlements. The commission's final report in 1919—never formally accepted by the Paris Peace Conference or the U.S. government—called for a serious modification of the "extreme Zionist program" and advised against the creation of a Jewish state in Palestine.

Palestine Mandate. In July 1922 the League of Nations approved Britain's mandate to Palestine, which went into force Sept. 22, 1923. The mandate instrument included a preamble incorporating the Balfour Declaration and stressing the Jewish historical connection with Palestine. Britain was made responsible for placing the country under such "political, administrative and economic conditions as will secure the establishment of a Jewish National Home...."

In the mid-1940s the push to lift restrictions—set forth in a 1939 British government White Paper—on Jewish immigration into Palestine gained support, especially in the United States. *(Jewish migration to Palestine, p. 106)*

In August 1945, President Harry S Truman called for the free settlement of Palestine by Jews to the point consistent with the maintenance of civil peace. Later that month Truman suggested in a letter to British Prime Minister Clement R. Atlee that an additional 100,000 Jews be allowed to enter Palestine. In December, both houses of Congress adopted a resolution urging U.S. aid in opening Palestine to Jewish immigrants and in building a "democratic commonwealth."

Anglo-American Committee. In November 1945, Britain, anxious to have the United States share responsibility for its Palestine policy, joined with the United States in deciding to create a commission to examine the problem of European Jews and Palestine. In the meantime, Britain agreed to permit an additional 1,500 Jews to enter Palestine each month. A 75,000 limit had been set by the 1939 White Paper.

In April 1946 the Anglo-American Committee of Inquiry recommended the immediate admission of 100,000 Jews into Palestine, and continuation of the British mandate until establishment of a United Nations trusteeship. Truman immediately endorsed the immigration proposal, but Britain stipulated prior disbandment of underground Jewish forces in Palestine.

The President in October released a communication sent to the British government in which he appealed for "substantial immigration" into Palestine "at once" and expressed support for the Zionist plan for creation of a "viable Jewish state" in part of Palestine. A British government spokesman expressed regret that Truman's statement had been made public because it might jeopardize a settlement.

United Nations. Britain turned to the United Nations in early 1947, when a London conference of Arab and Zionist representatives failed to resolve the Palestinian question. The United Nations set up an inquiry committee which ultimately recommended that Palestine be divided into two separate Arab and Jewish states, with Jerusalem and vicinity to be an international zone under permanent U.N. trusteeship.

The United States and the Soviet Union agreed on the partitioning of Palestine, and on Nov. 29, 1947, the U.N. General Assembly voted to divide Palestine. Britain—setting May 15, 1948, as the date its mandate would terminate—refused to share responsibility with the U.N. Palestine Commission during the transitional period because the U.N. solution was not acceptable to both sides.

Civil war broke out shortly after the U.N. decision was made. In March 1948 the United States voiced opposition to the forcible partitioning of Palestine and called for suspension of the plan. The United States urged a special session of the General Assembly.

In April the Security Council adopted a U.S. resolution calling for a truce and a special session of the General Assembly. But it was too late to stop the division of Palestine. On May 14, the British high commissioner left Palestine, the state of Israel was proclaimed and the General Assembly voted to send a mediator to the Holy Land to seek a truce.

The United States granted Israel de facto recognition immediately. The Soviet Union recognized the new state three days later.

Golan Heights Disengagement, May 1974

LEBANON
Qiryat Shemona
Jordan River
U.N. ZONE
El Quneitra
SYRIA
GOLAN HEIGHTS (Occupied by Israel)
ISRAEL
Tiberias ●
Sea of Galilee
Miles
0   10
JORDAN

Resolution 242

On Nov. 22, 1967, the U.N. Security Council unanimously approved a British resolution (Resolution 242) aimed at bringing peace to the Middle East. The resolution called for withdrawal of Israeli forces from occupied Arab areas; an end to the state of belligerency between the Arab nations and Israel; acknowledgement of and respect for the sovereignty, territorial integrity and political independence of every nation in the area; the establishment of secure and

---

"I would not hesitate if I saw clearly a fair and equitable solution to [the Middle East problem] to use the full strength of our own country and its persuasive powers to bring those nations to agreement."

President Jimmy Carter
May 1977

---

recognized national boundaries; a guarantee of freedom of navigation through international waterways in the area; and just settlement of the refugee problem. *(Text, p. 67)*

There has been considerable disagreement over the precise meaning of Resolution 242. The Arabs have contended that the document required total Israeli withdrawal from the Sinai Peninsula, the Gaza Srip, the Golan Heights, the West Bank of the Jordan River and the eastern sector of Jerusalem. But the Israelis have insisted that the phrasing of the resolution—withdrawal "from territories" and not "from the territories"—did not require a total pullback from the 1967 cease-fire lines.

No War, No Peace

Resolution 242 provided the basis for subsequent U.S. peace proposals. In a departure from previous U.S. policy, the Nixon administration agreed early in 1969 to a series of bilateral talks with the Soviet Union as well as four-power talks which included Britain and France. The talks were carried on sporadically throughout the year, but little was achieved.

Rogers Peace Plan

The major elements of the U.S. diplomatic position were outlined by Secretary of State William P. Rogers on Dec. 9, 1969. Rogers called on Israel to withdraw from Arab territories occupied in the June 1967 war in return for Arab assurances of a binding commitment to a Middle East peace. He also put on record for the first time more detailed peace proposals made by the United States in October during bilateral talks with the Soviet Union. The proposals were rejected by Israel and scorned by the Arabs.

Meanwhile, the United States continued to support the efforts of United Nations envoy Gunnar V. Jarring to mediate a settlement between the Arabs and Israelis. On Jan. 25, 1970, Nixon reaffirmed U.S. support for Israel's insistence on direct peace negotiations with the Arabs. On Jan. 30, he asserted that the United States was "neither pro-Arab nor pro-Israel. We are pro-peace."

The Arab-Israeli conflict was potentially more dangerous than the Indochina war and could result in a direct U.S.-Soviet clash, Nixon warned in a televised interview July 1, 1970. He reiterated that the United States would not allow the military balance to shift against Israel.

The United States had "not excluded the possibility" of participating in a Middle East peacekeeping role, Rogers said Dec. 23, 1970, but he ruled out any joint U.S.-Soviet force as "totally impractical."

In late 1971 and early 1972, the United States put forward a new proposal for indirect, American-mediated talks between Israel and Egypt on an interim peace settlement that included a troop pullback and reopening of the Suez Canal; but negotiations made little headway.

Fourth War

The "no-war, no-peace" stalemate held until October 1973, when Arab frustrations over the deadlock triggered the fourth Arab-Israeli war. On Oct. 6, Egyptian forces crossed the Suez Canal and Syria attacked the Golan Heights.

Benefiting from the element of surprise, Arab forces initially inflicted great damage to Israeli defenses, but Israel was soon on the offensive. The intensely fought war led to the rapid depletion of combatants' arsenals and the airlifting of arms first by the Soviet Union and then by the United States.

To avoid total defeat and humiliation of the Arabs—which would very probably have barred any peaceful resolution of the conflict—the United States and the Soviet Union joined in pressing for a cease-fire. Following a Kissinger trip to Moscow, a joint U.S.-Soviet resolution calling for an immediate cease-fire and implementation of the 1967 U.S. Security Council Resolution 242 was presented to the Security Council Oct. 21. Egypt and Israel agreed, and the cease-fire was to go into effect the next day.

U.S. Troop Alert

But the fighting continued and Egyptian President Anwar Sadat—concerned for the fate of his army—called on both the United States and the Soviet Union to send in troops to enforce the cease-fire. A worldwide alert of U.S. armed forces was called in the early morning hours of Oct. 25, reportedly in response to the possibility of a unilateral Soviet movement of troops into the Middle East to supervise the truce.

Secretary of State Kissinger said that U.S. forces had been alerted because of the "ambiguity" of the situation, after it had been learned that Soviet units had been alerted. The emerging crisis was defused when later that day the U.N. Security Council agreed to form a peace force that would not include the troops of the five permanent members of the Security Council, thereby excluding U.S. and Soviet forces.

Geneva Conference

The United States assumed a leadership role in attempting to bring about a peace settlement in the aftermath of the 1973 war. Kissinger negotiated a six-point cease-fire agreement which was signed by Egyptian and Israeli military representatives November 11, 1973, at Kilometer 101 on the Cairo to Suez road.

In late December 1973, largely through Kissinger's continuing efforts, the Geneva Conference was convened in accordance with U.N. Security Council resolution #338. (See p. 68) It recessed after only two days of largely ceremonial and propagandistic exchanges, but it symbolized the kind of semi-direct negotiations which have since then been the focus of attention.

Disengagement Agreements

Subsequent Kissinger shuttles produced troop disengagement accords between Israel and Egypt in the Sinai Peninsula (Jan. 18, 1974) and between Israel and Syria in the Golan Heights (May 31, 1974).

The January 1974 agreement between Egypt and Israel was hailed as a major breakthrough in Middle East diplomacy. The terms of the agreement were not very significant, but the fact that an agreement had been reached broke the tragic pattern of the Arab-Israeli conflict. A generation of wars, hatred and deep distrust had kept Arabs and Israelis from even entering negotiations. Kissinger succeeded in breaching these entrenched attitudes, because he focused negotiations on immediate and often minor issues.

In the meantime, the United States began to mend its relations with the Arab states. During a Kissinger visit to Egypt, Kissinger and Sadat agreed to resume U.S.-Egyptian diplomatic relations — broken since 1967. The resumption of U.S.-Syrian relations was announced in Damascus June 16, 1974, during a visit by President Nixon, whose Middle East tour also took him to Egypt, Israel and Saudi Arabia.

In March 1975, Kissinger sought to secure an agreement for a second-stage disengagement in Sinai as part of

---

Key Features of 1975 Pact

In Geneva on Sept. 4, 1975, Israel and Egypt formally signed a new Middle East accord, intended to provide another stepping-stone toward a final peace settlement between the Arab nations and Israel.

The key feature of the pact required the Israeli army to withdraw from the Sinai mountain passes of Gidi and Mitla. These areas were included in a new United Nations demilitarized zone. However, Israel still controlled 87 percent of the Sinai Peninsula, seized from Egypt in the 1967 war. (1967 map, p. 66; 1974, 1975 maps, p. 44)

Egyptian forces were allowed to advance to the eastern edge of the old U.N. zone established by the January 1974 accord. Egypt recovered possession of the Abu Rudeis oil fields along the Gulf of Suez, also held by Israel since 1967.

Egypt pledged that it would not resort to the threat or use of force or continue a military blockade against Israel in the straits of Bab el Mandeb linking the Red Sea to the Indian Ocean. The Egyptians also agreed to a provision stating that "nonmilitary cargoes destined to or coming from Israel shall be permitted through the Suez Canal," opening the waterway to Israel for the first time since 1956.

Both belligerents pledged that "the conflict between them in the Middle East shall not be resolved by military force, but by peaceful means," and that they "are determined to reach a final and just peace settlement by means of negotiations."

The agreement also limited military forces that each side was permitted to station adjacent to the U.N. buffer area, and called for the mandate of the U.N. peacekeeping mission to be renewed annually rather than for shorter periods.

As for the new U.S. role, a few hundred American civilian personnel began monitoring Egyptian and Israeli activities in the Sinai. The agreement resulted in two warning stations operated separately by Egypt and Israel and three other stations in the Mitla and Gidi Passes manned by American technicians.

---

his step-by-step approach to peace in the Middle East. But after 15 days of talks with Sadat and Israeli Premier Yitzhak Rabin, Kissinger returned on March 23 to the United States calling his efforts a failure. Kissinger and Ford made clear at the time that they held Israel primarily responsible for the breakdown in negotiations, although they subsequently avoided any public assessment of blame.

In response to the failure of the talks, the United States began a "reassessment" of its Middle East policies. Consideration of Israel's request for $2.5-billion in U.S. aid was suspended until completion of the reassessment, a thinly veiled form of pressure on the Israeli government to be more forthcoming in talks with Egypt.

The stalled negotiations began again as President Ford met with Sadat in Salzburg, Austria, and with Rabin in Washington during June 1975. The United States hoped that Egypt and Israel would reach an interim agreement and thus avoid the risks of failure in a resumed Geneva Conference. As a culmination of Kissinger's resumed shuttle

U.S.-Soviet Rivalry Over Naval Installations

Tit-for-tat superpower rivalry in the Indian Ocean advanced a notch July 28, 1975, when Congress approved a Pentagon proposal for constructing naval and air support facilities at Diego Garcia, a British-owned atoll 1,000 miles south of the Indian Peninsula. Action by both houses ended five years of bitter haggling with the White House, which argued that Diego Garcia was needed to match increased Soviet naval activity in the Indian Ocean and its outlying pockets—the Arabian Sea, the Persian Gulf, the Gulf of Aden and the Red Sea.

Diego Garcia was to replace another port facility the U.S. Navy had been using in the area. In December 1971, the United States secured docking privileges at the island sheikdom of Bahrain in the Persian Gulf. But after the October 1973 war, Bahrain announced its intention of canceling this agreement, which it did on June 29, 1977. U.S. military activity on Diego Garcia was opposed by India and Australia on the grounds that it could lead to a U.S.-Soviet naval confrontation in the relatively peaceful Indian Ocean. But the Ford administration held that the United States must protect vital sea lanes through which oil tankers ply from the Persian Gulf to the West.

At an Aug. 28, 1974, press conference, President Ford defended the administration proposition, saying, "I don't view this [Diego Garcia] as any challenge to the Soviet Union. The Soviet Union already has three major naval operating bases in the Indian Ocean. This particular proposed construction, I think, is a wise policy, and it ought not to ignite any escalation of the problems in the Middle East."

A Defense Department spokesman identified the Soviet installations as Umm Qasr in Iraq, at the head of the Persian Gulf; at Aden in South Yemen, on the southwestern tip of the Arabian Peninsula, and at Berbera in Somalia, on the east coast of Africa. Aden and Berbera flank the Gulf of Aden, the passage leading from the Arabian Sea to the Red Sea, and thence to the Suez Canal and the Mediterranean beyond.

Tass, the official Soviet news agency, scoffed at Ford's assertions, claiming that he had been misinformed by his staff. Tass also quoted testimony of William E. Colby, director of the Central Intelligence Agency, before the Senate Armed Services Committee. Colby had described the Soviet presence in the Indian Ocean area as "relatively small."

Legislative History

The Nixon administration first requested new construction funds for Diego Garcia in fiscal 1970 legislation; but the Senate Appropriations Committee refused to fund the project, and the matter languished until 1974. A Senate-House conference report on the fiscal 1975 military construction authorization bill included $14.8-million for the Navy and $3.3-million for Air Force projects on the island. Obligation of these funds, however, was prohibited pending the President's certification of need. The fiscal 1976 bill allowed an additional $13.8-million for the Navy, contingent upon action taken by Congress on the President's message.

A resolution barring the Diego Garcia improvements was introduced by Senate Majority Leader Mike Mansfield (D Mont.). His resolution was rejected on July 28, 1975, by a 43-53 vote. In floor debate, Mansfield called the $28.6-million Navy request "only a down payment" for deploying an Indian Ocean patrol fleet that could cost $8-billion and require $800-million annually in operating expense.

Armed Services Committee Chairman John C. Stennis (D Miss.) dismissed speculation that Diego Garcia would lead to a three-ocean navy. He called the request "reasonable," noting that the closest refueling station was 3,500 miles away, in the Philippines. Dewey F. Bartlett (R Okla.), who had led a Senate inspection of the Soviet facilities at Berbera in early July, claimed the Russians were developing a "significant" naval and air station there that "exceeds any other facility" outside Soviet borders.

The same day as Senate action, the House turned down by voice vote an amendment by Rep. Robert L. Leggett (D Calif.) to remove $13.8-million for Diego Garcia construction. Leggett, who also inspected Berbera, described the Soviet base as "modest."

The congressional green light enabled the Pentagon to enlarge its existing communications station at Diego Garcia by construction of a 12,000-foot runway for military planes, anchorage for a six-ship carrier task force and storage capacity for 640,000 barrels of oil, enough to fuel the task force for 28 days.

Bahrain Problems

The naval facility at Bahrain had also experienced congressional problems. At first the Senate balked at the idea, and a resolution deleting a provision to pay Bahrain for the leasing of docking facilities was introduced. The administration request for the funds was embodied in an executive agreement, and the resolution called for the agreement to be submitted as a treaty for Senate ratification. However, the resolution was defeated on a 30-59 vote June 28, 1972.

Reacting to U.S. support of Israel in the 1973 war, Bahrain rescinded the naval agreement on Oct. 20, 1973, accusing the United States of a "hostile stand against the Arab nations." After quiet negotiations, Defense Department sources revealed on Oct. 3, 1974, that Bahrain had shifted its policy and the United States would be allowed to retain the base. Reports indicated that Iran and Saudi Arabia put pressure on Bahrain, because they wanted a continued U.S. Navy presence in the Persian Gulf. But in June 1977 Bahrain finally did rescind the agreement.

The U.S. Middle East naval force consisted of one command destroyer and two additional destroyers, which rotated in and out of the Bahrain facility six months a year. The job of the mini-fleet was to show the flag in the Persian Gulf and on patrols along the south coast of the Arabian Peninsula and the east coast of Africa. A naval force now operates from Diego Garcia.

In 1979 the creation of a permanent naval force in the Indian Ocean was said to be under consideration. *(Rection to Yemen conflict, p. 57)* diplomacy, representatives of the two sides initialed a limited agreement Sept. 1. But it was recognized, at best, as only a hopeful first step toward a permanent overall peace settlement. *(Box, p. 41)*

Compared with the basic issues of recognition of Israel, the future of the Palestinians, permanent boundaries, the status of Jerusalem, and peace guarantees, the issues settled in the second Sinai troop disengagement accord were trivial. The tactic of avoiding basic issues succeeded again in producing an accord, but again the fundamental issues were not faced.

In one respect, however, the September accord did produce a major change. It introduced Americans, for the first time, into the midst of the Arab-Israeli conflict.

Congress approved, somewhat hesitantly, the stationing of American technicians between Israeli and Arab armies in the Sinai Desert to monitor military activities. The Israeli government made clear that its ratification of the agreement hinged on such congressional approval. But the combination of avoiding issues and injecting Americans left in doubt the direction of the path toward a permanent peace. As journalist Edward Sheehan recounted, "Perhaps Dr. Kissinger's greatest achievement is to have bought time, to have prevented war, to have erected the foundation for the pursuit of real peace. But the method he chose was simply too slow, and if clung to may imperil peace for the great future."[3]

Step-by-Step 'Shuttle Diplomacy'

The temptation to continue the step-by-step approach to peace arose partly from its initial success. The 1974 military disengagement agreements that Kissinger negotiated between Egypt and Israel in January and between Syria and Israel in May defused the explosive situation that existed after the 1973 war. But they accomplished much more. Although limited to military arrangement, the meeting between Israeli and Egyptian officers in the tent at Kilometer 101 produced the first agreement between Israel and an Arab state in 25 years—since the armistice of 1949, ending the Israeli war of independence. Scarcely a month before the Egyptian-Israeli accord was signed, representatives of the warring governments for the first time ever met face-to-face in search of a political settlement.

The experience of negotiating and agreeing, Professor Nadav Safran of Harvard observed, challenged deep-seated Arab and Israeli attitudes toward the very notion of settlement and mediation. It not only "cracked...mental molds that had made for rigidity, fatalism, and despair," but gave rise to "vested interest, intellectual or political, in depicting the other side's intentions and behavior in a favorable light," he wrote. Previously each side had placed the worst possible interpretation on every word, act or alleged thought of the other side—interpretations that became self-fulfilling prophecies. But now, Safran noted:

...The world [was] treated to the novel spectacle of Golda Meir and Moshe Dayan [Israeli defense minister] urging in the Knesset [Parliament] that there was no need to assume the worst about Sadat [Anwar Sadat, president of Egypt], arguing that he seemed to be genuinely desirous of peace and eager to turn his attention to the tasks of reconstruction and developing his country, and stressing

that he had scrupulously observed the terms of the agreement in letter and spirit.

On the other side, one could hear Sadat reassure his people that they need not worry about the possibility of Israel's sitting tight and trying to freeze the situation created by the disengagement agreement; and one could see him hopping from one Arab capital to another in an effort to allay this and other doubts and justify the "gamble" he took on the grounds that the United States and Israel had changed.[4]

While the initial Egyptian-Israeli accord established the minimum basis of trust necessary to pursue more basic issues, the second accord still did not come to grips with them. Whether or not an opportunity was thus lost, the nature of the issues placed limits on step-by-step diplomacy. The Carter administration had to face this reality in 1977.

Indeed, in retrospect, step-by-step diplomacy only set the stage for the Carter administration's efforts for an overall settlement to the Middle East conflict. Professor John Stoessinger assessed Kissinger's tactics in this way:

We cannot say with certitude whether the critics of the step-by-step approach...were justified in their assertions that Kissinger avoided the heart of the conflict by refusing to address himself to the Palestinian problem. What the record does indicate, however, is that Kissinger has managed to narrow the differences between Israel and the Arabs more successfully than any other mediator in the long history of that tragic conflict.[5]

Journalist Sheehan, who once suggested to Secretary Kissinger that he should have attempted to resolve the conflict himself, not just take a few small steps toward a future settlement, reported Kissinger's response as follows: "What were the alternatives? The conflict in the Middle East has a history of decades. Only during the last two years have we produced progress. It's easy to say that what we've done is not enough, but the steps we've taken are the biggest steps so far. They were *the attainable*—given our prevailing domestic situation."[6]

By the "domestic situation," Kissinger apparently had in mind the pressures applied by Israel's friends in the Congress and elsewhere whenever the demands being placed on Israel were thought to be excessive or unbalanced vis-a-vis the concessions being asked of the Arabs.

When Kissinger and President Ford began the "reassessment" of American Middle East policy in light of the March 1975 breakdown in shuttle diplomacy and alleged Israeli intransigence, the government developed three options for future Middle East strategy. The preferred option to emerge was, according to Sheehan:

The United States should announce its conception of a final settlement in the Middle East, based on the 1967 frontiers of Israel with minor modifications, and containing strong guarantees for Israel's security. The Geneva conference would be reconvened; the Soviet Union should be encouraged to cooperate in the quest to resolve all outstanding questions (including the status of Jerusalem) which should be defined in appropriate components and addressed in separate subcommittees.[7]

But Israel's supporters lobbied vigorously against this policy. The Jewish lobby on Capitol Hill produced a letter signed by 76 senators on May 21, 1975, strongly endorsing

---

3. Edward R. F. Sheehan, *The Arabs, Israelis and Kissinger* (Reader's Digest Press: 1976), p. 204.

4. Nadav Safran, "Engagement in the Middle East," *Foreign Affairs*, October 1974, pp. 48-49.
5. John G. Stoessinger, *Henry Kissinger: The Anguish of Power* (Norton: 1976), p. 221.
6. Edward R. F. Sheehan, *The Arabs, Israelis and Kissinger* (Reader's Digest Press: 1976), p. 201.
7. Ibid., p. 166.

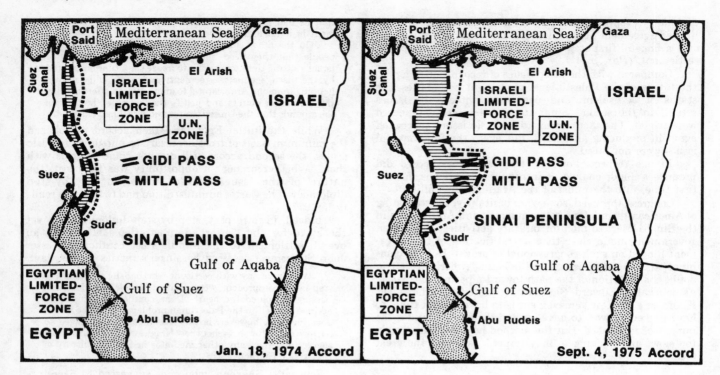

Israel's demands for "defensible" borders and massive economic and military aid.

It was a clear warning to Ford and Kissinger not to consummate the shift they were contemplating in American policies and strategies. Theodore Draper wrote in the April 1975 issue of *Commentary* magazine (published by the American Jewish Committee): "The consequences of attempting to impose a one-sided settlement on Israel, covered up by a less-than-convincing guarantee, could be traumatic for both Israel and the U.S."

In view of these developments, the preferred option to come out of the "reassessment" was shelved in late May. Sheehan wrote that Kissinger decided that "at some future date, when the president was stronger, when his prospects were more auspicious, he might go to the people with a plan for peace based upon the first option."[8] Consequently, Kissinger returned to shuttle diplomacy and by September had brought about a second disengagement agreement between Israel and Egypt in Sinai.

This agreement resulted in considerable tension among the various Arab parties to the conflict. Sadat was strongly denounced by Syria's Assad and by the PLO for agreeing to what amounted, in some views, to a separate though temporary peace with Israel. This dissension within the Arab camp became an important factor in the Lebanese civil war which escalated the following year, becoming, in a sense, an Arab civil war. *(See Lebanon chapter, p. 137)*

Brookings Report

In December 1975 the Brookings Institution, one of Washington's most prestigious think tanks, released a

broadly supported study entitled "Toward Peace in the Middle East." This study was frequently cited during the coming months as an outline of the policies the United States should pursue in attempting to bring about a comprehensive Middle East settlement, step-by-step diplomacy having apparently reached its end.[9]

The Brookings report was signed by 16 well-known Middle East specialists and scholars including a number of prominent American Jews. It was also signed by Jimmy Carter's prospective National Security adviser, Zbigniew Brzezinski, and by Brzezinski's selection as Middle East expert at the National Security Council, William Quandt.

In brief, the Brookings report contained the following recommendations:

- Israeli withdrawal to the 1967 borders with minor, mutually agreed modifications;
- Recognition of "the principle of Palestinian self-determination";
- Resolution, probably at a resumed Geneva Conference, of all outstanding issues, including Jerusalem, thus leading to peace between all of the parties;
- Implementation of the agreement in stages over a number of years;
- Arab recognition of Israel, conclusion of a peace treaty, and normalization of relations;
- Some arrangement for multilateral and bilateral guarantees for Israel's security, with the United States probably playing a unique role.

---

8. Edward R. F. Sheehan, "Step by Step in the Middle East," *Foreign Policy*, Spring 1976, p. 176.

9. The Brookings report became the central focus of an important series of hearings held by the Subcommittee on Near Eastern and South Asian Affairs of the Committee on Foreign Relations of the Senate during May, June and July 1976. The Brookings report along with considerable other useful information is printed in the report of these hearings entitled "Middle East Peace Prospects."

U.S. POLICY: AID, ARMS AND THE MILITARY BALANCE

Whether it produces a lasting peace or results in renewed turmoil, the Israeli-Egyptian treaty signed at the White House March 26, 1979, was likely to draw the United States further than ever before into the politics and conflicts of the Middle East.

The narrow purpose of the treaty was to end the 30-year state of war between Israel and its largest Arab neighbor. But the broader implication of the American-negotiated separate peace was that the United States would become both the protector and benefactor of the two nations. In addition to pushing the treaty negotiations to a successful conclusion, President Carter agreed to expand American security, economic and political commitments to Egypt and Israel.

In a letter to congressional leaders April 2, 1979, the president formally revealed the $4.8 billion package of loans and grants, mostly for military equipment, he had agreed to give the two countries. The only item in the package that had not been made public previously was $300 million in special economic assistance to Egypt. Included in the package was an $800 million grant to Israel to pay for constructing two airbases in the Negev desert to replace those in the Sinai that would be turned over to Egypt under the treaty, and $2.2 billion in arms sales loans. Egypt would receive $300 million in loans to improve its economy and $1.5 billion in arms sales loans.

The sale of weapons to Israel through long-term loans represented a major shift in American policy. Since 1973, Israel had been required to pay back only half the cost of weapons purchased from the United States. Also, the United States never before had loaned money to Egypt for weapons; Saudi Arabia had been financing most of Cairo's arms purchases.

Carter said total budget authority required for the additional aid would come to only $1.47 billion since most of the assistance would be in the form of guaranteed loans. Actual outlays from the Treasury would be $1.17 billion over four years, including $350 million in fiscal 1979 and $315 million in fiscal 1980.

The president emphasized three points about the aid:

• It was "evenhanded" and reflected "a careful assessment of the near-term burdens of the treaty balanced against the military and economic circumstances of each country. Our future influence in the Middle East depends on the perception by all affected countries that we do not unfairly support any one country."

• The aid package balanced "foreign policy needs and fiscal policy constraints." Carter said he made "every effort to limit United States funding in light of our current budgetary constraints."

• Warning against "peacemeal" action by Congress, Carter said the aid request was "a coherent, interrelated package which requires urgent congressional action." Delay "could critically disrupt the carefully negotiated timetable for treaty implementation."

Carter said the new aid request was "the most important foreign affairs proposal before the Congress."

Although the Egyptian-Israeli aid package met little opposition in Congress, where it was approved in the Senate by a 73-11 vote May 14 and in the House by a 347-28 vote May 30, there was widespread public opposition to further U.S. aid for the Middle East. Opinion polls taken shortly after the March 26 peace treaty signing indicated that Americans strongly opposed Carter's aid package.

Only two senators spoke at length against the bill. William Proxmire, D-Wis., complained that most of the money would be used to sell weapons to two nations that just signed a peace treaty.

"Military assistance is simply not the answer to achieving peace," Proxmire said. "This notion that we must provide military assistance to nations where that assistance is not directly related to the defense of this country is precisely what has led us down this long and bloody and reprehensible road of providing the weapons of death and destruction in the name of peace."

In response, Jacob K. Javits, R-N.Y., said the weapons would make Egypt and Israel secure against Arab nations that might want to disturb the peace.

Referring to other Arab nations, Javits said: "We have to build some kind of buffer against having the peace policy overrun by these warring forces, both economic and military, in order to give it half a chance."

In its report on the Egyptian-Israeli aid bill, the House Foreign Affairs Committee brushed aside criticisms that the package merely provided weapons to the two nations. "The security requirements of Israel and Egypt will not disappear as a result of the treaty," the committee said in its report. The aid package was responsive "to the legitimate self-defense requirements of both Israel and Egypt."

Background: Mideast Arms Race

"In the euphoria of a successful treaty, we may be tempted to pay any price," warned Proxmire. "But the payment should not include a new round of the arms race dressed as the dove of peace."

Although the new U.S. commitments to increase economic and military aid to Egypt and Israel caused apprehension among some that the arms race could be accelerated, it had been the four Arab-Israeli wars, along with interim clashes and inter-Arab feuding, that had sparked one of the world's most intense arms races. Since the quadrupling of oil prices that began during the 1973 war, Middle Eastern countries had found the means to purchase vast new arsenals of the most modern weapons. Western governments, anxious to pay for the costly oil, plunged into the Middle East arms market with gusto. None pursued the sale of weapons in the region with more enthusiasm and success than the United States.

In 1974, the Middle East took 57 percent of all arms exported. And the figure has steadily risen since then.

The Middle East accounts for the bulk of the steep rise in U.S. arms sales. From total sales of less than $1 billion in 1970, sales had jumped nearly ninefold by fiscal 1974, to a total of more than $8 billion. In the past few years sales have hovered around $9-$10 billion. France and England also have cashed in on the booming arms trade. The Arab countries have also decided to attempt to produce some arms themselves.

Money for Egyptian arms purchases and capital investments had, until the 1979 Israeli-Egyptian peace treaty, been provided largely by Saudi Arabia, Kuwait and smaller Persian Gulf states.

The Egyptians began complaining that the Soviets were dragging their feet in resupplying them with weapons lost during the 1973 war. Then as relations between Egypt and the Kremlin worsened, President Sadat began looking to the West. He had hoped to find the United States willing to supply Egypt with defensive arms, but until 1978, only a few cargo airplanes had been approved. Yet the Egyptian Ambassador to the United States, Ashraf Ghorbal, stated in a May 1977 interview that "If you are going to play . . . a very effective role, politically and economically, you must also help militarily."

U.S. Aid to Israel

U.S. military assistance to Israel entered a new phase after the 1973 war. Prior to that time, all U.S. assistance to Israel had been on either a cash sale or credit basis. But because of the magnitude of Israel's needs and the heavy toll the war had taken on the Israeli economy, the United States agreed to provide for the first time outright grants of military aid.

President Nixon Oct. 19, 1973, called on Congress to approve his request for $2.2 billion in military aid to Israel in order "to prevent the emergence of a substantial imbalance resulting from a large-scale resupply of Syria and Egypt by the Soviet Union." The U.S. decision to resupply Israel triggered the Arab oil embargo, but this did not deter the United States.

Of Israel's $2.5 billion aid request in 1975, $1.6 billion was to be for military assistance. The State Department held up the request to Congress during the "reassessment" period pending Middle East developments, but requested the aid in September in the wake of the new Sinai accord. Israel received in fiscal 1975 about $300 million in military assistance aid and $353 million in economic assistance. In 1976 Israel received about $714 million in economic assistance and $1.5 billion in military credits and grants.

By 1975 Israel's armaments were substantially in excess of what she had when the Yom Kippur war had broken out just two years earlier, from 1,700 to 2,700 tanks and from 308 combat aircraft to 486. Both the Arab and Israeli sides were clearly competing in a massive arms race, one which continued in 1977 and 1978 notwithstanding the constant talk of peace in the area.

This overwhelming U.S. support for Israeli arms assistance was in marked contrast to U.S. policy of less than a decade earlier. The United States, anxious to line up Arab allies in the cold war and to preserve its oil interests in that area, had been reluctant to supply Israel with weapons in the 1950s and early 1960s.

Tripartite Declaration

The first—and last—great power agreement to limit the flow of weapons to the Middle East was the U.S.-British-French declaration of May 25, 1950. In response to the Israeli argument that an arms race would threaten Israeli military superiority, the three powers declared their opposition to the "development of an arms race between the Arab states and Israel." The declaration was silent on arms races among Arab states.

From 1950 to 1955, the declaration had the effect of keeping Arab-Israeli arms rivalry at a low pitch. But Britain, the major arms supplier during this period, found itself drawn into an arms race between Egypt and Iraq, long-standing rivals in the Arab world. To maintain its oil interests in Iraq and to assure Iraq's association with the West in the cold war, Britain furnished aircraft and training to create an Iraqi air force. To assure Egypt's acceptance of continued British control of the Suez Canal, Britain created an Egyptian air force. Israel, realizing that the Tripartite Declaration was breaking down, began its search for arms suppliers.

Israel's success in finding arms was displayed in a February 1955 retaliatory raid into the Gaza Strip in which Egyptian forces suffered a number of casualties. Egyptian President Gamal Abdel Nasser sought Western arms to restore the military balance but was refused. After this refusal—coupled with the establishment of a U.S.-British-sponsored mutual defense treaty linking Britain, Iraq, Turkey, Iran and Pakistan—Nasser turned to the Soviets and convinced them Egypt could be useful in their efforts to destroy Western positions in the Middle East. Soviet bloc weapons began flowing to Egypt in September 1975.

France Arms Israel

Following disclosure of the Czech-Egyptian arms agreement, Israel intensified its search for an arms supplier in the West, approaching the Eisenhower administration in September 1955. After six months of delay, Israel was informed—through testimony by Secretary of State John Foster Dulles before the Senate Foreign Relations Committee, that it should rely for security not on U.S. arms but on the "collective security" of the United Nations. Turning then to Britain, Israel was advised by Prime Minister Anthony Eden to make concessions to the Arabs to avoid war.

France viewed the Soviet-Egyptian arms agreement in the context of its colonial war with the Moslem rebels in Algeria. Concerned that Soviet arms would find their way from Cairo to Algiers, France first sought an agreement from Nasser not to assist the Algerian rebels. When Nasser refused, France decided to honor Israel's request for arms. Arming Israel was viewed as a way to pin down Soviet-supplied weapons in Egypt. But, in the mid-1960s, France began to re-examine its arms sales policy to the Middle East in the light of the conclusion of the Algerian war in 1962. France began discussing arms sales with Arab countries—Jordan, Lebanon and Egypt. The apparent shift in French sales policy led to increased Israeli pressure on the United States to relax its restrictions on arms sales to Israel.

Another factor pushing Israel toward the United States was the disclosure in December 1964 and subsequent termination of secret West German arms sales to Israel. When the secret sales became known, Egypt threatened to recognize East Germany. The Egyptians' threat caused Bonn to cease abruptly its arms flow to Israel.

U.S. Arms to Israel

The shift in French policy, the termination of German arms and the continued flow of Soviet arms to Egypt, Syria and Iraq forced the United States in the early 1960s to reconsider its position on supplying weapons to Israel. In 1962, Israel obtained U.S. surface-to-air Hawk antiaircraft missiles and in 1965, Patton tanks; in 1966 an agreement was reached for the first sale of U.S. combat aircraft to Israel. The agreement called for the sale of 48 A-4 Skyhawk fighter-bombers to Israel, delivered in 1968. Pressure built up during the 1968 presidential campaign to supply Israel with the most advanced aircraft. Both party platforms supported efforts to end the arms race in the Middle East; but, in the absence of arms control, both called for providing Israel with the latest in supersonic aircraft.

Congressional Mandate

Similar support was shown on Capitol Hill. The fiscal 1969 foreign aid authorization act (PL 90-554) contained a provision calling on the president to negotiate the sale of supersonic aircraft to Israel to provide it with a deterrent force capable of "preventing future Arab aggression." In October 1968, President Johnson announced that he had instructed Secretary of State Dean Rusk to open negotiations for the sale of jets to Israel. The sale of 50 Phantom F-4s was announced by the administration in late December.

In the fiscal 1970-1971 Foreign Military Sales Act (PL 91-672), Congress called for arms control negotiations in the Middle East and expressed support for the president's position that arms should be made available to Israel and other friendly states in order to meet threats to their security. Also in 1970, in the fiscal 1971 defense procurement authorization (PL 91-441), Congress expressed "grave concern" over "the deepening involvement of the Soviet Union in the Middle East and the clear and present danger to world peace resulting from such involvement which cannot be ignored by the United States." The legislation authorized the transfer of an unlimited amount of aircraft and supporting equipment to Israel by sales, credit sales or guaranty.

By the mid-1970s, the increasing flow of arms sales to the Middle East had aroused growing concern in Congress. Sen. Edward M. Kennedy, D-Mass., June 18, 1975, urged a six-month moratorium on arms sales to the Persian Gulf to prevent hooking "these nations on the heroin of modern arms."

Congressional critics argued that the sales actually spur arms races rather than promote regional stability and that the United States is not able to control the use of the weapons once they have been sold. The critics also warned that the weapons can be used by totalitarian regimes to suppress legitimate interest groups within their own countries and that weapons sold to such countries as Saudi Arabia and Kuwait might one day be used against Israel.

By 1977, three Middle Eastern nations — Israel, Iran and Saudi Arabia — accounted for more than half of U.S. arms exports. Between 1973 and 1977, Iran had purchased $14.8 billion worth of U.S. weapons; Saudi Arabia, $12.3 billion; and Israel $5 billion. The difficulties of curbing the flow of advanced arms to these countries was underlined by a number of new commitments Carter had made to them in 1977 and 1978.

AWACS Sale to Iran

One of the first controversial arms policy steps taken by Carter was a proposal, formally submitted on July 7, 1977, to sell seven highly advanced flying radar command posts called AWACS (Airborne Warning and Control System) to Iran, at a total cost of $1.2 billion.

A provision of the 1973 foreign aid authorization act (PL 93-559) subsequently amended allows Congress to block arms sales worth more than $25 million by concurrent resolution passed within 30 days of the date the president proposes the sale to Congress. By informal agreement, the Senate Foreign Relations Committee and House Foreign Affairs Committee receive "pre-notification" of proposed sales 20 days in advance of the formal notification which starts the 30-day disapproval period.

AWACS is a Boeing 707 topped with a 30-foot diameter Frisbee-shaped radar dome and packed with communications equipment. The radar can pick up very low-flying airplanes up to 250 miles away that would be hidden from regular ground radar by the terrain. At $108.7 million a copy, it is the most expensive production-line aircraft in history.

Iran's interest in the plane had been common knowledge among foreign policy observers for at least a year when, on June 16, 1977, Carter sent Congress the pre-notification of a proposed sale: Iran would pay $1.2 billion for seven of the planes to be delivered starting in 1981. Formal notification would follow July 7 and Congress would have until Aug. 5 to kill the sale.

Opposition to the proposed sale was mobilizing on Capitol Hill for weeks before Carter formally notified Congress of the deal July 7. Critics charged the transaction would violate Carter's pledge that the United States would not be the first supplier of any qualitatively new weapon to a region. AWACSs highly advanced radar and communications gear would add a new dimension to the arms race in the volatile Persian Gulf area, they said.

Responding to the intensity of congressional opposition to the AWACS sale, Carter withdrew the proposal on July 28. He renewed his request on Sept. 7, with assurances that the deal had been modified to resolve most of the problems. To provide greater protection for the secret equipment, for instance, the new agreement stipulated that certain communications and coding gear would be removed from the plane.

Although a veto resolution was introduced in the Senate, the Foreign Relations Committee took no action by the Oct. 7 deadline. There also was no movement against the revised proposal in the House, thus allowing the sale to proceed. Nonetheless, the three-month battle between the administration and Congress over the Iranian arms sale served to highlight some important features of the legislative terrain that Carter would have to traverse in forthcoming foreign policy disputes concerning arm sales in the Middle East.

(As a perhaps somewhat wry footnote to this policy struggle, the new Iranian government in 1979 cancelled $7 billion of the $12 billion of military equipment and services that the deposed shah had wanted. Among the items the Iranian government said it would not need were the seven AWACS.)

1978 Middle East Jet Sales

Scarcely had the dust settled over the AWACS sale than smoke swirled up over an administration package deal to sell $4.8 billion worth of military aircraft to Israel, Saudi Arabia and, for the first time, Egypt. The weapons package proposal, announced Feb. 14, 1978, immediately became caught up in controversy not only over the administration's arms sales policy in general but also the U.S. role in shaping developments in the Middle East.

United States Assistance to the Middle East, 1946-1978[1]

(U.S. fiscal year — millions of dollars)

	1946-1952	1953-1961	1962-1973	1974	1975	1976	Transition Quarter[7]	1977	1978	Total Loans and Grants 1946-1978[2]
ISRAEL										
Economic[3]	86.5	507.1	662.2	51.5	353.1	714.4	78.6	742.0	791.8	4,009.4
Loans	—	248.3	535.1	—	8.6	239.4	28.6	252.0	266.8	1,553.0
Grants[4]	86.5	258.8	127.0	51.5	344.5	475.0	50.0	490.0	525.0	2,456.4
Military[4]	—	0.9	1,428.9	2,482.7	300.0	1,500.0	200.0	1,000.0	1,000.0	7,904.2
Credit Sales	—	0.9	1,428.9	136.4	200.0	750.0	100.0	500.0	500.0	4,454.2
Grants	—	—	—	1,500.0	100.0	750.0	100.0	500.0	500.0	3,450.0
Other[5]	135.0	57.5	279.2	47.3	62.4	104.7	12.6	.9	5.4	511.5
ALGERIA										
Economic[3]	—	4.6	176.6	—	4.6	6.1	2.1	5.4	4.1	202.7
Loans	—	—	11.6	—	—	—	—	—	—	11.6
Grants	—	4.6	165.0	—	4.6	6.1	2.1	5.4	4.1	191.1
Other[5]	—	—	55.5	72.2	123.8	87.6	—	82.3	492.8	1,063.2
EGYPT										
Economic[3]	12.3	302.3	582.8	21.3	370.1	464.3	552.5	907.7	943.0	4,168.5
Loans	10.7	131.2	453.9	9.5	298.8	351.7	443.6	796.8	797.1	3,313.7
Grants	1.6	171.1	128.9	11.8	71.3	112.6	108.9	110.9	145.9	854.8
Other[5]	7.3	30.6	38.9	9.0	38.1	7.8	—	—	1.2	123.6
IRAN										
Economic[3]	42.3	548.1	183.3	1.4	1.7	1.0	0.1	—	—	760.0
Loans	25.8	197.0	80.4	—	—	—	—	—	—	295.8
Grants	16.5	351.1	103.1	1.4	1.7	1.0	0.1	—	—	464.2
Military[4][6]	17.3	482.0	904.8	*	—	—	—	—	—	1,404.8
Loans	—	—	504.1							496.4
Grants	17.3	482.0	400.7	*	—	—				908.4
Other[5][6]	—	70.0	853.9	290.6	5.3	40.0	—	—	—	1,194.8
IRAQ										
Economic[3]	1.4	21.6	25.9	—	—	—	—	—	—	45.5
Loans	0.9	—	13.5	—	—	—	—	—	—	14.4
Grants	0.5	21.6	12.4	—	—	—	—	—	—	31.1
Military[4]	—	49.4	0.6	—	—	—	—	—	—	50.0
Grants	—	49.4	0.6	—	—	—	—	—	—	50.0
Other[5]	—	—	11.8	—	—	—	—	—	—	11.8
JORDAN										
Economic[3]	5.2	275.4	450.7	64.5	99.3	61.9	86.6	83.6	102.9	1,249.2
Loans	—	4.7	38.7	15.6	25.0	18.6	19.0	30.3	54.0	215.5
Grants	5.2	270.7	428.9	48.9	74.3	43.3	67.6	53.3	48.9	1,033.7
Military[4]	—	16.2	236.9	45.7	104.6	138.3	—	131.5	127.4	806.1
Credit Sales	—	—	69.0	—	30.0	82.5	—	75.0	71.0	327.5
Grants[5]	—	16.2	167.9	45.7	74.6	55.8	—	56.5	56.4	462.7
Other	—	—	16.7	7.9	—	—	—	—	—	24.6
KUWAIT										
Other[5]	—	—	50.0	—	—	—	—	—	—	50.0
LEBANON										
Economic[3]	3.6	95.5	32.3	5.7	2.9	0.1	—	29.8	32.9	181.1
Loans	1.6	17.9	14.1	—	—	—	—	6.8	7.6	33.4
Grants	2.0	77.6	18.2	5.7	2.9	0.1	—	23.0	25.3	147.7
Military[4]	—	8.4	27.0	0.2	0.1	0.1	—	25.0	0.6	50.2
Credit Sales	—	—	20.0	—	—	—	—	25.0	—	34.2
Grants	—	8.4	7.0	0.2	0.1	0.1	—	*	0.6	16.0
Other[5]	—	—	2.4	14.2	5.8	60.2	—	—	—	231.3
LIBYA										
Economic[3]	1.8	173.1	41.7	—	—	—	—	—	—	212.5
Loans	—	8.5	—	—	—	—	—	—	—	7.0
Grants	1.8	164.6	45.7	—	—	—	—	—	—	205.5
Military[4]	—	3.3	13.4	—	—	—	—	—	—	17.6
Grants	—	3.3	13.4	—	—	—	—	—	—	17.6
MOROCCO										
Economic[3]	0.3	290.4	525.4	20.0	23.7	45.1	4.0	26.8	36.2	952.8
Loans	—	192.9	274.6	—	8.0	24.8	—	8.0	8.8	505.7
Grants	0.3	97.5	250.9	20.0	15.7	20.3	4.0	18.8	27.4	447.1

	1946-1952	1953-1961	1962-1973	1974	1975	1976	Transition Quarter[7]	1977	1978	Total Loans and Grants 1946-1978[2]
Military[4]	—	2.4	110.2	3.6	14.9	30.8	0.2	30.8	44.2	244.3
Credit Sales	—	—	69.5	3.0	14.0	30.0	—	30.0	43.0	189.4
Grants	—	2.4	40.7	0.6	0.9	0.8	0.2	0.8	1.2	54.9
Other[5]	—	—	83.7	5.3	0.2	54.5	6.4	24.1	—	170.4
SAUDI ARABIA										
Economic[3]	4.7	27.9	—	—	—	—	—	—	—	31.8
Loans	4.3	—	—	—	—	—	—	—	—	4.3
Grants	0.4	27.9	—	—	—	—	—	—	—	27.5
Military[4]	—	63.1	232.2	0.2	*	—	—	—	—	292.4
Credit Sales	—	43.8	213.9	—	—	—	—	—	—	254.2
Grants	—	19.3	18.3	0.2	*	—	—	—	—	38.2
Other[5]	14.8	—	25.4	—	1.1	—	—	—	—	38.6
SUDAN										
Economic[3]	—	53.6	88.8	5.0	8.2	1.7	0.1	6.4	19.9	154.0
Loans	—	10.0	53.1	2.8	—	—	—	4.6	9.8	60.2
Grants	—	43.6	35.6	2.2	8.2	1.7	0.1	1.8	10.1	93.8
Military[4]	—	*	2.0	—	—	—	—	0.1	0.2	2.3
Credit Sales	—	—	1.5	—	—	—	—	—	—	1.3
Grants	—	*	0.5	—	—	—	—	0.1	0.2	1.0
Other[5]	—	—	23.5	18.1	—	2.7	—	3.3	—	41.4
SYRIA										
Economic[3]	0.4	44.9	45.1	—	104.6	34.9	78.7	99.7	105.4	480.6
Loans	—	23.6	29.4	—	99.4	32.9	78.5	89.0	93.4	413.5
Grants	0.4	21.3	15.7	—	5.2	2.0	0.2	10.7	12.0	67.1
TUNISIA										
Economic[3]	0.2	240.9	270.4	10.3	13.2	11.7	0.9	23.9	38.7	834.6
Loans	—	49.0	297.8	—	—	2.3	—	13.1	18.5	368.3
Grants	0.2	192.0	224.6	10.3	13.2	9.4	0.9	10.8	20.2	466.3
Military[4]	—	5.3	41.7	4.3	7.2	15.6	10.1	25.4	26.1	139.8
Credit Sales	—	2.6	2.2	2.5	5.0	15.0	10.0	25.0	25.0	87.5
Grants	—	2.7	39.5	1.8	2.2	0.6	0.1	0.4	1.1	52.3
Other[5]	—	—	27.5	—	—	8.4	14.3	—	—	50.9
TURKEY										
Economic[3]	237.3	1,093.2	1,479.1	5.5	4.4	—	—	0.2	1.2	2,705.8
Loans	97.2	301.9	1,123.1	—	—	—	—	—	0.4	1,445.9
Grants	140.1	791.3	355.9	5.5	4.4	—	—	0.2	0.8	1,259.9
Military[4]	325.6	1,587.7	1,954.3	190.8	109.1	—	125.0	125.0	175.4	4,984.2
Credit Sales	—	—	35.0	75.0	75.0	—	125.0	125.0	175.0	610.0
Grants	325.6	1,587.7	1,919.3	115.8	34.1	—	—	—	0.4	4,374.2
Other[5]	32.3	32.0	126.3	30.5	26.2	70.2	2.8	19.4	16.1	352.2
YEMEN ARAB REPUBLIC										
Economic[3]	—	16.0	31.8	4.0	6.9	7.4	2.7	17.1	7.7	91.6
Grants	—	16.0	31.8	4.0	5.5	7.4	2.7	17.1	7.7	90.2
YEMEN, PEOPLE'S DEMOCRATIC REPUBLIC OF										
Economic[3]	—	—	2.9	1.6	*	—	—	—	—	4.5
Grants	—	—	2.9	1.6	*	—	—	—	—	4.5

1 The table gives line categories under countries only where assistance was given. Egypt, for example, received no military aid during the 1946-1976 period.

2 Figures may not add up to totals due to rounding. Annual figures may not add up to cumulative totals because the fiscal year figures since FY 1955 represent new obligations entered into during those years on a gross basis; the cumulative figures for FY 1946-1976 are on a net basis, reflecting total obligations where funds obligated were not actually spent.

3 Economic aid totals include official development assistance, Food for Peace programs, Peace Corps and miscellaneous programs.

4 Military aid total includes the Foreign Assistance Act credit sales and grant programs,

transfers from excess stocks, other grants and loans under special programs.

5 Other includes Export-Import Bank loans, often made to the private sector within a country, Agriculture Department short-term credits, Overseas Private Investment Corporation direct loans and private trade agreements under PL-480, Title 1.

6 Iran received Export-Import Bank military equipment loans as follows: $120 million in 1971, $100 million in 1972, $200 million in both 1973 and 1974.

7 The figures listed in the column represent the dollar amounts allocated for the interim period between the old and new fiscal year budget, in this case July-Sept. 1976.

* Less than $500,000.

SOURCE: Agency for International Development, U.S. Overseas Loans and Grants and Assistance from International Organizations, July 1, 1945-September 30, 1978.

The sales that President Carter proposed to Congress were:

● For Israel, 15 F-15s, sophisticated long-range fighters to add to the 25 previously ordered. The new contract amounted to $480 million. Israel also ordered 150 F-16s, less sophisticated fighter/bombers, but only half were approved for $1.5 billion.

● For Egypt 50 F-5Es, short-range fighter/bombers that were priced at $400 million for the shipment.

● For Saudi Arabia, 60 F-15s costing $2.5 billion.

The proposed sale of America's most sophisticated jet fighter to Saudi Arabia set off a major battle between the large and influential community of Israel's supporters in the United States and persons — including administration officials — who argued that American policy in the Middle East must be more evenhanded.

In the end the latter group won as Congress refused to block the sale of the planes to any of the three nations. However, the fight principally was over the sale to Saudi Arabia. Few persons in the debate objected to selling Israel more planes, and the aircraft set to go to Egypt was an older type considered a less significant element in the Middle East arms balance.

In a statment Feb. 14 announcing the sales, Secretary of State Cyrus R. Vance said they were "directly supportive of our overall objectives in the Middle East," that they would help meet each country's security requirements and "will not alter the basic military balance in the region." The sale, Vance added, "will be consistent with the overriding objective of a just and lasting peace."

Although drawing less criticism than the proposed sales to Egypt and Saudi Arabia, the Israeli package was defended by the State Department on the grounds that it would enable Israel to plan for the continued modernization of its air force. "Our commitment to Israel's security has been and remains firm," Vance said.

"Egypt, too, must have reasonable assurance of its ability to defend itself if it is to continue the peace negotiations with confidence," the secretary of state added.

The sale to Cairo marked the first U.S. sale of weapons to that country in two decades. And the sale to Saudi Arabia was the first transfer to that country of the hottest U.S. fighter plane. Equally significant, the proposed sale to Israel was about half the number of fighter planes requested.

The administration's premise was that Saudi Arabia and Egypt had exercised a moderating influence on the Arab side of the Middle East conflict. This was more likely to continue and to affect other Arab states if the United States demonstrated its concern for the security of those countries by providing necessary defense equipment — according to this argument.

Opponents of the sale, prominent among them the American-Israel Public Affairs Committee (AIPAC), argued that U.S. arms sales to the two Arab states simply would feed Arab confidence that they could turn to military measures if Israel resisted their demands. Conversely, the shift in attitude of the United States, long Israel's arsenal against the Russian-supplied Arabs, could only heighten Israel's insecurity and make it less willing to compromise at the peace table.

Basic policy — not military minutiae — was at issue. But much of the debate also focused on the impact of the sales on the Middle East military balance.

The Military Balance

The prevailing assumption in the executive branch in 1978 was that most of Israel's military equipment was superior to most Arab equipment.

What Do They Have? U.S.-built Phantom and Skyhawk jets, which make up the bulk of the Israeli air force, carry many times the bombloads of most Arab planes over greater ranges. The U.S.-built electronic gear that is intended to blind enemy radars is assumed to be a match for the Soviet-built antiaircraft missiles in Arab arsenals.

Moreover, Israel has a substantial domestic arms industry which manufactures locally designed fighter planes, tanks and artillery that are superior to most of what the Arabs can buy from other countries.

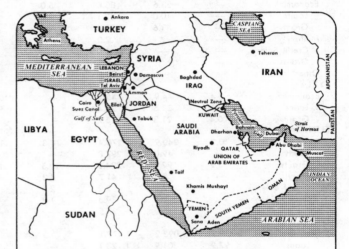

Balance of Forces in Middle East

	Modern attack planes[1]	Other combat planes[2]	Army[3]	Tanks[4]
Egypt	185	332	300,000	1,850
Iraq	150	199	160,000	1,400
Jordan	60	18	61,000	520
Libya	88	72	22,000	1,200
Saudi Arabia	90	37	45,000[5]	675
Syria	95	300	200,000	2,500
Other Arab States[7]	151	347	316,200	1,125
Total, Arab States	819[8]	1,305	1,104,200	9,270
Israel	590[9]	——	164,000[6]	3,135
Iran	514	80	220,000	2,840

1. Planes in or on order for ground attack squadrons. Excluded are 468 older planes, mostly Korean War vintage, with small bomb loads and short ranges.
2. Other armed planes in inventory or on order. Included are 709 interceptors and 468 older ground attack planes. Excluded are helicopters and small counter-insurgency planes.
3. Active-duty regular army troops, with two exceptions. The International Institute for Strategic Studies treats Israeli reserves as frontline troops; it does not so treat the 950,000 Arab reserves. Excluded from the table are the Arab states' various paramilitary units, except for the Saudi national guard, which is being organized and trained under U.S. supervision into mechanized infantry units. Also excluded is the 14,000 man Lebanese army, which has disintegrated.
4. Includes medium tanks (corresponding to U.S. battle tanks) in inventory or on order. Iraq has on order an unspecified number of Russian T-62 tanks.
5. Plus 35,000 in national guard.
6. 400,000 in 72 hours.
7. Algeria, Bahrain, Kuwait, Lebanon, Morocco, Oman, Qatar, Sudan, Tunisia, United Arab Emirates, Yemen Arab Republic (North Yemen) and People's Democratic Republic of Yemen (South Yemen).
8. Theoretically, the ground attack planes of the Arab states could carry about 2,700 tons of bombs in a single, combined mission (more than 85 percent of the payload carried by modern planes). More than 700 interceptors would be left for home defense.
9. Theoretically, the Israeli Air Force could carry about 3,100 tons of bombs in a single mission. But this would leave no planes for home defense.

SOURCE: International Institute for Strategic Studies, "The Military Balance-1977-78"

Opponents of U.S. sales to the Arabs warned that Israel's qualitative superiority was fading. With their new oil wealth, the Arab states were beginning to buy sophisticated equipment instead of the hand-me-downs with which they once made do. For instance, by summer of 1977 Arab states had in stock or on order about 150 Russian Mig 23s and about 130 French Mirage F-1s with much greater bomb loads and range than older Arab planes.

Already facing a substantial numerical inferiority, Israel cannot afford any erosion of its qualitative edge, according to this argument. To stay a jump ahead of modernizing Arab forces over a long haul would impose a crushing burden on the Israeli economy. It might even erode U.S. support for that country if Congress wearied of ever increasing military aid requests.

How Good Are They? The basic judgment of the executive branch agencies was that the Israeli military is far more effective than its Arab opposition on a man-for-man basis. Better training, more combat experience and a more widespread familiarity with modern technology are cited to explain Israeli advantage.

Not only is it assumed that Israeli pilots could outfly their Arab counterparts, but a similar disparity is assumed between the maintenance crews on the two sides. So a much higher proportion of the Israeli planes would be ready to fly if war broke out and they could fly more missions in a day than could the Arab aircraft.

This margin of superiority has been increasing, according to the State Department, because Egypt — by far the largest of Israel's potential foes — has curtailed its training exercises for want of spare parts for its equipment.

But former U.S. intelligence officials challenged this estimate in 1977 in testimony before the Senate Foreign Relations Subcommittee on the Near East and South Asia. The assumption was merely a political rationalization for decisions to pare down Israel's requests for military assistance, according to retired Air Force intelligence chief Maj. Gen. George Keegan.

"The Arabs are training, and they are training well," warned Dr. Joseph Churba, formerly the Air Force's senior Middle East intelligence analyst. "It was proven in the 1973 war that they are quite capable of handling sophisticated military technology if trained well." Churba resigned late in 1976 to protest allegedly anti-Israeli statements by Joint Chiefs of Staff Chairman Gen. George S. Brown.

What's the Bottom Line? "Israel has now, and will retain well into the 1980s, a substantial margin of military superiority — especially air superiority," according to a March 21, 1978, State Department letter to Rep. Gerry E. Studds, D-Mass.

In his May 1977 testimony to the Senate panel, Churba summarized the U.S. intelligence estimate at the time of his resignation late in 1976: "In the worst-case scenario — that is, a war simultaneously breaking out on several fronts — with a Soviet airlift [to the Arabs] and in the absence of an American airlift [to Israel] the Israelis would be able to defeat the combination of Arab armies in a period of one to three weeks, sustaining higher casualties the longer hostilities continue."

But Keegan insisted that this estimate assumed that Israel would continue to perform "miracles on the battlefield" in the face of mounting odds. "One failure in warning, one failure or delay in mobilization, and a number of small failures on strategy and tactics...at the outset of a war can mean the end of the Israeli state," he warned.

It was difficult to assess the impact of the sales on the Middle East military balance because the planes are inherently capable of performing a wide variety of combat missions.

How Much? How Far? To use any of the planes as bombers, a country must give up some of the plane's theoretical range. The weight and aerodynamic drag of bombs hung under the plane's wings increases fuel consumption. And the racks from which the bombs are hung could otherwise have been used for extra fuel tanks.

For instance, carrying no bombs, the F-5Es offered to Egypt can fly about 670 miles and return to base. Carrying about 1,000 pounds of bombs, this radius is reduced to 570 miles. Carrying a near-full load of 5,000 pounds the F-5E can reach only about 140 miles.

Even for a given mission, a plane's radius of action can vary. Planners must reduce the range to allow for the fuel-gulping evasive maneuvers necessary in combat. On the other hand, a nation can extend the range of its planes almost indefinitely by mid-air refueling from tanker planes.

In mid-1978 Saudi Arabia had four tankers and Israel reportedly had converted used jetliners into tankers. All three of the planes in the sale package were designed for mid-air refueling, but the necessary plumbing will be omitted from the exported planes.

Optional Equipment. What can be added on to a plane may be as important as what is built into it. And add-ons may be harder for the United States to control.

For instance, as built for the U.S. Air Force, an F-15 can carry only one bomb from each of its three underwing attachments (called "hardpoints"). But the manufacturer has built an adapter (called a "multiple ejection rack") that can carry six bombs from each hardpoint. There is considerable controversy over how easily Israel could duplicate these adapters or whether the Arab states could purchase copies from Soviet or European sources.

F-15

For about $17 million a copy the Saudis and Israelis were offered what is widely regarded as the world's finest fighter plane. Theoretically able to fly 2,000 mph, the F-15 has climbed seven miles within a minute of takeoff.

The plane's radar, whch can spot targets more than 50 miles away or flying at tree-top height, guides its four Sparrow missiles which can reach targets 20 miles away. For dogfights at close range, the plane carries a 20 mm cannon and four Sidewinder missiles that home in on a target's heat emissions. A highly accurate computer gunsight projects onto a teleprompter-like screen (called a "head-up display") so the pilot can read it without taking his eyes off the target.

For a fighter mission (hunting other planes) the F-15's range has been reported as up to 900 miles. But over shorter ranges, the plane could also carry 15,000 pounds of bombs. And the computer gunsight turns out to be an extremely accurate bombsight as well.

The Saudis have insisted that they do not plan to use the plane as a bomber. And the U.S. Air Force has told Congress that the plane would be wasted in that role. The F-16 can carry the same bombload over the same distance at half the pricetag. And while the F-15's radar can map ground targets, the F-16's is more accurate, having been designed for the purpose. Furthermore, in dense, turbulent air close to the ground, the F-15's big wings would bounce the plane around, cancelling some of the gunsight's accuracy.

The plane is designed for quick maintenance. Either engine can be replaced in 20 minutes. The mass of electronic gear is modularized: If a module fails, it is identified by built-in equipment and the ground crew simply replaces the module — there is no need to diagnose and repair the fault in the module.

F-16

According to Air Force testimony, the F-16, which was designed as a dogfighter, would be about the equal of the F-15 in close combat because of its agility and small size (about half as big as an F-15).

The F-15's chief advantage would be its long-range radar missiles that could destroy the F-16 from beyond the smaller plane's reach. The F-16's radar can search out to 50 miles and can detect very low-flying planes, but it cannot guide radar-controlled missiles (although the necessary additional equipment is available from the radar manufacturer).

The F-16 uses one engine of the type used in the F-15. For a fighter mission, it has a lower top speed (about 1,600 mph) and about the same range as the F-15. But it is half as expensive — about $7 million a copy.

Because the bombing mission was built into the plane's design, it can carry about 10,000 pounds of bombs for a greater range than the F-15. And its radar can pick out smaller ground targets more accurately.

F-5E

Designed expressly for export to U.S. allies, the F-5E combines respectable performance — about 1,000 mph top speed — with low cost and ease of maintenance. Its agility and small size make it a natural dogfighter and it is armed with cannon and Sidewinders. It has a small radar of about 20 miles range and, theoretically, can fly missions out to 650 miles.

Saudi Arabia and Jordan in 1978 had about 150 of the planes.

In recent years, the U.S. Air Force has used squadrons of F-5Es to mimic Russian Mig 21s in training exercises with front-line U.S. planes. Reportedly, the little planes have been surprisingly successful but this could be misleading — the exercises have been conducted under ground rules that stack the deck against the more advanced U.S. planes.

Mirage F-1 and Other Weapons

If the Saudis had been denied the F-15 they would probably have bought Mirage F-1s from France. In mid-1978 Egypt, Libya and Morocco already had (or reportedly had ordered) about 130 of these planes which can fly faster than the F-16 and can carry up to 9,000 pounds of bombs.

Opponents of the sales to Egypt and Saudi Arabia cited press reports that France and Egypt had agreed to build an F-1 production line in Egypt. But the State Department insisted that both governments had denied this.

Arab forces also had in mid-1978 about 130 Mirage III and Mirage V jets that usually carry about 2,000 pounds of bombs. They had about 200 Russian-built Sukhoi 7s that can carry 5,500 pounds of bombs for short distances and about 25 Sukhoi 20s that can carry 11,000 pounds.

The core of Israel's bomb-carrying capacity rested with its U.S.-built planes. These were 200 F-4 Phantoms that carry about 16,000 pounds each and 235 A-4 Skyhawks that carry about 10,000 pounds each. Israel also had about 30 Mirage IIIs and about 100 Israeli-built Kafirs, which are a much improved version of the Mirage III.

1979 Aid Package

Israel and Egypt have been the largest recipients of U.S. foreign aid. And the agreements relating to the 1979 peace treaty assured that these two nations would be the beneficiaries of the most massive American assistance effort since the Marshall Plan.

Since 1946 the United State has given Israel $12.4 billion in economic and military aid; Egypt has received $4.3 billion. Most of the aid has been granted since the 1973 war.

Since fiscal 1977 the United States has been supplying about $2 billion a year to Israel and $1 billion a year to Egypt. The commitments resulting from the peace treaty would almost double these amounts.

Although the total price tag for this additional aid is $4.8 billion over fiscal 1979-82, administration officials said actual budget outlays would be only $1.17 billion. The rest of the aid will be in the form of loans for arms purchases.

New Aid Commitments

The aid commitments made by the United States as part of the peace treaty agreements included:

ISRAEL:

● An $800 million grant to cover part of the cost of relocating in the Negev desert Israel's two air bases in the Sinai. Israeli officials have estimated the total cost of moving the bases at more than $3 billion. The $800 million grant will be spread over fiscal years 1979-80. In addition, the United States will provide "managerial and technical assistance" for the base relocation.

● Long-term loans to enable Israel to purchase $2.2 billion in arms from the United States; purchases are to include 200 tanks, 800 armored personnel carriers, air-to-ground missiles and artillery weapons. Terms for the loans are current market interest rates, a 10-year deferment on payment of principal, and then 20 years to repay the loan.

● A speed-up in the delivery of 75 F-16 fighter planes promised Israel in 1978. The planes had been scheduled for delivery in October 1981, but now will be delivered by January 1980.

● Expanded arrangements for cooperation between the United States and Israel on research and development of weapons.

EGYPT:

● Long-term loans to enable Egypt to purchase $1.5 billion in arms from the United States, including an unspecified number of F4 fighters, destroyers, tanks, armored personnel carriers, five Hawk air-defense systems and other equipment. The terms of the loan are the same as for Israel.

In a letter to Egyptian Defense Minister Kamal Hassan Ali, U.S. Defense Secretary Harold Brown said the arms sales represent "an expanded security relationship" between Egypt and the United States.

The terms for financing arms sales to both countries represent a major shift in American policy.

Most arms sales to nations other than Israel have been financed through a credit program under which the United

States appropriates 10 percent of the purchase price of an arms sale as a guarantee for the long-term loan.

But since 1973 Israel has received special treatment. The United States has forgiven up to half of the purchase price of arms delivered to Israel. Of the $7.5 billion worth of arms purchased by Israel between 1973 and 1979, the United States has forgiven payment on $3.5 billion. Beginning in fiscal 1977 the United States each year has provided $1 billion in arms sales financing, half of which has been forgiven.

In order to save money, the new aid program required Israel to pay back the full purchase price of all additional arms obtained from the United States. The sole exception was the $800 million in grants for relocating the Sinai air bases. The new program did not affect previous plans under the regular aid program to provide $1 billion in arms sales for Israel in fiscal 1980; half of this amount also will be forgiven.

The United States never before has granted Egypt credits for arms purchases. The new aid effort would, in effect, put Egypt and Israel on an equal basis for the financing of arms.

Existing Aid Program

The new commitments resulting from the treaty supplemented existing aid programs that have been running at the rate of nearly $1.8 billion a year for Israel and $1 billion annually for Egypt.

Israel has received both economic and military assistance, while nearly all of the Egyptian aid has been directed at reviving that nation's economy.

Since fiscal 1977 the United States annually has provided Israel $1 billion in arms sales credits and $785 million in a program called "security supporting assistance," or the "economic support fund." The program is designed to help the civilian economies of countries such as Israel and Egypt that have heavy military expenditures.

ISRAEL:

• Military Aid. Half of the $1 billion in arms sales credits is in loans, half in grants.

• Economic Aid. Two-thirds ($525 million) of the $785 million in economic aid is a direct cash grant, and the remainder is a long-term loan. Until fiscal year 1979, most of the money went for a program to permit Israel to purchase food and other imports from the United States. All of the money now goes to bolster the Israeli economy.

• Israel also receives a gradually diminishing amount of aid under Title I of the Food for Peace Program. That aid,

estimated at $5.4 million in fiscal 1979 and $1 million in 1980, enables Israel to buy American agricultural products at a discount by using Israeli currency.

EGYPT:

• Economic Aid. Egypt receives $750 million a year under the security supporting assistance program. Most of the money has gone to development projects, particularly to improve agricultural production in Egypt, and to purchase American food imports. A major new program proposed for fiscal 1980 would modernize Cairo's telephone system at a cost of $70 million. Some $500 million of the $750 million is in the form of grants, the rest in loans.

• Food for Peace. Egypt has received approximately $200 million a year since 1976 under various Food for Peace programs. Some $207 million was budgeted for fiscal 1979 and $219 million for 1980.

• Military Training. Egypt became eligible in 1976 for U.S. training of its military officers; $400,000 was budgeted for that program in 1979 and $1 million was requested for 1980.

SYRIA, JORDAN:

In addition to Egypt and Israel, the United States has also provided substantial aid to Syria and Jordan. The administration has tried, unsuccessfully, to get those nations to go along with the Middle East peace process. Since 1946 Jordan has received a total of $2.0 billion in U.S. aid, and Syria $500 million.

Half of the $283.7 million budgeted for Jordan in fiscal 1979 went for economic projects. Jordan also was to receive during 1979 $45 million in grants for military equipment and supplies, $85 million in financing for arms purchases, $2 million worth of military training, and $8.7 million in Food for Peace programs.

There have been signs that members of Congress have tired of providing major amounts of aid to Jordan since Amman has opposed the American initiatives for a Middle East peace.

The 1980-81 military aid bill (HR 3173) passed by the House March 29, 1979, would cut off further aid to Jordan unless the president "determines and certifies to the Congress that Jordan is acting in good faith to achieve further progress toward a comprehensive peace settlement in the Middle East and that the expenditure of such funds will serve the process of peace in the Middle East."

Syria receives $90 million in security supporting assistance (nearly all in loans) and $24 million in Food for Peace programs.

SUPERPOWER RIVALRY: SOVIET ROLE IN MIDDLE EAST

The 1970s have not been a good decade for the Soviet Union in the Middle East. In fact, the Arab Middle East, with its strong religious traditions, has never been hospitable ground for Soviet-style communism and atheism. It was not until the late 1950s when Egyptian President Gamal Abdel Nasser, feeling abandoned by the United States and Western Europe and confronted by an increasingly strong Israel, was forced to turn to the Russians for support and weapons. Soviet aid to Egypt, in turn, prompted Western Europe and eventually the United States to arm Israel and, to a much lesser extent, the conservative Arab states.

When Nasser died suddenly on Sept. 28, 1970, the two superpowers were entrenched as supporters and arms suppliers to their respective allies in the region. Under Nasser's successor, Anwar Sadat, however, relations between the Soviet Union and its major Arab ally, Egypt, began to deteriorate. On July 18, 1972, President Sadat ordered all Soviet military advisers and experts out of Egypt and placed all Soviet bases and equipment under Egyptian control. A week later, he explained that he took this decision because of the Soviet Union's "excessive caution" as an ally.

The October 1973 Middle East war further diminished Soviet influence in the area. In ending that war and for a few months thereafter, the Soviet Union was intimately involved in the peacemaking process. On Oct. 21, 1973, the two superpowers presented a joint resolution to the United Nations Security Council calling for a cease-fire in place and for implementation of a Security Council resolution calling for Israeli withdrawal from Arab lands occupied in the 1967 war. That resolution was adopted by the Security Council the next day.

Two months later, on Dec. 21, 1973, the United States and the Soviet Union co-chaired the first Arab-Israeli peace conference in Geneva. In addition to the two superpowers, the participants at the Geneva Conference were Egypt, Israel and Jordan. Syria boycotted the meeting. The conference lasted only two days and, despite innumerable proposals for subsequent meetings, had not reconvened as of mid-1979.

With the prospects of a comprehensive Middle East peace involving all parties to the conflict and the Soviet Union seemingly out of reach, U.S. Secretary of State Henry A. Kissinger embarked on his step-by-step shuttle diplomacy in early 1974. Kissinger's effort succeeded, to a great extent, in excluding the Soviet Union from any role in the peacemaking process.

During the next two years, Soviet-Egyptian relations continued to deteriorate as Sadat turned increasingly to the United States for support, Conservative Arab states, including Saudi Arabia and Jordan, remained firmly anchored to the United States and the West and suspicious of the Russians. There were serious crises in Soviet relations with even the two most important of the so-called Arab "radical" states, Syria and Iraq. Russian leaders were highly critical of Syria for intervening in Lebanon in 1975 against the leftists and Palestinians. Iraq, in the meantime,

was developing friendlier relations with the United States and the West.

By the time President Carter took office in January 1977, Soviet influence in the Middle East was at a low ebb. The Carter administration soon decided that the time was ripe for a comprehensive settlement in the area and that Kissinger's step-by-step approach had reached a dead end. This decision resulted in the Soviet-American statement of Oct. 1, 1977, calling for a Geneva Conference "not later than December 1977" to work out a full resolution of the Arab-Israeli conflict "incorporating all parties concerned and all questions."

Israel's and the American Jewish lobby's reaction to the Soviet-American statement was swift and visceral. Fearing that it would allow the PLO to participate, Israeli officials and their American supporters put sufficient pressure on the administration to scuttle the guidelines for Geneva. The Egyptian reaction to the guidelines was also negative. A Geneva Conference, with the Soviet Union as co-chairman, was no more appealing to President Sadat than it was to the Israelis, and the prospect of its reconvening has often been cited as a major reason for Sadat's decision to visit Jerusalem.

Soviet Role in Peacemaking Process

Excluded from any positive role in the Middle East peacemaking process, the Russian reaction to Sadat's visit to Jerusalem, the Camp David accords and the Egyptian-Israeli peace treaty was negative. Throughout that period, Sadat was routinely accused of betraying the Arab and particularly the Palestinian cause and of allying himself with the "reactionary" forces of Zionism and imperialism. The United States was denounced for encouraging an unworkable settlement that would benefit only Israel and warned that its meddling would result in increased turmoil and chaos in the area.

The Soviets also sought to improve their relations with the Arab rejectionists. There was, on the surface at least, greater amiability with Syria, Iraq, Libya and the other hard-liners. Contacts between the Soviet Union and Jordan increased and the Jordanian media began supporting a return to the Geneva Conference and a strong Russian role in the peacemaking process. Perhaps most significant were reports in early March 1979 of the possible establishment of diplomatic ties between the Soviet Union and staunchly anti-communist Saudi Arabia.

To many observers, Soviet opposition to the American-engineered Egyptian-Israeli peace process had less to do with Russian support for its allies in the Arab world or a desire to bring about a comprehensive settlement of the Arab-Israeli conflict than with Soviet frustration at being excluded from the peace efforts. With the United States assuming the major role of mediator in the conflict, it is argued, the Soviet Union had little choice but to improve its own ties with Arab opponents of a U.S.-backed settlement.

U.S.-Soviet Guidelines For a Comprehensive Peace

In a formal statement Oct. 1, 1977, the United States and the Soviet Union set forth the following guidelines for a comprehensive peace settlement in the Middle East:

Having exchanged views regarding the unsafe situation which remains in the Middle East, Secretary of State Cyrus R. Vance of the United States and Andrei A. Gromyko, member of the Politburo of the Central Committee of the Communist Party of the Soviet Union and Minister for Foreign Affairs of the U.S.S.R., have the following statement to make on behalf of their countries, which are the co-chairmen of the Geneva Peace Conference on the Middle East:

1. Both Governments are convinced that vital interests of the peoples of this area as well as the interests of strengthening peace and international security in general urgently dictate the necessity of achieving as soon as possible a just and lasting settlement of the Arab-Israeli conflict. This settlement should be comprehensive, incorporating all parties concerned and all questions.

The United States and the Soviet Union believe that, within the framework of a comprehensive settlement of the Middle East problem, all specific questions of the settlement should be resolved, including such key issues as withdrawal of Israeli armed forces from territories occupied in the 1967 conflict; the resolution of the Palestinian question, including insuring the legitimate rights of the Palestinian people; termination of the state of war and establishment of normal peaceful relations on a basis of mutual recognition of the principles of sovereignty, territorial integrity and political independence.

The two Governments believe that, in addition to such measures for insuring the security of the borders between Israel and the neighboring Arab states as the establishment of demilitarized zones and the agreed stationing in them of United Nations troops or observers, international guarantees of such borders as well as of the observance of the terms of the settlement can also be established, should the contracting parties so desire. The United States and the Soviet Union are ready to participate in these guarantees, subject to their constitutional processes.

2. The United States and the Soviet Union believe that the only right and effective way for achieving a fundamental solution to all aspects of the Middle East problem in its entirety is negotiation within the framework of the Geneva Peace Conference, specifically convened for these purposes, with participation in its work of the representatives of all the parties involved in the conflict, including those of the Palestinian people, and legal and contractual formalization of the decisions reached at the conference.

In their capacity as co-chairmen of the Geneva Conference, the U.S. and the U.S.S.R. affirm their intention through joint efforts and in their contacts with the parties concerned to facilitate in every way the resumption of the work of the Conference not later than December 1977. The co-chairmen note that there still exist several questions of a procedural and organizational nature which remain to be agreed upon by the participants to the Conference.

3. Guided by the goal of achieving a just political settlement in the Middle East and of eliminating the explosive situation in this area of the world, the U.S. and the U.S.S.R. appeal to all the parties in the conflict to understand the necessity for careful consideration of each other's legitimate rights and interests and to demonstrate mutual readiness to act accordingly.

It has become almost a truism that without the involvement of the Soviet Union there can be no comprehensive settlement in the Middle East. Craig R. Whitney reported in *The New York Times* on March 27, 1979, a day after the Egyptian-Israeli peace treaty was signed in Washington, that "a comprehensive Middle East peace, Western diplomats agree, is possible only with Soviet participation and support. And as long as the Russians and most Arab states remain opposed to the Egyptian-Israeli accord, it has no chance of becoming the first step toward a comprehensive peace."

Even a staunch supporter of Israel like Naham Goldmann had reached the same conclusion shortly before the Camp David agreements of September 1978. Goldmann, a former president of the World Jewish Congress and the World Zionist Organization, wrote in the fall 1978 issue of *Foreign Affairs* magazine that "any attempt to eliminate the U.S.S.R. from the area is, in my opinion, unwise and short-sighted. . . . The Soviet Union is certainly not strong enough to impose a peace agreement in the Middle East, but it is well capable of sabotaging any settlement reached without it. . . . Whatever may be achieved in the direct negotiations undertaken between the Israeli and Egyptian representatives will make necessary a reconvocation of the Geneva Conference, notwithstanding the reluctance of Israel and some Arab states."

The Geneva Option

By 1977, the Soviet Union was on the defensive and virtually excluded from American-led efforts to resolve the Arab-Israeli conflict. The Soviets had no diplomatic ties with Israel or Saudi Arabia and relations with Egypt, Syria and Iraq were going from bad to worse as these Arab countries turned to the United States. The Russians were doubtless relieved when the new Carter administration decided to scuttle the "step-by-step" approach in favor of a comprehensive peace in the Middle East.

On Oct. 1, 1977, the United States and the Soviet Union issued guidelines for a comprehensive peace. The joint statement seemed to indicate that the United States had reached the conclusion that lasting peace in the Middle East would be impossible without Soviet cooperation. In the declaration, both superpowers made concessions. The United States, for the first time, accepted the Arab-Soviet formula of "the legitimate rights of the Palestinian people," rather than the "legitimate interests." The Soviet Union, in turn, called for "withdrawal of Israeli armed forces from

U.S. Opts for More Assertive Mideast Role . . .

Seeking to dramatize its willingness to use military means to shore up U.S. allies in the Middle East, the Carter administration announced March 9, 1979, it would sell $400 million worth of jets, tanks and other arms to North Yemen without waiting for a congressional review of the deal.

The confidence of the pro-U.S. regimes in the region apparently was shaken by Washington's failure to shore up the shah's regime in Iran — which had been touted as a key U.S. ally and had been allowed to purchase almost unlimited amounts of U.S. military gear.

The administration hoped the arms deal with Yemen would demonstrate Washington's willingness to assist friendly governments in the Persian Gulf and Red Sea region — particularly Saudi Arabia — in meeting their external military threats.

At a March hearing on the president's decision to waive the congressional review process on the grounds of national security, some Democrats of a House Foreign Affairs subcommittee protested the presidential action. Only a few members, however, opposed the underlying administration decision to step up the transfer of U.S. arms to the region.

But one of the critics, Rep. Gerry E. Studds, D-Mass., maintained that the congressional quiescence to date reflected ignorance rather than support. As in Vietnam and Iran, he argued, the United States was misinterpreting purely local political problems as superpower showdowns. Turmoil in Iran and Yemen did not guarantee Russian advantages over the long run any more than Moscow had been able to capitalize on its earlier successes in Egypt and Somalia, he said.

More Assertive U.S. Role

The administration conceded that there were purely local aspects — regional, tribal and religious rivalries — to the chronic border warfare in the southern part of the Arabian Peninsula.

But it insisted there were broader political implications because of South Yemen's avowed Marxist orientation and its policy of abetting subversion in the neighboring non-Marxist Arab regimes. This alarmed Saudi Arabia, which, in turn, bankrolled the military modernization of North Yemen so that that country could act as its surrogate in waging war against South Yemen.

And the administration apparently felt that Yemen had taken on a larger significance because of recent events in Afghanistan, Ethiopia and Iran. Taken together, these events showed that the political tide around the rim of the Indian Ocean was flowing toward Moscow and away from Washington, the administration warned.

By mid-February 1979, the administration had opted for a more assertive role in the region. During a tour of major Middle Eastern countries friendly to the United States, Defense Secretary Harold Brown announced a series of arms transfers to demonstrate U.S. resolve to support its friends.

Included in the $400 million arms package for North Yemen were 12 F-5E fighters, 64 M-60 tanks and 100 troop carriers. According to the State Department, this sale had been agreed to in September 1978, but a formal announcement was deferred until the new Congress convened. Congress received informal notification of the sale Feb. 16, 1979.

Brown Middle East Trip

Brown's tour of the region had been planned months before the collapse of the shah's government. But even while the shah still ruled, Soviet gains in the area made 1978 a disturbing year for Middle East regimes that relied on American support.

● Ethiopian forces backed by a major Soviet airlift and Russian and Cuban advisers rolled back Somalia's attempt to capture the eastern Ethiopian province of Ogaden.

● North Yemen's president was assassinated on June 24; two days later the president of South Yemen was assassinated by a pro-Soviet organization.

● Afghanistan's Moscow-oriented government was ousted April 27 by an even more pro-Soviet group. On Dec. 4 the new Afghan prime minister arrived in Moscow to sign a 20-year treaty of cooperation.

After the revolution in Iran removed the regime that Washington long had relied on to police the region, Brown inevitably had the burden of assuring the other U.S. allies in the area that the United States still was a valuable friend.

The administration insisted that it realized the friendly governments in the region faced internal as well as external threats. But Brown insisted that U.S. allies did have legitimate military concerns to which Washington was sensitive. "No one should doubt our willingness and ability to be good friends in peace and war," he said in a Feb. 10 arrival speech in Riyadh, Saudi Arabia. The

territories occupied in the 1967 war," thus seeming to abandon its previous insistence on Israeli withdrawal from *all* those territories. The Soviet Union also did not insist upon a specific reference to the Palestine Liberation Organization's (PLO) participation in the Geneva Conference. Israel has steadfastly refused to enter into negotiations with the PLO.

In an article in the October 1978 issue of *Current History* magazine, O. M. Smolansky, professor of International Relations at Lehigh University, described the uproar over the joint Soviet-American declaration. "As is typical of the Arab-Israeli conflict, in short order emotion once again prevailed over reason. Subjected to groundless accusations of 'drawing the Soviet Union into the Middle East in order to *impose* a superpower solution on the reluctant parties, Washington quickly backed down. As early as October 5, Carter, Vance and Israeli Foreign Minister Moshe Dayan agreed on the details of a working paper which, to all intents and purposes, effectively dismantled the joint statement. Among other things, Israel was assured that such unacceptable subjects as 'ensuring the legitimate rights of the Palestinian people' could not be introduced to the Geneva conference's agenda without Jerusalem's approval."

. . . Yemen Arms Deal Aimed at Countering Soviets

United States could and would "provide the best training and equipment . . . [and] the extra strength needed to meet a foe from outside the region."

The various arms sales and military assistance moves discussed on the trip all had been under discussion for some time. But when confirmed and publicized by Brown, they added up to a dramatic commitment by the Carter administration to continue its military support of friendly regimes in the Middle East.

Justification for U.S. Involvement in Yemen

According to the administration, the scale of fighting between the two Yemens intensified dramatically in late February and early March. South Yemen troops, supported by Soviet-supplied tanks and planes, invaded North Yemen at four points. Up to 40 percent of South Yemen's armed forces were involved in the attack, which penetrated nearly 20 miles at one point. The administration insisted that South Yemen clearly was aided by the Soviet and Cuban advisers stationed in that country.

On March 6 the Arab League foreign ministers tried to arrange a cease-fire. To avoid alienating Syria, Iraq, Saudi Arabia and the Persian Gulf states, Moscow reportedly urged South Yemen to agree to a cease-fire, which it did on March 30.

In the meantime, the Carter administration had taken several highly visible actions to demonstrate support for its allies in the region.

● For the first time since enactment of the 1976 Arms Export Control Act, presidential authority was invoked under the act to waive the 30-day period for congressional review of the $400 million sales package. To further expedite the arms transfer, the administration approved the transfer to Yemen of similar equipment previously sold to Saudi Arabia.

● Additional weapons, including artillery and 1,500 anti-tank guided missiles, were approved for transfer to North Yemen. The value of this additional transfer fell below the threshold requiring congressional review under the 1976 act.

● The aircraft carrier *Constellation* and a flotilla of escorts sailed from the Philippines toward the scene of the conflict. In December 1978 the *Constellation* had been dispatched on a similar mission intended to signal continued U.S. support for the shah of Iran, but the ship was recalled before it entered the Indian Ocean.

● Two U.S. AWACS radar-warning and command planes were sent from Okinawa to Saudi Arabia to carry out what the administration called "passive radar surveillance." Since they were intelligence missions and not combat flights, the administration maintained, this did not trigger the War Powers Act.

● Saudi Arabia was offered a squadron of U.S. F-15 fighters to provide aerial defense for that kingdom if its own planes were sent to aid North Yemen, but the offer was declined for the time being. State Department officials told the House subcommittee that if the F-15s were sent, it would trigger the war powers provisions.

U.S. Advisers. Anxious to allay fears that the sales to North Yemen would be the first step toward direct U.S. involvement in that conflict, the administration stressed the limited role of the U.S. advisers who would be involved. According to the Pentagon, fewer than 100 U.S. citizens (70 of them military personnel) would be in North Yemen to train Yemeni troops in the use of the U.S. equipment. A small number of military advisers already was performing that role. They had been directed to stay away from combat zones. Up to 200 additional U.S. civilians in Saudi Arabia could be involved in the transfer of the F-5E fighters.

The administration stressed repeatedly that the decisions involving Yemen would be only the first steps toward an increased U.S. military presence near the Arabian Peninsula. The Egyptian-Israeli peace treaty raised speculation in Washington that such a presence might also be required by security guarantees offered by Carter.

Said to be under consideration was the creation of a permanent naval force in the Indian Ocean, to be called the Fifth Fleet. Currently, only two destroyers and a command ship are based in the region. The U.S. base on the British island of Diego Garcia, about 2,000 miles south of India, could provide a permanent anchorage for such a carrier task force. In 1975 Congress, after considerable controversy, had approved plans to expand the facilities at the Diego Garcia base.

Another option being discussed was the periodic movement of an Air Force fighter squadron through friendly countries in the Middle East. Occasionally, press reports have suggested that, in the wake of the peace treaty between Egypt and Israel, such a force might be welcome at one of the two large Sinai bases that Israel will turn over to Egypt under the treaty.

In less than a week, Smolansky continued, "the United States had succeeded in antagonizing both the Soviet Union and Israel. . . . Even more seriously, Washington's twin actions succeeded in making impossible the speedy convocation of the Geneva conference — an objective which, by then, had become one of the cornerstones of the Carter administration's Middle East policy. This 'feat' was accomplished because, in addition to alienating the Russians and the Israelis, the President's moves were received with hostility in Cairo and contributed to Egyptian President Anwar Sadat's decision to travel to Jerusalem."

The prospects of reconvening the Geneva Conference did not seem particularly auspicious as of mid-1979. Still, American officials, convinced that a comprehensive peace in the Middle East was impossible without Soviet cooperation, were dropping hints that an eventual return to Geneva might be necessary. Before any meeting could take place, however, the intractable problem of Palestinian representation at the conference had to be resolved.

At a summit conference in Rabat, Morocco, in October 1974, Arab leaders unanimously recognized the PLO "as the sole representative of the Palestinian people." Israel has refused to deal with the PLO under any circumstances. After the joint U.S.-Soviet statement of Oct. 1, 1977,

American officials had expressed the hope that the PLO could attend the conference as part of a single Arab delegation. Syria had insisted that the organization attend as a separate delegation. This issue was no nearer a solution in mid-1979 than it was in 1977.

While the Soviets wanted a return to the Geneva Conference under their co-chairmanship, Israel remained vehemently opposed to a meeting that would necessitate its dealing with the PLO. The United States would not oppose a reconvening of the conference provided that it was not merely a forum for propaganda. Perhaps the most surprising recent development was President Sadat's attitude toward a return to the Geneva Conference. In an interview published on May 20, 1979, in *The Observer* of London, Sadat stated: "We have no objections" to participating in a new Geneva Conference.

Egyptian-Israeli Negotiations

President Sadat's visit to Jerusalem in November 1977 seemed to be as great a shock to the Soviet Union as it was to most of the rest of the world. Aware that such a visit could well scuttle hopes for reconvening the Geneva Conference, Soviet leaders and the Soviet media nevertheless had little immediate comment on Sadat's visit to Jerusalem. The Communist Party newspaper *Pravda*, the Soviet press agency Tass and the government paper *Izvestia* merely reported Arab criticism of Sadat for almost a week after the visit without indicating the Russian position on the visit.

By the end of November, however, Soviet officials and the media were denouncing the trip. Sadat was accused of betraying the Arab and particularly the Palestinian cause for an unholy alliance with the "Zionists" and the "imperialists." Egypt, Israel and the United States were criticized for pursuing a "separate" and unworkable solution instead of the comprehensive path via Geneva. The "hegemonistic" United States was taken to task for abandoning its Oct. 1, 1977, pledge for a Geneva Conference and "egging on" Egypt and Israel in order to divide the Arab world.

Sadat's demands in his speech in the Israeli Knesset — peace in exchange for Israel's full withdrawal from all Arab territories seized in the 1967 Middle East war and recognition of the "legitimate rights" of the Palestinians, including their right to establish their own state — were identical to those of the Soviet Union and almost all of the other Arabs. Yet Sadat's visit to Jerusalem seemed to leave the Russians with two rather unpalatable choices.

One would have been to support Sadat on the basis of the demands he had made in the Knesset. Such a course, however, ran the risk of antagonizing Sadat's Arab opponents — and the Soviet Union's chief Arab allies — Syria, Iraq, the PLO, Libya and Algeria. It might also have obliged the Russians to join negotiations attended only by its main Middle East antagonists, Israel and Egypt, and dominated by the United States.

The Soviets chose the second alternative, joining their so-called "radical" Arab allies in criticizing the Egyptian leader, Israel and the United States. The Soviet Union, along with the United States, the United Nations, Syria, the PLO, Jordan and Israel had been invited by Sadat to a conference in Cairo in early December 1977. Syria, the PLO and the Soviet Union refused to attend, while Jordan declined the invitation because all the other parties had not accepted it. The conference was attended only by Egypt, Israel, the United States and a representative of the United Nations.

Until the Camp David agreements in September 1978, Russian strategy had consisted of publicizing the innumerable difficulties that beset the American-mediated negotiations between Egypt and Israel. The Soviets also encouraged the "steadfastness" of the hard-line Arab rejectionists. Overtures were made to Jordan and even to Saudi Arabia to convince the "moderate" Arabs to resist American pressure on them to join or at least support the peace process.

In the period between Sadat's visit to Jerusalem and the Camp David conference, the Soviet aim of isolating Sadat and his peace initiative within the Arab world received not inconsiderable help from Israel. Israel rejected U.N. Secretary General Kurt Waldheim's proposal for a quick reconvening of the Geneva Conference on Nov. 30, 1977. The Israeli government made it clear that it favored separate negotiations with the Arab countries and would under no circumstances accept the presence of the PLO in any negotiating forum. Subsequent statements by Israeli officials, particularly Prime Minister Menachem Begin, and the submission of an Israeli peace plan that was totally unacceptable to the Arabs, including the Egyptians, made the Soviet task of preventing other Arabs from joining the U.S.-Egyptian-Israeli talks much easier.

Camp David

By the summer of 1978, the Egyptian-Israeli negotiations seemed doomed. In August, however, President Carter invited Egyptian President Sadat and Israeli Prime Minister Begin to a summit conference at Camp David the following month.

On Sept. 3, the Soviet Communist Party newspaper *Pravda* declared that "the road of separate deals carries matters farther away from achieving a just Middle East settlement and hampers solution of key questions that are at the root of the Middle East crises." *Pravda* also warned that

> It would not be out of place to recall that the Middle East is in immediate proximity to the Soviet Union and other countries of the socialist community. The Soviet Union is far from indifferent to the direction events will take in the region.

Soviet criticism of the Camp David agreements was loud and immediate, unlike its restrained and apparently confused reaction to Sadat's visit to Jerusalem. Sadat was branded a "traitor" and a "supplicant." The Soviets charged that Israel had no intention of surrendering the West Bank, Gaza or the Golan Heights, and that the United States, having broken its promise on a resumption of the Geneva Conference, was now intent upon imposing a "separate solution" that would give its Zionist allies everything they wanted.

During October 1978, President Hafez Assad of Syria, the late President Houari Boumediene of Algeria and PLO Chairman Yasir Arafat visited Moscow. During all three visits, the Camp David formula was denounced. In return for promises of additional Soviet aid, Assad and Arafat both called for a reconvening of the Geneva Conference. The Algerians, along with the Libyans and Iraqis, opposed any direct negotiations with Israel, at Geneva or elsewhere, and there was no mention of a return to Geneva during Boumediene's visit.

Soviet condemnation of the Camp David accords continued through the winter. Contacts with Jordan increased and there were hints of an improvement in Soviet-Saudi relations. In its March 3, 1979, issue, the Lebanese weekly magazine *Al-Hawadess* published an interview with Saudi Foreign Minister Prince Saud. Prince Saud was quoted as saying:

> We would like to emphasize that the absence of diplomatic ties between us does not mean we do not recognize the Soviet Union or the importance of the role played by Soviet international policy. We have in the past expressed gratitude toward the positive stands taken by the Soviet Union regarding Arab questions.

Saudi Arabia had no diplomatic relations with any communist country in mid-1979.

Carter Visit

In addition to courting its hard-line Arab friends and heaping praise upon the policies of former antagonists such as Jordan and Saudi Arabia, the Soviet Union continued to denounce the "hegemonistic" plans of the United States. These denunciations were especially evident after President Carter announced in early March 1979 that he would visit Egypt and Israel to try to revive the stalled negotiations. The Russian media routinely attacked Carter's trip as a typical "imperialist" effort to protect American strategic interests in the area after the revolution in Iran and the departure of the shah.

After Carter's successful visit to the area and the day before the Egyptian-Israeli peace treaty was signed, Crown Prince Hassan, the brother of King Hussein of Jordan, warned that current American policy was encouraging "radicalization" and Soviet gains in the area. In an article in *The Washington Post* on March 25, 1979, Hassan wrote that

> the United States may be misreading the national interests of states such as Jordan when it assumes we can ensure our own basic security by joining short-term schemes, such as the Palestinian autonomy plan, that are based only on guaranteeing Israel's current security. The Camp David approach threatens to accelerate the destabilization process in the Middle East that is a function both of indigenous radicalization trends and global rivalries. We still hope that our friends in the United States would see this as clearly as we do.

Peace Treaty

Compared to that of the Arab world, the Soviet reaction to the signing of the Egyptian-Israeli peace treaty on March 26, 1979, was relatively restrained. The same criticism that had been voiced since Sadat's visit to Jerusalem and particularly since the Camp David accords was repeated. There were also warnings that the treaty would encourage the United States to form Egyptian-Israeli-American "military pacts" in the region. Israel, the Soviet media argued, would receive most of the increased supply of U.S. arms, while Egypt would be given only enough to enable it to become the "policeman" in the Middle East.

These same criticisms had been heard many times before the peace treaty was signed. There was considerable speculation that the rather low-keyed Russian response to the treaty signing was due to Soviet fear of further endangering the chances for U.S. Senate approval of a new Strategic Arms Limitation Treaty (SALT II). It was widely reported that President Carter, in his meetings with Soviet leader Leonid Brezhnev in Vienna in mid-June 1979, urged the Russians to refrain from disruptive tactics in the Middle East. The United States was particularly eager to discourage the Soviets from using their veto in the U.N. Security Council to prevent a renewal of the U.N. Sinai forces mandate when it expired.

Other Developments

There were several other Mideast developments involving the Soviet Union after the treaty was signed. One was the Soviet reaction to the invasion of North Yemen by its client state, South Yemen. The invasion put the Russians in a difficult position. Syria and Iraq, major Soviet allies, as well as conservative Saudi Arabia and the Persian Gulf states strongly urged a truce. South Yemen, armed and supplied by the Soviet Union, could not continue the war without Soviet approval. Moscow's desire for a united Yemen, under Soviet domination, was apparently less important to the Soviet Union than its good or improving relations with the rest of the Arab world. At Russian urging, South Yemen agreed to a cease-fire on March 30.

There have been indications of several Soviet gains in the Middle East since treaty signing. Contacts and cooperation between oil-rich Kuwait and Moscow have greatly increased. The Kuwaiti newspaper *Al-Hadaf* reported on May 24, that Saudi Crown Prince and First Deputy Prime Minister Fahd and Soviet officials had met in Morocco in early May.

In another development on the conservative Arab-Soviet front, Jordan's King Hussein was quoted by the Paris-based Arab magazine *Al-Mustaqbal* on June 16. In referring to Europe's role in solving the Middle East problem, Hussein remarked:

> These [European] countries might share our feelings and belief that the method which has been tried thus far is wrong and will not lead to any results, and that it is necessary to look for another method to be worked out, not only by the United States but also by the Soviet Union and most other countries on a general and comprehensive international level.

Even Egyptian President Sadat, isolated in the Arab world after the signing of the treaty, offered an olive branch to the Soviet Union at a political rally on May 15, 1979. While charging that the Soviet Union, and particularly Radio Moscow, "incites the actions of the Arab dwarfs around us and rejoices in the rupture of Arab relations" with Egypt, Sadat pledged that Egypt was nevertheless "completely prepared to reciprocate friendship with friendship" if the Russians so desired.

Despite its unequivocal condemnation of the Egyptian-Israeli peace treaty, the Soviet Union has had a few public contacts with Israel in recent months. In May, a Soviet delegation, headed by Aleksandr Bovin, a senior political commentator of *Izvestia* newspaper, visited Israel to participate in commemorative ceremonies marking the 34th year of the Nazi defeat in World War II. Hayim Margalit reported in *Al Hamishmar* on May 17, that Bovin had told him the previous day: "We do not want to participate in effecting a compromise which leaves Israel in the territories conquered in the war of June 1967. If Israel moves onto the road leading to a just peace and recognizes the legitimate rights of the Arab-Palestinian people, the Soviet Union will not hesitate to renew diplomatic relations with the State of Israel. The U.S.S.R. position is known to everyone — we support the existence of the State of Israel in conditions of security and completely reject blows of any sort against

Jewish civilian population as well as against Arab civilian population.

Just as in 1947 we supported the establishment of the State of Israel and support its existence today [Bovin continued], that is our position regarding the Palestinians. As for our position in the international organizations, you must understand the logic in our position. We condemn Israel in the United Nations, but we will not lend a hand in expelling Israel from the organization. Every country has the right to membership in the United Nations. In our own way we are saying to the State of Israel: Change your policy and then peace will come.

U.S.-Soviet Relations

The SALT II treaty seemed to have placed the Soviet Union in a dilemma similar to but more serious than the Russian predicament over South Yemen's invasion of North Yemen. If the invasion had succeeded, Yemen would have been unified under Soviet domination. Support for South Yemen, however, would have antagonized most of the Arab world. In that case, the Russians chose not to endanger their relations with the other Arabs and "persuaded" South Yemen to agree to a cease-fire.

Effect of SALT II

The SALT II treaty also posed potential problems for Soviet relations with the Arabs. Shortly after the treaty was signed in June 1979 it appeared likely that the Senate would not approve the treaty without amendments, which the Russians had said they would not accept, or at least without concessions or good-will gestures from the Soviet Union. But such concessions or good-will gestures, particularly if they involved a sizable increase in the immigration of Russian Jews to Israel, would complicate Soviet relations with the Arab world.

Uneasiness over the prospect of Soviet concessions began to surface in the Arab press. The Jordanian daily newspaper *Al-Akhbar*, for example, editorialized on June 14, 1979, that

The Soviet Union has shown more than self-restraint on the Middle East issue in the face of the unilateral U.S. policy in the Middle East. It has shown leniency to such an extent that it has jeopardized the confidence of its friends in the Middle East. It appears that it has done this as part of its leniency on a number of matters for the sake of the Strategic Arms Limitation Treaty.

Similarly, the Paris-based Arab newspaper *Al-Mustaqbal* reported on June 2, 1979, that Arab-Soviet relations "are currently experiencing a severe crisis. Nevertheless, both Soviet and Arab officials are maintaining strict secrecy over the matter. The chief reason for the crisis is the unprecedented increase in the migration of Soviet Jews to Israel and the report this week that the Soviet government intends to grant an emigration visa to every Soviet Jew who has applied for an exit visa during the past five years. This is to be done on the occasion of the signing of the SALT II treaty between the two superpowers.

Well-informed sources have told *Al-Mustaqbal* [the report continued] that the reason for the silence of Arab officials over this matter is the desire not to enter into public confrontation with the Soviet Union at present so as to insure that the Kremlin leaders will fulfill the pledge they have given to some Arab leaders, including Yasser Arafat, to oppose any attempt to lend the Egyptian-Israeli treaty any international legitimacy at the United Nations and to use its veto to prevent the extension of the U.N. forces' mandate in Sinai when it expires next July.

Except for Egypt, the Arab and Israeli reactions to the signing of the U.S.-Soviet SALT II agreement on June 18, was muted. The Arab media, while expressing some concern that the battle for ratification might involve Soviet concessions on Jewish emigration, were in general agreement that the Carter-Brezhnev meeting failed to bring the two superpowers any closer on the Middle East problem or on the methods of reaching a comprehensive peace. Similarly, the Israelis concluded that SALT II would have little effect on American support and Soviet opposition to the Camp David road to peace in the region.

In a commentary broadcast on Cairo Radio on June 20, Egypt was less restrained. The broadcast concluded that

As a result of the leaked reports on the talks between U.S. President Carter and Soviet leader Brezhnev, the U.S.S.R.'s official [refusal of] recognition of any participation in the peace efforts and its refusal to even recognize the efforts already achieved in this direction, it can be stated that the Soviet Union, which since the beginning of the conflict has persisted in issuing slogans and verbal propaganda and which has not offered a genuine step along the correct and peaceful path of resolving the crisis, does not want and is not pleased to see any form of peace prevail in the region.

Jewish Emigration

One issue that had been explored and would continue to be explored during Senate debate over ratification of SALT II and other aspects of U.S.-Soviet relations was Moscow's policy on Jewish emigration. That subject has been fraught with emotion for years. In passing the Trade Act of 1974, Congress added an amendment to the effect that no communist country would be eligible for U.S. trade concessions, including most-favored-nation status, if it "denies its citizens the right or opportunity to emigrate." Sen. Henry M. Jackson, D-Wash., the primary sponsor of the amendment, left little doubt that the amendment was directed against the Soviet Union's treatment of Russian Jews.

The Helsinki Agreement, signed Aug. 1, 1975, by the Soviet Union, the United States, Canada and most of the European countries, pledged the signatories to seek peaceful relations with each other, to respect human rights and to permit a freer exchange of people, ideas and information. Amidst accusations that the Soviet Union was denying emigration visas to dissidents, particularly Jews, Congress in May 1976 approved a bill that required the president to submit semiannual reports to Congress on the implementation of the Helsinki accords.

Congress' action in linking trade concessions with emigration in the 1974 Trade Act had a detrimental effect on both U.S.-Soviet détente and Jewish emigration. Soon after the act was approved, the Soviet Union rejected the terms imposed by the amendment, thereby cancelling a 1972 trade agreement with the United States. The number of Jews allowed to emigrate also fell dramatically from a high of 30,000 in 1973, the year before the amendment was enacted.

The problem in determining Soviet compliance with the Helsinki Agreement's provision on Jewish emigration has been the lack of information on how many of the more than two million Soviet Jews wish to emigrate. It is widely assumed that only a relatively small number wish to leave the Soviet Union and that an even smaller number of those wanting to emigrate would choose Israel as their destination. What is certain is that the rate of Jewish emigration has increased considerably in recent years.

In 1978, for example, almost 30,000 Jews were allowed to leave the Soviet Union. In a June 1979 report to Congress on compliance with the Helsinki Agreement, President Carter estimated that if the existing emigration rate continued, the number of Jews leaving the Soviet Union in 1979 could reach 50,000. And just before the Carter-Brezhnev summit conference in mid-June, there were a number of reports that Moscow would drastically ease visa restrictions for Russian Jews.

The Arab reaction to the increase in Soviet Jewish emigration was summed up by the Jordanian newspaper *Ad-Dustur* on May 27, 1979. The article, entitled "A question to the Soviet Union," noted that

certain signs emerge which suggest that there is a gradual change in Soviet policy regarding the problem of Jewish emigration. These signs prompt us to ask about the extent of the Soviet commitment to its stand toward the Arab question. The Arabs are highly appreciative of the Soviet stand which was and still is the essential factor on which Soviet-Arab friendship is based. Needless to say the reason for asking this question is due to the fact that a change in the Soviet policy toward Jewish emigration would directly affect the Soviet stand toward the Arab question. It is an established fact that Jewish immigrants using U.S. weapons have helped create the tragedy to which the Arabs are being subjected. These emigrants are also needed for Israel to continue its settlement plan in the occupied land. This plan is aimed at uprooting Pales-

tinians from their land and replacing them with Jewish emigrants. Like other peace-loving peoples, the Arabs understand the importance and necessity of détente between the two superpowers in this age. At the same time, however, the Arabs are aware of no stipulation whatsoever that supplying Israel with Soviet emigrants is a condition of this détente. The Arabs see no justification for this because the Arabs will necessarily have to bear the price.

Questions Remain

In mid-1979 a major question, for the United States as well as for the nations and peoples of the Middle East, was the likely Soviet response if the Senate rejected the SALT II treaty or insisted upon amendments unacceptable to the Soviet Union. In that event, Moscow would probably restrict the number of Russians Jews permitted to emigrate and might even, for a short time, cut off Jewish emigration completely. Senate failure to ratify SALT II was also likely to encourage much stronger Soviet opposition to American peace efforts in the Middle East.

Another important question was who would succeed Leonid Brezhnev, 72 years old and in ill health, when the Russian Communist Party leader died or was forced to retire. *Newsweek* magazine reported on June 25, 1979, that "a knowledgeable Soviet source" told the magazine that "Brezhnev has a year or a year and a half left, at most — not of life, but of ability to work and make decisions." There was considerable speculation but no reliable indications on the likely successor.

Most knowledgeable observers expected little immediate change in Soviet policy after Brezhnev's retirement or death. There was nevertheless a possibility that hard-liners like Mikhail Suslov might become more influential in Russian policy-making. Senate failure to ratify SALT II was likely to increase the chances for a less cautious and cooperative leadership after Brezhnev. Such a change would encourage greater tension and bipolarity in the Middle East.

ISRAEL AND THE ARABS: DECADES OF HOSTILITY

Since the establishment of Israel little more than a quarter of a century ago, Israel and its Arab neighbors have engaged in more or less continuing hostilities, punctuated by four major wars.

Having failed in 1947 to prevent the creation of a Jewish state in Palestine, the Arabs at first fought to destroy Israel and then to recover territories occupied by Israel in subsequent battles. Arab enmity has stiffened Israel's resolve to attain "secure and defensible borders," and this in turn has fostered Arab fears of Israeli "expansionism." The problem of the Palestinian Arabs, many of whom were made refugees during the 1948 and 1967 wars, has remained a continuing obstacle to peace.

The history of the Arab-Israeli conflict has been marked by a gradual movement toward Arab solidarity. Arab participants in the first war of 1948-49 distrusted each other almost as much as they distrusted the hated Zionists. By the time of the fourth war, in 1973, Arab unity had advanced to such a point that Saudi Arabia, the Persian Gulf states and several North African countries could join with Egypt, Syria and other "front line" Arab states (states bordering on Israel) in a common effort to recapture the territories lost to Israel in the 1967 war.

For its part, Israel has suffered growing isolation in the world community, most acutely since the 1973 war. Its refusal to give up Arab territories occupied in 1967 has cost the country many friends in the Third World, while the October 1973 Arab oil boycott forced Japan and most Western European governments to adopt a more pro-Arab stance. The Arabs' decision to use oil as a political weapon has also had an effect on U.S. policy in the Middle East. And by the mid-1970s, Palestinian nationalism had achieved considerably more sympathetic attention throughout the world.

The 1973 war gave the lie to the assumption that — despite U.S. backing for Israel and Soviet support for the Arabs — the two superpowers could avoid a confrontation during an Arab-Israeli war. The specter of superpower conflict arose as first the Soviet Union and then the United States felt compelled to resupply the belligerents with arms on a massive scale and later when the United States ordered its forces on worldwide alert following the threat of a possible Soviet troop movement into the Middle East.

By the time the first Arab-Israeli peace conference opened in Geneva in December 1973, it appeared that a permanent resolution of the Arab-Israeli conflict had become a real possibility at last. The 1973 war demonstrated the dangers of continued stalemate, while the Arabs' use of their oil weapon assured the interest of outside powers in promoting a peace settlement. But awesome issues remained to be resolved. While many Arab leaders might no longer demand the liquidation of the Jewish state, Arab insistence that Israel withdraw from all territories occupied in 1967 collides with Israeli insistence on secure and defensible boundaries. Even should a comprehensive agreement be reached regarding the West Bank, Sinai and the Golan Heights territories, the emotional issue of Jerusalem still might prevent a full settlement of the Middle East conflict.

The fate of the Palestinians also remains in dispute. On November 24, 1976, the United Nations General Assembly in a 90 to 16 vote (30 abstentions) called for the creation of a Palestinian state — something Israel has refused to contemplate — and for Israeli withdrawal from all occupied territories by June 1, 1977. Responding, Israeli U.N. Ambassador Chaim Herzog proclaimed, "The General Assembly has been hijacked by a group of Arab extremists."

When Carter assumed the presidency in January 1977, a world-wide consensus seemed to be emerging that the coming few years might be the best opportunity — and quite possibly the last — for peaceful resolution of the Middle East conflict. Secretary of State Henry A. Kissinger left office proclaiming the Middle East to be at a "moment of unprecedented opportunity." U.N. Secretary-General Kurt Waldheim and Kissinger's successor, Cyrus R. Vance, have also expressed this view. Both toured Middle East capitals early in 1977 for first-hand assessments and during Vance's first press conference he said that "it is critically important that progress be made this year" in the Middle East.

Despite the signing of the peace treaty with Egypt, the gulf separating Israel from the other Arab nations remains huge. Terence Smith returned from four years as Jerusalem correspondent for *The New York Times* noting that "I came home from those years deeply skeptical about the prospects for an early settlement in the Middle East. It is not that the political problem is beyond solution. That is basically a question of sovereignty versus security that two dispassionate lawyers could resolve. . . . But the *human* obstacles — the deep-seated mistrust on both sides, the fear of annihilation, the wounded national honor — these are the real stumbling blocks. They are the elements that have prevented a solution in the past and will continue to make one difficult to achieve in the future."[1]

Intangibles in the Conflict

The problem, Kissinger explained to the House International Relations Committee March 25, 1975, after the collapse of his Middle East negotiations, "was balancing tangible positions on the ground against less tangible assurances which have symbolic meanings and importance." The power of symbols in the Arab-Israeli conflict has, from the very beginning, baffled and thwarted diplomacy.

In the first phase of the conflict the issue was, simply, Israel's existence, an issue which scarcely lends itself to compromise. It was in this period, historian Bernard Lewis observed, that the question of direct negotiation became crucial for both sides. "By entering into direct negotiations with Israel, the Arab states would be giving her a vital token

---

[1] See "Israel Journal: 1972-1976. Reflections on a Troubled People," *Saturday Review*, 5 February 1977, p. 8.

of recognition," he wrote. "By refusing to negotiate they were maintaining their refusal to recognize her existence. For Arabs and Israelis alike the question of direct negotiation thus acquired a symbolic significance which it has retained for both sides ever since."[2]

Direct negotiations had symbolic significance, because the issue was Israel's existence. But from the beginning the existence of Israel has itself been a symbol. For nearly 2,000 years, Jews throughout the world have intoned the Passover slogan, "Next year in Jerusalem." For a scattered, persecuted, stateless people, the ritual could be little more than a fantasy, and its credibility scarcely grew with the passing ages.

But at the end of the 19th century, the Jews of Eastern Europe, oppressed by poverty and brutal pogroms, began to act on this fantastic hope. Modern Zionism grew from such unpromising ground, and within two generations the movement had carved out a sovereign state of its own. "If you will it, it is no dream," the Zionist leader Theodor Herzl had asserted, and soon the ancient dream of "next year in Jerusalem" was a reality. Most Israelis today insist that their sovereignty over the entire city of Jerusalem, whose Arab sector they conquered in the 1967 war, is "not negotiable." Soon after taking over as Prime Minister, Menachem Begin urged the United States to move the American embassy from Tel Aviv to Jerusalem.

Jerusalem symbolizes the Jews' ancient dream and in Jerusalem is a symbol of their recent nightmare. Yad Va'shem is the memorial center dedicated to recalling the Nazi holocaust and its six million Jewish victims. This unfathomable horror, as much as the Zionist ideal, is a foundation of the state of Israel, and, "In the rituals of government and diplomacy, Yad Va'shem is given a role parallel, and at times equal in its solemnity, to the role of national symbols that extol military glory, sovereignty, and independence."[3]

The trauma was real and could not fail to affect perceptions of reality, including the reality of being surrounded by Arabs condemning Zionism even if no longer specifically demanding the end of Israel. "The effects of the Nazi holocaust upon the national psychology," wrote Israeli author Amos Elon, "reached a new peak in the weeks preceding the Six Day War of 1967. Israelis, including many young people, were seized by abysmal fears; many were certain that another holocaust was being prepared for them by the rulers of Egypt, whose bloodthirsty statements were resounding hourly on the radio. Many impartial foreign observers have testified to the breadth of such feelings at the time, and how genuine the fears seemed."[4]

Ambivalence Toward the Arabs

Fears aroused by the Arabs may be complicated by less obvious sentiments. In an article in *Commentary,* Hillel Halkin, an American-born Israeli, recounted how scenes in occupied Arab communities prompted reflections on the way in which the Jew, while assimilating so much of European culture, preserved his identification with a lost land. The Jew clung to symbols which in biblical times were part of everyday life. Halkin wrote:

> The flat, round bread he ate with every meal, dipping it in oil or vinegar when there was nothing else, is now eaten once a year in the form of the Passover matzah.
> The headcovering worn out-of-doors to protect himself from the blazing Palestinian sun, blackens, shrivels into round little *yarmulke* of the synagogue; his blowing, toga-like robe becomes the fringed *tallit* or prayershawl.

Once or twice each year, on Rosh Hashanah or Tu B'shvat, he spends extravagant sums to buy exotic fruits of the Holy Land, dates and olives, almonds and figs....

But when the Europeanized Jew returns, after millennia, he finds "the Arab, the usurper, living there in his place, eating round, flat bread with every meal, covering his head with an elegant *kaffia* against the sun, wearing a long flat robe that ripples when he walks, eating figs and olives, almonds and dates for his daily fare, and living as a perfect matter of course the agricultural rhythms, the seedtimes and the harvests, of the Bible, Talmud, and prayerbooks. An upside-down world!"[5]

Whatever ambivalence such biblical scenes may stir in the Westernized Jew, another aspect of the Arab condition resonates with Jewish experience. The Arabs as a colonized people, like the Jews as a persecuted minority, have experienced powerlessness and humiliation at the hands of European civilization. Empathy with the Arabs finds only limited expression in Israel, and is not generally shared by Israeli immigrants from Arab countries, but the plight of the Palestinian refugees suggests parallels that are difficult to ignore. Especially since the 1967 occupation of the West Bank and Gaza Strip, with their refugee camps, Israelis have been forced to recognize their Palestinian enemies as suffering exiles craving a return to their homeland. The fact that the Palestinian diaspora resulted from the creation of Israel does not make it easier for Israelis to face the Palestinian problem.

Nationalism Versus Arab and Jewish Traditions

If Zionist attention to Arab nationalism was slow in developing, it was at least in part because that nationalism was still nascent. The kind of identification with the nation-state which Westerners take for granted did not characterize the Arab world, where loyalties were divided among Islam, the Ottoman state and local or kinship groupings. These divided loyalties left the Arabs vulnerable to domination by homogeneous European nations. When the Arabs finally reacted with a nationalism of their own, it had to contend with the deepest strata of their own culture.

Bernard Lewis compared this inner conflict with the great struggle at the birth of Islam, when monotheism fought the idols of pagan Arabia. Now, however, the struggle is "against a new set of idols called states, races and nations; this time it is the idols that seem to be victorious. The introduction of nationalism, of collective self-worship, is the best founded and least mentioned of the many grievances of the Middle East against the West."[6]

The Jews, like the Arabs, were late in embracing the kind of nationalism that evolved in Europe. For centuries they sustained a double identity in which they were Germans or Russians or Americans or Moroccans as well as Jews, and prided themselves on their universality as well as their uniqueness. This divided identity left them, like the Arabs, vulnerable to European nationalism, especially when it went berserk in Nazi Germany. There is terrible irony in the fact that Jews and Arabs now kill each other in the name

---

[2] Bernard Lewis, "The Palestinians and the PLO: A Historical Approach," *Commentary*, January 1975, p. 43.

[3] Amos Elon, *The Israelis, Founders and Sons* (1971), p. 200.

[4] *Ibid.*, p. 216.

[5] Hillel Halkin, "Driving toward Jerusalem: A Sentimental Journey through the West Bank," *Commentary*, January 1975, p. 51.

[6] Bernard Lewis, *The Middle East and the West* (1968), p. 70.

of the very nationalism which so long victimized both peoples.

The struggle of Israelis and Arabs to make nationalism dominant over traditional identities creates deep conflicts within each culture. The ambivalence is painful and often consciously denied; it is easier to confront an external enemy, projecting inner conflict onto hostile neighbors only too ready to reciprocate. Lebanese scholar Fouad Ajami wrote in *Foreign Policy* magazine: "Arabs and Israelis have yet to accept themselves, let alone one another. People cannot be at peace with others unless they are at peace with themselves."[7]

Both Jews and Arabs have felt their historical uniqueness primarily through their religious achievements. As their religions now yield to nationalism, they cling all the more fervently to the traditional spirit of historical mission. The burden of the past thus assumes extraordinary power in the politics of the Middle East. Each people, Ajami wrote, is "haunted by its own ghosts, and tormented by deeply felt historical grievances that seem to justify its own violence and insensitivity."

Arab-Israeli wars are not really between governments but between peoples, and the enmity between these peoples spring from depths that diplomacy can scarcely touch.

War of Independence (1948-49)

The first Arab-Israeli war stemmed from Arab refusal to accept a United Nations plan to partition Palestine into separate Arab and Jewish states. The U.N. had been drawn into the Palestine dispute following the failure of Great Britain, which held a League of Nations mandate over Palestine, to hammer out a Palestine solution that would be acceptable to both Arabs and Jews.

In May 1947 the U.N. General Assembly established an 11-nation special commission to study the Palestine problem. A majority of the commission recommended the division of Palestine into a Jewish state, an Arab state and an internationalized Jerusalem. The Zionists endorsed the majority approach. A commission minority recommended a federal state with autonomous Arab and Jewish provinces and limits on Jewish immigration. Although the Arabs initially insisted on absolute Arab sovereignty over Palestine, they ultimately endorsed the minority plan.

For a time it appeared that neither plan could command the necessary two-thirds support in the United Nations, but on Nov. 29, 1947, the General Assembly approved the partition plan by a narrow margin of 33 to 13 with 10 abstentions.

The Palestinian Arabs thereupon resorted to arms to prevent partition. In the civil war that followed, however, Palestinian Jews were able to win control over most of the territory allocated to them by the partition plan. Britain ended its mandate over Palestine on May 14, 1948, and the same day the Zionists proclaimed the establishment of the state of Israel. One day later, the armies of five Arab countries—Egypt, Transjordan, Iraq, Syria and Lebanon—invaded Palestine, and the first Arab-Israeli war began.

"The first Arab-Israeli war produced a shock from which the Arabs never truly have recovered—their defeat at the hands of the numerically inferior Jews," Harry B. Ellis wrote in a 1970 analysis prepared for the American Enterprise Institute, an independent research organization.[8]

Although the Arab states involved had 40 times as many people as the infant Jewish state, the Arabs, torn by dynastic rivalries, never placed their armies under effective joint command and were unable to agree on common objectives. Meanwhile the outnumbered Jews profited from their sense of cohesion and their paramilitary experience fighting the Palestinian Arabs during the mandate period. Their war

---

[7] Fouad Ajami, "Middle East Ghosts," *Foreign Policy*, spring 1974, p. 94.
[8] Harry B. Ellis, *The Dilemma of Israel* (1970), p. 29.

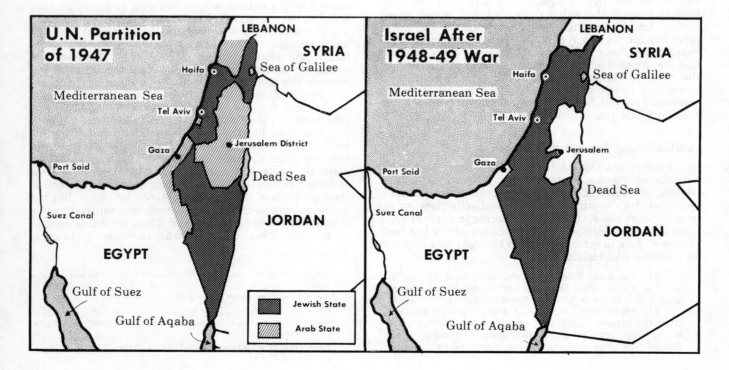

effort was augmented by the influx of men and equipment from abroad as the war went on.

The shooting war stopped on Jan. 7, 1949, and by Feb. 24 Egypt had separately signed an armistice agreement with Israel, followed by Lebanon in March, Jordan in April and Syria in July. Iraq refused to sign an armistice agreement and simply withdrew from Palestine.

When the fighting stopped, Israel held over 30 per cent more territory than had been assigned to the Jewish state under the U.N. partition plan. The Arab state envisaged by the U.N. plan never materialized; its territory was divided among Israel, Transjordan and Egypt. Israel gained about 2,500 square miles. Transjordan, which annexed the West Bank of the Jordan River and transformed itself into the state of Jordan, gained 2,200 square miles. Egypt took the Gaza Strip, about 135 square miles, which it held in the status of Egyptian-controlled territory. Jerusalem was divided between Israel and Jordan. U.N. mixed armistice commissions were established to police the frontiers, and several demilitarized zones were established between Israel and Egypt, Jordan and Syria.

The U.N. also created the United Nations Relief and Works Agency for Palestinian Refugees in the Near East (UNRWA) to assist Palestinian Arabs who had fled or been driven from their homes. It is thought that more than 700,-000 Palestinian Arabs—the exact number is disputed—who had lived in the area that came under Israeli control became refugees—38 per cent in the West Bank area, 26 per cent in the Gaza Strip, 14 per cent in Lebanon and 10 per cent both in Syria and Transjordan.

Although the refugee problem was widely regarded as a major obstacle to the conclusion of peace agreements between Israel and its Arab neighbors, Middle East specialist Nadav Safran, in *From War to War* (1969), held that other factors were more important in the refusal of Arab leaders to sign peace agreements. He quoted an interview with Azzam Pasha, first secretary general of the Arab League:

"We have a secret weapon which we can use better than guns and machine guns, and this is time. As long as we do not make peace with the Zionists, the war is not over; and as long as the war is not over there is neither victor nor vanquished. As soon as we recognize the existence of the state of Israel, we admit by this act that we are vanquished."[9]

In addition to this psychological reluctance to accept defeat, Safran cited other considerations for the refusal of Arab leaders to make peace, including their fear of an outraged public opinion that had been encouraged to expect an easy victory and their apprehension that "peace would legitimize Israel's entry into the Middle Eastern political arena and allow it to maneuver freely among the rival Arab states and with interested outside powers in order to promote its suspected expansionist designs."

Although the refusal to sign peace agreements left open the possibility of future offensive action against Israel, Safran concluded that "there was not, at this stage, an active Arab commitment to a resumption of hostilities or to the total destruction of Israel."

But the absence of formal peace agreements resulted in continuing tension and bitterness, heightened by the Arab boycott of Israel and the barring of Israeli shipping from the Suez Canal and the Gulf of Aqaba, Israel's sea lane to Africa and Asia.

In May 1950 the United States, Britain and France issued the Tripartite Declaration in which they pledged

9 Nadav Safran, *From War to War* (1969), p. 39.

themselves to limit arms shipments to the area and to oppose any attempt to alter the existing armistice lines by force. Yet the armistice lines were repeatedly violated by Arab commando raids into Israeli territory and retaliatory raids into Arab territory by Israel. The level of hostilities escalated, culminating in the second Arab-Israeli war of 1956.

Suez War (1956)

The immediate cause of the second Arab-Israeli war was Egyptian President Gamal Abdel Nasser's nationalization of the Suez Canal on July 26, 1956. Several events in the preceding year had emboldened Nasser to take this step: The British had withdrawn their 80,000 troops from the Suez Canal zone; the Soviet Union had agreed to supply large quantities of arms to Egypt on advantageous terms; and the United States, piqued by Nasser's opposition to the Baghdad Pact, had canceled its offer to help Egypt build the Aswan Dam.

Diplomatic efforts to settle the Suez Canal crisis foundered, and Britain and France—chief shareholders in the Suez Canal Company—determined to recapture the canal by force. They secretly enlisted Israel's participation in this effort.

On Oct. 26, 1956, the Israeli army invaded the Sinai Peninsula and in seven days had reached the Suez Canal. Egyptian troops were driven from the Gaza Strip and the Sinai. On Oct. 31, French and British air forces began bombing Egypt prior to invading the country. The United Nations speedily achieved a cease-fire and demanded the withdrawal of invading troops from Egypt.

Responding to intense international pressure from the United States and the Soviet Union, Britain and France withdrew the last of their forces from Egypt in December 1956. The last Israeli units were not withdrawn from the Sinai until March 1957, and then only under the threat that the United States would impose economic sanctions upon Israel if it failed to do so.

Meanwhile, a United Nations Emergency Force (UNEF) took up positions on Egyptian territory at the southern tip of the Sinai Peninsula and along the Gaza frontier. Israel gained free passage through the Gulf of Aqaba, and it warned that the removal of U.N. troops from Sharm el-Sheikh at the entrance of the gulf would constitute an act of war.

For a time Egypt also permitted Israeli cargoes on non-Israeli ships to transit the Suez Canal, but this concession was halted in 1959.

The 1956 war did not solve the Arab-Israeli territorial conflict and only temporarily altered the military balance in the area, since Russia immediately began replacing the military equipment lost by Egypt during the war. It did increase Arab hostility toward Israel, and as Nasser began to promote the concept of integral Arab unity this attitude intensified, since Israel was viewed as a physical barrier that split the Arab world.

The Arab-Israeli conflict became a "clash of destinies," in Safran's view, following the short-lived merger of Egypt and Syria in the United Arab Republic in February 1958. "Prior to the union with Syria, Egypt, along with the rest of the Arab League, stood for the application of the United Nations resolutions on partition and the return of the refugees, which admitted the right of Israel to exist; after the union, this line was abandoned for one that clearly intimated the liquidation of Israel under a variety of formulae, such as 'the restoration of the Arab rights in Palestine' or the 'liquidation of the Zionist aggression in Palestine,' " he wrote.[10]

Although it had suffered a clear diplomatic defeat, Israel following the 1956 war "enjoyed ten years undisturbed by the border belligerency of its major and most dangerous foe, Egypt," Ben Halpern wrote in *The Idea of the Jewish State* (1969).[11]

"The Negev, along the Sinai-Gaza frontier, was quiet, busy with civilian development. The continuing Suez blockade could be ignored because traffic flowed freely to and from Aqaba. While the UN Emergency Force was sketchily represented by troops in Gaza and Sharm el-Sheikh and by a light patrol along the Negev-Sinai line, no one—certainly not Israel—considered the Emergency Force a major factor in securing the border peace. Its chief function was to give the Egyptians an excuse for not reopening hostilities at a time when they felt unprepared," Halpern wrote.

Six-Day War (1967)

The Six-Day War of June 5-10, 1967, erupted after months of mounting tension. But its immediate cause was the failure of diplomatic efforts to lift the blockade of the Gulf of Aqaba declared on May 23 by Egyptian President Nasser.

The gulf had been opened to Israeli shipping by Israel's victory in the Suez War of 1956, and it had been kept open by the United Nations Emergency Force stationed since then at the gulf's mouth on the Red Sea. Nasser's request on May 18 for removal of the U.N. force, from the Gaza Strip as well as from the gulf outpost, was accompanied by movement of substantial Egyptian forces into the Sinai Peninsula, raising Tel Aviv's fears of the long-threatened Arab attempt to terminate the existence of the Jewish state.

The war substantially altered the power structure in the turbulent Middle East. Israeli planes in their first "preemptive" attack destroyed the bulk of the Egyptian air force while it was still on the ground. Israel's lightning move through the Sinai Peninsula broke the Egyptian blockade of the Gulf of Aqaba and once again put its soldiers on the banks of the Suez Canal. In the east, Israel's forces ousted Jordanian troops from the old section of Jerusalem and seized control of all Jordanian territory west of the Jordan River. The last move foreclosed the possibility that in the event of all-out war Israel could be cut in half; at some points, Jordan's territory on the West Bank extended to less than nine miles from the sea. Finally, Israel captured the Golan Heights, the heavily fortified borderland hills from which Syria had for two decades harassed Israel's northeastern settlements.

Israel's smashing victory not only stunned the Arabs and their Soviet backers; it left Israel in a position of strength. In contrast to 1956, when Israeli forces were withdrawn in response to strong Washington-Moscow pressure, Tel Aviv at once announced that Israel would remain in the occupied territories until decisive progress toward a permanent settlement had been made.

Meanwhile, the Soviet Union broke off diplomatic relations with Israel and began to rearm the Egyptians.

---

[10] Safran, *From War to War* (1969), p. 85.

[11] Ben Halpern, *The Idea of the Jewish State* (1969), p. 432.

Middle East After 1967 War

Mediterranean Sea
LEBANON
Haifa
SYRIA
Tel Aviv
Port Said
Jerusalem
Gaza
Dead Sea
ISRAEL
Suez Canal
JORDAN
Cairo
Suez
Elath
Aqaba
SAUDI ARABIA
Gulf of Suez
Gulf of Aqaba
EGYPT
Sharm el-Sheikh
Strait of Tiran
Occupied by Israel

Nasser, charging that U.S. aircraft had contributed to Egypt's defeat, severed diplomatic relations with Washington. Six other Arab states followed suit. With the Soviet Union providing military assistance to the Arab governments, the United States moved in to fill the vacuum created by the French government's 1967 decision to end its role as chief supplier of armaments to Israel.

On Nov. 22, 1967, the U.N. Security Council unanimously approved a resolution (Security Council Resolution 242) aimed at bringing peace to the Middle East. The document called for withdrawal of Israeli forces from occupied Arab areas; an end to the state of belligerency between the Arab nations and Israel; acknowledgement of and respect for the sovereignty, territorial integrity and political independence of every nation in the area; the establishment of "secure and recognized boundaries"; a guarantee of freedom of navigation through international waterways in the area; and a just settlement of the refugee problem. *(Text, box, next page)*

Although U.N. efforts to end the Arab-Israeli conflict once again foundered, this resolution has remained the basis for all subsequent peace initiatives. Prior to the 1967 war, the Arabs had insisted that Israel return all lands in excess of the territory assigned to the Jewish state by the 1947 U.N. partition plan. Since the 1967 war, however, the Arabs have gradually modified their demands, and now insist only that Israel adhere to the principles of the 1967 Security Council resolution which they say calls on Israel to return to its pre-1967 borders. This resolution, referred to in 1973 as resolution #338, became the basis for the Geneva Conference. *(p. 68)*

"War of Attrition"

Fighting was renewed in 1969 along the Suez Canal front after Egypt repudiated the cease-fire of 1967. This period, known as the "War of Attrition," was designed to

U.N. Security Council Resolution 242, Nov. 22, 1967

The Security Council
Expressing its continuing concern with the grave situation in the Middle East,

Emphasizing the inadmissibility of the acquisition of territory by war and the need to work for a just and lasting peace in which every State in the area can live in security,

Emphasizing further that all Member States in their acceptance of the Charter of the United Nations have undertaken a commitment to act in accordance with Article 2 of the Charter,

1. *Affirms* that the fulfillment of Charter principles requires the establishment of a just and lasting peace in the Middle East which should include the application of both the following principles:
    (i) Withdrawal of Israeli armed forces from territories occupied in the recent conflict;
    (ii) Termination of all claims or states of belligerency and respect for and acknowledgement of the sovereignty, territorial integrity and political independence of every State in the area and their right to live in peace within secure and recognized boundaries free from threats or acts of force;

2. *Affirms further the necessity*
    (a) For guaranteeing freedom of navigation through international waterways in the area;
    (b) For achieving a just settlement of the refugee problem;
    (c) For guaranteeing the territorial inviolability and political independence of every State in the area, through measures including the establishment of demilitarized zones;

3. *Requests* the Secretary-General to designate a Special Representative to proceed to the Middle East to establish and maintain contacts with the States concerned in order to promote agreement and assist efforts to achieve a peaceful and accepted settlement in accordance with the provisions and principles in this resolution;

4. *Requests* the Secretary-General to report to the Security Council on the progress of the efforts of the Special Representative as soon as possible.

wear the Israelis down and bring about territorial withdrawals. Although often violated, the cease-fire technically continued on the other fronts.

In June 1970, U.S. Secretary of State William P. Rogers proposed a cease-fire and a resumption of U.N. mediation efforts aimed at implementing the 1967 Security Council resolution to achieve a settlement based on withdrawal of Israeli forces from occupied territory and Arab recognition of Israel's right to exist within secure borders.

Egypt and Jordan, then Israel, agreed to invoke a cease-fire for 90 days, beginning Aug. 8, 1970, in their conditional acceptance of the Rogers peace formula. Once the agreement to seek a peace settlement was announced, however,

public protest arose in many parts of the Middle East. Arab guerrilla groups and the government of Syria and Iraq rejected the peace initiative and denounced Nasser for accepting it. In Israel, six members of the hawkish Gahal minority party quit the cabinet of Premier Golda Meir when she announced the government's acceptance of the Rogers peace plan. Palestinian commandos dramatized their opposition to peace negotiations through a spectacular series of commercial aircraft hijackings.

Hopes for a peace settlement were dashed Sept. 7, 1970, with Israel's announcement that it was withdrawing from the peace talks. Its ambassador had met only once with the United Nations mediator, Gunnar V. Jarring. Israel's decision followed its repeated charges (only later validated) that Soviet missile batteries had been emplaced in the Suez Canal cease-fire zone in direct violation of the standstill agreement. (It was these missiles which made possible the Egyptian army's crossing of the canal in October 1973.)

In late 1971 and early 1972, the United States put forward a new proposal for indirect, American-mediated talks between Israel and Egypt on an interim peace settlement that included a troop pullback and reopening of the Suez Canal, but negotiations made little headway. Meanwhile, in what was an apparent effort to disassociate his regime from Soviet military support, Egypt's President Anwar Sadat ordered the departure of 20,000 Soviet military advisers from his country.

Israel's determination to retain Arab territory occupied in 1967 until a final peace agreement would be agreed to by the Arabs gradually began to weaken the country's position in the international community and finally led to the fourth Arab-Israeli war in 1973.

Yom Kippur War (1973)

Unprecedented Arab solidarity and the emergence of oil as an Arab political weapon marked the fourth Arab-Israeli war, which began Oct. 6, 1973. The war broke out on Yom Kippur, the holiest day of the Jewish calendar, when Egyptian and Syrian troops in a surprise move broke through Israel's weakly defended forward fortifications and advanced into the Sinai Peninsula and the Golan Heights.

By seizing the initiative, and with the use of sophisticated new Soviet weapons, the Arab forces were able temporarily to dictate the conditions of battle most favorable to themselves. Whereas Israel excelled at a "war of rapid movement and envelopment," Safran wrote in the January 1974 issue of *Foreign Affairs*, the Arabs "forced the enemy to fight a set battle, where the undoubted courage of their own fighting men and their numerical superiority in manpower and equipment could be used to best effect."[12]

This "slugging type of war," Safran went on, "turned out to be extremely costly in men and especially in equipment to both sides," leading first the Soviet Union and then the United States to intervene as equipment suppliers to their client states.

Despite the success of the initial Egyptian and Syrian strikes into Israeli-occupied territory, Israeli forces subsequently succeeded in breaking through the Egyptian lines to the western bank of the Suez Canal and advancing to within 20 miles of the Syrian capital of Damascus. The United States and the Soviet Union then joined to seek a cease-fire

12 Safran, "The War and the Future of the Arab-Israeli Conflict," Foreign Affairs, January 1974, pp. 216-217.

through the auspices of the United Nations, and the Security Council adopted a cease-fire resolution Oct. 22. A cease-fire was to go into effect "no later than 12 hours" after adoption of the resolution, and this was to be followed, for the first time, by negotiations "between the parties concerned."

Just as the truce appeared to be taking hold, however, it was threatened by a renewal of tension between the two superpowers. On Oct. 24, the Soviet Union proposed to the United States that the two nations join together to supervise the truce. The proposal was rejected by the United States, which backed the creation of a U.N. observer force without big-power participation. In the early morning hours of Oct. 25, U.S. armed forces were placed on worldwide alert in response to the possibility of a unilateral Soviet movement of troops into the Middle East to supervise the truce. The crisis was defused later that day when Moscow agreed to a Security Council resolution establishing an international peace-keeping force without big-power participation.

Israel and Egypt Nov. 11 signed a six-point cease-fire agreement worked out by Secretary of State Henry A. Kissinger. The agreement was signed at a United Nations tent at kilometer 101 on the Cairo-Suez road by Israeli Maj. Gen. Aharon Yariv and Egyptian Maj. Gen. Mohammed Abdel Ghany el-Gamasy; it was the first face-to-face encounter between Israeli and Egyptian negotiators. The meeting resulted in an exchange of prisoners of war and the lifting of the Israeli siege of the city of Suez and the Egyptian Third Army.

Geneva Conference and "Shuttle Diplomacy"

The first Arab-Israeli peace conference opened in Geneva Dec. 21. The participants were Israel, Egypt, Jordan, the United States, the Soviet Union and the United Nations. Syria boycotted the meeting. The first round of the peace conference ended the following day with an agreement to begin talks on separating Israeli and Egyptian forces along the Suez Canal. Egypt and Israel signed a troop disengagement accord Jan. 18, 1974, and the troop withdrawal was completed March 4. Meanwhile, efforts to negotiate a similar agreement between Israel and Syria continued. Syria and Israel signed a similar agreement May 31. In early 1975, Kissinger sought a second-stage disengagement in the Sinai Desert, but after 15 days of shuttling between Egypt and Israel he declared March 23 that his efforts had failed and returned to the United States.

After the breakdown in the talks, Egypt formally requested a resumption of the full Geneva Conference. But it became widely recognized that a propaganda battle at Geneva might degenerate into war and the conference was indefinitely postponed.

When Kissinger returned from his shuttle talks he and President Ford unofficially indicated their displeasure with Israel's negotiating position, and the United States began a "reassessment" of its policy in the Middle East. Meetings between Ford and Sadat in Salzburg, Austria, June 1 and 2, and a visit by Israeli Premier Yitzhak Rabin to Washington June 11 and 12 led to a resumption of step-by-step negotiations for troop disengagements, resulting in a limited agreement initialed by both sides Sept. 1.

1973 War in Perspective

The 1973 war in the Middle East may be remembered as the war that broke the myths that three previous encounters between Israel and its Arab neighbors had built up. One casualty of the October 1973 fighting was the belief

---

U.N. Security Council Resolution 338, Oct. 22, 1973

The Security Council

1. *Calls* upon all parties to the present fighting to cease all firing and terminate all military activity immediately, no later than 12 hours after the moment of the adoption of this decision, in the positions they now occupy;

2. *Calls* upon the parties concerned to start immediately after the cease-fire the implementation of Security Council Resolution 242 (1967) in all of its parts;

3. *Decides* that, immediately and concurrently with the cease-fire, negotiations start between the parties concerned under appropriate auspices aimed at establishing a just and durable peace in the Middle East.

---

in Israeli invincibility which had prevailed since Israel's lightning victory during the Six-Day War in 1967.

It was clear when the fighting stopped in 1973 that the Israelis were on the brink of another military triumph prevented only by U.S. and Soviet intervention. But Israel's failure to win a decisive victory, the success of the initial Egyptian and Syrian strikes into Israeli-occupied positions in the Sinai Peninsula and the Golan Heights and the high toll of Israeli casualties (more than 2,500 killed compared to less than 700 in the 1967 war) laid to rest the assumption that the Israelis were supermen who could not be beaten in battle. Despite their later setbacks, the Arabs proved that they could fight and fight well. "No matter what happens in the desert, there has been a victory that cannot be erased," Egyptian President Anwar Sadat declared in a speech before his country's National Assembly on Oct. 16, 1973. "According to any military standard, the Egyptian armed forces have realized a miracle. The wounded nation has restored its honor, the political map of the Middle East has changed."

Although the 1973 outbreak of fighting seemed to catch both Israel and the world by surprise, Sadat had been saying for some time that he might be forced to resort to war. Besides the purely military objective of recapturing part of the territories lost to Israel in 1967, Sadat's primary motive for going to war was to refocus world attention on the Middle East. "Everyone has fallen asleep over the Mideast crisis," Sadat said in an interview with *Newsweek* senior editor Arnaud de Borchgrave in April 1973. "The time has come for a shock."[13]

When Arab unity was restored toward the end of 1976, a new Arab strategy began to emerge. By presenting a moderate image to the world, Sadat and most of the Arab leaders hoped to affect U.S. policy and create the conditions for resumption of the Geneva negotiations. Even the Palestine Liberation Organization (PLO) began to make gestures (however ambiguous) indicating a willingness to accept the existence of Israel if the bulk of the occupied territories would be turned over for the creation of a Palestinian state.

---

13 "The Battle Is Now Inevitable," *Newsweek*, April 9, 1973, p. 45.

Aware that the Carter administration's Middle East policies could largely determine Middle East events during the coming years ("The U.S. holds 99 per cent of the cards," Sadat has grown fond of repeating) a major effort was launched in 1977 to convince the United States that the Arabs no longer challenged Israel's existence but did question her occupation of Arab lands and her refusal to allow the fulfillment of "Palestinian rights." In February 1977, Sadat said in an interview in *Parade* magazine, "I want the American people to know . . . that never before have the prospects for peace been better. Not in the last 28 years — since Israel was created — have we had a better chance for a permanent settlement in the Middle East. We must not lose the chance."[14]

Israel's Growing Isolation

The Israelis were forced by the 1973 war and subsequent developments to take a new look at their Arab neighbors. For one thing, the war demonstrated that the Arabs were closing the technological gap that had in the past protected the vastly outnumbered Israelis. Unlike the 1967 war — when, during the first hours of fighting, Israel destroyed most of the Egyptian air force while still on the ground — Israeli planes in 1973 encountered opposition from Egyptian and Syrian MIGs and from anti-aircraft missiles supplied by the Soviet Union.

"This time [in 1973] they marshaled all their resources, including oil, to achieve their purpose," said Moshe Dayan, then Israeli Defense Minister. "They took the international climate into account, the role the Russians would play, the importance of the detente between the Americans and the

14 See George Michaelson, "Peace Prospects Are Better Than Ever; An Interview With Egyptian President Sadat," *Parade*, February 6, 1977.
15 Quoted in *New York Times*, Nov. 27, 1973, in the second of a series of four articles on changing Arab attitudes.

Russians. They realized that it was a changed world in 1973, and we have to realize it too."[15]

Another important change made evident by the 1973 war was Israel's growing isolation in the world community. The threat of an Arab oil boycott forced the Japanese and most West European governments to demonstrate a decidedly pro-Arab "tilt" during and after the October war. Western Europe consumes about one-fourth of the world's oil production and relies on the Arab states for nearly 70 per cent of its imports. In an attempt to appease the Arabs, the European Economic Community (Common Market), including the Netherlands and Denmark—generally considered to be pro-Israeli—issued a resolution on Nov. 6, 1973, calling on Israel "to end the territorial occupation which it has maintained since the conflict in 1967."

The Common Market declaration also pointed to the "recognition that, in the establishment of a just and lasting peace, account must be taken of the legitimate rights of the Palestinians." Japan, almost entirely dependent on outside sources of oil — 45 per cent of which comes from the Arab countries — also issued statements calling for an Israeli withdrawal. Numerous resolutions in the U.N. and other international bodies since the October War have indicated that developments of the 1970s tended to isolate Israel politically.

An especially hard blow to Israel was the loss of support in black Africa, where Israel had courted friendship since the 1950s through technical assistance programs. After the out-break of war in 1973 nine African states—Tanzania, Malagasy Republic, Central African Republic, Ethiopia, Rwanda, Cameroon, Dahomey, Upper Volta and Equatorial Guinea—broke off diplomatic relations with Israel. Togo and Zaire had previously severed their ties.

But most important, the new situation had a major impact on U.S. policy. In order to protect growing relationships with many of the Arab states as well as to preserve America's special ties with Israel it was the United States which began to encourage a general settlement.

PETROLEUM POLITICS: VOLATILE ARAB WEAPON

When the Arab governments in October 1973 embargoed oil to the United States and, together with other oil-producing states in the following months, quadrupled its price, a historic change began. Never in modern history had such an abrupt transfer of wealth and power taken place without war and in so short a time.

The most obvious consequence of high-priced oil was a redistribution of wealth. While industrial countries sank into recession, oil-producing states were suddenly gorged with money. Developing nations not blessed with oil staggered under the new cost of fuels and fertilizers needed to lift them from poverty — and yet the success of fellow Third World nations that used oil to gain wealth and power aroused new hopes that they, too, might somehow wrest a bigger share of the world's goods from the long-dominant West.

With the transfer of wealth went a shift in power. Not only did the major oil-producing states, especially Saudi Arabia, control a vital resource without which all Western economies would face collapse; they also had accumulated, by 1977, at least $150-billion in financial reserves and liquid assets. These petrodollars could, at least theoretically, be used to destabilize various currencies or weaken the economies of most Western countries. Assistant Secretary of State for Economic Affairs, Julius L. Katz, testified before Congress in January 1977 that the financial assets of the OPEC countries could total $300-billion by 1980, an unprecedented accumulation of financial muscle. In 1977, the current account surplus of the OPEC countries—the excess between income and expenditures — was $31.5-billion. The figure would have been considerably higher, in fact, were it not for the massive spending, development and arms sales programs being carried out by many of the OPEC countries.

States such as Iran and Saudi Arabia, to say nothing of petty sheikdoms along the Persian Gulf, are, of course, no match for the armed might of a United States or a Soviet Union. But by 1976 the discussion of using military might against the oil producers had subsided. Some Western journals, in the immediate aftermath of the oil embargo and price rises had featured scenarios in which American armed forces seized Middle East oil fields in the event of another embargo, or even as a means to prevent ruinous prices. Secretary of State Henry A. Kissinger warned that this would be a "very dangerous course," but did not entirely rule it out if "there's some actual strangulation of the industrialized world."

The Persian Gulf states eagerly buy hoards of modern weapons, which the United States as eagerly sells (a little less eagerly since President Carter took office), competing with its allies to recapture some of the funds the West is pouring into the coffers of the oil states. The new arsenals of the gulf could not block a seizure of oil fields, although they might raise its risks, especially if a country such as Iran developed nuclear weapons. But various Arab leaders have hinted that they would blow up their oil fields if any attempt were made to take them over by military force. And a Library of Congress study has indicated that the attempt itself would not be feasible.[1]

The greatest danger arising from military intervention, however, would be the uncertain response of the Soviet Union.

Shifting Power

It would be misleading, however, to formulate the shift in power in military terms. The "oil weapon" already has changed the balance of political and economic power between Israel and the Arab states. It has also wrought changes far beyond the Middle East. A mutual dependence has been built up between the Western industrialized countries and the Arab states. The U.S.-Saudi Arabian relationship is especially important.

During and after the 1973 Arab-Israeli war, disagreement over support for Israel created severe strains between the United States and its allies, who depend heavily on Arab oil; in another Middle East war these tensions might prove more damaging. The Western alliance was further strained by competition to secure scarce oil, a competition that could grow more intense with further restrictions in supply and increases in demand.

The damage oil prices have done to Western economies handicaps them in the arms race with the Soviet bloc and increases pressures for reducing the West's overseas commitments, including those in the Middle East and the Indian Ocean. As their monetary reserves grow to several hundred billion dollars, Middle Eastern governments will have much greater financial power to threaten Western economies.

Within industrial societies, the discontent fostered by inflation and unemployment may feed authoritarian movements in countries such as Italy and, if it grows worse, in more stable democracies. In developing countries, governments struggling against worsening economic problems may grow more repressive. In both rich and poor countries if political unrest grows with economic decline, leaders will find assertive foreign policies more tempting. A rising level of international tensions thus may coincide with a proliferation of nuclear weapons, and those weapons will be accessible to more states as they hasten to develop nuclear energy as a substitute for high-priced oil.

If the world can respond creatively to this sea of troubles, the oil crisis may prove, at least partially, a blessing in disguise. The exploitation of natural resources by industrial societies was growing at a dangerous rate, and the huge gap between rich and poor nations showed no sign of abating. Both are built into ways of life that were taken for granted until the new price of oil hit home. The impact of rising oil prices and demand lay at the heart of the 1979 energy crisis. The June 1979 OPEC price hike — the largest since 1973 — placed severe strains on the world economy.

---

1 "Oil Fields As Military Objectives: A Feasibility Study," Prepared by the Congressional Research Service of the Library of Congress for the Special Subcommittee on Investigations of the International Relations Committee of the House of Representatives, 21 August 1975.

Impact of 1973 Embargo

In early 1974, the world's money managers were close to a state of panic at the enormous imbalance in the international monetary system. The oil-producing countries had decreed huge increases in the price of petroleum, from an average of about $2.40 a barrel to more than $10. There seemed no way that oil consumers—the poor countries in particular—could afford to pay for their energy supplies, and no way that oil producers could spend their expected surpluses. On every hand, there were predictions of chaos and impending collapse of existing world monetary arrangements.[2]

Somehow the international community limped through 1974, and the sense of panic subsided. Optimistic statements about the resiliency of the world monetary system began to be heard. Early in 1975, Secretary of the Treasury William E. Simon told Congress that he believed "the international financial aspects of the oil situation are manageable." The sense of relief turned out to be premature, however. Among economists, there remained a deep concern about the condition of the monetary system; it was still subject to severe strains. Experts warned that a protracted imbalance of payments[3] would inevitably further slow economic growth in the industrial countries, bankrupt the less-developed countries, cause the banking system to collapse and throw the world into a massive recession or depression.[4]

By 1977 it was clear that rising oil prices had contributed to slower economic growth in many countries, that many countries, especially developing ones, were no longer good credit risks for the loans they required to purchase oil imports and that a world recession was possible should some countries begin defaulting on outstanding loans thus affecting the stability of the entire financial system.[5]

Business Week reported in 1977 that "The oil cartel's first big price hike tossed the world economy into the worst recession in 40 years—one from which it has not yet recovered. The OPEC-induced loss in output over the past three years is estimated at $550-billion. The external debt of the less developed nations has mushroomed to $170-billion. Even without the latest boost, the world is transferring $100-billion a year to OPEC."[6]

The member countries of OPEC, the Organization of Petroleum Exporting Countries, rang up a spectacular $97-billion foreign-exchange surplus in 1974. But massive spending programs and arms purchases have since recycled a substantial share of these funds back to Western economies. Late in 1976 it was reported that "The OPEC countries have surprised the world — and often themselves — by the speed with which they have been able to increase their imports."[7] In that first year of escalating oil prices, the industrial countries registered a $67-billion trade deficit, three times larger than in 1973. The less-developed countries saw their deficit more than double to $26-billion.

This seriously imbalanced situation has continued. It is hardest on less developed countries (the LDCs) who must pay for importing oil but have little to sell in return for recycling petrodollars. By 1977, LDC debt had skyrocketed to more than $170-billion with no end in sight.[8]

So far, "Private banking institutions, acting singly or in consortium, have continued to absorb and relend large sums of investible OPEC funds," President Ford reported just before leaving office.[9] But Princeton economist Peter B. Kenen said, "We have reached the point where to get back what you loaned in the first place you have to throw good money after bad."[10] Increasingly, doubt is being expressed about how long this situation can continue; how long the poorer countries can keep borrowing to pay their bills for imported oil.

"The continuation of sizable balance of payments deficits," which are mainly the result of the oil price increases, President Ford warned in January 1977, "poses serious financing and management problems for the countries concerned and is a major disruptive element in their development process."[11]

In general, oil exporting countries can "recycle" their huge surpluses in three ways: (1) by spending them on imports of consumer goods, military hardware, industrial equipment, food and other commodities; (2) by investing them, either in development projects at home or in foreign countries, and (3) by relending the money through official and private channels to oil-importing nations.

To a surprising extent, the exporting countries have done all three things since 1974. By 1977, U.S. exports to OPEC countries had increased nearly 400 per cent from 1973, to $13.5-billion.[12] *(See chart, p. 74)* OPEC nations are, in fact, greatly dependent upon products from the United States and other industrial countries. *(See graph, p. 85)*

At the same time, OPEC countries, and especially the Arab oil states, stepped up their investments in, and their loans to, Western enterprises. Arabs began to acquire substantial holdings in American real estate and industries and extended loans to several U.S. corporations. These developments were not entirely to the liking of many Western political leaders, who feared the possibility of Arab takeovers of huge national and multinational enterprises. So far, though, the Arabs appear to be more interested in secure placement of their capital management control. One reason is fear of possible freezing of assets should a major world crisis occur. Thus highly liquid investments were favored, even though they command lower interest rates. By 1977, though, there were indications of cautious movement into medium-term investment of one to two years.

Finally, a sizable amount of oil money found its way into international lending channels, both official and private. By 1977 U.S. banks were so crammed with short-term funds from OPEC states that some began discouraging them. Some banks in Switzerland began to charge a negative interest rate on certain types of deposits. In fact it was because the private banking system had acted as the intermediary for recycling petrodollar surpluses to debtor countries to finance their purchases of more oil from the

---

2 See "Arab Oil Money," *Editorial Research Reports*, 1974 Vol. I, pp. 365-381.

3 When income from abroad is less than a country's foreign spending on trade investments, tourism, military and foreign aid.

4 See, for example, Robert V. Roosa et al., "How Can the World Afford OPEC Oil?" *Foreign Affairs*, January 1975, pp. 201-202. Roosa was under secretary of the treasury for monetary affairs in the Kennedy and Johnson administrations.

5 During 1977 one of the best-selling fiction books had as its theme such an international banking collapse. It was written by a former international banker, Paul Erdman. *The Crash of '79* (Simon & Schuster: 1977). See review in *Business Week*, 7 March 1977, p. 10.

6 *Business Week*, 10 January 1977, p. 61.

7 Lawrence A. Veit, "Troubled World Economy," *Foreign Affairs*, January 1977, p. 265.

8 See David O. Beim, "Rescuing the LDCs," and Harold van B. Cleveland & W. H. Bruce Brittain, "Are the LDCs in over their heads?" in *Foreign Affairs*, July 1977.

9 *International Economic Report of the President*, January 1977, p. 10.

10 *Business Week*, 10 January 1977, p. 62.

11 *International Economic Report of the President*, January 1977, p. 19.

12 *Direction of Trade, Annual 1971-77*, International Monetary Fund.

Selected Consuming Countries'...

(Thousands of barrels per day and percent of imports)

	Total Imports	Major Arab Total	Major Non-Arab Total	Total Other[3]	Major Arab Oil Producers			
					Saudi Arabia	Kuwait	Libya	Iraq
United States	6,568	3,052	2,679	837	1,369	42	696	76
Percent	100	46.5	40.8	12.7	20.8	.6	10.6	1.2
Japan	4,510	2,431	1,403	676	1,423	373	3	153
Percent	100	53.9	31.1	15.0	31.6	8.3	.1	3.4
Canada	663	192	388	83	154	4	—	23
Percent	100	29.0	58.5	12.5	23.2	.6		3.5
Western Europe[2]	10,148	6,311	2,766	1,072	2,793	638	765	1,126
Percent	100	62.2	27.3	10.6	27.5	6.3	7.5	11.1
United Kingdom	1,323	801	300	222	282	227	26	180
Percent	100	60.5	22.7	16.8	21.3	17.1	2.0	13.6
West Germany	1,921	1,006	629	287	293	30	294	59
Percent	100	52.4	32.7	14.9	15.3	1.6	15.3	3.0
Italy	2,003	1,355	463	185	590	139	270	278
Percent	100	67.6	23.2	9.2	29.4	6.9	13.5	13.9
France	2,337	1,614	476	247	806	53	70	407
Percent	100	69.1	20.4	10.6	34.5	2.3	3.0	17.4
Netherlands	1,162	601	490	71	293	135	25	64
Percent	100	51.7	42.2	6.1	25.2	11.7	2.1	5.5
Belgium	618	370	199	49	248	31	2	38
Percent	100	59.9	32.2	7.9	40.1	4.9	.3	6.1
Spain	784	564	209	11	281	23	78	100
Percent	100	71.9	26.7	1.4	35.9	2.9	9.9	12.8

[1] Imports of crude oil and refined products traced to the original source. Figures may not add to totals because of conversion from metric tons to U.S. barrels.

[2] Includes United Kingdom, West Germany, Italy, France, Netherlands, Belgium and Spain.

[3] Includes all other Arab and non-Arab sources of oil.

OPEC countries—at the rate of about $10-billion annually by 1977—that the banks were increasingly worried about the quality of their loans.[13]

OPEC countries also have contributed increasing amounts to (1) a special oil "facility" fund set up by the International Monetary Fund to ease the balance-of-payments problems of consuming countries and (2) international development institutions, such as the World Bank and the regional development banks.

All these measures evidently helped forestall the drastic results predicted in early 1974, where estimates of the peak accumulation of OPEC reserves reached $600-billion and even higher. By 1975, U.S. bankers were making more optimistic projections, with the time and size of the peak surplus depending on such factors as the impact on consumption of high oil prices, the growth of alternative oil supplies, the degree to which alternative sources of energy such as coal and nuclear power are developed, the policies of consuming countries and the cohesiveness of the OPEC cartel (to say nothing of the chances of another war in the Middle East).

The First National City Bank in its June 1975 newsletter projected four different scenarios. The most pessimistic estimated a peak surplus of nearly $300 billion in 1981; the most optimistic placed the peak in 1977, at a level of about $130-billion, which rapidly fell to an actual deficit in OPEC balances by 1983. *(Graph of projected OPEC surpluses, p. 77)*

In 1977 the more pessimistic forecasts appeared to be the more accurate ones. Prices were continuing to go up. President Carter was predicting oil shortages within a few years, and some analysts were writing of a "more-or-less permanent annual OPEC surplus amount[ing] to about $38-billion."[14]—the surplus after spending on all the projects and schemes the OPEC countries had been able to put together since 1973.

Oil economist Walter Levy's predictions were coming true, it seemed. Back in 1975 he had written that "To the extent that oil imports are financed by a continued recycling of surplus oil revenues via investments or loans on commercial terms, oil importing countries will face pyramiding interest or individual charges on top of mount-

---

13 See *Forbes*, 1 July 1976, p. 76 and *Business Week*, 12 July 1976, p. 32; 17 January 1977, p. 65; and 28 March 1977, pp. 23-24.

14 Beim, *op. cit.*, p. 718. Beim is executive vice president of the Export-Import Bank of the United States.

... Dependence on Arab Oil, 1978[1]

United Arab Emirates	Algeria		Major Non-Arab Oil Producers					
		Iran	Venezuela	Indonesia	Canada	Nigeria	Soviet Union
331	538	525	249	502	278	1,123	2
5.0	8.2	8.0	3.8	7.6	4.2	17.1	—
472	7	807	1	594	—	—	1
10.5	.2	17.9		13.2			
3	8	114	262	—	—	7	5
.5	1.2	17.2	39.5			1.1	.8
645	345	1,658	91	—	—	665	352
6.4	3.4	16.3	.9			6.6	3.5
81	5	185	23	—	—	39	54
6.1	.3	14.0	1.7			2.9	4.0
131	199	347	18	—	—	208	56
6.8	10.3	18.1	.9			10.8	2.9
50	28	290	13	—	—	8	152
2.5	1.4	14.5	.7			.4	7.6
197	81	222	15	—	—	172	68
8.4	3.5	9.5	.6			7.3	2.9
78	6	286	4	—	—	197	2
6.7	.6	24.6	.4			16.9	.2
45	7	142	5	—	—	41	11
7.3	1.1	22.9	.8			6.6	1.8
63	19	186	13	—	—	—	9
8.1	2.4	23.7	1.7				1.2

SOURCE: Energy Information Administration, Department of Energy.

ing direct oil import costs."[15] Levy wondered then, and many continued to wonder, how long this could go on.

At some point in the future, it has been predicted, the private banking system will find itself unable to cope with the massive surpluses being acquired by OPEC members. And insofar as official efforts are directed at lending money to consuming countries to meet their rising energy costs, the problem is not solved but merely postponed.

Price Rise Impact on Industrialized Nations

The impact of the oil price rise has not been uniform on all the oil-importing countries. Among the industrial nations, the United States has fared better than most because of its lesser, though growing, dependence on imported oil and because of substantial export sales and arms sales. But even the United States by 1977 was running a $21.5-billion deficit to the OPEC nations in its trade account.

Western Europe fared worse, however. The combined trade deficits of Western European countries rose to $23.8-billion in 1974, up from $7.6-billion the previous year. Japan has had to resort to a $1-billion loan from Saudi Arabia to finance its oil imports, and Italy has received a series of credits from the European Economic Community (Common Market), the IMF and West Germany.[16]

Relative to other industrial countries, however, the United States may have benefited from the rising oil price—leading to speculation that possibly the U.S. was not so opposed to the developments that took place in 1973 and 1974. In a front-page Washington Post story on July 19, 1977, it was stated that "since the takeoff of oil prices in the fall of 1973, America's economic stature in the world has improved dramatically, reversing a long decline, while our competitors (and friends) in Western Europe and Japan have suffered. So much of American political rhetoric casts OPEC as an adversary intent on hurting us by embargo or price-gouging. Yet...the actual relationship more resembles a partnership, an intricate symbiosis in which the United States gains and gives, and so do the leading partners of OPEC.... Europeans have been talking for years about the

15 Walter J. Levy, "World Oil Cooperation or International Chaos," Foreign Affairs, July 1974, p. 697.

16 See "Italy's Threatened Democracy," Editorial Research Reports, 1975 Vol. I, pp. 1-20. West Germany, in contrast to its neighbors, enjoyed a trade surplus in 1974—some $20-billion.

economic advantages and the increased political leverage that America may have gained from OPEC."* In an article which partially supports this thesis, *Forbes* concluded that "...the Europeans are basically correct.... OPEC gained its power over prices through the maneuverings of the State Department."**

Effect on Less Developed Countries

Still, the most severe impact was felt by the poorer countries of the world—those without oil to sell or significant exports of other raw materials. These include 75 to 80 countries, or about three-fourths of the poorer nations. India, as the largest of the non-communist developing countries, is the foremost example of a nation being driven to the brink of bankruptcy by the energy price crisis. In the best of times, India has had a difficult job providing food and other basic necessities for its nearly 600 million people. The huge jump in oil prices has made the task virtually impossible. India's oil import bill in 1975 was about $1.5-billion, in contrast to only $300-million five years earlier.[17]

In recognition of India's plight, both Iran and Iraq offered New Delhi concessions in the form of loans and deferred payments for the purchase of petroleum. Such assistance was not likely in the long run to be sufficient to pull India out of the hole. This was also true for other countries whose commodity export earnings drop while their oil bills rise.

Economist Richard N. Cooper at Yale saw the debt burden on the less developed countries as creating a major international economic problem. "These countries are now hanging by their financial fingernails. They are top-heavy with external debt, and their financial position is extremely fragile," he wrote.[18]

A financial problem for the LDCs also poses a problem for the banking system in the West. American banks in particular have granted huge loans to various LDCs who between 1973 and 1977 increased their foreign debts by more than 150 per cent. Citibank in New York, for example, had 70 per cent of its portfolio in foreign credits of all types in 1977. In 1976, for the first time, bad debts abroad were greater than defaults on domestic loans for Citibank. "The real problem for banks in 1977 is going to be their exposure to less developed countries trying to finance oil deficits. Banks are in deep," *Business Week* reported in March 1977.[19]

Agence France-Presse, the French news agency, reported as long ago as 1973 that a number of developing countries "are finding it hard to honor their commercial debts, as a result of the world economic crisis." It cited the example of the African republic of Zaire, formerly the Belgian Congo, which has experienced declines in the prices of copper, diamonds, oil seeds, zinc, coffee, cocoa and cotton. Zaire's case is significant, because it points up a growing rift in the Organization of African Unity between the member states that produce oil and those that have to buy

	U.S. Trade with OPEC Members (in billions of U.S. dollars)		
	Exports	**Imports**	**Balance**
1972	2.6	2.7	− .1
1973	3.4	4.7	− 1.3
1974	6.4	16.1	− 9.7
1975	10.4	18.0	− 7.6
1976	12.2	26.6	−14.4
1977	13.5	35.0	−21.5

SOURCE: *Direction of Trade, Annual 1971-77*, International Monetary Fund

it. The oil consumers complain that the producers have turned a deaf ear to their pleas for economic assistance.[20]

Among the oil-exporting countries of the world, there is a wide divergence in their ability to make productive use of surplus revenues. In a 1975 study Hollis B. Chenery, vice president for development policy at the World Bank, put OPEC members into three categories:

• Countries with large reserves, small populations and little economic absorptive capacity. This group included the primary Arab oil producers — Saudi Arabia, Kuwait, Qatar and the United Arab Emirates. These countries accounted for most of the monetary imbalance that plagued the world — 83 percent of the 1976 surplus. Saudi Arabia ranked first, with West Germany and the United States in second and third place, for foreign-exchange holdings.

• Countries with substantial reserves but large populations and ambitious development programs which can absorb most of the new oil money. This group included Iran, Venezuela, Iraq and Algeria, all of which had reached a relatively sophisticated stage of economic development and were using up their oil money to finance the development effort. Need for money explained why these countries had been pushing for higher and higher oil prices while those in the first category had urged restraint.

• Countries with smaller reserves and large populations, whose development needs would eat up virtually every penny of the oil money flowing in. Nigeria and Indonesia were in this group.[21]

Coping with Petrodollars

The problem of recycling surplus oil revenues—"petrodollars"—and of cushioning the shock for consuming nations most seriously affected by high oil prices has been attacked in a number of ways. Two of the most important are the creation of the special oil facility within the IMF and the approval of a "safety net" fund by members of the Organization for Economic Cooperation and Development (OECD), a group of major non-communist industrial nations.

---

*William Greider and J. P. Smith, "A Proposition: High Oil Prices Benefit U.S."

**See "Don't Blame The Oil Companies: Blame the State Department," *Forbes*, 15 April 1976.

17 P. D. Henderson, *India: The Energy Sector* (1975), World Bank, pp. 107-115.

18 *Business Week*, 18 October 1976, p. 105.

19 *Business Week*, 28 March 1977, p. 34. One study found that "commercial banks increased their loans to non-OPEC developing countries by about $46-billion in the 1974-76 period, a sum that represented 42 per cent of total new financings. This compared with a 20 per cent share in 1971-73." See Robert A. Bennett, "Mountains of Debt Pile Up As Banks Rush Foreign Loans," *The New York Times*, 15 May 1977, p. 1 (financial section). Even French banks were becoming hostage to both Arab depositors and LDC borrowers. See *Business Week*, 17 January 1977, p. 65.

20 For background see "African Nation Building," *Editorial Research Reports*, 1973 Vol. I, pp. 355-372.

21 Chenery's analysis is contained in his article, "Restructuring the World Economy," *Foreign Affairs*, January 1975, pp. 242-263.

World Crude Oil Production, 1960-1978

(bpd = barrels per day)

Major Areas and Selected Countries	1960 1,000 bpd	1960 Per cent	1970 1,000 bpd	1970 Per cent	1973 1,000 bpd	1973 Per cent	1975 1,000 bpd	1975 Per cent	1976 1,000 bpd	1976 Per cent	1977 1,000 bpd	1977 Per cent	1978[4] 1,000 bpd	1978[4] Per cent
North America	7,845	37.3	11,373	25.1	11,452	20.5	10,550	19.9	10,389	17.9	10,546	17.6	11,232	18.5
United States	7,055	33.5	9,648	21.3	9,189	16.5	8,370	15.8	8,154	14.0	8,244	13.8	8,701	14.3
Canada	519	2.5	1,305	2.9	1,798	3.2	1,460	2.7	1,339	2.3	1,321	2.2	1,324	2.2
Mexico	271	1.3	420	.9	465	.8	720	1.4	897	1.5	981	1.6	1,207	2.0
Central and South America	3,470	16.5	4,758	10.5	4,666	8.4	3,585	6.7	3,553	6.1	3,530	5.9	3,548	5.8
Venezuela[1]	2,854	13.6	3,703	8.2	3,364	6.0	2,345	4.4	2,301	4.0	2,238	3.7	2,166	3.6
Ecuador[1]	7	*	5	*	204	.4	160	.3	187	.3	183	.3	202	.3
Other	609	2.9	1,050	2.3	1,098	2.0	1,080	2.0	1,065	1.8	1,109	1.8	1,180	1.9
Western Europe	289	1.4	375	.8	370	.7	550	1.0	776	1.3	1,260	2.1	1,679	2.8
United Kingdom	2	*	2	*	2	*	20	*	244	.4	744	1.2	1,082	1.8
Norway	0	0	0	0	32	.1	190	.4	279	.5	279	.5	356	.6
Other	287	1.4	373	.8	336	.6	340	.6	253	.4	237	.4	241	.4
Africa	289	1.4	5,982	13.2	5,902	10.6	4,990	9.4	5,849	10.1	6,236	10.4	6,120	10.1
Algeria[1]	185	.9	976	2.2	1,070	1.9	960	1.8	1,052	1.8	1,123	1.9	1,225	2.0
Libya[1]	0	0	3,321	7.3	2,187	3.9	1,480	2.8	1,929	3.3	2,064	3.3	1,993	3.3
Nigeria[1]	18	.1	1,090	2.4	2,053	3.7	1,795	3.4	2,071	3.6	2,097	3.5	1,910	3.1
Gabon[1]	—	—	110	.2	150	.3	225	.4	225	.4	222	.4	225	.4
Other	86	.4	485	1.1	442	.8	530	1.0	572	1.0	730	1.2	767	1.3
Asia-Pacific	554	2.6	1,340	3.0	2,272	4.1	2,215	4.2	2,528	4.4	2,787	4.6	2,843	4.7
Indonesia[1]	419	2.0	855	1.9	1,339	2.4	1,305	2.5	1,508	2.6	1,685	2.8	1,637	2.7
Other	135	.6	485	1.1	933	1.7	910	1.7	1,020	1.8	1,102	1.8	1,206	2.0
Middle East	5,269	25.1	13,937	30.7	21,158	38.0	19,590	36.9	22,235	38.3	22,430	37.4	21,603	35.6
Saudi Arabia[1]	1,319	6.3	3,798	8.4	7,607	13.7	7,075	13.3	8,367	14.4	9,014	15.0	8,530	14.1
Kuwait[1]	1,696	8.1	2,983	6.6	3,024	5.4	2,085	3.9	1,918	3.3	1,783	3.0	1,865	3.1
Iran[1]	1,057	5.0	3,831	8.4	5,861	10.5	5,350	10.1	5,940	10.2	5,699	9.5	5,207	8.6
Iraq[1]	969	4.6	1,563	3.4	1,964	3.5	2,260	4.3	2,442	4.2	2,493	4.1	2,629	4.3
Abu Dhabi[1] [2]	0	0	691	1.5	1,298	2.3	1,370	2.6	1,952	3.4	1,999	3.3	1,832	3.0
Qatar[1]	173	.8	367	.8	570	1.0	440	.8	498	.9	445	.7	484	.8
Other	55	.3	704	1.6	834	1.5	1,010	1.9	1,138	2.0	997	1.7	1,056	1.7
Total Non-Communist	17,716	84.3	37,765	83.3	45,820	82.3	41,695	78.5	45,331	78.1	46,789	78.0	47,025	77.5
Communist World[3]	3,310	15.7	7,610	16.7	9,865	17.7	11,650	21.9	12,728	21.9	13,213	22.0	13,683	22.5
Soviet Union	2,960	14.1	7,049	15.5	8,420	15.1	9,630	18.1	NA	NA	10,934	18.2	11,215	18.5
Other	350	1.6	561	1.2	1,445	2.6	2,020	3.8	NA	NA	2,279	3.8	2,468	4.1
Total World	21,026	100.0	45,375	100.0	55,685	100.0	53,120	100.0	58,059	100.0	60,002	100.0	60,708	100.0

* Production or percentage of production is negligible.
NA not available.
[1] Member of Organization of Petroleum Exporting Countries.
[2] Figures for 1976, 1977 and 1978 include all United Arab Emirate countries.
[3] Includes Soviet Union and other Warsaw Pact nations, China, Cuba and Yugoslavia.
[4] Estimate.

SOURCES: International Economic Report of the President, March 1975, January 1977; Energy Data Report, Energy Information Administration, June 1979.

The IMF's special oil facility was set up in mid-1974, over U.S. objections. The United States felt that such a fund, specifically designed to ease balance-of-payments problems caused by high oil prices, amounted to an endorsement of "exorbitant" price levels. The fund is financed by borrowings from oil producers and can be tapped by any of the IMF's member countries. When the fund went into operation in August 1974, its authorized capital was $3.2-billion. Subsequently, the amount was doubled to $6.2-billion.

The OECD's "safety net" fund of $25-billion was approved in March 1975 at the urging of Secretary of State Kissinger. It is made up of security pledges by participating nations under a formula based on national wealth. It is designed as a fund of last resort, to be used only when a member country has exhausted all other credit possibilities. Loans are limited to seven years at commercial interest rates. Because of rigid requirements governing loans, few requests were anticipated. However, the fund was expected to provide psychological security for industrial nations with tottering economies.

Also at Kissinger's urging, a 19-nation International Energy Agency (IEA) was created, consisting of most of the larger industrial oil-consuming nations. (Australia joined in 1979, bringing the number to 20.) The agency was intended to present a united front of oil users in negotiations with OPEC but had difficulty achieving its goal. Preliminary talks in Paris between the oil-producing and oil-consuming nations collapsed April 15, 1975. The United States, the European Economic Community and Japan insisted that the international conference planned for later in the year be confined to energy and related problems; Algeria, Saudi Arabia, Iran and Venezuela demanded that the agenda be broadened to include consideration of other raw materials and development aid. They were joined in this demand by some of the non-oil producing countries of the Third World.

At a May 27 meeting of the International Energy Agency in Paris, Kissinger reversed the U.S. position, proposing that stability of raw material prices be included in future meetings with oil-producing countries. "It has become clear as a result of the April preparatory meeting," he said, "that the dialogue between the producers and the consumers will not progress unless it is broadened to include the general issue of the relationship between developing and developed countries." The OECD met the next day and issued a "declaration on relations with developing countries," pledging greater cooperation and a resumption of talks with Third World countries which would deal generally with the problems of raw materials.

OPEC members themselves have made significant efforts to recycle their petrodollars, through bilateral lending arrangements and through contributions to international finance agencies. Abdlatif Al Hamad, director general of the Kuwait Fund for Arab Economic Development, told the Joint Development Committee of the World Bank and the IMF that OPEC members contributed $14.3-billion in development assistance in 1974, including a $3.1-billion loan to the IMF oil facility and $1-billion to the World Bank.

In this hemisphere, Venezuela, the world's fifth largest exporter of petroleum, has set up a $500-million fund in the Inter-American Development Bank for lending to the least-developed countries of the region. In addition, Venezuela has allotted $540-million to the World Bank, $540-million to the IMF oil facility and $100-million to the U.N. Emergency Fund, and was underwriting one plan to defer oil payments

Organization of Petroleum Exporting Countries' Revenues, 1970-1978[1]

(in millions of U.S. dollars)

Country	1970	1971	1972	1973	1974	1975	1976	1977	1978
Saudi Arabia	$1,200	$2,149	$3,107	$4,340	$22,600	$25,700	$33,500	$42,400	$35,800
Kuwait	895	1,400	1,657	1,900	7,000	7,500	8,500	8,900	9,200
Iran	1,136	1,944	2,380	4,100	17,500	18,500	22,000	21,300	20,500
Iraq	521	840	575	1,840	5,700	7,500	8,500	9,600	9,800
United Arab Emirates[2]	233	431	551	900	5,500	6,000	7,000	9,000	8,000
Qatar	122	198	255	410	1,600	1,700	2,000	2,000	2,000
Libya	1,295	1,766	1,598	2,300	6,000	5,100	7,500	8,900	8,600
Algeria	325	350	700	900	3,700	3,400	4,500	4,300	5,000
Nigeria	411	915	1,174	2,200	8,900	6,600	8,500	9,600	8,200
Venezuela	1,406	1,702	1,948	2,670	8,700	7,500	8,500	6,100	5,600
Indonesia	185	284	429	950	3,300	3,850	4,500	5,700	5,600
Total	$7,729	$11,979	$14,374	$22,510	$90,500	$93,350	$115,000	$127,800	$118,300

1 In November 1973, Ecuador became a member of the OPEC, and Gabon an associate member; they are not included in the above chart.
2 A federation of the Persian Gulf states was formed in 1971. Revenue figures for 1975 to 1978 included all UAE production; figures for 1973 and 1974 include only Abu Dhabi and Dubai; figures before 1973 are for Abu Dhabi alone, which is the largest oil producer among the members of UAE.

SOURCES: Petroleum Information Foundation (1970); Petroleum Economist, Vol. XLIII, No. 9, Sept. 1976, p. 338 (1971-72); Petroleum Economist, Vol. XLIV, No. 7, July 1977 (1973-76); Petroleum Economist, Vol. XLVI, No. 6, June 1979 (1977-78).

by Central American countries and another to stockpile coffee in the six coffee-exporting nations of the hemisphere.

During 1975 and 1976, additional sums from the oil producing countries were made available in various ways to countries which must borrow to pay their oil bills.

Private Channels

The glut of petrodollars is obviously more than official channels—governments and international agencies—can handle. A substantial portion of the oil wealth is finding its way back to the West through private means, in the form of loans, bank deposits, investments and purchases of consumer and industrial goods. Western businessmen have found themselves in fierce competition for the potentially lucrative markets of the Middle East.

The markets are obviously limited by what the national economies can comfortably absorb. Only so many cars and television sets can be sold in the tiny sheikdoms of Qatar and United Arab Emirates. In contrast, the sky was the limit — at least for a while — in Iran. In the largest business arrangement ever signed, Iran and the United States in March 1975 agreed to $15-billion, five-year pact for exchange of goods. Included in the agreement was a provision for the United States to build eight nuclear reactors in Iran. Britain, France and West Germany concluded large trade deals with the Iranian government. Iran also entered into trade agreements and joint ventures with numerous other countries, including some in the Communist bloc. But events leading up to the shah's abdication left Iran's economy in shambles and trade dropped off sharply.

Other OPEC countries were active, too. Eight nations — Algeria, Bahrain, Iraq, Kuwait, Libya, Qatar, Saudi Arabia and United Arab Emirates — contracted to acquire a fleet of supertankers that could cost upward of half a billion dollars in three years. Iraq placed an order for 10,000 Mercedes-Benz trucks and ordered $300-million worth of jet planes from Boeing. In 1977 it was estimated that Saudi Arabia had already placed orders for $27-billion with U.S. companies.

More unsettling was the rising level of armaments being purchased by Middle Eastern oil producers from the United States, Western Europe and the Soviet Union. U.S. arms sales to Iran alone in fiscal year 1974 amounted to $3.8-billion. Saudi Arabia has also become a multi-billion dollar arms purchaser in recent years. A report by the U.S. Arms Control and Disarmament Agency showed that 13 developing countries had spent more than 10 per cent of their annual budgets on weapons. Among the countries were Saudi Arabia, Iran and Iraq.[22] *(Arms sales, p. 45)*

Petrodollars were also being funneled to Western Europe and the United States for deposit in banks and for the purchase of government securities. Treasury Secretary Simon estimated that OPEC countries in 1974 bought $6-billion worth of government securities in the United States and put an additional $4-billion into private U.S. banks. Some observers thought the actual total could be as much as 50 per cent higher. Tens of billions have come into the United States since 1975.

Finally, OPEC businessmen have been investing increasing amounts in commercial and industrial firms and

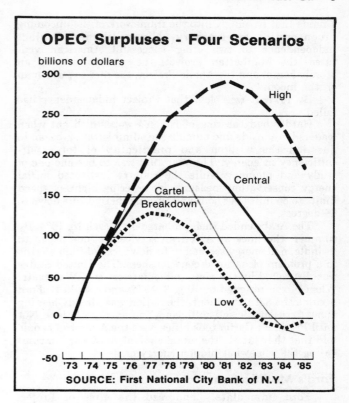

OPEC Surpluses - Four Scenarios

billions of dollars

SOURCE: First National City Bank of N.Y.

real estate interests in the West. In some cases, Arabs have offered loans to prop up sagging enterprises, as in the case of Iranian aid to Grumman Aircraft Corporation. More often, however, they have purchased shares in U.S. and European corporations, attempting in some isolated instances to acquire majority control.

Arab investment in Western corporations has been a source of growing controversy among government officials in America and Western Europe. In West Germany, where Iran owned 25 per cent of the Krupp steel works and tried to buy nearly 30 per cent of Daimler-Benz, Chancellor Helmut Schmidt expressed his misgivings. "In the long run," he said, "a sharper control by the state is unavoidable."[23] There was additional controversy on both sides of the Atlantic over attempts by the Arab Boycott Office to keep blacklisted "Jewish" banks and businesses in Western countries from participating in international transactions involving the Arabs.

Response to Embargo

The immediate response of the U.S. government to the Arab oil embargo in the fall of 1973 was to rally the nation in support of a crash program aimed at removing dependence on foreign oil in a few years.

When President Nixon addressed the nation on Nov. 7, 1973, he couched his remarks in terms of that ambitious and lofty objective. "Let us set as our national goal...that by the end of this decade we will have developed the potential to meet our own energy needs without depending on any foreign sources," he said. He called it Project Independence,

22 *World Military Expenditures and Arms Trade, 1963-1973,* Arms Control and Disarmament Agency, February 1975. See also Dale R. Tahtinen, *Arms in the Persian Gulf,* American Enterprise Institute, March 1974, "Resurgent Iran," *Editorial Research Reports,* 1974 Vol. I pp. 305-322, and "World Arms Sales," *Editorial Research Reports,* 1976 Vol. I pp. 325-341.

23 "German Press Review," West German Embassy in Washington, D.C., Jan. 29, 1975. See "Foreign Investment in America," *Editorial Research Reports,* 1974 Vol. II, pp. 561-580.

a name that fit snugly into the framework of the upcoming bicentennial anniversary. Nixon likened Project Independence to two other successful American ventures—the Manhattan Project, the race to develop an atomic bomb, and the Apollo Project, the race to put a man on the moon.

By 1977, it was clear that Project Independence had failed.

Hardly had the ring of Nixon's words died out when leaders both inside and outside the administration began to question the wisdom and practicality of total self-sufficiency in energy. The year 1974 was to become one of study and planning while the country instituted initial energy conservation measures by lowering highway speed limits to 55 miles per hour and turning thermostats down to 68 degrees.

The Arabs ended their embargo on March 18, 1974. By summer, the lines at American service stations began to dwindle, and energy seemed to be downgraded from a crisis to a problem of national consciousness. The United States was distracted by the more immediate crisis of Watergate. When Nixon resigned on Aug. 9, 1974, and Gerald R. Ford became the 38th President, the nation was already hearing about "reasonable self-sufficiency" in energy matters. Not until President Carter took office were the American people told that they faced "the moral equivalent of war" in combating the somewhat hidden energy crisis.

Ford's Modifications

Ford immediately endorsed the aims of Project Independence, but in one of his first important speeches as President, at the World Energy Conference in Detroit Sept. 23, he said that "no nation has or can have within its borders everything necessary for a full and rich life for all its people. Independence is not to set the United States apart from the rest of the world; it is to enable the United States to do its part more effectively in the world's effort to provide more energy."

Ford met no outcry at home against that move away from the original Project Independence goal of total self-sufficiency by 1980. To the contrary, informed opinion had found Nixon's goal unrealistic.

The Federal Energy Administration (FEA) formally unveiled its 800-page "Blueprint for Project Independence" on Nov. 13, 1974. Five days earlier, FEA Administrator John C. Sawhill had said, "Project Independence implies zero imports. I do not feel that this is either necessary or desirable as a goal for U.S. energy policy."

Widening U.S. Oil Gap

Whatever the original goals of Project Independence—their implementation remained vague and confused through the Ford presidency. There was no doubt that the Arab states had used the oil weapon tellingly against the American superpower. American domestic oil production peaked in 1970, meaning that, before the Arab embargo of October 1973, the United States had expected to import larger quantities of foreign oil to meet ever-increasing demands.

In 1972, the United States received 850,000 barrels of Arab oil per day, which represented 17.9 per cent of total imports. In 1973, Arab oil imports increased to 1,590,000 barrels per day, despite the beginning of the embargo. But the percentage of Arab oil to total imports dropped to 9.2 per cent.

In 1974, with the embargo still in effect until March 18, Arab imports dropped to 1,250,000 barrels per day, but the percentage of Arab oil went back up to 20.5 per cent. The percentage has grown ever since, and by 1977 the United States was importing more than nine million barrels of crude oil daily (about five times the amount imported in 1973 and about 50 per cent of U.S. consumption) with about 80 per cent coming from OPEC countries and about 50 per cent of this coming from the Arab states.

"Without constraints," President Carter warned in April 1977, "U.S. oil demand probably would grow at the postwar rate of 4 per cent per year, and reach 25 million barrels per day by 1985."[24] The CIA projection, quoted in *U.S. News and World Report,* May 2, 1977, and relied upon by the President, estimated that it was unlikely that this amount of oil would be made available to the United States at a reasonable price.[25]

With American demand continuing to rise at 4 per cent yearly, it was estimated in 1977 that oil imports would have to go up from nearly 9 million barrels per day in 1977 to 16 million barrels per day by 1985, assuming anticipated increases in domestic oil production prove to be accurate. In short, the oil embargo and U.S. efforts such as Project Independence had not altered the basic and growing American dependence on imported oil, and increasingly on imported Arab oil.

What actually happened was that the Arabs employed their oil weapon at the very time that the United States was beginning to rely more and more on Arab sources. The deepening reliance came about as supplies began to dwindle from Venezuela and Canada, historically the two

24 See "U.S. Leans More on Arab Oil," *Christian Science Monitor,* 13 June 1977, p. 1; "The National Energy Plan," Executive Office of the President, Energy Policy and Planning, 29 April 1977.
25 "The International Energy Situation: Outlook to 1985," Central Intelligence Agency, April 1977.

World Oil Production and Consumption 1977

Million barrels/day	Production	Consumption
United States	8.2	18.4
Canada	1.3	1.8
Western Europe[1]	1.3	11.4
Japan	—	5.1
South America[2]	3.5	2.2
Africa[3]	6.2	.6
Communist Countries[4]	13.2	11.9
Far East and Asia[5]	2.8	7.8
Australia	.4	.7
Middle East[6]	22.4	1.8

[1] Includes Austria, Denmark, France, West Germany, Italy, Netherlands, Norway, Spain and United Kingdom.
[2] Includes Argentina, Barbados, Bolivia, Brazil, Chile, Colombia, Ecuador, Peru, Trinidad, and Venezuela.
[3] Includes Algeria, Angola, Cameroon, Egypt, Gabon, Libya, Morocco, Nigeria, Tunisia and Zaire.
[4] Includes Sino-Soviet bloc countries, Cuba and Yugoslavia.
[5] Includes Australia, Brunei, Burma, India, Indonesia, Japan, Malaysia, New Zealand, Pakistan, Taiwan and Thailand.
[6] Includes Bahrain, Iran, Iraq, Israel, Kuwait, Neutral Zone, Oman, Qatar, Saudi Arabia, Syria, Turkey and United Arab Emirates.

SOURCE: Energy Information Administration, Department of Energy.

biggest suppliers of foreign oil to the United States. Canada announced plans to phase out all oil exports to the United States by 1983.

OPEC quadrupled its price between Jan. 1, 1973, and Jan. 1, 1974—from a posted price of $2.59 per barrel of Persian crude oil to $11.65. By 1977 the price was nearly $13 per barrel. The U.S. economy was caught in the two-edged vise of embargo and skyrocketing prices. An FEA report of August 1974 estimated that the five-month embargo cost 500,000 American jobs and a gross national product loss of between $10-billion and $20-billion.

The United States faced, anytime that OPEC was emboldened to hike its prices, such results as a further drain on consumer purchasing power, another spur to inflation, deeper deficits in balance of payments and the federal budget, and an ever-increasing menace to the world economic system. This situation explained why President Carter, soon after taking office, announced a comprehensive "National Energy Plan" designed to lessen American dependence on imported oil.

Exporting Countries' Unity

A central factor in the growing strength of Middle East states in the world oil market has been their increasing ability to act in concert. Increases in oil prices, new formulas for calculating royalty payments and taxes, agreements on participation in ownership and changes in prices to reflect devaluation of the dollar have been relatively recent breakthroughs for the Middle East oil countries.

These countries allowed foreign oil companies to exploit their oil reserves under concessions granted at various times between 1901 and 1935. These agreements required the companies to pay only a nominal royalty—an average of 21 cents a barrel in the Middle East, according to Charles Issawi in *The Washington Papers: Oil, the Middle East and the World.*[26] In return, the concessionaires were exempted from taxes and were free to determine production and pricing policy.

Issawi pointed out that these arrangements may have been fair enough in times when demand was slow, prices were fluctuating or dropping, prospects for discovering oil were uncertain and huge capital investments were needed. But during and after World War II, prices rose sharply, thus reducing the purchasing power of the fixed royalty and the government's share of the value of the oil.

Oil-producing countries pushed for a greater share, and by the early 1950s all the producing countries had negotiated agreements providing that revenues from oil production be divided between a country and a company or consortium on a 50-50 basis. These agreements—resulting in raising payments to 70-80 cents per barrel—multiplied the revenues of the Middle East governments almost tenfold between 1948 and 1960, from about $150-million to nearly $1.4-billion, according to Issawi.

OPEC and OAPEC

The Middle East countries had become acutely aware of the importance of maintaining a high price. Reductions in prices in the late 1950s by oil companies, without consultation with the producing countries, sparked a countermove by the world's five largest oil exporting nations.

26. Washington Paper #5, published for the Georgetown Center for Strategic and International Studies by Sage Publications, Beverly Hills/London.

U.S. Trade in Crude Oil

(*bpd* barrels per day)

Year	Exports Thousand bpd	Imports Thousand bpd	Net Imports Thousand bpd
1947	126	268	142
1948	110	353	243
1949	90	422	332
1950	96	488	392
1951	79	490	411
1952	74	575	501
1953	55	649	594
1954	38	658	620
1955	33	781	748
1956	79	937	858
1957	137	1,022	885
1958	11	953	942
1959	8	964	956
1960	8	1,019	1,011
1961	8	1,047	1,039
1962	5	1,126	1,121
1963	5	1,132	1,127
1964	3	1,203	1,200
1965	3	1,238	1,235
1966	5	1,225	1,220
1967	74	1,129	1,055
1968	5	1,293	1,288
1969	3	1,408	1,405
1970	14	1,323	1,309
1971	1	1,680	1,679
1972	*	2,222	2,222
1973	2	3,244	3,242
1974	3	3,422	3,419
1975	6	4,105	4,099
1976	8	5,400	5,392
1977	50	6,690	6,640

* Less than 500 barrels per day.

SOURCES: International Economic Report of the President, January 1977; Energy Information Administration, Department of Energy (1976 and 1977).

Iran, Iraq, Kuwait, Saudi Arabia and Venezuela in September 1960 established OPEC to keep oil prices from dropping further. The five countries agreed to prorate their future production, based on 1960 production levels, and to pool and prorate any future increases in world market demands. By 1974 OPEC also included Algeria, Ecuador, Indonesia, Libya, Nigeria, Qatar and the United Arab Emirates.

Early in 1968, Saudi Arabia, Kuwait and Libya formed another group, called the Organization of Arab Petroleum Exporting Countries (OAPEC). The membership had been broadened by 1974 to include Algeria, Bahrain, Egypt, Iraq, Qatar, Syria and the United Arab Emirates.

OPEC was successful in preventing further cuts in posted prices for oil on which taxes were calculated but failed to restore prices to their earlier level or to agree on a formula for prorating to limit output. A 1965 attempt to agree on a uniform production plan also failed, but OPEC did manage to achieve some important financial gains, according to Issawi. (A "posted price" is a fictitious, artificially high price set by producing countries for the purpose of boosting the royalty payments and taxes they receive.) *(Chart, this page)*

In the meantime, the 50-50 split of the oil profits came under increasing fire. As Simon pointed out in Senate testimony in May 1973, there had been virtually no increase in per-barrel payments in the 1950s and only a 12-cent-per-barrel increase in the 1960s. In the late 1960s, OPEC began its move toward increasing revenues.

An OPEC conference in Vienna in June 1968 produced a resolution that (1) cited the United Nations principle that all countries had the right to exercise sovereignty over their natural resources, (2) declared the desirability of exploitation of resources directly by the producing countries, (3) set forth a doctrine of "changing circumstances" to allow the countries to alter existing contracts and (4) expressed the right of governments to share in ownership.

OPEC also agreed on a minimum taxation rate of 55 per cent, establishment of more uniform pricing practices, a general increase in the posted or tax-reference prices in all member countries and elimination of allowances granted to oil companies.

Price Agreements

The 1968 conference marked the first significant step toward consolidation of OPEC power, and great strides have been taken since then. According to a January 1974 General Accounting Office (GAO) report on foreign sources of oil for the United States, OPEC members had negotiated eight agreements with oil companies that significantly increased the cost of crude oil.

Libya led the way toward exacting higher prices from the oil companies. In 1970, the companies held out for seven months while the Libyan government cut back production to force a price increase. The companies finally agreed to raise the posted price by 30 cents a barrel. Libya's success in obtaining higher prices provided incentive to the Persian Gulf states.

A triple victory was scored in 1971 with the negotiation of the Teheran, Tripoli and East Mediterranean agreements. The Teheran agreement, reached in February 1971, involved Abu Dhabi, Iran, Iraq, Kuwait, Qatar and Saudi Arabia.

Following on the heels of a 9-cents-per-barrel price hike negotiated in 1970, the Teheran agreement raised the basic posted price of oil 35-40 cents per barrel and contained a formula for a four-step increase in posted prices through 1975. Prices increased from about 86 cents per barrel in 1970 to about $1.24 per barrel in 1971—an increase of 43 per cent—with $1.50 as the goal by 1975.

The Teheran agreement also hiked the countries' taxes from 50 per cent to 55 per cent of the net taxable income and established a system for adjusting the posted price according to the oil's gravity.

The Tripoli agreement, negotiated by Libya in April 1971, and the East Mediterranean agreement, negotiated by Iraq in June 1971, used the Teheran agreement as their base. Additional elements included an increase in the basic posted price, a further increase for low-sulfur oil and temporary increases to reflect the geographical advantage resulting from the closing of the Suez Canal and the high freight rates prevailing for oil tankers.

Persian Gulf Crude Oil Prices [1]

(Dollars per barrel)

	Jan. 1, 1973	Jan. 1, 1974	Per cent Change, 1973-74	Jan. 1, 1975	Per cent Change, 1974-75	Jan. 1, 1976	Per cent Change, 1975-76	Jan. 1, 1977	Per cent Change, 1976-77
1. Posted price[2]	$2.591	$11.651	+ 350.0	$11.251	− 3.6	$12.376	+ 9.9	$12.995	+ 5.0
2. Royalty[3]	.324	1.456	+ 349.0	2.250	+ 54.5	2.475	+ 10.0	2.599	+ 5.0
3. Production cost	.100	.100	—	.120	+ 20.0	.120	—	.120	—
4. Profit for tax purposes (1-(2 + 3))	2.167	10.095	+ 366.0	8.881	− 12.0	9.781	+ 10.1	10.276	+ 5.1
5. Tax[4]	1.192	5.552	+ 366.0	7.549	+ 36.0	8.314	+ 10.1	8.735	+ 5.1
6. Government revenue (2 + 5)	1.516	7.008	+ 362.0	9.799	+ 39.8	10.789	+ 10.1	11.334	+ 5.1
7. Cost of equity oil (2 + 6)[5]	1.616	7.108	+ 340.0	9.919	+ 39.5	10.909	+ 10.0	11.454	+ 5.0
8. Cost of participation oil[5]	2.330	10.835	+ 365.0	10.460	− 3.5	11.510	+ 10.0	12.085	+ 5.0
9. Weighted average cost[5]	1.794	9.344	+ 421.0	10.240	+ 9.6	11.270	+ 10.1	11.836	+ 5.0
10. Weighted government revenue (9 - 3)	1.694	9.244	+ 446.0	10.120	+ 9.5	11.150	+ 10.2	11.716	+ 5.1

1 Prices shown are for Saudi Arabian light crude oil 34 degree API (American Petroleum Institute) gravity. Saudi light is used as a standard for Persian Gulf crude because it is the largest single type of crude produced there and represents a good average between higher-priced low-sulfur crude and lower-priced heavier oil.

2 The so-called "posted price" is a fictitious, artificially high price set by oil-producing countries for the purpose of producing the revenues—royalties and taxes—they receive from oil companies.

3 The Saudi royalty was fixed at 12.5 per cent of the posted price for the 1973 and 1974 dates, and at 20 per cent for the 1975 date.

4 The Saudi tax was fixed at 55 per cent of the profit for tax purposes (line 4) for the 1973 and 1974 dates, and at 85 per cent for the 1975 date.

5 The oil companies pay two different prices, and the weighted average cost per barrel falls between the cost for equity oil and the cost for participation oil. Participation oil is oil in which the oil-producing country has part ownership in the oil companies operating in the country. The oil companies—because of their exploration and development roles—have a right to a certain percentage of production at a cost something less than the market rate, which also is figured in the weighted average cost.

SOURCE: International Economic Report of the President, January 1977

Critics' Position

Some critics of Western negotiators have felt that these early agreements set the stage for spiraling Arab demands. In a controversial article in the winter 1973 issue of *Foreign Policy* magazine, oil economist M. A. Adelman of the Massachusetts Institute of Technology stated his belief that the steep price increases could be attributed to U.S. capitulation to OPEC during negotiations over the Teheran agreement.

"Without active support from the U.S., OPEC might never have achieved much," said Adelman. He called a January 1971 meeting of oil-importing nations the "turning point" and said that "there is no doubt that the American representatives and the oil companies assured the other governments that if they offered no resistance to higher oil prices they could at least count on five years' secure supply at stable or only slightly rising prices."

In testimony before the Senate Foreign Relations Subcommittee on Multinational Corporations Jan. 31, 1974, a vice president of Hunt International Petroleum Corporation, third largest independent oil-producing venture in Libya, offered a similar view. Henry M. Schuler called oil policy and negotiations since 1971 an "unmitigated disaster" which had created the "unstoppable momentum" within the Arab world for higher prices.

"If a political and economic monster has been loosed upon the world," Schuler stated, "it is the creation of Western governments and companies. Together we created it and gave it the necessary push, so only we, acting in harmony, can slow it down."

The GAO examination of the Teheran agreement negotiations noted that the oil companies had agreed among themselves to negotiate only on the basis of reaching a five-year settlement with all the producing countries, in order to avoid the leapfrogging effect of a series of agreements and to promote stability for those five years. But Libya and Algeria rejected any such joint bargaining. The negotiations, which lasted about a month, began under the threat of an oil production cutoff if OPEC demands were not met by a certain deadline.

Negotiations broke down at one point but, with the urging of U.S. government officials, the companies continued the negotiations and an agreement was finally signed Feb. 14, 1971.

In an April 1973 *Foreign Affairs* article, James E. Akins, U.S. ambassador to Saudi Arabia and former director of the State Department's Office of Fuels and Energy, dismissed charges that the United States had invited the threat of a cutoff of oil and thus had built up OPEC's bargaining position.

Akins asserted that, upon the protest of the State Department, leaders from Iran, Saudi Arabia and Kuwait had assured the United States that the so-called "threats" had been misunderstood, that they had been directed solely at the oil companies and that the oil would be available to consumers even if the negotiations broke down. He said that the State Department had also requested an extension of the deadline set by OPEC and an assurance that agreements reached with the companies would be honored for their full terms.

Dollar Devaluation

Another major agreement was negotiated in January 1972 in Geneva. Abu Dhabi, Iran, Iraq, Kuwait, Qatar and Saudi Arabia reached agreement with the major oil companies to increase the posted price to restore the purchasing power lost by the oil-producing countries because of the December 1971 dollar devaluation. According to the formula agreed upon, the posted prices would be adjusted every time the U.S. exchange rates differed from an index of nine major currencies by more than 2 per cent. Posted prices rose by 8.55 per cent in February 1972 and 5.69 per cent in April 1972.

A second Geneva agreement on dollar devaluation and oil was reached in June 1973. Oil companies agreed to raise immediately the posted price of crude oil from Iran, Iraq, Abu Dhabi, Qatar, Kuwait, Saudi Arabia, Libya and Nigeria by 6.1 per cent, making a total increase of 11.9 per cent since the February 1973 devaluation. The agreement, effective through 1975, also set a new formula under which posted prices would reflect more fully and rapidly any future changes in the dollar's value.

World Proved Oil Reserves

(Estimate at the end of 1976)

Major Areas and Selected Countries	Billion Barrels	Per Cent of Total
North America	69	10.3
United States	40	6.0
Canada	9	1.3
Mexico	20	3.0
Central and South America	22	3.3
Venezuela[1]	14	2.1
Ecuador[1]	2	.3
Other	6	.9
Western Europe	29	4.3
United Kingdom	19	2.8
Norway	7	1.0
Other	3	.4
Africa	65	9.7
Algeria[1]	7	1.0
Libya[1]	26	3.8
Nigeria[1]	20	3.0
Other	12	1.8
Asia-Pacific	22	3.3
Indonesia[1]	15	2.2
Other	7	1.0
Middle East	396	59.3
Saudi Arabia[1]	178	26.6
Kuwait[1]	79	11.8
Iran[1]	64	9.6
Iraq[1]	35	5.2
United Arab Emirates[1]	6	.9
Qatar[1]	31	4.6
Other	3	.4
Total Non-Communist	603	90.3
Communist World[2]	65	9.7
Soviet Union	40	4.0
Other	25	3.7
Total World	668	100.0

1 Member of Organization of Petroleum Exporting Countries (OPEC).
2 Includes Soviet Union and other Warsaw Pact nations, Cuba, China and Yugoslavia.

SOURCE: International Economic Report of the President, January 1977

Escalating Demands

The Teheran agreement was laid to rest in October 1973 when Iran, Saudi Arabia, Iraq, Abu Dhabi, Kuwait and Qatar announced a unilateral price hike after negotiations had broken down. The new level was a 17 per cent increase in the market price of crude — raising it to about $3.65 — and a 70 per cent increase in the posted price — bringing that up to about $5.11.

Yet another 70 per cent increase in prices, effective Jan. 1, 1974, was announced by these six Persian Gulf producers during a December 1973 meeting in Teheran. This brought the posted price to $11.65. Other petroleum exporting countries followed the initiatives of the Persian Gulf countries in raising their prices.

In 1974, a series of changes by oil-producing countries actually reduced the posted price slightly but increased the cost of oil by raising royalties and taxes. The actual prices charged the oil companies on terms that went into effect Jan. 1, 1975, were 9.6 per cent higher than a year earlier. OPEC froze those prices for nine months, until Oct. 1. *(See weighted average cost chart, p. 80)*

Further increases were expected in the last quarter of 1975. The shah of Iran, at a May 17 news conference in Washington, called for an increase to compensate for the loss of "between 30 and 50 per cent of our purchasing power because of world inflation." Western economists felt there was no justification for such a further increase, and President Ford warned June 25 that another price hike would be "very disruptive and totally unacceptable."

Largely because of the recession, but also because of conservation measures in consuming countries, demand for oil was falling in 1975. As a result, OPEC production dropped from 30.6 million barrels a day in 1974 to about 25 million in early June 1975, leaving its member countries with a surplus productive capacity of about 10 million barrels per day.

The oil-producing states with smaller revenues and larger development programs were beginning to feel the pinch from reduced sales. Western economists say that reduced prices would enable these countries to expand their output. In fact, by discreetly discounting its prices below the OPEC level, Iraq in early 1975 was producing at a rate 42 per cent above the same period a year earlier, while OPEC production in the same period fell by 16 per cent. In spite of this downward pressure on oil prices, experts expected some increase by the end of 1975 for the sake of keeping the OPEC cartel united and demonstrating its continuing effectiveness.[27]

Participation Agreements

Participation—part ownership by oil-producing countries in the oil companies operating in their countries—has become a significant issue in the world oil market. The concept was originated by Saudi Arabia's shrewd oil minister, Sheikh Ahmed Zaki al-Yamani.

A 1972 House Foreign Affairs subcommittee report on the Persian Gulf pointed out that many nationalists have found the concessionary system—which involved contracts between companies and exporting countries that enabled the companies to exploit oil deposits for a fixed period of time—degrading. They were said to believe that as con-

cessions approached their termination it was natural for the countries to begin to participate in all operations rather than remaining in the passive role of collecting revenues and royalties.

The attitude of many oil companies, according to the report, was that oil exporting countries held all the trump cards and participation was inevitable. They faced the dilemma of balancing the cost of yielding to demands too soon against the risk of holding out too long and perhaps precipitating nationalization.

Algeria had nationalized its natural gas fields in 1971 and taken over 51 per cent of oil concessions on behalf of its national company, thus breaking the favored position of French oil companies. Libya expropriated British Petroleum Company holdings in 1971. Iraq nationalized the Western-owned Iraq Petroleum Company in 1972.

In the OPEC participation agreement reached in December 1972, Saudi Arabia, Kuwait, United Arab Emirates and Qatar won an immediate 25 per cent interest in the companies' ownership which was to increase in steps up to 51 per cent by 1982. But these timetables were speeded up and by the mid-1970s, all the countries were heading for complete ownership, though actual management remained in the hands of Westerners.

Iran

In 1973, Iran took control of its oil industry. Shah Mohammed Reza Pahlavi had announced in June 1972 that Iran would extend the Western-owned consortium agreement of 1954 when it came up for renewal in 1979. However, in January 1973, the Shah declared that the agreement would not be extended unless the corsortium agreed to increase daily production from 4.5 million barrels to 8.3 million by 1977. But in March, the Shah nationalized the oil industry. A 20-year agreement was signed in May which provided for the National Iranian Oil Company to take control of all operations and facilities of the oil companies, with the consortium to have the role of technical adviser.

Libya

In June 1973 Libya nationalized a U.S. oil firm in retaliation for U.S. support of Israel. Libyan leader Col. Muammar al-Qaddafi told a rally that the United States "deserved a strong slap in the face." He warned: "The time might come where there will be a real confrontation with oil companies and the entire American imperialism."

The Libyan government acquired 51 per cent of the holdings of the Occidental Petroleum Company in mid-August 1973. Independent oil companies followed suit in sharing ownership, but the major companies held out. In September 1973 the revolutionary leader announced the unilateral takeover of 51 per cent of the operations of all the major companies. In February and March 1974, the government completely nationalized the operations of Texaco, Shell and subsidiaries of Standard Oil of California and Atlantic Richfield.

Oil Embargo

Oil production cutbacks and the embargo of exports to U.S. markets which began in late 1973 marked not only a peak in Arab unity but also the first formal use of oil as a political weapon to pressure the industrial nations into forcing Israel to return to its pre-1967 frontiers.

The potency of the weapon became highly visible within a short period. Arab oil exporting nations succeeded in dis-

---

[27] Wall Street Journal, June 27, 1975.

Monetary Reserves, Middle East Oil-Exporting Countries*

(in millions of U.S. dollars)

Country	1970	1971	1972	1973	1974	1975	1976	1977	1978
Algeria	$ 339	$ 507	$ 493	$1,143	$ 1,689	$ 1,353	$ 1,987	$ 1,917	$ 2,233
Egypt	167	161	139	363	356	294	339	534	605
Iran	208	621	960	1,236	8,383	8,897	8,833	12,266	23,152
Iraq	462	600	782	1,553	3,273	2,727	4,601	6,996	—
Kuwait	203	288	363	501	1,399	1,655	1,929	1,929	2,990
Libya	1,590	2,665	2,925	2,127	3,616	2,195	3,206	4,891	4,216
Saudi Arabia	662	1,444	2,500	3,877	14,285	23,319	27,025	30,034	19,407
Syria	55	88	135	481	835	735	361	546	—

* A country's international reserves consist of its reserves in gold, SDRs (special drawing rights which are unconditional international reserve assets created by the International Monetary Fund), its reserve position in the Fund (unconditional assets that arise from a country's gold subscription to the Fund's use of a member's currency to finance the drawings of others) and its foreign exchange (holdings by monetary authorities — such as central banks, currency boards, exchange stabilization funds and Treasuries — of claims on foreigners in the form of bank deposits, Treasury bills, government securities and other claims usable in the event of a balance of payments deficit).

SOURCE: Data from the International Monetary Fund's *International Financial Statistics,* June 1979.

rupting the lifestyle of every major industrial power, caused fissures in the Atlantic alliance, precipitated upsets in international money markets and prompted the United States to make an intensive search for a peace settlement in the Middle East.

1967 Boycott

An attempt at using oil as a political weapon had been made after the 1967 war, but it met with little success. Within two days of the outbreak of fighting in 1967, every major Arab oil producer except Algeria completely shut down production. But consuming countries turned to the United States, Venezuela and Indonesia, and the Arab countries soon broke ranks.

Three weeks after the embargo went into effect, Iraq began shipping oil to Turkey and France through a pipeline to Lebanon. By mid-July the major Arab oil producers had restored shipments to all countries except the United States, Britain and, in some instances, West Germany. The participating countries agreed in August to leave up to the individual countries the question of whether to continue the boycott, and by mid-September the only interruption to normal oil supplies was the continued closure of the Suez Canal.

Saudi Arabia's Role

Saudi Arabia—the top Middle East oil producer and holder of about one-fourth of the non-communist world's oil reserves—held the key to the success of a boycott. In 1967, Saudi Arabia had gone along reluctantly with the embargo because of pressure from Egyptian President Gamal Abdel Nasser. But the country had not enforced the embargo strictly and lifted it shortly after it was made voluntary.

However, Saudi Arabia, under conservative, pro-Western King Faisal, led the way in 1973. The formal decision to use oil as a weapon came Oct. 17, 1973, at an OAPEC meeting in Kuwait. The members agreed to cut production monthly by 5 per cent over the previous month's sales until Israel had withdrawn from the Arab territories it had occupied since the 1967 war and had agreed to respect the rights of Palestinian refugees.

The following day, Saudi Arabia announced that it would cut back its oil production by 10 per cent and would cut off all shipments to the United States if the United States continued to supply Israel with arms and refused to "modify" its pro-Israeli policy. Libya imposed an embargo Oct. 19.

On Oct. 29—the day after President Nixon requested $2.2-billion in emergency security assistance for Israel—Saudi Arabia announced a total embargo against oil exports to the United States. When four Persian Gulf states—Kuwait, Qatar, Bahrain and Dubai—joined the embargo Oct. 21, the Arab boycott of U.S. markets was complete.

The reasons for Saudi Arabia's turnabout rested with inter-Arab politics and Faisal's anti-Zionism. Nadav Safran, writing in the January 1974 *Foreign Affairs,* attributed Faisal's previous reluctance to use the oil weapon partially to a fear that Egyptian President Nasser, who died Sept. 28, 1970, and other Arab radicals might usurp control over when and how the weapon would be used.

Another factor, according to Safran, was that Saudi Arabia needed all the revenues it was receiving at that time and suspected the weapon could possibly be turned around and used against the Saudi regime.

In fact, according to an article by Benjamin Shwadran in the February 1974 *Current History,* the original purpose for the formation of OAPEC by Saudi Arabia, Kuwait and Iraq early in 1968 was to block the other Arab countries—particularly Egypt—from interfering with their economic interests.

But, as Safran pointed out, the circumstances in 1973 were quite different than in 1967. Saudi Arabia was receiving vastly increased revenues, and Nasser was no longer around to threaten Faisal's autonomy. Saudi Arabia's decision to use the oil weapon, coupled with substantial financial assistance to Egypt, was seen as a move to minimize the principal appeal of radical Libyan leader Col. Qaddafi—self-proclaimed heir of Nasser—and prevent the proposed union of Egypt and Libya.

Another factor was the failure of Saudi Arabia's quiet diplomacy aimed at nudging the United States into what it hoped would be a more evenhanded position in the Middle East. Faisal's reluctance to employ the oil option had been lessened considerably after Sadat's expulsion of Soviet military advisers from Egypt in July 1972 failed to bring a change in White House policy.

Saudi Arabia's final move came after a series of pleas to Washington to tone down its support of Israel. *The Washington Post* reported Oct. 20, 1973, that Faisal had sent at least two letters to President Nixon with pleas for a more evenhanded appearance. Petroleum Minister Yamani had made the same appeal during a visit to Washington in April 1973.

In a July 4 interview with two American reporters, Faisal delivered what was said to be his first public warning, when he stated that Saudi Arabia would like to continue its friendly ties with the United States but would find this "difficult" if the United States support for Israel remained at its existing level. The warnings continued, and the final decision to impose the embargo came only after Nixon's Oct. 19 request for money to rearm Israel.

Embargo Categories

The Arabs were systematic in their embargo, with countries being divided into categories. On the boycott list were nations considered to be friends of Israel. The United States was at the top. The Netherlands followed, because the Arabs were angered by what they saw as a pro-Israel stance and reports that the Dutch had offered to aid in the transit of Soviet Jewish emigrants to Israel. In late November, Portugal, Rhodesia and South Africa were officially placed on the embargo list. Shipments of oil to Canada were cut off because the Arabs feared the oil might be reshipped to the United States.

Exempted nations included France, Spain, Arab and Moslem states and—on a conditional basis—Britain. These nations were permitted to purchase the same volume of oil as they had purchased in the first nine months of 1973, but, since the fourth quarter of a year is normally a heavy buying period, these nations were also expected to feel the pinch.

All the remaining countries fell into the non-exempt category, which meant that they would divide what was left after the needs of the exempted nations had been met.

Embargo's Effect

In addition to the embargo, the Arab states continued their monthly reductions in production. The effects of the oil squeeze were soon felt in the consuming nations. Measures taken to cope with the oil shortage included gas rationing, bans on Sunday driving, reduced speed limits, increased prices, restrictions on energy usŗe, cutbacks in auto production and reductions in heating fuels.

Although estimates varied, the embargo was said to have resulted in the loss to the United States of about two million barrels of oil per day. However, Arab oil did leak through the embargo, reportedly from Iraq and Libya. In October, the United States began classifying data on its oil imports to prevent these leaks from being plugged up.

Hardest hit were Japan and Western Europe, areas most dependent on oil imports. Most of northern Europe suffered from the total embargo against the Netherlands, because the Dutch port of Rotterdam was Europe's largest oil-refining and transshipment center.

U.S. Peace Efforts

The embargo proved effective. Although Washington repeatedly denounced the Arab tactics and declared it would not submit to such coercion, the oil squeeze undoubtedly was the driving force behind U.S. peace-seeking efforts.

Secretary of State Kissinger shuttled relentlessly throughout the Middle East in attempts to mediate a settlement. A series of peace missions produced the Nov. 11, 1973, cease-fire agreement between Israel and Egypt, resumption of diplomatic relations between the United States and Egypt, the Dec. 21-22 first round of Geneva peace talks, the Jan. 18, 1974, Egyptian-Israeli disengagement accord and the May 31 disengagement agreement between Israel and Syria.

Atlantic Alliance

But in the meantime OAPEC's policies took a deep toll on an already troubled Atlantic alliance. The U.S. was unable to prevent its allies from bending to Arab pressure.

On Nov. 6, 1973, representatives of the European Economic Community (EEC), meeting in Brussels, adopted a statement calling on Israel and Egypt to return to the Oct. 22 cease-fire lines which had been drawn before Israeli troops completed the encirclement of Egypt's III Corps. They called on Israel to "end the territorial occupation which it has maintained since the conflict of 1967" and declared that peace in the Middle East was incompatible with "the acquisition of territory by force." Moreover, they declared that any settlement must take into account "the legitimate rights" of the Palestinian refugees.

Later in the month Japan followed suit. On Nov. 22, the Japanese cabinet announced that it might have to reconsider its policy toward Israel. The Arabs rewarded Western Europe and Japan by exempting them from the 5 per cent cut in December.

On Dec. 13, Japan switched from a neutral position to appealing to Israel to withdraw to the Oct. 22 cease-fire lines as a first step toward total withdrawal from occupied Arab territory. On Dec, 25, the January cutback was canceled and OAPEC announced that oil production would be increased by 10 per cent.

United Energy Policy

These statements by the EEC and Japan, while one-sided in favor of the Arabs, were in keeping with United Nations Resolution 242. That resolution, approved by the Security Council in 1967, had called for a return to pre-1967 boundaries in the Middle East and a respect for the sovereignty and territorial integrity of all states in the Middle East. *(Text, p. 67)*

What caused the real strain in the Atlantic alliance was Europe's refusal to forge a united energy policy. U.S.-French relations suffered the most because of France's moves to negotiate bilateral arms-oil agreements with the Arab nations. On Jan. 10, 1974, Kissinger declared that "unrestricted bilateral competition will be ruinous for all countries concerned."

On Jan. 9, the White House announced that Nixon had invited the foreign ministers of eight oil-consuming nations to meet in Washington to discuss world energy problems. The eight were Great Britain, Canada, France, Italy, Japan, the Netherlands, Norway and West Germany. Although all were not on the original invitation list, the foreign ministers of the nine EEC countries decided to attend. French Foreign Minister Michel Jobert, however, withheld his acceptance until less than a week before the conference.

The meeting convened Feb. 11, with representatives from Belgium, Britain, Canada, Denmark, France, West

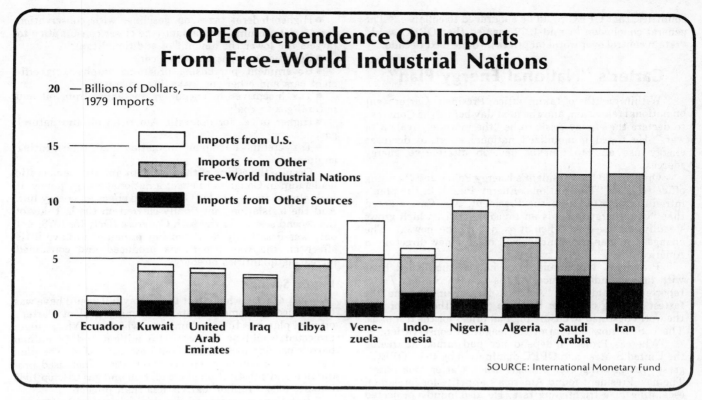

OPEC Dependence On Imports From Free-World Industrial Nations

20 — Billions of Dollars, 1979 Imports

15

☐ Imports from U.S.

▨ Imports from Other Free-World Industrial Nations

10

■ Imports from Other Sources

5

0

Ecuador | Kuwait | United Arab Emirates | Iraq | Libya | Vene-zuela | Indo-nesia | Nigeria | Algeria | Saudi Arabia | Iran

SOURCE: International Monetary Fund

Germany, Ireland, Italy, Japan, Luxembourg, the Netherlands, Norway and the United States. It was scheduled to end the next day but was delayed by a dispute between France and other EEC countries over the response to an American proposal for a joint effort to meet the energy crisis.

Their final communique contained several points opposed by France, including a proposal to formulate a comprehensive action program to deal with the energy situation, establishment of a coordinating group to prepare for a conference of oil-producing and oil-consuming nations, formulation of a group to coordinate development of the actions recommended by the conference and adoption of financial and monetary measures to deal with the balance-of-payments impact of oil prices.

Jobert charged that energy matters had been a "pretext" and that the conference's real purpose had been the "political" desire of the United States to dominate the relationships of Europe and Japan. Kissinger, however, called the meeting a success and said that it was possibly a major step toward "dealing with world problems cooperatively."

Embargo Lifted

With the progress made toward a peace settlement in the Middle East, the United States became increasingly insistent on an end to the embargo.

Kissinger told a Jan. 22, 1974, press conference that he had been given assurances by Arab leaders that when an Israeli-Egyptian accord was reached, the embargo would be lifted.

Egyptian President Sadat led the way to ending the boycott. On Jan. 22, Sadat said Arab oil states should take note of the "evolution" in U.S. policy toward the Middle East. Although he did not mention the embargo, he said

that "now that the Americans have made a gesture, the Arabs should make one too." And at a Feb. 24 press conference, Sadat said that the United States would now probably pursue a more evenhanded approach toward the Middle East.

OAPEC's formal announcement of an end to the embargo against the United States came at a Vienna meeting March 18. Libya and Syria, however, refused to end the boycott until later in the year.

OPEC's Strength

OPEC has remained a potent and effective cartel since 1974. There have been differences among the members about pricing and supply policies, but until December 1976, OPEC managed to maintain a unified price for oil, having made periodic price rises since the quadrupling in the 1973-1974 period. Meeting in Vienna in October 1975 OPEC raised oil prices by 10 per cent to $11.28.

During 1976 OPEC did not raise the price on its benchmark crude. At a meeting in Bali it was determined that the world economy was too fragile to withstand additional oil price increases. But when OPEC met again in December to consider 1977 prices, disagreements between the members could not be fully resolved. A two-tier pricing system emerged with 11 members deciding to raise prices by 10 per cent in January and an additional 5 per cent on July 1, 1977. Saudi Arabia and the United Arab Emirates limited their price rise to 5 per cent in January, pricing oil at $12.70 per barrel.

When OPEC met again in July 1977 it was agreed that the majority would not implement the additional 5 per cent price rise planned since December and that Saudi Arabia and the United Arab Emirates would raise their prices an additional 5 per cent bringing a single price structure back to OPEC and ending hopes, held by some in the industrial countries, that OPEC could be enouraged to collapse.[28] The general conclusion in mid-1977 seemed that OPEC would "retain control over world oil prices into the next decade."[29]

Carter's "National Energy Plan"

Within months of taking office, President Carter went on national television, and the next day before the Congress, to declare the energy crisis to be "the moral equivalent of war." He urged a mobilized national effort to decrease energy use and to quickly develop alternative energy sources.

On April 29 the President's Energy Policy and Planning office released "The National Energy Plan." In the plan's introductory letter from the President, Mr. Carter noted that "Our energy crisis is an invisible crisis, which grows steadily worse—even when it is not in the news.... The changes the plan recommends will mean a new direction in American life."

Presidents Nixon and Ford had accomplished little with Project Independence. As the London *Sunday Times* reported in mid-1976, "America has again become the fastest growing customer for Arab oil and the one force in the world destined to ensure high oil prices for the rest of us. The U.S. is now bottom of the league in conservation."[30]

Whereas Project Independence had aimed at freeing the United States from OPEC domination by 1980, OPEC's grasp was growing ever stronger when Carter took office. The new President found America's appetite for foreign oil escalating at a frightening rate. He also found a projected 1977 U.S. trade deficit of more than $25-billion brought on by the continuing rise in oil prices, and a serious curtailment of America's freedom of action in the world due to the fact that both oil and petrodollars had become potential economic and political weapons. In early August 1977, former Secretary of State Henry A. Kissinger not only warned of the oil weapon but added, "In another Middle East crisis the vast accumulated petrodollars could become a weapon against the world monetary and financial system."[31]

The President's energy goals to be reached by 1985, as stated in "The National Energy Plan," included the following:

- Reduce the annual growth of total energy demand to below 2 per cent;
- Reduce gasoline consumption 10 per cent below its current level;
- Reduce oil imports from a potential level of 16 million barrels per day to 6 million, roughly one-eighth of total energy consumption;
- Establish a Strategic Petroleum Reserve of 1 billion barrels [about a 10-month supply];
- Increase coal production by two-thirds, to more than 1 billion tons per year;
- Bring 90 per cent of existing American homes and all new buildings up to minimum energy efficiency standards; and
- Use solar energy in more than 2½ million homes.

To accomplish these goals, the President recommended such measures as:

- Higher federal taxes on gasoline, with conservation targets determining the amount (the closer consumption to targets the lower the amount of additional tax);
- Penalties on "gas guzzling" cars;
- Government purchasing programs emphasizing efficient cars and other energy-saving programs;
- Tax incentives to encourage switching from oil and natural gas to coal;
- Higher prices for domestic American oil and natural gas;
- Tax credits for home insulation and solar-heating equipment.

Despite the efforts of the President and the Democratic leadership in Congress to enact a national energy policy, it took almost two years for Congress to enact an energy bill. And the legislation that finally cleared on the last day of the second session of the 95th Congress (Oct. 15, 1978) not only was drastically rewritten but promised to have little effect on the way Americans produced and consumed increasing quantities of energy.

Import Savings

Just exactly what effect the energy bill would have was the subject of some dispute. A primary goal of Carter's original plan was to cut oil imports, which the White House projected would be between 11.5 million and 16 million barrels per day by 1985, without new legislation. The plan was to use a combination of conservation, increased production and substitution of coal for oil and gas to keep 1985 imports at 4.5 million barrels less than projected.

But Congress rewrote the original proposal. The tax section, for example, which accounted for 43 per cent of the savings projected by the White House, was substantially changed by Congress. Though Carter wanted to force industry to switch from oil and gas to coal, Congress provided only encouragement, but no punishment if industries chose not to comply. Carter also wanted stiff penalties for gas guzzling cars, but Congress weakened the penalties.

As those and other provisions were dropped or softened, the natural gas pricing section became the most controversial part of the bill. Carter had wanted to continue regulation, extending federal price controls to gas sold within producing states. The House agreed with Carter, but the Senate voted for deregulation of prices. The protracted conference between the two houses threatened the future of the entire energy package. But the administration and a few congressional negotiators finally came up with an agreement that doubled the price of newly discovered gas by 1985, when controls would be lifted.

The natural gas bill originally had not been counted on by Carter to contribute to savings of imported oil. But Department of Energy figures released after final passage predicted savings of from 1 million to 1.4 million barrels of oil per day from the natural gas provisions.

Total savings in imported oil from the legislation were estimated by the administration to range from 2.39 to 2.95 million barrels of oil per day by 1985.

Energy Crisis Deepens

Indeed, by 1979, the energy crisis loomed larger than it had when Carter assumed office. Energy consumption in the United States had continued to grow in 1978, increasing two per cent over 1977 consumption. About half of that energy was provided by oil and about 45 per cent of that was imported at increasingly high prices. To make matters worse, the civil war in Iran had brought that country's

28 See, for instance, "Can OPEC Be Broken Up?" in Forbes, February 15, 1977, p. 48 and Christopher D. Stone & Jack McNamara, "How to take on OPEC," New York Times Magazine, 12 December 1976, p. 38.

29 International Economic Report of the President, January 1977, p. 36.

30 James Poole, "The Next Oil Crisis," Atlas World Press Review, July 1976, p. 11.

31 The Washington Post, 4 August 1977, p. 2.

exports (about five million barrels a day to the non-communist world; the United States had been importing 900,000 barrels a day from Iran, or about five per cent of U.S. supplies) virtually to a halt in December 1978.

The ramifications for the U.S. economy of the impending (or existing, as some observers felt) energy crisis were widespread and unsettling. America's dependence on costly foreign oil imports — amounting to $42.7 billion in 1978 — fueled inflation and could lead to increased unemployment and a slower growth rate or even recession in the nation's economy. Oil imports accounted for a substantial share of the U.S. trade and balance of payments deficit and contributed significantly to the decline in the dollar's value with respect to other currencies.

All of these factors led Energy Secretary James R. Schlesinger to warn in February 1979 that the situation was "prospectively more serious" than the Arab oil embargo of 1973-74.

However, other administration officials and some economists questioned the severity of the crisis, and there was skepticism among the general public as well.

America's energy problems had been further compounded by the Dec. 17, 1978, announcement by OPEC that its oil prices would increase 14.49 per cent in 1979. The increase voted by OPEC in the price of Arabian light was initially scheduled to be implemented in four stages, starting with a 5 per cent increase on Jan. 1, 1979, which would bring the price to $13.335 a barrel. Then, on April 1, the price would be increased another 3.809 per cent, to $13.843. That increase would be followed on July 1 by a 2.294 per cent increase, bring the price to $14.161. On Oct. 1, the scheduled increase of 2.691 per cent would bring the price to $14.542 a barrel.

However, on March 27, 1979, members of OPEC voted to raise the price of crude oil by an additional 9 per cent and to give individual members permission to add surcharges. Throughout the spring and summer of the year, numerous OPEC governments announced oil price increases.

Although Iran in April announced (along with a 13 per cent price hike over the OPEC base level set in March) that it had increased its output of oil back up to 4.7 million barrels a day, Saudi Arabia almost simultaneously said that it would reduce its production by one million barrels a day. The country had been producing up to 10 million barrels a day in January, but had been reducing production to about 8.5 million barrels a day. Moreover, a report released April 15 by the Senate Foreign Relations Subcommittee on International Economic Policy predicted that Saudi Arabian oil production in the 1980s would be at lower levels than previously expected, a situation that could trigger a "fierce political and economic struggle among the consuming countries." Production in the 1980s will be limited to not more than 12 million barrels a day, the report predicted. Previous government estimates of Saudi production for that period were 14 million to 16 million barrels a day.

Faced with this impending crisis, members of the International Energy Agency agreed March 2, 1979, to cut back their oil imports by 2 million barrels a day, or about five per cent of their current consumption. The decision was reached at a two-day meeting in Paris of the governing board of the agency. Assistant Secretary of State for Economic Affairs Richard Cooper said the United States would shoulder about half of the cutback, or about five per cent of U.S. consumption.

1979 Administration Proposals

U.S. energy officials estimated in early 1979 that the country's share of the international oil shortage — estimated at about 2 million barrels a day — could rise to 800,000 from 500,000 barrels a day by the end of the year. To cope with the anticipated shortage and increased prices of oil imports, the administration proposed a number of measures. These included:

● Decontrolling the price of domestically-produced oil to encourage conservation and to bring up U.S. oil prices to the world level. Under the 1975 Energy Policy Act, the President would gain powers to raise oil prices without congressional approval on June 1, 1979. On April 5, Carter announced plans for gradual decontrol, but the proposal ran into strong opposition in Congress, where many members argued that it would fuel inflation.

● Raising the price of gasoline. On March 2, 1979, the Energy Department announced it was putting into effect a regulation that would allow oil companies to increase gasoline prices. The impact, said Schlesinger Feb. 28, could mean that the price of unleaded gasoline could rise to $1 a gallon in a year. By mid-1979, that prediction had come to pass in many parts of the country.

● Instituting gasoline rationing and mandatory energy conservation measures. On Feb. 27, the administration requested congressional approval of emergency standby authority to ration gasoline, restrict weekend gas sales, ban decorative lighting and impose lower thermostat settings. Although the Senate approved Carter's gas rationing proposals, the House defeated the standby rationing plan in May. Both chambers approved the plan for restricting thermostat settings.

"Our national strength is dangerously dependent on a thin line of oil tankers stretching halfway around the earth" to the Persian Gulf, Carter warned in his April 5 address. He called on Americans to drive less and support other conservation efforts. The nation's energy problem is "serious — and it's getting worse," Carter said. "There is no single answer. We must produce more. We must conserve more."

Carter's boldest move was the plan to let the price of oil rise. Decontrol was to be phased in starting June 1, when existing law gave the President new authority over prices. That law automatically ends all controls in 1981.

The oil price decontrol proposal was coupled with an excess profits tax, the proceeds of which would go to low-income families to help with higher energy costs; to mass transit programs; and to a new "energy security fund" for research and development.

Spurring the effort to raise domestic prices was the promise Carter made to world leaders at a Bonn economic summit in July 1978. He said then he was "determined" that U.S. oil prices would equal world levels by the end of 1980. His hope was to stem further increases in the U.S. trade deficit by reducing oil imports. The estimated $42.7 billion that the United States paid for imported oil in 1978 was the major factor in the nation's growing trade deficit, which had risen from about $10 billion in 1976 to an annual rate of almost $45 billion in 1978.

Carter also on April 5 announced several moves to help make more energy supplies available. They included:

● Reduction of red tape delaying pipelines and other energy projects.

● Expedited approval of permits for the Standard Oil Company of Ohio (Sohio) pipeline from California to

Texas. The administration would support federal pre-emption of state laws holding up the pipeline.

● Increased production from federal lands, including private exploration of the National Petroleum Reserve in Alaska, a move that required congressional approval.

● Removal of restrictions on the export of Alaskan oil to provide flexibility for securing energy supplies.

Other plans included: waiver of fees on crude oil imports, about 21 cents a barrel at the time; tightening of tax credits to oil companies drilling in foreign countries (legislation was required); and a one-year delay in a rule, scheduled to go into effect Oct. 1, 1979, which would require the lead content in gasoline to average less than .5 grams per gallon. The standard instead would be .8 grams a gallon. The administration said the delay would prevent loss of 350,000 barrels a day.

Outlook

In mid-1979, in the aftermath of the peace treaty between Israel and Egypt, a big and unanswered question was what steps the Arab oil producers might take to increase pressures on those two nations — and the United States — to meet Arab demands for a full peace settlement. The oil embargo and price rises that followed the 1973 war were a strong reminder of the leverage that the Arab oil producers could exercise. Following the Camp David agreements and the Iranian revolution, some of the more militant OPEC nations began to raise the prices unilaterally. Officially, the surcharges were said to be temporary increases that reflected the tight world market created by the cutback in Iranian production. However, in the first six months of the year, the overall world price had increased more than 30 per cent, despite the December 1978 OPEC agreement on a phased 14.5 per cent increase.

On the other hand, by 1979 there were numerous constraints on the use of oil power. The 1978-79 OPEC price rises increased the risks of pushing the industrial nations into a recession. The prospects for a slowdown in worldwide economic growth were further exacerbated by ceilings placed on oil production by Saudi Arabia and others. (Mexico, too, has said it favored a slow development of its oil reserves.) Part of this has been due to problems of developing OPEC members' ability to absorb this revenue, as well as apprehensions that too rapid economic growth could result in political and social upheavals such as occured in Iran.

At the same time, the world's dependence on Arab oil could be lessened by the development of oil fields in Mexico, the North Sea, the Alaskan North Slope and other areas. Indeed, rather paradoxically, the steep OPEC price increase following the 1973-74 embargo encouraged competitive production elsewhere. One result of this — in addition to inflation and the decline of the dollar's value — was a 1978 price of oil that, measured in real terms, was only about as much as the 1973 levels. Moreover, in 1978, the OPEC countries plowed back most of their revenues into expenditures in the oil consuming nations, sharply reducing the petrodollar surplus. (The surplus was expected to grow considerably in 1979.)

In the foreseeable future, the most likely prospect was for still higher oil consumption by the United States and other industrial nations (in 1978, the IEA-member nations consumed an average of 34.7 million barrels of oil daily, of which U.S. consumption accounted for 18.7 million barrels, or 54 per cent. However, a leveling off or even a reduction of oil use also was possible in view of continued oil price increases; lower production by Arab oil-producing nations; conservation measures; and increased use of alternative energy sources. In May 1979, the IEA predicted that the amount of OPEC oil available for export would decline from 33 million barrels a day in 1985 to 31 million barrels a day by 1990.

Meanwhile, meeting in Geneva, OPEC oil ministers voted June 28, 1979, to let the price of a barrel of crude oil rise to a range of from $18 to $23.50. The 24 per cent increase in the base price (officially $14.55 a barrel at the time, although individual nations had raised their prices substantially beyond that figure) was the largest since the 1974 increases.

The price range was a compromise between Saudi Arabia, the cartel's largest producer and most conservative member, and price radicals, such as Libya, which wanted much higher prices. Saudi Arabia, Qatar and the United Arab Emirates planned to charge $18 a barrel, with additional surcharges up to $23.50 a barrel for high quality oil. Some observers speculated that the OPEC decision reflected a decline in Saudi Arabia's influence over the organization, since that nation — which contained a third of OPEC's total oil reserves — had pressed for a less steep increase.

Reacting to the OPEC price hikes, the United States and six other major industrial nations (France, Britain, Canada, Japan, West Germany and Italy) agreed June 29 in Tokyo to cut future oil imports. Each country agreed to set its own target, with the United States pledging to hold imports to 8.5 million barrels a day through 1985.

By decreasing the demand for oil the countries hoped to curb OPEC's ability to increase prices. A communique by the seven leaders, released at the end of the economic summit meeting, said they "deplore" the price hikes announced by OPEC. But, in a nod to Saudi Arabia's attempts to keep increases moderate, the communique stated, "We recognize that relative moderation was displayed by certain of the participants.

"But the unwarranted rises in oil prices nevertheless... are bound to have very serious economic and social consequences."

The critical oil price/supply situation was somewhat alleviated in July, with the announcement that Saudi Arabia would temporarily increase its production and reports that Iraq would do likewise.

Nonetheless, Treasury Secretary W. Michael Blumenthal warned, "There is considerable danger we will now enter 1980 facing oil bills that present a severe challenge to our ability to stabilize our economies and maintain respectable rates of growth. The choice is not between growth and inflation. It is between growth with oil conservation and low growth with high inflation."

A POTENT, EFFECTIVE FORCE ON U.S. POLICY

In May 1975, 76 members of the United States Senate sent President Ford a special letter. "We urge you to make it clear, as we do, that the United States, acting in its own national interests, stands firmly with Israel in the search for peace in future negotiations, and that this promise is the basis of the current reassessment of U.S. policy in the Middle East."

The letter was the result of a major campaign by the American Israel Public Affairs Committee (AIPAC) urging the Senate to make "a significant contribution to the reassessment of American policy in the Middle East," as AIPAC's influential newsletter reported.[1]

The policy "reassessment" resulted from a breakdown in Secretary of State Henry A. Kissinger's "shuttle diplomacy" earlier that year, for which Kissinger and Ford publicly blamed Israel. As journalist Edward R. F. Sheehan later reported, "Kissinger's much trumpeted 'reassessment' of American policy in the Middle East was his revenge on Israeli recalcitrance." The letter of the 76 senators, Sheehan noted, "was a stunning triumph for the lobby, a capital rebuke for Kissinger in Congress." "It was," wrote Sheehan, "the Israeli lobby that dealt reassessment its *coup de grace*."[2]

What is popularly thought of as the "Israeli lobby" is, beyond doubt, one of the most powerful influences on U.S. Middle East policy in the nation's capital. Still, it is often credited with an undeserved omnipotence. It is doubtful if former Senator James Abourezk's (D S.D.) assertion that the lobby has the "ability to accomplish virtually any legislative feat involving military or economic assistance to Israel" is true. More accurate is the understanding that AIPAC has the ability to maximize pro-Israeli sentiments while often promoting what many consider anti-Arab policies. The billions of dollars in aid that Israel receives from the United States is an example of this maximizing influence. The 1977 legislation restricting compliance with the Arab economic boycott of Israel is an excellent example of this latter power.

Moreover, the "Israeli lobby" is not in reality a foreign agent required to register with the Justice Department and the Congress. It is a lobby financed and supported primarily by the American Jewish community. AIPAC's ability to stir the grass roots throughout the United States when support is needed is well known. While AIPAC and the Israeli government are in close and constant contact, it would be an exaggeration to say that Israel controls AIPAC. There have been instances where AIPAC has promoted policies or used tactics not fully supported by the Israelis.

In short, AIPAC is a unique institution mirroring the unique relationship between the American Jewish community and the state of Israel.

Effectiveness

During the past few years, AIPAC, which serves as the coordinator for the efforts of nearly all Jewish organizations, has been very active on a number of issues including:

● Amendments to the 1974 Trade Reform Act linking trade benefits to Communist emigration policies and limiting U.S. loans and credits to those countries.

● Requiring stringent restrictions on the sale of Hawk surface-to-air missile batteries to Jordan.

● A resolution calling for re-examination of U.S. membership in the United Nations if Israel were expelled.

● A bar on future U.S. support for the United Nations Educational, Scientific and Cultural Organization (UNESCO) because of its anti-Israel actions.

● Financial assistance for refugees from the Soviet Union and other Eastern European countries, with Israel receiving 80 per cent of the money.

● An agreement by the Ford administration not to supply weapons to Egypt during 1976 except for six C-130 transport planes.

● An amendment by Senator Abraham Ribicoff (D Conn.) to the Tax Reform Act of 1976 penalizing those American firms that complied with the Arab boycott of Israel by denying certain tax benefits on foreign source income; along with other anti-boycott legislation passed by the 95th Congress in 1977.

● Passage of a fiscal 1979 foreign aid bill that included $1.785 billion in military and economic aid for Israel, the same as appropriated in fiscal 1978.

Congressional Anxiety

In a 1976 year-end summary, AIPAC reported that during the 94th Congress it had "vigorously countered" the "moves to 'reassess' America's relationship with Israel." "On the basis of this fine record of congressional support for closer U.S.-Israel cooperation, we are confident that the 95th Congress will demonstrate the same awareness of fundamental U.S. interests by supporting a secure, viable Israel,"[3] AIPAC noted in October 1976.

There has developed, however, a growing uneasiness in Congress regarding the Middle East predicament and it has been reflected in a level of criticism of AIPAC unheard of just a few years ago. Most of this criticism is quiet and almost always "off-the-record." However, journalists Rus-

"What's good for American society is terribly important to the Jewish community."

—Hyman H. Bookbinder, Washington Representative, American Jewish Committee

1 *Near East Report*, 28 May 1975, p. 93.
2 Edward R. F. Sheehan; *The Arabs, Israelis, and Kissinger* (Reader's Digest Press: 1976), pp. 165, 173, 176.

3 *Near East Report*, 27 October 1976, p. 179.

sell Warren Howe and Sarah Hays Trott uncovered substantial criticism when researching their book *The Power Peddlers, A Revealing Account of Foreign Lobbying in Washington.*[4]

Assessments of the strength of the Jewish lobby depend largely on the perspective of the assessor. Few, however, would agree with the president of Hadassah, the Jewish women's organization, who termed the Jewish lobby a "myth" created by journalists.

Senator Abourezk, of Lebanese origin who had been one of the few members of Congress espousing Arab interests before his retirement in January 1979, has said he is "envious" of the Jewish lobby. Abourezk told a Denver audience in March 1977 that "The Israeli lobby is the most powerful and pervasive foreign influence that exists in American politics." Others disagree. "There is a lot of mythology about the Jewish lobby," said Richard Perle, an aide to Senator Henry M. Jackson (D Wash.).

In any event, the lobby's effectiveness was tested by the Carter administration. President Carter, within a few months after entering office, outlined some clear differences between the United States and Israel concerning resolution of the Middle East stalemate. *(Carter policy, p. 3)*

Even before Carter outlined his views, columnist Joseph C. Harsch wrote that there is "a desire and intention on Mr. Carter's part to regain the control over aid and support to Israel which President Eisenhower asserted and kept." "It will come down to a test of strength in Washington between the White House and the Israeli lobby," Harsch concluded. "The lobby has won most rounds since the days of Lyndon Johnson. Which will win this new round? It will be a fascinating test of Mr. Carter's political skill and strength."[5]

Mideast Jet Sales

One of the first tangible indications of the Carter administration's desire to pursue a more "evenhanded" Middle East policy was its proposal to sell $4.8 billion worth of military aircraft to Saudi Arabia, Israel and Egypt. The proposed sale to Saudi Arabia set off a major lobbying effort by the large and influential community of Israel's supporters in the United States that ultimately proved unsuccessful when Congress in May 1977 approved the sale. *(Jet sales, p. 47)*

A victory for the Carter administration but a bitter defeat for Israel and U.S. Jewish organizations passionately opposed to the weapons package, the Senate's 44-54 decision May 15 to turn down a resolution (S Con Res 86) blocking the sales was preceded by 10 hours of emotional debate on the heavily-lobbied issue.

Sales critics objected to linking Israel's supplies to the Saudi contracts and asserted that the Carter policy would "sap the morale" of the Jewish state.

Contract supporters argued that the United States now must be "evenhanded" in relations with both Israel and Arab states because of the complex weave of U.S. economic and strategic interests in the Middle East.

"We must have the courage, we must have the guts to face a changing world," said Ribicoff, referring to Saudi influence on international economic policies and Middle East peace efforts resulting from its oil riches. Ribicoff has been a longtime supporter of Israel.

4 Doubleday, 1977. See Chapter Six, "The Mideast Conflict."
5 Quoted in Mazin Omar, "A Test for Carter's Mettle," *The Middle East* (London), April 1977, p. 10.

Although Ribicoff and other administration supporters stressed that their position did not imply any lessening of support for Israel — that "commitment is unshakable," said Muriel Humphrey (D Minn.) — sales opponent Jacob K. Javits (R N.Y.) told the Senate the vote might not be read that way.

"The Israelis and Americans who feel as I do are likely to read the signal that is going to go out from this chamber quite differently. . . . The vote today may raise doubts now for the first time in 30 years respecting our commitment given the overtone and context of the debate," he said.

Pressure by the administration began to build May 12, the day after the deadlocked Foreign Relations Committee voted to send the resolution to the floor without a recommendation, when President Carter sent every member of the Senate a letter stating that a rejection of the aircraft for Egypt would be a "breach of trust" with Egyptian President Anwar Sadat who "has turned away from a relationship with the Soviet Union" to work with the United States in the search of peace.

The White House also disclosed that Carter was calling many in the Senate to argue his case. Members of the Cabinet and others in the administration also were reported to have contacted undecided senators before the vote.

On the opposite side, the American Jewish Committee and other pro-Israeli organizations were swamping Senate offices with telegrams, Mailgrams, letters and phone calls as the vote approached, according to aides. Outside the Senate chamber itself, the reception lobby was choked with lobbyists on both sides of the issue.

It was the pressure from Jewish organizations, however, that prompted Sen. Mike Gravel (D Alaska) and others to state publicly that their votes had become a "litmus test" for future support from Jews, although they had supported Israel on every issue in the past.

"This vote, if it is not done properly, kisses away in the future all kinds of financial support that would inure to a candidate for office," said Gravel. More troublesome, he added, the vote "will cost me some very important personal friendships."

Earlier George McGovern (D S.D.) warned the U.S. Jewish community's members that if they "press the case for Israel to the point where America loses its capacity to influence the Arab leadership . . . that may set in motion a backlash both in the Middle East and in the United States that can only harm the Israeli cause."

Bob Packwood (R Ore.) defended the lobbying, insisting that Jews have an understandable interest in the homeland of their forefathers as do Poles, Greeks and blacks. "It is with sorrow and disgust, therefore, that I hear the State Department time and again refer to the Jewish lobby or the Israeli lobby in a tone suggestive of a group which puts the interests of another country ahead of the United States."

AIPAC

Organization

AIPAC's origins are in the American Zionist Council which originally promoted support for Israel's creation and welfare. The present name was adopted in 1954 and until 1975 the organization was headed by I. L. (Si) Kenen. By 1979, it functioned as an umbrella lobbying organization with a staff of more than 20, an annual budget of about $750,000 and four registered lobbyists — an executive director, Morris J. Amitay, who replaced Kenen, legislative director Kenneth Wollack, and legislative liaisons Richard Straus and Ira Forman.

AIPAC's money comes from individual donations ranging from $25 to $5,000, which are not tax-exempt. More than 15,000 members contribute to AIPAC. Presidents of most of the major Jewish organizations sit on its executive committee and the Washington representatives of more than a dozen of these organizations meet weekly at AIPAC's offices. AIPAC does not contribute to candidates or rate members of Congress.

Separately incorporated from AIPAC is Near East Research Inc., a non-profit organization supported by subscriptions to its weekly newsletter, *Near East Report,* and individual donations. It conducts research on the Middle East and the Arab-Israeli conflict. Si Kenen, who in 1979 remained as honorary chairman of AIPAC, was its initial editor in chief and he contributed a column to *Near East Report.*

The newsletter, quartered with AIPAC near Capitol Hill, has an estimated readership of 30,000 and is legally separate from AIPAC. But Amitay is a contributing editor and his organization pays for mailing about 4,000 copies to every member of Congress, embassies, executive branch officials and United Nations delegations. The popular perception of the newsletter throughout Washington is that *Near East Report* is AIPAC's newsletter.

Operations

"The basic axiom of our work," said Amitay, "is the basic support for Israel that already exists. There is a broad base of support that shapes congressional feeling and the administration's. It makes our job a lot easier."

More and more, AIPAC's job is to counter the lobbying of pro-Arab groups and what Wollack has called the "petro-diplomatic group," which have greater financial resources but less power, in the view of AIPAC. The organization basically is a one-issue lobby. "We are pro-Israel — I don't deny that," explained Amitay. "But we make our case on the basis of American interests. . . .Our point of strength is not that we're so highly organized, but that so many people are committed to Israel. We have a lot of non-Jewish support. I'm very glad we don't have to rely just on Jews; if we did, we would be an ineffective group."

Amitay said the organization does "what all lobbies do" — informing Congress and the executive branch on the issues of importance to it — U.S.-Israeli relations, peace negotiations and military and economic assistance. It testifies for itself and on behalf of other Jewish groups, as it did on the proposed arms sale to Jordan. It provides members of Congress with information and encourages its members to communicate their views. "We keep in touch with other Jewish organizations," Amitay said, "but we're not a button-pressing organization" when it comes to mobilizing their members.

Amitay, since taking over in 1975, has greatly expanded AIPAC's Capitol Hill operations. Jews, Amitay explained, were ". . .concerned that after the Yom Kippur war [in 1973] that the United States' effort to improve relations with Arab states not be at the expense of the security of Israel." Under Amitay AIPAC has moved into new, roomier headquarters a short distance from the Capitol.

Publicly, and for obvious reasons, AIPAC has kept its distance from the Israeli Embassy in Washington. Amitay asserted that "We maintain no formal relationship or substantive connection with the Israeli Embassy." Many in Washington take issue with the assertion of complete separation. However, the relationship appeared to be close and often intimate — Amitay visits Israel regularly.

Evaluation

Commenting on the lobby's impact, Amitay said, "I think we've had some effect." Capitol Hill staffers have been more generous in their appraisal. "AIPAC is very effective," said a former staffer in the Senate minority leader's office. "They have a good grass roots operation, which is vital. It can deliver letters, calls to members from their home state. At any given moment, it can mobilize."

"It's effective with very little in the way of resources," said an aide to a Democratic senator.

A House source called AIPAC's involvement "helpful" in preventing the sale of anti-aircraft equipment to Jordan. Besides its Senate testimony, it mailed information to members of Congress on the possible impact on Israel of the sale. It also described this in mailings to Jewish groups across the country. One House aide estimated that it helped round up an additional 40 cosponsors to a resolution (H Con Res 337) opposing the sale, which had more than 125 cosponsors.

Though widely acclaimed, AIPAC also has its detractors. One Washington professor often consulted by the Israeli Embassy on political matters acknowledged, when questioned about AIPAC, that "in the past two years I've heard more anti-lobby sentiment than in all the years before." And a former Foreign Service officer who worked on Middle East matters for a Democratic senator felt "AIPAC often does with a sledgehammer what should be done with a stiletto."

Other Groups

Other major Jewish groups play a less direct political role than AIPAC, leaving much of the explicit lobbying to it and devoting more of their time to issues besides Israel. Beyond their relatively small Washington operations, they have influence as sources of information to their members and the public through mailings and publications and as forums for political figures.

American Jewish Committee

"I'm concerned that there could be an impression that the Jewish community is interested only in Israel," said Hyman H. Bookbinder of the New York-based American Jewish Committee. "If we have to list our priorities, it is my top priority, but we also pursue a variety of other issues." He listed the extension of the Voting Rights Act, voter registration by postcard, housing issues and civil rights as among those his two-person office follows. And they keep up with executive branch actions, and comment on regulations and proposals.

Behind that course is Bookbinder's belief that "we can't expect people to be interested in our issue and in the security of Israel unless we're interested in theirs. What's good for American society is terribly important to the Jewish community." A long history of scapegoating, he said, shows that "when there are social ills, Jews get it."

Additional Support

B'nai B'rith's Anti-Defamation League also has a Washington representative, David A. Brody, a registered

AIPAC's Tough Executive Director

Morris J. Amitay, known around Washington as Morrie, became in 1975 AIPAC's second executive director in its 23-year existence. Amitay brought to his job a Jewish heritage, foreign affairs experience in the State Department and five years as a legislative assistant in Congress.

He replaced I. L. (Si) Kenen, who retired at age 70. AIPAC's new and roomy office on North Capitol Street near Capitol Hill keeps its front door locked and scrutinizes visitors on a monitor for security reasons.

Kenen once told an interviewer that he rarely went to Capitol Hill to lobby, because support for Israeli causes already was so strong. Amitay conducts a different operation, although support in Congress remains firm. "I'm trying to change things here from essentially a one-man operation to having many qualified people," Amitay said in an interview when he first assumed his position. "We hope for a greater presence on the Hill."

AIPAC by 1977 had expanded to four registered lobbyists and a budget in excess of half a million dollars. The budget had been increased to about $750,000 by 1979.

"Until a few years ago, this was a public affairs organization," Amitay continued. "Now it's a nuts-and-bolts operation, analyzing legislation, gathering information, keeping up with the issues." Though AIPAC has grown since Amitay assumed the directorship, the organization has remained tightly controlled. "I put a premium on working quickly, on a quick response. That's why I like being fairly small and un-bureaucratic," he has said.

Amitay is known as a tough, no-nonsense partisan. He is a highly efficient, though sometimes abrasive fighter who knows how to pull the right congressional levers. He is considered a much more controversial personality than his predecessor.

Journalists Russell Howe and Sarah Trott in their study of Washington lobbyists have focused on the personality difference between Amitay and Kenen. "Kenen stands in contrast to Amitay, the New Yorker whom he chose as his successor and who enjoys boasting of AIPAC power and the facility with which it procures 'confidential' documents from senatorial offices," the two authors have written. "Amitay seems to detect Hitlerian tendencies in all who disagree with Israel. Kenen, in contrast, attended the 1975 convention of the National Association of Arab Americans.... When pointed out in the audience..., he drew some laughs but did not appear to mind. Few could imagine Amitay submitting to this experience."[6]

6 *The Power Peddlers: A Revealing Account of Foreign Lobbying in Washington* (Doubleday: 1977), p. 280.

lobbyist. The league, too, is particularly interested in domestic issues, not just Israel. Bookbinder and Brody, as well as individuals active in other major Jewish organizations, are on AIPAC's 70-member executive committee.

But the amount of lobbying that any of them do is limited by law because of their tax status; contributions are exempt. "We obviously work with each other, cooperate and share information," Bookbinder observed. "But every Jewish group bends over backwards to comply with the law. So we welcome an explicit operation like AIPAC."

An aide to a Republican senator insisted that Middle East issues are not lobbied only by Jewish groups, because broader questions than just Israel usually are involved. On the proposed arms sale to Jordan, for example, Americans for Democratic Action, the AFL-CIO and other unions worked against it, he said. Non-Jewish groups were active as well in barring U.S. payments to UNESCO in late 1974.

Among the other Jewish organizations which work closely with AIPAC in Washington are the American Jewish Congress, various religious groups, the Institute for Jewish Policy Planning and Research, the National Council of Jewish Women and Hadassah.

Since the 1973 Mideast war, debate about Israeli positions and about U.S. Middle East policy has caused serious tensions even within the American Jewish community. A new organization, "Breira" which in Hebrew means "alternative," has acted as a catalyst for debate on both Israeli and American policies. The Jewish establishment has vigorously challenged Breira which at times has voiced an opinion separate from AIPAC on Capitol Hill. For example, following Sadat's visit to Jerusalem, the Washington chapter of Breira issued a public statement urging that "all Israeli settlements set up outside Israel since Sadat's visit should be withdrawn at once, and Israel should announce that all post-1967 settlements are temporary and subject to negotiation."

Effectiveness

"When I have a question, I'll call one of those groups," said one aide who has worked for more than 10 years for several House members. "It's an educational situation, though, not overt lobbying like AIPAC, which keeps members constantly informed." An aide to a Democratic senator said he feels that these Jewish groups fill a need by being active in social programs, but, in his view, are "necessarily less effective" as an influence on Middle East policy because they are not one-issue-oriented.

Bookbinder believes the nationwide personal contacts the organizations' members have with influential members of Congress and executive branch officials are as important as any Washington operation.

Citizen Support

In the view both of people on Capitol Hill and of representatives of Jewish organizations, the so-called Jewish lobby gains much of its power from citizen activism — both Jewish and non-Jewish — and widespread public backing for the longstanding U.S. policy of support for an independent Israel.

Jewish Community

"The influence of the Jewish lobby is not a result of people walking the halls of Congress, but of people back home," said Perle. "What happens in Washington is really

The Jewish Community's Relations with Carter

Although there is no doubt that the security of Israel is the ultimate "consensus position" for American Jews, some questioned certain of the policies of Israeli Prime Minister Begin, particularly on the West Bank settlements issue. In 1977 and 1978, many were equally apprehensive about the Carter administration's policy of "evenhandedness." In response, Carter sought to reassure leaders of the Jewish community of the continued U.S. commitment to Israel's existence and security by meeting with 40 Jewish representatives on July 6, 1977. Three months later, however, the October 1977 joint U.S.-Soviet statement calling for a Geneva conference with some kind of role for the Palestine Liberation Organization provoked an angry outcry from many Jewish Americans, who deluged the White House with critical telegrams and letters. "The assurances with which we walked out of the [July 6] meeting have turned to new doubts and new fears," said Rabbi Alexander M. Schindler, then chairman of the Conference of Presidents of Major Jewish Organizations.

By late October, however, the possibility of a confrontation between the Carter administration and the Jewish lobby had lessened somewhat. Carter met with a largely Jewish congressional delegation and pointed to places where the U.S.-Soviet statement had made concessions in Israel's favor. Delegation members said afterward that they were convinced that Carter had not swerved from his commitment to Israel. Nonetheless, an Oct. 13, 1977, Harris poll indicated that 60 percent of Jews interviewed gave Carter a negative rating, with an overwhelming 69.4 percent expressing disapproval of his Middle East policies. "There is a tension in the community that is almost electric," said Mark A. Siegel, an administration aide appointed to serve as a liaison with the Jewish community. Particular criticism on the part of many Jews had been directed at Zbigniew Brzezinski, Carter's national security adviser, over what were considered his critical remarks about Israel.

In early March 1978, a new element was injected into the shaky relations between Carter and the Jewish community with the resignation of Siegel, who said he had withdrawn from defending and explaining the administration's Middle East policy to Jewish groups "because I couldn't articulate it any more." Close on the heels of Siegel's resignation came the revelation of the administration's proposed jet sale package, which deepened the confrontation.

In June, the administration took steps to mend fences by appointing Edward Sanders, a Los Angeles lawyer and past president of AIPAC, to serve as a principal adviser on matters affecting the American Jewish community.

The September Camp David summit and resulting accords went a long way toward quieting the growing anti-Carter sentiment in the U.S. Jewish community. The agreements represented "a magnificent achievement in the cause of peace, made possible by major concessions from both sides under the wise and determined leadership of President Carter," said Theodore R. Mann, chairman of the Conference of Presidents of Major American Jewish Organizations.

Much of the praise and optimism was based on the assumption that Carter would continue to play an active role as mediator. That assumption, however, was questioned by some Jewish spokesmen in December 1978. They charged that the administration had abandoned its evenhanded position and had become an advocate of Egypt's position.

There was widespread praise from the Jewish community over Carter's role in obtaining the March 26, 1979, Egypt-Israel peace treaty — and equally strong support for the $4.8 billion aid package for the two nations. However, there was also apprehension about Carter's comment that the United States would "immediately start working directly" with the PLO, although he repeated the administration's previous position that such talks depended on PLO recognition of Israel's right to exist and endorsement of UN Security Council Resolution 242 as the basis for Middle East peace negotiations. There was also criticism of the administration's efforts to woo Saudi Arabia as a "moderating" influence. Nonetheless, an editorial in the March 28, 1979, *Near East Report* concluded, "Without Carter there would have been no treaty signing between Israel and Egypt, and whatever lay ahead for Israel and Egypt or for Carter, the American president earned his day in the sun. All Americans can be proud of his accomplishment."

modest compared to what happens in the district. A newspaper story or an event in the Mideast can trigger an immediate response." Still, those familiar with AIPAC know how quickly a telephone or telegram campaign can be mobilized if AIPAC gives the signal.

According to 1973 census statistics, there are about 5.7 million Jews in this country, 2.8 percent of the population. But with their higher political participation, they account for about 4 percent of the vote nationally, wrote Stephen D. Isaacs in his book, *Jews and American Politics*. The electoral college system serves to further multiply that power, especially since Jews are concentrated in states with the greatest electoral votes.

An aide to Rep. Stephen J. Solarz (D N.Y.) noted that the "American Jewish community is very active and very well informed, especially in foreign policy matters, and it will make its views known." While this community is generally considered more liberal than the public at large on most issues, it draws some support from conservatives who have anti-communist views and reservations about detente.

Bookbinder defined the Jewish lobby as "the totality of Jewish influence in America. If AIPAC went out of life tomorrow, it wouldn't mean the death of the Jewish lobby." He noted the influence of academics, the business community, professionals, and socially and politically active individuals, including contributors to cultural and social causes as well as political campaigns.

"The idea of Jewish giving in return for support for Israel is very, very unfair," Bookbinder continued. "Compared to giving of others, like labor, corporations, environmentalists, the anti-war movement, Jewish giving is relatively unstructured and untargeted."

John Thorne, former press secretary to Senator Abourezk, indicated the Jewish lobby is "better organized and more effective than the oil lobby, because it's scattered all over the country. Its power is due to pressure from constituents."

Public Opinion

Coupled with Jewish activism is public support for the U.S. policy, in effect since before Israel's founding in 1948, that the existence of Israel is in the U.S. national interest. Opinion surveyor Louis Harris documented that support in a poll concluded in January 1975 and described in a *New York Times Magazine* article April 6. He found that 52 per cent of the public sympathized with Israel, up from 39 per cent in 1973 right after the Yom Kippur War, with only 7 per cent expressing sympathy for the Arab side. Sixty-six per cent of the public favored sending Israel whatever military hardware it needed, but no American troops. On what Harris called the "pivotal" question—whether the United States should stop military aid to Israel if this were necessary to get Arab oil—64 per cent of the public was opposed.

In an April 1978 Gallup survey, 44 per cent of Americans who had heard or read about the situation in the Middle East said their basic sympathies were with Israel and 10 per cent with the Arab nations. Nearly half, however, were not aligned with either side (33 per cent) or had no opinion on the situation (13 per cent).

Congressional Support

"Traditionally, the bastion of pro-Israel sentiment has been the Congress," one scholar concluded in a 1976 study of "The Arab-Israeli Battle on Capitol Hill."[7] The *Jerusalem Post's* Washington correpondent, commenting on the new faces in the 95th Congress, agreed. "Pro-Israel support in Congress," Wolf Blitzer wrote in December 1976, "has traditionally been a crucial factor in balancing the more 'even-handed' slant in the administration, influenced by Arabists in the State Department."[8] A longtime pro-Israeli observer further notes that "Had it not been for Israel's support in Congress, things would have been quite gloomy."[9] Si Kenen has been quoted as saying that "Without the lobby, Israel would have gone down the drain,"[10] dramatizing the importance of AIPAC in influencing the Congress.

A combination of local activism and public opinion, as well as the deep feeling that U.S. interests in the Middle East are served by support for Israel, is reflected in Congress, whose membership matches closely the Jewish population at large.

The number of Jewish members increased to 27 in the 95th Congress from 23 in the 94th and only 14 in the 93rd. That was 5 per cent, just a little more than the voting strength of Jewish citizens. The 96th Congress had seven Jewish senators: Rudy Boschwitz (R Minn.), Jacob Javits (R N.Y.), Carl Levin (D Mich.), Howard Metzenbaum (D Ohio), Abraham Ribicoff (D Conn.), Richard Stone (D Fla.) and Edward Zorinsky (D Neb.). There were 23 Jews in the House.

Explanation

Aides to key members of Congress argue that Jewish lobbying is not solely responsible for the support on Capitol Hill. A Senate aide who has worked on Jewish issues has said, "It is fundamentally misleading to talk about attitudes up here toward the Mideast and Israel in terms of Jewish lobbying. Seventy-five per cent of the Senate is pro-Israel for a whole lot of reasons."

An aide to a Republican senator said that the "interest and support on the Hill for Israel comes from the belief that it is vital to the U.S. national interest. American interests lie in the Middle East; extract Israel from the picture and things are not changed."

Staff Network

Augmenting the support for Israel is what has been called a "network" of staff aides who are interested in Jewish matters, particularly Israel.

They have included such people as Richard Perle in Senator Jackson's office, Albert Lakeland in Javits' office and aides to other senators, among them Birch Bayh (D Ind.), Ribicoff, Metzenbaum and Frank Church (D Idaho), chairman of the Foreign Relations Committee. Senator Stone, one of Israel's strongest supporters, has assumed the chairmanship of the Subcommittee on Near Eastern and South Asian Affairs of the Senate Foreign Relations Committee.

In the House, a partial list of the staff "network" has included aides to Speaker Thomas P. O'Neill Jr. (D Mass.), Sidney R. Yates (D Ill.), Charles A. Vanik (D Ohio) and Stephen J. Solarz (D N.Y.).

In his book, Isaacs quotes Amitay, a former aide to Ribicoff, as saying in 1973, "There are now a lot of guys at the working level up here who happen to be Jewish, who are willing to make a little bit of extra effort and to look at certain issues in terms of their Jewishness, and this is what has made this thing go very effectively in the last couple of years."

As head of AIPAC, Amitay took a somewhat different view of the importance of any Hill network. "The talk of a Hill network is highly over-rated," he said. "It doesn't exist as such. It's not a question of the staff getting members of Congress to do things; it is the bosses who get the staff people interested."

Staffers who made up to so-called network described it in terms of people knowing each other from working on common issues. They denied that they may constitute an "Israel lobby" in their own right. "Staff people are important, just because of the way senators operate," said one aide. "But they are important on any issue, not just Jewish ones. Strongly held views on Israel are due to constituents — no staff can create that kind of concern."

Assessments

The success of the Jewish lobby thus has been attributed to a combination of U.S. national interest, widespread public support, community activism and an effective Washington operation. Former Senate Majority Leader Mike Mansfield (D Mont.) has said, "It's a strong lobby. But there are other strong lobbies, too." A longtime House

7 Mary A. Barberis, "The Arab-Israeli Battle on Capitol Hill," *Virginia Quarterly Review*, Spring 1976, p. 204.

8 Wolf Blitzer, "Many Friends Among the New Faces in Congress," *Jerusalem Post Weekly*, 21 December 1976.

9 *Ibid.*

10 *The Power Peddlers, op. cit.*, p. 271.

aide observed, "Compared to some pressures, the Jewish lobby palls in comparison."

Bookbinder stressed that legislative successes were not the result of heavy-handed lobbying. "In the areas where we don't have substantial non-Jewish support, we don't make our case," he says. "Most of the Jewish community would like to have a federal welfare program or a multi-billion-dollar food assistance program, but we don't have that power.

"I'm concerned about a feeling that the Jewish lobby uses strong-arm, pressure-type tactics. That's nonsense.... There is a very small staff of professionals; we don't wine and dine members of Congress; we have no former congressmen on our payrolls; we don't give parties or have a direct political operation funding or rating people. It's just a bunch of fairly good, devoted people."

An aide to an influential Republican senator said he believes the claims of a powerful Jewish lobby were "way overrated and blown up" by State Department officials and Arab interests to suggest that Congress is "blinded and myopic" toward Israel. "Lobbies will win when they have the facts to support them," he observed.

The Israel lobby has facts—sometimes slanted—at its fingertips. AIPAC has both a director of research and a director of information and the instant availability of concise, hard information can often be translated into power and influence. *Near East Report's* indexed pamphlet *Myths and Facts: A Concise Record of the Arab-Israeli Conflict* is widely distributed and often the source of information on Capitol Hill.

Nonetheless, criticism of AIPAC has apparently begun to hurt. Some of AIPAC's supporters have called for a more low-key style but have expressed doubts that Amitay would be able to conform.

The coming years would be ones of great challenge for this key Washington lobby which was likely to be deeply enmeshed in the politics of American involvement in the Middle East.

OPENING DOORS THAT WERE PREVIOUSLY CLOSED

In the view of Middle East Arabs and their American kinfolk, they have spent a quarter century anguishing on the sidelines while the Zionist lobby has called the plays that have helped thrust the United States into the deadly game of Middle East politics—on Israel's team.

But, since the October 1973 Middle East war, American supporters of the Arab cause have felt that at last they are getting into the game. Richard C. Shadyac, an Arab-American trial lawyer from Annandale, Va., who is a past president of the National Association of Arab Americans (NAAA), put it tersely: "The day of the Arab-American is here. The reason is oil."

Thomas Ruffin, former executive director of the NAAA, summed up the goal of the newly emerging Arab lobby. "We are not asking the United States government to take a pro-Arab, anti-Israeli position. We are asking that it weigh all aspects of the Middle East, that it adopt a balanced, even-handed approach in foreign policy."

Whether they consider it a tilt toward the Arabs or a bending back from Israel, American supporters of the Arab cause believed they witnessed a shift in U.S. policy. The shift began in the aftermath of the 1973 war, with its oil embargo and its oil price hikes. Until then, Arabists had viewed American policy, in tandem with that of the Soviet Union, as maintaining the status quo in the Middle East, meaning to them that the United States was doing nothing to remove Israel from occupied Arab lands and to bring about a "just settlement" of the Palestinian question.

But then Secretary of State Kissinger mediated initial troop disengagement accords between Egypt and Israel, and Syria and Israel. In the spring of 1975, he tried for further agreements among the belligerents. That mission came to naught, and an obviously annoyed President Ford commented, "If they [the Israelis] had been a bit more flexible . . . I think in the longer run it would have been the best insurance for peace." The White House announced a total reassessment of Middle East policy, covering "all aspects and all countries."

All this was an unfamiliar tune to Arab lobbyists, but it was music to their ears. Many Arab-Americans supported Gerald Ford for the presidency in 1976 on the basis of the shift in U.S. Middle East policy, especially in view of Carter's clearly pro-Israeli stands designed to attract the more numerous Jewish vote. Yet, by mid-1977, Carter's Middle East views were being applauded by many Arab-Americans. Joseph Baroody, then president of NAAA, may have captured the consensus when he said that "right now we're prepared to give Carter the benefit of the doubt. Until he gives us good reason to think he's not being even-handed, we'll assume he is being even-handed."

Complex Problem

Thus the stated objective of the Arab lobby is simple. Its leaders all speak of a "balanced, even-handed approach." But to carry that message beyond the White House to other American institutions, principally Congress, as well as the populace at large, presents a complex problem. Arab lobbyists must present their case effectively to the American establishment—its political, financial and communications power structure.

At any table where American sympathy and support are the stakes, Arabs hold that they sit down with a shorter stack of chips than do their Jewish counterparts. It has been estimated that there are two million Americans of Arab origin or heritage in the United States, compared with almost six million Jewish-Americans. And the Arabs claimed they spent far less on their cause in the United States than did their opponents, mainly because, they said, they had fewer funds and fewer sources of money.

But the real problem for the emerging Arab lobby has been mobilizing Arab-Americans to become active. Baroody said that "Arab-Americans have always been a group that quickly assimilated. There hasn't been an Arab-American consciousness, we never thought of ourselves as a group in that sense." But as with other ethnic affiliations, being Arab-American has come into style. The 1967 and 1973 Middle East wars stimulated Arab-American identification much the same as they did with American Jews. And the conflict of "dual loyalty" might have to be faced by Arab-Americans, just as by Jewish-Americans, should the Arab oil-producing states clamp another oil embargo on the United States.

The question has arisen as to how the Arabs can square away their pleading poverty with the piles of "petrodollars" Arab nations have amassed since the 1973 war. Hatem I. Hussaini, former assistant director of the Arab Information Center in Washington who became the first director of the Palestine Liberation Organization (PLO) Washington office in 1978, said, "Only recently have Arab nations begun to think about Arab information in this country. Arab governments think that diplomacy—visits by heads of states, prime ministers—is more important than publicity campaigns in the United States."

Dr. M. T. Medhi, founder of the Action Committee on American Arab Relations, said that "The Arab governments are really not part of the 20th century. They have hundreds of problems of their own. . . . Hardly any of them have come to power as a result of elections and free campaigns. So they do not quite understand the need for spending money in America to change public opinion."

"I hope we are becoming known as the Arab lobby...the Arab-American lobby that is."

—Joseph Baroody, former president, National Association of Arab-Americans

Lebanese editor Clovis Maksoud who came to the United States in 1975 as an Arab League emissary, recommended then that the Arab League information offices either be revamped or closed down in view of their ineffectiveness.

"We can't represent Arabs the way the Jewish lobby can represent Israel," said Baroody. "The Israeli government has one policy to state, whereas we couldn't represent 'the Arabs' if we wanted to. They're as different as the Libyans and Saudis are different, or as divided as the Christian and Moslem Lebanese."

A similar observation was offered by John P. Richardson, public affairs director of NAAA, who commented that Arab-Americans tended to have more varied and less clear perceptions of their identity than American Jews who are at least united on their support for Israel's existence.

Ugliness and Finery

Many observers of and activists in the Arab lobby believe that one of the major hurdles it must clear is overcoming the derogatory image of the Arab in the American mind, which they attribute to a large extent to the American media. "One of our most serious problems is image," said NAAA's public relations director Richardson. The group has been working with the media to point out the negative stereotypes perpetuated in television, cartoons, movies and so forth.

Writing in the Dec. 13, 1978, issue of *The Christian Century*, mass media specialist Jack G. Shaheen, professor at Southern Illinois University, concluded: "Television entertainment programs suggest that the Arab world consists of several stock characters. One is the oil-rich desert sheik, possessor of camels, Cadillacs and retinues; he is rich, irresponsible, backward and sex-mad.... Another Arab type is the terrorist or participant in political intrigue.... The Arab woman is seldom shown. A chattel of little importance, always veiled, she apparently has no function but to secure food and serve as member of a harem.

"Viewers are never shown the positive contributions Arabs have made to Western culture in mathematics, astronomy, medicine, physics and literature."

The Arab caricature image, wrote columnist Meg Greenfield in the Dec. 5, 1977, issue of *Newsweek*, "is one of the very few 'ethnic jokes' still indulged by our cartoonists and stand-up comics. It is somehow considered permissible where comparable jokes are not, and I do not think this is wholly owing to the absence of a big enough Arab-American political constituency to raise hell. There is a dehumanizing, circular process at work here. The caricature dehumanizes. But it is inspired and made acceptable by an earlier dehumanizing influence, namely, an absence of feeling for who the Arabs are and where they have been."

Greenfield (and others) observed that the widely televised visit of Egyptian President Anwar Sadat to Jerusalem in late November 1977 "transformed more than the political landscape of the Middle East. He has surely also transformed, or at least substantially altered, the American perception of the Arab and his cause. Unlike the set pieces to which we have become accustomed—the oil-rich sheik, the terrorist, the ululating crowd—Sadat was neither alarming nor strange.... He spoke as a man of the twentieth century. He bore his national and religious heritage with pride and confidence, but without swagger or put-them-to-the-sword rhetoric and posturing.... [W]hen the plane touched down in Jerusalem, Sadat stepped into American political reality, just as surely as he stepped onto Israeli soil."

"... U.S. foreign policy toward the Middle East is ... injurious to our national well being."

—Joanne McKenna, president, National Association of Arab-Americans

Signs of Change

But there have been indications of rising influence of Arab governments and Arab-Americans in Washington. Arab nations have begun to spend considerable sums to retain the services of public relations firms and top-level political and legal experts. In addition, many large U.S. corporations are sympathetic to the Arab cause because of their interest in investments and business activities in the Middle East.

"It's still tough to present the Arab view, but for the first time we see a glimmering of a real debate in Congress over Middle Eastern policy," said NAAA's Richardson. "We are gradually being heard here. Now ambassadors of Arab countries are making regular trips to the Hill to meet privately with members of Congress."

Richardson's observation was vividly borne out during the debate over the proposed sale of fighter jets to Egypt, Israel and Saudi Arabia in the spring of 1978. Lobbying on both sides of the issue was intense, with Cabinet ministers and members of the Saudi royal family appearing on Capitol Hill almost daily to present reasoned arguments on behalf of the sale. During Senate and House committee deliberations on the jet package, representatives of NAAA testified along with the American Israel Public Affairs Committee (AIPAC), a group long familiar on Capitol Hill.

"It's just amazing how things are changing here in town," said Richardson at the time of the jet sale debate. "When AIPAC is invited to testify on something on the Hill, the committees are pairing us with them. We may not be able to match Morrie [Amitay of AIPAC] on everything he does, but at least we're in there. People are looking for an Arab point of view."

And, too, with the shift in the United States' traditionally Israel oriented foreign policy in the Middle East to accommodate growing diplomatic and financial involvement with Arab nations, the Arab-American populace—though small—has assumed new importance. "Traditionally, they have not been involved much in social activism. They are more entrepreneurial," said Richardson. "Now they are beginning to take some interest in political activity."

In Congress, the number of Arab-Americans has grown from none in 1966 to five in 1979: Reps. Abraham Kazen Jr., D-Texas; Anthony (Toby) Moffet, D-Conn.; Nick Joe Rahall, D-W Va.; James Abdnor, R-S.D.; and Mary Rose Oakar, D-Ohio. Until his retirement in 1979, James G. Abourezk, D-S.D., represented Arab-Americans in the Senate.

More significant than the growing number of Arab-Americans in Congress, however, has been changing attitudes among other influential members not of Arab ancestry. For example, Sen. Abraham Ribicoff, D-Conn., has spoken out against the Israeli government's West Bank settlements policy and has sometimes been critical of Jewish lobbying efforts. Ribicoff also supported the administration's proposed jet sale to Saudi Arabia, although he said his position did not lessen his support for Israel.

Both Sens. Jacob K. Javits, R-N.Y., and Richard Stone, D-Fla., strong supporters of Israel, have visited Saudi Arabia and have said they were impressed by the Saudis. Numerous other members of Congress have also visited the Arab nations at their invitation, and although they have not been won over to the Arab point of view, many of them have urged a more even-handed U.S. Middle East policy. At least six senators have met with PLO leader Yasir Arafat in Beirut. One of them, Sen. Charles McC. Mathias Jr., R-Md., said he found Arafat "very well informed."

One indication of the Arab lobby's growing strength came in May 1978. The NAAA considered that a major victory had been won when the Senate voted to support the administration's proposal to sell a package of jet aircraft to Egypt, Saudi Arabia and Israel. During the spring, the organization had circulated a position paper on the sales; NAAA witnesses were also invited to testify, along with AIPAC, at congressional hearings. "The political conclusion to be drawn from the vote is that the Israel lobby lost its first major fight and its apparent veto over American policy toward the Arab world," NAAA stated jubilantly. "[T]he vote . . . confirmed that the Israel lobby is subject to political limits. This reality opens the door to a more constructive and balanced American approach to the Middle East."

The NAAA

A multiplicity of domestic organizations promotes the Arab cause in the United States, but it is clear that one has had mounting importance since the 1973 war — the National Association of Arab-Americans.

Established in 1972 "to fill the absence of an effective political action group" on the national level, the NAAA staked itself out as the umbrella group for Arab-Americans (most of whom are of Lebanese ancestry) unable to identify with pro-Arab activists who leaned "too much to the left." In 1979, there were 20 local chapters and numerous affiliated groups (mainly cultural).

NAAA has attempted to act as the major Arab lobby, according to its former president Joseph Baroody. "Our basic support is among affiliates. There are 1,100-1,200 Arab-American organizations in this country. Virtually all of them are cultural, religious, or charitable, but many of them have affiliated with us for political reasons."

Michael Saba, the NAAA executive director from August 1976 to July 1977, emphasized relations with what he termed "affinity groups" and grass-roots lobbying. Responding to some criticism that the organization's efforts had not been sufficiently political, Saba replied that "We look to AIPAC as an organization that's done incredible things in this country and has mounted programs very significant in terms of American foreign policy. As a potential counter we need first to get our members more involved. The Jews relate more to the issues of the Middle East. We have to show our people that we can represent their interests."

Until 1975, NAAA was a small and relatively weak organization. In 1979, it was still small, with a membership of about 2,000 individuals and groups and a paid staff of six, but its influence had grown. The group's lobbying effort received a boost in 1977 when it hired Richardson — a well-respected and articulate Middle East expert of British and Norwegian descent who had headed American Near East Refugee Aid Inc. — as its public affairs director. Richardson registered as the group's lobbyist in 1978.

All members of the NAAA are Americans. "We don't accept money from any Arab country, though, the good Lord knows, there have been times when we could have used it," a former executive director said. While Arab governments do not contribute directly to NAAA, it does appear they help out by sponsoring such things as sessions at the annual convention and by taking out advertisements in the annual journal.

The group's annual budget was about $250,000 in 1979. Dues ranged from $25 to $100; about 70 percent of the budget was funded by U.S. corporations. Dues and contributions are not tax deductible, nor is the organization tax exempt. Among NAAA publications are a biweekly political affairs newsletter, *Focus*, a series of issues papers called Counterpoint, and a quarterly cultural and educational newsletter. In addition to the membership, publications are sent to members of Congress, journalists and other interested organizations.

The group works closely with U.S.-Arab chambers of commerce; participates in U.S. trade missions to the Middle East; provides assistance concerning international and domestic legal issues; and has established a nationwide "hot line" to alert the membership to upcoming congressional votes on critical issues.

NAAA presidents serve for one-year terms without compensation. They are selected by a 50-member board which meets about four times a year to set policy. In 1978, Dr. Hisham Sharabi, a history professor at Georgetown University and a Palestinian by birth, succeeded Baroody as NAAA president. In 1979, Joanne McKenna, a native of Cleveland of Lebanese ancestry who had been active in NAAA affairs since the group was established, became the organization's president.

Meeting with Ford

NAAA was little known in government circles until 1976, when, on June 26, in a session that Ruffin termed "very historic," 12 NAAA representatives met with President Ford at the White House. It was only the second time such a meeting with an American president had taken place. (A small group of Arab-Americans met with President Lyndon B. Johnson at the time of the 1967 Arab-Israeli war.) The NAAA arranged the Ford meeting through Kissinger, who, Ruffin said, was interested in the NAAA's presenting its views to the chief executive.

A four-page position paper was presented to Ford by the then-NAAA president, Edmond N. Howar of Washington, D.C. He told Ford that the NAAA supported the president's initiatives in the Middle East, especially the administration's total reassessment of foreign policy in the region. However, Howar said the organization was concerned that certain fundamental problems not be overlooked. Ford was presented with these six points: a demand for Israeli withdrawal from territories occupied in the June 1967 war; protection of the rights of Palestinians; U.S. recognition of the Palestine Liberation Organization; special status for Jerusalem; a complaint about Israeli military incursions into Lebanon; and an expression of concern that congressional attitudes "are keeping more petrodollars from being invested in the United States."

Emphasis on "Americanism"

In speaking to Ford, as it did elsewhere, the NAAA stressed its American roots and its claim that its lobbying efforts were for objectives in the best interests of the United States. Ruffin said, "We don't speak on behalf of any Arab country or any Arab leader. In relation to U.S. policy, first and foremost we are Americans. We would not be pro-Arab if that hurt the United States. The reason why we are against the pro-Israel policy is that it hurts the economic and social well-being of the United States."

Said president McKenna at the annual NAAA convention in May 1979: "The fact is that we, the two million Americans of Arabic descent, are indeed Americans. When we talk about the United States of America, we are not talking about somebody else's country, we are talking about *our* country.... We have a constitutional mandate to utilize our freedom of speech to inform and enlighten our fellow Americans.... The condition of U.S. foreign policy toward the Middle East is ... injurious to our national well being."

The NAAA is "an organization of Americans, acting in the interest of the United States," said Abourezk, who added that he supported the association as long as it maintained an American posture and did not become a tool of Arab nations. "We try assiduously to stay out of inter-Arab politics," commented public affairs director Richardson. "It's not our job to tell the Arabs what to do. Our principal job is to influence *American* Middle East policy."

"We will not be involving ourselves in any inter-Arab or intra-Arab politics," said McKenna. "Our business is the United States government."

Obstacles to Action

NAAA has set for itself the goal of awakening the sense of Arabic heritage in two million Arab-Americans beyond the confines of Middle East food and music. There has been considerable success so far, but even NAAA's leaders freely admit there's a long, long way to go before there is an effective Arab lobby in Washington that can match the efforts of American Jews.

"Arab-Americans are more difficult to mobilize politically than are Jews," said Richardson, noting a number of reasons for this, among them the fact that much of the Jewish population is concentrated in large urban centers with electoral clout and the fact that many Arab-Americans take a somewhat conservative position on political issues, not wishing to "rock the boat." And, too, he said, due to the negative stereotype, some Arab-Americans view their ethnic identity as a political liability. The NAAA has tried to overcome the tendency of its members to avoid political activity by encouraging Arab-American participation on local boards and governments as well as to increase the federal government's awareness of the needs and interests of the U.S. Arab community.

Pushing the Cause

Championing the Palestinian cause has become one of NAAA's important priorities. "I don't think there's any way to come up with a settlement in the Middle East without dealing face-to-face with the Palestinians," Baroody has said. In April 1977, representatives of NAAA visited the Middle East, meeting with various Arab officials including Yasir Arafat of the PLO. Since then, NAAA

Other Domestic Lobby Groups

Additional facets of Arab lobby activity in the United States include educational and cultural organizations. The Chicago-based Federation of Arab Organizations encompasses small social and cultural Arab clubs throughout the nation. The American Friends of the Middle East, headquartered in Washington, D.C. provides education counseling to help place students from the Middle East in U.S. universities. Also in Washington, the Middle East Resource Center and the Middle East Research and Information Project (MERIP) provide information generally considered pro-Arab.

Another organization, the Association of Arab-American University Graduates (AAUG), has become more visible during the past few years in addition to NAAA. Not especially active in Washington, AAUG has not attracted the attention of journalists and politicians. But it has become an influence. "AAUG — they're more the academics and intellectuals," Baroody noted. "They identify more with internal Arab politics," Saba said.

Another component of pro-Arab activity in the United States encompasses organizations working to provide assistance to Palestinian refugees. Prominent among them is American Near East Refugee Aid Inc. (ANERA), a nonprofit organization funded by the Agency for International Development, corporations, foundations and individuals interested in aiding Palestinian refugees and other persons in the Middle East.

ANERA came into existence after the June 1967 war. Among the activities the organization has supported were the Industrial Islamic Orphanage in Jerusalem, the Palestine Hospital, Gaza College, the YWCA of East Jerusalem, Arab Women's Society of Jerusalem and the Association for the Resurgence of Palestinian Camps.

Over the past few years, ANERA has raised a few million dollars in the United States, of which 82 percent, mostly in cash grants but a small part in pharmaceuticals, has gone to the Palestinian organizations. The other 18 percent has been spent on administration and travel.

---

board members have traveled frequently throughout the Arab world.

At its sixth annual convention in May 1978, NAAA delegates adopted a package of resolutions strongly denouncing what was characterized as an Israeli policy of military expansion in the Middle East. The resolutions called on President Carter to recognize the PLO as the sole voice of the Palestinian people; to halt the arms trade with Israel until Israel guaranteed the human rights of Palestinians and all other minorities living in Israel; and to renew negotiations for a "just and lasting peace." Speaking at the convention, Najeeb A. Halaby, a former administrator of the Federal Aviation Administration, past president of Pan American Airways and international businessman, portrayed the NAAA as an American moderator to help solve the Middle East crisis. "First, I believe that the best thing we can all do is to try to isolate the zealots on both sides who have made such a mess for themselves and for us in that part of the world," he said.

In the wake of the September 1978 Camp David summit, a group of five NAAA members headed by Dr. Sharabi in December visited eight Arab states and talked with six Arab heads of state and PLO leader Yasir Arafat. The Arab leaders, the NAAA group said on its return to the United States, "were eager to have their perspective understood in Washington and welcomed the visit of the NAAA delegation, whom they looked upon as unofficial American interlocutors with the White House and the administration."

On their return, the group immediately requested meetings with administration officials, including President Carter. They saw Harold Saunders, assistant secretary for Near East and South Asian Affairs, and William Quandt, head of the Middle East desk at the National Security Council. "We are not carrying messages between the two sides," Dr. Sharabi maintained. "We are citizens of Arab ancestry with privileged access in the Arab world and we feel that we have a role to play." Sharabi also expressed disappointment that Carter had declined to meet with the group.

That it was still an uphill fight for Arab-Americans to be heard in Washington was demonstrated by the seventh annual NAAA convention in May 1979. Both Carter and Secretary of State Cyrus R. Vance declined invitations to address the convention. Although the theme of the meeting was "Arab-American Awakening," a number of speakers emphasized the need for keeping Arab lines to Washington open. "From the Arab point of view," said Dr. Sharabi, "it would be a strategic mistake to allow a wedge to be driven between the U.S. and the Arab countries. . . ."

U.S. Middle East policy, particularly the Egyptian-Israeli peace treaty, was castigated by the majority of the speakers, who urged the Carter administration to start a dialogue with the PLO or "efforts toward peace in the Middle East may soon reach an impasse," in the words of Rep. Paul Findley, R-Ill.

Arab Governments

In addition to the NAAA — the major domestic lobby group — Arab governments themselves have developed substantial influence in Washington, spurred largely by the influx of petrodollars into the country. (In 1979 it was reported that Saudi Arabia alone had invested between $40 and $60 billion in the United States, most of it in U.S. Treasury securities.)

Lobbying on behalf of the Arab countries has been carried on by the Arab Information Centers, an arm of the Arab League, which provided at least $500,000 a year for AIC operations. The main Arab Information Center is in New York City; there are offices in Washington, Chicago, Dallas and San Francisco. Speakers and films are provided by the AIC for interested American university, church and civic groups. In 1975, the AIC began publication of a biweekly newsletter, *The Arab Report*, which it sends to members of Congress, journalists, television commentators and public opinion-makers. Also published is *The Palestine Digest*, principally a collection of news articles, editorials and speeches sympathetic to the Arab cause.

More effective than the AIC, however, have been the individual Arab governments and their representatives. There was little doubt that, following the 1973 oil embargo, officials and businessmen from Arab nations had begun to carve out a comfortable niche for themselves in U.S. government circles. By the mid-1970s, there was a growing awareness both within this country and in the Arab nations that their economic interdependence had necessitated cultivation of closer political relationships. In 1977, Saudi Arabia sent an information team to the United States; and others, particularly the Egyptian press office under the lead of press minister Mohamed Hakki and Egyptian ambassador Ashraf Ghorbal, were making impressive efforts to gain the ear of members of Congress and the administration.

A key figure in the new Arab prominence was Saudi Ambassador Ali Abdallah Alireza, who, according to Nick Thimmesch, in a May/June 1979 *Saturday Evening Post* article on Arabs in Washington, "has a reputation for being effective, energetic and savvy." Unlike his predecessors, Alireza has traveled around the country to make speeches and persuade businesses to invest in Saudia Arabia's massive development effort.

"The Arab nations have mobilized a vast network of influential lawyers, Washington lobbyists, public relations experts, political consultants and a host of other highly paid specialists" on behalf of their cause, commented a June 20, 1976, article in *Parade* magazine. Among them was Frederick Dutton, a well-known liberal Democrat who served in the Kennedy administration, hired by Alireza to serve as counsel and lobbyist for the Saudi embassy, reportedly at a $270,000 annual salary. The law firm of Clark Clifford, former Secretary of Defense, was paid $150,000 a year to represent the commercial interests of Algeria; and the law firm of former Senator J. William Fulbright, D-Ark., was receiving annual compensation of $25,000 for representing the interests of the United Arab Emirates as well as $50,000 annually from Saudi Arabia.

Another group mentioned in a June 24, 1979, *New York Times Magazine* article by Judith Miller ("The Arab Stake in America") was the U.S. Arab Chamber of Commerce, a private organization that has sponsored lobbying sessions — attended by Commerce Secretary Juanita M. Kreps and Treasury Secretary W. Michael Blumenthal — in several cities across the nation to promote U.S.-Arab trade.

Indeed, by mid-1979, it appeared that the Middle East lobbying scene in Washington had been substantially transformed, despite the small number of Arab-Americans and the rather late start of the Arab governments. "Until lately, the Arabs didn't even know where the Hill was," said Dutton. Now there seems to be an openness on the Hill. That is encouraging the development of an Arab lobby."

Commented Seth P. Tillman, former aide to Fulbright and a resident fellow at the American Enterprise Institute in Washington, "We have had a politically powerful pro-Israeli lobby in the United States for some 20 years, which has asserted that U.S. and Israeli interests are totally synonymous. Now, a pro-Arab lobby is beginning to emerge, and I believe that the interplay of lobbying by special interests, rather than merely by one side, may neutralize those interests and enable our national interests in the area to emerge."

"We have a lot of catching up to do," said NAAA's Richardson in June 1979. "The potential is there, but there's no product in political institutional terms. Our people and resources are strained, and we're still mainly reacting to events instead of initiating action. But our efforts will be helped when Congress sees us as a useful source of information. And that's beginning to happen."

COUNTRY PROFILES

LONGSTANDING STRUGGLE FOR NATIONAL SURVIVAL

Ever since its creation in 1948, Israel has been trying to impress on the Arabs that it had come to Palestine to stay and that the Jews had considered their age-old dream of a Jewish state on sacred soil to have come true. Not until 1979 did Israel have official recognition from an Arab state of its existence.

The recognition came from what had been Israel's most formidable Arab adversary and was negotiated by an Israeli leader who just two years earlier had been considered by many to be an unlikely candidate for peace honors. Ironically, he probably was the only one who could have done it.

On March 26, 1979, Israeli Prime Minister Menachem Begin sat down amidst pomp and circumstance on the lawn of the White House in Washington, D.C., and affixed his signature to a peace treaty with Egypt, worked out over 16 months under the aegis of U.S. President Jimmy Carter. The trek towards peace began Nov. 19, 1977, when Egyptian President Anwar Sadat stepped onto Israeli soil and told the Knesset, the Israeli parliament, he wanted to make peace with Israel.

A principal impetus for Sadat's initiative was his desire to regain the Sinai Peninsula, which Egypt had lost to Israel in the third of four wars they had fought. For Israel, Begin obtained peace with one of the nation's staunchest enemies. Although it still had to face the enmity of the other Arab states, the defection of Egypt from a previously united Arab goal of destroying Israel was a source of great comfort to the beleaguered Jewish state, about the size of New Jersey in a land of Texas-sized nations. Without Egypt's military support, the other Arab states were not considered much of a match for Israel.

As of 1979, the peace treaty with Egypt had not brought peace between Israel and other Arab states. In fact, the peace treaty with Egypt included an agreement to negotiate further over the two major issues left unsettled in the document signed on the White House lawn — the fate of the 25-mile-long Gaza Strip pointing at Israel from the Sinai and the fate of the West Bank of the Jordan River, which Israel insisted on calling by its Old Testament names of Judea and Samaria. Israel had captured the entire Sinai, West Bank and the Golan Heights on the Syrian border in the 1967 war with Egypt and the other Arab states. Israel appeared invincible in that war, but in the next conflict, beginning on Yom Kippur in 1973, Israel barely managed to hold onto its spoils. And in 1979 it was bargaining over two of them.

Ten weeks after the White House treaty signing, Israeli and Egyptian representatives, with Americans mediating, sat down at a bargaining table again to begin what some observers expected to be an even more grueling round of negotiations.

Internal Problems

Preoccupation with the Egyptian peace talks obscured other problems that Israel faced, ones that had become almost as urgent in mid-1979. In May 1977, after ruling for 29 years since the founding of Israel, the Labor government had been replaced by the right-wing, nationalist opposition,

Israeli Prime Minister Menachem Begin

the Likud, headed by Begin, a former underground leader in the fight to establish the Jewish nation.[1]

Begin had sacrificed some of his support in the Israeli parliament by signing the peace treaty and agreeing to bargain over the West Bank. The problems that led to his election in 1977 — a worsening economy, increases in taxes, inflation, unemployment, emigration and social unrest — still existed two years later and threatened to dissolve his coalition government. Polls showed he was in trouble with the electorate.

Israel's gross national product increased by only one per cent in 1977, compared with 2 per cent the previous year. Thirty per cent of the $13.2-billion gross national product in 1977 was tied to defense. The 1978 percentage was estimated to be closer to 40 per cent, partly because of projected costs of pulling military forces out of the Sinai and relocating bases during the three-year phaseout of Israeli control there.

The Israeli pound plummeted in relation to the U.S. dollar, from 10.5 pounds to a dollar in 1977 to 24 pounds to the dollar in 1979. Israelis remained among the most highly taxed people in the world, paying nearly half their income in taxes in the average brackets. Inflation was a major problem, running higher than 40 per cent in 1978 and expected to climb in 1979. For the first time, Israel had reason to worry about unemployment, with the rate running between 3 and 3.5 per cent in 1979.

---

1 Begin's history in the underground Irgun, which often resorted to terrorist tactics, is detailed in J. Bowyer Bell's *Terror Out of Zion* (St. Martin's Press: 1977) and also in his own book, *The Revolt*, written in 1948 and republished by Nash Publishing in Los Angeles in 1972. Begin was once asked how it felt to be the father of terrorism in the Middle East. His response: "In the Middle East? In the whole world!" (noted in "Book World," *The Washington Post*, June 26, 1977, p. E5).

Israel was still heavily dependent upon U.S. military and economic assistance. In return for the peace treaty, the United States in March 1979 agreed to give at least $3 billion in grants and loans to Israel over the next three years in addition to its existing aid program of $1.8 billion.

For Israel, giving up the Sinai meant giving up 15 per cent of the country's oil supply. Adding to its energy problems was the decision by the revolutionary government in Iran not to sell any more oil to the Jewish state and Israel's failure to obtain a firm commitment from Egypt for continued supplies of Sinai oil. Israel thus could become dependent on the oil-tight United States.

Dwight James Simpson, professor of international relations at San Francisco State University, pointed out another problem facing Israel — its population mix. If the trend of the 1970s continued, he said, Jews could be a minority in Israel by the year 2000 if Israel retained control of the West Bank and Gaza Strip.[2]

Signs of Stress

The strain showed in demographic figures. In 1974, the number of Israelis emigrating to other countries rose to 18,000, almost double the average annual exodus since the founding of the state. The number of immigrants in 1974 dropped to 32,000, compared with 55,000 in 1973. But the birth rate, indicating perhaps an instinct to preserve the nation, rose from 66,000 births in 1973 to 84,000 in 1974.

By 1977, official figures indicated that as many people were leaving the country as were coming. Unofficial figures showed the emigration rate in excess of the immigration rate. In January 1977, *The New York Times* reported that "a quarter of a century after the Zionist dream of a Jewish state was fulfilled, one out of every 10 Israelis [350,000] has left home" and about 300,000 reside in the United States. Though many of these Israelis insist they are only living abroad temporarily, most have probably left Israel for good, the *Times* reported. According to the Israeli consul general in New York, "They are living here but their soul is in Israel."[3]

There are 1.1 million Arabs living in the disputed territories of the Gaza Strip and the West Bank. Egypt wants the Gaza Strip back and autonomy for the West Bank Arabs, perhaps to allow them to form a Palestinian state of their own. Israel had refused to grant the West Bank full autonomy and has wanted to maintain overall control over the Arabs living there. There are another 600,000 Arabs living elsewhere within Israel, more than triple the number living in the same area in 1948. By comparison, despite rigorous efforts to increase Jewish population the number of Jews only quadrupled during the same period. Simpson reported that emigration of Jews from Israel has been increasing in recent years while immigration has decreased. By 1979, it barely exceeded emigration. The Jewish growth rate is less than 1.5 per cent, while the Arab growth rate is 3.7 per cent. The overall population of Israel is only 3.7 million and there are estimates that up to 400,000 Israelis are living abroad. Thus, Jews outnumbered Arabs only 2.6 million to 1.7 million.

One aspect of Israel in 1979 was not much different than in previous years. The Israeli Air Force still was conducting strafing missions across the northern border into Lebanon to retaliate against terrorist activities. In addition, Jews and Arabs residing in Israel were still getting into serious squabbles and the government was still constructing Jewish settlements within the occupied West Bank, even as negotiators sat down to determine the fate of the area.

Possibilities for Peace

The stalemate at the end of the 1973 war provided, many thought, the best opportunity yet to try to end the 25 years of hostilities between Israel and its Arab neighbors. But what would Israel's place be in a peaceful Middle East? Would it remain a tiny outpost of Western culture in the heart of the Moslem world? Or would it slowly be absorbed, like the medieval crusader states, in the civilization of the Middle East? Would the pre-Israeli pattern of relations between oriental Jews and Arab societies ultimately reassert itself? Or would Israelis play a leading role in the transformation of Arab societies?

Instead of attempting an overall settlement to the Arab-Israeli conflict after the 1973 war, Secretary of State Henry A. Kissinger embarked on a step-by-step approach involving what came to be termed "shuttle diplomacy." He eventually achieved two disengagement agreements in the Sinai between Egypt and Israel and a separation of forces agreement between Israel and Syria. But he was severely criticized for not capitalizing on the opportunity to attempt a comprehensive settlement, including a solution for the nagging Palestinian problem.

Former Under Secretary of State George Ball wrote in February 1976 of his "deep regret as I watched the United States turn its back on a serious effort to solve the problem in favor of a tactical maneuver that bought time at the expense of ultimate peace."[4] Journalist Edward Sheehan wrote that Kissinger achieved his success by avoiding "the very essence" of the problem, the Palestinians.[5]

During peace negotiations in the spring of 1975, the United States suspended consideration of Israel's new $2.5-billion aid request pending "reassessment" of its Middle East policies, exerting thinly veiled pressure on Israel to be more forthcoming with concessions to Egypt.

By the time the Carter administration took office in January 1977, there was general agreement that step-by-step diplomacy should be replaced with an effort for an overall settlement. But the questions concerning the form of such a settlement and how to reach agreement on it remained illusive and highly controversial.

And though Vice President Walter Mondale publicly assured Israel in June 1977 that "we do not intend to use our military aid as pressure on Israel," doubts remained about what forms of pressure the United States might again resort to if Israel refused to make the concessions decided necessary by the new Carter administration in Washington to achieve a peace settlement.

Constant wars in the past enabled Israelis to concentrate on urgent, less complicated questions. Indeed, the militancy of the Arab world in some ways helped Israelis avoid the ambiguities that would accompany any peace process.

European nations and Japan, heavily dependent on Arab oil, had grown increasingly impatient with Israeli occupation of Arab territories taken in the 1967 war. In June 1977, the European Economic Community formally went on

2 Dwight Simpson, "Israel After Thirty Years," *Current History*, January 1979.
3 James Feron, "The Israelis of New York," *New York Times Magazine*, 16, January 1977.
4 George Ball, "How not to handle the Middle East," *Atlantic Monthly*, February 1976.
5 See Edward F. R. Sheehan, *The Arabs, Israelis, and Kissinger* (Reader's Digest Press: 1976).

record supporting the creation of a "Palestinian homeland" and repeating its insistence that Israel withdraw from the territories occupied 10 years earlier. Third World countries began to show growing hostility in the United Nations. Only Bolivia, the Dominican Republic and the United States voted with Israel in unsuccessfully trying to prevent Yasir Arafat, head of the Palestine Liberation Organization, from being the first non-governmental representative to address the United Nations General Assembly.

Israel's reponse to its growing isolation was a reaffirmation of its tradition of emphasizing self-reliance. Digging in for what then Prime Minister Yitzhak Rabin foresaw as "seven lean years," the government devalued the Israeli pound by 43 per cent in November 1974, sharply curtailed the market for consumer goods and maintained even higher levels of military mobilization than before the war. Numerous small devaluations followed — often on a monthly basis — while Israel's military strength continued to increase.

For a short time, Israeli spirits were lifted by the July 4, 1976, raid on Entebbe Airport in Uganda by Israeli soldiers who freed 103 hostages being held by Palestinian terrorists. But such psychological lifts did not alter the basic political and economic realities of Israel's predicament.

Many felt the Israeli people, by choosing Begin as their leader, were preparing for a difficult time with the United States. Others saw Begin's victory as less of a positive vote for him and more of a protest vote against the Labor Party for its indecisiveness on both domestic issues and international matters. Still others saw Labor's defeat as caused by Israel's increasingly difficult economic problems and the series of scandals which just a month before the election brought about Prime Minister Rabin's resignation after revelation of his wife's illegal bank account in Washington, D.C., where he had served many years as ambassador. Veteran foreign affairs writer Tad Szulc suggested that the emerging outline of a Carter administration plan for a Middle East settlement that might eventually be imposed on Israel contributed to Begin's democratic coup d'etat.[6]

Israeli Politics

There were many early predictions that Begin's election would cause difficulties in Israel's relations with the United States. Writing on the Israeli government of 1978, Simpson said, "The Israeli political scene, never notable for its decorum, has begun to resemble (in the words of one close observer) a 'bearpit.' One of the contributing causes of the continuing high level of turmoil is the Prime Minister himself. Menachem Begin, a former terrorist, has an abrasive personality; his temper has a low boiling point; he seems utterly convinced of his own rightness; and he frequently manages to appear either patronizing or contemptuous of those who oppose his policies. In addition, Begin is in poor health; he has a chronic heart ailment and diabetes."[7]

Amos Perlmutter, American University professor and author of *Politics and the Military in Israel: 1967-1977*, wrote: "A political system that was already changing dramatically is now replete with bitterness and ironies. Begin, long one of the most uncompromising nationalists in the country, is suddenly accused of making almost traitorous compromises with Sadat, while moderates like Yigal Allon, the conciliatory former foreign minister, is in the

position of becoming one of Israel's leading militants. A new and profoundly powerful rejectionist coalition is emerging."[8]

Perlmutter noted that the Camp David negotiations in September 1978 split the Herut Party, the largest element in the ruling Likud coalition government. And the opposition Labor Party had never recovered from the rifts that led to its defeat in 1977, he said. The political situation in the Knesset was so volatile that Begin could not predict with any assurance that the long, dangerous and sensitive dealings at Camp David would be ratified in Israel. As it turned out, the parliament ratified the accord by an overwhelming 95-18 vote, but only after 28 hours of debate that revealed the acrimony and doubts within the Knesset.

Several times on the road from Camp David to the March 22 vote in the Knesset the settlement appeared to be breaking down, in part because of Begin's tough bargaining, failure by the Israeli Cabinet to approve what its negotiators had agreed to, and disagreement on both sides about how binding the negotiations at Camp David were on the rest of the talks and even about what was agreed to at Camp David. In December, even as Begin was to share the Nobel Peace Prize with Sadat, the entire process appeared doomed as Begin attempted to walk the fine line of reassuring Israelis about what he was not giving up while at the same time attempting to appear to U.S. and Egyptian negotiators to be willing to bargain. Intensive U.S. efforts, including a three-day Carter journey to the Middle East to practice his own brand of "shuttle diplomacy" brought about a last-minute agreement and Knesset ratification.

Israeli Settlements

In the aftermath of the treaty, Begin faced the possibility of more trouble with his Israeli countrymen than he had experienced with Sadat. The treaty called for removal of cherished Israeli settlements from the Sinai as the Israeli presence was phased out. Carter told a Sept. 28, 1978, press conference that the ban on new settlements that was agreed to at Camp David meant a ban on any new settlements in the West Bank and Gaza Strip while negotiations were going on and during the five-year progress toward self-government for the Arabs envisioned by the accords. Begin disagreed, saying the agreement to a ban on new settlements was valid only until the treaty was signed. Subsequently, the Israeli government allowed construction of new settlements on the West Bank to begin in June 1979. Arab land had to be confiscated for the settlements, and minor incidents between the Jews and Arabs threatened to put an unbearable strain on the already sensitive relations between the two peoples.

Zionist Background

Like the United States, Israel is a country founded and developed by immigrants from many different ethnic and cultural backgrounds. The Jewish population of Israel today is almost as hybrid as that of the United States. Since the founding of the state in 1948, more than 1.5 million immigrants have come to Israel from 101 countries. Israel encourages this "ingathering" of Jews from all parts of the world, counting on their common Jewish heritage to help cement their union with other Israelis—a task that presents serious difficulties. This devotion to "ingathering" is the es-

---

6 See "How Carter Fouled the Israeli Election," *New York* Magazine, 6 June 1977. A review of the situation leading up to Begin's victory is in Bernard Avishai, "A New Israel," *The New York Review*, 23 June 1977.

7 Simpson, op. cit.

---

8 Amos Perlmutter, "Dateline Israel: A New Rejectionism," *Foreign Policy*, Spring 1979.

sence of Zionism, which might be called the founding "religion" of the Israeli nation. But even Zionism is coming under question in the changing temper of modern Israel.

Zionism is rooted in the reformist zeal that swept over eastern Europe in the latter part of the 19th century. It emerged from a ferment of nationalist, socialist, populist and utopian ideas that were inflaming the youth of that time and place. As nationalists, the Jews were not unlike other minority groups within the Russian and Austro-Hungarian empires that chafed under foreign rule. The Jews had a special impetus, however, because of anti-Semitic persecutions.

Zionism began with a small group that in 1882 formed an organization called Lovers of Zion.[9] These young Jews conceived the idea of sending groups of colonists to Palestine, then a neglected backwater of the Ottoman Empire, to establish Jewish communities in the land of their forbearers. A pamphlet distributed at that time projected the rationale of the new movement: "Everywhere we are rejected," it stated. "We are pushed out from everywhere. We are considered aliens.... [But] Judea shall rise again. Let our own lives be an example to our people. Let us forsake our lives in foreign lands and stand on firm ground on the land of our forefathers. Let us reach for shovels and plows...."[10]

Palestine at that time had a Jewish population of around 25,000, mostly descendants of refugees from the Spanish Inquisition and pious pilgrims who had come to the Holy Land to pray and die. They were very poor, very religious, and lived closed in on themselves in the largely Moslem cities. The resident Jews looked with hostility on the new arrivals, whom they considered dangerous radicals and religious renegades, while the newcomers were equally repelled by a lifestyle that seemed to contain the worst aspects of the ghetto life from which they had fled.

Earliest Settlements

The new arrivals moved beyond the squalid cities to the sparsely populated coastal plains, "a silent, mournful expanse, ravaged by centuries of warfare, fever, piracy and neglect."[11] This was the ancient land of the Philistines. Ruins of antiquity lay under shifting sand dunes. Much of the area was malarial swampland, the result of clogged waterways. Despite the unpromising scene and the difficult climate, a succession of immigrants succeeded over the next few decades in founding several dozen communities. Land was purchased from absentee owners with funds that came largely from philanthropy, including large sums given by Baron Edmond de Rothschild in Paris. Many could not stand the rigors and left, but those who stuck it out managed to establish a viable agriculture, although they came to depend increasingly on Arab farm labor.

The settlement of Jewish Palestine, later Israel, was marked by a series of waves of immigration, known by the Hebrew word *aliyah*, meaning ascension (to Zion).[12] The first *aliyah*, 1882-1903, brought some 20,000-30,000 Jews to Palestine. The second *aliyah*, 1905-1914, which brought 35,000-40,000, was the formative one that set the tone for

the nation-to-come, the one that produced the first leaders of independent Israel.[13] These immigrants came as unattached young men and women, in their late teens or early 20s, burning with zeal to create a utopia. They believed that only through socialism could a society be created free of the evils of selfishness, materialism, exploitation and the aberrations that produced anti-Semitism. "What had so dismally failed in Russia (in the abortive revolution of 1905) some now hoped would succeed in one of the more destitute corners of the Ottoman Empire—a safe haven for Jews, and a new paradise to boot. A kingdom of saints, a new world purged of suffering and sin."[14]

Although not religious in the traditional sense, they were driven by an intense, near-mystical devotion to their cause. Working the soil for them was not merely a pioneering necessity, but a sacred mission. They scorned all luxury, wearing the plainest clothes and eating the simplest food.

Founding of Kibbutzim

"The immigrants of the second *aliyah* brought with them to Palestine not only their powerful ties to Jewish history and traditions as well as to contemporary political and social movements...in their countries of origin, but also ideologies and principles concerning the nature and institutions of the Jewish community and society they intended to create." This wave of immigrants "did in fact later become the political, social, economic, and ideological backbone of the Jewish community in Palestine, and large sectors of life in Israel today are organized around institutions created by immigrants arriving in the Second *Aliyah*."[15]

These were the founders of the kibbutz, which author Amos Elon has described as "the single most powerful cultural force of the entire Zionist enterprise." The first kibbutz was founded in 1910 on swampland near Lake Tiberias in the Jordan Valley; it was the cheapest land available. The new collective community was named Deganiah ("God's Wheat"). "Life was hell in this burning pesthole, and yet it was marvelously exciting. The average age of the group [of founders] was 20. They were like an extended family. They took their meals together in the communal dining hall and...talked and danced the hora and sang sad Russian songs until dawn."[16]

The kibbutz idea appealed to the most ardent idealists among the new pioneers, and soon other agricultural collectives of similar mold were established. Although the kibbutzim never held at any time more than 10 to 12 per cent of the Jewish population, they created the national ideal of the tough, vital, selflessly dedicated, sun-bronzed farmer-soldier and patriot. The kibbutz provided the nation's governing elite and some of its best soldiers. Tales of their heroism in defending Israel's borders and in its wars are legend; although only 4 per cent of the Israeli population has lived on kibbutzim in recent years, Kibbutzniks accounted for one-fourth of the fatalities in the Six-day War.[17]

Immigration

World War I brought Jewish immigration to a halt. Furthermore the Turkish regime, which was on the side of

9 From Zion, the name of a hill in Jerusalem on which King David's palace stood.

10 Amos Elon, *The Israelis: Founders and Sons* (Bantam edition: 1972), p. 92. The formal founding of the Zionist movement took place at an international congress held at Basel, Switzerland, in 1897, under the leadership of Theodore Herzl, an Austrian journalist whose book, *The Jewish State*, published in 1896, had a powerful influence in marshaling support for the Zionist idea.

11 Elon, *ibid.*, p. 109.

12 Detailed accounts of the various *aliyah* movements can be found in *Encyclopedia of Zionism and Israel* (Herzl Press, McGraw Hill: 1971).

13 Among them were David Ben Gurion and Ben Zvi, later prime minister and president.

14 Elon, op. cit., p. 137.

15 Judah Matras, "The Jewish Population: Growth, Expansion of Settlement and Changing Composition," *Integration and Development in Israel* (1970), S. N. Eisenstadt, Rivkah Bar Yosef, Chaim Adler, editors, p. 310.

16 Herbert Russcol and Margalit Banal, *The First Million Sabras* (1970), p. 57.

17 The kibbutznik's good performance as soldiers is attributed in part to the hardiness engendered by kibbutz life and in part to the communal methods of child rearing which emphasized love of the land and intense group-loyalty to one's peers.

the Central Powers, expelled many Jews who had come from Allied nations. Other Jews left voluntarily because of deteriorating economic conditions. During the war the Jewish population of Palestine dropped from 85,000 to 56,000. But a third *aliyah* soon got under way, encouraged by the Balfour Declaration of Nov. 2, 1917, in which the British government, by then the occupying power in Palestine, expressed sympathy for the Jewish dream of a homeland.

Between 1919 and 1923, the third *aliyah* brought 35,000 Jews to Palestine. They included mainly new contingents from Russia, similar in their drives and conditioning to the prewar pioneers.

A new wave—the fourth *aliyah*, 1924-1931, brought some 82,000 immigrants, mainly middle-class Jews from Poland. "An economic depression, combined evidently with anti-Semitism, touched off widespread economic, social and political sanctions and discrimination against the Jews in Poland and subjected them to increasing pressure toward emigration."[18] Another factor was newly enacted U.S. legislation restricting immigration from eastern Europe.[19] The new quotas enacted by Congress reduced the potential flow to the United States. This was also a period when Palestine's immigration from Asian and African countries rose from less than 5 per cent of the total during the third wave to 12 per cent during the fourth.

The fifth *aliyah*, 1932-1938, was massive; in all, 217,000 Jews came to Palestine in those years. The rise of Nazism in Germany and its expansionist moves in central Europe occasioned the first sizable influx of immigration to Palestine from Germany and Austria, as well as from Czechoslovakia, Hungary and Greece. The Nazi threat also accounted in large part for a renewed flow, totaling 91,000, from Poland. Unlike the pioneers, who were young, unattached and fired up about working on the soil, the *aliyah* of the 1930s included a number of settled middle-class families, headed by mature men who had made their mark in business and in the professions. Some of them came with appreciable amounts of capital. This group established a number of industries, commercial enterprises, financial organizations and cultural institutions that are still important in Israeli society.

Throughout the entire period of Jewish settlement, large numbers had left Palestine. Nevertheless by the end of 1938 the Jewish population had risen to 413,000. There followed a slowdown of immigration due to Arab demonstrations and a general strike in protest against the large influx of Jews. The British government, ruling Palestine under terms of a 1920 mandate from the League of Nations, responded to that protest by ordering a reduction in immigration quotas and restricting Jewish land purchases.

This policy, set forth in a government White Paper on May 17, 1939, remained in force throughout World War II. Nevertheless, 75,000 Jews entered Palestine during the war years, 29,000 of them coming in illegally. They were mainly Polish, German, Romanian and Czech, but they also came from the Soviet Union, Bulgaria, Hungary, Austria, Yugoslavia and Italy. Jewish immigration from Middle Eastern countries also rose. Menachem Begin, who became Israel's Prime Minister in 1977, reached Palestine in 1942

while in the Polish army. By the end of the war, the Jewish population of Palestine stood at 564,000.

The next wave drew mainly from the 200,000 homeless Jews—Russian, Polish and German—who were living in so-called "displaced persons" camps after World War II. In the years 1946-48, 61,000 came to Palestine, nearly one-half of them slipping through a blockade imposed by the British to halt further immigration.[20] The ban on immigration drew protests throughout a world haunted by the disclosure of Hitler's death camps, and provided an additional ingredient to fuel a three-sided civil war developing in Palestine among the Jews, British and Arabs. A hard-pressed Britain notified the United Nations in 1947 it could no longer continue its role in Palestine and withdrew its forces the following year. With the ending of the British mandate, Jewish Palestine declared its independence, took the name Israel and abolished all restrictions on Jewish immigration.[21] A census of November 1948 recorded a Jewish population of 716,678, of whom 35 per cent were native-born.

A mass immigration then began that lasted until 1951. Within three years the population doubled to 1.4 million, 75 per cent of it foreign-born. The Jews came not only from the displaced persons camps but from other locations in Poland and Romania, which had lifted restrictions on Jewish emigration. And for the first time there was a large flow from non-Western countries. "This immigration changed the character of the Jewish population of Israel considerably," Judah Matras has written. In 1977, more than half of Israel's population was from North Africa.

Post-World War II Immigration

Altogether in the 13-year period, 1948-1960, nearly one million Jews from 40 countries entered Israel to stay, and nearly one-half of them were from Asia and Africa. Together with a high birth rate, this flow accounted for a population growth in that period from 649,000 to 1.9 million. "The number of children under 10 years of age almost quadrupled, the Jewish population of Asian birth increased fivefold, and that of African birth increased 15-fold. Substantial previously unsettled areas of Israel were populated, the number of settlements more than doubled, and the rural population almost quadrupled."[22]

There has not since then been an immigration flow of this magnitude, although the stream continues, mainly from the Soviet Union. Despite the great emotional and financial support for Israel among American Jews, the exodus of Americans for settlement in Israel has always been modest, although it did pick up somewhat after the 1967 war.

From 1949 through 1972, a total of 25,797 American Jews emigrated to Israel, according to figures provided by the Israeli Embassy in Washington. Those who go there to settle may be given immigrant status, which may lead to Israeli citizenship, or some form of resident status.

In the years 1965 through 1968, 2,066 American Jews were given immigrant status; from 1969 through 1971, another 1,583; and in 1972, another 502. However, in 1969-71, a total of 12,920 American Jews were classified as potential immigrants—that is, they were given some sort of

---

18 Matras, op. cit., p. 311.

19 The Quota Act of 1920, revised and continued by the Immigration Act of 1924, imposed country-by-country quotas beyond the western hemisphere, greatly favoring emigrants from Britain, Ireland and Germany at the expense of most of the other.

20 The 1939 White Paper stated that after five years "no further Jewish immigration will be permitted unless the Arabs of Palestine are prepared to acquiesce in it." See "Palestine Crisis," *Editorial Research Reports*, 1948 Vol. I, p. 168.

21 Under the 1950 Law of Return, every Jew has the right to emigrate to Israel and to become a citizen of that country.

22 Matras, op. cit., pp. 320-321.

residence status after going to Israel. The figure for that category in 1972 was 3,361.[23]

Israel is now looking hopefully to the Soviet Union's three million Jews as the remaining large pool for supplying it with immigrants. A lowering of Soviet barriers to Jewish emigration accounted for an influx to Israel of more than 90,000 by the end of 1974. "We must prepare to absorb 250,000-500,000 newcomers in the next five years," said Minister of Immigration Nathan Peled in January 1973. "The final figure," he added, "depends largely on the policy of the Soviet Union." (Soviet policy, p. 54)

Unifying and Divisive Forces

The heavy Jewish immigration was a prime necessity for realization of the Zionist dream, but it has presented many problems and it accounts for many of the tensions in Israeli society today. Its basic contributions were in producing the desired Jewish majority and providing manpower for defense, for economic expansion and for colonizing empty areas of the country. The post-1948 immigration alone accounted for the founding of 500 villages. Recent emigres from the United States and the Soviet Union have been a particular boon because they have tended to be well-educated and to possess needed skills; 40 per cent of them are in the professions. The Americans also brought in moderate amounts of capital; in 1971 alone, according to the immigration minister, new arrivals accounted for an investment of $150-million in various enterprises.

Israel's efforts to court immigrants of this caliber have caused resentment among earlier settlers and native-born Israelis who do not enjoy the same advantages. Housing is a particular sore point because of its scarcity. Couples who have been on a waiting list for an apartment for many months or years find it unfair that the new arrivals are so promptly settled into new quarters. The oriental Jews, many of whom arrived penniless a decade or more earlier, recall that they were first quartered in tents, and even now many of them live with their families in crowded slums. There were also complaints that immigrant students were pushing native-born Israelis out of the universities. Immigrants' duty-free privileges for bringing in household goods added another grievance.

For the newly arrived Americans and Russians, on the other hand, the favored quarters given them were usually below the standard to which they were accustomed. There have been occasions when new arrivals from Russia have refused assignment to quarters in new towns or villages in development areas distant from the pleasures and excitement of the big cities. Israel apparently has its share of bored ex-urban housewives in fine, new, well-equipped homes, located in culturally barren "new towns."

Efforts to Equalize Schooling

Two institutions serve as the main vessels of Israel's melting pot—the schools and the army. The country provides 12 years of free, compulsory education. There are two types of public schools—general and religious. The anomaly of tax-supported religious schools in the public system of a secular state is a tribute to the power of a small but high-pressure ultra-orthodox religious minority that has always held the balance of power in a coalition government. In 1977 this religious minority gained more power than ever as part of the Begin coalition government. Zevulun Hammer, of the National Religious Party, became Minister of Education.

Basic curricula are the same in all schools, but the religious schools naturally stress the religious aspects, and they keep up the ancient rituals that sustained Jews over the many years of wandering and persecution in the Diaspora. Such schools serve to counteract the assimilationist effect of public schooling by perpetuating the religious, and often political, conservatism of their founders.

Parents may send their children to either type of public school—or to private school, some of which are run by various Christian denominations. There is little coeducation between Israeli Arabs and Jews. By 1972, the Arabs had 225 kindergartens, 277 elementary, 66 secondary and 25 postsecondary schools of their own, and there were 500 Arabs attending Israeli universities. Educational attainment of the Arab population is much lower than the norm, and the university dropout rate is high. Centralization of school administration has necessarily prevailed in the early years of nationhood, but efforts to decentralize are under way. Kibbutzim are free to operate schools in their own manner; these naturally make an effort to inculcate the young with the values of collectivization.

As in the United States, the schools have been set the task of attacking poverty and cultural alienation by equalizing educational opportunity for children from widely diverse home backgrounds. In the early years of the nation, the problem of the "educationally disadvantaged" was overlooked in the scramble to provide the physical facilities and staff to handle the sudden accretions of school population. About 15 years ago, the schools began developing special programs for children known as te'unei tipuah, meaning "requiring care." These were chiefly children of poorly educated or illiterate parents who had lived in poverty in Moslem countries before emigrating to Israel. Many suffer a language barrier in the schools. Hebrew is the official language of the country and therefore the language of its schools.

The language problem apparently has had a direct effect on the literacy rate in Israel, averaging a high 87.6 per cent overall. The Arab population is only 64 per cent literate while the Jewish population is 90 per cent literate, a sign that the Israeli education ministry has not been able to break through the language barrier.

An indication of the failure is the decline of school attendance among children from Moslem countries as they reach higher grades. This group constitutes 63 per cent of kindergarten attendance, 60 per cent primary, 43 per cent secondary and 13 per cent university attendance. Tuition is lowered according to family income, even dropped, to encourage this group to stay in school beyond the compulsory-attendance years. University tuitions have gone up considerably for everyone, however, in recent years.

The problem is not only economic but cultural. In some of the smaller towns and villages, where nearly the entire population is of Moslem-country origin, there is no opportunity for integrating children of Eastern and Western European and American background in the classroom. Ex-

---

23 The two organizations chiefly responsible for raising funds for Israel in the United States are the United Jewish Appeal and the Israel Bond Organization. UJA headquarters in New York is a tax-exempt organization under United States laws. It raises money for Jewish causes within the United States as well as contributions on a "people-to-people" basis for rescue, rehabilitation and recovery programs within Israel. Accordingly, UJA made direct contributions of $250-million in 1973 and $500-million in 1974 within Israel. The bond organization sells bonds and securities for the state of Israel, and funds are used for development programs, a spokesman for Israel Bond headquarters in New York said. These bond sales provide significant sums toward the overall development budget—for agriculture, industry, roads, civil aviation, harbors, refineries, pipelines, etc. Recent figures showed bond sales of $502-million in 1973 and $281-million in 1974.

perienced teachers are reluctant to serve in these cultural backwaters. The sense of alienation of these people from the Israeli mainstream therefore tends to deepen. Educational television, recently introduced, is being directed toward ameliorating this situation.

Army Life, Role of Women

Army service has been a welding influence because it is a near-universal experience and because the army itself, as an institution, stands so high in the regard of the people. There have been, however, concerns raised within Israel about the dedication of the current Israeli fighting forces, coupled with a recent change in service for women that critics said would become a draft dodger's dream and could destroy the entire idea of equal service that had made the Israeli army an effective fighting force.

The change was a fulfillment of a promise that Begin had made to a minor party in order to get the necessary support he needed to form a coalition government in 1977. All Israeli youth, of both sexes, are eligible for military service at age 18. Physical or educational handicaps are not necessarily a barrier to acceptance. Men serve three years and women for two years. The only exceptions had been for religious scruples or, for women, marriage.

The religious scruples exemptions were widened under the change, barely passed by the Knesset. In effect, the changes allowed a woman to avoid military service if she avows Jewish orthodoxy, such as keeping a kosher diet.

The Israeli army is unusual in that it depends more on the individual motivation of the soldier than on ritualistic forms to maintain discipline. It is egalitarian in spirit; there is little saluting and no hazing of green recruits. Everyone enters as a private. Officers come up from the ranks and are often addressed by their first names. They wear minimal insignia, and all uniforms are cut from the same cloth, though in recent years more medals and awards have been given out.

Army service does not have as alienating an effect on recruits as it might in other nations. Israel is a small country. Soldiers thus serve close to home and get frequent passes for home visits. The hitchhiking soldier is a familiar weekend sight. Furthermore, the army continues to be an important part of his life pattern well into middle age. He remains a member of the reserves until he is 55; as such he is back in the army for about 40 days every year and is subject to call-ups for emergencies at any time.

The generation gap in Israel has taken the odd form of a cooling off rather than a heating up of passionate rebellion in the young. The women's liberation movement, as it is known in the United States, has made little headway. Equal rights for women are written in the law and are regarded as a truism in Israel. But it was the pioneer woman of the past who shucked off the cares of homemaking and child rearing on the kibbutz to toil as an equal beside pioneer man. Young women in Israel today feel equal, there is an easy camaraderie between the sexes and career opportunities are open. But most of them opt for marriage and babies in their early 20s, and their employment tends to be in service jobs traditionally reserved for females. Even in the army their function is to do work that releases the male soldier for combat.[24] Although one of the nation's best

known prime ministers, Golda Meir, was a woman — a pioneer woman—there have been few others of her sex in government.

For many years, the old guard has complained of a decline in idealism among Israeli youth. The complaint is that they are too concerned about "making good" in their personal lives. Actually the young are impatient with the oft-told tales of their elders about the heroic deeds of the pioneer past, and especially with sentimental nostalgia for the good old days. And many do not want to hear more about the holocaust, when so many Jews went passively to their deaths. "Why didn't our army save them?" an Israeli child asked when told of the Jewish tragedy.

This is a question from the new Israeli, confident, secure in his nationhood and no longer marked by the emotional hang-ups of the minority Jew. It has taken three generations, David Schoenbrun wrote, to produce the true Israeli. The early settlers, though they rebelled against the ghetto mentality, were nevertheless marked by it and inevitably passed on some of the malaise to their children. But the grandchild of the early settlers cannot conceive of anything but a free Israeli living on his own land. He is patriotic, but his attitude is "Why the fuss?" He is not interested in the old philosophic issues over which the pioneers wrangled—questions such as "What is a Jew?"

The change in outlook may spell the end of a distinctive style of Jewish humor, just as the adoption of Hebrew as the national language tossed aside the highly expressive Yiddish as a language of the ghetto Jew. "Sabra humor hardly excels in the kind of biting yet humane self-irony that is the hallmark of traditional [Yiddish] humor," wrote Elon. "It is cooler, a bit distant, or abstract, in the shaggy-dog style. In his humor, the sabra is critical, not of himself, but of the pathos of the older generation."[25]

Strains in the Social Order

There are strains in Israeli society that spell far more serious trouble ahead than the so-called generation gap, which is actually more a matter of manner than a clash of values. Three situations are potentially explosive. One is the social-cultural-economic gap between the oriental Jews and the so-called Ashkenazi, whose background and outlook is Western. Another is the tension between the ultra-religious and the secular Israelis, which has not abated over the years of their testy coexistence. The third has to do with Israel's relations with the Arabs, both those within Israeli borders and the Arab world outside which has sworn eternal enmity to the very existence of a Jewish national state. This situation has become more pressing because of the issue of what to do about the "administered" — occupied — territories.

The tension between the oriental and Western Jew is sometimes compared with that of the black and white people in the United States. This is partly because the oriental Jew is darker skinned than the European Jew and falls low on every modern index of social well-being —income, education, occupational status, quality of housing, etc. The black-white analogy was stressed when a group of dissident oriental Jews took the name of Black Panther and began to demonstrate in the classic manner of civil rights activists. Like American blacks, the oriental Jews claim the system is stacked against them.

Concessions to religious orthodoxy have put a curiously theocratic overlay on secular Israel. Civil marriage is for-

---

24 Army chieftains told journalist David Schoenbrun that the army did not press induction on women who did not want to serve or whose families objected, as many religious families do. Although the army takes in low I.Q. or near-illiterate males and gives them basic education, it does not have enough teachers to give intensive education to all, "so we don't take women if they're a problem."—David Schoenbrun, *The New Israelis* (1973), pp. 144, 153.

25 Elon, *op. cit.*, p. 321.

bidden, in effect banning mixed marriage. Divorce laws are strict. Blue laws close down many facilities, including public transit, on the Sabbath. But the effect of such laws is hardly more than a nuisance compared with the pressures of the religious minority on major policies such as those pertaining to the occupied territories. The religious orthodox are chauvinist about this question and unbudging in their righteousness. They claim a Talmudic justification for holding on to the acquired lands, a belief also held by Prime Minister Begin. Religious influence in Israel substantially increased when the Begin government took power in June 1977. Begin's Likud Party relied on two smaller religious parties to form a government. The religious parties demanded certain Cabinet seats and social reforms. For the first time in Israel's history the National Religious Party was assigned the Ministry of Education. This meant that Israel's political system allowed a minority of 15 to 20 per cent to determine many ways of life for Israel's secular majority of 70 to 80 per cent.

All issues and all tensions come back to the Arab question. Despite the terrorist attacks by Palestinian guerrillas and the retaliatory attacks on bordering Arab countries, Israel has maintained a relatively peaceful relationship with the Arabs within its borders. The Israeli policy is to try to integrate the Arabs into the Israeli economy, winning their cooperation by the demonstrated benefits to be gained by a rising standard of living while allowing them to maintain a separate cultural identity as a minority within the Jewish state. As it has worked out, the booming Israeli economy has come to depend more and more on Arab labor. To some Israelis, the dependence on Arabs to do the kind of manual labor the pioneers once gloried in is a negation of the Israeli ethos and the beginning of decadence.

But the relationship with "Israel's Arabs" has been questioned in recent years. Demonstrations in March 1976 spread from the occupied West Bank into Israel proper. There were six deaths of Israeli Arabs that month.

Increasingly, it seems, the once docile Arabs of Israel are identifying as Palestinians, seeing themselves aligned on political and national matters with other Arabs, and especially with the West Bank Palestinians.[26]

"Deep mistrust underlies the entire relationship between Israeli Jews and the country's Arab minority," CBS News reported at the time of the March demonstrations. "Most Israeli Arabs, as a result of Israel's policy of unofficial apartheid, live apart in their decaying and neglected villages, ignored by the Jewish minority.... Every Arab citizen of Israel knows that at some point, no matter how qualified he may be, his path will be blocked by a closed door, that there's a line he cannot cross."[27]

This situation with the Arabs has not helped Israel's world image as a thriving democracy. Chaim Weizmann, Israel's first president, was quoted as saying in November 1947, the day after the U.N. vote to establish a Jewish state, "I am certain that the world will judge the Jewish state by what it shall do with the Arabs." Beginning in 1967, Israel found itself not just having an Arab minority to deal with, but in control of some 1 million Arabs in the occupied territories. Israel's occupation of these Arab-claimed lands remained a central element in the continuing Arab-Israeli conflict.

Contributing to the strains in the relationship between the Israelis and the Arabs were reports that emerged in the late 1970s of Israeli mistreatment of Palestinian Arabs.

A *Sunday Times* story in June 1977 alleged that "Torture of Arab prisoners is so widespread and systematic" in the occupied territories "that it cannot be dismissed as 'rogue cops' exceeding orders. It appears to be sanctioned as deliberate policy."[28] Israel vehemently denied the charges in a detailed, case-by-case report. And the *Sunday Times* did acknowledge that "Very few if any of the Arab countries would emerge unstained from a comparable inquiry into methods used there by police and prison authorities." Still, there remained reports of brutal treatment and suppression.

West Bank Occupation

After the signing of the peace treaty with Egypt, the future of the area known as the West Bank (and also the Gaza Strip located along the coast some 35 miles south of Tel Aviv) remained an unresolved problem in Israel. Dozens of Israeli settlements already dotted the area at the signing of the treaty. In defiance of what the United States and Egypt thought were bans on any more settlements, a Zionist official announced plans for 20 more in five years, and overnight construction of several settlements soon after emphasized Israel's determination to hold onto the West Bank.

For his part, Begin has shown no erosion of his determination, stressed during his election campaign, to hold onto the West Bank (Samaria and Judea) as historical and sentimental rights of the Israelis. The West Bank never legally belonged to Jordan, Begin believed, so Israel took nothing from Jordan in the 1967 war and therefore was not obligated to give anything back. His view was that the 1947 partition of Palestine gave that area to the Palestinians. Jordan's illegal annexation of the West Bank, however, prevented a Palestinian state from ever being legally formed, so as long as Israel occupies the area, it can decide the area's fate.

In the peace talks, Israel agreed to discuss the possibility of granting the Palestinians self-government over the most mundane portions of life on the West Bank, and to pull Israeli troops out of the section. But Israeli citizens would be allowed to move freely within the area, buy land and establish settlements. Under no circumstances would Israel accede to creation of a Palestinian state there.

The political impasse over the West Bank could not be blamed entirely on Israel's intransigence, however. Jordan, under pressure from the other Arab states, refused to discuss the matter with Israel, repeating its claim that Israel occupied its territory illegally. And the Palestine Liberation Organization (PLO), a terrorist group that has harassed Israel for several years, had not accepted the existence of a Jewish state, and in turn, has not been recognized by Israel. In fact, one Israeli negotiator in the talks with Egypt was forced by his government to "clarify" a statement he had made referring to "the PLO." He meant to say "the Palestinians," he said.

Secret meetings have been held in Paris between PLO members and Israeli officials formerly associated with the Labor Party, but little has come of them. So even if Israel decided to rid itself of the West Bank and even of the Gaza Strip, the question would remain, to whom would it give

---

26 For background on Israel's Arab minority see Sabri Jiryis, *The Arabs in Israel* (Monthly Review Press: 1976).

27 Tom Fenton reporting from Israel, CBS Evening News, 29 March 1976.

28 "Israel and Torture," *Sunday Times* (London), 19 June 1977.

Statistics on Israel

Area: 7,993 square miles.

Capital: Jerusalem; Tel Aviv is the diplomatic capital recognized by the United States.

Population: 3,689,000 (1978 est.)

Religion: Predominantly Judaism; Arab minority is largely Moslem; also Christian Arabs who are chiefly Greek Catholic and Greek Orthodox.

Official Language: Hebrew. Arabic is spoken by 15 per cent of the population. English is widely used.

GNP: $13.2-billion, $3,666 per capita (1977 est.).

them? And there was not even universal agreement in Israel that it should hold onto the West Bank. Yehoshafat Harkabi, for instance, one of Israel's leading Palestinian experts, stated in March 1977, "I personally would like to see Israel get rid of the West Bank. It's corrupting our soul."[29]

The Economy and Preparations for War

Within weeks of the treaty signing, the U.S. Congress approved a $1-billion authorization bill as the first of several loans and grants to Israel for its military needs, underscoring the reality that even though Israel had signed a peace treaty, the dominance that military needs had on its economy had not abated. And despite a concerted effort to become self-sufficient in weapons production during the past several years, the congressional action underscored Israeli dependence on the United States for its weapons and supplies.

But military needs did not comprise the only Israeli dependence on U.S. funds. In its first 30 years of existence, Israel received more than $12-billion in military and civilian aid from the United States. Half of that was in the form of grants, not to be repaid. The measure following the treaty authorized $800-million in grants for defense items and building air bases in Israel to replace two given up in the Sinai under the treaty agreement and $200-million in military sales loans. Israel already had an arrangement to buy $2.2-billion in defense goods and services from the United States.

Although it had been assumed for several years that Israel had developed the capacity for producing nuclear weapons, the nation never confirmed that it had. It was no secret, however, that Israel had developed into an arms supplier nation, expecting to increase its income from arms sales from $500-million in 1976 to $1-billion in 1978. But there was a limit to what Israel could do for itself, as *The Washington Post* noted in a 1977 article. "It is not possible for Israel, with its limited resources, to contemplate forever matching the Arab world, tank for tank, and plane for plane [Foreign Minister Moshe] Dayan has advocated a 'two-layer' military capability. 'Conventional weapons of a limited number' and a 'nuclear capability.' "[30]

The Jerusalem Post, in May 1977, listed fighter planes, machine guns, tanks, missile boats, mortars, and all kinds of ammunition among Israeli production.[31] This need for self-sufficiency grew in part, the *Post* said, from concern that American aid to Israel could not be counted on indefinitely. "Any Israeli who expects the U.S. to continue pumping $2-billion per year into Israel — mostly for arms — is living in a dream world," the newspaper said. It quoted one source as saying, "The bubble is going to burst, and we have to ensure that our security is not totally jeopardized when it happens."[32]

Israelis could take solace, however, that as much as the peace treaty committed Israel to link its future with Egypt, it also tied the United States irrevocably to Israel's well-being. President Carter told Congress in a speech following the Camp David talks that the Middle East was strategically vital to the United States. "That is why we cannot be idle bystanders, why we have been full partners in the search for peace," he said.

English author Henry Fairlie, writing in the generally pro-Israeli *New Republic* weekly, said that "if America does not ensure the survival of Israel, the American people will endure a despondency of spirit beside which the defeat in Vietnam will appear as one restless night; not merely because America helped create the nation, but because the invisible Jew would once again be on their backs. The Jew has to have a nation, in order for us not to see him where he is not."[33]

The Future

Though Israel's problems have multiplied enormously since the pre-1967 war period, the Zionist vision of a Jewish state remains alive and strong, regardless of any treaties that might be signed with former enemies.

Israelis clearly voted for change when they voted for Begin in 1977. He brought a considerable change of style, policies and beliefs. For decades, Labor Party leaders had condemned Begin, for both his personal history and his policies. David Ben-Gurion, in fact, was said never to have spoken directly to Begin in the Knesset, but only to have referred to him with loathing as the leader of the opposition.

Some observers saw Begin as a determined Zionist with an uncompromising background who would nevertheless modify his positions on becoming prime minister. And when he accepted territorial and political compromises, many pointed out, there would not be any major right-wing opposition to challenge him as would have been the case had Labor retained power. No doubt, after two years of Begin's government and a treaty with Egypt, many of these observations had proved correct.

Begin, generally believed to be inflexible, began showing signs of flexibility almost as soon as he took office. The tough bargainer he turned out to be could be viewed as no more than apropos for a nation that had been struggling more than 30 years for survival and would have to continue struggling even after signing a peace treaty with its most threatening foe.

29 *Christian Science Monitor,* 8 March 1977.
30 *Washington Post,* 30 April 1977, p. A16.

31 Hirsh Goodman, "The Army Imbroglio," *Jerusalem Post International Edition,* 31 May 1977, p. 12.
32 Ibid.
33 *The New Republic,* 28 May 1977.

SHAH'S 37-YEAR REIGN COMES TO AN END

After months of civil disturbances, mass demonstrations and crippling strikes, Shah Mohammed Reza Pahlavi left Iran Jan. 16, 1979, for an "extended vacation," bringing to an end his 37-year reign. The Shah, long championed by the United States as a guardian of stability in the turbulent Middle East, left behind a country in chaos — a populace steeped in Islamic tradition but swept by the winds of modernization — a state without authority; an economy in shambles; rival factions battling for supremacy.

Within several weeks the Shah's monarchy had been replaced by religious rule, called an "Islamic republic" by the nation's new leader, a 77-year-old doctrinaire Shiite Moslem, the Ayatollah Ruhollah Khomeini. The ayatollah (or Moslem leader), having been in exile since Moslem-led anti-Shah protests in 1963, had made no secret of his intentions for Iran. In an interview published in December in the London-based magazine *The Middle East*, Khomeini had stated: "The purpose of a future Islamic republic — and it is the will of the Iranian people — will be to eliminate Western influence in our country. By the same token, our purpose is to break the hold of Western domination, in all its forms, in Iran. This Western influence is found in all walks of Iranian life. Since the entire Iranian nation has risen up against this state of affairs, nobody can now expect this movement to be stopped."

And from the moment of his triumphant return to Iran — when he was greeted by an estimated million persons lining his route from the airport to central Teheran — Khomeini set out to achieve his goals.

The new government acted through edicts issued by Khomeini from his headquarters at the holy city of Qum, about 80 miles south of the capital, Teheran. Orders came down to reimpose Islamic customs on the Iranians who had been steadily assimilating Western ways. Khomeini would have them eschew everything from Western forms of justice, independence from religious rule and women's rights to alcohol, pork and movies. He also moved to break the strong ties that bound the Shah's government so closely to the United States, the very epitome of Western culture. Long before his fall, the Shah had been labeled by dissidents as the "American Shah."

"The purpose of a future Islamic republic . . . will be to eliminate Western influence in our country."

—Ayatollah Ruhollah Khomeini

But in trying to shake off all vestiges of Westernization, the Khomeini government was, in fact, trying to overturn customs the Iranians had adopted during the 40 years since the Shah's father began the Westernization push over the opposition of the Moslem religious leaders. And they were customs that would not die easily. Khomeini's wish that women resume wearing dark veils (chadors) and foresake Western dress led to street demonstrations by women, forcing Khomeini to back off for the moment. There were other signs of disenchantment among moderates, liberals, leftists and secular groups in Iran as the euphoria of the Shah's abdication and Khomeini's return began to wear off.

On June 2 part of the influential and long-banned political group that had aided Khomeini in the overthrow issued a public letter rebuking Khomeini. Contrary to his promise to stick to ecclesiastical affairs, the open letter of the National Democratic Front, a splinter of the National Front, said, "Your idea is one of intermingling clergy and politics. That is fine, but being a clergyman you will not accept any hows and whys because that would be going against the will of God. Thus, the nation will not have the freedom to voice grievances. Isn't this dictatorship? Criticisms get crushed immediately by the issuance of an order from the office of the Imam [the leading ayatollah]."

The letter continued: "Why do people, in the name of religion, threaten writers and stop publications, burn bookshops, remove teachers because of following some ideology? They have even brought about discord through the radio and television which gives false news and provocative ideas." It added, "every problem from meat, electricity and water to the more important internal and foreign policies is under your discretion. . . . It is our moral and humanitarian duty that we should fight against all excesses and not let tyranny overwhelm us yet again."

A tug of war was going on at the time between the clique of Khomeini operatives known as komitehs who were running revolutionary courts and councils and performing other government tasks in the name of Islam, and the government of Mehdi Bazargan, 73, installed by Khomeini as the prime minister of the post-revolutionary government to deal with the affairs of state. Bazargan also voiced his disenchantment with Khomeini.

A primary stimulus for the revolution supposedly had been the excesses of the Shah's dreaded secret police force, SAVAK, generally believed to have held upwards of 100,000 political prisoners. Stories of brutal torture, repression and death at the hands of SAVAK fanned anti-Shah sentiment.

But in the first four months of Khomeini's rule, there were reports of the execution of several hundred persons, most connected with the Shah government or SAVAK, and the imprisonment of thousands of others. The trials often were hasty, secret and presided over by the komitehs and outside the control of the Bazargan government. The death penalties were carried out within hours, with no right of appeal. The Khomeini people replied to critics that they were operating under Islamic law, not Western justice.

Several government officials, including vital oil ministers, had resigned by that time in protest of the subservience of the Iranian government in Teheran to the komitehs. Leftist groups began voicing discontent with Khomeini.

And there were protests outside the country. The U.S. Senate adopted a resolution condemning the summary executions. U.N. Secretary-General Kurt Waldheim and Amnesty International also protested.

In a national referendum, only the second in Iran's history (the first had been held in 1963 by the Shah to approve his "White Revolution" of modernization) held the end of March 1979, 97 percent of the Iranian people approved the "Islamic Republic." A new constitution, to replace the one in force since 1906 and to embody many Islamic laws, was promised the people.

The Iranian people went to the polls in early August 1979 to choose an assembly to draw up the new constitution. The assembly was to meet later in the month and ratify the new constitution within 30 days. The constitution was then to be presented to the populace for their approval. This was to be followed by the election of a parliament, which was then expected to elect Iran's president.

According to news reports, early unofficial returns indicated that candidates of Ayatollah Khomeini's Islamic Republican Party had won a majority of the seats that had been decided as of Aug. 5, 1979.

Internal Dissension

The economy in Iran was still stagnant, with unemployment reaching 3.5 million, or more than 30 percent of the labor force. An estimated 200,000 persons marched through Teheran on May 1 to protest that situation. The Khomeini-Bazargan government also faced unrest in the center of the oil-producing section of Iran along the Persian Gulf and the border with Iraq.

As in any other religion, the Shiite sect of Islam had its conservative and liberal factions and all shades between. At about the same time secular interests were causing him trouble, Khomeini also faced dissension from other ayatollahs in Iran.

All this occurred within days of massive demonstrations set for June 5, 1979, to commemorate Khomeini's jailing in 1963 by the Shah on charges he was fomenting a rebellion. Mass demonstrations had taken place in 1963, but turned bloody as thousands were killed in the suppression by government troops.

At the 1979 demonstrations, Khomeini delivered a speech warning opponents of the ruling Moslem clergy that they would be destroyed just as the Shah was destroyed if they persisted.

The Shah's Legacy

Part of Khomeini's problems in mid-1979 were the direct result of actions taken by the Shah, most of them during the decade of the 1970s. The Shah had used his nation's oil riches to build Iran into an influential nation. But he also knew that the known oil reserves in Iran would be depleted by 1990 at the rate of production his oil wells were pumping.

As the world's second largest oil-producing nation, Iran did have powerful influence in the Organization of Petroleum Exporting Countries (OPEC) of which it was one of the few non-Arab members. The Shah was able to wield that power following the 1973 war in the Middle East and the ensuing oil embargo that OPEC nations imposed on Israeli supporters. That began the spiral of oil price increases that continued right through his fall from power. Before October 1973, Iran's oil revenues were $2.5 billion a year. Five years later, the revenues were $20.5 billion and the government was projecting annual revenues of $25.7 billion through 1983.

As oil consumption by Western industrialized nations grew, so did their dependence on OPEC nations and thus so grew the Shah's power and influence. According to Central Intelligence Agency figures, the United States depended on Iran for 9.1 percent of its crude oil imports in August of 1978, compared with 5.9 percent in September 1973. During the same period, Britain's dependence grew slightly from 16.5 percent to 16.8 percent; West Germany from 10.8 to 21.1, France 7.8 to 12.9 and Italy from 11 to 12.7. Japan, during the same period, looked elsewhere for its supply, dropping its dependence on Iran from 31.9 to 16.4 percent.

The Shah used his nation's oil income to buy into Western economies. He arranged a $100 million deal with Germany's legendary Krupp empire for a 25 percent interest in Krupp's steel and engineering division and made a similar deal for partial control of power generating machinery manufacturer Deutsche Babcock and Wilcox, A.G.

The Shah made other deals to buy into ventures in most parts of the world. He even considered making a $300 million loan-purchase investment in then-ailing (partially because of high fuel prices) Pan American World Airways. That deal was dropped.

The United States had been a major source of imports for Iran. U.S. exports to Iran increased about sevenfold from 1973-78. They included about $200 million in military goods and $600 million in commercial trade in 1973, rising to $2 billion military and $3.6 billion commercial in 1978. At the time of the Shah's fall, Iran owed $7.2 billion to foreign leaders, including $2.2 billion to U.S. banks.

Never realized, of course, were the Shah government's projected revenues and expenditures for the five-year period from 1979 to 1983. According to Theodore H. Moran, a former member of the State Department Policy Planning Staff, the government had projected revenues of $42.1 billion per year during that period, $25.7 billion from oil and gas. Its borrowing would have been down to $2.1 billion during the period, from the $4.5 billion in the 1977-78 budget.[1]

Moran said the government planned to allocate its revenue in four principal areas: $13.5 billion on economic development projects (such as a Teheran subway and nuclear power plants), $12.6 billion on defense (the 1977-78 budget was $12.6 billion for economic and $8 billion for defense), $10.1 billion for social welfare, and the rest in the general and miscellaneous category, about equal to 1977-78.

Regardless of how they were to be earmarked, the figures showed that the Shah's government was projecting a dependence on oil and gas revenues at 61 percent, up slightly from the 59 percent they comprised in the $34.1 billion in revenues budgeted in 1977-78.

Even under an austerity budget that had been planned as a fallback, Moran pointed out, revenues from the oil and gas exports would have to remain at no less than 4 million barrels a day. Not until June 1979 when Khomeini was undergoing his own severe test did the production reach

---

1 Theodore H. Moran, "Still Well-Oiled," *Foreign Policy*, Spring 1979, p. 27.

that level. And that was still far less than the nearly 6 million barrels a day that were being pumped out of the Iranian oil fields before strikes shut down the wells late in 1978 and helped contribute to the Shah's fall. A 3.8 percent price increase in May 1979, coupled with previous increases under the Shah and agreed-upon OPEC hikes, assured revenue nearly equal to the revenues realized from pumping 6 million barrels the previous year, however.

But the spring unrest among the Arabs in the Iranian oil fields demonstrated how vulnerable Iran's continued oil production was and, in turn, how vulnerable any Iranian leadership was as long as it depended that much on one resource.

Broadening the Base

The Shah had been impatient to transform his country from an impoverished agricultural land almost totally dependent on oil to an industrialized nation that, after the oil was gone, would be able to maintain its new living standards.

The Shah decreed that Iran's income from other sources should equal its oil income within 10 years, leading to a government prediction that by 1988 Iran would have a gross national product as large as France's was in 1975 and larger than Britain's, although some economists viewed such projections with skepticism. Iran's 1978 GNP was estimated at $89 billion, not even one-fifth as large as France's, but impressive nonetheless, since it had been only $15 billion six years earlier.

Western governments, faced with huge new payments deficits to oil-producing countries, were more than eager to cash in on Iran's development program. Non-military imports to Iran more than trebled during 1974, to $10 billion. The United States negotiated a $15 billion, five-year trade pact under the aegis of Secretary of State Henry Kissinger who called it "the largest agreement of this kind that has ever been signed by any two countries."

Massive sales of weapons to Iran also eased the U.S. balance-of-payments burdens imposed by higher oil prices. The Shah's huge military budget rose 44 percent in 1974 to a total of nearly $8 billion, about 60 percent of its purchases from the United States. Cash sales of military goods from the United States jumped from $472.6 million in fiscal year 1972 to nearly $2.2 billion the following year. In 1974, the sales nearly doubled, to $4.3 billion. Sales varied since then, but from 1973 through 1978, Iran bought more than $19 billion worth of military equipment just from the United States. Iran became the single largest purchaser of U.S. arms. And in that six-year period, the arms purchases from the United States alone equaled half the revenues the Iranian government had budgeted in the last year of the Shah.

Prior to the Shah's fall, the United States had agreed to sell Iran an additional $12 billion in arms. A small amount of that had been delivered by early 1979. More than $7 billion was subsequently canceled by mutual agreement, primarily at the behest of Iran's new revolutionary government, with the remaining $4 billion worth subject to negotiation.

Strategic Concerns

Why did Iran want such an arsenal? It was not enough to worry Russia, and more than enough for defense against Iran's other neighbors. Pakistan, wounded by the loss of Bangladesh, was too concerned about India to make trouble

---

Statistics on Iran

Area: 636,293 square miles.
Capital: Teheran.
Population: 35,000,000.
Religion: 98 percent Moslem, with great majority members of the Shia sect; 5% of Sunni sect. Minority groups include Jews, Bahais, Zoroastrians and Christian Armenians and Assyrians.
Official Language: Persian or Farsi. Kurdish, forms of Turkic, Arabic spoken by leading minorities.
GNP: $89 billion (1978 est.), $2,100 per capita (1978 est.).

---

for Iran, with whom in any case it had friendly relations and common interests. Turkey had no recent or outstanding dispute with Iran and was preoccupied with Cyprus. Afghanistan was too underdeveloped to challenge Iran; Iraq had only a third of Iran's population; the other Persian Gulf states were much smaller. In the longer perspective of Iranian history, the Shah's fascination with modern weapons may have found some justification. The country was full of minorities — Arabs, Turks, Kurds, Qashqais, Baluchis, Turcomans, Lurs — with turbulent pasts and no deep love for the government in Teheran. Some of these groups have brethren in neighboring countries, and the great powers had not hesitated to encourage local or tribal rebelliousness in order to bring pressure on the central government. Other groups in Iran — religious, ideological, socio-economic (e.g., the bazaar merchants in Teheran) — had risen against the government in the past.

From the beginning of the 19th century until after World War II, Iran was squeezed between the Russians to the north and the British in India. By balancing their rival imperialisms, Iran preserved at least nominal independence, although British influence was felt by Iranians to be pervasive in their own country. The withdrawal of Britain from India in 1947 and the subsequent waning of British power east of Suez forced Iran to seek another balance to Russian pressures, and the United States gradually assumed that role.

No matter how many weapons he bought, the Shah obviously could not withstand a Soviet attack — he had to rely on the Americans to deter that. But Soviet influence with Iran's other neighbors troubled him. He expressed this concern in an interview in October 1973:

> The Cold War is over. But the question with Soviet Russia will always be the same and, when negotiating with the Russians, Iran must remember the chief dilemma: to become Communist or not?... There exists what I call the USSR pincer movement. There exists their dream of reaching the Indian Ocean through the Persian Gulf.[2]

The Shah's fears had historical validity. Soviet attempts to absorb parts of his country after World War II could never be far from the Shah's mind. That Soviet move, which the United States prevented, continued to provide validation for the assertion by Soviet Foreign Minister Vyacheslav Molotov to Nazi Foreign Minister Joachim von Ribbentrop, in November 1940, that "The territorial aspirations of the Soviet Union lie south of Soviet territory in the direction of the Persian Gulf."

2 Interview with Italian journalist Oriana Fallaci, quoted in *The Economist*, May 17-23, 1975, Survey, p. 74.

A 1973 coup in Afghanistan had proved less pro-Russian than the Shah feared, and his March 1975 agreement with Iraq may have reduced the reliance on Moscow of that country's radical government. In exchange for the end of Iranian support of the Kurdish rebellion, Iraq probably gave Iran private assurances that it would cut back its support of potential rebels in Iran and on the Arab side of the gulf.

The conservative government in Oman, at the southern tip of the gulf, enjoyed the support of Iranian troops and planes in its miniature war on Dhofar Province against guerrillas backed by the avowedly Marxist regime in South Yemen. It was a minor skirmish in a primitive society inhabiting some of the most desolate territory on earth, but it served the Shah as a symbol of hegemony.

His solicitude for the stability of the gulf made the Shah, in the eyes of some Western strategists, the natural ally of the West in the region. In its May 1975 survey of the Persian Gulf region, *The Economist* noted the Shah's effort to make Iran a "countervailing power against Soviet influence" in the region, and particularly his interest in helping to patrol the sea routes through the northwestern Indian Ocean. "There are excellent reasons why he should be helped to do this," *The Economist* said.

These sea routes are the most unprotected parts of the Western economic system, and so long as inflation continues it is unlikely that the American or British or French navies will be able to afford to give them adequate supervision. The Shah's interest in the Indian Ocean complements the West's very neatly, and it should be the aim of the governments in Washington and London and Paris to coordinate the two as closely as possible.[3]

In the same survey, *The Economist* outlined possible Western military action in the Persian Gulf to seize oil fields if either intolerable oil price increases, or a new embargo sparked by the Arab-Israeli conflict, left the West no choice. This scenario and similar ones in American magazines located the hypothetical invasion in Saudi Arabia, not Iran. But the Shah had made clear that he wanted protection of the gulf to be left entirely to the states of the region with no interference from *any* outside powers.

His efforts to establish regional cooperation at least raised the question whether the arms Iran was purchasing in the West might someday be used to protect Persian Gulf oil from the West. The mere possibility could make Western powers more hesitant to try a military response to future oil price increases and thus, in effect, raise the price level, which they would consider tolerable.

The Shah's longstanding ties to the United States and his continuing reliance on this country to counter Soviet pressures made scenarios of Iranian-U.S. conflict highly speculative as long as his regime was in power. His government had a remarkable record of stability in a region notorious for instability. The ongoing economic and social transformation of Iran, however, had the proportions of an earthquake. For all his eagerness to accelerate technological change, the Shah had gone to extremes to prevent political change.

He had divided and intimidated all opposition to his regime, and this policy had been so consistent that any liberalization could have been interpreted by Iranians as a sign of weakness and an opportunity to rebel. The result was to prevent national debate on the most fundamental issues. But fundamental questions were being posed by changes in Iranian civilization, and the silence only hid historical forces whose power would one day be felt.

In the traditional absence of formal political institutions entrusted with the advancement of the national interest, Iran's shahs had often been the sole embodiment of central authority and the principal architects of national policy. Since the turn of the century they had adamantly opposed any encroachment on their sovereignty by representative government. Because the last shah was no exception, he provoked vociferous criticism from the left and aroused mild irritation among American policy makers who had been largely responsible for underwriting his ascendance. "It's not democratic leadership, but it's decisive leadership," a State Department official had said.

In the Shah's opinion, democracy itself was an irritation, a poor substitute for divine inspiration. His public candor before his people was possible, he once had explained to an American television audience, because he did not "fear and tremble before them" or "look at the polls to see if they're up or down two degrees."[4] Absolute monarchy was apparently easier to defend in a country that had experienced it for over a thousand years. At 59, the Shah himself was an amalgam of technocracy and royalty who was often portrayed as being ruthless yet religiously inspired. In an interview with the prominent Italian journalist Oriana Fallaci, the Shah confided to her: "I believe in God, and that I've been chosen by God to perform a task."[5]

U.S.-Iranian Friendship

If the Shah had been ordained by God, he had also received able assistance from the secular powers of the United States. U.S. friendship with Iran dated from 1946, when official U.S. protests to the Soviet Union led to Soviet troop withdrawals from northern Iran.

But his gratitude for American support by no means diminished his desire for an independent foreign policy, even when that policy conflicted with Washington's. He amply demonstrated that independence, and celebrated a national holiday, by nationalizing the Western-held Iran Oil Participants Ltd. on March 21, 1973, the Iranian new year. Iran did not join the oil embargo imposed by the Arab states during their 1973 war against Israel, whose government Iran recognized. But the Shah enthusiastically championed the increases in oil prices that began with the embargo.

Iran could not be labeled an American "client" state. But its interests seemed to coincide with America's own interests in the Middle East insofar as Iran's strength, rather than Russia's, tended to fill the "vacuum" left by the withdrawal of British forces "east of Suez" in 1971. Defense Department official James H. Noyes told a House Foreign Affairs subcommittee in 1973 that the United States had definite "security interests" in the Persian Gulf. The bulk of U.S. arms support went to Iran because it was perceived to be the most stable and responsible guarantor of those interests, he said. Reliance on this concept of regional defense as a substitute for deterioration of the Central Treaty Organization[6] as a credible deterrent against potential Soviet aggression had logically contributed to the U.S. Iranian policy.

---

3 Ibid., p. 11.

4 On "Sixty Minutes" (CBS-TV), Feb. 24, 1974.
5 *The New Republic*, Dec. 1, 1973, p. 16.
6 The organization had its origin in a pact of mutual cooperation signed at Baghdad initially by Iraq and Turkey and soon afterward by Britain, Pakistan and Iran, in 1955 at U.S. urging, to cover an area between the reaches of the North Atlantic Treaty Organization and the Southeast Asia Treaty Organization. Iraq withdrew in 1959. The United States was an associate member.

25 Centuries of History

The Shah's festivities in 1971 to commemorate his country's 25th century as a continuous civilization served to remind the world of Iran's antiquity and cultural heritage. Ancient Persia, or Iran *(see box)*, extends back even farther than that time span, as Old Testament chronicles attest. However, the sixth century B.C. was when Cyrus the Great established the greatness of the Persian Empire which, with Darius' subsequent conquest of Babylonia and Egypt, extended from the Nile Valley almost to Asia Minor.

The empire shrank under the weight of Greek and Roman conquests and internal disintegration. By the seventh century A.D. it was beset by Arab invaders who brought with them the religion of Islam and foreign rule. The Arabs were gradually deposed, but the religion remained. Today more than 90 percent of Iran's people belong to the Shia sect of Islam, the state religion. Together with the Arabs and the Turks, the Iranians played a major role in shaping Islamic civilization. Within the world of Islam, however, the Shia sect is a minority, retaining a formal priesthood and influential clerical establishment and differing in many ways from the orthodox Sunni majority.

Modern Iranian history begins with a nationalist uprising in 1905, the granting of a limited constitution in 1906 and the discovery of oil in 1908, which intensified a British-Russian rivalry that had already (in 1907) divided Iran into spheres of influence. During World War I the country underwent actual occupation by British and Russian soldiers, although it officially remained neutral in the war. The war interrupted the sporadic growth of constitutionalism. In 1919 Iran made a trade agreement with Britain that formally affirmed Iranian independence but in fact established a British protectorate over the country. After Iran's recognition of the new communist government, Moscow renounced the imperialistic policies of the czars toward Iran and withdrew any remaining Russian troops.

A second revolutionary movement, directed largely by foreign influence in Iranian affairs, was initiated in 1921 by Reza Khan, the Shah's father and founder of the Pahlavi dynasty. In 1925 he was placed on the throne and made a start toward modernizing his country. But his flirtation with the Nazis led to another British and Russian occupation in 1941 and forced him to abdicate in favor of his son. Separatist Azerbaijani and Kurdish regimes, established under Soviet patronage in northern Iran, crumbled after Soviet forces were withdrawn in 1946 under pressure from the United States and United Nations.

Nationalism, Mossadegh and Oil

With the Soviet crisis over, Iran was left with the subtle but disturbing presence of the British. The most onerous symbol of British influence in Iran's domestic affairs, and one which served to bolster Iranian nationalism, was the Anglo-Iranian Oil Company. This consortium of British and American interests antagonized both the political right and left in Iran. The domestic political climate was further aggravated by deteriorating economic conditions resulting from the allied occupation during World War II. By 1951, the moderate center had rallied around the Shah, who had then been on the throne for 10 years without real power.

Hopeful of avoiding civil war, the Shah sought an accommodation with the oil industry. But the more radical demands prevailed. The communist-backed Tudeh Party, largely middle class with strong support in the army, and

---

Iran or Persia?

Iran is the ancient name for the country and its people. The word Persia gradually evolved from European usage of the word Fars, an ancient province in which the Iranian people were first known to have lived. In a spirit of nationalism in 1935, the Iranian government asked all foreign governments to use the name Iran rather than Persia.

---

the rightist National Front, a heterogeneous collection of groups led by the "opposition" nationalist leader in parliament, Dr. Mohammed Mossadegh, demanded nationalization of the oil consortium. Finally, on March 15, 1951, the Iranian Parliament voted unanimously for nationalization, and on April 27 named the 73-year-old Mossadegh as premier. Given the prevailing atmosphere, the Shah had little choice but to accede.

Britain and the United States took a dim view of those events, while the Soviet Union did curiously little to exploit the unrest. The British strenuously rejected Iran's claim of the sovereign right to nationalize. Secretary of State Dean Acheson later recalled that the United States feared that "Britain might drive Iran to a Communist *coup d'etat,* or Iran might drive Britian out of the country."[7] Although Iran did neither, what did happen was unsatisfactory to all parties. The oil industry refused to cooperate with the new national ownership lest it set an example in the Middle East. Consequently, oil production virtually stopped for the next several years.

New evidence brought to light by Senate Foreign Relations Committee hearings on multinational companies in March 1974 indicated the extent of oil company and U.S. government collusion in reacting to Iran's unsettling decision to nationalize and to the growing instability of the Mossadegh regime. Declassified State Department files made public at the hearings revealed concern as early as 1951 over monopolistic practices of American oil companies in the Middle East, including Iran, and urged that such practices be ended. The Justice Department responded with an antitrust suit. The suit was quashed, however, when in 1953 the National Security Council invoked claims of "national security." According to testimony from a former Exxon executive before the same subcommittee in April 1974, Secretary of State John Foster Dulles encouraged the industry's presence in Iran to prevent the country from falling under Soviet influence.

Internal Stability

By 1953, stability was restored in Iran. Mossadegh was deposed on Aug. 19 by royalist sympathizers with the apparent backing of the CIA. Whether by chance or by design, the outcome was that the Shah gained power and the foreign-owned oil industry returned. With Mossadegh imprisoned and his National Front allies in parliament reduced to marginal effectiveness, the Shah's retribution was quick and decisive. The Tudeh Party was smashed and hundreds of its members in the army's lower ranks were rooted out, as were the sympathizers in all significant interest groups and associations. It remained for the Shah to consolidate his strength by rewarding his supporters—chief-

---

7 Dean Acheson, *Present at the Creation* (1969).

ly in the officer corps—and make peace with the nationalist-minded clerical authorities. The oil companies were free to renegotiate more favorable terms, and Iran could expect continued financial assistance from the United States in addition to $45 million it had received immediately upon Mossadegh's ouster. For the remainder of the decade, the government applied itself to economic development.

But reform programs were not introduced until after 1961, when the results of two contrived national elections incited virulent criticism, bringing about the resurgence of the National Front and threatening the stability of the government. In January 1963, the Shah announced the "white revolution," an ambitious plan to give social growth equal priority with production. The plan promoted women's suffrage, literacy and health, nationalization of natural resources, sale of state-owned factories and profit-sharing for workers. With the addition of eight new principles by 1975 to the original 1963 six-point declaration, the final charter for reform included 14 basic objectives.

The cornerstone of the "white revolution" was land reform. In most developing countries the concentration of land in the hands of a few wealthy owners is a serious obstacle to social reform, and Iran was no exception. In some regions a single landowner might own 50 villages—as many as 100 in parts of Azerbaijan. Predictably, the landed classes, with allies among the Shiite clergy, incited violent demonstrations in June 1963. Predictably, too, the Shah crushed them instantly. After that, reforms mollified those with moderate demands and repression silenced the others.

Regional Foreign Policy [8]

In foreign affairs, Iran's traditional preoccupation with the Soviet Union gradually gave way to a greater concern for what it perceived to be the more menacing threat of Arab socialism. But in 1955, Arab socialism was still in its infancy while the Soviet Union was foremost in mind. Without an adequate defense capability of its own, Iran that year joined the Baghdad Pact. Up to 1955, postwar relations with Russia had been officially cordial as both countries chose to ignore the Soviet-inspired insurgency in the northern provinces in 1945-46.

But Iran's participation in the Central Treaty Organization provoked a furious propaganda attack from Moscow. Above all, the Russians feared Iran would permit the United States to station nuclear missiles on Iranian soil, as Turkey had done when it joined the organization. Iran assured the Kremlin in 1959 that it would not do so. Russia ceased its propaganda activity against Iran, and relations between the two countries steadily improved thereafter. Beginning in 1962, the year Iran assured the Kremlin that no foreign missiles would be allowed on Iranian soil, Iran and the Soviet Union entered into a series of extensive commercial ventures, the most significant being the 1966 agreement whereby Russia built Iran's first steel mill, at Isfahan, in exchange for large quantities of natural gas piped from southwestern Iran to the Soviet interior.

Ironically, in strengthening its ties to the Soviet Union during this period, Iran also managed to improve its relations with the United States. After it joined the Baghdad Pact in 1955, Iran was dissatisfied with the low level of arms shipments it received and soon wanted a stronger defense commitment than the United States was willing to provide. But the American attitude changed considerably as Iran's relations with the Soviet Union began to thaw, especially in 1958, when Iran announced its intention to seek a nonaggression pact with the Russians. Instead, the result was a friendship treaty with the United States in 1959. By skillfully playing off both sides to its advantage, Iran had substantially improved its position with the great powers by 1960.

But by that time Iran had calmed its fears of Soviet belligerence only to replace them with equally intense suspicions of Arab socialism in the Persian Gulf. When, in July 1958, a military group overthrew the Hashemite monarchy in Iraq, relations between Baghdad and Teheran quickly deteriorated. Up to that point, Iran had maintained reasonably good relations with radical Arab regimes in Syria and Egypt, and with conservative monarchies and sheikdoms in Saudi Arabia and Oman. But the cumulative effect of the Iraqi coup was to nurture fear that other friendly monarchies would fall.

After witnessing the U.S. reluctance to back its CENTO partner, Pakistan, against India over Kashmir in 1965, Iran began to entertain serious doubts about the value of its defense alignment with the United States. It drew the conclusion that it would have to rely on its own strength to protect Iranian interests in the Persian Gulf. Unlike Iraq, Kuwait and Saudi Arabia at the head of the gulf, which have pipelines to transport their oil to the Mediterranean Sea and the West, Iran must export its oil entirely by water through the gulf and the Indian Ocean. The measure of Iran's heavy reliance on uninterrupted sea transport is the measure of its vulnerability. Since the British departure from the gulf, this very dependence on the Persian Gulf for access to the Indian Ocean seemed to dictate that Iran would become its *de facto* guardian.

Problems of Gulf Stability

The evolution of Iranian military and economic power changed Iran's regional policy from a reactive one to an assertive one. "Iran has gone out of her way to impress both local and outside powers with her ambitions and her potential for realizing them," stated the London-based International Institute for Strategic Studies.[9] These impressions were forcefully conveyed by a series of successful military ventures conducted during the four years between the announcement and implementation of Britain's withdrawal east of Suez. The Labor government of Prime Minister Harold Wilson announced in July 1967 that Britain must abandon its historical role east of Suez and the following January set a timetable for withdrawal of military forces from Singapore, Malaysia and the Persian Gulf by the end of 1971. Before 1968, British troops had left Adan, a seaport fortress vital to British interests in the Indian Ocean since the 19th century.

Iran's first move came in April 1969 and grew out of a longstanding dispute with Iraq over navigational rights in the Shatt al-Arab, a broad estuary which is of strategic importance to both countries, especially for Iran as an access route to its oil facilities.[10] Iran contested Iraq's nominal control of the waterway when it sent a freighter with jet fighter escort through the mouth of the estuary and successfully defied Iraqi threats of retaliation, which never materialized.

---

8 See "Iran: The Making of a Regional Superpower," pp. 470, 471 in A. L. Udovitch (ed.), *The Middle East Oil, Conflict and Hope* (Lexington, N.Y., 1976).

9 "The Soviet Dilemma in the Middle East, Part II: Oil and the Persian Gulf," by Robert E. Hunter, *Adelphi Papers* of the International Institute for Strategic Studies, October 1969.

10 Iran has since moved the bulk of its refineries to a safer site near the desert-edged part on Kharg Island.

Finally in March 1975, in return for an end to Iranian support of the Kurdish rebellion, Iraq accepted the Iranian claim that the deep-water line in the Shatt al-Arab defined the boundary.

Another dispute, also resolved by gunboat diplomacy, was Iran's subsequent seizure of Abu Musa and the two Tumbs, three gulf islands near the Strait of Hormuz. After protracted and futile negotiations with the British over its claims to the islands, Iran landed troops there on Nov. 30, 1971, despite the protests of the Arab littoral states. To placate the Arabs, Iran dropped its ancient territorial claim to the large gulf island of Bahrain after a U.S.-sponsored referendum revealed that the Bahrainians preferred their independence to Iranian dominion.

It has been suspected that when the Shah pressed his claims to Bahrain, he did so with the sole purpose of relinquishing them with apparent magnanimity, as he did in May 1970, to obtain his real objective, the three islands in the strait.[11] Hence, by the end of 1971, with the passing of the last vestige of Pax Britannica, Iran had consolidated its position in the Persian Gulf. Success, however, was bought at the price of encouraging speculation about Iranian expansion. But both the United States and the Soviet Union and the littoral state generally seemed content with Iran's frequent denials of territorial ambition. Nevertheless, in view of the rapid arms buildup in the gulf, weaker littoral states could not cling to that belief with certainty.

Growing Unrest

Serious mass demonstrations in 1976 protesting the Shah's ordered change from the Islamic calendar to one based on the coronation of Cyrus the Great portended the future of Iran. There had not been such public disorder in over a decade. Yet neither the Shah nor observers of Iran realized its significance.

All eyes were on other possible sources of opposition and observers felt secure in what they saw. Only remnants of the Tudeh Party survived; the several hundred remaining members badly splintered among Soviet and Maoist factions. The Kurdish tribesmen in Northwest Iran, unlike their Iraqi brethren, had been comparatively docile since 1946.

In addition to close historical bonds that tied the Persian military to the monarch, the Shah was directly responsible for the army's rising pay and stature. Although the Shah enjoyed their loyalty, there was always some fear that one day a military elite would rise against its creator.

And the urban middle class, comfortable with its prosperity, was not considered a threat. It apparently did not want to risk its prosperity by doing anything more than criticizing the regime, even if the rising inflation was pinching.

The Shah and observers also felt secure in the belief the Shah had neutralized the opposition of the religious hierarchy to the process of modernization by denying them effective political power and by imprisoning some of their leaders. One of the most vociferous, the Ayatollah Ruhollah Khomeini, had, after all, been in exile in neighboring Iraq since 1963.

But all was not quiet. Religious opposition to the Shah's rapid move toward modernization had provided the initial impetus for anti-Shah demonstrations and

"I am going on vacation because I am feeling tired."

—Shah Mohammed
Reza Pahlavi

Khomeini had served as a national symbol behind which Iranians could rally. But the Shah's opponents came from virtually every class and shade of opinion. Criticism of his methods of dealing with domestic affairs was steadily growing. All the money being spent on defense and the Shah's other lavish purchases did not go unnoticed by the populace.

And an Iranian economist at the International Monetary Fund told Editorial Research Reports during the Shah's reign that in his country "development is always linked to torture." A United Nations panel documented gross violations of human rights in Iran, and *U.S. News & World Report* reported on Aug. 6, 1973, that "about 70 persons have been executed for subversion in the last several months." The secret police (SAVAK) already had become a ubiquitous and efficient means of intimidation, according to Iranian political dissidents. It was reported that students suspected demonstration leaders of being paid police informers, because only they could afford to be so daring. Reports of SAVAK atrocities abounded over the following years.

In March 1975, the Shah dropped even the pretense of a two-party system. The majority Iran Novin Party and the opposition Mardom Party were combined into a new "National Resurgence" movement. The new and only party was called Rastahiz. The regime organized a campaign to turn out votes in the June 20, 1975, elections in which the new party put up 700 candidates for 268 seats in the national assembly and 30 in the senate. Although the Majles (Parliament) functioned as a rubber stamp for the Shah's programs, his government was anxious to give voters the impression of participating in politics. Premier Amir Abbas Hoveida, head of the National Resurgence, had told Iranians that those who failed to vote would have to explain their failure to the party, which would regard it as a breach of discipline.[12]

In his 1961 autobiography, the Shah had written: "If I were a dictator rather than a constitutional monarch, then I might be tempted to sponsor a single dominant party such as Hitler organized or such as you find in Communist countries. But as a constitutional monarch, I can afford to encourage large-scale party activity free from the straitjacket of one-party rule or the one-party state." But the change to a single party was not granted deep significance by traditionally cynical Iranians, who hitherto had jokingly boasted that Iran had not one but two puppet parties.

While this cynicism had prevented the Shah's reforms from dashing expectations among the upper classes—since

11"The Persian Peninsula, Iran and the Gulf States: New Wealth, New Power" (1973), a summary of papers presented at the 27th annual conference of the Middle East Institute.

12 *New York Times*, June 16, 1975.

they are practiced at political indifference[13] — some intellectuals and critics had labeled the Shah's reforms cosmetic substitutes for real changes. They said the real purpose of land reform, for example, was never to redistribute land but to break the back of the aristocracy. When modernization is conducted from the top, it invariably thwarts political participation from below.

Protests Escalate

Following the mass religious demonstration in 1976, Iran was relatively quiet, but pockets of unrest occurred throughout 1977, primarily in opposition to the Shah's activities of repression, centered in SAVAK.

The unrest of 1977 soon escalated into the riots of 1978, beginning in the holy cities of Qum and Tabriz. The first riot began in January, apparently when a government-inspired article in the Teheran newspaper, *Etelaat*, accused Khomeini of conspiring with communists against the Shah regime. The article impugned the ayatollah's character.

Khomeini supporters protested the article with a demonstration in Qum, dominated by the nation's Shia clergy, and army troops fired into the crowd. The victims became the first of an estimated 10,000 deaths resulting from the year's rioting. The level of violence spiraled upwards as the demonstrators rioted in protest to the shootings and the Shah forces put down the riots with increased fervor. Shiite mourning ceremonies, traditionally held every 40 days, would honor those killed in earlier demonstrations, fomenting more demonstrations and more deaths to be mourned at the next ceremony.

Universities in Iran were closed in June, not to reopen again in 1978. Their students joined in the demonstrations. Outbreaks occurred with increasing frequency and intensity, with Khomeini taking an active part in encouraging the demonstrations from his exile in Iraq. One of the most violent demonstrations occurred in September when the government imposed a ban on unauthorized rallies. An estimated 10,000 persons marched in defiance in Teheran on Sept. 7 and the Shah's troops again fired into the crowd, killing hundreds. That action led to more riots throughout Iran the following day, leading the Shah to declare martial law.

The Iraqi government, concerned with maintaining good relations with Iran, meanwhile told Khomeini to leave that country. On Oct. 6, he moved to a locale near Paris and set up his headquarters, attracting even more worldwide attention than he had enjoyed in Iraq.

The government in Iran continued its crackdown on the demonstrations and the Carter administration in turn stepped up its pronouncements in support of the Shah.

Another destructive riot occurred in Teheran in early November and the Shah, in one of the first of several acts of appeasement to follow, installed a military government and renewed a pledge to hold national elections in June 1979, ostensibly to allow Iranians to choose their own ruling government.

Later in November, one of the most decisive blows was struck against the Shah when various groups of Iranian workers staged strikes in sympathy with the anti-Shah demonstrators. The most important were the oil workers, whose walkout soon produced a fuel shortage, causing serious damage to the economy of the beleaguered nation.

On the Dec. 10 and 11 holy days of mourning for Shia Moslems, an estimated million persons marched through

[13] See Marvin Zonis' *The Political Elite of Iran* (1971), and J. A. Bill's "Plasticity of Informal Politics," *Middle East Journal*, spring 1973.

the streets of Teheran in protest against the regime, causing the army to withdraw to the northern sector of the city.

Final Efforts at Appeasement

The size of the anti-Shah movement now apparent, the Shah made several last-minute efforts at appeasement, trying to mollify the protestors who accused him and his government of lavish spending, corruption and repression. He granted amnesty to Khomeini, but he also pledged to continue his controversial industrialization reforms. The demonstrations and strikes continued and even civil servants began defying orders to return to work.

The oil industry was gradually shut down, denying the government $20 million a day in revenues and imposing hardships on the Iranian people. The mosques of the Moslem clergy were being used for meeting places and also provided a communications network for the demonstrations and strikes, coordinating with the edicts from Khomeini who had by then become a symbol of the growing revolution.

The Shah then offered to step down as head of the government, but not as Shah, and appointed Shahpur Bakhtiar, 62, as premier. Bakhtiar, a member of the National Front that had always opposed the Shah, quickly attempted his own appeasement with such moves as proclaiming that no more Iranian oil would be sold to Israel or South Africa, turning over the Israeli Embassy to the Palestine Liberation Organization, and openly criticizing American policy adopted by the Shah. Bakhtiar promised to end SAVAK, prosecute corruption and reduce the influence of the military.

It was all too late. Bakhtiar was even denounced by his own party for accepting the premiership from the Shah, whom the party declared head of an illegal government. Riots continued and more deaths resulted, but strikers trickled back to work in response to appeals from opposition leaders.

The Shah tried again to appease, ordering members of his royal family to turn in their millions of dollars in Iranian holdings to the Pahlavi Foundation, a family trust and charitable organization under his absolute control.

None of the appeasement worked. With the end near, the Shah announced, "I am going on vacation because I am feeling tired," and flew to Egypt on Jan. 16 on the first leg of an odyssey that was not expected to return him to Iran. And even that last grand act of appeasement failed to work.

The Shah had left his government in place, still in the hands of Bakhtiar. Violence continued and there was a threat of a military coup to oust Bakhtiar. Bakhtiar appointed a nine-member regency council to carry out the Shah's duties and tried to enlist members of the opposition to join it. They, including Mehdi Bazargan, refused. Khomeini on Jan. 13 announced he had formed his own Council of the Islamic Revolution which would replace Bakhtiar and serve as a transition to the Islamic Republic he would establish in Iran. Bakhtiar said he was determined to remain in office.

As Khomeini and Bakhtiar wrestled over the power in Iran (Khomeini threatened to fly to Teheran to take over and Bakhtiar shut down the airports) the United States, which depended upon Iran for 5 percent of its oil needs by then, ironically announced it would send Iran 200,000 barrels of diesel fuel and gasoline for government and military vehicles.

Appeasement by the United States also was too late. In a serious misreading of the threat to the Shah, the U.S.

intelligence agencies had maintained as late as the end of September 1978, that the Shah regime was stable. The Carter administration continued to support the Shah. On Dec. 14 Carter told interviewers: "We obviously support him fully. . . . We have treaty agreements with Iran. We have strong defense agreements with Iran. We look on Iran, as do their neighbors, as being a stabilizing factor." When Bakhtiar was installed, the Carter administration gave him its full support, too, even in light of the by then obvious opposition in Iran to anything even remotely connected with the Shah.

Khomeini returned triumphantly to Iran on Feb. 1 and his supporters succeeded in overthrowing Bakhtiar's government 10 days later.

The ayatollah's return came after two days of bloody fighting, and increasing incidents of troops fraternizing with demonstrators forced the military to declare its neutrality and withdraw to its barracks. Bakhtiar then resigned and fled to France. Bazargan was installed to replace him, but the ayatollah kept his hands on the reins of government, determined to bring about the Islamic Republic he had promised. Khomeini made clear his plans for Iran did not include extensive dealings with the United States. He named the entire U.S. Senate (because of its resolution) and President Carter as enemies of Iran and said, "We have no need for the United States. It is they who need us . . . as a source of oil, for which their greed never ceases."

The U.S. State Department projected Iranian commerce with the United States at no more than $1.5 billion in 1979, symbolically bringing an end to an era.

SADAT'S CAMP DAVID GAMBLE: PEACE AND MONEY

On May 27, 1979, Egyptian President Anwar al-Sadat donned a white admiral's uniform trimmed with gold braid and service ribbons and stepped off a plane at El Arish, capital of the Sinai Peninsula. The moment was filled with symbolism.

It was during his service as a colonel at El Arish that Sadat received a call from Gamal Abdel Nasser in 1952 to return to Cairo to help plot the overthrow of King Farouk. Sadat had not been back to El Arish since then; he could not have returned during the previous 12 years because Israel controlled the city and nearly all of the 24,000-square-mile peninsula.

It was while wearing a similar uniform on June 5, 1975, that Sadat boarded an Egyptian destroyer and led a ceremonial parade of ships south through the newly cleared Suez Canal. The commercial ships that followed were the first to pass through the canal since its closing on June 6, 1967, during the Six-Day War that humiliated Egypt

Between June 5, 1975, and May 27, 1979, Sadat had transformed his nation from leadership of the 22 Arab countries and an outspoken critic of Israel — which occupied six per cent of Egypt's land — to a nation that was viewed with enmity by its Arab neighbors for negotiating a peace treaty with its former belligerent that guaranteed repossession of all but a 28-mile strip of Egyptian soil.

Within that four-year period, Sadat had not only set in motion a profound alteration of the lifestyle of his country; he might in fact have determined its political and economic future, for good or ill.

By signing a peace treaty with Israel before settling the issues of the West Bank, Gaza Strip and Golan Heights — all traditionally Arab land but controlled by Israel since the 1967 war — Egypt incurred the wrath of its Arab neighbors, most of whom broke off diplomatic relations and threatened to end trade with Egypt in an attempt to isolate it from the Arab world. Sadat was gambling that by 1980 or 1981, he would be successful in negotiating with Israel over the three disputed areas to the satisfaction of the Arab nations, who would then end their enmity.

If those negotiations failed to appease the other Arabs, Sadat was gambling that new and stronger ties with non-Middle Eastern nations, primarily the United States and China, would provide economic compensation and international political support. He was also counting on the prospect that new oil discoveries in Egypt and the fields recovered under the Israeli agreement to return the Sinai would make it independent of oil imports and economic assistance from the Organization of Petroleum Exporting Countries (OPEC), which was comprised primarily of Arab nations threatening a boycott of trade.

Above all, Sadat was gambling that all those changes would benefit his country, that they would put it on the road to modernization and prosperity. Despite its political leadership in the Arab world, Egypt had not experienced the riches that transformed many of its Arab neighbors into money-laden oil-producing powers, and its economy was in deep trouble. And, too, Sadat was gambling on his own survival as Egyptian president. Under the 1971 constitu-

Egyptian President Anwar al-Sadat

tion, he would be up for re-election for a third six-year term in 1982.

Three months before the 1975 Suez reopening, Egyptian workers demonstrating in Cairo and Alexandria against the country's grave economic ills, had chanted at Sadat, "Hero of the crossing [a reference to Oct. 6, 1973, when Egypt retook part of the Sinai] where is our breakfast?" Two years later, in January 1977, 79 people were killed in rioting that was sparked by the government's attempt to remove food subsidies in an effort to bring about essential economic reforms. Those incidents just before and after Sadat's well-displayed triumphs showed just how mercurial the Egyptian political climate was and how much it was tied to the stability of the Egyptian economy. The rioting in 1977, the worst internal upheaval in decades, cast doubt on the government's ability to carry out the economic measures demanded by international lending institutions to pull Egypt's economy from potential bankruptcy.

In an effort to strengthen his political position, Sadat in February 1977 called on Egyptian voters to ratify a law-and-order decree outlawing demonstrations, strikes and sit-ins as well as membership in "organizations that are opposed to the regime." Within the next two years he disbanded the majority Center Party and established a new group, the National Democratic Party, in an effort to better control the People's Assembly, Egypt's parliament. The move apparently did not work to his satisfaction, despite his rising popularity stemming from the 1973-79 negotiations with Israel, and consequently, Sadat called for national elections after the treaty was signed in March 1979. At the same time, he issued an edict barring any debate on the peace treaty during the campaign.

In 1979, it appeared that the indirect linkage of peace with Israel, regaining the Sinai and a switch of alliance from Arab to West to the improvement of the Egyptian economy could determine Egypt's political future.

In the mid-1970s, Sadat had told his country and his financial and political supporters that he expected to pull Egypt out of the economic doldrums by around 1980. He expected to do so in part with revenues from the enlarged Suez Canal (to be completed in 1981) to accommodate larger tankers and from canal fees from a new user, Israel; from oil discoveries (aided by the addition of the Sinai oil fields); and from capital investment from the West.

Looking back just a few years Sadat may have underestimated the difficulties in returning Egypt to a Western economic as well as political orientation. "The problem is that we declared an open door policy before we provided basic infrastructural prerequisites,"[1] Dr. Ahmed El Ghandour, Deputy Minister of Economy and Economic Cooperation said in 1976. Reporting on the situation, Andrew Lycett noted that soon after Sadat's reversals in 1974, "enthusiastic capitalists were flying in from all corners of the globe." "But it did not take long for them to become disillusioned," Lycett added. "Egypt was in a bigger mess after her years of tutelage to the Soviet Union than even President Sadat must have imagined. Her debts were huge. Her bureaucrats were not geared to dealing with enterprising businessmen and talking in terms of growth."[2]

Two years later Professor Alvin Z. Rubinstein of the University of Pennsylvania wrote: "Egypt's economic, social and political problems are worsening. Not without justification, Egypt is referred to as the Bangladesh of the Middle East. The meaning is clear: unless effective steps are taken soon to control population, attract investment capital and increase production, domestic pressures may get out of control."[3]

Terrain

Egypt is at the geographical center of the Arab world. Situated at the northeast corner of Africa, it lies at the crossroads of Europe and the Orient, of North Africa and Southwest Asia, a location which accounts for its prior history of foreign domination. Its location on Israel's western border and its central role in the Arab world enhance its importance to U.S. policy in the Middle East.

Occupying an area slightly larger than California, Nevada and Arizona combined, Egypt stretches northward to the Mediterranean Sea. To the east is Israel and the 1,200-mile coast of the Red Sea. The Sudan lies to the south and Libya to the west.

Egypt includes the Israeli-occupied Sinai Peninsula, seized by Israel during the 1967 war. The 1949 armistice agreements between Israel and the Arab states also granted Egypt administrative jurisdiction over the 28-mile-zone Gaza Strip, another area that Israel subsequently occupied.

Since ancient times, Egypt's lifeline has been the Nile River, which flows from Uganda and Ethiopia through upper Egypt, northward to the Mediterranean. Despite a 2,140-mile coastline and 2,100 miles of inland waterways, much of Egypt is an arid wasteland. The 100-mile-long Suez Canal, opened in 1869, links the Red Sea to the Mediterranean. Egypt's major ports are Alexandria, founded in 332 B.C. by Alexander the Great, and Port Said and Suez, both on the Suez Canal.

The ribbon-like Nile Valley, the Nile delta and a few oases provide Egypt's only arable lands. Less than 3 per cent of the country is cultivated, and 0.7 per cent is covered with inland water. The Aswan high dam, however, is expected eventually to increase cultivable land to 13,000 square miles.

The Nile Valley divides two other regions of Egypt: the Arabian Desert to the east and the Libyan Desert to the west. The eastern desert is distinguished by wadies, trenchlike formations that were once important means of communication between the north and the Red Sea. Mountains along the Red Sea in this region rise to above 7,000 feet. The Libyan Desert in Egypt's western area is broken at three places by oases, created by seepage from the Nile.

The Nile Valley nonetheless dominates the country. While Egypt has an overall population density of 93.2 persons per square mile, the figure leaps to 2,631 per square mile in the pencil-thin valley. The largest cities are concentrated there and in the Suez Canal Zone.

Cairo, Eygpt's capital and Africa's largest city with more than eight million people, is located inland along the northern end of the Nile. Although it is still partly a city of Arabic grandeur, it suffers the problems of overcrowding, urban rot and pollution. In parts of Cairo there are a quarter million people per square mile, one of the highest densities in the world. Alexandria's population is more than two-million.

People

The population of Egypt was estimated at 40,500,000 in March 1979, with a growth rate of 2.58 per cent, continuing the one-million-a-year increase of the past several years. Egypt's high birth rate was a major factor contributing to its serious economic difficulties. If population continued to grow at the 1979 rate, Egypt would have more than 70 million inhabitants by the year 2000. And the population would have doubled in less than 26 years.

Exacerbating the problem was the fact that the urban growth rate was even higher. Nearly all the nation's population was concentrated along the life-supporting Nile River, and industrialization in the capital of Cairo was attracting an exodus from the rural areas into the city that, along with its environs, already held nearly 25 per cent of the nation's population.

Ninety per cent of Egyptians are of eastern Hamitic stock, resembling their dark, stocky ancestors who have inhabited the area since the beginning of historic times. Greeks, Italians and Syro-Lebanese, living primarily in the north, constitute the other 10 per cent of the population. Unlike several of its Arab neighbors, Egypt does not have a significant nomadic population.

Illiteracy remains high in Egypt, with only about 53 per cent of the population functionally literate. Eighty-five per cent of the school age population enter school the first year and 75 per cent of those complete the sixth grade. Ninety per cent of the Egyptians are Sunni Moslems. The other 10 per cent are comprised almost entirely of Coptics, continuing the Christian creed retained since the early days of Christianity when Egypt was among the first countries to adopt the religion. Islam was introduced into Egypt in the sixth century.

Along with the first move toward peace in 1975, the educational system began changing a school curriculum

---

1 "Egypt Economic Survey," *African Development*, November 1976, p. 7.
2 Ibid.
3 Alvin Z. Rubinstein, "Egypt's Search for Stability," *Current History*, January 1979, p. 19.

that fostered opposition to Israel to one that by 1979 included no derogation of Jews.[4]

Economy

Egypt has long relied on the Nile for its life support. With few other natural resources, the Egyptian economy continues, as it has for centuries, to be based on agriculture. Nearly half the population is directly engaged in farming, and many other people work in agricultural processing and trade. Egypt's agricultural products are the net earners of foreign exchange. Although Egypt was called the granary of Rome in ancient times, its main cash crop today is cotton, which accounts for nearly half of export earnings.

Egypt's mild climate allows for multiple cropping, thereby doubling the country's yearly agricultural yield. Farming practices are inefficient by modern standards, but production continues to grow. Produce and commodities are raised primarily for the market, and there is little subsistence farming.

Faced with a rapid population growth rate and limited resources, the Egyptian government has funneled its major efforts into increasing industrialization as a means of raising productivity and the standards of living. In the early 1960s, the government nationalized all major foreign and domestic industries. Today many of these industries and all public utilities are run by organs of the central government. Most agriculture and trade, however, remain in the hands of private owners. Significant gains have been made in textile, chemical, cement, food processing, petroleum refining and construction industries.

In the mid-1970s, however, Sadat reversed the state socialism trend initiated by his predecessor in the presidency, Nasser. In April 1974 Sadat issued a statement on Egypt's long-term economic and social objectives. It was called "The October Paper" to symbolize Sadat's belief that the October War had ushered in a new era for Egypt. The paper candidly criticized some of Egypt's problems and failings and promoted decentralization and regionalism, not further centralization. Concretely, Sadat has offered incentives for foreign investment and a free-trade zone at Port Said. Also in 1974 the Egyptian State Council ruled illegal the confiscation of private property under Nasser, and certain lands and properties were returned to their former owners.

De-Nasserization of the Egyptian economy complemented Sadat's political initiatives toward the West, especially the United States, as well as his objective of attracting Western capital, essential to building Egypt's industrial base. An inflation rate of 25 per cent accompanied a rise in the per capita income from a low $200 in 1975 to an estimated $280 in March 1979. About 600,000 workers enter the labor force each year.

Egypt's balance of trade remained desperate in 1979. It exported $2.225-billion, according to 1978 estimates, while importing $5.325-billion, for a deficit of $3.1-billion. Saudi Arabia had helped make up part of the deficit through $500-million in annual grants, but the Israeli peace pact threatened continued aid from that nation, leaving the budget-conscious United States to make up the balance. At the same time, Egypt was paying interest and principal on outstanding loans of about $15-billion. Chronically short of cash, Egypt has been forced to spend one-fourth of its national budget on the military.

Another 25 per cent of the nation's budget went for subsidies to keep food prices artificially low, a practice that has made it difficult for Egypt to attract international monetary aid and the capital investments it so sorely needs. The 1977 riots in Egypt were the direct result of Sadat's efforts to reduce those subsidies in order to get the country's financial house in order. His lack of success highlighted some of the economic reform problems the nation faced. On the other hand, reflecting some optimism in Egypt's abilities to surmount its problems, the International Monetary Fund decided in mid-1978 to sign a three-year extended credit facility with Egypt.

The discovery of oil resources in Egypt in the mid-1960s thrust the country into a field of growing importance. Oil concessions had been granted to Phillips Petroleum and American International Oil Co. in 1963. Since 1966, oil production has increased with the development of fields in the Gulf of Suez and the Western Desert. The Sinai oil fields at Abu Rudeis were returned to Egypt after the 1975 second Israeli-Egyptian disengagement agreement. Together with its other oil and the additional fields Egypt is to regain with the Israeli pull-out from the Sinai, Sadat was expected to be able to meet his prediction of producing a million barrels a day by 1980. Part of the Sinai agreement called for Egypt to sell some of the oil to Israel, although it was not a firm commitment.

A critical food shortage has been a major contributor to Egypt's recurrent trade deficit. The country has required $1-billion a year in foreign currency to feed its population. In spite of government efforts to boost wheat output, population growth continued to outstrip increases in food production, making Egypt even more heavily reliant upon food imports. Capital goods constituted another sizable portion of Egyptian imports. Cotton continued to be the main export item, although rice, petroleum and manufactured goods have assumed increasing importance. In its favor, in view of Arab hostility, however, was the fact that less than 10 per cent of Egypt's foreign trade has been with other Arab nations.

Much depended upon what assistance the United States was willing to give Egypt to bolster its economy and how much foreign trade Egypt could attract with other nations. Prior to the Israeli agreement, Egypt had been able to count on $1- to $2-billion in aid each year from the oil-rich Arab states — assistance which, in Alvin Rubinstein's opinion, contributed more to the balance-of-payments deficit than it did to development. "What Egypt desperately needs is an Arab 'Marshall Plan,' a $10-billion to $15-billion commitment over the next five years to permit sound planning and reassure investors," he wrote.[5] Unless Sadat could persuade his fellow Arabs to contribute as a result of achieving an acceptable West Bank settlement, however, such a plan appeared to be highly unlikely.

Soviet Bloc Trade

Communist countries became Egypt's main trading partners after 1967. That arrangement had gained its initial footing in 1956 when West European countries boycotted Egyptian trade as a result of the Suez crisis. Communist countries since have purchased as much as 50 per cent of Egypt's exports. Thirty-five per cent of Egypt's imports come from communist countries, primarily the Soviet Union, East Germany and Czechoslovakia until recently.

4 The Washington Post, June 10, 1979.

5 Rubinstein, op. cit., p. 20.

Statistics on Egypt

Area: 386,659 square miles, including 22,500 square miles occupied by Israel.
Capital: Cairo.
Population: 40,500,000 (March 1979 est.)
Religion: 90 per cent Moslem, 10 per cent Coptic Christian and others.
Official Language: Arabic; English and French widely known by educated Egyptians.
GNP: $11.7-billion, $280 per capita (1978).

U.S. Trade

Before Egyptian-U.S. relations were broken off during the 1967 war, Egypt imported more goods from the United States than from any other country. Egypt received nearly $700-million in American Food for Peace program wheat in 1949-67, largely meeting Egypt's demands for that commodity. The country received no U.S. assistance of any kind from 1968 through 1971, then began to receive modest aid sums again in 1972. From World War II through 1974, Egypt received more than $900-million in American economic loans and grants.

The resumption of diplomatic ties between the two countries on February 28, 1974, opened the way for renewed and expanded trading relations. Sadat's turn toward the West in the aftermath of the 1973 war quickly resulted in Congress voting $250-million in Egyptian aid for fiscal year 1975. During fiscal 1977, Sadat's Egypt received over $900-million in economic aid plus an extra amount sought by the Carter administration after the January 1977 rioting highlighted Sadat's serious problems.

By 1979 annual U.S. aid to Egypt was running at about $950-million. In fact, the U.S. aid program to Egypt had grown from a standing start in 1974 to the largest assistance program in the world. By 1977, for example, more American assistance went to Egypt than to the rest of Africa and Latin America combined. John J. Gilligan, administrator of the U.S. Agency for International Development (AID), visited Egypt in June 1977 and predicted that the American commitment to sustaining the massive aid program would continue for "a long time to come." "Egypt is a powder-keg," he added. "If we don't help to stabilize the economic situation here we're going to have a highly volatile situation over a long period of time."[6]

Egypt's prospects for establishing a favorable trade balance remained uncertain in 1979. Before the 1967 war, revenues from tourism and the Suez Canal had offset most of the trade deficit. Tourism subsequently declined, but had picked up again by the end of the 1970s, to the point that the 800,000 tourists it attracted each year taxed its capacity to handle them. The peace pact with Israel contained an agreement to drop travel restrictions between the two nations, opening a possibility for even heavier tourism. With help from outside private investors, Cairo already had launched a decade-long program of major hotel construction.

Early History

Egypt's recorded history, the longest continuous account in the world, dates from 3200 B.C. From then until

6 *The Washington Post,* 28 June 1977, p. 1.

333 B.C., Egypt was a united kingdom under various dynasties of pharaohs. During that period, the great pyramids were built to propel the pharaohs, believed to be divine, back to heaven. After 333 B.C., the country's territory alternately increased and diminished according to the conquests of foreign occupiers.

Egypt's choice location made it a prime target for foreign invaders. It has been successively occupied by Asian barbarians, Assyrians, Persians, Alexander the Great, Greco-Egyptian Ptolemies, Romans, Moslems, Turks, Tunisians, Ottoman warriors and Napoleon Bonaparte.

Although the invasion of Egypt was a phase of Napoleon's war against the English, France's domination of the country from 1798 to 1801 ushered in the modern period of Egypt, which emerged from a long, dark age. Bonaparte's army included scientists, medical doctors and teachers. A French officer unearthed the famed Rosetta Stone, and Jean Francois Champollion, the first Egyptologist, deciphered its hieroglyphics, providing the key to Egypt's ancient glories—about which Egyptians for many centuries had known very little. Thus many Egyptians look upon the French emperor as the father of modern Egypt.

Political disorganization after French withdrawal in 1801 gave rise in 1805 to the reign of Mohammed Ali, founder of the last Egyptian dynasty, who continued the modernization movement.

Suez Canal

The first survey for the Suez Canal was made by French army engineers directed by Napoleon himself, who spent several days on the Isthmus of Suez setting up the study. After that, little was done for half a century until another Frenchman, Ferdinand de Lesseps, who had served as a diplomatic officer in Cairo, undertook to make the long-discussed canal project a reality.

He had to overcome major financial and political obstacles. Initially de Lesseps raised half the capital for construction in France. Ironically, de Lesseps' principal opponent was the British government, which, suspicious of French intentions, fought the canal project with every means at its disposal, short of war. Finally, after 10 years of construction work, the canal was opened on Nov. 17, 1869, creating the short route between Europe and the Indian Ocean and western Pacific. The canal soon became one of the world's busiest waterways. Great Britain turned into the chief guardian of the canal, a vital defense and trade lifeline between the mother country and India and other Asian colonies.

British Occupation

The ruling dynasty was interrupted in 1882 by British occupation of Egypt. In 1914, occupation eased and Egypt became a British protectorate. In 1922, Egypt was returned to a kingdom under King Fuad and later King Farouk. Ties to Britain remained, however. Under a 1936 mutual defense treaty, Britain maintained a military base in the Suez Canal Zone and, together with Egypt, continued to administer the Sudan.

World War II

One of the most important campaigns of World War II was fought on Egyptian soil. Germany's elite Afrika Corps, under Field Marshal Rommel, drove across North Africa into Egypt, reaching El Alamein, only 60 miles from the huge British naval base at Alexandria and, beyond it, the

Suez Canal. After vicious fighting in the summer and fall of 1942, the British stopped Rommel's advance and subsequently chased him out of Egypt. El Alamein was the high mark of German expansion. After that campaign, Hitler's armies knew only retreat.

Egypt itself did not declare war on Germany and Japan until 1945. Egypt was among the founding members of the United Nations and became a member of the Arab League in 1945.

Creation of Israel

Egypt was among the Arab states that bitterly rejected the U.N. decision in 1947 that partitioned Palestine, creating Israel and leading to the first Arab-Israeli war in May 1948. The armistice agreement of 1949 gave administration of the Gaza Strip to Egypt.

Republic Proclaimed

Arab failure to eradicate the new Jewish state, coupled with ongoing minor disputes with Britain, fed a wave of opposition to King Farouk. The underlying tension erupted Jan. 26, 1952, when dissidents burned and looted foreign establishments in Cairo and killed many British residents. On July 23, 1952, a military junta seized the government. The "free officers" led by Lt. Col. Gamal Abdel Nasser forced the abdication of Farouk. On June 18, 1953, the monarchy was abolished and Egypt was proclaimed a republic.

The new government was headed by Gen. Mohammed Naguib, a war hero from the Palestinian invasion. Disagreement among the ruling group of military officers eventually brought about the ouster of Naguib. Nasser assumed leadership of the government April 18, 1954, and became president Nov. 14, 1954.

The new regime's reformist, socialist outlook and the personal magnetism of Nasser quickly gained esteem from the Arab world. To set the stage for Arab unity along a moderate, socialist line, the government undertook measures to divide aristocratic landholdings, raise the cultural and economic level of the farmer and urban worker, increase industrialization and reduce the degree of foreign participation in the country's commercial enterprises and other affairs.

The last move led to Egypt's rejection of Western efforts to formulate a Middle East defense strategy. The West then turned to Egypt's chief rival, Iraq, and the Baghdad Pact resulted in 1955. The United States never joined the alliance, although it promoted it, because of U.S. hesitance to alienate Egypt. Egypt countered the Baghdad Pact, signing an arms agreement with Czechoslovakia and mutual defense treaties with Syria, Saudi Arabia and Yemen, each opposed to Iraqi policies, and recognizing Communist China.

End of Occupation

Strong Egyptian nationalist feelings also led to Egyptian pressure on Britain to evacuate the Suez Canal. On July 27, 1954, Britain agreed to withdraw all its troops within 20 months. The 74-year occupation ended June 13, 1956. The diplomatic antagonism and disagreement over plans for the construction of the Aswan Dam led the United States July 19, 1956, and Britain July 20 to withdraw their promises of aid for the dam. On July 26, 1956, in retaliation, Nasser nationalized the Suez Canal, controlled by the British and French.

Egyptian relations with Britain and France rapidly deteriorated while, on another front, tension mounted with Israel. Israel invaded the Sinai Oct. 29, 1956, and soon after, Britain and France attacked and bombed Egypt, with the announced intention of ending Egyptian-Israeli fighting. The Soviet Union threatened to intervene when the canal was blocked; and combined Soviet and United States pressure forced the British, French and Israelis to withdraw.

Egypt interpreted President Eisenhower's policy of assistance to Middle East nations to maintain their independence as an attempt to block Arab unity under Egyptian leadership. Accordingly, U.S.-Egyptian relations declined. Meanwhile, civil conflict in Syria between nationalists and communists increasingly diverted Egypt's attention to its Arab neighbor.

Syrian unrest was resolved when Syria, attracted by Nasser's leadership and Egypt's support of Arab nationalism, agreed to unite with Egypt in the United Arab Republic. The union was established Feb. 1, 1958. Economic and political incompatibility undermined the U.A.R., leading to Syria's secession Sept. 30, 1961, after a Syrian military coup. Egypt alone continued to carry the name U.A.R. until 1971.

Formation of the U.A.R. raised fears in Jordan and Lebanon of Egyptian expansion. That fear, coupled with Nasser's hostility toward Lebanese President Camille Chamoun's pro-West policies and Lebanese civil unrest, led to Lebanon's request for U.S. Marines July 14, 1958. Marines arrived July 15. Meanwhile, British forces were sent to Jordan in response to a similar request. The Lebanese unrest eventually subsided, and American and British forces were able to withdraw by November.

1967 War

After 1957, there was relative quiet along the Egyptian-Israeli border. In 1966, tensions once again began to mount as retaliation raids increased. In May 1967, Nasser ordered U.N. forces out of the cease-fire zone set up in 1956, closed the Strait of Tiran to Israeli cargoes and moved troops into the Sinai.

War broke out June 5 between Egypt and Israel. Jordan, Syria and Iraq soon joined the battle against Israel. Within six days, Israel made sweeping conquests, defeating Egypt and occupying the Sinai Peninsula, the Gaza Strip and areas in Syria and Jordan. The Suez Canal was closed. By June 11 all parties had accepted a U.N. cease-fire.

Sadat's Succession

The Arab world was shaken by Nasser's death following a heart attack Sept. 28, 1970. Anwar Sadat, vice president under Nasser, was elected to succeed him in a nationwide plebiscite Oct. 15, 1970. Sadat pledged to pursue Nasser's policies.

A merger between Egypt and Libya, announced during the summer of 1972 to take effect Sept. 1, 1973, ran aground because of Egypt's hesitancy about association with Libya's increasingly extremist policies. In July 1973, Sadat firmed up an alliance with Saudi Arabia and chose close relations with his eastern neighbor instead of ties to Libya.

Sadat surprised the world when he emerged as a strong leader. He embarked on new directions—reversing Nasser's politics of state socialism, moving Egypt away from dependence on the Soviet Union and toward friendship with the United States and dropping the holy war call for annihilation of Israel as the only basis for a lasting peace.

1973 War

In a surprise attack Oct. 6, 1973, Egyptian forces crossed the Suez Canal into the Israeli-occupied Sinai, and Syrian troops invaded the Golan Heights. Israelis, caught unaware while observing the holy day of Yom Kippur, suffered substantial initial losses. Two weeks later, Israel, however, had turned the tide of the battle and driven back its Arab enemies. U.N., American and Soviet efforts brought about a cease-fire Oct. 25, but not until the situation had posed the danger of a U.S.-Soviet confrontation. Egypt and Israel signed a six-point armistice Nov. 11.

Although neither the Arab states nor Israel emerged clearly victorious from the war, the successful Arab oil boycott weakened Western support for Israel and appeared to increase Egypt's chances of regaining the Israeli-occupied lands lost in the 1967 war.

Egypt re-established its presence in the Sinai for the first time since 1967 and looked upon the crossing of the canal and the initial Israeli reverses as a vindication of Egyptian arms. All this gave Sadat new stature. He was emboldened enough to have his deputies sit down with Israeli officials, for the first time since 1949, to sign the armistice agreement and then a disengagement of forces accord in January 1974. The Egyptian foothold on the East Bank enabled Sadat to clear the Suez Canal of mines, sunken ships and other debris and to reopen it on June 5, 1975.

Government

Egypt's government is headed by a strong president who in turn appoints vice presidents, a prime minister, his Cabinet and the governors of Egypt's 24 governorates, or provinces. When Nasser held the office between 1954 and his death in 1970, he dominated nearly all aspects of Egyptian life, but Sadat has not equaled that wide-ranging dominance.

Under the constitution, approved by the people Sept. 11, 1971, executive authority rests with the president, who is also chief of state and supreme commander of the armed forces. He is popularly elected to a six-year term after nomination by the People's Assembly. Sadat has been elected twice, most recently in September 1976, but in unopposed elections where the people were only asked to validate the choice of Egypt's single party, the Arab Socialist Union. After his latest victory, though, Sadat began experimenting with a more liberal, democratic system.

Three "forums" were developed within the Arab Socialist Union party representing left, right and center. According to Rubinstein, that action "inadvertently opened a Pandora's box." He added, "At first, Sadat did not interfere when a fourth party, the New Wafd, was established on Feb. 4, 1978. Like its predecessor [the Wafd], the New Wafd had a broad following among intellectuals, small landowners and the lower middle class. Its leader, Fuad Serageddin, was a voice from the pre-revolution past. He criticized corruption in government and the poor handling of the attempt by Egyptian commandos to free a hijacked Egyptian airliner in Cyprus on Feb. 19. Sadat became increasingly edgy. With the specter of isolation in the area haunting him as a result of his peace initiative, he decided to take no chances with his internal base and to nip criticism in the bud."[7]

The result was a new referendum on May 21, 1978, that effectively outlawed the Wafd and any other political critics. It received 99 per cent approval. In August, Sadat announced formal creation of the National Democratic Party under his leadership that augmented his control of the country. Although the June 7, 1979, parliamentary election was the first multi-party election since 1952 and attracted 1,683 candidates for 382 seats, Sadat's party benefited from his edicts that there would be no criticism in the campaigns of the peace treaty with Israel, the previous referenda or little else of import. Additionally, according to *The Washington Post*, "two parties ostensibly in the opposition, the Socialist Labor Party and the right-wing Socialist Liberals, . . . made a pact with Sadat's party to protect each other's most prominent figures from uncomfortable challenges."[8] Not surprisingly, Sadat's party retained a comfortable majority.

Besides the power of veto, the Egyptian president holds emergency powers to issue binding decrees when the People's Assembly delegates such authority by a two-thirds majority. The assembly is a unicameral legislative body elected for an indefinite term by universal adult election. The body serves mainly as a forum for discussion and for automatic approval of government proposals.

Foreign Policy

Egypt's ties to the West were weakened by the 1956 Suez crisis and the 1967 war, and communist ties were correspondingly increased. Major goals of Egyptian foreign policy during these Nasserist years included Arab nationalism, Arab socialism and the victory of Arab states over Israel.

Although Sadat signed a 15-year treaty of friendship with the Soviet Union, he astonished the world on July 18, 1972, when he summarily expelled 20,000 Russian military advisers and technicians from Egypt and placed all Soviet bases and equipment under Egyptian control. In a four-hour speech, Sadat said Moscow's "excessive caution" as an ally led him to the decision. A few years later the friendship treaty was totally abrogated by Egypt and Egyptian-Soviet relations have turned very sour.

In response, the Soviets worked to build up Iraq and Syria as rivals to Cairo's influence and established cordial relations with Libya President Muammar Qaddafi, who turned vociferously against Sadat after Egypt backed off from union with Libya. Sadat lashed out at Russian-Libyan arms deals, complaining that he did not understand Soviet policy, which cut off arms supplies to Egypt and refused Sadat a period of grace in amortizing a $5-billion debt for previous military purchases.

As Sadat cooled relations with Moscow, he turned more and more to Washington. He publicly embraced Secretary of State Kissinger after the latter's "shuttle diplomacy" resulted in the Israeli-Egyptian disengagement of forces on the Suez Canal front in January 1974. On Feb. 28, 1974, Egypt and the United States resumed diplomatic relations, broken off during the 1967 war. Sadat began to rely on the good offices of the United States to bring about a general Middle East settlement, rather than on the Geneva Conference, of which the Soviet Union was a cosponsor.

The Arab use of the oil weapon in the 1973 war stimulated American interest in a Middle East settlement.

---

7 Rubinstein, op. cit., 21.

8 *The Washington Post*, June 7, 1979, p. A40.

When President Nixon toured the Middle East in June 1974, he made Cairo his first call. Sadat and Nixon signed a friendship pledge. In June 1975, Sadat and President Ford met in Austria to explore possibilities for a peace settlement, with Sadat always hopeful of prying the United States loose from unqualified support of Israel.

But presidential parleys were only window dressing for the key role the United States was to play in mediating the Sinai accord of 1975. After Kissinger's shuttle diplomacy failed to produce a new interim agreement in March, the dejected secretary returned to Washington, where he and Ford launched a "total reassessment" of U.S. Middle East policy. They wondered publicly about what would have happened had Israel been "a little more flexible."

The United States went to work to persuade Israel to accept a new pact as a stepping stone to eventual peace, in the process relieving some of the tensions that again had built up after the spring diplomatic setback. Pleased with the new approach, Sadat, for one, was willing to give the United States another chance. Accordingly, Kissinger went back to the Cairo and Jerusalem negotiating tables in August and ended that round triumphantly with a new Sinai agreement, signed Sept. 4 at Geneva.

Sadat visited the United States in both 1975 (when he addressed a joint session of Congress) and 1977, the first Arab head of state to visit Jimmy Carter's Washington. Before the latter journey he spoke out in a *Parade* magazine interview. "I want the American people to know," he declared, "that never before have the prospects for peace been better. Not in the last 28 years — since Israel was created — have we had a better chance for a peace settlement in the Middle East."[9] For the first time Sadat had begun speaking of a complete normalization of relations with Israel, including eventual diplomatic relations.

But during his visit not only the Arab-Israeli predicament was on Sadat's mind. He courted President Carter on both economic aid and arms. He further discussed how American and Egyptian interests in Africa were similar and how Egypt could play a role in holding back communist advances on the continent. Indeed, within weeks of his return to Cairo, President Sadat dispatched Egyptian pilots to Zaire to help repulse Soviet and Cuban-supported forces invading Zaire's Shaba province from neighboring Angola.

Peace Initiatives

It was clear to Sadat that he needed a settlement of the hostilities with Israel. Without it his economic and political plans were sure to collapse eventually and his friendship with the United States could be jeopardized. Furthermore, Sadat was aware that the Arab world could be unstable and unpredictable.

After the second Sinai disengagement, Egypt's relations with Syria plummeted as the Lebanese civil war mushroomed and engulfed the entire region. Not until the Riyadh and Cairo summits in late 1976 was some semblance of unity restored among the Arab confrontation states. But all parties were aware that unless progress could be made toward an overall Middle East settlement, disunity and instability would resume.

In fact, in July 1977 serious fighting broke out between Libya and Egypt. Sadat vowed to teach Libya's leader, Muammar Qaddafi "a lesson he will never forget." For the

previous few years Sadat had repeatedly accused Qaddafi of attempting to overthrow Sadat's regime. Sadat had also expressed considerable anxiety about the quantities of Soviet arms being bought and stored in Libya; but according to Qaddafi, he was only serving as the arsenal for eventual war against Israel.

Four months later, Sadat took a giant step aimed at assuring that war with Israel would not reoccur. In November 1977 he threw all Arab diplomatic caution to the wind and became the first Arab leader to visit Israel, thus giving the 30-year-old Jewish state the stamp of recognition, but at the same time alienating Egypt from its Arab neighbors.

Israel and Egypt had been discussing peace off and on since 1973, focusing on the fate of the Sinai, but the talks had not progressed very far. Sadat felt that his visit to Israel would provide the psychological inducement that he believed was needed to end the stalemate and lead to a comprehensive settlement. The reaction to his visit was overwhelmingly favorable in both nations. Israeli Prime Minister Menachem Begin returned the visit, meeting Sadat at Ismailia Dec. 25-26, 1977.

Camp David Accords

Despite the psychological boost, the two nations were unable to achieve concrete results until President Carter invited Sadat and Begin to Camp David to thrash out their differences in the seclusion of the mountaintop retreat. After 13 days of marathon negotiations in September 1978, they were able to sign an agreement committing themselves to an outline for a settlement of the Middle East conflict and an Egyptian-Israeli peace treaty.

A major snag, the first of many, developed when Carter and Sadat announced that the agreement at Camp David included a promise by Begin not to allow any more settlements in the disputed areas of the West Bank and Gaza Strip. Begin replied that he had made no such agreement.

Sadat also faced harsh criticism from his Arab neighbors who denounced him for making any agreement with Israel without receiving a commitment that Israel would cede the occupied West Bank to Palestinian Arabs. Sadat had tried but failed to achieve that linkage. The two nations had agreed, however, that talks would begin on that issue and the Gaza Strip after a peace treaty was signed.

The Camp David accords almost collapsed several times over disagreements about what had been agreed to and how far-reaching the accords were. In a move interpreted as a protest against Israeli intransigence, Sadat refused to go to Oslo, Norway, in December 1978 to collect the Nobel Peace Prize he shared with Begin. His official reason was that he could not in all conscience accept an award for peace until a peace treaty had been signed.

Adding to Sadat's problems over the treaty, the militant Arab states of Syria, Algeria, Libya and South Yemen, along with the Palestine Liberation Organization (PLO) met in Damascus soon after the Camp David session to criticize Sadat for making a separate peace with Israel.

Carter set up a ministerial-level "mini-summit" at Camp David in February to end the stalemate, and with encouragement from those talks he announced on March 5, 1979, that he would fly to the Middle East in a dramatic effort to mediate the remaining crucial differences separating the two leaders. In his own form of shuttle diplomacy, Carter flew first to Egypt to talk with Sadat, who agreed to some compromise, and then flew to Israel to obtain matching concessions from Begin.

9 "An Interview With Egyptian President Sadat," *Parade* magazine, Feb. 6, 1977, p. 8.

Sadat's concessions came in the face of a PLO call for an oil embargo against Egypt if a bilateral treaty were signed. Other Arab leaders joined in the denunciation of Sadat. Nonetheless, the Egyptian president agreed to exchange ambassadors with Israel early in 1980, without tying the exchange to his previous demands that Palestinian self-rule on the West Bank should be achieved first. After some dramatic last-minute efforts, the two sides agreed on March 12 to the final wording of a treaty. They signed the pact at a White House ceremony on March 26.

To some observers, the attraction of U.S. aid played a substantial role in bringing about the treaty. Carter promised the two nations $4.8-billion in aid and arms sales in exchange for signing. Egypt would get about $2-billion in arms, including 34 F4 Phantom jet fighters — some to be delivered in time for display at Egypt's October parade celebrating its gains in the 1973 war with Israel. The United States already had agreed to sell Egypt 50 F5 fighters, contingent on Saudi Arabia underwriting the $525-million cost, but in the wake of Arab nations' hostile reaction to the treaty, the Saudis said they would reconsider the financing. If they decided negatively, Sadat said he would ask the Unitd States to foot the bill. In addition to planes, Egypt was to get tanks and other weapons from the United States.

The reaction of the other Arab nations to the bilateral treaty was swift. Meeting in Baghdad, 18 of the 21 Arab countries agreed to a total economic boycott of Egypt and a severing of diplomatic relations with it. Only Sudan, Oman and Somalia declined to go along, at least for the time being. The hope was expressed at the meeting that isolation of Egypt from the rest of the Arab world would bring about a revolution that would depose Sadat and abort the treaty. To help kindle the flame of revolution, several Arab nations announced intentions to withdraw their huge amounts of funds on deposit in Egypt. Egypt countered by freezing its relations with the Arab League and refusing to pay its dues and recalling its ambassadors from the 18 belligerent Arab countries.

Sadat lambasted the Baghdad action, calling it "emotional, hysterical, and insulting to Egypt." He said, "Egypt is not and has never been a traitor. I did not achieve peace for the sake of materialism; I wanted to put an end to an unending situation. When I can save my people from the misery of war, there is no price tag involved."[10]

---

10 *Time* magazine, April 16, 1979, p. 57.

IRAQ: A CAUTIOUS PATH TOWARD MODERNIZATION

Unlike many of its oil-rich neighbors, Iraq has taken a cautious approach toward modernization. Its economy has a rather austere socialist character with limited attention given to consumer goods and luxury imports. Missing is the boomtown atmosphere so pervasive in other developing countries.

Characteristic of this step-by-step approach toward development has been the government's attempt to extend 20th century technology to Iraqi farmers, thereby strengthening the country's agricultural base. Iraq's goal has been to have a developed economy based on oil, industry and agriculture rather than one dependent solely on oil. Iraq has deliberately opted for low oil production in order to pace its development.

Iraq also has shown signs of a more pragmatic, moderate approach to its foreign policy. Although Iraq is the only Arab country with a 15-year "friendship pact" with the Soviet Union, relations between the two states have been limited by Iraq's intense nationalism. An internal crackdown on pro-Soviet communists (21 were executed in May 1978 for attempting to overthrow Iraqi President Ahmed Hassan al-Bakr) and an effort to establish closer economic ties with the West have served as evidence of Iraq's tilt toward moderation. Iraq has also improved relations with Saudi Arabia and Kuwait.

Fear of communist subversion has been cited as a factor in Iraq's moderating trend. There has also been speculation that Iraq wants to assume a leadership role in the Persian Gulf region to fill the vacuum left by the removal of the shah of Iran.

But whether Iraq would be able to fill the role of regional leader remained uncertain. Iraq was still a politically divided country. A 1976 study on the Middle East concluded: "Although the government seems more firmly in control of society than any previous one, political life still exists within a space narrower than that of Iraq as a whole. There is still more than one sense in which Iraq is not yet a unified political society. Political activity is mainly concentrated in the towns of the Tigris valley. . . . Even within the cities, the consensus which supports the government is limited and weak. Power tends to lie, as in Syria, in the hands of new men from small provincial towns who have come up through the main channel of social mobility, the army; in the present regime, in those of a group from the northern Tigris town of Tikrit. They rule in uneasy partnership with technocrats, civilian ministers, and officials of high education and special qualifications, but with no independent basis of political power."[1]

Terrain

Iraq occupies a strategically significant position in the Middle East. In addition to having vast oil resources which made it in 1978 the third-largest producer in that region, Iraq is located on the Persian Gulf and shares borders with two powerful non-Arab countries—Turkey and Iran. Iraq's

1 A. L. Udovitch, ed., *The Middle East: Oil, Conflict and Hope* (Lexington, 1976), p. 285.

Iraqi President Saddam Hussein

other neighbors are Kuwait, Saudi Arabia, Jordan and Syria.

Historically known as Mesopotamia—"the land between the rivers"—Iraq includes the twin river system of the Tigris and Euphrates. Eighteen per cent of Iraq's approximately 172,000 square miles is agricultural; 10 per cent is seasonal and other grazing land, and 4 per cent is forested; the remainder is primarily desert.

People

Arabs, the dominant group in the Iraqi population of more than 13 million, occupy most of the central, western and southern regions of the country. Other ethnic groups include the Kurds, Assyrians, Turkomans, Iranians, Lurs and Armenians. The bulk of a once-significant Jewish community which had totaled about 150,000 emigrated from Iraq to Israel in the late 1940s.

About 95 per cent of Iraqis are Moslems. It has been estimated that approximately 75 per cent of the Arabs belong to the Shia sect, along with 50-60 per cent of the Kurdish population. The remainder belong to the Sunni sect. Other religious communities include Christians, Jews, Bahais, Mandaeans and Yezidis.

Kurdish Rebellion. The Kurds are a non-Arab Moslem people who inhabit the mountains of northern Iraq, northwestern Iran and southeastern Turkey and who spread out into tiny pockets of Syria and the Soviet Union. They make up about 20 per cent of Iraq's population. Ever protective of their own identity and traditions, the Kurds, beginning in 1961, launched intermittent guerrilla warfare that fought Iraqi forces to a standstill. In 1970, the rebels won from the Baghdad government a promise of Kurdish autonomy within four years. In March 1974, the autonomy proposals were presented by the Kurds and rejected by the Iraqis.

The Kurds demanded virtual veto power over legislation in Baghdad affecting Kurdistan and the inclusion of rich oil fields in their region. The central government called the demands tantamount to secession.

Fighting erupted on an even bloodier scale, reportedly involving thousands of casualties. Baghdad employed tanks and jet aircraft, and the Kurdish "Pesh Merga" forces led by Gen. Mustapha Mulla Barzani were aided by Iran, which supplied the insurgents with wire-guided antitank missiles and sent two artillery battalions into Iraq. By his action, the shah hoped to undermine the left-wing Baathist regime in Baghdad, with which Iran feuded almost constantly.

But a year later, the Iranian-Iraqi rapprochement isolated Barzani, who, on March 22, 1975, with his army crumbling around him, said, "We are alone with no friends." On March 30, the general fled into Iran. By early April, Iraqi forces had completed their takeover of rebel mountain strongholds, meeting no further resistance. In a report published May 3 in Teheran, Barzani was quoted as saying, "The battle for Kurdish autonomy is futile, and the struggle will never be resumed."

The fate of the Kurds was sealed by a public kiss of peace between Vice President Saddam Hussein of Iraq and the shah of Iran on March 6 at Algiers — an embrace that choked off Iranian support of the Kurdish cause.

The fiercely independent Kurds, within two weeks, fell victim to international politics far beyond their reach, largely the shah's ambitions to end border disputes with Iraq and to bring about regional cooperation in the Persian Gulf that would exclude outside powers. Iraq's long dependence on Soviet arms was expected to be reduced by the termination of the Kurdish civil war.

Economy

Oil dominates the Iraqi economy. Though no official statistics have been published, it is estimated that Iraq's oil reserves are fourth among the OPEC countries. In 1978, Iraq ranked third among Middle East oil producers and its oil revenues were estimated at about $9.8 billion, a figure approximating the total GNP only a few years earlier.

In June 1972, Iraq nationalized the Western-controlled Iraq Petroleum Company, which had dominated almost the entire oil production of the country. In February 1973, the Iraqi government announced an agreement with the company on terms of the nationalization and compensation. Later, in 1973, Iraq nationalized two American oil firms, Mobil and Exxon, to chastise the United States for its support of Israel in the 1973 war.

Services, agriculture, industry and trade—in that order—contribute to Iraq's GNP in addition to oil. Though oil dominates the country's revenues and provides nearly all the foreign exchange, agriculture occupies most of the population.

Iraq's agricultural development program aims at self-sufficiency, but it will be a number of years before the country can hope to approach this goal. Presently, about 55 per cent of Iraq's population has been estimated as living by agriculture or stock-rearing. Besides being the largest supplier of dates in the world, Iraq also produces wheat, barley, rice, millet, cotton and tobacco.

Early History

Mesopotamia is one of the famous place names of ancient history. The Sumerians founded city-states there about 3000 B.C. Other civilizations which flourished between the Tigris and the Euphrates Rivers were the Babylonian and the Assyrian.

After 500 B.C., Persia, and later Macedonia, dominated the area. In the seventh century A.D., Mesopotamia was overrun by the Arabs, who established a capital at Baghdad, storied setting for *The Tales of the Arabian Nights.* Mongol invasions followed in the 12th and 15th centuries. In the 16th century, the area fell to the Ottoman Turks, under whose rule it remained until World War I.

It is held that the Garden of Eden once stood between the two rivers, and it was there that Nebuchadnezzar created the splendors of Babylon. King Hammurabi established the first recorded code of justice.

Iraqi Independence

Iraq began its move toward modern statehood during World War I, when the Turkish Empire, a belligerent on the Austro-German side, began to fall apart. Turkey's entry into the war in late 1914 prompted a British expedition to the Turk-controlled territory which was to become the state of Iraq. The move eventually led to British occupation of the area and Britain's receipt of a League of Nations mandate for the territory in April 1920.

Hashemite King Amir Faisal, driven by the French from his throne in Syria in July 1920, was elected to the Iraqi throne by a referendum and crowned in Baghdad in August 1921. Iraq became independent Oct. 3, 1932, but the Hashemite family continued to rule Iraq as a constitutional monarchy, following a generally pro-British, pro-Western policy.

In 1955, Iraq signed a mutual defense treaty—called the Baghdad Pact—with Britain, Iran, Pakistan and Turkey. Although the United States promoted the pact and provided members with assistance, it never became a formal partner. The main reason for this ambivalence was that Iraq and Egypt were rivals for leadership of the Arab world; and the United States, in the hope that Egypt could eventually be persuaded to join the pact, did not want to alienate Egypt by formally allying itself with Iraq. An alliance with Iraq also would have created problems for U.S. relations with Israel.

Military Coups

The Hashemite monarchy was ousted July 14, 1958, by a leftist military coup in which King Faisal II was killed. The leader of the coup, Brig. Gen. Abdul Karim Kassim, seized control and began reversing the country's policies, including renunciation of the Baghdad Pact, establishment of relations with the Communist bloc countries and purchasing of Soviet military equipment.

Kassim was assassinated in another military coup in February 1963, when a group of "free officers," primarily members of the Arab Socialist Resurrection Party (Baath Party), took over. The Baath regime was unable to consolidate its power and was ousted in another coup in November 1963. The new regime pursued a neutral East-West policy and turned its efforts to strengthening relations with other Arab states, especially Egypt.

The Baath Party came back to power when yet another military coup took place in July 1968. A Revolutionary Command Council took control and chose Maj. Gen. Ahmed Hassan al-Bakr as president and prime minister.

Ultimate power was granted to the command council. A Council of Ministers was set up with administrative and legislative responsibilities.

Statistics on Iraq

Area: 172,000 square miles.
Capital: Baghdad.
Population: 13,171,000 (1978 est.)
Religion: 95 per cent Moslem, 5 per cent other.
Official Language: Arabic; Kurdish minority speaks Kurdish.
GNP: $19 billion, about $1,550 per capita (1978 est.).

The provisional constitution adopted in July 1970 called for the establishment of a national parliament, but set no date for its creation. Bakr crushed a coup on July 30, 1973, which aimed at overthrowing the Baath regime. After a swift trial, the government executed 36 coup leaders. In the trial's aftermath, the president announced plans for the formation of a 100-member National Council, to be implemented later and to which the Revolutionary Command Council was to appoint the membership and turn over its legislative powers.

Iraq's vice president, Saddam Hussein, emerged as the new strongman of Baghdad politics. It was he who helped bring about the detente with Iran in the spring of 1975.

In July 1979, Iraqi President Bakr, who had been in ill health for several years, announced he was resigning in favor of Hussein, who had been considered the most powerful figure in the country's politics for several years.

Foreign Relations

Iraq broke off diplomatic and consular relations with the United States on June 7, 1967, after the outbreak of the Arab-Israeli war. Iraq retained several diplomats in Washington in an "interest section" established under the aegis of the Indian embassy. The United States had the same option since the 1967 break but did not exercise it until July 1972, when two foreign service officers were sent to Baghdad to open a similar "interest section."

Iraq has maintained close ties with the Soviet Union, its principal arms supplier. In April 1972, Iraq signed a 15-year treaty of friendship and cooperation with the Soviets, similar to the 1971 Moscow-Cairo treaty (abrogated in 1976). Although details of the treaty have been vague, it was generally considered to be a significant development in the Persian Gulf region, with the Soviets acquiring a strong foothold for naval operations in the Indian Ocean. On Aug. 31, 1974, President Ford named Umm Qasr in Iraq, at the head of the gulf, as one of the ports the Soviets were using for their Indian Ocean fleet. Moscow has repeatedly denied it was building up bases in the region. In June 1977 Iraq agreed in principle to buy from France more than 70 French Mirage F-1 fighter-bombers in a move to diversify its Soviet-equipped air force.

Iraq's leftist Baath regime and its alliance with Soviet Russia have been eyed suspiciously by its conservative neighbors—Iran, Saudi Arabia and the gulf emirates—which have been steadfast in their determination not to be swept up by missionary socialism. Both Kuwait and Iran have fought limited border wars with Iraq.

During 1975 and 1976 Syria moved infantry units and tanks to its border with Iraq because of Iraq's unhappiness over Syrian intervention in Lebanon and the longstanding dispute between the two countries over the waters of the Euphrates. However, signs of improved relations appeared in October 1978 when, for the first time in five years, Syrian President Hafez Assad visited Iraqi President al-Bakr. The two leaders discussed the Egyptian-Israeli accords. *(p. 163)*

Iran and Iraq each won major concessions as the two patched up their differences in the March 1975 agreements. The shah summarily dropped his support of the Iraqi Kurds, enabling the Baghdad government to crush their war for independence. In turn, Iraq yielded to Iran on the borders issue, notably rights to the Shatt al Arab waterway, where the Tigris and Euphrates converge before entering the Persian Gulf. Iraq acceded to Iran's demand that the boundary between the two countries follow the midcourse of the Shatt.

It is still unknown as to exactly what course Iraqi relations with the new regime in non-Arab Iran will follow. Iraq did recognize the new Iranian government the day after it seized power in February 1979. However, it is also known that Iraq expelled the Ayatollah Khomeini in 1978 after having given him asylum since his exile in 1963. In addition, Khomeini is a Shiite Moslem. The Shiite Moslems comprise 75 per cent of the Arab population in Iraq, but Iraq rulers come from the Sunni sect of Moslems and the Shiites feel they are disadvantaged. Whether the tension between the two sects would lead to discord between Iraq and the new government was uncertain.

In the spring of 1973, Iraq occupied some Kuwaiti border posts in clashes with that sheikdom, causing Saudi Arabia to send 20,000 troops into Kuwait for a short period in order to bolster the state's defense. At the time, Iraqi Foreign Minister Murtada Abdul Baki said there was no legal basis for the existing frontier between Iraq and Kuwait, adding that Iraq "wants to become a Persian Gulf state—that is the crux of the border dispute with Kuwait." Later, Iraq claimed it had withdrawn from the outposts, an assertion denied by Kuwait.

Iraq has had a 13-year argument over Euphrates water with Syria, which also has a radical Baath regime. Although the matter should be technical, the approach of the two countries has often been spiteful. In April 1975, the Arab League Council referred the water dispute to a seven-nation technical committee. The gulf's conservative states looked with favor on Iraq's new willingness to arbitrate differences, hoping that Baghdad, growing richer from its increasing oil production, was temporizing its missionary zeal and that the gulf region was entering into a tranquil phase.

Iraq, like Libya, has remained ideologically opposed to any settlement with Israel. Iraq dispatched troops to Lebanon in 1978 during Israel's incursion into that country. Iraq joined with other members of the Arab League in adopting political and economic sanctions against Egypt following the March 1979 signing of the Egyptian-Israeli treaty.

A PRO-WESTERN KINGDOM WITH A DURABLE LEADER

When President Carter, Israeli Prime Minister Menachem Begin and Egyptian President Anwar Sadat met at Camp David, Md., in September 1978 to hammer out what they hoped would provide a "framework" for a comprehensive Middle East settlement, a pivotal Arab figure was not in attendance. He was King Hussein of Jordan, to whom as a boy the Hashemite crown was passed more than a quarter century earlier. The king — whose survivability in the face of political turmoil and numerous assassination attempts had become almost legendary — refused to participate in the negotiations aimed at determining the fate of the occupied West Bank and the role of the Palestinians, who comprised a majority of the population even on the East Bank which Hussein controlled.

Without Jordan's participation, there was little chance that an overall peace settlement, and particularly a solution to the West Bank and Gaza Strip areas, could be found. But Hussein was the first to break off diplomatic relations with Egypt following the signing of the bilateral Egyptian-Israel peace treaty in March 1979; and he has repeatedly denounced the Camp David formula for achieving a settlement. As a result, the king — who has been considered a pro-West Arab moderate — found new favor with Arab hard-liners, while relations between the United States and Jordan became strained.

The question of participating in the West Bank negotiations is a central one to Hussein's desert kingdom. The hub of the king's turmoil has been the West Bank region — occupied and later annexed by the current monarch's grandfather, King Abdulla, after the 1948 war, and then occupied by Israel since the 1967 war. Since then, major elements within the Palestine Liberation Organization (PLO) have demanded that this area, along with the Gaza Strip, become a separate Palestinian state in any prospective peace settlement. Even if this were to occur, some form of affiliation with Jordan would seem likely. The longer-range problem is thus whether the Palestinians might come to overpower the Hashemites who are the ruling elite of Jordan. Few in Jordan have forgotten the 1970 civil conflict in which it took behind-the-scenes United States intervention and the threat of Israeli aid to assure Hussein of his throne.

Jordanian-Palestinian Links

Longstanding Jordanian policy linking the Jordanian and Palestinian causes reached a nadir in October 1974, when 20 Arab heads of state, meeting in summit at Rabat, Morocco, relieved Hussein of all authority to negotiate for the return of the Israeli-held West Bank. Faced with such Arab unanimity, Hussein could do little but capitulate to the decision to elevate the PLO to quasi-government status. Two weeks after the Rabat decision, PLO chief Yasir Arafat went to New York in triumph to address the United Nations General Assembly. Hussein's 1972 proposal for a United Arab Kingdom which would allow for two separate regional governments with Hussein retaining overall federal authority appeared to have been decisively rejected.

Jordan's King Hussein

But the 1975-76 Lebanese civil war saw a partial eclipse of the Palestinians who had come under increasing pressures for more conciliatory policies from Egypt, Saudi Arabia and Syria. In May 1975, President Sadat became the first Egyptian leader to visit Jordan. A month later, Hussein was host to Syrian President Assad. Since then Syrian-Jordanian relations have blossomed and there has even been talk of a regional federation involving both countries. During 1976, President Sadat, in a clear step back from the Rabat decisions, declared that the contemplated Palestinian state would have to be linked in some way to Jordan. President Carter, in his discussions of a "Palestinian homeland," has also foreseen such a linkage.

Terrain

The arid land of Jordan lies between Syria to the north, Iraq to the east, Saudi Arabia to the south and east and Israel to the west. Nearly landlocked, it has a 16-mile coastline on the Gulf of Aqaba, where its only major port, Aqaba, is located. It also shares the Dead Sea with Israel.

About the size of Indiana, Jordan covers 37,300 square miles of territory, 2,200 square miles of which were occupied by Israel during the 1967 war. Only 11 per cent of the land is forested. The remaining 88 per cent is primarily desert.

A great gorge divides the country, forming the Jordan River Valley in the north, the basin of the Dead Sea and Lake Tiberias in the center and the dry bed of the Wadie el Araba in the south. On the East Bank of the Jordan River, plateaus rise toward the vast Syrian desert, which covers most of the area. On the small West Bank, the land is hilly and receives sufficient rainfall for cultivation.

People

In 1977, Jordan's population was estimated to be 2,896,000, including the people living on the Israeli-controlled West Bank of the Jordan River and in East Jerusalem. Nearly all Jordanians, 98 per cent, are of Arab stock. Circassians and Armenians account for the other 2 per cent, although these ethnic groups long ago adapted to the preponderant Arab culture of the country.

Following the greatest concentration of rainfall, most of the people reside along the Jordan River, where sufficient rains allow for normal cultivation. Approximately one-third of the population lives in the Israeli-occupied West Bank, which was a portion of Palestine until Jordan seized the area during the Arab-Israeli war of 1948. More than 850,000 registered refugees live on the East Bank. The population is nearly evenly divided between rural and urban living, with 50 per cent of the people in the countryside, 44 per cent in the cities and 6 per cent nomadic or semi-nomadic.

Islam is the overwhelming majority religion in Jordan. Sunni Moslems comprise 95 per cent of the population, and Christians constitute the remaining 5 per cent.

Economy

Jordan's rapid economic expansion during the 1960s has been cited as an outstanding example of a well-planned and well-administered assistance program. With few natural resources and limited arable lands, Jordan as late as 1958 was a country with no industry, with an underdeveloped tourist trade, with a large unemployed or under-employed refugee population and with a need for adequately paved roads.

Using assistance from the United States, the United Nations, the International Bank for Reconstruction and Development, Great Britain and West Germany, Jordan expanded all major sectors of its economy, more than quadrupling its gross national product (GNP) between 1954 and 1967.

Irrigation projects increased the amount of arable land. Light industries were established. Shipping and port facilities were set up at Aqaba. Phosphate deposits in the Dead Sea were exploited. And tourism was encouraged with the restoration of historic sites and the construction of better roads and more hotels.

The Arab-Israeli war of 1967 and the ensuing years of civil unrest were major setbacks to the economic strides of the 1960s. During the 1967 war, Jordan lost the fertile West Bank and hence agricultural income. As a result of the war, it also was burdened with additional Palestinian refugees. However, by maintaining employment levels and consumer demand and by stepping up government spending, Jordan was able to limit the war's impact. Economic revival and military expenditures fed a newly increased demand for imports. Agriculture improved also, except in the Jordan River Valley, where sporadic clashes between Jordanian and Israeli forces kept production down.

Fighting between the Jordanian army and Palestinian guerrillas in 1970 and 1971 also hampered economic growth. The government's steadfast policy against the guerrillas led to Libya's and Kuwait's withdrawal of respective $26-million and $39-million annual subsidy payments to Jordan. The United States moved to offset the loss.

By 1972, economic activity had returned to its pre-1967 levels. During the 1973-75 three-year-plan period, real growth was estimated at around 7 per cent annually. The ambitious 1976-80 five year plan called for investments of approximately $2.4 billion and envisioned an economic growth rate of 12 per cent.

Agriculture is the life source of the Jordanian economy, rivaled only by phosphate production. Although the country is not totally self-sufficient in foodstuffs, it produces considerable amounts of wheat, fruits, vegetables, olive oil and dates. Jordan's exports, primarily fruits, vegetables and phosphate rock, have fallen far below its imports. In 1973, exports totaled $43 million, while imports totaled $330 million; by 1977, the country's trade deficit stood at $1.2 billion (with imports of $1.4 billion and exports of $256 million). Jordan's principal export markets are neighboring Arab countries — primarily Lebanon, Syria and Kuwait — and Eastern Europe (phosphates).

The United States had been Jordan's major supplier from 1971 until 1975, when the Federal Republic of Germany assumed that position, supplying 11 per cent of Jordan's imports. By 1977, however, the United States regained the position as Jordan's major supplier, providing 15 per cent of the country's imports.

The Jordanian government has continually offset its unfavorable balance of trade and its deficit budget spending with subsidies from Arab neighbors and with assistance from the United States and the United Nations. Between 1949 and 1973, Jordan received $753 million in economic assistance and $235 million in military assistance from the United States, most of which was given in grants. In 1978, U.S. economic assistance to Jordan totaled $102.9 million, with military aid (grants and sales) totaling $127.4 million. Other countries and international organizations had provided an estimated $222.7 million in economic assistance that year. In addition, the Arab nations at the November 1978 Baghdad summit voted substantial additional subsidies to Syria, Jordan and the PLO. *(See Arab reaction chapter)*

Inflation, a growing shortage of skilled manpower and a limited domestic market, combined with perceived unreliable access to the export markets of neighboring Arab countries were major obstacles to Jordan's economic growth in 1979. The cost of living in 1977 rose 14.3 per cent and was running at an annual rate of 12 per cent as of October 1978.

Early History

In ancient times, Jordan was part of various empires and civilizations, but not until after World War I did it exist as a separate nation. The Old Testament recounts its settling by Gilead, Ammon, Moab and Edom and by the Hebrews under Joshua in the 13th century B.C. Arabian Nabataeans, Greeks, Romans, Moslem Arabs and Crusaders successively held the area until the Ottoman Empire extended its domination over much of the Arabian Peninsula, including what is Jordan, in the 1500s.

British forces and their Arab allies ousted the Turks from Palestine and Transjordan in 1918, and the area came under the brief rule of King Faisal I as part of the Kingdom of Syria. Faisal's ejection by the French in 1920 placed Transjordan under loose administration by Britain. The regions presently known as Israel and Jordan had been awarded to Britain as the mandate for Palestine and Transjordan under the League of Nations mandate system. The French got similar mandates for Syria and Lebanon.

When Faisal's brother, Abdullah ibn-Hussein, moved into the area, threatening to vindicate Arab rights and attack the French in Syria, Britain created a partially autonomous kingdom for him, the Emirate of Transjordan. In May 1923, Britain recognized the independence of Transjordan under British tutelage within the mandate system of the League of Nations.

Under King Abdullah, Transjordan moved forward economically and politically and created the Arab Legion under British command. By arrangement, Transjordan accepted financial assistance from Britain and agreed to accept advice on financial and foreign affairs and to allow Britain to station forces in the country.

The British mandate over Transjordan ended May 22, 1946. On May 25, 1946, the kingdom became the independent Hashemite Kingdom of Transjordan, taking its name in part from the Hashemite family whose original patriarch was a disciple of Mohammed and the "guardian of Mecca."

When the British mandate over Palestine ended May 14, 1948, and the state of Israel was proclaimed, Transjordan forces joined the Arab attack on the new nation. Its forces took control of areas of central Palestine, including the West Bank and the Old City Sector of Jerusalem. In addition, nearly 500,000 Palestinian Arabs fled to Transjordan and Transjordan-occupied territories.

The armistice agreement of April 3, 1949, between Transjordan and Israel left the Arab nation in control of about 2,165 square miles of new territory on the West Bank. The country was renamed the Hashemite Kingdom of Jordan in 1950 to include the occupied lands annexed by King Abdullah.

On July 20, 1951, King Abdullah was assassinated by a Palestinian extremist in Jerusalem. His eldest son, Talal, was proclaimed his successor on Sept. 5, 1951, but mental disorders led to his removal by Parliament in August 1952. Talal's eldest son, Hussein, assumed power under a regency until his 18th birthday, May 2, 1953, when he was crowned king.

During 1955 and 1956, anti-Western sentiment in Jordan led to the country's severance of several ties to the West. The British commander of the Arab Legion was dismissed, and a mutual defense treaty with Britain was ended by mutual consent.

Scattered rioting erupted against Jordan's joining the Baghdad Pact, and Jordan later decided to remain outside the defense alliance. British troops left the country by 1957.

Domestic turmoil struck the country in the spring of 1957. King Hussein survived a military plot to overthrow his government, but only after public rioting, an extended Cabinet crisis and rumors of foreign intervention had disrupted the country. Political parties were dissolved at that time by royal decree.

Federation with Iraq

On Feb. 14, 1958, the Arab Union of Iraq and Jordan was proclaimed as a countermove to Egypt's merger with Syria. The Iraqi revolution of July 1958 spelled the end of the federation, however, and the Arab Union was formally dissolved Aug. 2, 1958. The Iraqi coup led King Hussein to accuse communists and the United Arab Republic of conspiring to overthrow his regime and to undermine the independence of Jordan. Hussein requested British and American assistance to meet the threat. Accordingly, British troops were stationed in Jordan from July 17 to Nov. 2, 1958, and American economic assistance was greatly increased.

Toward the end of 1966, Jordan faced another crisis, due to Palestinian guerrillas, notably from the Syria-based al-Fatah or al-Asefa organizations, who streamed across the Syrian-Jordanian border en route to raiding Israel. Israeli

---

Statistics on Jordan

Area: 37,300 square miles, including 2,200 square miles occupied by Israel.

Capital: Amman.

Population: 2,896,000 including approximately 769,540 under Israeli occupation on the West Bank and in East Jerusalem (1977 est.).

Religion: 95 per cent Sunni Moslem; 5 per cent Christian.

Official Language: Arabic.

GNP: $1.2-billion, $562 per capita (1977 est.).

---

reprisal raids on Jordan put pressure on the country to cut off the flow of commandos. Clashes on the border with Syria resulted from Jordan's attempt to stem the infiltration. Relations with Syria were eventually broken off over the issue in May 1967.

Notwithstanding the guerrilla problem, Jordan maintained its support of the Arab cause against Israel. It affirmed its solidarity with Syria when Israeli forces massed on the Syrian border later in 1967. Jordan also committed itself to a defense pact with Egypt.

1967 War

Jordan's defense treaty with Egypt committed the country to join the fight against Israel when the 1967 war erupted June 5. Within two days, Jordan lost all of the West Bank to Israeli forces, including the whole city of Jerusalem. Among the Arab states, Jordan suffered the heaviest losses of the war: more than 6,000 dead or missing and an influx of 200,000 additional Palestinian refugees. Although Saudi Arabia, Kuwait and Libya stepped in with economic assistance to offset the losses, Jordan's economy suffered a major setback from the war.

Following the war, guerrilla commandos of the Palestinian resistance movement, the *fedayeen*, expanded their activities within Jordan, Syria and Lebanon. In Jordan, particularly strong activity was aimed at the overthrow of King Hussein in order that the war against Israel could be continued. By the beginning of 1970, tension between the government and the guerrillas had led to sporadic fighting.

An agreement, whereby Jordan agreed to fully support the continued war effort against Israel, and the guerrilla groups agreed to restrain their members and honor Jordan's internal security, soon proved unsuccessful. Two weeks of fighting in June 1970 came to an end only through the efforts of an Arab mediation committee. Occasional clashes continued.

In September 1970, tensions erupted again when the *fedayeen* set out to disrupt the United Nation's peace talks among Jordan, Egypt and Israel. As part of the effort, one *fedayeen* group, the Popular Front for the Liberation of Palestine, hijacked three commercial planes belonging to the United States, Britain and Switzerland and flew the planes and 400 hostage passengers to a desert airstrip outside Amman. Several days later, the *fedayeen* blew up the planes and released the hostages in exchange for the release of fellow *fedayeen* members held captive in Switzerland, West Germany and Britain.

Heavy fighting broke out in mid-September 1970 between the Jordanian army and the *fedayeen* in Amman, the new headquarters of the guerrilla movement. A Syrian tank force crossed into Jordan Sept. 18 to aid the *fedayeen*, but fears of an enlarged conflict subsided several days later when the Syrian forces, repelled, withdrew.

Foreign ministers of surrounding Arab states met in Cairo Sept. 22 to try to resolve the crisis. King Hussein and guerrilla leader Yasir Arafat signed an agreement in October calling for substantial concessions by the *fedayeen*, but tensions continued into 1971. By April 1971, King Hussein had strengthened his position and ordered the *fedayeen* out of Amman. Despite commando protests, other Arab governments refused to intervene, and in July 1971, the Jordanian army crushed the last guerrilla strongholds.

The Palestinian guerrillas threatened reprisals for Jordan's action. Members of the Black September organization claimed responsibility for the assassination of Jordanian Prime Minister Wasfi al-Tal in November 1971 and for an unsuccessful attempt on the life of Jordan's ambassador to London.

Later, Hussein appeared to have mitigated his strong feelings against the Palestinian guerrillas. In a royal decree issued Nov. 13, 1974, he freed 100 political prisoners held in Jordanian prisons—an apparent gesture to Arafat, who addressed the United Nations General Assembly the same day. Most of the prisoners were members of Arafat's al Fatah.

On May 6, 1975, during a U.S. tour, Hussein said at the Citadel in Charleston, S.C., that Israel, as a condition for a permanent Middle East peace, must accept "the legitimate rights of the Palestinians in their homeland." The king repeated the assertion during other U.S. stops.

During the past few years Hussein has continued to play an ambiguous role on the Palestinian issue. While constantly supporting the rights of the Palestinians, he has expressed the hope that whatever Palestinian entity emerges will be linked to Jordan and not become an irredentist force in the area. As Hussein told journalist Stanley Karnow in an interview in early 1975 not long after the Rabat decision, "My feeling is that the ties between Palestinians and Jordanians are very, very strong, and they will be involved with each other if there is peace."[1]

Proposed Federation

King Hussein March 15, 1972, set forth plans for a "United Arab Kingdom." Under the federation, the Gaza Strip, the Israeli-occupied West Bank and the East Bank would have been united under Hussein. Each bank would have had a parliament under a federal parliament. While Israel's reaction was mixed, the Arab world thoroughly denounced the proposal at that time. The federation never materialized, but the continuing discussion of a Palestinian entity linked in some way to Jordan could possibly result in a rethinking of some aspects of this plan.[2]

1973 War

At the outbreak of the Yom Kippur war on Oct. 6, 1973, Jordanian troops were put on the alert. But when the forces did not engage in the fighting, King Hussein came under dual pressure to modify his position. While the United States asked for Jordan's assistance in quickly ending the war, Arab leaders urged Hussein to send troops to fight Israel. Jordan finally entered the war Oct. 13 after an appeal

from Saudi King Faisal, who had heavily contributed to Jordan's budget.

On Oct. 17, 1973, King Hussein called for peace in the Middle East, although he affirmed his intention of not yielding an inch of territory to Israel and of continuing to work for the recovery of occupied Arab lands. Jordan Oct. 22, 1973, accepted the U.N. truce and began to disengage its forces.

Government

Jordan is a constitutional monarchy under King Hussein I. The constitution was promulgated in January 1952. Executive authority rests with the king and the Council of Ministers. The king signs and executes laws and retains veto power unless overridden by a two-thirds vote by both houses of the National Assembly. His other powers include appointment and dismissal of all judges, approval or rejection of all constitutional amendments, declaring war and commanding the armed forces. Cabinet decisions, court judgments and the national currency are issued in his name. He is also immune from all liability for his actions.

The king appoints the Council of Ministers, which is headed by a prime minister. The Cabinet is responsible to the Chamber of Deputies, which can demand its resignation on a two-thirds vote of "no confidence."

The constitution established a bicameral legislature: the 60-member Chamber of Deputies, which is elected by universal suffrage every four years, and an upper house (Senate) composed of 30 members appointed by the king for four-year terms. Representation in the lower house is divided equally between the East and West Banks. Of the 60 seats in the lower house, 50 are allocated to Muslims and 10 to Christians.

Following the Arab summit conference in Rabat in October 1974, during which Hussein agreed to recognize the PLO as the sole legitimate spokesman for Palestinians, the king dissolved the parliament and appointed a new Senate in which the number of Palestinians was substantially reduced. Two years later, in February 1976, the king reconvened the lower house to ratify a royal decree amending the constitution to postpone lower house elections for an indefinite period because of continued Israeli occupation of the West Bank.

Foreign Policy and Middle East Peace

King Hussein's two major foreign policy goals have determined most of his other policies. First, he has emphasized the need to maintain a strong linkage with the United States. Second, he must ensure himself against those forces who wish to topple his kingdom. This has meant fostering a working alliance with Syria, Saudi Arabia and other Arab states while working to achieve a relationship with the Palestinians that will produce stability rather than turmoil in the area. In an interview in *Newsweek* in March 1977, Hussein looked to the uncertain future: "My duty is to develop my country, its human resources, armed forces and security and intelligence services, to face the tremendous threats that lie ahead," he said. "The road is strewn with mines to sabotage the peace process. . . . Reality shows that Geneva is not a panacea. And over-optimism will be our greatest problem."

Jordan has followed a consistent pro-West foreign policy, although it has never recognized Israel and has supported the Arab cause against the Jewish state. Since the 1967 war when Israel occupied the West Bank, a

---

1 Stanley Karnow, "An Interview with King Hussein," *The New Republic*, 22 February 1975, p. 20.

2 See Chapter 1 in John K. Cooley, *Green March Black September* (Frank Case: London, 1973) for a detailed discussion of this plan and of Hussein's motives.

primary objective of Jordan's foreign policy has been the recovery of that land.

Since the Rabat decision in 1974 elevating the PLO to spokesman for the occupied West Bank, King Hussein has followed a dual policy. He has retained ties to the West Bank leadership while endorsing the need for restoration of Palestinian rights. Whatever comes of the West Bank, Hussein has been striving to protect his country from any regional forces which could threaten his rule. There are many who have argued that an independent West Bank, PLO-run Palestinian state would represent more of a threat to Jordan than to Israel. As mentioned previously, after the Rabat decision, Hussein reorganized the Jordanian government to exclude most Palestinian representatives. When the National Assembly temporarily reconvened in February 1976 with West Bank representatives, the PLO charged Hussein was attempting to undermine it.

Since 1974, relations between Hussein and PLO leader Yasir Arafat have improved considerably, as have relations with Syria, Iraq and other Arab nations (with the exception of Egypt as a result of the 1979 peace treaty). Jordan and the PLO agreed to begin a dialogue in an effort to normalize relations that had been severely strained since the 1970 Jordanian-PLO clash in Jordan. Hussein and Arafat met at Mafraq in northern Jordan in September 1978, and official talks between Jordan and the PLO began in Amman in December following the Baghdad summit. On March 17, 1979, Hussein and Arafat moved a step closer to reconciliation with a joint declaration against the Egyptian-Israeli peace treaty. Following a four-hour meeting, both leaders confirmed the decision of the November 1978 Arab summit in Baghdad to reject Egypt's decision to negotiate with Israel. They agreed to set up a joint committee to coordinate opposition to the peace treaty. In addition, the king permitted the PLO to open offices in Amman, although he continued to oppose allowing the PLO to re-establish guerrilla bases in Jordan.

Despite strains caused by Jordan's rejection of the Camp David formula for a Middle East peace settlement, U.S.-Jordanian relations have remained close.

Nonetheless, speaking to reporters March 20, 1979, Hussein said disagreement over the Egyptian-Israeli peace treaty had caused a deep estrangement in Washington-Amman relations. And he warned that the pact could also result in a deterioration in U.S. relations with other Arab nations "for a long time to come." On numerous occasions the king has pointed out that "Jordan was mentioned 17 times in the Camp David agreements, and yet no one at Camp David even gave us a phone call to ask what we thought of them."

Although Hussein initially expressed admiration for Sadat's decision to hold direct talks with Begin, he has since Camp David expressed reservations about Egypt's decision to engage in a negotiating process that did not have a predetermined outcome.

Hussein has repeatedly emphasized that he remained committed to a negotiated solution of Arab-Israeli issues based on United Nations Security Council resolution 242 that called for a comprehensive settlement and a return to the 1967 boundaries. The major Jordanian objections to the Camp David accords were that they did not explicitly guarantee the restoration of Arab sovereignty over East Jerusalem, the West Bank, Gaza and the Golan Heights, and full Israeli withdrawal from those territories, and that they offered no assurances regarding the ultimate solution to the Palestinian problem.

Of Carter's role in the Middle East negotiations, Hussein said in late March 1979, "I think he is indeed sincere about peace. But after a good beginning, his methods and approach are badly misguided and will soon be disrailed. President Carter originally spoke of a comprehensive settlement. Now he has switched to a different course, the dangerous road to a partial settlement."

REBUILDING A WAR-RAVAGED COUNTRY

Lebanon, where orderly government until the mid-1970s rested on a delicate balance between its Christian and Moslem populations, was plunged into a ruinous civil war in April 1975. By the time the war was brought under control in November 1976, it had resulted in approximately 50,000 deaths (including the American ambassador, Francis E. Meloy in July 1976), destruction of the Lebanese army, the economic destruction of a country frequently described as the "Switzerland of the Middle East" and the domination of the country by neighboring Syria.

By mid-1979, the Syrians were still in Lebanon, but were attempting to extricate themselves from what became known as "Syria's Vietnam"; a United Nations peacekeeping force was in place to supply a buffer zone between the Israelis and the Palestine Liberation Organization (PLO) guerrillas still using southern Lebanon as a staging area for terrorist activities inside Israel; and the small militias of Lebanon's political factions were still disrupting all efforts at compromise and peace.

Other nations, in a rare unity of purpose, were trying to do what they could to restore peace and stability in the country. Although they may have preferred different routes, the Arab nations, Israel, the United States, France and the United Nations all had the same goal in mind. For its part, the United States believed a solution lay in strengthening the Lebanese army, which could bring about law and order, reduce the anarchistic tendencies of the populace and set the stage for reconstructing the Lebanese economy to which the United States already was contributing.

But it also was clear that the Lebanese had not yet developed the means to control their own destiny. By mid-1979, the Lebanese army had been rebuilt to a force of 18,000 (an army of 40,000 was envisioned), but it paled beside the nearly 30,000 Arab League troops (more than 22,000 of them from Syria) inside the country and the 4,500-member United Nations peacekeeping force stretched across southern Lebanon. The predominance of foreign forces in Lebanon was highlighted on June 27, 1979, when Israeli and Syrian jets staged a dogfight over the nation in the first Middle East air battle since the two nations fought over the adjacent Golan Heights in 1974. The Israelis were confronted by the Syrians in 1979 as they made raids — their 10th of the spring — on PLO guerrilla bases in Lebanon.

Complex Lebanese Politics

Though comprised of three major groups—Christians, Moslems, and Palestinians—the Lebanese political landscape is complex, with each group itself subdivided into numerous factions which at various times during the civil war fought with each other. A Beirut newspaper editor has commented, "...here we are with three armies, two police forces, 22 militias, 42 parties, nine Palestinian organizations, four radio stations, and two television stations." [1]

Lebanese President Elias Sarkis

For decades the Phalange Party led by Pierre Gemayel has been the strongest, most cohesive political group. These Christian rightist forces have sought the preservation of their privileges stemming from the 1926 Constitution and the unwritten 1943 National Covenant. They also have sought to rid the country of the Palestinian guerrillas. The Maronite Catholics, in particular, have been resentful of the Palestinians whom they had blamed for Israel's massive retaliation strikes against Lebanon, including a number of commando assaults on Beirut, in the early 1970s. The hatred was expressed in a sign posted outside the Palestinian Tal Zaatar refugee camp near Beirut which was to be destroyed in an historic 52-day siege during the summer of 1976: "It is the duty of every [Christian] Lebanese to kill a Palestinian." [2] Gemayel and other Christian leaders have called for the redistribution of the approximately 400,000 Palestinians in Lebanon among the less populated Arab countries. Former President Suleiman Franjieh, in his September 19, 1976, farewell address, placed total blame for the war and the country's destruction on the Palestinians.

Another important Christian leader is former President Camille Chamoun, whom President Franjieh appointed as foreign minister in June 1976, in a move characterized by Moslem Premier Rashid Karami as "unconstitutional and

1 Norman F. Howard, "Tragedy in Lebanon," *Current History*, January 1977, p. 2. For background information on the Lebanese situation through mid-1978, see "Middle East Peace Prospects" Hearings before the Subcommittee on Near Eastern and South Asian Affairs of the Senate Foreign Relations Committee, May, June, July 1976, pp. 121-183.

2 Howard, *ibid.*

groundless" and designed to thwart a smooth transfer of power to the new president, Elias Sarkis. [3]

But even traditional alliances have become blurred since the end of the civil war. Syrians have fought with Palestinians inside Lebanon; Lebanese Moslems and Israelis have made alliances; some Christians have allied with Israelis in the south; others have allied with Syrians in the north; Christians have fought other Christians; Palestinians have fought each other; and fledgling Lebanese government troops have had to confront all of the factions.

Franjieh's son, Tony, considered Syria's main Christian ally in Lebanon, was killed in a fight between warring Christian factions in mid-1978, leading to a flareup of fighting in Beirut, the heaviest since the civil war. The primary foes became the Syrian forces and the Christian militia. More than 200 persons were reported killed. Syria demanded that the Arab League forces be increased in all sectors of Lebanon, that the Lebanese army be reorganized to give Moslems equality with the commanding Christians and that the size of the Christian militia be reduced. In response, President Sarkis, citing a lack of cooperation by all the political elements in Lebanon, said in July 1978 that he would resign if Syria insisted on its demands. He was persuaded by representatives of most of the elements and by foreign governments to remain in office.

Until his assassination on March 16, 1977, Druze sect leader Kamal Jumblatt, a wealthy feudal boss over much of Lebanon's mountain country, led the nation's socialist-leftist-Palestinian coalition. Jumblatt's forces sought various political changes which would have resulted in a more equitable distribution of power between Christians and Moslems and a foreign policy more in line with Arab national goals, the main concern of the Palestinians. The Palestinians, comprising about four-fifths of the military force available to the leftists, were somewhat reluctantly drawn into the war late in 1975 in an effort to protect their privileges in a country in which they did not really belong.

One analyst gave the following description of the Palestinian entrance into the war, an action that precipitated, within a few months, the Syrian intervention:

> Despite PLO efforts to stay out of the conflict, the PLO leadership under Yasir Arafat reasoned, not illogically, that if the Christians defeated the indigenous left, the Palestinians would be their next target. Not surprisingly, therefore, by late 1975 the radical Popular Front for the Liberation of Palestine (PLFP) had become deeply implicated in the war on the leftist side. Arafat's Fatah joined the struggle openly in 1976, with disastrous results both for the Palestinians and for Lebanon. In March, 1976, for instance, Arafat reported that 16,000 Palestinians had been killed and 40,000 wounded. Rivalries among various Palestinian groups also intensified.... Many Palestinians apparently lost sight of their central goal: Salah Khalaf, Fatah's second-in-command, for instance, declared that the road to Palestine (Israel) ran through Jounieh, the Christian center north of Beirut. By summer, 1976, the PLO had suffered severe blows to its political prestige, and its forces were on the verge of total defeat at the hands of Syria. [4]

Syrian Intervention

During the early part of 1976, Syria became more and more politically involved in the Lebanese conflict. On January 22, the battered Christian forces accepted a cease-fire along with a Syrian-sponsored peace plan and reform package. President Franjieh at the time stressed that the reforms—which provided some additional power for the Moslems—could only be accepted after the Palestinians had in effect disarmed and started to adhere to the 1969 Cairo agreement which was designed to regulate their activities in Lebanon.

But within six weeks the peace plan failed. Franjieh came under heavy pressure from factions of the disintegrating army and the leftists to resign, but he refused. It was at this point that Syria became involved on the Christian side by adamantly refusing to support Jumblatt's mounting demands that Franjieh step down. A Saiqa (Syrian-controlled Al Saiqa forces) communique revealed Syria's feelings that "Jumblatt wants to rekindle the fire of sedition and sabotage of Syrian [peace] initiative." [5]

On April 10, the parliament voted 90-0 to amend the Constitution to permit the early election of Franjieh's successor. After some delaying tactics by Franjieh; the election took place on May 8, some two months before the scheduled balloting.

The Syrians pressed hard for their candidate, Elias Sarkis, governor of Lebanon's central bank. Jumblatt supported Raymond Edde, who was outspoken in his opposition to Syrian involvement in Lebanon. A general strike was called by the leftists in the hopes of preventing Sarkis' election. The election eventually took place, with mortar rounds falling near the temporary parliament building.

Franjieh, however, refused to leave office and Jumblatt urged "popular resistance" to Sarkis' election which he termed "a flagrant distortion of the wishes of the Lebanese people." [6]

As the year went on, little was resolved politically and the war intensified. A de facto partition of the country gradually came into effect as the Christian militias controlled a small enclave extending from eastern Beirut north to Tripoli. Sarkis took over the presidency on September 23, and by early October Syrian and Lebanese Christian forces had succeeded in overcoming leftist resistance in most areas of Lebanon.

Syria had gradually shifted her support to the Christians during 1976 when the left showed signs of victory. In April Syrian army regulars entered Lebanon, and on June 1 the Syrians intervened in force with a build-up to 30,000 men and 500 tanks. In June, a senior Syrian official called Arafat "a fool" for opposing the Syrian intervention, and Syrian President Assad placed the entire blame for the war on the PLO in July. [7] In September the Syrians opened a general offensive to crush the Palestinians and end the fighting. It was at this point that the Saudis and Egyptians decided a major Arab peace effort had to be made.

Saudi Influence

Arab leaders went to Riyadh, Saudi Arabia, on October 17 and 18 for a meeting, sponsored by the Saudi king, which was to mark the beginning of the end of the civil war in Lebanon. One major impetus behind their action was the desire of the Arab leaders to settle their own problems and prepare for resumption of negotiations with Israel following the U.S. presidential elections in November.

3. *Ibid.*, p. 4.
4. *Ibid.*, p.3.

5. *Ibid.*, p. 4.
6. *Ibid.*
7. *Ibid.*, p. 30.

At the Riyadh meeting, Assad and Egyptian President Sadat agreed on the establishment of a definitive cease-fire commencing October 21 and to be maintained by a 30,000-man Arab "deterrent" force under control of President Sarkis but which in fact would consist mainly of the Syrian forces then in Lebanon. Libya and Iraq wanted only limited Syrian participation in the force, but the plan was approved during an Arab League summit meeting in Cairo late in October. By November the war had largely ceased, though periodic fighting continued into 1979. The assassination of Jumblatt in March 1977 was a particular shock to the left and Palestinians.

Some estimates of the death toll during the 19 months of heavy fighting go as high as 60,000. Proportionally, this would be 75 times as many people killed during the civil war as were Americans killed during the eight years of fighting in Vietnam. The hatreds that existed before the conflict had thus been exacerbated, since nearly every family had experienced personal tragedy. For the left, the situation was especially bitter, for the country was dominated by Syria, and the Maronite majority remained in control of the social, economic and political systems.

But the Christians, too, faced a very anxious future. They remembered their near defeat in early 1976 before the Syrian intervention. To preserve their way of life, they were prepared, if necessary, to partition the country — a step Syria, the leftists in Lebanon and the entire Arab world opposed. Nevertheless, the Christians in 1977 began constructing an international airport (the Pierre Gemayel International Airport) in territories they controlled, and they had already set up the skeleton of a telephone and telex system for use should the Moslems ever cut off the regular facilities.

"Regionalization," a plan for de facto partition of Lebanon, was being pushed by the more extreme Camille Chamoun followers, and less so by the Phalangists. Chamoun's son, Dory, second in command of the Liberal Party, explained in April 1977 that "You can't force these people [the Lebanese] to live together now; there is too much tension between them. The tension must be reduced, and the only way it can be done is by creating regions that govern themselves under a federal system. It's the only way to preserve national unity." he added. [8]

Southern Lebanon

The focus of most of Lebanon's warring factions since the end of the civil war, except for periodic destructive clashes in Beirut, has been the area south of the Litani River to the Israel border, an area of more than 300 square miles or nearly one-tenth of all of Lebanon. While the Syrians were managing to keep general peace in the rest of the country, the Israelis had let it be known they would not tolerate the Syrian army near their border with Lebanon, nor would they accept the return of Palestinian guerrilla forces to what had been called "Fatah Land" for the al-Fatah, the strongest Arab guerrilla organization in the country. The Palestinians did return in 1978, however, and carried out damaging terrorist raids against Israel. The Israelis retaliated in March 1978 by invading southern Lebanon with 20,000 troops and taking control of the entire area, except for the city of Tyre, in an attempt to rid the area of the PLO. A March 19 United Nations resolution called for replacement of the Israeli troops with a UN force and Israel complied.

---

8. *The New York Times*, 10 April 1977.

Statistics on Lebanon

Area: 4,000 square miles.

Capital: Beirut.

Population: 2,600,000 (June, 1979 est.)

Religion: 55 per cent Christian, 44 per cent Moslem and Druze (based on 1932 official census); by the mid-1970s, Moslems believed to constitute a slight majority.

Official Language: Arabic; French is widely spoken.

GNP: $3.7-billion or $1,200 per capita (1979 est.).

Indicative of the inability to satisfy all the factions in Lebanon, however, was a statement by PLO Leader Yasir Arafat to Lebanese Prime Minister Selim al-Hoss that his forces would honor the truce, while George Habash, leader of the Iraqi-backed Popular Front for the Liberation of Palestine (PFLP), said his followers would not. The PFLP opposed any settlement with Israel, thus becoming known as the "rejection front."

The Israeli alliance with Christian forces in the area had begun in 1977 with what the Israelis called "The Good Fence." Israel not only supplied Christian forces with medical aid, food, and in some cases even jobs in Israel; it had also supplied arms to be used against the Palestinians in the later stages of the war. In March 1977, the Palestinians went on the offensive in southern Lebanon, apparently getting a green light from the Syrians after Chamoun's forces rejected Syrian demands that the Christians break off their cooperation with Israel.

Efforts to rebuild the Lebanese army as the first step in reasserting government control in the south began in June. After the 3,000-man nucleus of a new army had been organized, the PLO and Syria reached an agreement to bring Lebanese army forces into southern Lebanon to halt the fighting between Christians and Palestinians. One reason the Palestinians seemed eager for some kind of end to the southern Lebanon fighting was fear of a possible Israeli attack against the Palestinian guerrillas, especially after the election of the Likud Party in Israel, headed by Menachem Begin, who had a reputation of being militant.

But the Lebanese army was no match for all the factions in southern Lebanon, and the Palestinians soon returned to the area as a base for continuing their terrorist activities inside Israel. Israeli forces raided the PLO bases until finally they decided to take control of the entire area south of the Litani River.

In the spring of 1979, after suffering repeated raids by Israelis, Arafat announced the PLO would leave Lebanon and conduct its raids from Jordan, even though it had been banished from Jordan years earlier because of its terrorist activities. That did not end southern Lebanon's troubles, however. Maj. Saad Haddad, head of a Christian militia, said his pro-Israeli group would establish an independent "Free Lebanon" along a six-mile-deep border with Israel in defiance of UNIFIL (UN Interim Force in Lebanon) and the 500-man Lebanese army unit that had moved into the area to restore government control with Israeli approval. Haddad, whose forces had controlled that area since the end of the civil war, said the Lebanese army was pro-Syrian and had been infiltrated by Palestinian guerrillas. If the PLO ever intended to leave Lebanon, it was slow in doing so and Israeli raids continued through mid-1979.

Rebuilding The Country

Direct economic losses since the beginning of the civil war in 1975 — that is, physical damage alone — have been estimated at more than $3-billion, with indirect losses exceeding $15-billion, most of the losses occuring during the civil war itself. Whether Beirut would ever again become a financial center for international businesses and a playground for the jet set of the Arab world remained a major question, even were the country to be structurally rebuilt.

In an effort to show solid support for the Lebanese government of Sarkis, the United States committed itself to military and economic aid to Lebanon. Its policy was based on rebuilding the Lebanese army to the point that it could reestablish stability and respect for the government, while at the same time helping the nation to reconstruct its economy.

In the first two years following the end of the war, the United States gave Lebanon $70-million in relief and rehabilitation assistance. In 1978, U.S. economic aid to Lebanon totaled $36.9-million. Continuing the aid programs in the hopes that Lebanon would reestablish itself, the Carter administration planned assistance of $52-million in 1979, $38-million in 1980 and $10-million in 1981. These figures included very tentative projections of military aid scaled down from $42.5-million in 1979 to $32.5-million in 1980.

With that money and funds from other sources, the Lebanese government announced it would try to buy the airport the Phalangists had built for $50-million, rebuild Beirut's commercial center with a $167-million loan from Kuwait and undertake other reconstruction with $150-million it hoped to obtain from international sources. [9]

Terrain

Lebanon is situated on the eastern shore of the Mediterranean Sea and is bounded on the north and east by Syria and on the south by Israel. With an area of about 4,000 square miles, it is smaller than the state of Connecticut. It has a maximum length of 135 miles and is 20 to 35 miles wide.

Lebanon's terrain is predominantly mountainous. Behind a narrow coastal plain rise the high Lebanese Mountains, which are separated by the fertile Beqaa Valley from the Anti-Lebanon Mountains along the Syrian-Lebanese border. Lebanon's only important river, the Litani, flows into the sea north of Tyre. About 64 per cent of the land is desert, waste or urban; 27 per cent is agricultural and 9 per cent forested.

People

As of 1979, the only census conducted in Lebanon had been taken in 1932 when the country was under a French mandate. Because of the age of the census and the upheavals wrought by the civil war and its aftermath, there are no accurate figures for the makeup of the Lebanese people. In addition to the tens of thousands of deaths due to fighting, thousands of others have emigrated and many of those have returned, some re-emigrating as new flareups occurred. It has been estimated that more than 200,000 persons moved within Lebanon or left as fighting erupted in the south. Lebanon was estimated to have lost one million people as a result of the war, down to a population of 2.45-million in

1977. [10] Estimates are that the growth rate since has been between 2.3 per cent and 3 per cent, resulting in an estimated range from 2.5-million to 2.6-million in mid-1979.

Part of the problem of estimating population stemmed from the number of Palestinians who have immigrated to Lebanon from Israel and Arab nations. Although there were 182,000 Palestinians officially registered in December 1971, estimates of their numbers by the end of the decade ranged from 200,000 to 400,000. The population is considered to be 93 per cent Arab and 6 per cent Armenian. Before the war, about one-third of the total population lived in the capital city of Beirut.

Religious divisions not only are of great political importance in Lebanon: the government is officially structured to take those differences into account. But the structure is based upon a 1932 census that showed that 55 per cent of the population was Christian and 44 per cent was Moslem and Druze, an offshoot of Shia Islam. The French thus gave a controlling position to the dominant Maronite Christians, who have traditionally supplied the president of the nation while Sunni Moslems have provided the prime minister. The president of the chamber of deputies (parliament) has been a Shiite Moslem.

But the Lebanese Moslems contended, and Western estimates agreed, that the setup was outdated and that Moslems had become the majority in Lebanon, by a reverse ratio of 55 to 45 per cent. The estimates were that the Shiites comprised the largest religious sect in Lebanon, the Sunnis next, then the Maronites, Greek Orthodox, Druze and last, the Greek Catholics. It was, in fact, Moslem demands for a stronger voice in government to reflect their new majority that helped spark the civil war. Arabic is the official language, although French is widely spoken.

Economy

Because of the unrest that has kept the government from functioning efficiently, the Lebanese government, three years after the official end of the civil war, was still unable to provide a precise picture of its economy. Western analysts estimated Lebanon's gross national product at $3.7-billion in current prices in 1979, or $2.6-billion in constant prices. The $2.6-billion figure would be compared with the nation's pre-war GNP of more than $3-billion. Two-thirds of the 1973 GNP was drawn from services, primarily banking, commerce and tourism. Although economic figures were imprecise, one government report at the end of 1978 estimated unemployment at 90,000 and businesses that had restarted since the war at only 100,000. At the same time, there were only 10 American companies in Lebanon, compared with the prewar figure of 250. [11]

Before the war, Beirut served as a major transhipment point to the Arab interior, handling more than $900-million worth of goods annually. In the first six months of 1978 it handled only $135-million. But money was reported pouring into the country, primarily from Kuwait, which was backing Arab efforts to buy up Lebanese land as a counter to the wealthy Lebanese Christians, who were doing the same thing in an apparent attempt to establish rights as landowners in advance of whatever settlement of Lebanon's problems should eventually be made.

9. *Christian Science Monitor*, Feb. 15, 1978.

10. Central Intelligence Agency estimate in *National Basic Intelligence Handbook*, January 1977.
11. *The New York Times*, Dec. 2, 1978.

Transit trade was a major element in Lebanon's pre-war, free-enterprise economy. There were 75 banks and 120 legitimate labor unions, organizations generally banned in other Arab countries. Beirut also was an important gold and foreign exchange market. Although no oil has been found in Lebanon, Tripoli and Saida served as terminals of oil pipelines from Iraq and Saudi Arabia. Beirut, the country's chief seaport, also had a modern jet airport. International communications facilities included a satellite ground station and a cable linking Lebanon and France.

Lebanon had the highest literacy rate in the Arab world, 86 per cent, and a high percentage of skilled labor, but 49 per cent of the labor force still derived its living from agriculture. Principal products were cereals, vegetables, fruit and livestock. Lebanon was not self-sufficient in food and depended on imports for a substantial part of its food supply. The last export-import figures compiled showed Lebanese exports at $355-million in 1972, compared with $850-million in imports.

Lebanon's huge deficit was covered by large net receipts from such sources as transportation and tourism and private capital inflow, all seriously hurt since the start of the war. There were some signs in 1978 that the economy was well on its way to rebuilding, barring any new disruptions. Lebanon's chamber of commerce had noted that in the first half of 1978, flights at Beirut's airport, an indicator of business and tourist activity, were up nearly 40 per cent over the same period in 1977, the first year after the war.

History

In ancient geography, much of present-day Lebanon was part of Phoenicia. In later centuries Lebanon served as a Christian refuge, and during the Middle Ages it became part of the crusaders' states. It was absorbed into the Ottoman Empire in the 16th century. After World War I, Lebanon and Syria were divided into separate entities administered under French mandate. Lebanon gained its independence in 1943. French troops were withdrawn in 1946.

Since that time, Lebanon's history has been marked by recurrent political unrest and friction with Syria. President Bichara el-Khoury (1943-52) was deposed by a popular movement in 1952. Moslem opposition to the pro-Western policies of President Camille Chamoun (1952-58) led to an open revolt in May 1958, which was aggravated by Lebanon's Arab neighbors. At the request of the Lebanese government, the United States sent troops into Lebanon in July to help restore order. The revolt dwindled, and the U.S. forces were completely withdrawn by Oct. 25, 1958, after the inauguration of Fuad Chehab as president and the formation of a coalition government.

Both Chehab (1958-64) and his successor, Charles Helou (1964-70), pursued neutralist policies that were generally acceptable to both Arabs and the West. An attempt to overthrow the government by the Syrian Popular Party, which sought union with Syria, was put down in December 1961. President Franjieh was elected Aug. 17, 1970.

Although Lebanon participated in the 1948 Arab war against Israel, it generally has tried to keep its distance from the Arab-Israeli conflict. But the Palestine problem has contributed to internal instability.

In December 1968, an Israeli airliner in Athens was attacked by Arab terrorists who were said to have come from a Palestinian refugee camp in Lebanon; Israeli commandos retaliated with a raid on the Beirut airport. Lebanon's effort to restrict commando activities led to armed clashes in the country in 1969. Continued commando raids in 1970-71 brought further Israeli reprisal raids.

An Israeli raid on Palestinian commando groups in Beirut and Saida April 10, 1973, resulted in the resignation of Lebanese Premier Saeb Salam. He was succeeded by Amin Hafez, a former Palestinian who was reported to have strong ties with guerrilla organizations. Hafez, who resigned briefly during fighting between the Lebanese army and Palestinian commando groups in May 1973, finally gave up his post June 14, 1973, under pressure from Sunni Moslems who charged that his government did not adequately represent their sect. Franjieh June 21, 1973, called on Rashid al-Solh to form a new government. He survived until May 1975, when major riots forced his resignation and Franjieh called on Rashid Karami to form a cabinet that would appease warring factions.

Government and Politics

Lebanon is a parliamentary republic whose governmental system is based on the Constitution of May 26, 1926, and the National Covenant of 1943, an unwritten agreement providing for the distribution of public offices among the country's religious groups.

The Chamber of Deputies, Lebanon's unicameral parliament, has 99 members who represent the country's nine religious communities in proportion to their national numerical strength. Members are elected by universal adult suffrage. Elections are held every four years or within three months after parliament is dissolved by the president. The last parliamentary elections were held in April 1972.

Executive power is vested in a president, who is elected by a simple majority of the Chamber of Deputies for a six-year term. He appoints members of the cabinet, who are subject to a parliamentary vote of confidence.

Political activity in Lebanon is organized along sectarian lines, and political parties generally are vehicles for powerful political leaders whose followers are often of the same religious sect. Political stability is dependent on the maintenance of balance among religious communities.

Lebanon had one of the largest Communist parties in the Middle East. The party, which was legalized in 1970, had an estimated 6,000 members and sympathizers before the civil war. Palestinian refugees and Arab guerrilla organizations continue to exert substantial political pressure. But, Lebanese politics since 1976 have been dominated by Syria.

Within days of a meeting between Sarkis and Syrian President Hafez al-Assad in Damascus in May 1979, Prime Minister Selim Hoss, whose "technocrats" government had served longer than any other in Lebanon since independence, announced his resignation in favor of a "national reconciliation." A new Cabinet, presumably, would be composed of the leaders of the Lebanese factions that have been at war with each other throughout the decade.

Hoss and the Lebanese Cabinet had resigned a year earlier, in April 1978, in another attempt to form a unified government, but the traditional rivalries prevented any agreement on a new Cabinet. Sarkis renamed Hoss prime minister the same month and reinstated the Cabinet in May.

According to an article in the June 1979 issue of *Middle East* magazine, "Most Lebanese agree . . . that even if some kind of formal solution is put together, real national reconciliation will not be so easily achieved. For the bitterness and social dislocation which has resulted from the civil war will remain. Wounds reopened so many times take a long time to heal and whatever the composition of the new government, it will face almost insuperable problems."

Foreign Relations

Lebanon's dependence on trade demands good relations with other countries. Lebanese Christians are especially interested in friendly ties with Western countries, particularly the United States, and Lebanese foreign policy has been generally pro-Western. In its relations with the Communist bloc, Lebanon has pursued a more or less neutral line.

Although Lebanon is an Arab state and a member of the Arab League, it has sought to avoid major involvement in the Arab-Israeli conflict. Many Lebanese Christians would welcome peace with Israel—partly for the trade which peace would permit, but also as a contribution to Lebanon's internal stability. How the de facto alliance between Lebanese Christians and Israel would affect Lebanon's future was uncertain in mid-1979.

Under the National Covenant of 1943, Christians are prohibited from seeking foreign protection or attempting to bring Lebanon under foreign control or influence, while Moslems are prohibited from trying to bring Lebanon into any form of Arab union.

In reality, however, by 1979 Damascus, Syria, had become in effect the capital of Lebanon, and outside forces had as much to say about the future of the country as did the Lebanese. With the same old rivalries continuing, the Lebanese army still too weak to have much effect in reestablishing stability and the Syrians' disenchantment with their own ability to achieve a solution in Lebanon, the little nation remained a tinderbox.

The New York Times, in reporting on the Hoss resignation, quoted an unnamed Western diplomat as saying, "Anybody with a gun can light the fuse in Lebanon today. There are at least 70,000 armed men out there with guns and clashing political ideologies who can do it." [12]

---

12 *The New York Times,* May 20, 1979, p. E3.

EVANGELICAL BLEND OF ORTHODOX AND RADICAL

Col. Muammar al-Qaddafi has pursued Arab unity with singular fervor, turning Libya into a suitor whose persistence only repels less ardent Arab states. The colonel has turned east to Egypt, then west to Tunisia, but has failed to forge a union of his nation with either one. Although both of his neighbors would welcome a share of Libya's oil wealth, they are scared off by Qaddafi himself, at once aggressive, radical and erratic, and never shy about heaping scorn on Arab leaders who spurn his overtures.

During the past few years, relations between Egypt and Libya have become tense. In August 1976 President Sadat of Egypt moved troops to guard his border with Libya. In April 1977, Egypt convicted and hanged Libyan terrorists said to be involved in assassination plots and sabotage. That same month a Libyan mob sacked the Egyptian consulate in Benghazi. Actual fighting broke out between Egypt and Libya in July.

Although open hostilities have since ceased, Egyptian-Libyan relations have become increasingly strained as Egyptian-Israeli relations have improved.

Qaddafi has failed to command leadership in Arab affairs, because, among other things, he breaches no softening of his blend of strictly orthodox Islam and radical socialism. Remaining true to the hard-line "rejectionist" ideology, Qaddafi has vigorously opposed a negotiated settlement with Israel and has called for the annihilation of Israel as a state. The Libyan leader has made the concept of Arab unity nearly a religion, but he has failed miserably in bringing it about.

On Feb. 10, 1974, Qaddafi was quoted as saying that he would arm and train revolutionaries to overthrow the governments of Tunisia, Egypt and Algeria if Arab unity could not be achieved by "normal means"—a statement his aides said was misinterpreted, but one accepted at face value by leaders in Tunis, Cairo and Algiers.

Over the years, Qaddafi has been accused of aiding revolutionary movements from the Philippines to the Irish Republican Army, as well as movements in neighboring countries, the most publicized being Chad. In another well-publicized venture, Libyan troops suffered a humiliating defeat when it came to the aid of Ugandan President Idi Amin in his final days.

All of this has continued, according to Egypt's Sadat, with the encouragement and support of the Soviet Union. Although Libya's military stockpiles have been supplied over the years by the Soviet Union, and its ties to the Soviets may be growing closer in response to Egypt's rapprochement with the United States, Libya is said to retain a non-aligned policy. Qaddafi reportedly has supported revolutionary movements not as a Marxist, but as a revolutionary purist.

Terrain

Located on the north central coast of Africa, Libya has a coastline of about 1,100 miles on the Mediterranean Sea. It is bounded by Egypt on the east, Sudan on the southeast, Tunisia and Algeria on the west and Niger and Chad on the South.

Libyan Leader, Col. Muammar al-Qaddafi

Libya's area of 679,536 square miles—about 2½ times the size of Texas—is approximately 95 per cent desert or semi-desert. There are two small areas of hills and mountains in the northeast and northwest and another zone of hills and mountains rising more than 10,000 feet, in the Saharan south and southwest.

Only 2 per cent of the total land area, largely in the narrow coastal strip, is arable; another 4 per cent is semi-arid grazing land. Libya has no permanent rivers, although large subterranean water reserves are fairly widespread. Rainfall, always scanty, falls about once every three years. A hot, dry, dust-laden wind called the *ghibli* is a recurrent threat to crops.

People

Libya had an estimated population of 2.6 million in 1977, with an average annual growth rate of 3.7 per cent. Ninety per cent of the people live in less than 10 per cent of the area, chiefly in the coastal regions. About 20 per cent of the people live in the co-capitals of Tripoli and Benghazi.

Libya's population is 97 per cent Arab and Berber, with some Negro stock. The population includes some Greeks, Maltese, Jews, Italians and Egyptians. About 97 per cent of the people are Moslems, nearly all of whom belong to the orthodox Sunni sect. Arabic is the official language.

Economy

Oil is Libya's principal product and main source of revenue, accounting for 99 per cent of its exports. Since the first major discovery of oil in 1959, Libya's economy has expanded rapidly. But by 1978, oil revenues alone had jumped to $8.6-billion from $1.6-billion in 1972, making Libya one of the richest countries in the world on a per capita basis, even though petroleum production had not increased substantially, hovering around two million barrels per day.

Proximity to Europe and the closing of the Suez Canal in 1967 were major factors in Libya's rapid rise as an oil producer. Unlike other Middle East oil states that gave one huge concession to a major foreign oil company, Libya granted concessions to many companies of different nationalities—mainly U.S., British and West German. On Sept. 1, 1973, Libya nationalized 51 per cent of the assets of all foreign oil companies operating in the country. On Feb. 11, 1974, Libya totally nationalized three U.S. oil firms—Texaco, California-Asiatic Oil Company, a subsidiary of Standard Oil of California, and Libyan-American, a subsidiary of Atlantic-Richfield Company.

Although overshadowed by oil, agriculture is the second-largest sector in the Libyan economy. Libya is not self-sufficient in many kinds of food. Major crops include barley, wheat, olives, dates, citrus fruits and peanuts. Sheep and goats are the chief livestock. An estimated 36 per cent of the labor force was engaged in agriculture in 1971.

History

Libya was conquered by the Arabs in the seventh century, ruled by Turkey from 1553 to 1911 and administered as an Italian colony from 1911 until World War II. After Italian forces were expelled from the area in 1943, Libya was administered by the British and French.

Libya was the first nation to achieve independence under the auspices of the United Nations. In November 1949, the U.N. General Assembly adopted a resolution calling for the independence of Libya not later than Jan. 1, 1952. Libya declared its independence Dec. 24, 1951, as a constitutional and hereditary monarchy under King Idris I, a local ruler who had led Libyan resistance to Italian occupation.

King Idris was deposed Sept. 1, 1969, by a military junta which abolished the monarchy and proclaimed a Socialist Libyan Arab Republic. Col. Qaddafi, the leader of the coup, became chairman of the Revolutionary Command Council, the nation's chief governing body. A provisional constitution promulgated in December 1969 proclaimed Libya "an Arab, democratic and free Republic which constitutes a part of the Arab nation and whose objective is comprehensive Arab unity."

One of the early objectives of the new government was the withdrawal of all foreign military installations from Libya. In 1970, the British withdrew from their military installations at Tobruk and El Adem, and the United States withdrew from Wheelus Air Force Base near Tripoli.

Qaddafi in April 1973 proclaimed a new "popular revolution" involving a five-point reform program. The program called for suspension of existing laws and promulgation of new ones; implementation of Islamic thought, distribution of arms to loyal citizens; purging of political deviationists, including those who preached communism and capitalism, and a campaign against bureaucratic inefficiency. "Popular committees" were set up throughout the country to serve as the main instrument of the revolution.

In 1977, the country's name was changed to the "Socialist People's Libyan Arab Jamahiriya" and all power was vested in the General People's Congress. The Revolutionary

---

Statistics on Libya

Area: 679,536 square miles.
Capital: Tripoli, Benghazi co-capitals.
Population: 2,607,000 (1977 est.).
Religion: 97 per cent Moslem.
Official Language: Arabic.
GNP: $11.9-billion, $6,000 per capita (1979).

Command Council was abolished, but its members were named members of the Secretariat of the new Congress and serve in an advisory capacity. Qaddafi, as secretary general of the Secretariat, remained chief of state.

Foreign Relations

Under Qaddafi, two themes have dominated Libyan foreign policy: Arab unity and anti-imperialism.

In September 1971, Libya joined Egypt and Syria in a loose political confederation. On Aug. 2, 1972, Qaddafi and Egyptian President Anwar Sadat announced that "unified political leadership" had been established between their two countries and pledged to achieve a full merger by Sept. 1, 1973. But Qaddafi and Sadat differed on major issues, including their approach to Israel, and on Aug. 29, 1973, the two leaders signed a compromise agreement under which they pledged only to establish a union by gradual stages.

But as the merger plan collected dust and eventually died, relations between Egypt and Libya grew increasingly hostile. In February 1974, Qaddafi said he would turn Libya into "a school where we will teach how a people can take up arms to stage a revolution." His threat was aimed at Sadat, among others. In the spring of 1975, Tripoli began threatening to sever relations with Cairo, and the controlled Libyan press described Sadat and his wife as a "20th century Anthony and Cleopatra." Sadat countered the insult by saying Qaddafi was "100 per cent sick and possessed by the devil." In June, Cairo newspapers reported that Egypt had imposed new restrictions on travel to Libya, requiring special permits and banning tourist travel. Since then the relationship has progressively deteriorated.

Plans to implement a merger between Libya and Tunisia also foundered. Tunisian President Habib Bourguiba declined a merger offer from Qaddafi in December 1972, but on Jan. 12, 1974, Libya and Tunisia announced an agreement to unite their two countries in a single nation to be known as the Islamic Arab Republic.

Algeria and Morocco strongly opposed the decision, however, and Tunisia subsequently announced that the proposed union required further consultations with Libya. It also invited Algeria, Morocco and Mauritania to join the union. A referendum on the merger, planned for Jan. 18, 1974, was postponed. As in the case of Egypt, Qaddafi's hard-line policy toward Israel appeared to be a major stumbling block to union. Finally, on March 29, 1975, Bourguiba explained away the union, saying that Tunisia could enter a merger only if a popular referendum were held and that the Tunisian constitution did not provide any referendum procedures.

In its relations with the superpowers, Libya has been critical of both the United States and the Soviet Union, but has benefited by various relationships with both. It has denounced American support for Israel, and it refused to go along with the March 18, 1974, decision of seven other Arab oil-producing states to end the oil embargo against the United States. (Libya lifted the embargo at the end of 1974.) Libya has criticized the Soviet Union, as well as the United States, for practicing imperialism. It also has charged the Soviets with duplicity in their arms deals with Arab states, while Marxism has been attacked as an atheistic doctrine that is incompatible with Arab thought. Still, Libya's relationship with the Soviet Union has caused Sadat in Egypt to see Libya as one of Moscow's agents in attempts to penetrate Africa with Soviet influence.

Politically, Libya has pursued a policy of neutralism between East and West, but its major trading partners lie in the Western bloc: West Germany, Italy, the United States, the United Kingdom and France. France, the Soviet Union and Czechoslovakia are its chief arms suppliers; U.S. arms sales to Libya were suspended in September 1969.

In December 1978 the Carter administration approved the sale of cargo-carrying trucks to Libya, signaling a slight easing of tensions. Earlier in 1978 the State Department had blocked a proposed sale of heavier duty trucks on the grounds that they could be used to haul tanks. Libya reportedly has provided written assurances that the cargo trucks will not be used for military purposes.

During a May 1975, visit to Libya by Soviet Premier Alexei N. Kosygin, the two countries signed a major arms deal, variously estimated at $800-million by the Russians, $1-billion by U.S. intelligence sources and $4-billion by the Egyptians. Libya and the Soviet Union have expanded this arms relationship in recent years. Egypt has begun openly expressing fear that Soviet influence in Libya and Ethiopia might seriously threaten the Sudan, Egypt's ally.

But Qaddafi has insisted he was only stockpiling arms to serve as an arsenal for the Arab states in case of a new Arab-Israeli war.

In mid-1977 Qaddafi began attempts to mend his fences with Arab leaders. Libya and Egypt, for some months, halted propaganda attacks against each other and Libya ended the expulsion of Egyptians living there. Qaddafi also appealed to the United States to send a full ambassador to Tripoli.

Although U.S. officials have indicated in 1979 that there were signs of a more "positive" attitude on Libya's part, the two countries still had a long way to go before there could be a major improvement in relations. From the U.S. viewpoint, three major obstacles stood in the way of better relations: Libya's support of international terrorism, interference in the affairs of its neighbors and resistance to the achievement of a Middle East peace settlement.

Libyan money has been finding its way to a variety of causes. It is generally believed that Libya contributes substantially to Palestinian groups most opposed to any settlement with Israel. Libya has also endowed a chair at Georgetown University in Washington, D.C. Other funds were used to support the film "Mohammed, Messenger of God." In short, Qaddafi has mixed oil, petrodollars and Islamic fanaticism into a blend of political and cultural chauvinism.

THE EMIRATES: DESERT POVERTY TO OIL RICHES

Not long ago, the desert sheikhdoms that dot the western and southern shores of the Persian Gulf[1] were remote and backward lands peopled by camel herders and pearl fishermen. The place names of Kuwait, Qatar, Bahrain, Abu Dhabi, Dubai and Sharjah had minuscule impact on world consciousness.

But that was before the dramatic increase in demand for oil, coupled with OPEC price hikes. Since 1973-74, when OPEC began increasing the price of oil dramatically, the Persian Gulf states have become significant forces in the world economy, with Kuwait and Abu Dhabi enjoying per capita incomes equal to or exceeding those of the Western industrialized nations. Oil revenues have produced substantial funds to invest overseas and at the same time have attracted foreign industries to help in developing rapidly expanding internal economies. While oil still forms the main source of their income, the gulf states are working at creating diversified economies which can continue to provide a high standard of living after the oil reserves have been depleted. Bahrain, which by 1979 had nearly exhausted its oil supplies, and Qatar have been the most active in developing alternate industries.

The need for reliable supplies of imported oil has underscored the strategic importance of the gulf states, especially since the 1978-79 revolution in Iran. More than ever the United States, Europe and Japan are concerned with maintaining the political and social stability of the Persian Gulf region. This interest has been complicated by the sometimes opposing interests of the United States and the Persian Gulf countries, as occured in the case of the U. S.-supported Egyptian-Israeli peace negotiations which the gulf states viewed with some apprehension. The failure of the United States to provide greater support to the shah of Iran has also led to a reassessment of the value of America as an ally. While the smaller gulf states feared an increase in the Soviet presence in the Persian Gulf area, they were no longer sure they could rely on the United States during a crisis.

The gulf nations' international politics are carried out against a backdrop of sometimes intense regional rivalries. The small emirates and gulf states are in many ways dependent on Saudi Arabia for policy guidance, yet they are determined to avoid Saudi domination. All of the nations in the gulf region have essentially similar goals, but they differ on how to achieve them.

Bahrain

Area: 260 square miles.
Capitol: Manama.
Population: 305,000 (1977 est.).
Religion: Moslem, evenly divided between the Sunni and Shia sects, Sunni predominates in urban centers, Shia in rural areas.
Official language: Arabic; English is widely used.
GNP: $660-million; per capita income $2,400.

Terrain

The emirate consists of about 35 desert islands in the Persian Gulf — with a total territory one-fifth the size of Rhode Island — which lie 15 miles east of Saudi Arabia and the same distance west of the emirate of Qatar. Bahrain is the main island. Other important islands are Muharraq, Sitra, Umm Na'san and the Howar group. The beaches are mud flats.

People

The majority of the population consists of Moslem Arabs, nearly a third of whom are non-Bahrainian Arabs, Indians, Iranians and Pakistanis. Bahrain is the only gulf state that boasts a native population that outnumbers imported workers. Most of the population inhabits Bahrain, the largest island and the one from which the emirate derives its name. The largest city is Manama, the capital (90,000). The predominant Moslem religion is evenly divided between the Sunni and Shia sects. The ruling family is Sunni.[2]

Economy

Bahrain discovered oil in 1932, one of the first Persian Gulf states to do so, but its reserves are almost depleted and its oil income is declining. Bahrain's economy is not as strong as those of its Arab neighbors; it has restrained internal spending and attempted to diversify. The development of industry has been encouraged and banking has become an important activity, particularly since the war in Lebanon forced many financial institutions to flee Beirut. A large refinery on Sitra Island is kept busy refining Saudi Arabian oil moved through underwater pipeline from the mainland. The government has developed an aluminum

PERSIAN GULF STATES

Map showing: KUWAIT, SAUDI ARABIA, IRAN, BAHRAIN, QATAR, Persian Gulf, Ras Al Khaimah, Umm Al Qawain, Ajman, Dubai, Sharjah, Abu Dhabi, Fujairah, to Oman, OMAN, UNITED ARAB EMIRATES. Statute Miles 0 50 100 150

---

1 Many of the Arab states term the sea between Iran and Saudi Arabia the "Arab Gulf." Popular usage in the U.S. continues to refer to it as the "Persian Gulf."

2 For a revealing description of life in Bahrain see Part III in Linda Blandford's *Superwealth, The Secret Lives of the Oil Sheikhs* (Morrow, N.Y.: 1977).

processing plant, the first in the Arab world, and is at work on a gas liquefaction project.

Banking has been encouraged through special legislation allowing foreign banks to set up Offshore Banking units (OBUs) to handle international financial matters. By the end of 1977 nearly 40 banks had obtained government permission to establish OBUs.

Manama was declared a free transit port in 1958 and the port city of Mira Solman is being developed to handle containerized cargo. The international airport at Muharraq is the most important in the Persian Gulf. British Airways and Gulf Air have headquarters there.

A substantial number of American and European companies have offices and installations in Bahrain. An American engineering and construction firm, Brown and Root Inc. of Houston, Texas, maintains the largest headquarters, supplying offshore oil-drilling rigs to oil companies. Other important foreign companies include Gray Mackenzie shipping lines and Grindlay's, a British bank.

The only agriculture is on the northern end of Bahrain Island, where dates, rice and vegetables are grown. The fields are irrigated from underground springs. Once-important pearl fishing is now in decline. The building of dhows and the making of sailcloth and reed mats are minor but old industries.

History

Archaeologists and historians relate Bahrain Island to the ancient Sumerian civilization center of Dilmun, known as the "earthly paradise," dating back to 2600 B.C. The archipelago is mentioned for its strategic and commercial importance by Assyrian, Persian, Greek and Roman geographers and chroniclers.

Portuguese sailors captured the islands from local Arab rulers in 1521. After Portuguese dominance ended in 1602, Bahrain was conquered by a series of Arab tribes until a paramount family, the al-Khalifas, established themselves as sheikhs of Bahrain in 1782. The family still rules.

Isa bin Sulman al-Khalifa

In 1820, the British established hegemony over the islands, taking over responsibility for defense and foreign policy. In return for this protection from large Arab tribes, the sheikhs promised to refrain from "prosecution of war, piracy or slavery."

In August 1971, Bahrain declared independence from Britain and signed a treaty of friendship with the former mother country. Bahrain joined the United Nations and the Arab League. Choosing to remain totally independent, Bahrain rejected a proposed federation with neighboring Qatar and the United Arab Emirates.

Government

The ruler is Emir Isa bin Sulman al-Khalifa, born in 1933. He enjoys almost absolute power. In 1970, an 11-member Council of State was created, responsible to the emir and serving at his pleasure. Elections were held to a small National Assembly in December 1973, but the assembly was dissolved within two years.

Royalties from oil, while declining, still account for between 70 and 80 percent of Bahrain's national income, with the rest coming primarily from custom duties. The government provides extensive social services including free medical treatment and free primary, secondary and technical education. Bahrain's reputation for having good schools and a high literacy rate has been one of the reasons Western companies are attracted to the islands.

Foreign Relations

Bahrain still has strong ties to Britain, which, with Saudi Arabia, is its main trading partner.

The U.S. Navy had docking facilities at Jufair. In October 1973, Bahrain suspended the naval agreement, charging Washington with ignoring its warning concerning the United States' "hostile stand against the Arab nations." After quiet negotiations, the Bahrainians allowed the Navy to return in 1974. The arrangement ended in 1977, but U.S. Navy ships are still allowed to dock at Bahrain from time to time. *(Box, p. 42)*

Because of its size and location Bahrain must maintain close relations with Saudi Arabia, but there has been resistance to any overt domination by the Saudis. In particular, controversy has arisen over a causeway, financed by Saudi Arabia, that is to link Bahrain with the Saudi mainland. Some Bahrainians have expressed fears that the causeway could increase Saudi influence in Bahrain.

In an interview with *U.S. News & World Report* in April 1979, Prime Minister Khalifa bin Sulman al Khalifa criticized the United States for failing to be consistent in supporting the shah of Iran before he was deposed and for breaking ties with the Nationalist Chinese on Taiwan. The prime minister expressed his concern over the security of the Persian Gulf and said he was worried that the United States might be passing up its last chance to have a major impact in the area if it failed to maintain close ties with Saudi Arabia.

Kuwait

Area: 7,780 square miles.
Capital: Kuwait.
Population: 1,130,000.
Religion: About 95 percent Moslem.
Official language: Arabic; English is widely spoken.
GNP: $16.5-billion; per capita income, $15,480.

Terrain

Kuwait is slightly smaller than New Jersey. It is located on the northeastern corner of the Arabian Peninsula, bordered on the north and west by Iraq, on the east by the Persian Gulf and on the south by Saudi Arabia. The terrain is mainly flat desert with a few oases. There are no rivers. The heat is torrid in summer; winter brings severe dust storms.

People

Native Kuwaitis today make up less than half the population. Most of them are Arabs, principally of the Suni sect. Non-Kuwaitis make up almost 80 percent of the national work force.

The majority of the population consists of immigrants who do not enjoy Kuwaiti nationality and are not allowed to vote. Nearly one quarter of the population is Palestinian and there are significant numbers of Indians, Pakistanis, some Egyptians, Arabs from neighboring countries and a small number of British and Americans.

Most of the population lives in Kuwait town.

Economy

Tiny Kuwait is an opulent strip of desert which boasts of a standard of living second to none in the world, thanks to its one and only export, crude oil and petroleum products. The country is the second smallest in the Arab League and the richest — its per capita income is the highest in the world.

The government owns the Kuwait Oil Company which for many years was owned jointly by the British Petroleum Company and the Gulf Oil Corp. On Jan. 1, 1973, the government of Kuwait acquired a 25-percent share of the company. This rose to 100 percent in 1976.

With an estimated 70 billion barrels of oil, Kuwait has more proved and probable petroleum reserves than any other country in the world except Saudi Arabia. In 1978 oil production hit an estimated two million barrels per day, with known reserves expected to last another 50 years.

Kuwait has practiced a policy of oil conservation and has limited production to less than capacity in order to make the supplies last longer into the future. In addition, the government has been emphasizing the need to establish new industries which will enable the country to become self-sufficient in the long run. While much oil wealth has been invested abroad, particularly in securities, real estate and banks, more money is now being spent to develop the country's internal economy.

History

The name Kuwait is derived from "kut," meaning a small fort. In the early 18th century, the territory was settled by three Arab clans, and in 1756 Sheikh Sabah Abdul Rahim founded the al-Sabah dynasty, which rules to this day.

As one recent visitor amusingly tells the story, "After a shocking drought in the desert in 1710 some of the more aristocratic Bedouins went down to the Gulf for a sight of water. They wandered around until they settled on a convenient spot, Kuwait. Someone had the bright idea of sending one of their clever young men off to see the nearest Turkish governor to get permission to stay put, on condition they kept quiet. His mission was a success; his name was al-Sabah. His family has been top dog ever since; everyone else who was around at the time is 'heritage.'[3]

The ruling prince of the nominally Ottoman Turkish province made a treaty with Great Britain in 1899 because he feared the Turks wanted to make their authority effective. One British aim was to prevent the German kaiser from building the terminus of the Berlin-Baghdad railway on Kuwaiti territory on the Persian Gulf. When war broke out with Turkey in 1914, London recognized Kuwait as an independent state under British protection.

British troops twice have gone to Kuwait's rescue when it was troubled by larger neighbors, the first time repelling attacks from Najd (now Saudi Arabia) by Wahhabi fanatics. A 1922 treaty settled the matter and set up the neutral zone southeast of Kuwait—later a rich oil area (with 4 percent of the world's oil reserves) over which Kuwait and Saudi Arabia share sovereignty.

---

3 *Ibid.,* p. 212. See Chapter IV in Blandford's book for a description of Kuwait today.

Great Britain granted Kuwait full independence in 1961, which led to Iraq's claiming the tiny state as a province. When Baghdad threatened to invade, the Kuwaitis asked for British military aid, which was promptly dispatched, and Iraqi action was deterred. Iraq recognized Kuwait's independence in 1963, the same year the sheikhdom was admitted to the United Nations.

Government

Kuwait is a constitutional monarchy with Sheikh Jaber Al-Ahmed al-Sabah as emir. He is assisted by a Cabinet of 14 ministers (10 appointed and four elected) headed by a prime minister. The constitution, dating from 1962, provides for a 50-member National Assembly, elected by all natural-born literate Kuwati males over 21. In August 1976 the National Assembly was suspended. The emir promulgates laws and decrees, and has taken over full legislative powers.

Life Styles

Because of Kuwait's vast oil riches, poverty hardly exists in the country. Kuwait is a curious mixture of capitalist intake of money and socialist output of services. Citizens are provided free education, free medical services, free telephones and virtually free housing, and they pay no taxes. The literacy rate of over 80 percent is one of the highest in the Arab world.

Jaber Al-Ahmed al-Sabah

However, Kuwait often is an economic paradise for the native-born only, even though foreigners comprise 60 percent of the population and 80 percent of the labor force. Each Kuwaiti citizen is guaranteed a job and a minimum annual income of about $8,500, a spectacularly high figure outside the Western world. Yet the immigrants — Palestinians, Iraqis, Egyptians, Indians, Iranians and Pakistanis — often earn no more than $2,500. Only Kuwaiti citizens receive subsidized housing and can own land on which a house can be built. It is exceedingly difficult for foreigners other than Arabs to obtain Kuwaiti citizenship. However, most aliens complain little, probably because they do better in Kuwait than they would have done in their home countries.

Kuwait has a higher proportion of the latest American automobiles than any other country outside the United States, and they are driven over wide, well-surfaced roads. The government built the modern city of Rikka in the desert 25 miles south of Kuwait town. The city has 5,000 duplex housing units valued at $13,000 each.

The sheikhdom boasts of twice as many air-conditioning units as people and one millionaire for every 230 persons. In short, modern Kuwait is a garish, *nouveau-riche* land.

Kuwaiti efforts to employ its oil riches to transform a hot, sleepy land into a modern state are largely the work of Sheikh Abdullah al-Salem al-Sabah, who died in 1965. Abdullah believed that the country could not develop unless it shed its tribal structure and its wealth was distributed among its people.

Foreign Policy

During the 1967 Arab-Israeli war, Kuwait joined in the ineffectual oil embargo ordered by Arab states against Western nations. Kuwait cut off shipments to the United States and Britain on June 6, 1967. At the time, Britain was getting 23 percent of its oil requirements from Kuwait. However, Kuwait did not break off diplomatic relations. Kuwait, a member of the Organization of Petroleum Exporting Countries (OPEC), also took part in the effective 1973 oil boycott.

Kuwait's conservative ruling family has expressed alarm over Soviet inroads in the Persian Gulf — the arming of Iraq by Moscow and the use of an Iraqi port at the head of the gulf by Soviet warships. Yet Kuwait has diplomatic relations with both the Soviet Union and China and has recently begun acquiring Russian arms and some military advisers.

Some years ago Kuwait considered forming a federation of nine neighboring sheikhdoms as a means of thwarting the possibility of the sheikhdoms toppling to revolutionary movements. While nothing came of the plan, Kuwait's prime minister and crown prince Sheikh Sa'ad al-Abdullah al-Sabah has been active in developing cooperation and coordination among the Arab states. Sa'ad has expressed the opinion that the security of the gulf states should be left to the people of the area and that it would be unacceptable for any country from outside the region to interfere in its affairs.

Kuwait has traditionally been friendly toward the Palestinians. The government supplies funds to the Palestine Liberation Organization (PLO) and has indicated that it would not support any Arab-Israeli peace settlement that is not acceptable to the Palestinians.

Qatar

Area: 4,000 square miles.
Capital: Doha.
Population: 200,000.
Religion: Mostly Sunni Moslems of the Wahhabi sect.
Official language: Arabic; some English is spoken.
GNP: $2.4-billion; per capita income, $11,400.

Terrain

Qatar, pronounced "gutter" in Arabic, occupies a thumb-shaped desert peninsula stretching north into the Persian Gulf. On the south it borders the United Arab Emirates and Saudi Arabia. Qatar is about the size of Connecticut. The peninsula is a low, flat, hot, dry plain, consisting mostly of limestone with sand on top. On the west coast is a chain of hills, the Dukhan Anticline, and beneath it is oil, which gives Qatar its importance.

People

The population is composed of Qataris, Arabs from neighboring states and Iranian immigrants. Less than half the population is native born. About 80 percent of the people are located in and around the capital city of Doha on the east coast; Doha has an estimated population of 130,000. There is a sprinkling of Bedouin nomads.

Economy

The oil resource accounts for nearly all of Qatar's national income. Discovered in the Dukhan range in 1940, oil was brought into production in 1947. Development of offshore fields and improved techniques in the 1960s greatly increased output. The country produced an estimated 480,000 barrels of oil per day in 1978.

One-fourth of the oil revenue is reserved for the ruler. The rest is spent on public development and services. Oil royalties bring in more than $2-billion per year.

Using oil monies, the government has built a seawater distillation plant, doubling water supply, and two power stations. There have been some government-aided exploitation of the gulf fishing potential, experimentation in natural gas recovery and the introduction of domestic refining. The government has built a steel mill at Musay'id (Umm Sa'id) and is developing a petrochemical industry. Economic plans call for a mix of heavy and light industry and a diversified economy to provide an alternate income to that produced by oil revenues. Various shipping lines call at Musay'id, and the port is being expanded to nine berths. There is also some vegetable growing and herding of camels and goats.

History

The Qataris long were ruled by the Persians, and they paid the governor of Bushire an annual bounty for the right to fish for pearls. Qatar became independent of Persia in the 19th century under Thani, founder of the al-Thani dynasty.

Thani was succeeded by his son, Mohammed, who signed an agreement in 1868 with Great Britain which provided protection to the sheikhdom. Mohammed's son, Qasim, died in 1913 at the age of 111, and Qasim's son, Abdullah, renewed the accord with the British in 1916.

From 1947 to 1960, Qatar was ruled by Emir Ali, who was forced from his throne by his son, Ahmed, with the help

Khalifa ben Hamad al-Thani

of a British gunboat in Doha harbor. In turn, in 1972, Ahmed, who spent most of the country's fortunes on himself and the large royal family, was deposed in a bloodless coup by his cousin, Emir Khalifa ben Hamad al-Thani.

Qatar declared its independence on Sept. 1, 1971, after the British announced they were pulling back their forces from the Persian Gulf by the end of that year. Along with Bahrain, Qatar considered entering into a large federation with the United Arab Emirates, but the plan eventually was dropped.

Emir Khalifa is assisted by a 23-member advisory council, including 20 elected members. The state is run under a strict religious law, but it is not as severe and puritanical as that in Saudi Arabia. Qatar, for example, permits movie houses and women drivers, two items banned by its larger neighbor. Qatar has introduced a free educational system and free medical services.

Foreign Relations

After the British abandoned their protectorate status over Qatar, the two countries signed a new treaty of friendship. In September 1971, Qatar joined the Arab League and the United Nations. Since the fall of the shah of Iran, Qatar looks to Saudi Arabia to provide for its security.

In 1975 a three-year, $250-million industrial plan was announced to lessen the country's total dependence on oil. Qatar continues to be interested in joining some kind of regional federation. In March 1976, the emir issued an appeal for a Gulf common market to prevent duplication of economic development in the area and to coordinate the trade of Gulf nations in world markets.

Development projects that were underway in 1979 include additional desalination plants, an enlarged harbor at Doha, refrigerated storage facilities for the fishing industry, and a gas liquefaction plant.

United Arab Emirates

Membership: A federation of the sheikhdoms of Abu Dhabi, Ajman, Dubai, Fujairah, Ras al-Khaimah, Sharjah and Umm al-Qaiwain.
   Federal capital: Abu Dhabi.
   Area: 32,278 square miles.
   Population: 760,000 (1977 est.).
   Religion: Moslem.
   Official language: Arabic.
   GNP: $9.7-billion; $13,900 per capita income.

Terrain

Six of the emirates are strung along the southern rim of the Persian Gulf. Fujairah faces on the Gulf of Oman, a part of the Arabian Sea. The United Arab Emirates (UAE) is bordered by Qatar, Saudi Arabia and Oman. The approximately 32,000 square miles of largely undefined borders are the size of South Carolina. Most of the region is a low, flat desert where temperatures sometimes reach 140 degrees Fahrenheit. At the eastern end, along the Oman border, are the Western Hajar Mountains.

People

The population is made up of Arabs, Iranians, Baluchi and Indians. Only 25 percent of Abu Dhabi's population of 235,000 is native. The UAE's total population, including foreigners, is over 700,000.

Seven States

Abu Dhabi, the largest of the seven states, is mostly desert, but it has the largest oil deposits. Settlements include the towns of Abu Dhabi, Dalma' and Das Island, and Al Jiwa and Al Burayami oases. There are airfields at Abu Dhabi and Das Island.

Dubai, including the town of Dubayy, has a population of about 200,000, and possesses one of the few deepwater ports in the area, Port Rashid. It has a police force, municipal council, elementary schools and a small hospital.

Sharjah includes Sharjah town (Ash Shariqah), and has a population of about 20,000. There are a medical mission, schools, steamer and air services. There are red oxide mines on Abu Musa Island.

Ajman, which has only 100 square miles, is the smallest of the emirates. The population is 22,000.

Ras al-Khaimah is comparatively large and fertile, and has a town and several villages. No oil has been discovered there.

Umm al-Qaiwain (22,000) includes Falaj al 'Ali oasis.

Fujuairah (26,000) consists of a few small villages.

Economy

The emirates are highly competitive among themselves. Abu Dhabi and Dubai, the two most important, are the chief rivals.

Until oil was discovered in Abu Dhabi in the early 1950s, Dubai ranked first, because it was a commercial center, home of the entrepot trade, which included the smuggling of illicit gold to India and Pakistan. Dubai billed itself as "the Hong Kong of the Middle East."

Dubai began pumping oil in 1969, joining Abu Dhabi in production of the resource. In July 1974, Sharjah became the third of the seven states to produce oil. The emirates pumped almost two million barrels of oil per day in 1978. In 1976, the UAE's oil revenues reached $7-billion.

Before oil, Abu Dhabi lacked paved roads, telephones and apartments.

After oil, the emirate began building a city, including a wide boulevard atop a new sea wall along the coast. Abu Dhabi built an international airport. After oil, Dubai started construction of its own international airport. After oil, Sharjah began its own international airport, not far from the other two. Abu Dhabi, Dubai and Sharjah all are building their own cement factories. Each of the seven states has its own radio station, and there are two television stations in the federation.

Aside from oil, the economy is based on fishing and pearling, herding, date-growing and trading.

Several of the emirates—Ras al-Khaimah, Ajman, Sharjah, Fujairah and Umm al-Qaiwain—have produced large and varied issues of postage stamps aimed at catching the eye of the world's stamp collectors. Colorful sets highlight and honor events and personalities with no connection to the desert sheikhdoms—American baseball greats Babe Ruth and Ty Cobb, historical and contemporary figures Benito Juarez and Charles De Gaulle, the Olympic games, antique automobiles.

Banking is an important business. In a 1974 survey on the Persian Gulf, *Newsday,* the Long Island newspaper, reported there were 165 branch banks in the UAE, about one for every 1,400 residents. Tiny Ajman had six banks alone.

Newsday also found that Abu Dhabi in 1974 put $675-million into bonds—guaranteed loans at 8, 8.5 or 9 per cent—to the Spanish Highway Authority, the Korean Development Bank, the Austrian Central Bank, the Industrial Fund of Finland, the Republic of Ireland, the Paris Airport Authority, the European Investment Bank and the World Bank. Morgan Guaranty Trust of New York handles a large portion of Abu Dhabi's $240-million in direct investments in telephone companies, textiles, gas and electric companies, food companies and merchandising companies. Of course, investments since 1974 have leaped.

History

The emirates were formerly known as the Trucial States or the Trucial Oman because of their ties to Great Britain by truce and treaty.

The dominant Arab tribe was the Qawasim, made up of competent sea traders until they were overrun by Wahhabis from the interior of the Arabian Peninsula in 1805. They then became pirates. The British sent in a naval fleet after two of their commercial ships were plundered, leading to the general treaty of peace in 1820. The sheikhs also signed with Britain the perpetual maritime truce in 1853 and the exclusive agreements in 1892, which gave Britain control over their foreign policy.

After Great Britain in 1968 announced its intention to withdraw the Union Jack from the gulf by the end of 1971, the Trucial States, Qatar and Bahrain initiated plans to form a confederation. But the latter two sheikhdoms finally decided in favor of independent sovereign status.

In December 1971 the United Arab Emirates was formed. Ras al-Khaimah did not join the federation until February 1972.

Government

The president of the UAE is Zayed ibn Sultan al-Nahayan, emir of Abu Dhabi, who became head of the federation at its inception.

Zayed ibn Sultan al-Nahayan

The Supreme Council, made up of the seven ruling emirs of the member states, is the highest legislative authority. There is also a Federal Council, in which each state is represented and which holds executive powers. Matters that are not of federal concern are left to the individual rulers.

The UAE is a loose federation which shares common roads, telephone and postal systems. Concerned about their own identity and the possible future ambitions of larger Arab and non-Arab nations in the region, the seven states joined together chiefly to form a common foreign and defense policy. But the union has not been without problems. The smaller states have at times felt that Abu Dhabi has a greater voice than it should in federation decisions. The gap in wealth between the member nations has also caused internal dissent. These and other developments led to a crisis that caused a change of government in May 1979, when Sheikh Rashed al-Maktum of Dubai was appointed prime minister. Sheikh Rashed has said that his government would work to reduce the gap between the rich and poor of the federation. Some observers felt the change in government signaled a change in policy for the UAE, with more emphasis on improving the standard of living of the people and less concentration on overseas investments.

Foreign Relations

The UAE boundaries are vague, and there have been border disputes with Saudi Arabia. But relations between the two have remained good. After independence in December 1971, the UAE was admitted to the United Nations and the Arab League.

The United States, Britain and the European nations are the UAE's principal trading partners. The federation joined in the oil boycott against the industrial nations in October 1973. Since then the UAE has basically followed Saudi policy on oil matters.

Like Saudi Arabia, the UAE has a special relationship with the United States. In December 1976, celebrating its fifth birthday, a public relations campaign was carried out to acquaint the American people with the history and aspirations of the UAE. A major section appeared in *Time* magazine and full-page ads appeared in major newspapers.[4]

In May 1977 Sheikh Zayed restated that on OPEC matters he would always support the Saudi positions. On the Arab-Israeli conflict, he had this to say in light of Menachem Begin's victory in Israel earlier in the month: "The Arabs fought four wars against those who are now described as moderates. Will the hawks be more extremists than them?" Asked how he now viewed prospects for a Middle East settlement, he answered: "I am not pessimistic.... The more obstinate the enemy becomes the more unified the Arabs tend to be. Arab calculations can be more realistic and with less wishful thinking. I told the PLO representative who [recently] handed me a message from Yasir Arafat that maybe such a disease will cure the whole body."[5]

4 For instance *The New York Times*, 19 December 1976, p. E 5.

5 *Events*, 3 June 1977, p. 5.

A CONSERVATIVE ISLAMIC BASTION, BUILT ON OIL

On the surface, Saudi Arabia is an Alaska-sized wasteland. But that vast, sun-scorched lid covers at least 173 billion barrels of oil, one-fourth of the world's proven reserves. The guardian of the land and the mind-staggering treasure beneath it is the Saudi king, supported by a royal family that counts some 4,000 princes.

The fact that governing Saudi Arabia is a family affair was tested when an assassin's bullet killed 69-year-old King Faisal on March 25, 1975, the birthday of the prophet Mohammed and a holy day for the devout monarch, a champion of Islam and the Arab cause. Continuity was assured when the austere, shrewd Faisal was succeeded within minutes of his death by Crown Prince Khalid, his half-brother. The new monarch, in turn, elevated another half-brother, Fahd, to the crown princedom. The new order was rapidly agreed to by the five senior royal princes, then by the entire royal family.

Faisal was shot down by a nephew, 27-year-old Prince Faisal Ibn Musaed, while the king was holding court in his palace. The family announced quickly that the murderer was "deranged" and that he acted alone, thus assuring the country that there was no plot to incite a general insurrection. Later, a religious court found Prince Faisal to be sane, and in keeping with the precepts of the Koran, the Moslem holy book, he was beheaded on June 18, 1975, in a public square in Riyadh, the Saudi capital.

Not long ago it often was written that Saudi Arabia was a remote feudal kingdom, a 20th century anachronism. Faisal ruled by the Koran alone, and he held a weekly court during which his subjects could approach him to present their problems. But by the time of his death, ending a 10-year reign, Faisal had turned his country from a poor, nomad-populated desert into a financial giant bursting into the modern world while clinging to the most conservative Islamic principles.

Booming Oil Economy

Since the oil-price rises, engineered by the Organization of Petroleum Exporting Countries (OPEC) beginning in 1973, Saudi Arabia has become a politically active and powerful country. The country's growing income—far outstripping its ability to spend on modernization—has given Saudi Arabia a financial power which it exercises through foreign aid (more than 10 per cent of the country's GNP, mainly channeled to other Arab states) and through investments (mainly in Western, industrial states). It produces one-third of OPEC's oil.

Saudi income from oil reached an annual level of $55.8-billion by mid-1979 and every time OPEC raised the price of oil by $1 a barrel, Saudi Arabia's oil income rose by another $3.1-billion a year. And it was that low only as long as the nation held production to its self-imposed ceiling of 8.5 million barrels a day, below its capacity for sustained production of more than 10 million. The more the price rose, the less Saudi Arabia had to pump to cover the cost of its imports. At the $18 price they were charging in mid-1979

Saudi Arabian King Khalid

(compared to prices as high as $23 a barrel set by other OPEC members), the country had to produce only slightly more than 3 million barrels a day to cover the $20-billion in imports it bought in 1978. In July 1979, it was announced that the Saudis were temporarily increasing oil production by an estimated one million barrels a day. *(p. 88)*

In May 1975 Saudi Arabia approved a five-year modernization plan budgeted at $142-billion, the equivalent of five years of its annual income at the time.

Saudi imports rose to $20-billion in 1978 and exports jumped to $34-billion, leaving the country with an enviable $14-billion trade surplus. (U.S. involvement in the Saudi economy amounted to 24 per cent of its imports and 14 per cent of its exports.) Increasingly, Saudi Arabia has turned to investing its funds abroad. By 1979 it counted $60-billion in foreign assets, primarily in Europe and the United States. Of the U.S. funds, a large share was in U.S. Treasury securities.

Most of the Saudis' $2-billion-a-year foreign aid had gone to Egypt, but after that country signed a peace treaty with Israel, Saudi Arabia acquiesced to demands of its Arab neighbors and reduced its aid to Egypt.

Saudi Riches

There have been problems associated with having so much money. Saudi Arabia found it had to be careful how it used its funds, for its decisions now affected not only the economies of the world, but world politics as well. Saudi Arabia's riches have created somewhat of a dilemma for the nation. There are potential conflicts between oil conservationists, religious conservatives and foreign policy makers in the country.

David E. Long, a State Department analyst, described the dilemma. "The conservationists believe lower production will boost oil prices, thereby dampening total world demand and further forcing consumers to shift to other forms of energy. This would slow the depletion rate of Saudi Arabia's principal marketable resource. But setting production rates to meet only domestic financial requirements would jeopardize worldwide political stability, in which the Saudis have a major stake. . . . If the world economy were to suffer as a result of Saudi oil cutbacks, the Saudis would suffer too. As devout guardians of the Muslim holy places, Mecca and Medina, the Saudis feel a special responsibility to protect the Islamic way of life. One of the greatest threats to that way of life, in the Saudi view, is the expansion of communism or indeed any kind of radical, atheistic ideology. Only a healthy West can contain that threat."[1]

Louis Turner and James Bedore pointed out Saudi Arabia's "Catch 22" when they wrote: "The growing dependence of the United States on imported oil means that any increase in OPEC prices immediately worsens the American balance of payments; this then hits the value of the dollar, which hits the value of Saudi holdings; the Saudis cannot compensate for this by raising the price of oil because the whole circular process then starts all over again."[2]

Saudi Arabia's importance in the world also has made it more vulnerable. It has only 80,000 men under arms, and although its oil riches have bought it some of the world's most sophisticated weaponry — including a $2.5-billion contract for 60 U.S. F-15s, considered the world's most advanced airplane — it could not be expected to successfully defend itself for long. It has been said that if the Soviet Union wanted to defeat Western Europe, it need not march across Europe; it would do better to march on Saudi Arabia. Japan and the United States are nearly as dependent as Western Europe is upon Saudi oil.

Long said the determinants of Saudi oil policy boiled down to three factors: "(a) the need to generate oil revenues at a level compatible with the country's total economic development; (b) the need to ensure regional and international political and economic stability; and (c) the need to maintain a predominant influence over price-setting through [OPEC]."[3]

Terrain

Saudi Arabia extends over four-fifths of the Arabian Peninsula in a strategic location stretching from the Persian Gulf to the Red Sea and the Gulf of Aqaba. It shares borders with Jordan, Iraq, Kuwait, Bahrain, Qatar, United Arab Emirates, Oman, Yemen Arab Republic and the People's Democratic Republic of Yemen. Several of these borders are undefined. It faces non-Arab Iran across the Persian Gulf and Egypt, the Sudan and Ethiopia across the Red Sea. And it faces the Sinai Peninsula across the Gulf of Aqaba.

Saudi Arabia's 1,560-mile coastline provides the only access to water for the otherwise arid wasteland. Recently dams have trapped floodwaters for irrigation and city needs. Extinct volcanoes and lava beds scar much of the terrain.

Only 1 per cent of the territory is arable, cultivated or pasture land. Less than 1 per cent is forested.

Saudi Arabia has five major regions. The holy cities of Islam, Mecca and Medina and the diplomatic capital of Jidda are located in Hijaz, adjoining the Red Sea. The mountainous Asir, where peaks rise above 9,000 feet, lies to the south along the Red Sea. Najd occupies the central part of the country where the capital, Riyadh, is located. The Eastern Province, known as al-Hasa, is the area containing the country's rich oil fields. The main feature of the rugged Northern Provinces is the trans-Arabian pipeline which crosses that area, Jordan, Syria and Lebanon en route to the Mediterranean Sea.

In the north, the Syrian desert stretches downward toward the 22,000 square miles of the Al-Nufud desert. In the south is the vast Empty Quarter, over 250,000 square miles of sand, a nearly uninhabited desert.

People

Although no official census figures are available Saudi Arabia's population has been estimated to be as high as 9.4 million.[4]

Previously, nearly all Saudis were nomadic or semi-nomadic, but rapid economic growth following the development of the country's oil resources has lowered that figure to an estimated 20 per cent.

Saudis are ethnically Arabs, although there are some small groups of non-Arab Moslems. These minorities are Turks, Iranians, Indonesians, Indians and Africans who came on pilgrimages and remained in the Hijaz Province. Saudis recognize no color line, and mixed racial strains are common.

Nearly all Saudis are Moslems practicing the puritanical Wahhabi interpretation of Sunni Islam. A small Moslem minority, belonging to the less rigid Shia sect (which dominates Iran), resides in the Eastern Province.

Economy

When it comes to oil, Saudi Arabia is the land of superlatives. In 1979 it ranked as the world's largest oil exporter, holding by far the largest proven oil reserves, mostly located in its barren Eastern Province. Employing 10 per cent of the labor force, the oil industry accounts for nearly all of the country's exports and foreign exchange. More than 95 per cent of government revenues are derived from oil royalties and taxes. As Dr. Mansoor Alturki, Deputy Minister of Finance and National Economy, noted in an interview, "Oil is our only resource."

Oil was discovered in Saudi Arabia during the 1930s, but exploitation of the rich fields was delayed until after World War II. Standard Oil of California was granted a 66-year concession in 1933 for the Arabian-American Oil Company (Aramco). Later, the company was jointly owned with Texaco, Standard Oil of New Jersey and Mobil Oil on a 30-30-30-10 basis. In 1949, another concession in the Saudi Arabian-Kuwait neutral zone was granted to Pacific Western Oil Company, later Getty Oil.

During 1950, two major developments in the oil industry strengthened the significance of the product for the country. First, a 753-mile pipeline was opened to carry crude oil out of the country across Jordan and Syria to the Mediterranean, where it could be easily shipped abroad.

1 David E. Long, "Saudi Oil Policy," *The Wilson Quarterly,* Winter 1979, p. 86.

2 Louis Turner and James Bedore, "Saudi Arabia: The Power of the Purse-Strings," *International Affairs,* July 1978, p. 419.

3 Long, op. cit., pp. 85, 86.

4 Estimates of Saudi Arabia's population vary from a low of 5 million to more than 9 million, due partly to Saudi secrecy and the difficulty in estimating foreigners in the country.

Second, Saudi Arabia and Aramco signed an agreement to share Aramco's profits on a 50-50 basis, thereby greatly increasing Saudi Arabia's return on its natural resource. This agreement was the first instance of what later became a common arrangement between oil companies and Middle East governments.

Oil production expanded rapidly in the early 1970s to meet rising world demand. In 1969, oil flowed at 3 million barrels a day. By 1974, that figure had nearly tripled to 8.48 million barrels. During 1975 the production capacity had risen to 10 million barrels a day and when the upheaval in Iran halted that country's 6-million-barrel production at the beginning of 1979, Saudi Arabia produced at capacity to help make up for the shortfall. It quickly dropped back to its 8.5 million ceiling when Iranian production resumed in the spring, however. In light of the Saudis' reluctance to produce at capacity and the fuel conservation campaign they were promoting, it was not likely Saudi Arabia would step up production significantly in the 1980s. A 1977 CIA study reached that conclusion and accordingly forecast a serious worldwide shortage of oil in that decade.[5] A U.S. Senate report in 1979 predicted that Saudi oil production in the 1980s would be no more than 12 million barrels a day, far short of the 14 million to 16 million expected to be needed. The situation, it said, could trigger a "fierce political and economic struggle among consuming countries."

The shortfall was likely even though the Saudi Arabian ambassador to the United States, Shaikh Ali A. Alireza, told a New York business audience that "The kingdom is still discovering more new oil reserves each year than the amount being taken out. And there are strong grounds for anticipating major new petroleum and other mineral reserves will be found with the more deliberate approach now being taken to exploration."[6]

In 1973, Saudi Arabia signed an agreement with Aramco, under which Saudi Arabia acquired a 25 per cent share of the ownership of the oil company. By 1975 the Saudi government assumed 60 per cent ownership and the share leveled off at that point.

Regardless of ownership, Aramco continues to dominate the Saudi Arabian oil industry and is crucial to the economies of the Western countries and Japan. Aramco represented the largest single American investment in any foreign country; as of 1979, nearly 20,000 Americans remained to manage the company.

The presence of Aramco has radically transformed the Saudi Arabian economy. Before the exploitation of oil, the economy revolved around simple exchanges between the nomads who raised camels, sheep and goats and the sedentaries who were mostly farmers and merchants. The revenues derived from tourists on pilgrimages to the holy cities yielded the greatest single source of income. Farming was poor due to extremely hot and dry conditions.

Aramco has stimulated the kingdom's economy and given rise to an industrial class. Government revenues from the oil companies have been funneled into internal improvements of transportation, communication and health and educational facilities. Agriculture has improved somewhat with the control of locust invasions. Dams have been built to retain seasonal valley floodwaters. Some irrigation systems have been built, and fishing practices are being modernized. Several industrial plants have also been built. The five-year plans offer hope that Saudi Arabia will develop a diversified economic base which will allow the country to remain modernized even when the oil runs out or the world shifts reliance to another energy source.

A serious shortage of Saudi manpower has been the main obstacle to rapid growth. As a result, more than a million and a half foreigners have flocked to Saudi Arabia or have been recruited and lured with tempting financial offers. In a 1976 report on U.S. interests in the Middle East it was pointed out that "All the hard manual work involved in the frenzy of construction which now grips the country is done by imported laborers, mostly Yemenis, while the architectural, technical and other required skills are supplied by Europeans, Americans, 'northern Arabs' or Pakistanis. The schools are staffed by Egyptians and the oil industry is run by Americans."[7]

In 1978, 75 per cent of the population was still engaged in farming and stock-raising. Farming remains the principal occupation. For internal use, Saudi Arabia produces grains, vegetables, livestock and dates, which are a significant part of the diet.

Saudi Arabia must still import essential foodstuffs such as rice, flour, sugar and tea. Its other imports are machinery and building equipment, acquired mainly from the United States, Japan, West Germany and Great Britain. Besides oil and natural gas, also found in the oil fields, its exports include dates, skins, wool, horses, camels and pearls. Saudi Arabia exports mostly to the Common Market, but significantly also to Japan and the United States.

With the massive amounts of capital being expended in the five-year plans, Saudi contracts have been eagerly sought by numerous companies and governments. The Saudi ambassador to the United States, Alireza, noted late in 1976 that "American companies have been awarded contracts within just the last year for over 27-billion dollars worth of work and goods to be completed in the years ahead. . . . And that is only a beginning."[8] More have been awarded since. The second five-year plan included such undertakings as a $24-billion desalinization program and an increase by 40 per cent in the country's irrigable acreage.

A United States-Saudi Arabian Joint Commission on Economic Cooperation was created in 1974. Jointly managed by the U.S. Treasury Department and the Saudi Ministry of Finance and National Economy, technical projects involving hundreds of millions of dollars have been agreed on.

Among the massive Saudi Arabian projects, according to *New York Times* reports, have been a $10-billion city of 100,000 people near Riyadh, reportedly to manufacture arms; $23- to $45-billion to create two industrial cities, at Jubail and Yanbu, for 170,000 and 120,000 residents, respectively; a $1-billion oil refinery at Jubail, to be built jointly by Shell Oil Co. and the Saudi oil company, Petromin; a $4.5- to $7-billion airport complex twice the size of Manhattan outside of Jiddah; and $3.4-billion to build a new campus for the University of Riyadh on the capital's outskirts. In addition, the U.S. Army Corps of Engineers is involved in Saudi Arabian projects totaling

5 *The International Energy Situation: Outlook to 1985,* Central Intelligence Agency, April 1977.

6 Speech before the National Foreign Trade Council, Waldorf Astoria, New York City, 16 November 1976.

7 A. L. Udovitch (ed.), *The Middle East: Oil, Conflict and Hope* (Lexington Books, 1976), p. 433.

8 Alireza speech, op. cit.

more than $15-billion, the *Times* reported.[9] Large portions of the projects involved American companies. In fact, since 1975, the Saudis had signed $25-billion worth of contracts with about 330 U.S. firms, $4.8-billion in 1978 alone.

The American-Saudi relationship is based not only on oil, but also on the accumulating petrodollars, Saudi geography and the Saudi family's political moderation. Indeed, the Washington-Riyadh axis has become a central one in world politics and finance. As the Saudi ambassador in Washington described the relationship that has evolved, "The strategic significance of the partnership between our two countries has grown with each decade.... Indeed, it has now become one of the key links in the prosperity and stability of the entire international economy and the strength of the Free World's security system."[10] And Richard Nolte, a former American ambassador to Egypt, serving in 1977 as executive director of the Institute of Current World Affairs, concluded that "The amicable 44-year relationship with Saudi Arabia has become a matter of prime importance to the United States. This is true for economic and political reasons, and most crucially for reasons of United States security. Our national interest requires that this relationship . . . be supported and strengthened."[11]

Both the Saudi ambassador and Nolte went on to express fears that congressional efforts to pass anti-boycott legislation could seriously injure American relations with Saudi Arabia and cost the United States billions of dollars in contracts and increasing unemployment. But in the spring of 1977 a compromise was reached between Jewish organizations, business organizations and the Carter administration on legislation which appeared to be reluctantly accepted by most Arab states, including Saudi Arabia.

The fear reappeared in 1979, however, in the aftermath of the Egyptian-Israeli peace treaty. Crown Prince Fahd — heir apparent and leader of the kingdom in political affairs — had been due to visit the United States again in March 1979. He had visited last in May 1977 and President Carter had repaid the visit in January 1978. Fahd cancelled his second visit three weeks ahead of time, however, in what some observers saw as a protest of the Middle East settlement then about to be signed. The White House attributed the cancellation to Fahd's health problems. The Saudi Embassy, denying this explanation, said that both countries agreed to a delay to allow more time to study issues to be discussed.

Defense Secretary Harold Brown and Carter's foreign policy adviser, Zbigniew Brzezinski, made separate trips to Saudi Arabia later to offer assurances about the Israel-Egypt pact. But Secretary of State Cyrus R. Vance acknowledged at a congressional hearing May 8 that the relations between the two countries had deteriorated because of the treaty. He did say, however, that Saudi Arabia had decided to go ahead with its previous commitment to provide the funds for a $525-million sale of 50 F-5E jet fighters to Egypt by the United States despite Saudi Arabia's agreement with other Arab nations to punish Egypt economically for signing with Israel. However, as of mid-1979, it was still uncertain whether Saudi Arabia would in fact underwrite Egypt's purchase of the jets.

---

9 *New York Times:* "Saudis Aren't Hoarding All the Money," 29 May 1977; "Saudi Plan for 2 Industrial Cities...," January 1978; "Saudis to Build Weapons Center; ...," 18 February 1978; "Saudi Arabia Building A Mammoth Airport," 24 April 1978; "Saudis Set $3.4 Billion Contract," 5 June 1978.

10 Alireza speech, *op. cit.*

11 "The Saudi Connection and the Arab Boycott," *New York Times,* 18 February 1977.

Statistics on Saudi Arabia

Area: 829,995 square miles; some borders poorly defined.

Capital: Riyadh; diplomatic capital located at Jiddah.

Population: 6-7 million (1979 est. — highly uncertain).

Religion: 100 per cent Sunni Moslem.

Official Language: Arabic.

GNP: $63-billion (1978 est.), $10,000 per capita.

History

Saudi Arabia takes its name from the Saudi family, which has ruled it patriarchically, with only a few lapses, since the mid-1700s. To check the kingdom's rapid expansion in the early 1800s, Egypt invaded Saudi lands and occupied areas of the inner Arabian Peninsula from 1818 to 1840, until internal problems drew the Egyptian forces home. Ottoman-Egyptian occupation gave rise to the rival Rashid family, which ruled the area in the late 1800s, sending the Saudi king and his son into exile.

The son, who came to be known as Ibn Saud, returned in 1902 to reconquer his patriarchal lands. He waged a successful 30-year campaign and eventually took all of the inner Arabian Peninsula, proclaiming himself king. He drew his support from fanatic Wahhabi Moslems, whom he urged to fight in the name of their faith. But their ties to the Wahhabi traditions were to create obstacles for Ibn Saud.

On the eve of World War I, Ibn Saud conquered what is now the Eastern Province, a move that led to close contact with Great Britain. In 1915, the situation compelled him to sign an agreement which placed Saudi lands under Britain as a protectorate. But the country took no part in the war; and another treaty, signed in 1927, canceled the protectorate and declared Saudi Arabia's absolute independence.

When Ibn Saud was unexpectedly even-handed with the non-Moslems his armies had conquered, and even took a moderately favorable view of modernization, introduced by contact with the West, he was opposed by some of the conservative Wahhabi Moslems who rejected Western ways and technology. In 1929, leaders of the armies he had led accused him of betraying their faith and traditions and launched attacks against Saudi tribes. The civil war was brought to an end in 1930, when British forces captured the rebel leaders in Kuwait and delivered them to Ibn Saud. The king then set out to proclaim the complete independence of Saudi Arabia and the supremacy of Islam within the kingdom.

Role in Conflicts

The modern kingdom of Saudi Arabia dates from 1932. On Sept. 24, 1932, Ibn Saud issued a royal decree, unifying the dual kingdoms of Hijaz and Najd and their dependencies. Since 1934, the kingdom has known only peace and security.

During the second world war, Saudi Arabia retained a neutral stance, but its pro-Allies inclination was readily apparent. In 1945, Ibn Saud nominally declared war on Germany, an action which ensured Saudi Arabia's charter membership in the United Nations. Also in 1945 the importance of Saudi Arabia's oil and location were recognized when President Roosevelt met with Ibn Saud on board an American warship in the Mediterranean. The same year, Saudi Arabia joined the Arab League, but the country's religious conservatism limited its interaction with other Arab states in the pursuit of Western modernization.

Ibn Saud's death in 1953 placed his eldest son, Saud, on the Saudi throne, and his second son, Faisal, was named heir apparent. The dissimilarity between the two sons, Saud's traditionalism and Faisal's penchant toward moderate modernization, fed an increasing rivalry between them. Faisal was granted executive powers in March 1958. On Nov. 2, 1964, Saud was deposed by a family decision, and Faisal became king.

Saudi Arabian relations with Great Britain were strained between 1952 and 1955 over a possibly oil-rich oasis in Muscat and Oman, a sultanate with alliances to Britain. When Saudi tribal forces moved against the oasis at Al Buraymi, British-led forces from Oman countered. An attempt to settle the dispute broke down, and British-led forces from Muscat and Oman and Abu Dhabi reoccupied the oasis. During the 1956 Suez crisis, Saudi Arabia broke off ties with Britain, and relations were not resumed until 1963.

During 1961, Saudi Arabia sent troops into Kuwait in response to a request from its ruler after Iraq claimed sovereignty over the country. The troops remained there until 1972.

Continued hostility between Saudi Arabia and Egyptian President Gamal Abdel Nasser dominated Saudi-Egyptian relations during Nasser's tenure. In 1958, Nasser accused King Saud of plotting his assassination. Thereafter, Egyptian propaganda vehemently attacked the Saudi royal family and the country's form of government. Tension again resulted in 1962, when Egypt and Saudi Arabia backed opposing sides in the Yemeni civil war.

Since World War II, the United States has been the dominant foreign influence in Saudi Arabia, although the United States has refrained from involvement in the country's internal affairs. Between 1952 and 1962, the United States maintained an air base at Dhahran on the Persian Gulf. That arrangement was not renewed in 1961, partly due to Saudi Arabia's opposition to American aid to Israel. Both King Saud and King Faisal took strong stands against communism, warning against its influence in Arab and Moslem countries.

Egypt's defeat by Israel during the Six-day War in 1967 apparently did not disappoint King Faisal, due to strained Egyptian-Saudi relations. But aware of Arab nationalist sentiments, Faisal called for the annihilation of Israel and sent troops to Jordan, although they did not engage in extensive fighting.

On Sept. 4, 1973, Saudi Arabia foreshadowed its major role in the Yom Kippur War, when King Faisal said via U.S. television that American support of Zionism "makes it extremely difficult for us to continue to supply the United States' petroleum needs and even to maintain our friendly relations." On Oct. 8, after the outbreak of fighting, Saudi forces were placed on alert. A small contingent of forces crossed into Syria, although they were never reported as fighting.

Saudi Arabia's major role in the war was its lead in employing its rich oil resources as a political weapon. During the 1967 war, Saudi Arabia had reluctantly joined the Arab effort to withhold oil only after extensive pressure from Egyptian President Nasser, and lifted the embargo as soon as possible. But it joined with 10 other Arab oil-producing nations Oct. 17, 1973, in reducing by 5 per cent each month the amount of oil sent to "unfriendly" countries. The next day, Saudi Arabia independently cut oil production by 10 per cent to bring pressure on the United States. On Oct. 20, it announced a total halt of oil exports to the United States, action which only Abu Dhabi already had taken. This step—which caused some discussion in the United States of the need for possible military intervention to keep oil flowing—followed President Nixon's announcement that the administration was requesting an unprecedented $2.2-billion in emergency aid for Israel. This new Saudi willingness to use the oil weapon has been attributed, first, to the country's additional latitude gained from increasing wealth and, second, to its increased ability to guide the oil weapon following the death in 1970 of Nasser and the subsequent improvement in Egyptian-Saudi relations.

However, after the United States acted as a mediator in bringing about troop disengagement accords between Egypt and Israel in the winter of 1974, and while Secretary of State Henry A. Kissinger was spending much of that spring in quest of a similar agreement between Syria and Israel, the Saudi Arabians assumed a moderate position in the Organization of Arab Petroleum Exporting Countries (OAPEC). At a meeting in Vienna on March 18, 1975, Saudi Arabia was joined by Algeria, Egypt, Kuwait, Abu Dhabi, Bahrain and Qatar in lifting the five-month oil embargo against the United States. Only Libya and Syria dissented from the decision. Simultaneously, Sheikh Yamani announced Saudi Arabia would hike his country's oil output by one million barrels a day and ship the increase to the United States.

Saudi Arabia has continued to argue against large OPEC price rises insisting that the stability of the Western world's financial system could be severely undermined. In December 1976, Saudi refusal to go along with the full amount of an OPEC price rise resulted in a two-tier pricing system and Saudi increases in the amount of oil produced. But oil minister Yamani accompanied this small break with OPEC with a warning: "Don't be too happy in the West," he declared. "We expect the West to appreciate what we did, especially the United States." This close linking of oil and politics, of oil with the Arab-Israeli conflict, raised considerable anxiety in America and renewed concern about Arab blackmail. "The oil business," the liberal *New Republic* noted, "no longer is a business at all. It has become a political enterprise ruled by a council of clever extortionists."[12]

Clement Martin, chief of the Federal Energy Administration's international division, summed up Yamani's message to the West in this way: "They are definitely sending a signal to the United States that the political use of oil is still a major arrow in their quiver.... They have said, 'Look, over the past couple of years we've been very supportive of your efforts to bring about Middle East peace and stability. We have bankrolled the moderates in Egypt; we have bankrolled the Jordanians; we have encouraged the Syrians in the Lebanon situation.... Now it's your turn, United States, to take the next step.... Unless we have some real progress in a year or so the moderates will be in real trouble.' "[13]

Since Yamani's warning, the Saudis have grown more cautious and have often denied the linkage between oil, petrodollars and politics. Nevertheless, it is a linkage that

---

12 "Not So Friendly Saudis," *The New Republic*, 1 & 8 January 1977, p. 3.
13 *Ibid.*, p. 4.

poses many problems for the United States and one which is sure to remain central in the coming years.

Government

Saudi Arabia's government is patriarchal, though major decisions are usually made by consensus. There is no parliament or formal constitution, although the Koran, the basis of Islamic law, restrains Saudi kings, as does unwritten tribal law and custom. The king reigns as chief of state and as head of government. The judiciary branch consists of the Islamic Court of First Instance and Appeals. King Faisal acted as his own prime minister and foreign minister.

The new King Khalid, at age 61 ascending the throne upon the assassination of Faisal on March 25, 1975, has long been regarded as a weaker figure than his half brother, Faisal. Khalid underwent open heart surgery in Cleveland, Ohio, in 1974 and, until his ascension had not been active in state affairs in recent years. For these reasons Crown Prince Fahd, another half-brother, has become power behind the throne in the new reign. Fahd was serving as interior minister at the time of Faisal's murder. Khalid's continuing poor health could result in Fahd assuming the throne at any time.

Not all 4,000 Saudi princes on the civil list play an active role in governing the nation, but at least a few hundred of them do. Saudi monarchs have been clever in splitting military power between the 47,000-man regular army and the 33,000-man national guard. Prince Sultan heads the army and Prince Abdullah runs the militia. Both are half-brothers of King Khalid. The Saudi family always has been careful to cultivate its bonds with the two other great families in the country, the Sudairis and the as-Sheikhs, who helped the Saudis overrun most of the Arabian Peninsula between 1750 and 1926. Members of the two lesser families usually hold important posts in the government.

The Saudi state in 1979 appeared to rest on three major pillars. The first was the alliance between the house of Saud and the important families of the major tribes. The second was Aramco, although 60 per cent owned by the Saudi government, still a symbol of the U.S.-Saudi partnership. And the third was religion. Every Saudi leader has assumed not only the kingly throne but also the office of imam of the Wahhabiya — thus becoming the spiritual as well as the temporal leader of the Saudi people.

Foreign Policy

Saudi Arabia has maintained close relations with the United States since they were established in 1940. The relationship has been mutually advantageous. The Saudis have sold the United States oil and have provided a moderating influence in the Arab world. In return, the United States has assisted Saudi Arabia in bolstering its defenses and developing its resources.

The 1979 Egyptian-Israeli treaty, however, placed the Saudis in a difficult position. To the United States' surprise, the Saudis joined in the denunciation of the treaty and approved political and economic sanctions against Egypt.

Also significant were hints at that time of an improvement in Saudi-Soviet relations, despite the fact that the Saudis had no relations with communist states and vehemently opposed communist influence in the Moslem world.

The Saudis' fears of Soviet inroads in the region appeared to have been well-founded. During the 1977-78 battle over control of Somalia — which lay on the key shipping route through the Gulf of Aden — Saudi Arabia reportedly provided $300- to $360-million to Somalia to help it and the Moslem Eritrean Liberation Front expel Soviet advisers. But when the Soviets responded by sending in equipment and supporting an influx of Cuban troops to help Ethiopia in its fight against Somalia, Saudi Arabia and its money were no match.

On its own peninsula, Saudi Arabia could depend upon only the United Arab Emirates, Qatar, Bahrain and Kuwait as long as their governments were stable, but that has not always been the case. Insurgents have been causing trouble in neighboring Oman, and across the Persian Gulf the Saudi sense of security was damaged by the fall of Iran and the rapid buildup of Soviet-supplied arms in Iraq.

Troubling Saudi Arabia most in 1979, however, were conflicts in Yemen. The Saudis supported North Yemen in its battle to stave off a takeover by the Soviet-supported South Yemen. With the United States, the Saudi government pledged more than $200-million to North Yemen to help it defend itself. In March 1979, the United States rushed $390-million worth of weapons to North Yemen. A U.S. Navy task force was sent to the Gulf of Aden in a display of American support for North Yemen and Saudi Arabia. To avoid alienating the states in that region, the Soviets persuaded South Yemen to agree to a cease-fire. *(Details, p. 56)*

With a standing army of only 45,000 men and a 35,000-man national guard, Saudi Arabia has had to turn increasingly toward sophisticated arms for its defenses. "As with the Horn of Africa, the difficulties for an under-populated country like Saudi Arabia of converting money into military influence are clearly demonstrated," wrote Turner and Bedore. "The simple answer has been to enter the arms market in a major way." Regardless of advances in that area, they said, the Saudi air force would "remain dependent on foreign maintenance personnel through the 1980s at the very least. The crucial importance of spare parts and maintenance will give foreign powers such as the United States some leverage over the Saudis. . . ."[14] That was illustrated when the Saudis agreed, as a condition of being allowed to buy the F15s, not to deploy them near Israel nor to increase their range or bombing capacity.

The size of Saudi Arabia's military force was a problem illustrated dramatically when the trouble in Yemen early in 1979 led Saudi Arabia to place its troops on alert and to recall the 1,200 Saudi troops serving in an Arab League peacekeeping force in Lebanon.

The extremist policies of Libyan President Muammar al-Qaddafi led to expanded Saudi cooperation with Egypt in an effort to keep Arab policies in a moderate line and to enhance the late King Faisal's personal leadership role in the Arab world. During the summer of 1973, when Egypt still faced a possible merger with Libya, Saudi Arabia worked hard with Egypt to firm up their own alliance. The Libyan merger did not materialize. Saudi Arabia subsidized Egypt for revenues lost with the 1967 closing of the Suez Canal, which was reopened to shipping in 1975. In 1977, the Saudis made a five-year commitment to subsidize the Egyptian army's development, and although that commitment was weakened by the Egyptian-Israeli treaty, Saudi Arabia continued to funnel aid to Egypt, including $100-million in 1979 for Egypt's purchase of jeeps and trucks from the United States.

---

14 Turner and Bedore, op. cit., p. 415.

POLITICAL TURMOIL AND A DELICATE BALANCING ACT

Well into his ninth year as president of the most durable government modern-day Syria had seen, there were signs in mid-1979 that Hafez al-Assad had spread himself too thinly. He had served long in a land that had counted a dozen coups between its independence in 1945 and Assad's own armed but bloodless seizure of power a quarter century later in November 1970.

Being the leader of one volatile country would have been enough, but Assad was — in fact if not in name — head of two nations, Syria and Lebanon. Much of Syria's army was committed as a peacekeeping force in Lebanon, a country that had been on the verge of anarchy for much of the 1970s. It had become popular in the press and in government circles to refer to Lebanon as Syria's "Vietnam," a reference to the United States' long, divisive and unsuccessful attempt to bring order to Southeast Asia.

Syria's involvement in Lebanon, as well as corruption and inefficiency within its own government, had crippled it financially. It had become heavily dependent upon foreign aid at a time economists said it already had the second-largest industrial capacity in the Arab world and had the potential to become a rich country.[1] Eighteen months of assassinations of Syrian officials at the rate of about one a month were capped in June 1979 by the mass slaying of 50 military cadets in a classroom in Aleppo. The officials and cadets were mainly of Assad's own minority religious sect in a nation of Sunni Moslems who believed in the "greater Syria" dream Assad once professed. The assassins were believed to be members of the militant Sunni group called the Moslem Brotherhood.

The Moslem Brotherhood action was especially threatening because Assad had reached power by virtue of being a member of the Alawite Moslem sect, which still comprised only 11 per cent of the Syrian Moslems. The Sunnis traditionally had looked down upon the Alawites, a factor that kept the latter group impoverished. Their only route out of poverty often was through the army and by virtue of numbers they soon became the military's ruling power. Assad staged his 1970 coup in his role as commander of the air force when he refused to commit his forces to combat with Jordan. He brought into power with him other Alawites, an action that did not endear him to the majority of the Syrians. With religious unrest toppling governments in neighboring Lebanon and Iran, public dissatisfaction with the $1-million-a-day cost of "Syria's Vietnam," and low military morale because of the frustrating and dangerous occupation of Lebanon (more than 1,000 Syrian troops were killed in the 1978 conflict with Lebanese Christians), Assad's position was not considered very secure by mid-1979. In addition, there were widespread but unconfirmed reports that Assad was suffering declining health.

Syria experienced an economic boom similar to those of its oil-rich Arab neighbors until 1976 when it became deeply involved in the Lebanese civil war. For Syria, Lebanon's occupation had many ramifications beyond the

Syrian President Hafez al-Assad

question of Lebanon's future. Syria's financial stock plummeted, it became snared in a tug of war between the opposing ideologies of the nations providing the foreign aid it badly needed, and it appeared to have lost the pre-eminence it once held in the pan-Arabism movement. The guerrilla activity of the Moslem Brotherhood and its potential threat to the Assad regime was linked to Syrian involvement in Lebanon.

One journalist quoted historian Albert Hourani as saying on the eve of Syrian independence in 1945 that there was no feeling of Syrian nationalism because the name "Syria" had long been applied to the land occupied by Lebanon, Israel and Jordan as well as Syria. "This is one important reason why officials in Damascus traditionally tended to place the Palestinian cause above that of Syrian well-being," the journalist wrote.[2]

As a result, it was not surprising that when Syria sent its troops into Lebanon in 1976 it did so on behalf of the Moslems, reformers, leftists and Palestinians. But when the left's position became dominant, Syria broke its "greater Syria" aspirations, switched sides and began aiding the Maronite Christians, whose leadership of Lebanon was being contested.

Many theories were advanced for the switch. One explanation, offered by Hourani, held that while Syria's security lay in a peaceful Lebanon next door, it did not necessarily lie in providing a haven for Palestinians who would continue their guerrilla activity against Israel. Syria was well aware that Israel, much stronger militarily, would

1. *The Washington Post*, 1 October 1978.

2. Michael Tannenbaum, "Politics and the Sword in Syria," *The New Leader*, Oct. 9, 1978, p. 11.

not tolerate that situation and might attack Syria and invade and control Lebanon.

Whatever its reasons for switching alliances, Syrian relations with other Arab countries (with the exception of Jordan) became strained due to Syria's involvement in Lebanon. However, by the end of 1976, Syrian relations with most Arab countries, especially with Saudi Arabia and Egypt, had dramatically improved.

This improvement in relations with the two nations soon proved to be mercurial, however. Syria was one of the leaders of the Arab nations that blacklisted Egypt for signing a separate peace with Israel without resolving two prime concerns of Syria's — the Golan Heights along its border with Israel and the fate of the hundreds of thousands of Palestinian refugees that formed the core of Syria's Lebanon quagmire. Saudi Arabia meanwhile had emerged as the leading Middle East moderate while Syria, Libya, Algeria and South Yemen formed, with the Palestine Liberation Organization (PLO), the "Steadfastness and Confrontation Front" sworn to press for severe diplomatic and economic punishment of Egypt.

In its pursuit of militant Arab nationalism, Syria often has reached out with an abrasive hand to sister Arab states. It joined with Gamal Abdel Nasser of Egypt to create the United Arab Republic in 1958, but was relegated to the role of junior partner, with most of the power emanating from Cairo. In 1961, the Syrian army staged a coup that took the country out of the union.

As self-appointed protector of the Palestinians and their cause, Syria sent armored units into Jordan in 1970 during the clash between King Hussein's troops and Palestinian forces. (Fearing U.S. intervention, however, Syria withdrew quickly.) And Syria's leftist military regimes and its dominant Baath Party long vowed to "liberate" Saudi Arabia by destroying its "reactionary" Saudi family.

Jordan and Saudi Arabia have, since 1970, moved with caution to improve their relations, and Saudi Arabia has renewed its massive foreign aid to Syria, accounting for the majority of $520-million in aid from Arab nations in 1978.

Syria and Israel

Embittered by the triumph of Israeli arms in the 1948 war, Syria became the first Arab nation to use oil as a weapon eight years later. When Anglo-French-Israeli forces attacked the Suez, Syria responded by blowing up its own oil pipelines. Syria suffered its most devastating blow from Israel in the 1967 war, when Israel destroyed two-thirds of the Syrian air force on the ground and seized the Golan Heights.

Benefiting from a degree of domestic calm and relative political stability, Assad moved Syria from a posture of belligerence to one of pragmatism in dealing with other Arab countries. He prayed beside King Faisal in Damascus' Omayyad Mosque in January 1975 and accepted a $250-million gift from the Saudis. Assad has received some airplanes from Persian Gulf princes. Since 1975 Saudi aid has increased.

After the 1973 war, Syria was six months slower than Egypt in coming to any terms with the Israelis; but, after U.S. Secretary of State Henry Kissinger traveled from capital to capital for a full month, Syria and Israel signed a disengagement of forces agreement on May 31, 1974 — the first time the two enemies had put pen to the same document since 1948. However, Syria still adamantly called for return of all occupied territories, especially the Golan Heights. And although Syria has battled the PLO in Lebanon, it has continued to champion the PLO cause internationally.

At the same time, along with Egypt and Saudi Arabia, Syria has engaged in what has been described as a peace phase — symbolized by regular extensions of the U.N. peacekeeping force mandate that separates Syrian and Israeli troops on the Golan Heights; and by talk of a limited peace with Israel. A break with Egypt after its peace agreement with Israel and a strain in relations with Saudi Arabia had not altered Syria's role in the peace phase in mid-1979. Assad has emphasized the peace he envisioned would not include actual recognition of Israel nor any form of economic or cultural relations.

Syria had long avowed its neutralism between East and West, yet inched into the Soviet orbit by its acceptance of massive amounts of Russian weaponry, only to make openings to the West again in the aftermath of the 1973 war. Assad did some serious soul-searching before agreeing to welcome President Nixon to Damascus in June 1974. The visit resulted in the two countries' establishing full diplomatic relations, broken since the 1967 war. Since then, small amounts of U.S. aid have been granted Syria.

Terrain

Syria contains some of the most arable land in the Middle East, a growing industrial sector and a refining facility that, although damaged during the 1973 Arab-Israeli war, is important to Iraqi as well as Syrian oil. However, successive government upheavals have upset the cohesiveness of Syrian development programs.

A land of Middle East contrasts, Syria extends southward and eastward from the Mediterranian Sea over alternate stretches of fertile valley, plain land, desert and mountains. Lebanon and Israel are to the west, Jordan to the south. Iraq lies to the east and Turkey to the north. In earlier times, greater Syria included Jordan, Lebanon and Israel. About the size of North Dakota, modern Syria covers 71,586 square miles, including 500 square miles occupied by Israel. Approximately 48 per cent of the land is arable, and 29 per cent is used for grazing. Forests cover 2 per cent of the country and deserts the remaining 21 per cent.

The country is divided into seven distinct regions. A fertile belt, site of Syria's major port, Latakia, borders the Mediterranean. Further east, mountains extend southward to the Anti-Lebanon range, peaking with Mount Hermon at 9,232 feet. The central region of Syria includes the fertile valley of the Orontes River and the arable plains of Aleppo, Hama and Homs. The Syrian desert occupies the southeast portion of the country, site of historic Palmyra. The Euphrates River valley extends northward from the desert; the rich Ghutah valley, surrounding Damascus, extends southward. At the southernmost tip of the country lies the black, hilly region of Jebel Druze, where mountains reach 5,900 feet. The Trans-Arabian pipeline cuts through Jebel Druze.

Syria's standing as one of the most cultivable lands in the Middle East results from its access to major sources of water—the Euphrates and Orontes Rivers and their tributaries.

People

In 1978, Syria's population was estimated at 8,100,000. Nearly all the people, 90 per cent, are Arabs, descendants of the Arab branch of the Semitic family. Another 9 per cent are Kurds, a group racially akin to the Iranians. Other

Statistics on Syria

Area: 71,586 square miles, including about 500 square miles occupied by Israel.
Capital: Damascus.
Population: 8,100,000 (1978 est.).
Religion: 87 per cent Moslem, 13 per cent Christian.
Official Language: Arabic, also Kurdish, Armenian, French and English.
GNP: $6.6-billion, $844 per capita (1978 est.).

ethnic groups include Armenians and nomadic Bedouins. The great majority of Syrians are concentrated in the fertile areas around Aleppo, Hama and Homs, around Damascus and on the coastal plains of Latakia.

Most Syrians are Moslems, 70.5 per cent of the people following Sunni Islam. Another 16.3 per cent belong to other Moslem sects, primarily Shia and Ismaili. President Assad is a member of the Alawite sect of the Shias. Christians, mostly Greek, Armenian and Syrian Orthodox, comprise 13.2 per cent of the population. Jews have dwindled in recent years to a negligible group.

Economy

Syria's economy is more balanced than those of most Arab states. About half its total gross national product comes from services, including oil refining, and the other half is about equally divided among agriculture, industry and petroleum production. Two thousand years ago, the fertile valleys of western Syria allowed it to serve as the granary of the eastern half of the Roman Empire. Today, agriculture, primarily cotton, still is a primary factor in the Syrian economy. Although agriculture provided only about 22 per cent of the GNP in 1977, half the nation's labor force was employed at least indirectly in agriculture. Nonetheless, Syria is a net importer of agriculture products. (Total exports were $1.076-billion in 1978 and imports were $2.6-billion.)

A warm climate, much like that of Arizona, and a rainy season from November until April enhance Syria's agricultural capability. Main crops are cotton, wheat, barley and tobacco. Fertile plains provide pasture land for sheep and goat raising, another major occupation.

Syria has stepped up efforts to improve its agricultural output. With Soviet Union help, a giant dam was built on the Euphrates River to provide irrigation and power. In addition to doubling Syria's irrigated land, the Tabqa Dam was expected to not only provide all of Syria's power needs, but also to enable the nation to export some to neighboring countries.

Industrial growth occurred after World War II, following the declaration of Syrian independence in 1945. Today, major industries include textiles, petroleum, food processing, beverages and tobacco. Among the nation's fastest-growing industries are flour milling, oil refining, textile production and cement. Syria's current five-year plan places major emphasis on industrialization.

Syria issued nationalization decrees Jan. 3, 1965, in an effort to halt the flow of capital from the country. Another decree, issued March 4, 1965, nationalized six Syrian oil companies, the American-owned Socony-Mobil Oil Company and the Standard Oil Company of New Jersey and a Royal Dutch Shell affiliate. That effort, which was successful in controlling 95 per cent of industrial production, 50 per cent of commercial transactions and 15 per cent of the agricultural land by July 1965, soon lost momentum. When President Hafez al-Assad came to power in 1970, the trend was reversed. Small entrepreneur firms have sprung up with government encouragement.

A petroleum industry has grown up around Syria's modest oil reserves, located in the northeast parts of the country. When negotiations between the government and American, French and German oil companies failed to develop a plan for exploitation, the government stepped in to perform the task. With Soviet assistance, the government has developed the fields at Karatchouk, and an Italian-built pipeline carries the crude oil to Tartous for refining.

The country's major refinery, at Homs, was built by Czechoslovakians. Syria's oil production increased by nearly half between 1977 and 1979, from 120,000 barrels a day to 170,000, a modest production level by Middle East oil standards. Syrian oil is considered low-grade, but with an estimated 3.8 billion barrels of recoverable reserves, Syria's reserves should last 61 years at the 170,000-barrel-a-day pumping rate. In 1974, oil exports replaced cotton as the nation's main export and by 1979 oil accounted for 58 per cent of export earnings. That figure was expected to decline, however, as Syrian domestic consumption increased. Consequently, oil production was not expected to play as major a role in Syria's long-range economic planning.

Oil refining and transhipments might play a major role in long-term economic planning, however. The trans-Arabian pipeline cuts through Syria en route to Mediterranean ports and Syrian refinement of Iraqi oil, a source of considerable revenues, was resumed in 1979, after a cutoff by Iraq in 1976, with a new rapprochement between the two nations.

In 1978, Syria's GNP was $6.6-billion, or about $844 per capita. Military expenditures have been a continuing drain on the economy, accounting for nearly half of the ordinary yearly budget. To meet budgetary expenses, the government relies mainly on taxes and pipeline transit fees. The government is also encouraging tourism with an eye to increasing its revenues. The economy has suffered a lack of cohesiveness from repeated government upheavals, but the Syrian pound is strong and becoming more valuable with respect to the dollar as the Syrian economy improves and foreign investment increases.

In a full-page advertisement in the January 30, 1977, issue of *The New York Times*, Assad noted that since he assumed the presidency in 1970 "the Syrian economy has moved forward with vigor and vitality unprecedented in the modern history of our country." Assad has opened the door to private and foreign investment, and the fourth five-year plan (1976-1980) is focused on expansion of basic industries; growth of food processing, textile, chemical and engineering industries; along with continuing infrastructural improvements.

But Assad's optimism was a bit premature. In 1977 and 1978, Syria's GNP growth rate, which had been averaging about 13 per cent, suddenly plunged to less than 6 per cent. The economic expansion had produced an increased consumer demand that could not be met, and, as the nation imported more goods, the balance of trade deficit grew to $500-million with inflation soaring to 30 per cent. Government actions to stem the undesirable tide brought a drastic reduction in economic growth and led to a revision of the

1976-1980 five-year plan. In 1979 the plan envisioned a GNP per capita increase of 12 per cent per year and aimed at self-sufficiency rather than an increase in exports.

Syria exports cotton, fruits, vegetables, grain, wool and livestock, mostly to Italy, Belgium and West Germany. Syria's exports to the United States have been confined largely to small quantities of carpet wool. Its imports, machinery and metal products, textiles, fuels and food-stuffs, come mainly from the Soviet Union, West Germany, Italy and France. Imports from the United States have been primarily pharmaceuticals, agricultural machinery and tires, although in drought years wheat shipments have been significant.

Early History

The history of Syria, one of the longest-inhabited areas of the world, reflects the country's strategic position between Africa, Asia and Europe. In ancient times, its location made it an important battlefield as well as a prime trade route. Its present capital, Damascus, first settled about 2500 B.C., was successively dominated by Aramaean, Assyrian, Babylonian, Persian, Greek, Roman, Nabatean and Byzantine conquerors.

In 636 A.D., Damascus came under Moslem occupation. Shortly thereafter, it rose to its historic peak of power and prestige as the capital of the Omayyad Empire, which stretched from India to Spain from 661 to 750. From 1260 to 1516, Damascus was a provincial capital of the Mameluke Empire, before coming under a 400-year rule by the Ottoman Turks in 1516.

World Wars

The modern state of Syria began to emerge during World War I, when Turkey's entry into the war gave opportunity for the expression of Arab nationalist aspirations. Syria, still under Ottoman domain, became a military base and fell in 1918 to British forces. At the conclusion of the war, Syria temporarily was ruled by an Arab military administration. At this time, the Sykes-Picot Agreement of 1916, dividing the Middle East between Britain and France, and the Balfour Declaration of 1917, favoring the establishment of a Jewish homeland, were signed, documents whose intentions and pledges were to prove irreconcilable.

Following the San Remo Conference in April 1920, which gave France a mandate over Syria and Lebanon, French troops occupied Syria, dethroning King Faisal (later to become king of Iraq) who had assumed power in March 1920. The grant by Britain of independence for Egypt in 1922 and Iraq in 1932 put pressure on France to recognize Syria's independence. Negotiations with Syrian nationalists in 1936 resulted in such an agreement, but by 1938, France had still not ratified the treaty.

Free French and British forces seized Syria in June 1941. Arab nationalists, with British assistance, eventually procured a pledge of independence from the Free French forces. In April 1945, when the French troops withdrew, a republican government, under President Shukri al-Kuwatly, elected in 1943, assumed full control of the country. Meanwhile, Syria had already become a founding member of the United Nations and of the Arab League.

Military Coups

Over the next 25 years, Syrian government was marked by successive changes of leadership. President Kuwatly's government was overthrown by a bloodless military coup led by Col. Husni al-Zayim, chief of the Syrian army, on March 30, 1949. Zayim reasoned that the change of government had been necessitated by Syria's poor military showing in the war with Israel in 1948. Five months later, reaction to the repressive military rule resulted in a second coup, which yielded power to Syria's elder statesman and former president, Hashim al-Atasi. That government was ousted in December 1949 by a third military coup. The new, harsh regime, headed by Lt. Col. Adib al-Shishakli, failed to consolidate support, and on Feb. 25, 1954, the government was returned to a democratic regime under Hashim al-Atasi. Kuwatly was re-established as president on Sept. 6, 1955.

Kuwatly's ascension to power gave voice to groups favoring union with Egypt as a first step toward a united Arab state that would merge the Arabic-speaking Middle East states. On Feb. 1, 1958, President Kuwatly and Egyptian President Gamal Abdel Nasser signed an agreement in Cairo proclaiming the United Arab Republic. The two countries were united under one president, Nasser, and defended by one army. A Syrian plebiscite Feb. 21, 1958, gave overwhelming approval to the new merger. But geographic separation, Nasser's imposition of higher taxes and import limitations, nationalization of commercial firms, and Egyptian domination of the union eventually undermined the merger. A revolt by the Syrian army Sept. 28, 1961, established a new civilian government and led to Syria's secession from the U.A.R. and the establishment of the independent Syrian Arab Republic. The government faltered, troubled by an ongoing conservative-Socialist rivalry.

Baath Party

In March 1963, a pro-Nasser military faction, led by Lt. Gen. Louai al-Atasi, seized the Syrian government. The Arab Socialist Resurrection Party, the Baath Party, proclaiming "unity, freedom and socialism," assumed predominant control of the government, thereby ending its 20-year clandestine existence in Syria and other Arab countries. Lt. Gen. Amin al-Hafez became premier and de facto president. On April 17, 1963, an agreement was signed in Cairo for the union of Egypt, Iraq and Syria, but disagreements between the parties developed, and the tripartite federation failed to materialize. The fall of the Baath Party in Iraq in November 1963 doomed tentative plans for an alternative Syrian-Iraqi union.

President Hafez was ousted Feb. 23, 1966, by a dissident army faction within his own party that claimed Hafez had betrayed Baathist principles and assumed dictatorial powers. Following the "rectification," executive and legislative powers were assumed in full by the Baath Party.

Arab-Israeli Wars

Syria was an active participant in the Arab-Israeli war in 1967, although it was quickly defeated. Israeli forces overran Syrian positions and captured the Golan Heights. Syria joined other Arab states in refusing to negotiate a peace settlement with Israel. The nation remained a leader in Arab efforts to resolve the status of Palestinian refugees, many of whom are located in Syria. During the war, Syria severed diplomatic relations with the United States because of American support for Israel. It boycotted the conference of chiefs of Arab states, held Aug. 29 to Sept.1, 1967, believing more forceful measures should be taken to neutralize Israeli gains.

In November 1970, the ruling civilian Baath Party was supplanted by the ruling military faction of the party. Hafez al-Assad was brought to power by the coup and subsequently was elected president. This followed Assad's refusal, a month earlier when head of the Syrian air force, to order his men into action against Jordan in a skirmish that almost toppled King Hussein and resulted in a regional war. Israel (with U.S. approval) was poised to attack the Syrian tanks had they entered the Jordanian capital, Amman.

Since 1970 the new Baathist regime has embarked on a more pragmatic course than its civilian predecessor, pursuing a more liberal economic policy and playing down ideological tenets.

Syrian troops joined Egyptian forces in a two-pronged surprise attack on Israel Oct. 6, 1973. Initial Syrian gains along the Golan Heights were eventually offset by Israel. A week after the fighting began, Israeli forces had penetrated six miles into Syria, attacking Latakia and Tartous and heavily damaging the oil refinery at Homs. On Oct. 23, Syria accepted the U.N. cease-fire resolution of Oct. 22, conditional upon complete Israeli withdrawal from occupied lands. On Oct. 29, President Assad said Syria accepted the Oct. 25 U.S. cease-fire after the Soviet Union gave guarantees that Israel would withdraw from all occupied territory and recognize the rights of the Palestinians. Assad added that Syria would resume the war if these conditions were not met.

Syria was more reluctant than Egypt to take steps beyond the cease-fire, and confrontation between Israeli and Syrian forces on the Golan Heights continued for six months. The two belligerents engaged in sporadic air, artillery and tank duels. Finally on May 31, 1974, at Geneva, the two signed an agreement which set up a U.N.-policed buffer zone between the two armies and called for the gradual thinning out of forces. The two countries also exchanged prisoners of war. The fate of POWs had been an emotionally charged issue in Israel.

Government

Syria's government has been under a left-wing military regime since March 1963, when the Baath Party seized power. Executive power rests in the president and Council of Ministers, legislative power in the People's Assembly and judicial authority in special religious as well as civil courts, relying on Islamic and civil law. A new constitution was promulgated in 1973.

Assad, running unopposed, was elected for his second seven-year term as president Feb. 8, 1978, by 3.9 million Syrian voters.

The Arab Socialist Resurrection Party, the Baath Party, dominates the political scene. The Baath Party Regional Command is particularly powerful. A "national front" cabinet was formed in March 1972, comprising mostly Baathists, with some independents and members of the Syrian Arab Socialist Party, the Arab Socialist Union and the Syrian Communist Party. Communists are mostly sympathizers and number only 10,000 to 13,000. Outside of the "national front" cabinet, little influence is exerted by groups other than the Baath Party. The greatest threat to the Baathist regime lies within the factionalism of the party itself.

Foreign Relations

Syria has long sought to maintain its independence from foreign influence. In line with this goal, successive governments have articulated a policy of non-alignment with Western alliances or the communist world. But Western-Israeli ties, which Syria views as an obstacle to Arab unity, and Soviet arms supplies and assistance, which have greatly aided Syria in its ongoing conflict with Israel, have moved Syria away from neutrality and toward Soviet influence.

Syria is a major proponent of Arab unity, subject to the preservation of Syrian interests. It fully supports the immediate withdrawal of Israeli troops from lands occupied during the 1967 war and the restoration of Palestinian rights. Syria has frequently been on the side of more stringent Arab measures against Israel.

During the Six-day War in 1967, Syrian-American diplomatic ties were severed. In keeping with Assad's more pragmatic approach to external affairs, the two countries renewed full relations during President Nixon's visit to Damascus June 16, 1974.

Assad's moderate approach paid off economically. By mid-1975, there was a steady flow of investment from the conservative Arab oil powers, making its ally, Egypt, envious and its enemy, Israel, more apprehensive. With Saudi Arabian aid, Syria was able to recover from the 1973 war damage which had been estimated at somewhere between $350-million and $1.8-billion. Although modest in comparison to Arab assistance, the United States aid that resumed in 1975 averaged more than $85-million a year. Syria's attacks on Christian strongholds in Lebanon in the fall of 1978 nearly cost it $90-million in economic aid that the Carter administration had earmarked for Syria for fiscal 1979. A congressional compromise allowed the State Department to use its discretion to give Syria as much as $90-million. However, the administration planned to pare that back to no more than $60-million in each of the following two years.

U.S. estimates have put total aid to Syria from Arab nations at $520-million, with nearly 60 per cent of the total from staunchly anti-communist Saudi Arabia. The Arab aid flow resumed its normal rate following a sharp curtailment in response to Syria's invasion of Lebanon against the Palestinians in 1976. The Soviet Union also was thought to be contributing millions in aid, mainly tanks, missiles and advisers. In all, the nearly $850-million in aid Syria received from foreign nations amounted to nearly 13 per cent of its GNP, a factor that sharply reduced Syria's options in conducting its foreign relations.

According to one news analysis, Syria's reliance on foreign aid from diverse sources "all but rules out such proposed moves as joining a Soviet-supported military pact with other members of the hard-line group, renouncing the principle of negotiations with Israel or cooling relations with the United States and conservative Arab countries."[3]

Outside the Arab world, the United States, France, West Germany and Italy, as well as Syria's Soviet-bloc friends, are engaged in investment or aid projects in the country. The World Bank, among international organizations, has been lending money to the Syrians.

Intervention with Syrian forces in the Lebanese conflict began in April 1976, and became massive in June. Within a few months, nearly 30,000 Syrian troops had been deployed in Lebanon in an effort to cripple the Palestinians and leftists under the leadership of Yasir Arafat and Kamal Jumblatt. Egypt was outraged and the Soviet Union turned on its friend. Soviet Leader Leonid Brezhnev, in a July 11 letter to Assad, stated, "We insist that the Syrian leadership should take all possible measures to end its

---

3. *The Washington Post, ibid.*

military operations against the resistance and Lebanon's national movement."[4] Arafat, in turn, accused Damascus of "bloody butchery."[5]

Tempers cooled, however, particularly after Syria attacked Christian strongholds in Lebanon in 1978, a form of proof that Syria had not forsaken fellow Arabs. Syria's efforts to establish close links with Jordan, begun in August 1975, had moved forward by mid-1977 to the point where economically, at least, the two countries were fast becoming one unit.

A potentially more significant foreign policy move was Syria's efforts to merge with Iraq, signaling a change in the long-standing belligerency between the two nations. The merger move was initiated as a response to the Israeli-Egyptian peace agreement at Camp David in September 1978. Meeting in Baghdad in late October 1978, the presidents of the two countries agreed to merge military forces to counter the dangers they saw in the Camp David accords. By mid-1979, however, the merger had gotten little beyond reopening the border and the oil pipeline from Iraq to the sea.

Even if the two nations did merge their military forces, the estimated army of 440,000 troops, 4,500 tanks and more than 730 combat aircraft that would be created[6] was not thought to be enough to match Israel's military power. As one analysis put it, "The Syrians realize that, with or without Iraq, their country would be clobbered."[7]

The Syrian-Iraqi union effort came as somewhat of a surprise, since the Baath political party that ruled both nations had suffered a deep ideological split in 1966, and relations had subsequently cooled. Iraqi Vice President Saddan Hussein referred to the split early in 1979 in explaining a delay in merger plans: "It is not possible to achieve union between the two states without first having achieved the union of the party."

Each nation had accused the other of launching party-based terrorist activities across their borders, and Syria had blamed Iraqi terrorists for the assassinations of Syrian officials. The blame appeared to shift, however, around the time of the ambush of the cadets, when Syria swiftly executed 15 reputed members of the Moslem Brotherhood on charges of carrying out the assassinations.

The U.S. government had cause to worry about the unrest Assad faced in 1979. Still only tepid, the relations between the United States and Syria had continued to improve since the Yom Kippur War even though Assad had repeatedly charged that Kissinger and the United States were attempting to divide the Arabs to Israel's benefit. In 1977 Assad also charged the United States with fomenting the Lebanese civil war "in order to get all Arab countries drowned in it."[8] However, Assad did meet with President Carter in 1977. The meeting took place on neutral ground — Geneva — during Carter's first international trip soon after taking office.

Washington is well aware that Syria plays an important, possibly a crucial, role in influencing the outcome of the Arab-Israeli dispute. According to *Time* magazine, "The prospect of Assad's downfall is a chilling thought for Washington. . . . Chances are that his replacement would be someone amenable to the zealous wishes of the Moslem Brotherhood — most likely meaning stronger opposition to any negotiations with Israel and greater hostility to Egypt's lonely approach to peace."[9]

4. See Mary Costello, "Arab Disunity," Editorial Research Reports, 29 October 1976, p. 792.
5. U.S. News & World Report, 21 June 1976.
6. Time magazine, Feb. 12, 1979, p. 45.
7. Baltimore Sun, 31 May 1979.

8. The Washington Post, 26 June 1977.
9. Time magazine, July 9, 1979, p. 39.

BIRTH OF ISLAM TO SEARCH FOR NEW DESTINY

The greatest historical achievement of the Arabs was the development and spread of Islam. It was an astonishing achievement.

In the Arabian peninsula on the fringe of the civilized world, a lone prophet in the seventh century converted the pagan Arabs to a faith which they carried, within a century, to distant Spain and the steppes of central Asia. This was not merely the propagation of a religious doctrine; the compartmentalization of religion as a separate aspect of life has always been unthinkable in Islam. Respected Arabist William R. Polk notes that "Islam must be thought of as at once a religion and a social order.... Islam, the religion of the overwhelming majority of the Arabs, permeates every aspect of society."[1]

As it conquered Persia and pushed back the Byzantine Empire, Islam absorbed much of both cultures but transformed what it borrowed into a new and distinctive world view and way of life. At its height in the ninth and 10th centuries under the Abbasid caliphate in Baghdad, this flourishing culture included Christians, Jews and Zoroastrians among its creators, Greek philosophy among its intellectual stimulants and Persian administration and statecraft among its political principles. But it was dominated by the religion and language of the Arabs, whom Mohammed led out of Arabia. "Mohammed," English scholar Peter Mansfield writes, "was undeniably one of the few men who have permanently changed the world.... Through him this small race of lean and hungry camel-riding nomads, who provoked a blend of contempt and fear in the contemporary civilized world, became one of the most potent forces in the history of mankind."[2]

Even in the decadence that followed, the Crusaders that began to arrive in 1096 found a culture far more sophisticated than the Europe they had left behind. Later waves of Moslem expansion were to carry the message of Mohammed to India and even Indonesia and the Philippines; under the Ottoman Empire the armies of the prophet reached, in 1529 and again in 1683, the gates of Vienna.

Arabs' Decline

Historians trace the beginnings of Arab decline as far back as the 10th century, although the fall of the Abbasid caliphate to invading Mongols in 1258 is the customary benchmark for the end of Islam's classical period.

Turks migrating from central Asia converted to Islam and soon dominated its armies. They gained *de facto* political power in Baghdad in the 11th century, and after the fall of the caliphate, Turkish minorities increasingly dominated the governments of the Middle East. The major creative cultural impulse within Islam, meanwhile, passed from the Arabs to the Persians, whose Indo-European language, written now in Arabic script and enriched by Arabic vocabulary, provided the dominant literary medium for this next phase of Moslem history. The Arabs were eclipsed in the civilization they had launched long before

---

Who Is An Arab?

It is not easy to define accurately the term "Arab." The British geographer W. B. Fisher, in his book *The Middle East: A Physical, Social and Regional Geography,* stated: "From the point of view of the anthropologist, it is impossible to speak with accuracy either of an Arab or of a Semitic people. Both terms connote a mixed population varying widely in physical character and in racial origin, and are best used purely as cultural and linguistic terms respectively." Thus the so-called "Arab" countries are those in which Arabic is the primary language and which share a common culture.

As Islam spread from the Arabian Peninsula, what took place has been described as the "twin processes of arabization and islamization"—closely linked but not identical. As Peter Mansfield writes, "Arabization began some two centuries before the Prophet Mohammed, with the overflow of Arabian tribes into Syria and Iraq, and reached its greatest impulse during the first decades of the Arab Empire. Islamization lasted much longer and still continues today, especially in Africa. The consequence is that although Arabic language and culture retain a special and predominant place in the world of Islam, only about one-fifth of the one-sixth of mankind who are Moslems are Arabic-speaking."[4]

Currently the Arab countries are Egypt, Syria, Jordan, Lebanon, Iraq, Saudi Arabia, Yemen Arab Republic, South Yemen, Kuwait, a series of tiny sheikdoms along the Persian Gulf, and the North African states known collectively as the Mahgreb—Algeria, Morocco, Tunisia and Libya. Islam is the predominant religion in all of these countries. But that in itself does not define an Arab country. Turkey, Iran, Afghanistan and Pakistan are Islamic, but not Arab, nations. The restive Moslem Kurds, who inhabit areas of Iraq, Iran and Turkey, have their own culture and religion and are also not Arabs. And there are Christian minorities in Arab countries—some with ancestral roots antedating Moslem conquests and others converted by missionaries—who speak Arabic and consider themselves Arabs.

---

the Ottoman Turks in the 16th century brought almost the entire Arabic-speaking world under their control.

"Through a millenium of Turkish hegemony," historian Bernard Lewis writes, "it came to be generally accepted that Turks commanded while others obeyed, and a non-Turk in authority was regarded as an oddity."[3] It would be a mistake to read back into the past, however, an Arab

---

1 William R. Polk, *The United States and the Arab World* (Third Edition), (Harvard University Press: 1975), p. xi.

2 Peter Mansfield, *The Arabs: A Comprehensive History,* (Crowell: 1977), p. 22.
3 Bernard Lewis, *The Middle East and the West,* (Harper Torchbooks: 1966), p. 20.
4 Mansfield, op. cit., pp. 45-46.

resentment of foreign rule such as the 20th century takes for granted. Modern nationalism is a recent import from the West into the "Arab world," where religious, local and family identities had more political significance than ties to the diverse and scattered peoples who spoke the Arab language. In its heyday, the Ottoman Empire brought glory to the community of the faithful, and the fact that the sultans were Turks did not make their state illegitimate in the eyes of the Arabs.

By the 18th century, however, the Ottoman Empire had decayed from within and no longer could protect Moslems from the advancing civilization of the "infidel" West. The ease with which Napoleon occupied Egypt in 1798 shocked Moslems' faith in their superiority over the West, and the next century saw Arab peoples increasingly dominated by European power and wealth.

The early history the Arabs had ill prepared them for this fate. In its formative century, their religion had swept all before it, and even conquerors of the Arabs had bowed before the revelation of their prophet. Islam, like the Judaism and Christianity it recognized as predecessors, was distinguished by the ultimate importance it attached to history. But unlike those older Semitic faiths, which had early been forced to cope with defeat and persecution, Islam took shape amidst triumph after triumph, a historical experience that seemed to confirm that the Koran was, indeed, God's final revelation.

What is the modern Arab, then, to make of his own recent history? Even after political liberation, Bernard Lewis observes, "the intelligent and sensitive Arab cannot but be aware of the continued subordination of his culture to that of the West." Lewis continues:

> His richest resource is oil—but it is found and extracted by Western processes and machines, to serve the needs of Western inventions. His greatest pride is his new army—but it uses Western arms, wears Western-style uniforms, and marches to Western tunes. His ideas and ideologies, even of anti-Western revolt, derive ultimately from Western thought. His knowledge even of his own history and culture owes much to Western scholarship. His writers, his artists, his architects, his technicians, even his tailors, testify by their work to the continued supremacy of Western civilization—the ancient rival, once the pupil, now the model, of the Muslim. Even the gadgets and garments, the tools and amenities of his everyday life are symbols of bondage to an alien and dominant culture, which he hates and admires, imitates but cannot share. It is a deeply wounding, deeply humiliating experience.[5]

Two World Wars

The faint beginnings of Arab nationalism can be traced back into the 19th century, when it was strongest among Christian Arabs, who did not identify with the larger Islamic community and who were more susceptible to Western ideas. The British occupation of Egypt in 1882 sparked development of a local nationalism there, but until the First World War, the Moslem faith still supplied the predominant bulwark against the encroaching West.

As a popular movement, Arab nationalism began during World War I. The defeat of the Ottomans provided the Arabs with an opportunity to pursue political ambitions which they had habitually left to Turks, and the presence of

5 Lewis, *op. cit.*, p. 135.

victorious European armies stirred new fears and aspirations.

At the beginning of the war, most Moslem Arabs favored the Turks against the Allied powers. But in 1916, the British organized the Arab revolt in the desert, immortalized by the adventures and writings of T. E. Lawrence. Bedouin troops then supported the British forces advancing through Palestine and Syria. Their leaders had been promised Arab independence after the war, but once the war ended the imperialist powers were reluctant to give up their advantages in the area. Instead of the hoped-for independence, the Arabs of the former Ottoman Empire found themselves divided into a series of states under British or French mandates. The mandates, as formalized by the League of Nations between 1922 and 1924, provided that the British and French would administer and develop the territories until they were ready for independence.

Under the terms of the mandates, the British were given control of Palestine (which then included today's Jordan and Iraq). Through British efforts both Transjordan (the area to the east of the Jordan River) and Iraq became ruled by Arab kings—under the constant supervision of British advisers and troops. Palestine was run by a British commissioner who, under the League of Nation's mandate, was to allow development in the area of a national home for the Jews. Syria, which then included what is now Lebanon, was administered by the French, who took over by forcing out the Arab king and partitioned the area. In Egypt, the British in 1923 recognized Egyptian independence but retained advisers and the right to station troops to oversee the Suez Canal. Iraq's independence came with the end of the British mandate in 1932.

The situation in the Arabian Peninsula, now Saudi Arabia, was different. The strength of the Ottoman Turks had never penetrated deeply there. There was a major rivalry for power between Hussein, king of the Hejaz, and Ibn Saud, king of Riyadh. The French and British were content to let them fight it out, and in 1927 Ibn Saud became sovereign over the whole area.

In the period between the wars, Saudi Arabia, while independent, was too inward-looking to lead the move for Arab unity that had begun during the war. The other states, under their tutelary rulers, were concerned with achieving a greater degree of independence from occupying powers rather than with working for pan-Arab nationalism.

The unification movement was reawakened by World War II. The Arab countries in 1939 were more than half-way between the complete servitude of 1914 and the total independence they would come to achieve. The war removed the French from Syria and Lebanon and the Italians from Libya, leaving Britain the only colonial power in the Middle East. Arab nationalism revived and intensified, and the eventual end of the British role appeared inescapable.

Near the end of the war, the Hashemite Arab leaders of Iraq and Syria proposed plans to unite several Arab countries under their leadership. The plans were opposed by both the non-Hashemite Arabs and the British. They instead backed the formation of a loose federation of the Arab states which would safeguard national sovereignties but at the same time enable them to work for the common interest. For the British, the plan appeared to have the advantage of giving them a mechanism through which they could pursue their interests in the Middle East. The loose federation grew out of two conferences among Egypt, Saudi Arabia, Yemen, Transjordan, Syria, Lebanon and Iraq and became known as the Arab League.

The Arab League

The birth of the first pan-Arab organization in 1944 stirred high hopes among many Arabs, but its capacity for action turned out to be considerably smaller than many had hoped. The League had largely a negative function in its early years. The seven original states were unequal in wealth and prestige and had differing political goals. None wanted to sacrifice its own sovereignty to a federal ideal, and there were destructive personal rivalries among the rulers of Egypt, Saudi Arabia, Jordan and Iraq.

The one area in which members of the League were in complete agreement in the early years was opposition to growing Jewish claims in Palestine. After the United Nations voted to partition Palestine in 1947, the Arab League made a joint declaration of war against the new state of Israel. But then, instead of acting in a truly coordinated fashion, each Arab state tried to help a particular client group among the Palestinian Arab population which they believed would help them to pursue their own goals. This uncoordinated and conflicting effort led to the defeat of the Arabs in the first Arab-Israeli war, bitter feuds among the Arab governments and the influx of hundreds of thousands of unwanted Palestinian Arab refugees into other Arab countries. *(Arab-Israeli Wars, p. 62)*

The move against Israel led to the end of any British influence in the Arab League, and the Arab defeat nearly led to the end of the League itself. It was resuscitated by the signing of a mutual security pact designed to protect Syria from the ambitions of the Hashemite kings.

Neither the mutual security pact nor other collective actions by the League were of great practical value. Nevertheless, the League did perform some useful functions for the Arab world. In his book *From War to War*, Middle East authority Nadav Safran speculated that the League "gave the idea of pan-Arabism an institutionalized expression that made it part of Arab daily life." During the 1950s it also was responsible for useful administrative and cultural initiatives.

The Arab League has remained an important Arab forum, though one where rival Arab countries often display more disunity than unity. As of June 1979, the Arab League had 21 members including the Palestine Liberation Organization (PLO). Notably, when Syrian forces were used, beginning in mid-1976, to quell the destructive Lebanese civil war, they did so under the colors of the Arab League.

The League has set up more than 20 specialized agencies and institutions and has sponsored other projects like the Arab Common Market and various funds and financial organizations. Its two most notable successes have been the Economic Unity Council and the Boycott of Israel Office. Following the signing in March 1979 of the Israeli-Egyptian peace treaty, Egypt was expelled from the League.

Postwar Developments

The factionalism and failure of the Arab League to meet its primary goals were reflected in the larger history of the Arab world during the post-World-War-II period.

As the British systematically gave up their remaining control, the political histories of the newly independent nations were characterized by dictatorships, coups, assassinations and abdications. Moreover, the Arab countries were continually interfering in each others' affairs.

Egypt alone attempted to instigate or support revolutions in Syria, Lebanon, Iraq, Jordan, Saudi Arabia and Yemen. Egypt became involved in a full-scale war with Yemen and at one point had as many as 70,000 troops there. Almost all of the Arab countries at one time or another were involved in machinations intended to bolster one state against another. Arab unity was a byword. Until 1973, however, attempts to achieve fruitful pan-Arab cooperation were failures.

For much of the postwar period, Egypt, the most populous state, sought to be the dominant country in the Arab world. The monarchy was overthrown by a military dictatorship in 1952. The dictatorship was headed by Gamal Abdel Nasser, a vigorous and charismatic figure, between 1954 and 1970. Nasser preached Arab nationalism, but his feuds with other leaders often made him a divisive force. His successor, Anwar Sadat, at first seemed a weak figure by comparison; but after the 1973 Arab-Israeli war and until the March 1979 Israeli-Egyptian peace treaty, Sadat began to emerge as a more constructive worker for Arab unity.

Britain relinquished its role in what was then called Transjordan in 1946. Emir Abdullah of the Hashemite clan became king. He was assassinated in 1951 by a Palestinian because of the fear that he was attempting to achieve peace with Israel. He was succeeded briefly by his son and then, in 1953, by his grandson, Hussein, who took over at the age of 18. Hussein has remained on the Jordanian throne since then, though his kingdom has faced a number of serious crises. Generally, Hussein has been more pro-Western and moderate than other Arab leaders and it is usually said that Jordan will be the second country to make peace with Israel—its position within the Arab world not allowing her to go first. Hussein's regime has faced sharp conflicts with other Arab nations in the past because of the problems posed to the state by the existence of a large number of Palestinian refugees who fled in 1948 and in 1967 from areas controlled by Israel. A civil war broke out in Jordan in 1970 when the PLO attempted to take over the country but was defeated by the King's largely Bedouin army and the threat of Israeli military intervention supported by the United States.

Saudi Arabia was ruled from 1964 until his assassination in 1975 by King Faisal, son of King Ibn Saud, who had unified the country in 1927. The world's richest oil reserves had been discovered there in 1933, but the country remained an economically backward land of desert tribes. Fearful of challenges to its power, the royal family did not even develop an army. In recent years Saudi Arabia has become the financial capital of the Arab Middle East. Saudi political influence has multiplied enormously since the Yom Kippur War and the steep rise in oil prices, making the U.S.-Saudi alliance one of the central political facts of world politics.

The postwar political history of other major Arab countries has been more complex. Syria and Iraq are cases in point. By some counts there had been 20 coups d'etat in Syria before the current ruler, Gen. Hafez al-Assad, seized power in 1970. Assad's position was unsure, and he did not have the freedom of action of his Egyptian counterpart, Sadat, during negotiations following the 1973 Arab-Israeli war. Iraq was also bedeviled by a series of coups after the Hashemite king was murdered in 1958. *(For more detailed political histories of the major Middle East nations, see individual country profiles starting on p. 101)*

During the postwar period, there were several unsuccessful attempts to form federations of Arab states. Syria and Egypt in 1958 united in a common government to form the United Arab Republic. The federation was ended by a Syrian coup in 1961. Nasser threatened but was powerless to act; Syria's nearest point was 130 miles from Egypt. Subsequent efforts to unite Syria and Iraq while they were both controlled by the Baath Party also fell apart. Syria, Egypt and Libya in 1971 formed a loose Federation of Arab Republics. Subsequent plans for an actual merger of neighboring Libya and Egypt collapsed in 1973, when Sadat turned from Libya to Saudi Arabia for support.

Most recently Jordan and Syria have begun steps toward a form of limited unification. In addition, Syria's post-civil war control over Lebanon may mark a revived Syrian quest for regional hegemony. There has even been discussion of a possible federal link between Syria, Lebanon, Jordan and a new state of Palestine which some hope will be created out of territories now occupied by Israel. Egypt and Syria, after more than a year of at times bitter hostility, agreed in December 1976, to a joint political command. They were joined a few months later by Sudan, Egypt's southern neighbor.

Palestinian Issue

Since 1948, the existence of Israel has been a constant irritant to the Arab world and has led four times to all-out warfare.

Ironically, Israel has been at once both an aid and a detriment to Arab unity. Whenever inter-Arab relations were seriously strained, common hostility to Israel was a unifying force. But the existence of Israel, physically separating Egypt from Syria and Iraq, impeded Arab attempts at unity.

A major offshoot of the wars was what came to be known as the Palestinian refugee problem. The war that followed the partition of Palestine led to the displacement of more than 700,000 Palestinian Arabs who had lived in the area. Since then, controversy has continued over whether the Arabs fled of their own accord or were forced out by Israeli design. The Israelis contend that the Arab leaders first fled the country and that the populace followed after receiving broadcast orders from their absent leaders to leave. The Arabs point to acts of Israeli terrorism, such as the massacre of 200 Arabs by the dissident Irgun group at Dir Yassin in April 1948, as the explanation for the mass exodus.

Whatever the cause, the refugees left, and the Israelis, not wanting to saddle the new state with a large dissident minority, did not want them back. The Palestinians became refugees in Jordan (about 50 per cent with most going to the West Bank area), the Gaza Strip (about 25 per cent) and Syria and Lebanon (most of the remainder).

Proposals for settling the problem have been put forward since 1948. The basic document still is a paragraph of the U.N. General Assembly's Resolution 194, adopted Dec. 11, 1948, which provided: "That the refugees wishing to return to their homes and live at peace with their neighbors should be permitted to do so at the very earliest practicable date, and that compensation should be paid for the property of those choosing not to return and for loss of or damage to property which, under principles of international law or in equity, should be made good by the governments or authorities responsible." A Conciliation Commission for Palestine attempted to work out a settlement in 1949 and 1951, but negotiations broke down, because the Israelis wanted to receive only a limited number of the refugees and the Arabs opposed a refugee settlement which recognized a Jewish state.

The Arab states also did not want to absorb the Palestinians. Many were settled in dreary United Nations refugee camps which grew into permanent Jordanian, Syrian and Lebanese towns; there were 63 such camps in 1974. The Arab leaders refused to absorb them, on the grounds that their lands lacked resources and were already overpopulated and that resettlement would imply the permanence of Israel. In addition, the compensation issue was never settled, and the Palestinians received nothing for the homes, orange groves, farms and businesses which were taken over by the Israelis. The festering situation led to the birth of numerous Palestinian terrorist groups, most of which now belong to the Palestine Liberation Organization, which since 1974 has become widely recognized as representing the Palestinians.

The refugee problem increased after the 1967 war when Israel occupied the Gaza Strip and the West Bank where the majority of refugees lived. While most of the Palestinians remained under Israeli occupation, others fled, some for the second time in one generation, across the Jordan River or into Lebanon.

In January 1978, there were an estimated 4 million Palestinians in the world, 1,275,000 living in the occupied West Bank and Gaza, 1.1 million in Jordan, 500,000 in Israel and 600,000 in Syria and Lebanon, with the remainder scattered throughout the world. *(See box in Palestinian chapter, p. 29)*

As of 1977, slightly less than a third of the Palestinians, about 1.6 million, were still registered as refugees with the United Nations Relief and Works Agency (UNRWA). The UNRWA-registered refugees were distributed as follows:

Jordan	550,000	Gaza	325,000
Israeli-occupied		Lebanon	185,000
West Bank	280,000	Syria	170,000

Soviet Involvement

The end of World War II and colonialism found many Arab nations economically underdeveloped but with strong anti-Western feelings. As a result, a number of Arab leaders turned to the Soviet Union for help in modernization. The arrangement was a two-way street; the U.S.S.R., which had been unable to gain a foothold in neighboring Turkey or Iran, was eager to develop clients in the strategic southern Middle East.

Russian postwar involvement in the area grew to major proportions after 1955, when the U.S.S.R. took over the role formerly held by Britain and the United States as munitions supplier and financier to Egypt. It also became heavily involved in the less stable nations of Syria and Iraq. Russian aid to Arab nations ranged from building the Aswan Dam in Egypt to port construction to supplying large numbers of weapons and economic and military advisers. In return, Russia received military facilities in Egypt, Syria, Iraq, Algeria and the Yemen. It aided both revolutionary and reactionary states and achieved good relations with most Arab countries; a major exception was anti-Communist Saudi Arabia.

The dependence of the Arab countries on Soviet aid increased substantially after the disastrous Arab defeat in the 1967 Arab-Israeli war. The Egyptian arsenal that was rebuilt was more sophisticated and extensive than the one destroyed in 1967. Then, in an unexpected move on July 18, 1972, President Sadat ordered the bulk of Soviet military personnel to leave the country. The decision was partly motivated by the "no war, no peace" policies of the Soviet

Union and partly by Egyptian chaffing at Soviet attempts at dominance. ("No war, no peace" is a phrase used frequently to describe Soviet Middle East policy. It means that the Soviet Union preferred Arab-Israeli tension but was unwilling to help the Arabs force Israel to withdraw from Arab territories occupied in 1967.)

Egypt, however, was careful to avoid a complete break with Russia, and the value of the aid it had received was clearly indicated by the results of the 1973 war; Arab armies had profited greatly from new sophisticated training, and new Russian weapons left Israel far more vulnerable than it had anticipated. *(Soviet involvement, p. 54)*

The Ramadan War* and the "Oil Weapon"

While the Arabs were united in a common opposition to Israel during the period 1948-73, they were rarely able to translate this unity into effective human action. An Arab League boycott of Israeli goods was one of the only fruitful, though largely symbolic, joint actions taken until 1973. That year, the Arab countries were finally able to unite in a coordinated surprise attack on Israel and to use the "oil weapon" against Israel's supporters.

An oil embargo against pro-Israeli nations had been briefly tried after the 1967 war but had never really worked. It had been undertaken by King Faisal of Saudi Arabia under pressure from Nasser. Faisal was not a Nasser sympathizer; oil was allowed to "leak" to the West, and then the embargo was quickly ended.

By 1973, the situation was different. Nasser had died in September 1970 and his successor, Sadat, quietly set about a policy of "de-Nasserization." He eased restrictions on foreign capital, ended nationalization of industry and asked help from Saudi Arabia in economic development. In September 1973, plans for a political union with Saudi Arabia's enemy, Libya, foundered. As a result, Faisal, apparently at some point in mid-1973, indicated to Sadat a willingness to use his country's vast oil resources to gain leverage against Israel. By that time, with Westerners predicting an "energy crisis," oil was a much more potentially powerful weapon than it had been in 1967.

On Oct. 6, Egypt and Syria went to war and fought with conspicuously more success than in 1967. The earlier defeats had been immensely humiliating to Arab pride, and the comparative success in 1973 enabled the Arabs to recoup much stature in their own eyes. Sadat called the war "the first Arab victory in 500 years." The emotional impact of the success apparently led the Arabs to close ranks as they never had before. At a November 1973 meeting in Algiers, an oil embargo was proclaimed in retaliation for massive American military and financial aid to Israel. Since then, the fear of a future embargo coupled with the increased financial power of the Arab world due to ever-spiralling oil costs has acted as a stimulus to proposals to settle the Arab-Israeli conflict along lines more favorable to Arab interests. *(See Middle East Oil chapter, p. 70)*

A Senate Foreign Relations Committee staff report, "The Middle East Between War and Peace," released March 10, 1974, gave much of the credit for newly achieved Arab unity to Sadat. It said, "That unity has been made

possible largely by the personality of President Sadat. Nasser was a charismatic leader, whom other Arab leaders—especially one supposes, King Faisal—would not have wanted to win a war. The fact that President Sadat is moderate and uncharismatic, without pretensions to the leadership of the Arab world, makes him a safe ally."

Another theory for the new unity was expressed by Nadav Safran in the January 1974 issue of *Foreign Affairs*. He postulated that the "second circle" Arab countries which did not have common borders with Israel had become concerned by the vast growth of Israeli power and territory after 1967, which now had the potential to affect them directly. "Their support for countries of the 'first circle,'" Safran said, "became an investment in their own security."

The solidarity, achieved as a result of the 1973 war, brought the likelihood of continued Arab cooperation, but the outlook was unclear. A possibly major divisive factor was Libya, whose revolutionary head, Col. Muammar el-Qaddafi, was the one leader of an Arab state to hold to the old position that the Arabs should not come to terms with Israel under any condition but should continue to fight for its destruction. Iraq was also a question mark, although in 1975 it began to seek rapprochement with its neighbors.

Moreover, even if the Arab countries did continue to operate cooperatively, it was unclear how many initiatives they would take outside of the area of oil. The Senate Foreign Relations Committee report commented: "There has been one common characteristic of just about every discussion of the peace conference we have had, with both officials and private citizens, in Egypt, Saudi Arabia, Kuwait, Lebanon, and now Syria: a pervading sense on the Arabs' part of it all being somebody else's responsibility and that somebody else is the United States. They themselves are passive, skeptical and pessimistic."

The picture of the Arab as "passive" is also part of the Arabs' self-image, an image fostered by colonialism and deepened by humiliation in wars with Israel. Determination to break free of that sense of impotence has been one of the most powerful drives behind Arab terrorism. Ironically, that same self-image of passivity has long plagued the Jews, especially after the extermination of six million of them in Hitler's holocaust, compelling Israelis to compensate with demonstrations of prowess. The attitudes of both sides thus reinforce each other in escalating conflicts.

The stalemate at the end of the last, largest war, however, may provide an opportunity to break out of that vicious circle. Arab armies took the initiative in the war and fought with anything but passivity. The Israelis, by the end of the war, were again demonstrating their military prowess, but with results that showed that military power could not bring the peace they need. Both sides in the war paid a terrible price in human lives and are still paying the heavy economic price of continuing confrontation.

Since that bitter stalemate, the leaders of Egypt and Jordan have said they will recognize Israel's existence in exchange for a return to its pre-1967 borders. Jordan's King Hussein called this an "historic change" in the Arabs' position. [6] But that recognition of Israel also depends, Hussein and other Arab leaders said, on Israel's willingness to "recognize the legitimate rights of the Palestinians in their homeland." The Palestinians meanwhile are divided about the possibility of living peacefully with Israel, no matter what its boundaries. It appeared that a pragmatic majority might be willing to coexist with Israel should they be

---

* The war that began on October 6, 1973 has different names. In Israel and the U.S. it is best known as the Yom Kippur War since it began on the Jewish Day of Atonement. The Arabs call it the War of Ramadan, since it began during their month-long period of daytime fasting. A "neutral" term is the October War. Throughout this book Yom Kippur War is used in deference to popular usage in the U.S.

6 *The New York Times*, May 7, 1975.

allowed to create a Palestinian state in the area of the West Bank and Gaza Strip. Israel, however, continued in 1979 to oppose creation of an autonomous Palestinian state.

1978-79 Developments

The September 1978 Camp David accords that were intended to provide a framework for settling the Palestinian question on the West Bank and Gaza Strip as well as the basis for an Egyptian-Israeli peace treaty produced both dissension within Arab ranks and at the same time a hardening of the Arab "rejectionists'" position on Israel. One result of the accords, and the ensuing Egyptian-Israeli peace treaty signed in March 1979, was the increasing economic, political and military isolation of Egypt from the rest of the Arab world. Rather than augmenting Sadat's stature as the leading Arab statesman and a principal spokesman for the Arab cause, he was accused of being a "traitor" by many Arab governments.

At the same time, the Camp David accords produced a degree of unity among the other Arab countries. This was apparent in the reconciliation of Syria and Iraq in late October 1978, when the two governments agreed to work toward a "full military union" against Israel because of the "great dangers looming over the Arab nation" after Camp David. Saudi Arabia and Iraq have also increased bilateral cooperation, particularly in security matters; moreover, while U.S.-Saudi relations have grown cooler, Iraq has pulled somewhat away from its Soviet friendship.

There was also more unity than expected at an Arab summit conference held Nov. 2-5, 1978, in Baghdad, Iraq. The conference, attended by 21 Arab states and the PLO was widely viewed as a victory for the hard-liners. Among the measures adopted at the meeting were a condemnation of the Camp David accords and the approval of a $3.5 billion-a-year war chest to help subsidize Syria, Jordan and the PLO. It was further agreed that, upon conclusion of the Egyptian-Israeli peace treaty, Egypt's membership in the Arab League would be suspended, the League's headquarters would be moved from Cairo, and all Egyptian firms dealing with Israel would be subject to the Arab boycott. Egypt did not attend the Baghdad conference. Of particular concern to Egypt, which depended on Saudi Arabian economic assistance, and to the United States, which had been working to enlist the support of the more moderate Arab states, was the fact that Saudi Arabia and Jordan supported resolutions adopted at the meeting.

On the other hand, another effect of the Camp David accords and the peace treaty was to put pressure on the moderate states, thereby causing strains in Arab unity. While Arab moderates have been critical of Egypt's withdrawal from the Arab-Israeli struggle, they have been reluctant to take drastic action against Sadat. In an address to his people Oct. 10, 1978, King Hussein of Jordan said: "Most Arabs still hope that Arab Egypt will not reach the point of no return and isolate itself from its history, its Arabism and even from itself."

Without a comprehensive peace agreement acceptable to all parties in the region — and particularly an agreement on the future of Palestinians — it appeared that the Middle East would remain a dangerously unstable area. The conflict in Lebanon, which erupted in 1975 and which intensified following the 1979 peace treaty, was another destabilizing factor, as was the 1978-79 upheaval in Iran. The war in Lebanon was unlikely to be ended until a solution to the Palestinian problem was found. The volatile situation in Iran has put considerable pressure on the moderate and conservative governments in Saudi Arabia and the Gulf sheikdoms.

Especially since 1973, depleting oil and accumulating petrodollars have brought great changes to the Arab Middle East. Some countries, such as Egypt, Jordan and Syria, still had serious — and deepening — economic problems. Others, especially Saudi Arabia and Kuwait, were troubled by the difficult task of preserving their Arab way of life while modernizing at a rate dependent only on how fast the West could sell them the required goods and technology.

In sum, in 1979, there were forces of both stability and revolution in the Arab world. And though the West, primarily the United States, had the dominant involvement at the moment, it appeared certain that the Soviet Union would continue to demand a role in Middle East developments. Much would be determined by whether the Egyptian-Israeli peace treaty would ultimately hinder or advance the cause of a comprehensive peace in the region.

APPENDIX

PARTICIPANTS IN THE MIDDLE EAST DRAMA

Following are biographical sketches of some of the leading 20th century political personages in the Arab world, Iran and Israel. The list also contains several persons from countries outside the Middle East, but who exerted influence on Middle East events.

Abd-ul-Ilah (1913-1958). Regent of Iraq (1939-53); then crown prince. Educated at Victoria College, Alexandria. Became regent when his cousin and nephew, King Faisal II, succeeded to throne at age 3. Known for loyalty to boy-king, opposition to violent nationalism, support for cooperation with West. Relinquished powers to Faisal II when he reached majority in 1953. Assassinated with the king in Baghdad uprising July 14, 1958.

Abdullah ibn Hussein (1882-1951). Emir of Transjordan (1921-46); Hashemite king of Jordan (1946-51). Born in Mecca, second son of sharif Hussein (later king of Hejaz). Educated in Turkey. Played outstanding role preparing Arab revolt against Turkey in World War I. In 1920, boldly occupied Transjordan; recognized as emir by British, who held mandate. Established Transjordan as entity separate from Palestine, extracting pledge from British that Jews would not settle in his emirate. His unachieved ambition to unite Transjordan, Syria and Iraq into a Hashemite bloc embittered Saudi Arabian dynasty.

In World War II, sent his army, the Arab Legion, to assist British troops in Iraq and Syria. In 1946, rewarded with independence by British, renamed country Jordan and became king. After Palestine partition, in 1948 Arab-Israeli war, Abdullah's army captured Old Jerusalem and held central Palestine for Arabs. When territories annexed to Jordan, Abdullah drew wrath of Egypt, Saudi Arabia, Syria, which sought an Arab Palestine. Jordan, more impoverished by arrival of Palestinian refugees; Abdullah's enemies multiplied, and he was assassinated in Aqsa Mosque, Jerusalem, July 20, 1951, by young Palestinian Arab.

Abdullah al-Salem al-Sabah (1895-1965). Emir of Kuwait in 1961 at time British withdrew protection over emirate and recognized Kuwait's independence. When Iraq threatened to make Kuwait a province, Abdullah sought and got British aid, which deferred Iraq action. Using vast oil wealth, Abdullah modernized country, shared riches with people to give Kuwait one of world's highest living standards.

Ali, Kamal Hassan (born 1920). Egyptian defense minister and military commander. Appointed assistant defense minister in 1975; named defense minister in October 1978.

Allenby, Edmund Henry, 1st Viscount (1861-1936). British field marshal. His World War I campaigns in Palestine, Syria broke centuries-old Turkish rule over Arabs. While Allenby was high commissioner for Egypt (1919-25), Egypt was recognized as sovereign state (1922).

Amitay, Morris (born 1936). Executive Director of American Israel Public Affairs Committee (AIPAC) popularly known as the Israeli or the Jewish lobby in Washington. Contributing Editor to the weekly newsletter *Near East Report*. Born in New York City. Graduated from Columbia University and Harvard Law School. State Department foreign service officer (1962-1969). Congressional assistant before going to AIPAC in 1975. Home in Rockville, Maryland, bombed in July 1977.

Arafat, Yasir (born 1929). Native of Palestine, became head of Palestine Liberation Organization, alliance of Palestinian organizations. Trained as guerrilla fighter, he associated with Al Fatah, militantly nationalist Palestine organization, in 1950. As PLO chief, represents the more than three million Palestinians in Israel, occupied territories and in Arab states surrounding Israel. PLO has become widely recognized since 1974. Arafat condemned the separate peace treaty between Egypt and Israel that was signed March 26, 1979.

'Arif, Abdul Rahman (born 1916). Baath Party leader; president, premier of Iraq. Became president when younger brother, President Abdul Salem 'Arif, was killed in helicopter crash April 13, 1966. Abdul Rahman 'Arif made attempts to end Kurdish revolt in northeast Iraq. When 1967 Arab-Israeli war broke out, sent troops to Sinai, Jordan; cut off oil supplies to West; severed diplomatic relations with United States, Britain, West Germany. Arab defeat, Kurdish troubles, economic problems led to his overthrow in bloodless coup July 17, 1968; living in exile.

'Arif, Abdul Salem (died 1966). Headed Baathist army coup overthrowing Iraq dictator Abdul Karim Kassim, who was executed, and making 'Arif Iraqi president. Improved relations with oil companies; dropped Iraqi claims to Kuwait. Killed in helicopter crash near Basra April 13, 1966.

al-Assad, Hafez, Lt. Gen. (born 1928). President of Syria since 1971. Became defense minister in 1965; headed "Nationalist" faction of Baath Party, which favored less strong ties to Soviet Union and more moderate Marxist economy. After unsuccessful February 1969 coup, led successful coup in November 1970, assumed presidency March 1971. Considered moderate by Syrian standards. Improved relations with Saudi Arabia and other conservative Arab states. A bitter foe of Israel, launched war against Jewish state in Golan Heights in October 1973, but entered into troop disengagement with Israel in 1974. Accepted massive Soviet military aid, Soviet advisers in Syria. Took Syria into the Lebanese conflict in mid-1976 and since then has exerted great influence over Lebanese developments and over the PLO. Elected for second 7-year term as president in February 1978.

al-Atasi, Hashim (born 1875). Became president of Syria after August 1949 coup; ousted in another coup in December 1949. Further army revolt in February 1954 led to restoration of constitutional rule and al-Atasi to presidency; after elections, was succeeded by al-Kuwatly as president in 1955.

al-Atasi, Louai (born 1926). Syrian army officer, government official. Educated at Syrian Military Academy. In March 1963 led pro-Nasser military faction which seized Syrian government. As president of Revolutionary Council, helped establish Baath Party predominance, ending its 20-year clandestine existence. Since 1969 in exile in Egypt.

al-Atassi, Nureddin (born 1929). Syrian medical doctor and government official. Led "Progressive" faction of Baath Party, favoring strong ties to Soviet Union and strong Marxist economy. Became president in 1966; deposed by Hafez al-Assad in November 1970 bloodless coup.

Bakhtiar, Shahpur (born 1914). Iranian prime minister and opposition leader. Appointed by the Shah in January 1979 to form a new civilian government; expelled from membership in the National Front. Resigned on February 12, 1979 when forces loyal to the Moslem leader Ayatollah Khomeini took over the government.

al-Bakr, Ahmed Hassan (born 1912). President of Iraq (1968-79). Seized power in bloodless coup on July 17, 1968, and assumed presidency and premiership. Under his regime, Iraq sought to end Kurd revolt by granting measure of autonomy; but after Iraq and Iran, which armed Kurds, settled differences, Bakr government militarily quashed revolt in March 1975. In June 1973, regime defeated an attempted military coup, resulting in execution of 36 officers. In April 1972, a 15-year friendship treaty with Soviet Union was signed; in June 1972 Iraq Petroleum Company was nationalized. Resigned for health reasons July 1979.

Balfour, Arthur James, First Earl (1848-1930). British government official. As foreign minister, decided in favor of Zionist aspirations for creating a Jewish national state in Palestine, embodying it in Balfour Declaration of November 1917.

Barzani, Mustapha Mulla (1904-79). General and leader of Kurdish revolt against Iraq. Declared war on Baghdad government in 1974 after turning down offer of limited autonomy. Revolt crushed by Iraqi armed forces in March 1975; Barzani fled into exile in Iran.

Bazargan, Mehdi (born 1905). Iranian prime minister appointed by Moslem leader Ayatollah Khomeini in February 1979 to head the post-revolutionary government.

Begin, Menachem (born 1913). Became Prime Minister of Israel in June 1977. Long-time opposition leader whose surprise election victory cast considerable doubt over what compromises Israel might be willing to make on the Palestinian problem and in regard to the West Bank and Gaza Strip territories. Former leader of the underground terrorist organization *Irgun Zeva'i Le'umi*. Signed peace treaty with Egypt on March 26, 1979, at the White House in Washington, D.C.

Ben Bella, Ahmed (born 1916). Algeria's national hero and first president. Leader of nationalist movement against French. Exiled and imprisoned several times. After Algerian independence in 1962, was elected president Sept. 15, 1963. Pushed Socialist measures. Overthrown in bloodless coup June 19, 1965; in confinement until July 1979 when President Bendjedid released him.

Bendjedid, Chadli (born 1929). Algerian president. Former member of the general staff of the National Liberation Army and member of the Council of the Revolution; attained the rank of colonel in 1969. Elected president in February 1979, succeeding Boumediene who died at the end of 1978.

Ben-Gurion, David (1886-1973). Zionist leader and Israeli government official. Born in Plonsk, Poland; went to Palestine in 1906 as laborer. Started Labor Party. During World War I was expelled from Palestine by Turks; went to New York, where he formed Zionist Labor Party. Joined Jewish Legion, part of British forces in Palestine. From 1918, lived in Tel Aviv, and headed Labor Party.

Convinced Jews must have state, organized Haganah as fighting force. At Tel Aviv May 14, 1948, read publicly declaration of Israel's independence. In new state, became prime minister and defense minister, holding both posts until 1963 except for one interlude. His main aim was to bring in all Jews to Israel willing to come; nearly one million immigrants came in first decade.

Sent troops into Suez Canal conflict of 1956. Resigned as premier in June 1963 but remained member of Knesset until 1970.

Ben-Zvi, Isaac (1884-1963). Second president of Israel (1952-63). Born in Ukraine. Studied at Kiev University, Imperial Ottoman University, Istanbul. Went to Palestine in 1907, helped found Hashomer (Jewish self-defense organization). After exile by Turks in 1915, went to New York where, with Ben-Gurion, established Hehalutz (Pioneer) movement and Jewish Legion. Founder and chairman of Vaad Leumi (National Council of Palestine Jews). Signed Israeli declaration of independence. Elected to Knesset in 1949 and president Dec. 8, 1952, upon Chaim Weizmann's death.

Bernadotte, Folke, Count (1895-1948). Swedish humanitarian appointed U.N. mediator between Arabs and Jews at time of Palestine partition. Assassinated by Jewish extremists in Jerusalem Sept. 17, 1948.

al-Bitar, Salah (born 1912). Syrian politician. Helped create Socialist Baath Party, which became Syria's ruling party, and short-lived United Arab Republic (Syria and Egypt). Led pro-Nasser coup in Syria which on March 8, 1963, resulted in Bitar becoming premier, holding that post at various times until 1966. In exile in Lebanon.

Boumediene, Houari (1925-78). Second president of Algeria (1965-78). Educated in Arabic studies at universities in Tunis and Cairo. Fought against French in war for Algerian independence; became chief of National Liberation Army in 1960. After independence, became defense minister under Ben Bella in 1962, vice premier in 1963 and president in July 1965, when Ben Bella was ousted and jailed. Followed policy of democratic centralism; set up elections in which 700 communes elected councils of workers and militants.

Bourguiba, Habib Ben Ali (born 1903). First president of Tunisia, since 1957. Educated at Sadiqiya College, Tunis; law degree, University of Paris. Founded nationalist Neo-Destour Party in 1934; jailed and exiled several times by French. After France granted Tunisia independence, was elected president in 1957; re-elected in 1959, 1964, 1969. Favored social reform at home, association with West in foreign affairs. Incurred enmity of military Arab states when he urged moderate approach to Israel. Elected president for life by National Assembly in March 1975.

Bunche, Ralph J. (1904-71). American official at United Nations. Negotiated 1949 armistice between Israel and Arab states, receiving Nobel Peace Prize for it. Directed U.N. peacekeeping efforts in Suez in 1956.

Carter, James Earl (born 1924). Became 39th President of the United States in January, 1977, and within months began discussion of a comprehensive Middle East settlement to include Israeli withdrawal to approximately the 1967 boundaries, creation of a "Palestinian homeland," and establishment of real peace and normal relations between Israel and her Arab neighbors. Presided over signing of an Egyptian-Israeli peace treaty on March 26, 1979, at the White House in Washington, D.C.

Chamoun, Camille (born 1900). President of Lebanon (1952-58). Educated at College des Frères and Law School, Beirut. After election to presidency, his pro-Western policies led to open Moslem revolt, aggravated by radical Arab neighbors. At his request, United States sent Marines into Lebanon in July 1958 to help restore order. In July 1975, became defense minister in "rescue cabinet" formed to end bloody Moslem-Christian clashes over Palestinian refugee issue in Lebanon. Heads National Liberal Party.

Chehab, Fuad (1903-73). President of Lebanon (1958-64). Educated at Damascus Military School, St. Cyr Military Academy, France. Served as commander-in-chief, Lebanese army; prime minister, interior minister, defense minister. As president, pursued neutralist policy acceptable to Arabs and West. Put down attempt to overthrow government by Syrian Popular Party, which sought Lebanese union with Syria.

Dayan, Moshe (born 1915). Israeli soldier, politician. Hero of Young Israel during building of Jewish state. Learned guerrilla warfare as member of "night squadrons" fighting Arab rebel bands in Palestine. A leader of Haganah, volunteer defense force, was jailed by British in 1939; released to serve in British army in World War II. In Syrian campaign against Vichy French, lost eye from sniper's bullet. Chief of staff for all Israeli forces (1953-58); prepared plans for invasion of 1956 Sinai war. Elected to Knesset; became defense minister and executed battle plans which defeated Egypt, Syria, Jordan in 1967 Six-day war. Quit cabinet in 1974 after criticism mounted over initial Arab victories in 1973 war. In 1977 became foreign minister to the new Begin government drawing much criticism from his Labor party from which he resigned while keeping the seat in Parliament he won on the Labor list.

Dulles, John Foster (1888-1959). U.S. secretary of state (1952-59). Architect of Eisenhower administration Middle East policy, which turned United States into a major Middle East power broker after departure of French and British left vacuum in area. Held that without U.S. economic and military assistance, Middle East states could not maintain independence and would come under Soviet hegemony.

Eban, Abba (born 1915). Educated at Cambridge University, England. Deputy prime minister of Israel (1963-66); foreign minister (1966-74). Worked to maintain strong U.S.-Israeli ties; architect of several Middle East peace plans. In August 1977 traveled U.S. discussing Israel's positions at behest of Prime Minister Begin.

Eisenhower, Dwight D. (1890-1969). 34th President of the United States (1953-61). Under his leadership, United States entered Middle East affairs with economic and military aid on large scale. On request from Lebanon government, sent Marines into that country in 1958 to maintain order when Lebanon was threatened by internal revolt and radical Arab states, an application of the Eisenhower Doctrine aimed at maintaining independence of Middle East states and preventing Soviet dominance of area.

Eshkol, Levi (1895-1969). Finance minister of Israel when Ben-Gurion resigned premiership in 1963; succeeded him as prime minister (1963-69). Under his leadership, Israel crushed Arab states in Six-day War of 1967.

Fahd ibn Abdul Aziz (born 1922). Saudi Arabian crown prince and first deputy premier. Served as education minister, interior minister. Raised to crown prince by Saudi royal family after his half-brother, King Faisal, was assassinated in March 1975. Believed to be real power behind older half-brother, King Khalid.

Fahmy, Ismail (born 1920). Egyptian foreign minister (1974-77) and politician. Appointed foreign minister in April 1974. Resigned post November 1977 in apparent opposition to President Sadat's trip to Israel.

Faisal ibn Abdul Aziz al-Saud (1906-75). King of Saudi Arabia (1964-1975). Became crown prince when brother, King Saud, ascended throne in 1953. Served as prime minister, foreign minister, defense minister, finance minister. Became king in March 1964 when Saud was legally deposed. Supported pan-Arab and pan-Islam solidarity. Pressed for economic and educational advances domestically.

A Moslem ascetic, called for Israel to evacuate Islamic holy places in Jerusalem and all occupied Arab territory. An anti-Communist, fostered ties in United States and supported conservative Arab regimes. However, during 1973 Arab-Israeli war, enforced oil embargo and oil-price hike against United States, Western Europe and Japan. Assassinated by a nephew March 25, 1975, at palace in Riyadh.

Faisal I (Faisal ibn Hussein) (1885-1933). King of Iraq (1921-33). Horrified by Turkish anti-Arab actions, was a leader of Arab revolt, assisted by British and Lawrence of Arabia, against Ottomans in World War I. In effort to consolidate Arab state in Syria, was king of Syria briefly in 1920 until expelled by French who held Syrian mandate. With British help, elected to second throne in Baghdad, 1921. Identified himself with strengthening and liberating his kingdom.

Faisal II (1936-58). King of Iraq (1939-58). Inherited throne at age 3 upon accidental death of King Ghazi. Crowned May 2, 1953. During five-year reign, Iraq pursued anti-Communist course, culminating in Baghdad Pact (Britain, Iran, Iraq, Pakistan, Turkey) in 1955. Pact aimed at thwarting possible Soviet intrusion into Middle East. Assassinated with most members of royal family in Baghdad revolution July 14, 1958, which resulted in Iraq being declared a republic.

Faisal ibn Musaed. Saudi Arabian prince. At age 31, killed his uncle King Faisal, at royal palace, Riyadh, March 25, 1975. Tried by religious court and beheaded in Riyadh public square June 18, 1975.

Farouk I (1920-65). King of Egypt (1936-52). Educated in Egypt and England. Reign marked by quarrel with dominant Wafd Party and with British over fate of the Sudan. Standing was damaged by disastrous campaign against Israel in 1948 and corruption connected with arms purchases. Military coup of July 1952 forced abdication. Went into exile in Italy, where he died in Rome March 18, 1965.

Franjieh, Suleiman (born 1910). President of Lebanon (1970-76). In crisis of 1975 between rightist Christians and leftist Moslems, had trouble finding formula for a government placating all sides. Refused to leave presidency, even after petition from Parliament and military assault on his residence, until his official term of office expired in September 1976. Followed as president by Elias Sarkis.

Fuad I (1868-1936). King of Egypt (1922-36). Proclaimed king when Britain relinquished protectorate over Egypt in 1922. Reign was marked by struggle between Wafd Party and palace parties centering around king. Interested in charitable and education matters, prime mover in establishing first Egyptian university of Western type, the Fuad I (now Cairo) University, in 1925.

Gemayel, Pierre (born 1905). Leader of Phalangist party in Lebanon. Pharmacist educated in Beirut and France. Member of Parliament since 1960 who held office in most Lebanese governments. Ran for presidency in 1970 but withdrew in favor of neutral candidate Suleiman Franjieh.

Ghazi (died 1939). King of Iraq (1933-39). Pleasure-loving monarch; reign considered inglorious. However, oil production began in 1934; revenues enabled progress in industry, irrigation, communications under series of able government ministers. Died in road accident.

Habash, George (born 1925). Palestinian leader of "rejection front" which refuses to consider the possibility of coexistence with Israel. In 1970 his Popular Front for the Liberation of Palestine (PFLP) became known for its daring and brutal hijacking of foreign planes. PFLP held responsible for triggering the Jordanian civil war in 1970 and for helping spark the Lebanese civil war in 1975.

Hafez, Amin (born 1911). Syrian army officer, politician. Prime minister (1963) and head of state (1963-66); ousted in coup by pro-Nasser and Baath Party followers. In November 1978 in exile in Iraq.

Hassan II (born 1930). King of Morocco since 1961. Absolute monarch; dissolved National Assembly in 1965. Steered Morocco clear of radical Arab policies; cultivated friendship with United States and Western Europe. Rule limited by 1970 constitution. Survived coups in 1971, 1972.

Helou, Charles (born 1911). Lebanese journalist and government official. Educated at St. Joseph College and Ecole Francaise du Droit, Beirut. Was minister of justice and health. President of Lebanon (1964-70). Steered neutralist course between West and neighboring Arab militants.

Hoveida, Amir Abbas (1919-79). Iranian government official. Educated at Paris and Brussels universities. Served as general managing director of National Iranian Oil. Prime Minister 1965-77. Replaced by Jamshid Amuzegar in August 1977. Executed on April 7, 1979, by a firing squad during the revolutionary trials held in Iran.

Hussein, Saddam (born 1937). President of Iraq since July 1979, succeeding Bakr who resigned for health reasons. Former vice chairman of Revolutionary Command Council.

Hussein ibn Ali (1854-1931). Emir of Mecca (1908-16); king of Hejaz (now Saudi Arabia), (1916-24). During World War I, negotiated with British, leading to Arab revolt against Turkey. Opposed mandatory regimes imposed on Syria, Palestine, Iraq by Versailles Treaty. Kingdom attacked by Ibn Saud of Wahhabi sect; Hussein forced to abdicate in 1924; Ibn Saud later proclaimed king of Saudi Arabia. Hussein exiled to Cyprus. Hussein's son Ali was king of Hejaz briefly; another son, Abdullah, became king of Jordan; a third son became King Faisal I of Iraq.

Hussein Ibn Talal (born 1935). King of Jordan since 1953. Educated at Royal Military Academy, Sandhurst, England. Crowned May 2, 1953, after father, King Talal, was declared mentally ill. Opened kingdom to powerful Egyptian and republican influences. In 1956, abrogated Jordan's treaty with Britain. Accepted U.S. economic aid.

With more than half his subjects Palestinians, supported Nasser in war against Israel in 1967, losing half his kingdom (West Bank of Jordan River) to Israel. Sought to treat indirectly with Israel to recover lost lands. When Palestinians sought to create state within a state, September 1970 civil war broke out, Hussein crushing Palestinian guerrilla enclaves. At Rabat summit conference of Arab League in 1974, right to negotiate for return of West Bank was taken from Hussein and given to Palestine Liberation Organization. Hussein denounced the Egyptian-Israeli peace treaty signed in March 1979 and broke off relations with Egypt.

Ibn Saud (1880-1953). First king of Saudi Arabia (1932-53). To create kingdom, overcame British policy maintaining status quo in Persian Gulf and made war on King Hussein of Hejaz, forcing him to abdicate and leading to merger of Hejaz and Nejd Kingdoms into Saudi Arabia. Worked to consolidate his realm and improve relations with old enemies in other Arab states. In 1933 granted 60-year oil concession to a U.S. oil company which became known as Aramco. Oil royalties greatly enriched his treasury. In 1940s, launched veritable social and economic revolution in Saudi Arabia. In 1945, helped form Arab League.

Idris I (born 1890). King of Libya (1951-69). As emir of Cyrenaica, fought Italian occupation of Libya; was declared constitutional monarch when Libya was made independent state in 1951. Deposed in coup Sept. 1, 1969, led by Col. Muammar el-Qaddafi, who declared Libya a Socialist republic.

Isa bin Sulman al-Khalifah (born 1933). Emir of Bahrain (head of state). Declared independence of Bahrain after Britain quit Persian Gulf in 1971. Considered, then rejected, union of Bahrain with Qatar and United Arab Emirates.

Jumblatt, Kamal (1917-1977). Leader of leftist forces in Lebanese civil war assassinated in March 1977. Strong supporter of Palestinian cause and of reforming Lebanon into a secular state.

Kamel, Mohammed Ibrahim (born 1927). Egyptian foreign minister (1977-1978). Appointed foreign minister by President Sadat in December 1977 to replace Ismail Fahmy who resigned over Sadat's trip to Israel. Kamel was involved in peace talks with Israel but resigned on Sept. 18, 1978 in protest over signing of the Camp David accords. Retained in Foreign Service with ambassadorial rank.

Karami, Rashid (born 1921). Lebanese government official. Educated at Fuad al-Awal University, Cairo. Several times prime minister; last time, in May 1975, called upon to form "rescue cabinet" to restore order to Lebanon after three months of intermittent street fighting between leftist Moslems and rightist Christians in Beirut, April-June 1975. Deputy in Parliament as of 1979.

Kassim, Abdul Karim (died 1963). Iraqi dictator (1958-63). As army general, led military revolution July 14, 1958, which, in one day, saw bloody killing of young King Faisal II and most of royal family. Republic was proclaimed; Kassim was named prime minister. Took Iraq out of Baghdad Pact; improved relations with Soviet Union, Communist China. Attempted assassination of Kassim in October 1959 failed; 13 former officials and army officers were executed.

Suppressed with great severity Kurdish revolt in 1961. Laid claim to Kuwait after its independence in 1961, but British sent troops to Kuwait's aid, deterring Iraqi action. Coup by "free officers" of Baath Party resulted in execution of Kassim in 1963.

Katzir, Ephraim (born 1916). Elected by Knesset as president of Israel in 1973. Succeeded by Yitzhak Navon in 1978 when his term as president expired.

Khalid ibn Abdul Aziz (born 1913). King of Saudi Arabia since March 1975. Educated at religious schools. Represented Saudi Arabia at various international conferences. Became vice president of Council of Ministers, 1962; elevated to crown prince, 1965; succeeded to throne when King Faisal was assassinated.

Khalifa bin Hamad al-Thani (born 1937). Emir of Qatar (head of state). Assumed power after deposing cousin, Emir Ahmad bin Ali bin Abdullah al-Thani, in bloodless coup Feb. 22, 1972. Headed program of social and economic improvements made possible by oil revenues. Joined in oil embargo against West in 1973.

Khalil, Mustafa (born 1921). Egyptian prime minister since October 1978, when he was appointed by President Sadat to replace Mamdouh Salem who resigned the same day; also holds position of foreign minister as of February 1979. Former secretary-general of ruling Arab Socialist Union which merged with Sadat's National Democratic Party.

Khomeini, Ayatollah Ruhollah (born 1900). Shiite Moslem leader of Iran who returned to the country on Feb. 1, 1979 from a 15-year exile to establish an Islamic republic. His forces formed a Council of the Islamic Revolution to replace the Shah-appointed Bakhtiar government. In March he ordered a national referendum to seek support for the new Islamic Republic.

el-Khoury, Bichara (1860-1964). Lebanese government official. In 1943, while Lebanon was under Free French, was elected president. Insurrection followed after French arrested el-Khoury and other government officials, leading to restoration of Lebanese government and transfer of powers to it by French.

In 1946, French relinquished Lebanese mandate and country became independent. During el-Khoury presidency, Beirut grew rapidly and became free-money market and trade center, Tripoli and Saida on Mediterranean became terminal points of oil pipelines from Iraq and Arabia. Abuse of power made regime unpopular; el-Khoury was deposed in popular movement in 1952.

Kissinger, Henry A. (born 1923). U.S. Secretary of State (1973-1977). During 1973-75, through on-the-scene diplomatic efforts, mediated troop disengagement agreements between Egypt and Israel in Sinai and between Syria and Israel on Golan Heights. In 1977 began writing his memoirs, lecturing, and teaching at Georgetown University.

Kuwatly, Shukri (1891-1967). Syrian government official. Opposed to French mandate in Syria, emerged as nationalist leader in 1920s and 1930s. While Syria was under Free French, was elected president in 1943; secured French withdrawal and Syrian independence in 1946. Regime discredited by failure of economic policy and of Arab policy in Palestine. Overthrown in 1949 coup, went into exile; returned to Syria and public life in 1954. Advocated broad Arab union led by Egypt; elected president again in 1955, serving until 1958, when United Arab Republic of Egypt and Syria was inaugurated.

Lawrence, Thomas Edward (1888-1935), known as Lawrence of Arabia. British scholar, soldier, author. Injected new life into Arab revolt against Turks in World War I; and, dressed in Arab garb, fought successful battles (1916-18) with Arab army led by Emir Faisal. In conjunction with British forces. Allies captured Jerusalem in December 1917, and Damascus in October 1918. As member of British delegation to Paris Peace Conference, opposed separation of Syria and Lebanon from rest of Arab states into French mandate. Wrote *Seven Pillars of Wisdom*, an account of his experiences in desert. Died of injuries received in motorcycle accident in England in May 1935.

Mansour, Hassan Ali (died 1965). Helped form New Iran Party from centrist groups in 1963; became prime minister 1963. Died from gunshot wounds inflicted by a student Jan. 21, 1965.

Meir, Golda (1898-1978). Israeli government official. Native of Kiev, Russia, was brought to United States in 1906; immigrated to Palestine in 1921. Active in labor movement, World Zionist Organization and in Hagannah struggle to set up Jewish state.

After Israeli independence, was ambassador to Soviet Union, minister of labor, minister of foreign affairs, prime minister (1969-75).

Maintained inflexible policy vis-a-vis Arab states; during 1973 war, led country as Arabs won initial success, later reversed by Israeli counter-offensives. However, Labor Party lost seats in parliamentary elections Dec. 31, 1974, and she was unable to form new government after several tries as criticism mounted over initial Israeli reverses in 1973 war. Relinquished premiership in March 1975.

Mohammed Reza Pahlavi, (born 1919). Shah of Iran. Educated in Iran, Switzerland. Became Shah in 1941 upon abdication of father, Reza Shah Pahlavi. The Shah's 37-year reign as monarch ended when he left Iran on January 16, 1979, for an "extended vacation," a few weeks before the Moslem leader, Ayatollah Khomeini returned to the country to set up a new Islamic republic.

Mossadegh, Mohammed (1880-1967). Iranian government official. As prime minister, was largely responsible for act nationalizing Anglo-Iranian Oil Company in 1951. Efforts to obtain what amounted to dictatorial powers led to strained relations with shah. Overthrown by military coup in April 1953; later sentenced to three-year prison term for treason.

Naguib, Mohammed (born 1901). Egyptian soldier, government official. Became president of Egypt when it was declared republic in 1953. After power struggle with Nasser, was deprived of presidency in 1954.

Nasser, Gamal Abdel (1918-70). Egyptian soldier, government official. Educated at Military College, Cairo. As head of Revolution Command Council, made up of 11 army officers, led revolt which resulted in deposing King Farouk and establishing republic. After power struggle with President Mohammed Naguib, became president in 1956.

Negotiated withdrawal of British troops from Suez Canal Zone in 1954 and nationalized canal in 1956. Action resulted in Anglo-French-Israeli military intervention; after United States forced Allied withdrawal, Nasser emerged with unparalleled prestige in Arab world. Created 1958 United Arab Republic (Egypt, Syria) and was president of it until Syria seceded in 1961.

Avidly opposed Israel, which defeated Egypt in 1967 war. Defeat led to detente between Nasser and conservative Arab states, which had distrusted his revolutionary objectives. Received revenues from Saudi Arabia, Kuwait and arms from Soviet Union. At home, pursued course of social justice, redistribution of land, improved medical care, education. Construction of Aswan Dam was made a symbol of his achievements. After September 1970 conference in Cairo that ended Jordanian civil war, died of heart attack.

Navon, Yitzhak (born 1921). President of Israel. Born and educated in Jerusalem; elected to the Knesset in 1965 where he served as member of the House until his election to the presidency on April 19, 1978.

al-Nimeiry, Gaafer (born 1929). Sudanese army general, government official. Seized power in coup in May 1969; became first elected president in 1971. Has put down several coups, summarily executing at least 14 persons accused of plotting takeover.

Pasha, Nuri (Nuri as-Said) (1888-1958). Twelve times prime minister of Iraq. Known for suppression of communism. Formed defensive alliance with Turkey in 1955 which, when joined by Iran, Pakistan, Britain, became Baghdad Pact, aimed at possible Soviet aggression in Middle East. Killed along with King Faisal II in Baghdad uprising July 14, 1958.

Peres, Shimon (born 1923). Leading figure in Israeli Labor party associated with the small group known as "Rafi" built by Ben-Gurion, Peres, and Moshe Dayan. Became acting prime minister in April 1977 when Yitzhak Rabin resigned due to scandal. Considered a hard-liner within Labor party. Considered leader of opposition since the defeat of Labor in the May 1977 election in which Peres was Labor's choice for Prime Minister.

Qabus bin Said (born 1942). Sultan and absolute ruler of Oman. Overthrew father, Sultan Said bin Taimur, in 1970, known as one of century's most tyrannical despots. Qabus known for limited attempts to modernize country, which is isolated, inaccessible, feudal.

Qaddafi, Muammar (born 1942). Chairman of Revolutionary Command Council of Libya. Regarded as heir to radical mantle of Egypt's late President Nasser. Educated at University of Libya and Libyan Military Academy. In 1969, led coup which overthrew King Idris. Evicted United States, Britain from Libyan bases. Nationalized oil industry. Unable to forge Arab unity through merger of Libya with Egypt, then with Tunisia, which backed out of union in fear of Qaddafi's radicalism. Known for implacable enmity to continued existence of Israel. Strong supporter of Palestinian "rejection front" and other radical Arab movements.

Rabin, Yitzhak (born 1922). Israeli soldier, government official. Was army chief of staff responsible for planning overwhelming victory in 1967 war. Served as ambassador to Washington. Became prime minister in 1974 when Golda Meir retired. Held Israel to hard line in peace maneuvering of 1974, early 1975. Resigned as Prime Minister in April 1977 just one month before the Israeli election after a scandal involving an illegal bank account held by his wife in Washington.

Rashid ben Saeed (born circa 1910). Emir of Dubai, vice president of federation of United Arab Emirates. Used oil revenues to modernize Dubai, improve port, build international airport.

Reza Shah Pahlavi (1878-1944). Shah of Iran (1925-41). Gained throne after coup deposing Ahmad Shah. Autocratic ruler who ignored constitutional safeguards. Built Trans-Iranian Railway, developed road system. Sought machinery and technicians from Germany, which led to World War II occupation of Iran by British, Soviet troops. Abdicated in 1941 in favor of son, Mohammed Reza Pahlavi.

Rogers, William (born 1913). American Secretary of State (1969-1973) whose name is associated with the 1969-1970 "Rogers Plan" which aimed to bring about a Middle East settlement based on Israeli withdrawal from occupied territories in exchange for peace.

al-Sabah, Jaber Al-Ahmed (born 1920). Emir of Kuwait. Assumed the throne upon the death of Sabah al-Salem al-Sabah at the end of 1978.

Sadat, Anwar (born 1918.) Educated at Military College, Cairo. Was deputy to Nasser in organizing secret revolutionary brotherhood which overthrew monarchy. Was speaker of National Assembly, twice vice president. Became president when Nasser died in 1970. Sadat surprised world by becoming strong leader. In 1972, ordered 20,000 Soviet military advisers out of Egypt. Became Arab world hero in 1973 war when Egypt won initial victories over Israelis. Agreed to troop disengagement accords in Sinai, first reliance on United States to mediate general Middle East peace agreement. Moved country away from radical socialism of Nasser to attract Western capital and alleviate grave economic problems. In June 1975, reopened Suez Canal after eight-year closure. In March 1979 signed a separate peace treaty with Israel, incurring the wrath of its Arab neighbors.

as-Said, Nuri *(see Pasha, Nuri).*

Salam, Saeb (born 1905). Lebanese government official. Foreign affairs minister, defense minister. Prime minister (1952, 1953, 1960-61, 1973). Resigned last time during crisis over Israeli raids on Palestinian commando groups in Beirut, Saida. Deputy in Parliament as of 1979.

Sarkis, Elias (born 1924). Elected by Lebanese parliament on May 8, 1976, to be president. But assumed office only on September 23rd when President Franjieh stepped down at the legal end of his term. Supported by Syrians over the candidacy of Raymond Edde.

Saud IV (1902-69). King of Saudi Arabia (1953-64), succeeding his father, King Ibn Saud. Expanded father's modernization program, with emphasis on educational and medical services. In foreign affairs, continued friendship with United States and all Arabs, suspicion of communism and firm opposition to Israel. Abdicated in 1965 after royal family transferred powers to brother, who became King Faisal.

Saud ibn Faisal (born 1940). Foreign Minister of Saudi Arabia said to be a possible Saudi king in the future.

Saunders, Harold (born 1930). In 1977 serving as Director of the State Department's Bureau of Intelligence and Research. Formerly member of the National Security Council and Deputy Assistant Secretary of State dealing with Middle Eastern affairs. While in this position he testified before Congress in November 1975, that "In many ways, the Palestinian dimension of the Arab-Israeli conflict is the heart of that conflict." This statement became known as "The Saunders Statement."

Shah of Iran *(See Mohammed Reza Pahlavi).*

Sharett, Moshe (1894-1965). Headed foreign policy department, Jewish Agency for Palestine; a founder of Israel. Prime minister (1953-55).

Shazar, Zalman (1889-1974). Born in Mir, Russia. Educated at Academy of Jewish Studies, St. Petersburg, Universities of Freiburg and Strasbourg. Long a leader in World Zionist movement. First education minister of Israel; president (1963-73).

al-Shishakli, Adib. Became president of Syria in 1949 after coup. Known as harsh leader; lost power in 1954 after Syria returned to democratic regime.

al-Solh, Rashid (born 1926). Lebanese government official. Educated American University and St. Joseph's College, Beirut. Became premier in 1973; resigned in 1975 after criticism of his handling of bloody Christian-Moslem riots put Lebanon on brink of civil war. Deputy in Parliament as of 1979.

Strauss, Robert S. (born 1918). Chief U.S. Middle East negotiator. Appointed by President Carter April 24, 1979, as U.S. ambassador-at-large for negotiations on Palestinian autonomy in the West Bank and the Gaza Strip. Former chief trade negotiator for the Carter administration (1977-1979).

al-Tal, Wasfi. (1920-71). Jordanian government official. Educated at American University, Beirut. Thrice prime minister. Assassinated in Cairo in November 1974 by Black September, Palestinian terrorist organization, in reprisal for crushing Palestinian strongholds in Jordan.

Talal (1909-72). King of Jordan (1951-52). Jordanian Parliament declared him mentally ill, deposing him in 1952. Spent rest of life in mental institution in Turkey. Succeeded by his son, King Hussein.

Truman, Harry S (1884-1973). 33rd President of United States (1945-1953). After World War II, prevailed upon British to loosen restrictions on immigration of Jews to Palestine; worked in United Nations for creation of Israel; recognized Israel as state 11 minutes after its creation in May 1948.

Vance, Cyrus R. (born 1917). Attorney and international affairs specialist who was appointed by President Jimmy Carter Secretary of State. Vance's background in the Middle East was minimal but the month after taking office he made his first visit to the area. Then on July 31st he returned to the Middle East for a 12-day visit which took him to all of the confrontation countries plus Saudi Arabia and included indirect contacts with the PLO.

Weizman, Ezer (born 1924). Israeli defense minister from 1977. Commanding officer of Israeli Air Force (1958-66); Army deputy chief of staff (1966-69) and former businessman until appointed defense minister in 1977.

Weizmann, Chaim (1874-1952). Born in Russia, educated in Germany. Lecturer in chemistry at University of Manchester, England. Headed British Admiralty Laboratories that created synthetic acetene for explosives in World War I. Rewarded with Balfour Declaration, British white paper which stated national homeland for Jews should be created in Palestine. President of World Zionist Organization (1920-31). In 1947, headed Jewish Agency delegation to United Nations on Palestine question. Elected first president of Israel (1948-52).

Yamani, Sheikh Ahmed Zaki (born 1930). Educated at University of Cairo, New York University, Harvard. Minister of Petroleum and Mineral Resources since 1962 for Saudi Arabia. Leader in formulating participation agreements with oil companies in Arab states, in devising oil embargo of 1973-74 against West and in setting oil prices in councils of Organization of Petroleum Exporting Countries (OPEC).

Zayed ibn Sultan al-Nahayan (born circa 1916). Emir of Abu Dhabi, president of federation of United Arab Emirates since it was formed in December 1971. Used vast oil wealth to modernize his sheikhdom and provide social programs for its people.

MIDDLE EAST DEVELOPMENTS BETWEEN 1945 AND 1979

1945

March 22. Arab League founded in Cairo. Egypt, Iraq, Lebanon, Syria, Saudi Arabia and Transjordan are members.

Aug. 16. President Harry S Truman calls for free settlement of Palestine by Jews to the point consistent with the maintenance of civil peace.

Nov. 13. Truman in Washington and British Foreign Secretary Ernest Bevin in London announce agreement on creation of a commission to examine the problem of European Jews and Palestine; Bevin says Palestine will become a United Nations trusteeship eventually to have self-government.

Nov. 22. Palestine Arab leaders form a 12-man Higher Committee to present their views to the Arab League.

Dec. 10. Truman appoints six-man committee to represent the United States on a joint Anglo-American Committee of Inquiry to study the question of Jewish immigration into Palestine.

Dec. 12. Senate Foreign Relations Committee approves, 17-1, a resolution (S Con Res 49) urging U.S. aid in opening Palestine to Jews and in building a "democratic commonwealth." The resolution is adopted by the Senate Dec. 17 and the House Dec. 19.

1946

Jan. 7. Anglo-American Committee of Inquiry holds opening Washington session.

Jan. 30. Britain announces it will permit 1,500 Jews to enter Palestine each month during the inquiry by the Anglo-American committee. (This monthly quota was in addition to the 75,000 permitted by a 1939 British government White Paper.)

Feb. 2. Arab strike in Palestine; Arab Higher Committee protests against British decision to permit additional Jews to enter Palestine.

Feb. 25. Soviets tell Iran they will retain some troops in Iran after the March 2 deadline for foreign troop withdrawal set by the 1942 Anglo-Soviet-Iranian Treaty.

March 2. Arab League spokesman tells the Anglo-American committee the league will oppose creation of a Jewish state in Palestine; it calls for creation of an Arab state in Palestine.

March 5. United States protests Soviet retention of troops in Iran.

March 22. Britain and Transjordan sign a treaty ending British mandate.

April 5. Soviet Union and Iran reach agreement on Soviet troop withdrawal by May 6.

April 30. Anglo-American Committee of Inquiry report is released with recommendations for the imme-diate admission of 100,000 Jews into Palestine and continuation of the British mandate until establishment of a U.N. trusteeship.

May 2. Arab League protests the report by the Anglo-American Committee and the Arab Higher Committee warns Britain that the "national struggle" will be resumed if the committee's recommendations are adopted.

July 25. Anglo-American committee in London proposes tripartite partition of Palestine into Jewish, Arab and British-controlled districts.

Aug. 7. Britain announces plans for a blockade of ships carrying Jewish immigrants to Palestine and diversion to Cyprus of ships of immigrants in excess of the 1,500 monthly quota.

Sept. 10. London conference on Palestine opens with Arabs present but Jews boycott.

Sept. 20. Committee appointed to study Arab proposals for Palestine; Jews agree to end boycott of London conference.

Oct. 4. Truman releases appeal sent to Britain for "substantial immigration" into Palestine "at once" and expressing support for the Zionist plan for creation of a "viable Jewish state" in part of Palestine; British government expresses regret that Truman's statement was released because it might jeopardize a settlement.

1947

Jan. 27. London conference on Palestine reconvenes with Arab delegates and Zionist observers.

Feb. 14. London conference closes without agreement on a plan for Palestine; conference informed of Britain's decision to refer Palestine question to the United Nations.

April 28. A special session of the U.N. General Assembly to study the Palestine question opens. A Political and Security Committee of the U.N. General Assembly votes May 13 to establish an inquiry committee.

May 14. Andrei A. Gromyko, Soviet delegate to the United Nations, proposes that Palestine be divided into two independent states, if the Arabs and Jews cannot agree on one Arab-Jewish state.

June 16. U.N. Palestine inquiry committee opens hearings.

Aug. 31. U.N. committee issues majority report recommending Palestine be divided into two separate Arab and Jewish states by Sept. 1, 1949, with Jerusalem and vicinity maintained as an international zone under permanent U.N. trusteeship; minority report calls for federated Arab-Jewish state in three years.

Sept. 1. Zionist leaders approve majority plan of U.N. Palestine inquiry committee; Arab Higher Committee denounces plan and threatens military action.

Sept. 20. British cabinet announces acceptance of U.N. Palestine inquiry committee's majority report.

Oct. 9. Arab League Council recommends member nations station troops along Palestinian borders to prepare for action if British troops evacuate.

Oct. 11. U.S. representative to the United Nations committee on Palestine endorses proposal to partition Palestine. Soviet Union endorses proposal Oct. 13.

Nov. 29. U.N. General Assembly votes, 33-13, with 10 abstentions, to partition Palestine into separate, independent Jewish and Arab states, effective Oct. 1, 1948, with the enclave of Jerusalem to be administered by the U.N. Trusteeship Council; Arab members denounce decision and walk out.

Dec. 5. United States places embargo on arms shipments to the Middle East because of violent disorders which followed U.N. decision.

Dec. 8. Arab League pledges to help Palestine Arabs resist any move to partition Palestine.

1948

Jan. 15. Britain and Iraq sign a 20-year alliance.

March 19. United States proposes to the U.N. Security Council suspension of the plan to partition Palestine and urges special session of the General Assembly to restudy issue.

March 25. Truman calls for truce between Jews and Arabs.

April 1. U.N. Security Council adopts U.S. resolution calling for a truce and a special session of the General Assembly to reconsider Palestine question.

May 13. Arab League proclaims existence of a state of war between league members and Palestinian Jews.

May 14. State of Israel proclaimed at 4:06 p.m., effective at midnight.

May 14. Midnight. Israel comes into existence; British mandate for Palestine ends as British high commissioner sails from Haifa.

May 15. 12:11 a.m. (6:11 p.m. in Washington). President Truman recognizes Israel, eleven minutes after its independence. Simultaneously, five Arab League states—Transjordan, Egypt, Iraq, Syria and Lebanon—invade Israel. Egyptian planes bomb Tel Aviv.

May 17. Soviet Union recognizes Israel.

May 25. Israel's President Chaim Weizmann visits Truman and appeals for a $90-million to $100-million loan to arm Israel and assist immigration.

May 27. Truman says Israel's loan application should be sent to the World Bank and the U.S. Export-Import Bank.

June 11. Four-week Arab-Israeli truce goes into effect.

June 30. Last British troops pull out of Palestine.

July 8. U.N. mediator Count Folke Bernadotte reports Arabs had refused to extend truce.

July 18. Truce renewed.

Sept. 17. U.N. mediator Bernadotte assassinated, allegedly by Jewish terrorists; Dr. Ralph J. Bunche named to succeed him.

Sept. 20. Bernadotte's final proposals for Palestine —including recognition of Israel—are published; Arab League announces establishment of an Arab government for Palestine—a move denounced by Transjordan and Iraq as amounting to recognition of Palestine's partition.

Oct. 22. Israel and Egypt agree to halt renewed fighting and comply with a cease-fire ordered by the U.N. Security Council Oct. 19.

Nov. 16. U.N. Security Council approves resolution calling for armistice.

Dec. 11. U.N. General Assembly sets up new Palestine Conciliation Commission.

1949

Jan. 6. Israel and Egypt announce a cease-fire on all fronts to begin Jan. 7. Israel withdraws its troops from Egypt Jan. 10.

Jan. 13. U.N. mediator Bunche meets with representatives of Israel and Egypt to negotiate an armistice.

Jan. 24. Egypt and Israel extend the cease-fire indefinitely.

Jan. 25. In the first Israeli election to be held, Prime Minister David Ben-Gurion's party wins the largest number of seats in the Knesset (legislature).

Jan. 31. The United States extends full diplomatic recognition to Israel and Transjordan following a flurry of diplomatic activity during which a number of Western nations including France on Jan. 24 and Britain Jan. 29 recognized Israel.

Feb. 1. Ending its military governorship of Jerusalem, Israel formally incorporates the city as part of the new state.

March 7. Egypt signs an agreement on the Suez Canal with the British-owned Suez Canal Co. calling for 80-90 per cent of the company's jobs to be manned by Egyptians and for Egypt to receive 7 per cent of profits.

March 11. Transjordan and Israel sign a "complete and enduring" cease-fire agreement to be binding even in the event of a failure to reach agreement on other points.

March 21. The first meeting of the U.N. Palestine Council Commission to settle the question of Arab refugees opens in Beirut, Lebanon.

April 5. Armistice talks between Israel and Syria run aground because of Israel's refusal to negotiate with representatives of Syria's new military government, which took over the country in a coup March 30.

April 20. While consenting to internationalization of the Holy Places in Jerusalem, Israel again rejects internationalization of the entire city.

April 26. Transjordan announces that the correct name of the country is Jordan, or Hashemite Jordan Kingdom.

April 26. In response to Jordan's statement on April 7 that a "greater" Jordan may evolve, Syria closes its Jordanian border and warns against attempts to annex its territory.

April 28. Israel rejects a proposal to return Arab refugees to their homes in the new state.

May 11. Israel is admitted to the United Nations after a vote of 37-12 in the General Assembly. Great Britain abstained from voting. On announcement of the final vote, delegates of six Arab states walk out of the meeting.

July 20. Syria and Israel sign an armistice agreement setting up demilitarized zones in contested areas and calling for both countries to keep their forces behind the frontiers.

July 27. U.N. mediator for the Middle East, Dr. Ralph J. Bunche, reports that "the military phase of the Palestine conflict is ended."

Sept. 13. The U.N. Palestine Conciliation Commission issues a draft statute whereby the United Nations would control Jerusalem, neither Israel nor the Arab states could have government offices there, and neither would control the city except for local administration of areas where their citizens lived. Holy places would be under permanent international supervision. Israel rejects the statute Nov. 15.

Oct. 28. Israel threatens to quit U.N. Palestine Conciliation Commission negotiations unless Arab states agree to direct Arab-Israeli negotiations, rather than indirectly through the commission.

Dec. 9. The U.N. General Assembly adopts a resolution placing Jerusalem under administration of the Trusteeship Council. The resolution is opposed by the United States, Britain and Israel.

Dec. 16. Israeli Prime Minister Ben-Gurion announces that Jerusalem will become the country's capital Jan. 1, 1950. Transfer of government offices from Tel Aviv to Jerusalem's New City has been going on for some time.

1950

Jan. 15. Secretary of State Dean Acheson defends Britain's arms shipments to Iraq, Jordan and Egypt on the grounds that the West must have the friendship of the Arab states.

Jan. 30. Truman requests $27,450,000 for U.S. contribution to the U.N. relief and public works program for Palestinian Arab refugees.

March 9. Turkey becomes the first Moslem state to recognize Israel.

March 15. Iran recognizes Israel.

March 24. Jordan breaks off non-aggression pact talks with Israel.

April 1. Arab League Council votes to expel any member making a separate peace with Israel.

April 4. U.N. Trusteeship Council approves a statute for internationalization of Jerusalem.

April 13. Israel rejects Arab League terms for peace negotiations which included a return to 1947 U.N. partition boundaries.

April 20. Arab League secretary condemns Anglo-American policy in the Middle East and urges Arab states to turn to the Soviet Union.

April 24. Jordan formally annexes Jordan-occupied eastern Palestine, including the Old City of Jerusalem.

April 27. Britain recognizes Jordan-Palestine merger and changes its recognition of Israel from de facto to full recognition.

May 25. Truman reveals agreement with France and Britain, reached at the London foreign ministers' conference, to sell arms to Mideast states—Israel as well as the Arab states—on a basis of parity between Israel and Arab countries if purchasers promise there will be no renewal of the Palestine war.

June 2. Israel and Jordan formally notify the United Nations of their rejection of the Trusteeship Council's plan for internationalization of Jerusalem.

June 14. Trusteeship Council concedes failure of five-month attempt to internationalize Jerusalem and turns the problem back to the General Assembly.

June 17. Five members of the Arab League—Egypt, Saudi Arabia, Syria, Lebanon and Yemen—sign a collective security pact.

June 21. Arab League pledges not to use arms purchased from the United States, France, Britain or other countries for purposes of aggression.

Nov. 21. In response to Egyptian demands for Britian's immediate withdrawal from the Suez Canal Zone and the Anglo-Egyptian Sudan, British Foreign Secretary Bevin tells Parliament that British troops will remain until the 1936 Anglo-Egyptian treaty is altered "by mutual consent."

1951

Feb. 7. The U.N. Mixed Armistice Commission breaks down as small-scale guerrilla fighting breaks out on the Israeli-Jordanian border.

March 7. General Ali Razmara, Iranian Premier since June 26, 1950, is assassinated by a religious fanatic who belonged to a group favoring the nationalization of Iran's oil industry. Razmara had angered members of that group by his support of U.S.-suggested economic reforms. He is succeeded March 11 by Hussein Ala, a strongly pro-West official who has served as a former ambassador to the United States.

March 20. The Iranian Senate votes unanimously in favor of nationalizing the country's oil industry. Later in the day, martial law is proclaimed in Teheran to stem Communist political terrorism over the oil issue.

April 28. The Iranian Parliament votes unanimously to sanction government expropriation of the British-owned Anglo-Iranian Oil Co. With favorable Senate action April 30, the oil nationalization bill becomes law.

May 18. The U.N. Security Council adopts a resolution calling on Israel to halt the Hulek border zone drainage project that allegedly set off border clashes between Israel and Syria. Criticizing Israeli aerial attacks on Syria, the resolution denounces the use of force by both countries to settle their differences. Israel halts work on the drainage project June 6.

June 1. President Truman sends a personal message to Iran's Premier urging prompt negotiations between Iran and Britain on the oil question.

June 12. Iran's Premier, responding to President Truman's message of June 1, stands firm on the decision to nationalize the country's oil industry.

July 5. The International Court of Justice at The Hague hands down a 10-2 decision on Britain's dispute with Iran over nationalization of the Anglo-Iranian Oil Co. The decision calls for Iran to re-instate the Anglo-Iranian Oil Co. to full control of its assets and operations. Iran's ambassador to Britain says his country will "ignore" the recommendations and proceed with the take-over of the oil company.

July 9. President Truman sends a personal message to Iranian Premier Mossadegh urging him to examine the International Court proposal as a basis for settling the oil dispute. Truman offers to send W. Averell Harriman to Iran to mediate the British-Iranian dispute. Mossadegh accepts that offer July 11.

July 14. Disclaiming all previous obligations, Iran opens sales of its oil on an equal basis to old and new clients of the Anglo-Iranian Oil Co.

July 20. Jordan's King Abdullah is assassinated, reportedly by a member of a faction opposing his annexation of parts of Palestine. The King's son, Prince Talal, is crowned King Sept. 6 in Amman.

July 24. Secret plans for Iranian-British negotiations over the nationalization of the Anglo-Iranian Oil Co. are sent to London after formulation during eight days of talks between Iranian officials and U.S. envoy Harriman.

Aug. 2. Britain and Iran formally agree to begin negotiations over the nationalization dispute.

Sept. 1. The U.N. Security Council calls on Egypt to end its three-year-old blockade of the Suez Canal to ships carrying cargoes bound for Israel. Egypt refuses Sept. 2 to comply with the request until Israel obeys previous U.N. resolutions dealing with the partition of Palestine, repatriation and compensation of Arab refugees, and internationalization of Jerusalem.

Sept. 13. The U.N. Palestine Conciliation Conference with Israeli and Arab delegates opens in Paris.

Sept. 17. Averell Harriman refuses to relay Iran's ultimatum calling on Britain to resume negotiations within two weeks on Iran's terms or to have British nationals expelled from Abadan, Iran, site of an Anglo-Iranian Oil Co. refinery.

Sept. 21. Israel says it will sign non-aggression pacts with each of its four Arab neighbors, but warns that negotiations should not continue if Arabs will not meet in the same room with Israeli delegates. Israel offers to compensate Arab refugees and to make contributions to their resettlement in Arab countries but is unwilling to accept repatriation of the refugees in Israel.

Sept. 25. Iran orders the last 300 British oil technicians to leave the country by Oct. 4.

Oct. 3. Britain's 300 oil employees depart leaving Western Europe's largest oil supply source in the hands of untrained Iranians.

Oct. 8. Egypt announces plans to expel British troops from the Suez Canal and to assume full control of the jointly administered Anglo-Egyptian Sudan. The next day, Britain declares it will neither vacate the Suez Canal nor withdraw its administrators from the Sudan.

Oct. 16. Tension builds in the Suez Canal zone as eight persons are killed and 74 wounded during fighting between British troops and Egyptian rioters. A three-day state of emergency is proclaimed throughout Egypt. Meanwhile, the Parliament approves the change of King Farouk's title to "King of Egypt and the Sudan" and extends the Egyptian constitution to apply to the Sudan.

Oct. 23. Iranian Premier Mossadegh meets in Washington, D.C. with President Truman who stresses the importance of Iran's oil to the West. Truman appeals for new efforts to reach an amicable settlement with Britain.

Oct. 27. Egypt formally notifies Britain that the 1936 Treaty of Alliance and the 1889 agreement on joint administration of the Sudan are both considered broken. In the Sudan, the legislature rejects the decision to place the country under the Egyptian crown.

Oct. 31. Lebanon's Chamber of Deputies orders the government to undertake negotiations with oil companies to revise concession agreements. The American-owned Trans-Arabian Pipeline Co. comes under fire from the deputies for "smuggling" oil to Israel and Jordan and for not employing the promised quota of Lebanese citizens.

Nov. 2. Britain continues to amass additional troops in the Suez Canal to strengthen its garrison there.

Nov. 5. Egypt refuses to discuss the Suez Canal dispute until British troops leave the area.

Nov. 15. Britain proposes self-rule for the Sudan with the voters of that country deciding in a year or two whether to unite with Egypt.

Nov. 18. British troops and Egyptian police battle in Ismailia, killing 11.

Nov. 21. Citing the "rigid positions" on both sides, the U.N. Palestine Conciliation Commission ends mediation efforts between Israel and the Arab states.

Dec. 2. Following a bloodless military coup in Syria, Army Chief of Staff, Col. Adeeb Shishekly, becomes President, after the resignation of President al-Atassi. Col. Fawzi Silo is appointed Premier Dec. 3.

Dec. 10. Reportedly in response to President Truman's appeal, Iran ends a six-month boycott of the International Court of Justice's proceedings on nationalization of the Anglo-Iranian Oil Co. and agrees to contest the Court's ruling.

Dec. 13. Egypt recalls its ambassador to Britain in protest against Britain's "aggression" in the Suez Canal zone.

Dec. 24. The Federation of Libya, an Arab kingdom created by the United Nations, becomes independent. By agreement, Britain and the United States will retain their military bases in the country.

1952

Jan. 18. British troops and Egyptian guerrillas battle for four hours at Port Said.

Jan. 25. British troops disarm Egyptian police in Ismailia along the Suez Canal. Fighting breaks out, killing 42 persons.

Jan. 26. Martial law is imposed in Egypt following widespread rioting and burning in Cairo. More than 20 persons are dead. Extensive damage to American, British and French property is estimated to total over $10 million.

Feb. 7. Britain issues "strongest condemnation" of the violence in Egypt Jan. 26 that killed British nationals and destroyed British property in the Canal Zone.

Feb. 16. Jordan signs a collective security pact with other Arab League countries.

March 18. Iranian Premier Mossadegh accuses President Truman of delaying an American loan to his country pending acceptance of British proposals for settling the oil nationalization dispute.

April 2. Britain's submission of a new constitution for the Sudan, during renewed British-Egyptian talks on the Sudan, brings an immediate Egyptian protest. The Sudanese Parliament, welcomes the new constitution April 23, and asks for an amendment allowing the Sudanese to determine whether they wish union with Britain, Egypt or neither.

May 3. Britain, proposing a solution to the dispute with Egypt over the Suez Canal and the Sudan, offers to evacuate British troops from the base in the Suez Canal, but denies recognition of King Farouk as ruler of the Sudan until the Sudanese people are consulted.

July 22. Canceling its year-old decision calling for restoration of property to the British-owned Anglo-Iranian Oil Co., the International Court of Justice at The Hague rules it has no jurisdiction in the dispute over Iranian nationalization of the oil company.

July 23. Egyptian King Farouk flees the country following a military coup that empowers Maher Pasha as Premier. Farouk abdicates July 26 and goes into exile in Italy. The King's infant son, King Fuad II is proclaimed ruler of Egypt and the Sudan by the cabinet.

Aug. 11. Declaring that King Talal, suffering from mental disorders, is unfit to rule, the Jordanian Parliament proclaims Crown Prince Hussein the new King.

Aug. 11. Iranian Premier Mossadegh is granted full dictatorial powers by the Senate. The Chamber of Deputies had approved the dictatorial powers Aug. 3.

Sept. 7. General Mohammed Naguib assumes leadership of Egypt.

Sept. 18. Ending a nine-year rule, Lebanon's President el-Khoury resigns in the face of general strikes to protest political corruption. Parliament elects Foreign Minister Camille Chamoun President Sept. 23.

Oct. 7. Iranian dictator Mossadegh demands $1-billion from Britain before talks can resume on the question of nationalizing the Anglo-Iranian Oil Company.

Oct. 22. Iran severs diplomatic ties with Britain after Britain's rejection Oct. 14 of Iran's demand for $1-billion from the Anglo-Iranian Oil Co.

Oct. 29. Egyptian President Naguib and delegates of the Sudanese independent parties sign a final agreement to work for political development of the Sudan.

Nov. 7. Israel's first President, Dr. Chaim Weizmann, dies. The Israeli Parliament, (Knesset), Dec. 8 names Itzahk Ben-Zvi to succeed him as President.

1953

Jan. 19. The Iranian Parliament votes to extend Premier Mossadegh's dictatorship powers for one year, rejecting his bid for a 2-year extension.

Feb. 12. British and Egyptian officials sign an agreement in Cairo establishing immediate self-government in the Anglo-Egyptian Sudan and calling for self-determination by the Sudanese people within three years. The Sudanese must choose to unite with Egypt, become independent or follow another path.

May 2. King Faisal II of Iraq is crowned on his 18th birthday, thus ending the 18-year regency of his uncle Emir Abd-ul-Ilah.

May 10. Egyptian President Naguib tells his nation to prepare for a "big battle" to achieve their goal in the British-Egyptian dispute over the Suez Canal.

June 29. President Eisenhower notifies Iran that the American public is opposed to additional U.S. aid

to that country while the oil dispute between Iran and Britain continues.

Aug. 16. The Shah of Iran seeks sanctuary in Iraq after his unsuccessful attempt to dismiss dictator Premier Mossadegh.

Aug. 19. A revolt by Iranian Royalists and troops loyal to the Shah ousts Premier Mossadegh. Announcing plans to return to Iran, the Shah names Maj. Gen. Gazollah Zahedi as premier. The Shah returns Aug. 22.

Sept. 1. President Eisenhower sends personal assurances to newly appointed Iranian Premier Zahedi of U.S. readiness to send financial and economic aid to Iran. The message is followed by a grant of $45-million on Sept. 5.

Oct. 19. The United States submits a plan to the U.N. Security Council aimed at helping Arab refugees and easing tensions in Palestine. It calls for development of the irrigation and power resources of the Jordan River.

Oct. 28. The United States resumes economic aid to Israel after that country agrees to halt work on a power project on the Jordan River.

Nov. 7. The United States, in the face of growing anti-American Arab sentiment, denies that economic aid would be withheld if the Arab states did not agree to a special T.V.A.-type development of the Jordan River.

Nov. 14. Jordan rejects the U.S. proposal for development of the Jordan River resources.

Nov. 29. The Sudan's first general elections yield a decisive victory to forces seeking union with Egypt.

Dec. 21. An Iranian military court convicts former Premier Mossadegh on all counts of attempted rebellion. Instead of the death penalty, the court imposes a three-year solitary confinement sentence after the Shah's request for clemency.

1954

Feb. 25. Egyptian President Naguib resigns after the Egyptian legislature refuses his appeal for absolute power, but he returns to power Feb. 27.

Feb. 26. A Syrian army revolt ousts President Shishekly. Former President Hashim Atassi succeeds him Feb. 28.

April 17. Egyptian Col. Gamal Abdul Nasser becomes Premier in a new organization of the government, replacing Premier Naguib. Nasser had served as Premier for two days in February following Premier Naguib's brief ouster.

June 5. Following a visit to the United States by Turkish Premier Menderes, it is announced that Turkey will receive $200-million in military aid from the United States.

June 11. Egypt announces an agreement with Saudi Arabia to place both countries' military forces under a unified command.

July 27. Egypt and Britain sign an agreement ending the dispute over the Suez Canal. Britain will remove its forces from the area within 20 months, but will retain the right to use the Canal base in the event of aggression against an Arab state or Turkey.

Oct. 9. Israel attends a meeting of the Israel-Jordan Mixed Armistice Commission, thus ending a seven-month boycott.

Oct. 21. The Iranian Parliament votes to restore that country's oil production.

Nov. 2. Jordan summons the ambassadors of Britain, France, and the United States to ask their governments to halt Israel's unilateral diversion of the Jordan River.

Nov. 14. Egypt's ruling military junta quietly deposes General Naguib whose powers had been turned over to Gamal Abdul Nasser April 17.

1955

Feb. 24. Iraq signs a mutual defense treaty (Baghdad Pact) with Turkey despite Egyptian protests.

April 4. Britain joins Baghdad Pact.

April 21. French Premier Faure and Habib Bourguiba, leader of the militant Tunisian nationalists, reach agreement on autonomy for the French protectorate of Tunisia.

June 29. U.N. efforts to initiate negotiations between Egypt and Israel over the dispute in the Gaza Strip break down.

Aug. 16. The Sudanese Parliament unanimously calls for the evacuation of British and Egyptian troops from the Sudan within 90 days.

Aug. 26. As fighting in the Gaza Strip increases, Secretary of State Dulles suggests a plan under which internationally guaranteed borders would be established with U.S. participation.

Aug. 30. Secretary of State Dulles says the United States has offered to sell arms to Egypt.

Sept. 23. Pakistan joins Baghdad Pact.

Sept. 28. Assistant Secretary of State Allen arrives in Cairo to discuss Premier Nasser's announcement that Egypt would exchange cotton for Soviet arms.

Oct. 12. American and Israeli sources disclose that the Soviet Union may be willing to sell arms to Israel as well as to Egypt. The announcement followed a request Oct. 11 by Israel for the United States to match Soviet arms to Egypt.

Oct. 12. The Soviet Union warns Iran that its intention to join the Baghdad mutual security pact is "incompatible" with peace in the Middle East.

Oct. 20. Egypt and Syria sign a mutual defense treaty, triggering Israeli requests for an Israeli-American security pact. Israel cites recent Egyptian arms purchases from Czechoslavakia.

Oct. 31. Israel appeals to the Soviet Union not to foster a new war in the Middle East by arming the Arab states.

Nov. 3. Iran joins Baghdad Pact.

Nov. 22. The five Baghdad Pact countries announce the establishment of a permanent political military and economic organization, the Middle East Treaty Organization, to be based in Baghdad. Members are Britain, Iran, Iraq, Pakistan, and Turkey.

Nov. 26. The Soviet Union accuses Iran of violating their mutual treaty obligations by participating in the Baghdad Pact. Iran rejects the protest Dec. 6.

Dec. 12. Arab ambassadors from eight countries tell Secretary of State Dulles that U.S.-Arab relations are being strained by the behavior of Israel.

Dec. 14. The Jordanian government resigns to protest British pressure to join the Baghdad Pact. As rioting breaks out in additional protest to the British pressures, King Hussein dissolves Parliament, Dec. 20.

Dec. 15. In light of recent clashes between Israeli forces and the Syrian Army, Egyptian Premier Nasser warns Israel that further aggression may prompt a full Egyptian-Syrian military response.

Dec. 26. Egypt, Saudi Arabia and Syria unify their military power by placing troops under one commander, the Egyptian Minister of War.

1956

Jan. 13. Lebanon and Syria agree on a bilateral defense pact.

Jan. 19. The Sudan joins the Arab League. Egypt, Iraq, Jordan, Lebanon, Libya, Saudi Arabia, Syria and Yemen are other members.

Jan. 30. Israel urges the United States and Britain to allow it to buy arms.

Feb. 6. Secretary of State Dulles, not excluding "the possibility of arms sales to Israel," suggests that Israel look for security in the United Nations and the 1950 Anglo-American-French Three-Power agreement.

Feb. 14. Israel agrees to halt work temporarily on the Jordan Valley Project to allow for U.S. attempts to gain Arab cooperation on joint continuation of the project.

Feb. 16. It is disclosed that the United States is sending tanks to Saudi Arabia, an action Israel calls "regrettable" to the balance of power in the Mideast.

Feb. 28. French Premier Guy Mollet offers Algerian rebels a choice between all-out war or a cease-fire. Guerrilla warfare, staged by the nationalist rebels seeking Algerian independence has continued over the past 16 months.

March 3. Agreeing to honor the 1948 treaty of friendship with Britain, Jordan announces it will grant Britain bases in Jordan.

March 9. Jordan rejected a bid by Egypt, Syria and Saudia Arabia to replace British subsidizing of Jordan's defense forces.

March 10. Ending a two-year period of relative quiet on their border, Jordan stages raids on Israel.

March 12. Egypt, Saudia Arabia and Syria agree to unite their defenses against Israel.

March 15. France sends two Army divisions into Algeria.

March 17. France recognizes Tunisia's independence.

April 10. Yemen joins the military alliance of Egypt, Saudi Arabia and Syria.

April 18. The United States becomes a full member of the Economic Committee of the Baghdad Pact. The next day, the U.S. agrees to set up a military liaison office at the permanent headquarters of the Baghdad Pact.

April 19. Israel and Egypt agree to a U.N. cease-fire.

April 21. Egypt, Saudi Arabia and Yemen establish a five-year unified military command under an Egyptian leader.

May 6. Jordan and Egypt announce plans to unify their armies.

May 8. The French Resident Minister, Robert Lacoste, says French troops in Algeria will total 330,000 by June and that he will request 40,000-50,000 more forces.

May 9. Secretary of State Dulles states the United States' reason for not wanting to sell arms to Israel. He explains that Washington seeks to avoid a Soviet-American confrontation in the Middle East and to avoid incidents that could bring about a global war.

May 12. As the United States confirms its sale of arms to Saudi Arabia, 12 more jets arrive in Israel in a second shipment from France which has tacit U.S. approval.

May 16. Britain announces that six of its former bases in the Suez Canal are now under Egyptian control.

May 21. Lebanon and Jordan agree to coordinate their defense plans.

May 31. Jordan and Syria sign a military agreement.

June 7. Iranian troops seize Soviet oil concessions in Khuryan, Iran.

June 13. Britain turns over full responsibility for the defense of the Suez Canal to Egypt. On June 18, Britain declares its 74-year occupation of the Canal ended.

June 24. After an uncontested election, Gamal Abdul Nasser becomes Egypt's first elected president, having received 99 per cent of the vote.

July 20. Following disputes over funding the Aswan Dam, the United States refuses to loan Egypt funds for the project and Britain withdraws its offer to supplement the American loan. Egyptian officials are surprised and angered by the move.

July 27. Egyptian President Nasser nationalizes the Suez Canal and imposes martial law there in retaliation for American and British withdrawal of support for the financing of the Aswan Dam. Income from the canal will be funnelled into building costs of the dam.

July 28. Britain freezes assets of Egypt and the Suez Canal held in Britain.

July 31. Secretary of State Dulles arrives in London to discuss British and French proposals for international supervision of the Suez Canal.

Aug. 9. President Nasser announces the creation of a National Liberation Army made up of the National Guard and youth organization volunteers.

Aug. 14. The United States creates a Middle East Emergency Committee to supply U.S. oil to Western Europe in the event that shipments from the Middle East are discontinued during the present crisis.

Aug. 16. In London, 22 nations open conference on the Suez canal crisis. Eighteen nations agree Aug. 23 to ask Egypt to negotiate for international operation of the Suez Canal. On Aug. 28, Nasser agrees to meet with a five-nation delegation.

Sept. 11. After initial efforts at negotiations fail to settle the Suez crisis, Britain and France agree to apply economic pressure to force Egypt to accept international control of the canal. The United States rejects the plan "under present circumstances."

Sept. 14. Egypt takes over complete control of the Suez Canal.

Sept. 21. The Suez Conference in London concludes with a draft plan for a Suez Canal Users' Association. The following day, Britain issues invitations to 18 nations for a third conference on the Suez Canal situation.

Sept. 30. Lebanon calls for talks between Syria, Jordan, Egypt and Lebanon to mobilize forces in retaliation against Israeli reprisal raids.

Oct. 1. Fifteen nations, including the United States, Britain and France, set up a Suez Canal Users' Association.

Oct. 8. Egypt and the Soviet Union again reject proposals for international supervision of the Suez Canal.

Oct. 12. In the face of increasing clashes between Israel and Jordan, Britain warns Israel that it will stand by its 1948 mutual defense treaty with Jordan.

Oct. 25. Egypt, Syria and Jordan sign an agreement to place their armed forces under the joint command of an Egyptian general.

Oct. 30. Aerial warfare breaks out between Israel and Egypt. Egypt warns Britain and France that it will also fight to keep the Suez Canal. This provokes a British-French ultimatum warning that troops will be sent to the Suez unless Egyptian and Israeli troops withdraw 10 miles from the canal and cease fighting by a designated time. Egyptian President Nasser rejects the ultimatum. The same day, Egypt reports that British and French planes are bombing Egyptian cities and other targets in an effort to force an Egyptian evacuation of the Suez.

Oct. 31. Israel accepts the British ultimatum on the condition that Egypt also agrees. Meanwhile, British and French troops are readied on Cyprus in the event that they are ordered to move against Egypt.

Nov. 1. Egypt breaks off diplomatic relations with Britain and France and seizes their property in Egypt as bombing of military targets continues. Jordan also severs ties with France and tells Britain that it will no longer be allowed to use ground or air bases in Jordan for further attacks on Egypt.

Nov. 2. The City of Gaza surrenders to Israeli forces.

Nov. 3. France and Britain reject the U.N.'s call Nov. 1 for a cease-fire in Egypt.

Nov. 5. The Soviet Union warns that it is prepared to use force "including rockets" to restore the Mideast peace. The Soviets call for joint Soviet-American action against "aggressors," a proposal the United States rejects as "unthinkable."

Nov. 6. As Israel ends its Sinai campaign, France and Britain agree to a cease-fire in Egypt. The same day, British and French parachute troops capture Port Said.

Nov. 7. The U.N. General Assembly calls on Britain, France and Israel to withdraw their forces from Egypt.

President Eisenhower in a personal note to Israeli Prime Minister Ben-Gurion expresses U.S. "concern" that "Israel does not intend to withdraw." Israeli rejection of the U.N. appeal would, says the President, "impair friendly cooperation between our two countries."

Nov. 9. Iraq breaks off ties with France and announces it will boycott any future meeting of the Baghdad Pact attended by Britain.

Nov. 10. The Soviet Union calls for the withdrawal of British, French and Israeli troops from Egypt and warns that Russian volunteers will be allowed to join Egyptian forces unless the withdrawal takes place. On Nov. 14, the United States says it would oppose any such Soviet intervention.

Nov. 21. Token British, French and Israeli troop withdrawals from Egypt begin. Eisenhower, according to sources, is reported to have sent private messages to the British and French governments urging complete troop withdrawal.

Nov. 30. The United States puts into operation its emergency oil plan to supply Europe with 500,000 additional barrels of oil a day.

Dec. 17. Britain implements gas rationing due to the cut-off of Middle East oil.

Dec. 22. The last British and French troops withdraw from Egypt.

Dec. 24. Egypt demands reparations from Britain, France and Israel for war damages.

Dec. 26. Clearance of sunken vessels and mines in the Suez Canal begins.

Dec. 31. Secretary of State Dulles says the United States has a "major responsibility" to prevent Soviet expansion in the Middle East. The same day, the Syrian Ambassador to the United States says that Arab states will not welcome American protection against the Russians.

1957

Jan. 4. The Suez Canal opens halfway, for medium-sized shipping.

Jan. 5. President Eisenhower addresses a joint session of Congress to urge support for a declaration, dubbed the Eisenhower Doctrine, calling for American action to counter Communist actions in the Middle East.

Jan. 7. Britain announces that its air force troops are protecting the Aden protectorate against recent incursions from Yemen.

Jan. 15. Egyptian President Nasser undertakes an "Egyptianization" process. Only natural citizens will be allowed to hold shares of Egyptian-based companies. British and French banks and insurance companies are nationalized.

Jan. 21. Turkey, Pakistan, Iran and Iraq, the four Moslem nations of Baghdad Pact, endorse the Eisenhower Doctrine.

Jan. 23. Israel sets a prior condition for complete withdrawal of its troops from Egypt: Egyptian assurances that the Gaza Strip and Sharm el Sheikh will not be used for hostile actions.

Jan. 28. Yemen says peace will not be restored in Aden until its claims to the Western and Eastern Aden protectorates are recognized. Britain is accused of not yielding Aden because of hopes to find oil there.

Feb. 6. Saudi Arabian King Saud, meeting in Washington with President Eisenhower during a 10-day state visit, says the Eisenhower Doctrine "is a good one which is entitled to consideration and appreciation."

Feb. 17. A small Egyptian cargo vessel completes the first full course of the Suez Canal since ships were halted in November 1956.

March 1. Israel agrees to withdraw its troops from the Gaza Strip and the Gulf of Aqaba on "assumptions" that the U.N. Emergency Force will administer Gaza until a peace settlement is reached and that free navigation of the Gulf will continue.

March 7. The last Israeli forces withdraw from Egyptian territory.

March 13. Jordan and Britain cancel their 1948 treaty of alliance. British troops are to withdraw within six months.

March 15. As the situation in the Middle East appears to be worsening, Israeli Foreign Minister Golda Meir flies to Washington to confer with U.S. officials. In contravention of U.N. resolutions, Egypt March 14 sent civil administrators into Gaza and on March 15 announced that Israel would not be permitted to use the Suez Canal. Saudi Arabia halted Israeli use of the Gulf of Aqaba March 15.

March 19. Vice President Richard M. Nixon visits Tunisia as part of a 22-day, 19,000-mile African tour.

March 22. The United States announces it will join the Military Committee of the Baghdad Pact.

April 8. The United States and Saudi Arabia sign an agreement extending the U.S. lease on the Dhahran air base by 5 years.

April 13. Syria attacks Jordan.

April 24. As internal political turmoil continues in Jordan, a U.S. statement, authorized by President Eisenhower and Secretary of State Dulles, warns that the United States regards "the independence and integrity of Jordan as vital." On April 25, the United States orders the 6th Fleet into the eastern Mediterranean.

April 24. Egypt reaffirms its intention to unilaterally operate the Suez Canal and issues a declaration on the conditions for management and operation of the canal.

May 5. King Hussein announces that the battle against leftist elements in Jordan has succeeded.

May 13. Britain accepts Egypt's conditions for British passage through the Suez Canal.

June 10. A rift arises in Jordanian-Egyptian relations as Jordan charges that an Egyptian military attache is plotting against Jordanian officials. His recall is requested. Egypt complies.

June 29. The United States signs an agreement with Jordan, extending $10-million in military supplies and services.

July 9. In the most violent encounter since November, Syria and Israel battle for almost 10 hours before a fourth U.N. intervention halts the fighting.

July 19. British-led forces step in to suppress a tribal revolt in Muscat and Oman on the Arabian Peninsula. On July 24, British planes attack military targets controlled by rebel tribesmen in Oman after the rebels refused to heed a British warning.

July 26. Egyptian President Nasser accuses the United States of intriguing to overthrow his government.

July 26. Tunisia's National Constituent Assembly deposes the Bey of Tunis and declares Tunisia a republic, the third along with Egypt and Nigeria in Africa. The Assembly elects Premier Habib Bourguiba President.

Aug. 13. Following Syrian accusations of U.S. efforts to overthrow that government, Syria ousts three American embassy officials. On Aug. 14, the United States expels Syrian diplomats.

Aug. 20. British troops complete their withdrawal from Oman, following recognition Aug. 11 of the Sultan of Oman's authority by the rebels.

Aug. 29. Lebanon affirms its support of the Eisenhower Doctrine.

Sept. 5. The United States announces plans to send arms to Jordan, Lebanon, Turkey, and Iraq.

Sept. 7. Affirming his doctrine on the Middle East, President Eisenhower says the United States will take action to protect pro-West Middle East countries if they are threatened by Syria.

Sept. 12. Saudi Arabian King Saud, in Washington, calls on U.S. officials to modify the U.S. stance toward Syria.

Oct. 3. Egypt says it will help defend Syria if necessary. Lebanon echoes that sentiment Oct. 11.

Oct. 10. Syria accuses Turkey of aggression on the Syrian-Turkish border.

Oct. 21. Turkey accepts Saudi Arabia's offer to mediate the dispute between Turkey and Syria. Syria Oct. 23 refuses to accept that proposal.

Nov. 12. The Shah of Iran instructs his cabinet to present a bill to parliament to bring Bahrain, a British oil protectorate, under Iranian jurisdiction.

Dec. 28. Tunisian President Bourguiba declares that British troops must leave the country no later than March 20, 1958.

1958

Jan. 18. Israel and Jordan agree that the 1948 agreement calling for demilitarization of Mt. Scopus should be followed.

Jan. 30. Secretary of State Dulles, addressing the Baghdad Pact countries meeting in Ankara, Turkey, tells the delegates that the Eisenhower Doctrine commits the United States to the Mideast as effectively as would membership in the Baghdad Pact.

Feb. 1. Egypt and Syria merge into the United Arab Republic. Citizens of the two countries approve the merger, nearly unanimously, in plebiscites Feb. 21.

Feb. 11. Yemen agrees to federation with the U.A.R.

Feb. 12. Tunisia demands the removal of all French forces from the country. The demand followed France's attack Feb. 8 on a Tunisian border town as reprisal for Tunisia's "cobelligerence" in the French-Algerian conflict.

Feb. 14. Iraq and Jordan form the Arab Federation with Iraqi King Faisal II serving as head of the two-state federal union. King Hussein retains sovereignty in Jordan. The federation is approved Feb. 17 by the Iraqi parliament and by the Jordanian parliament Feb. 18.

Feb. 17. The Sudanese government discloses that Egypt has demanded that the Sudan relinquish common border lands north of the 22nd parallel, in exchange for a small strip of land south of that parallel. The Sudan requests U.N. consideration of the Egyptian actions.

Feb. 19. France announces plans to establish a 200-mile long, 15-mile wide "no man's land" along the Tunisian-Algeria border. Tunisian President Bourguiba strongly protests the plan Feb. 27.

March 3. Morocco proposes the union of Tunisia, Algeria and Morocco as a means of resolving the crisis in Algeria.

March 20. Tunisian President Bourguiba announces his intention to cooperate with France and thanks the United States and Britain for their efforts to resolve the tension between his country and France.

March 25. Israeli Premier Ben-Gurion voices optimism for an Arab-Israeli peace, provided other powers will guarantee Israel's borders.

April 3. Jordan seizes control of petroleum supplies within its boundaries.

April 21. At the first conference of independent African states, Egypt, the Sudan, Libya, Tunisia, Morocco, Ethiopia, Ghana and Liberia adopt a common foreign policy based on "nonentanglement" with the United States and the Soviet alliances.

May 13. Rightist French civilians and Army officers in Algeria rebel and form an Algiers Committee of Public Safety in order to maintain French rule there. Leaders demand the return to power in France of Gen. Charles de Gaulle.

May 24. The United States and Britain caution Tunisia and France against further clashes as fighting between French and Algerian forces spreads to Tunisia.

May 24. As a state of siege continues in Lebanon, the U.N. Security Council meets to discuss Lebanon's complaint that the U.A.R. has caused the continuing anti-government rioting that started May 10.

June 1. Gen. Charles de Gaulle becomes premier of France after a paralysis of the French National Assembly **and after a rebellion by right-wing French living in Algeria force the resignation of Premier Pierre Pflimlin.**

June 11. The U.N. Security Council votes 10-0 to send U.N. observers to Lebanon to guard against the smuggling of arms or troops into that country.

June 11. The International Bank for Reconstruction and Development announces an agreement by which the Suez Canal Company shareholders will be compensated for their losses under the accords of the treaty signed in Rome April 29.

June 17. Secretary of State Dulles pledges American troops, if necessary, to quell Lebanese rebel warfare.

June 17. France agrees to evacuate all bases in Tunisia except the one at Bizerte.

June 29. Heavy fighting breaks out again in Lebanon.

July 4. Lebanon orders the departure of six U.A.R. diplomats accused of inciting the Lebanese revolt and financing the fighting.

July 14. The government of Iraq is overthrown by revolutionaries who kill King Faisal and Premier as-Said, seize Baghdad and proclaim a republic. Brig. Gen. Abdul Karim el-Kassim is named Premier. In reaction to the coup, King Hussein of Jordan announces his assumption of power as head of the Arab Federation of Iraq and Jordan. Hussein and Lebanese President Chamoun each appeal for U.S. military assistance because of the Iraqi coup.

July 15. President Eisenhower dispatches 5,000 Marines to Lebanon. He tells Congress, in a special message, that the troops will protect American lives and help defend Lebanon's sovereignty and independence. Meanwhile, martial law is proclaimed in Iraq.

July 15. At a meeting of the U.N. Security Council, the United States says its troops will remain in Lebanon only until U.N. forces can guarantee Lebanese "continued independence."

July 17. British paratroopers land in Jordan at the request of King Hussein.

July 19. The U.A.R. and the new Iraqi regime sign a mutual defense treaty.

July 19. British commandos land in Libya in support of the government against rumors of an Egyptian plan to overthrow it.

July 20. Jordan severs relations with the U.A.R. due to its recognition of the new Iraqi regime.

July 22. Iraq's new Premier el-Kassim declares his government's intention to increase cooperation with the West, especially in oil production.

July 24. Iraq and the U.A.R. set up committees to work out closer cooperation between those countries in political, economic, military and educational fields.

July 28. Secretary of State Dulles, committing the United States to partnership in the Baghdad Pact, assures Britain, Turkey, Iran and Pakistan that the United States will not fail to act in defense of their independence and integrity.

July 31. General Fuad Chehab, sympathetic to the Lebanese rebels, is elected President of Lebanon by Parliament over the strong objections of Premier Said.

Aug. 2. The United States recognizes the new government of Iraq. Britain recognized the government Aug. 1.

Aug. 2. Jordan announces the formal dismemberment of the Arab Union of Jordan and Iraq, in light of the new regime in Iraq.

Aug. 2. Iraq says it has not renounced the Baghdad Pact, nor will it buy arms from the Soviet Union at this time.

Aug. 5. Newly elected Lebanese President Chehab sends a message to President Eisenhower assuring efforts to "maintain the traditional friendship" between the countries.

Aug. 8. An emergency meeting of the U.N. General Assembly opens in New York to discuss the Middle East crisis, following a month-long conflict between the Soviet Union, Britain and the United States over the form of the special summit conference.

Aug. 13. President Eisenhower presents the U.N. General Assembly with a "framework of a plan of peace" in the Middle East. It includes provisions for a U.N. peace-keeping force in the region and for an "Arab development institution on a regional basis, governed by the Arab states themselves." At the same session, the Soviet delegate asks the Assembly to call for an immediate U.S. troop withdrawal from the area, as U.S. forces begin withdrawing from Lebanon.

Aug. 21. The General Assembly unanimously adopts an Arab resolution calling on Secretary General Hammarskjold to take the necessary steps to restore order in Jordan and Lebanon and thereby "facilitate the early withdrawal" of foreign troops. In the next few days, tension in the Mideast appears to lessen.

Sept. 19. An Arab nationalist government-in-exile, the "Republic of Algeria" government, is formed in Cairo. Ferhat Abbas, a leader of the Nationalist Liberation Front, is named Premier. Six Arab states recognize the government, while France denounces it.

Sept. 22. Lebanon's pro-West cabinet resigns. Rashid Karami, a rebel leader, becomes premier Sept. 24. The United States Sept. 27 assures Karami of continued U.S. support.

Oct. 1. Morocco and Tunisia are admitted to the Arab League composed of the U.A.R., Iraq, Jordan, Saudi Arabia, Libya, Lebanon, the Sudan, and Yemen.

Oct. 3. During his fourth visit to Algeria since assuming power, French Premier de Gaulle outlines a 5-year plan for creation of a peaceful and prosperous Algeria closely linked to France, but maintaining a distinct "personality."

Oct. 15. Tunisia severs diplomatic ties with the U.A.R. following a dispute over alleged U.A.R. interference in Tunisian affairs.

Oct. 25. The last U.S. forces leave Lebanon following a 102-day stay.

Nov. 17. A bloodless military coup, headed by Lt. Gen. Ibrahim Abboud, ousts the Sudanese government.

Nov. 18. Moroccan King Mohamed V orders the evacuation of all Spanish, French and U.S. troops and/or bases, thereby rejecting a U.S. bid to maintain military bases for another seven years.

Dec. 1. 19 months of martial law end in Jordan.

Dec. 6. The Soviet Union protests Iran's acceptance of a military agreement with the United States.

1959

Jan. 9. West Germany recalls its ambassador to the U.A.R. following the establishment of consular relations between the U.A.R. and East Germany.

Jan. 13. U.S. arms shipments arrive in Tunisia.

Jan. 17. Egypt and Britain resolve their two-year dispute generated by the Suez crisis in 1956. Terms of the agreement are not disclosed.

Feb. 10. It is reported in Washington that Soviet arms shipments to Iraq have doubled that country's military strength since last November.

Feb. 15. Iran announces its decision to stay within the Western alliance. It the past week, the Soviet Union had urged Iran not to sign a mutual defense treaty with the United States. The U.S., Britain, Turkey and Pakistan had countered, sending personal messages to the Shah urging him to sign further economic and defense agreements. Turkey, Iran and Pakistan sign mutual defense treaties with the United States March 5.

March 20. U.A.R. President Nasser denounces Soviet interference in Arab affairs and protests Soviet Premier Khrushchev's remarks the day before calling Nasser's hostility toward Iraq "hotheaded." Nasser on March 11 had accused Iraq and foreign Communist agents of attempting to divide the Arab world.

March 24. Iraq withdraws from the Baghdad Pact, which is left with four members—Britain, Turkey, Iran and Pakistan.

March 24. President Eisenhower praises Jordanian King Hussein for his resistance to outside pressures on his country.

April 14. Jordan's King Hussein arrives in Washington on an official visit for talks with President Eisenhower.

June 1. The U.S. embassy in Iraq announces the termination of U.S.-Iraqi military assistance agreements.

June 6. Jordan's King Hussein protests to the United Nations Syria's closing of their common border, which occurred after fighting sparked by Palestinian commandos.

July 13. Communist demonstrations in Kirkuk, an Iraqi oil center, nearly erupt into civil war. After the Iraqi army bombs the rebels, the government regains control.

July 21. Jordan and the U.A.R. agree to resume diplomatic relations, an action coupled with the reopening of the Syrian-Jordanian border.

Aug. 13. The Arab League, meeting in Bhamdun, Lebanon, supports reinforcement of the boycott of Israel.

Aug. 18. With the departure of Iraq from the Baghdad Pact, the organization is renamed the Central Treaty Organization (CENTO), with Britain, Iran, Pakistan and Turkey remaining as members. The United States supports the organization, holds memberships in certain committees, but is not an official member.

Aug. 26. Jordan offers citizenship to all Palestinian refugees.

Sept. 4. After four days of talks, U.A.R. President Nasser and Saudi Arabian King Saud agree to resume relations with Britain and to seek to end Communist penetration in Iraq.

Sept. 6. The U.A.R. announces an end to foreign control of banks in Syria, directing that 70 per cent of banks' stocks and board of directors seats must be held by Arabs.

Sept. 16. De Gaulle tells Algerians that within four years of the restoration of peace there, they will be allowed to determine their future by a free vote. They may choose between association with France and independence.

Oct. 5. U.A.R. Foreign Minister Fawzi tells the U.N. General Assembly that Israel will be permitted to use the Suez Canal after the Palestine refugee problem is resolved.

Oct. 9. President Eisenhower commends Iranian Premier Eghbal, in Washington for a meeting of the CENTO Council of Ministers, for his country's resistance to Communist propaganda.

Oct. 10. The United States and Turkey agree to establish an intermediate range ballistic missile base in Turkey.

Nov. 12. A spokesman for Saudi Arabian King Saud announces that the King disapproves of keeping U.N. troops in the Gulf of Aqaba.

Nov. 16. Iraq's Premier Kassim favors "Fertile Crescent" plan to unite with Syria and Jordan.

Dec. 1. Britain and U.A.R. reestablish diplomatic relations after 3-year break.

Dec. 14. President Eisenhower addresses the Iranian Parliament during a 6-hour stop-over visit.

1960

Jan. 18. The U.A.R. announces that the Soviet Union will finance the second stage of the Aswan Dam.

Jan. 24. Algerian rightists rebel against the liberal Algerian policies of French President de Gaulle. Tanks and troops seal off Algiers and the rebellion finally collapses.

Feb. 2. The United Nations asks the U.A.R. to withdraw forces from the Israeli-Syrian demilitarized border zone following air fights between Israeli and Syrian planes Feb. 1.

Feb. 11. Jordanian Foreign Minister Musa Nasir says the Arab states are "completely united" on a "declaration of war" against Israel if Israel attempts to divert the Jordan River to irrigate the Negev desert.

March 7. It is disclosed that at the Feb. 28 meeting of the Arab League, Jordan rejected a U.A.R. proposal to establish a "Palestine entity," claiming instead the allegiance of its Palestine refugees for Jordan's King Hussein.

March 9. As Premier Ben-Gurion leaves Israel for visit in the United States, Secretary of State Christian Herter assures Arab leaders that his visit will not undermine U.S.-Arab bloc relations.

March 14. Ben-Gurion meets with West German Chancellor Konrad Adenauer, the first meeting between leaders of those two countries.

March 27. Iraqi Premier Kassim announces plans to raise an "Army of the Palestine Republic" to train Palestinians for a war to restore their homeland.

March 27. It is disclosed that the U.A.R. has refused a Soviet offer to protect its borders against possible attack.

April 8. U.N. Secretary General Dag Hammarskjold protests U.A.R. seizure of ships carrying Israeli supplies and products through the Suez Canal. Hammarskjold says he will renew persuasive efforts to end such actions.

July 23. Iran recognizes Israel. The new diplomatic ties lead to a break-off July 27 in Iran-U.A.R. ties and Iran is put under an economic boycott by the U.A.R. July 28.

Oct. 22. Arab representatives at the second Arab Petroleum Congress protest price reductions by oil companies and ask for improved concessions.

Nov. 17. Jordan and Iraq agree to resume diplomatic ties in December. Relations had been cut off in July, 1958, following the Iraqi revolution.

Dec. 21. Saudi Arabian Prince Faisal resigns, returning complete control of the government to his brother, King Saud. Saud had relinquished executive power to Faisal early in 1958.

1961

March 16. It is disclosed that a U.S.-Saudi Arabian pact of 1957, which called for the setting up of a U.S. military base at Dhahran, will not be renewed. On April 11, Saudi Arabian King Saud explains that the decision was partially due to American aid to Israel.

April 22. Rightist Algerians, headed by four retired French generals, launch a second, right-wing revolt in Algeria. The attempted coup is aimed at preventing peace talks between France and Algeria's Moslem rebels and to keep Algeria part of France. The insurrection collapses April 26.

June 19. Great Britain grants independence to Kuwait, but signs a treaty with the new nation assuring British protection if requested.

June 26. Kuwaiti Sheik Abdullah al-Salem al-Sabah says he will fight to maintain Kuwait's independence after Iraq claims that Kuwait is an "integral part" of Iraq.

June 27. A state of emergency is declared in Kuwait. U.A.R. President Nasser supports Kuwait's independence.

July 20. The Arab League unanimously admits Kuwait to membership. Iraq walks out of the meeting, accusing the League of aiding "British imperialism."

Aug. 27. Ferhat Abbas resigns as Prime Minister of the Algerian Provisional Government and is succeeded by Ben Yusuf Ben Khedda.

Sept. 19. British protective forces in Kuwait are replaced by troops sent by the Arab League to assure Kuwait's sovereignty against Iraqi claims.

Sept. 29. Following a coup Sept. 28 by dissident Syrian army units, the revolutionary command sets up a civilian government for Syria and announces independence from the U.A.R. Jordan and Turkey recognize the new Syrian government.

Oct. 1. President Nasser announces in Cairo that the U.A.R. has broken ties with Jordan and Turkey for their recognition of new Syrian government.

Oct. 13. Syria is reseated at the United Nations, regaining the seat it gave up when it merged with the U.A.R. The New Syrian government was recognized by the Soviet Union Oct. 7 and by the United States Oct. 10.

Dec. 11. Adolf Eichmann, former Nazi SS lieutenant colonel and head of the Gestapo's Bureau of Jewish Affairs, is convicted on 15 counts of war crimes and genocide. He is sentenced Dec. 15 to death by hanging. He had gone on trial in Israel April 11.

Dec. 26. U.A.R. President Nasser dissolves his country's union with Yemen, formed in 1958, thus reducing the United Arab Republic to only the state of Egypt.

Dec. 27. British naval craft are ordered into the Persian Gulf to resist Iraq's possible seizure of Kuwait.

1962

Jan. 23. Morocco and Algeria establish a joint commission for a "United Arab Maghreb," a North African union.

Feb. 14. President Kennedy says U.S. use of the Saudi Arabian air base at Dhahran will terminate in April 1962.

March 9. Egyptian President Nasser issues a constitution for the Gaza Strip, under Egyptian administration since 1948.

March 16. Iraqi Premier Kassim and Syrian President Kodso endorse close Iraqi-Syrian cooperation.

March 18. The Provisional Government of Algeria signs a cease-fire agreement with France to end fighting and violence which has continued since 1954. Ben Bella and four other Algerian rebel leaders are released in France.

March 28. Syrian army leaders oust the new Syrian government which was elected after the break with Egypt in the fall of 1961. The Syrian army leaders declare their intentions to work closely with Egypt and Iraq.

April 13. Syrian President Kodsi, ousted by an army coup March 28, is reported returned to office. Kodsi tells Syrians April 14 that he will seek a union of "liberated Arab states, beginning with Egypt."

May 22. Syria nationalizes all foreign banks.

May 31. Former Nazi Adolf Eichmann is hanged in Israel following conviction on charges that he committed crimes against humanity while heading Nazi efforts to annihilate Jews.

June 2. Iraq orders the departure of the American ambassador and recalls its ambassador to the United States following U.S. accreditation of an ambassador from Kuwait.

July 1. Algerians vote in a special referendum on the question of Algerian independence. Overwhelmingly, citizens vote for an independent Algerian cooperation with France. On July 3, de Gaulle recognizes Algeria's independence.

Aug. 7. Great Britain and the U.A.R. sign an agreement to transfer funds and compensate British nationals for property seized during the Suez crisis of 1956.

Aug. 27. Syria asks the Arab League to condemn the U.A.R. for alleged interference in Syrian internal affairs.

Aug. 29. Saudi Arabian King Saud and Jordanian King Hussein agree to merge military troops and economic policies.

Sept. 26. The U.S. State Department announces that the U.S. will sell short-range defensive missiles to Israel.

Sept. 30. Despite urging by the secret French nationalist Army in Algeria for the French population to remain in Algeria, all but 250,000 of nearly one million are reported to have left.

Nov. 6. Saudi Arabia breaks off diplomatic ties with the U.A.R. following charges that U.A.R. planes bombed Saudi Arabian villages near the Yemen border. The U.A.R. is reportedly cooperating with the revolutionary government in Yemen.

1963

Feb. 8. The Iraqi air force overthrows the government of Premier Kassim. Kassim is killed by a firing squad. A Nasserite and conspirator in the coup, Colonel Abdul Salem Arif, is appointed provisional president.

March 1. Iraq's Revolutionary Council guarantees "the rights" of Kurds, a dissident faction residing in northern Iraq that has been seeking autonomy within Iraq.

March 8. A coup by pro-Nasser and Baath Party followers ousts the Syrian government. The U.A.R. and Iraq governments threaten war if other nations interfere in the Syrian revolt.

March 12. Syria's new Premier Salah el-Bitar voices hopes of a federation of Syria, Iraq and Egypt under one president.

March 20. Israel's parliament (Knesset) endorses a government statement urging the West German government to forbid its scientists to aid the U.A.R. in the development of offensive missiles "and even armaments banned by international law."

April 1. Following pro-Nasser rioting, a state of emergency is declared by the Syrian Revolutionary Command Council.

April 10. U.A.R. Prime Minister Aly Sabry outlines the new federation between the U.A.R., Syria and Iraq, to be called the United Arab Republic. Later it is announced that the federation proposal will be submitted to national plebiscites to be held Sept. 27, 1963.

April 13. U.A.R. and Saudi Arabia agree to end their support of opposing factions in the Yemeni civil war.

April 20. Street demonstrations break out in Jordan in support of Jordan's joining the new U.A.R. federation.

April 23. Israeli President Itzhak Ben-Zvi dies at 78.

May 14. The U.N. General Assembly unanimously elects Kuwait as the body's 111th member.

May 21. In violation of an agreement reached in April, U.A.R. President Nasser declares that U.A.R. troops will not leave Yemen until royalist factions have been put down.

June 10. The Iraqi government announces war against troops seeking Kurdish autonomy within Iraq.

July 22. U.A.R. President Nasser renounces an agreement to unite Egypt, Syria and Iraq and denounces the Syrian Baath Party.

Aug. 9. Iraq and Syria, in agreement on ending disputes over Arab unity, urge U.A.R. President Nasser to join them in improving inter-Arab unity.

Aug. 21. The Arab League meets to consider a unified stance in support of Syria against Israel as fighting breaks out near the Sea of Galilee. Iraqi forces are placed "at the disposal of" Syria. U.A.R. troops are on alert for possible support of Syria.

Aug. 23. U.N. Secretary General U Thant announces Israeli and Syrian acceptance of a cease-fire.

Aug. 25. Israeli and Jordanian troops clash in Jerusalem before the U.N. truce observers persuade both sides to agree to a cease-fire.

Sept. 2. Iraq and Syria agree to seek "full economic unity" and to jointly work to strengthen their defenses.

Sept. 4. U.N. Secretary General U Thant reports that despite U.N. efforts to restore peace, the civil war in Yemen continues one year after the outbreak of hostilities.

Oct. 20. Iraq announces that Syrian troops are aiding government troops against the Kurdish rebels.

Nov. 12. Syrian Premier el-Bitar resigns and a new Syrian government is set up with Major General Amin el-Hafez as the president of the Revolutionary Council.

Nov. 18. Iraq's President Arif announces that his forces have overthrown Iraq's civilian Baathist government. Arif becomes president and chief of staff of the army. The new government announces Nov. 21 that it will seek to fulfill the April agreement between Iraq, Syria and Egypt on the formation of a union and offers Nov. 22 to settle differences with "the Kurds, our brothers."

1964

Feb. 10. Iraq's President Arif announces a cease-fire agreement, apparently concluding the Kurds' struggle for autonomy within Iraq.

March 24. The Soviet Union announces the signing of a five-year treaty of friendship with Yemen and discloses promises of increased economic aid.

March 28. Saudi Arabian King Saud signs over his full powers to his half-brother Crown Prince Faisal. King Saud took the action to reduce his own position to that of a figurehead after unsuccessful attempts to regain the powers he gave to Prince Faisal during his prolonged illness.

April 14. In talks with President Johnson in Washington, Jordanian King Hussein stands firm on Arab intentions to dam two tributaries of the Jordan River in order to block Israel's plans to divert the Jordan River for irrigation purposes.

April 28. Syria's Revolutionary Council cancels its military treaty with Iraq.

May 3. Iraqi President Arif introduces a new provisional constitution which has as its main goal the union of Iraq with the U.A.R.

May 26. Iraq and the U.A.R. sign an agreement providing for joint command of their troops in time of war.

June 2. After two days of talks in Washington, **Israeli Premier Levi Eshkol and President Johnson issue** a communique calling for joint efforts to apply nuclear power capabilities to desalinization of sea water. In the communique, the United States reaffirms its support of the "political integrity" of all Middle East nations.

July 13. Yemen and the U.A.R. sign an agreement to coordinate political, economic and cultural ties "as a step toward complete unity."

July 14. Iraq nationalizes all private and foreign banks, insurance companies and 30 industrial and commercial businesses.

Aug. 18. The Lebanese Parliament elects Minister of Education Charles Helou as president to succeed President Fuad Chehab, who retired.

Aug. 22. Libyan Premier Mahmud Mutasser announces that both the United States and Great Britain have agreed to give up their military bases in Libya.

Sept. 11. After seven days of talks, chiefs of state of 13 Arab nations issue a final communique urging immediate Arab efforts on water projects to cut off the Jordan River from Israel in an effort to thwart Israeli plans to dam the Jordan for irrigation purposes.

Oct. 3. The economic ministers of Algeria, Morocco, Tunisia and Libya sign a protocol creating machinery for economic cooperation.

Nov. 2. The Saudi Arabian cabinet and consultative counsel proclaim Crown Prince Faisal the King of Saudi Arabia, thus dethroning King Saud.

Nov. 7. The Sudanese Cabinet rescinds the state of emergency in effect since 1958.

Dec. 24. Syria announces that it will not grant oil and mineral exploitation concessions to foreigners.

1965

Jan. 3. Syria nationalizes, in whole or part, 107 principal industries, reportedly to stem the flow of capital from the country.

Jan. 12. At the conclusion of four days of talks in Cairo, premiers of 13 Arab nations issue a comminique disclosing common policy toward nations henceforth recognizing Israel or aiding in her "aggressive military efforts." The policy is regarded as directed primarily at West Germany.

Jan. 26. Iranian Premier Mansour dies of gunshot wounds inflicted by a student Jan. 21.

Jan. 22. The Lebanese Parliament approves construction of a pumping station on the Wazzani River aimed at diverting the Jordan River from Israel.

Feb. 10. West Germany temporarily halts military aid for Israel in the face of Arab threats to recognize the East German government if the military aid continues. Israel's parliament, the Knesset, Feb. 15 denounces West Germany's "surrender to blackmail" by the U.A.R.

Feb. 17. The State Department acknowledges that the United States was a secret partner in the West German-Israel military aid agreement.

Feb. 24. After East German leader Walter Ulbricht arrives in Cairo despite West German protests, West Germany suspends its economic assistance to the U.A.R. and cancels its program of guarantees for private investments there.

March 1. East Germany and the U.A.R. sign a $100-million economic aid agreement during Ulbricht's seven-day visit.

March 4. Syria nationalizes nine oil companies: six Syrian, two U.S. affiliates, and one joint British-Dutch company. Procedures for compensation are outlined.

March 16. U.A.R. President Nasser is elected to another six year term.

April 21. Tunisian President Habib Bourguiba criticizes Arab policy toward Israel and proposes broad terms to end the Arab-Israeli conflict. He calls for the opening of direct negotiations between Israel and the Palestinian Arabs on the basis of the 1947 United Nations plan for partition of Palestine into Jewish and Arab states; and for cession of one-third of Israel's territory for a Palestine Arab nation. Bourguiba says the land he would have Israel give up was earmarked for an Arab sovereignty by the 1947 U.N. plan but won by Israel during the Arab-Israeli war of 1948. Israel rejects Bourguiba's plan April 25. The U.A.R. rejects the proposals April 27 and "strongly denounces the issuance of such a proposal from the head of an Arab state." The Arab League rejects the plan April 29 during a meeting boycotted by Tunisia.

May 12. Israel and West Germany establish full diplomatic relations. The U.A.R. breaks diplomatic ties with West Germany. Nine other Arab states later follow suit in breaking off ties with Bonn.

June 1. Syria declares that the only Palestinian solution is the elimination of Israel. Syrian President Amin el-Hafez terms the Arab unified military command ineffectual.

June 4. Syrian President Hafez accuses other Arab nations of planning to leave Syria alone to face Israel in a showdown over diversion of the Jordan River.

June 22. The State Department announces U.S. plans to ship surplus farm products to the U.A.R. in fulfillment of an agreement that ends June 30. The aid had been suspended six months before because of anti-American incidents in the U.A.R.

July 15. The chief of the Israel General Staff says Israeli raids on Syria have deterred that country's plan to divert the Jordan River from Israel.

July 20. Lebanon's Prime Minister Hussein Oueini unexpectedly resigns. He is replaced by ex-Prime Minister Rashid Karami July 22.

Aug. 23. The Arab Socialist Baath Party in Syria establishes a National Council (legislature) to consolidate the party's political control. The new provisional legislature re-elects Hafez as chairman of the Presidency Council, Sept. 2.

Aug. 24. Saudi Arabian King Faisal and U.A.R. President Nasser sign an agreement ending the civil war in Yemen. The accord, reached during talks between the two leaders Aug. 22-24, calls for an immediate halt to hostilities, for Saudi Arabia to end military aid to the royalists, and for the U.A.R. to withdraw its troop support of the revolutionary republicans. Repre-sentatives of the opposing factions had agreed Aug. 13 to end the three-year civil war.**

Sept. 17. Heads of state of 12 Arab nations meeting in Casablanca call for "a cease-fire in the war of words" between the Arab states and for abatement of interference in each other's internal affairs.

Nov. 7. The Iraq government reestablishes free enterprise, announcing that it will reconsider socialism. Iraq will also adopt new approaches to the Kurdish rebel problem.

Nov. 10. In response to Syrian statements that the Khuzistan province in southwest Iran is part of the "Arab homeland," Iran closes its embassy in Syria and recalls its ambassador.

Nov. 24. Kuwait's Emir al-Sabah dies and his younger brother Sabah al-Salem al-Sabah is proclaimed the new ruler.

Dec. 29. The State Department confirms that the United States has been supplying Jordan with 50-ton Patton tanks.

1966

Jan. 3. The United States and the U.A.R. sign a $55-million aid agreement. The accord is the first major diplomatic overture between the two nations since relations became strained a year before.

Feb. 22. U.A.R. President Nasser warns he may station U.A.R. troops in Yemen for five years if necessary in order to establish a republican regime there.

Feb. 24. The United States acknowledges that Saudi Arabian King Faisal has asked for diplomatic and military support if the U.A.R. renews fighting in Yemen.

Feb. 25. Following a coup Feb. 23 by left wings of the military and of the Baath Party, Syria announces that the military junta in power has named Nureddin Attassi chief of state. Attassi had been ousted from office by a coup in December 1965.

March 19. For U.S. food shipments to continue to Egypt the United States says Egypt must reduce its cotton production. Egypt has been exchanging cotton for arms from the Soviet Union.

April 16. Iraqi Major General Abdul Rahman Arif is elected by a joint session of the cabinet and the national defense council to succeed his brother as president. Former president Abdul Salem Arif died in a helicopter crash April 13.

May 1. U.A.R. President Nasser warns that his country will attack Saudi Arabia if "any aggression or infiltration" into Yemen comes from Saudi territory.

May 18. Israeli Premier Eshkol urges the big powers to limit the arms build-up in the Middle East.

May 19. It is reported in Washington that the United States agreed in February to sell several tactical jet bombers to Israel. This is the first such weapons sale to be disclosed.

May 25. Jordanian King Hussein lays the first stone of the Mokheiba Dam. The dam is part of an Arab effort to divert the Jordan River from Israel.

June 22. At a news conference in Washington during a three-day visit, Saudi Arabian King Faisal says Israel is not his country's enemy, but Zionists have transplanted Arabs from Palestine.

June 29. Iraqi Premier al-Bazzaz announces a plan for local autonomy for the Kurdish tribes in northern Iraq, an attempt to end the five-year civil strife.

July 25. The U.N. Security Council discusses the Israeli-Syrian border conflict for the 214th time in 18 years.

Sept. 27. The United States announces that it will sell $100-million in vehicles to Saudi Arabia for modernization of the army.

Oct. 10. Jordanian King Hussein warns against excessive Egyptian interference in "Syrian affairs," saying Jordan will not allow the Syria-Jordan border to be closed. Hussein also says that his country would attack Israel if war developed between Israel and Syria.

Nov. 4. Syria and the U.A.R. sign a mutual defense treaty which provides for joint command of their armed forces.

Nov. 24. U.A.R. customs authorities seize Ford Motor Co. assets in the country allegedly due to a dispute over Ford's obligation to pay customs duties on cars assembled and then sold in the U.A.R.

Nov. 29. Jordan's King Hussein charges Soviet fomentation of tension in the Middle East following a week of anti-government demonstrations and riots.

Dec. 7. Syrian Chief of State Attassi calls on Jordanians and Palestine Arabs to overthrow Jordan's King Hussein and offers them arms.

Dec. 8. Syria impounds the assets of the Western-owned Iraq Petroleum Company over claims to back royalties and higher pipeline transit fees. When the company rejects Syrian demands of doubled transit fees and export fees, the company's oil pipeline is closed.

1967

Feb. 19. Iran and the Soviet Union sign a defense agreement whereby Iran will purchase $110-million in arms and supplies.

Feb. 27. Jordan and West Germany resume diplomatic ties that were broken in 1965 when West Germany recognized Israel.

March 2. The Western-owned Iraq Petroleum Company announces plans to pay an additional 50 per cent rental fee for the use of a pipeline through Syria.

April 20. Iraq and Kuwait call home their ambassadors as fighting erupts along their common border.

May 15. The U.A.R. alerts its military forces because of mounting tension with Israel. Syria also announces that its military forces are ready for action.

May 19. The U.N. Emergency Force in the Middle East pulls out, ending a 10-year commitment for peacekeeping in that area. The withdrawal had been requested by the U.A.R.

May 20. The U.A.R. declares that a state of emergency exists along the Gaza Strip.

May 22. The U.A.R. closes the Strait of Tiran to Israeli ships and to ships carrying strategic cargo bound for Israel.

May 23. The United States and Israel each issue strong warnings against the U.A.R.'s blockade of the Strait of Tiran, entrance to the Gulf of Aqaba.

May 23. The U.S. 6th Fleet is ordered toward the eastern Mediterranean. Meanwhile the Soviet Union warns that it will resist any aggression in the Middle East.

May 23. Following the explosion of a bomb on the Jordan-Syria border, Jordan orders the shutting down of the Syrian embassy and the departure of Syria's ambassador to Jordan.

May 24. The U.A.R. has reportedly mined the Strait of Tiran and the Gulf of Aqaba.

May 26. Israeli Foreign Minister Abba Eban meets in Washington with President Johnson on ways to restore order in the Middle East. On his way to Washington, Eban made stops in London and Paris to confer with officials there.

May 29. Egyptian and Israeli troops open fire on the Gaza Strip.

May 30. Jordan and the U.A.R. sign a mutual defense pact.

June 3. Israel appeals to the Soviet Union to help bring peace to the Middle East.

June 5. Arabs and Israelis fight in the Egyptian section of the Sinai Peninsula and in Jerusalem. Israel destroys Egyptian, Syrian and Jordanian air forces in surprise early morning attacks. After 36 hours of battle, Israelis capture the Jordanian sector of Jerusalem.

June 6-7. The U.A.R., Syria, Iraq, Sudan, Algeria, and Yemen sever diplomatic relations with the United States.

June 6. Kuwait and Iraq cut off oil supplies to the United States and Britain.

June 6. The U.A.R. closes the Suez Canal, charging that U.S. and British planes are aiding Israel. The U.S. strongly rejects the charges.

June 7. In a sweeping seizure of territory, Israel takes over the Old City of Jerusalem, Mt. Scopus, Bethlehem in Jordan, the Sinai Peninsula between the Negev Desert and the Suez Canal, Sharm el Sheik, the Gaza Strip, and announces the breaking of the blockade of the Gulf of Aqaba.

June 7. The U.N. Security Council adopts a resolution calling for an immediate cease-fire in the Middle East. Israel announces it will accept the cease-fire if the Arab states do. The cease-fire is accepted by Jordan June 7, the U.A.R. June 8 and Syria June 9-10.

June 8. Israeli planes erroneously attack an American vessel in the Mediterranean, killing 10 and wounding 100. Israel apologizes for the error.

June 9. Claiming the sole responsibility for Egypt's defeat by Israel, President Nasser resigns. Later the National Assembly rejects his resignation.

June 10. The Soviet Union severs diplomatic ties with Israel, pledging assistance to Arab states if Israel refuses to withdraw from conquered territory.

June 11. Israel and Syria sign a cease-fire agreement.

June 12. Israel announces that it will not withdraw to the 1949 armistice boundaries and calls for direct negotiations between Israel and Arab nations.

June 15. Libya asks the United States and Britain to remove their military bases and troops immediately.

June 19. President Johnson, in a nationally televised speech, sets forth five points for peace in the Middle East: right of each country's national existence, fair and just treatment of Arab refugees, freedom of innocent maritime passage, limitation of arms build-up, and guaranteed territorial integrity for each Middle East country. Meanwhile at the U.N., Soviet Premier Kosygin calls for the condemnation of Israel, the withdrawal of Israeli forces from occupied Arab lands, and Israeli reparations to Syria, Jordan and the U.A.R. for damages incurred during the war.

June 23. President Johnson and Soviet Premier Kosygin meet for 5 1/2 hours at Glassboro State College in New Jersey to discuss the Middle East, Vietnam and arms control. They meet again for over four hours June 25, but later President Johnson says that "no agreement is readily in sight on the Middle East crisis." Kosygin, at a televised news conference, says the first step to peace in the Middle East is Israel's withdrawal to positions behind the 1949 armistice lines.

June 27. President Johnson announces $5-million in U.S. emergency aid for victims of the Arab-Israeli war.

June 28. Israel proclaims the unification of all of Jerusalem under Israeli rule.

July 4. U.N. Secretary General U Thant asks Israel and the U.A.R. to accept U.N. supervision of the cease-fire in the Suez Canal zone. The U.A.R. agrees July 10 and Israel accepts July 11.

July 13. President Johnson defines an "urgent need" for a "maximum number" of Arab refugees to be permitted by Israel to return to their homes.

July 17. Israel tells the General Assembly that the Arab states must recognize Israel's "statehood, sovereignty and international rights" before peace talks can begin.

Aug. 3. Israel and the U.A.R. agree to a U.N. proposal to halt for one month navigation through the Suez Canal.

Aug. 9. It is reported that the Sudan will obtain arms from the Soviet Union, Yugoslavia and Czechoslovakia.

Aug. 23. The Shah of Iran, ending two days of talks with President Johnson in Washington, arranges the purchase of a second squadron of the latest U.S. fighter jets.

Sept. 1. Arab heads of state, meeting in Khartoum, agree to seek a nonmilitary solution to the tensions with Israel. Meanwhile, Israel rejects a Yugoslav peace proposal calling for a return of Israeli troops to pre-June 5 positions, free passage of Israeli ships through the Strait of Tiran and free cargo movement through the Suez Canal.

Sept. 24. Israel announces it will move settlers into occupied Syria and the captured Jordanian sector of Jerusalem. The United States expresses its "disappointment" with that decision Sept. 26.

Sept. 27. Israeli Foreign Minister Eban suggests the economic cooperation of Israel, Lebanon and Jordan, the demilitarization of the Sinai, and the establishment of a "universal status" for the "holy places" of Jerusalem.

Sept. 29. Rejecting Israel's suggestion of direct negotiations, Egypt's Foreign Minister Raid accuses the United States of violating its pledge of territorial integrity for each Middle East state.

Oct. 3. Israel repudiates the 1949 armistice treaty and declares that a new treaty must be negotiated.

Oct. 22. Israel announces plans to build an oil pipeline between Elath on the Gulf of Aqaba and Ashdod on the Mediterranean to circumvent the Suez Canal.

Oct. 24. The United States announces it will fill arms orders, placed before the June war, to Israel and five pro-West Arab states.

Oct. 26. Mohammed Reza Pahlavi, crowns himself Shah of Iran and his wife, the Empress Farah, as Iran's first crowned queen.

Nov. 5. Jordan's King Hussein tells an American television audience that his country is ready to recognize Israel's right to existence.

Nov. 22. The U.N. Security Council unanimously adopts a British proposal (Resolution 242) for bringing peace to the Middle East. Under the plan, Israel would withdraw from all conquered territory, each country would agree to recognize the territory of the other states, and free navigation through international waterways would be assured.

Nov. 23. U.A.R. President Nasser says he will continue to deny Israeli ships access through the Suez Canal and that Israeli withdrawal from occupied lands is not open to negotiation.

Nov. 28. Britain declares the independence of South Arabia, which is renamed the People's Republic of South Yemen. British troops complete their evacuation of Aden Nov. 29. The country had been a British colony since 1839.

Dec. 24. Iraq and the Soviet Union agree to cooperate in the development of oil deposits in southern Iraq.

1968

Jan. 7. President Johnson confers with Israeli Premier Levi Eshkol on his Texas Ranch. It is later disclosed that Johnson promised Eshkol more Skyhawk A-4 fighter-bombers.

Jan. 11. Israel expropriates a section of the former Jordanian sector of Jerusalem, promising compensation for the private land owners.

Feb. 14. The United States announces its intention to resume arms shipments to Jordan.

Feb. 15. Significant fighting between Jordan and Israel erupts along their common border. U.S. embassies in both states are successful in negotiating a cease-fire after eight hours of fighting. The next day, Jordan's King Hussein calls for an end to terrorist activities originating within Jordan against Israel because, he says, such raids prompt Israeli retaliation.

Feb. 27. South Yemen, in an effort to remove "vestiges of colonial rule," dismisses all British military and administrative officers.

March 20. Continuing to reject direct negotiations with Israel, the U.A.R. nonetheless indicates its willingness to implement the British proposal adopted by the United Nations on Nov. 22, 1967.

April 10. U.A.R. President Nasser says his country is "fully prepared to support and arm the Palestine resistance movement" in its terrorist activity against Israel. Iraq April 13 announces the formation of a committee to raise funds for the Arab guerrillas.

April 25. Iraq announces an agreement to resume diplomatic relations with Britain, broken during the June war of 1967.

May 28. Israel pays the United States $3-million for the families of Americans killed by an erroneous Israeli bombing of a U.S. vessel June 8, 1967.

June 1. Martial law is proclaimed in Beirut, Lebanon, following an unsuccessful assassination attempt on President Chamoun.

July 5. Israel rejects plans for a U.N. peacekeeping force in the Israeli-occupied Sinai Peninsula, endorsed the day before by the U.A.R., in place of direct negotiations for a peace settlement with Arab states.

July 6. Nine Persian Gulf sheikdoms agree to a loose form of federation.

July 15. Arab guerrilla leaders meeting in Cairo agree to coordinate their activities against Israel.

July 17. The fourth coup in 10 years deposes Iraq's government. Ahmed Hassan al-Bakr is named president and premier July 31.

Aug. 11. Reportedly easing its position on a Middle East settlement, the U.A.R. says it will agree to a demilitarization of the Sinai Peninsula, will lift demands for the return of Arab refugees to their homeland, will agree to internationalizing the Gaza Strip and will grant Israeli cargoes access throught the Suez Canal and Israeli vessels through the Strait of Tiran.

Oct. 8. Israeli Foreign Minister Abba Eban offers a nine-point peace plan at the United Nations. The proposal calls for Israeli withdrawal from occupied territory following the establishment of "permanent" boundaries between the Arab states and Israel. The U.A.R. rejects the plan Oct. 9, but agrees Oct. 10 to accept a timetable worked out by U.N. special representative Jarring for implementing the British peace proposal adopted by the Security Council Nov. 22, 1967.

Oct. 27. After night-long shelling between Egypt and Israel, Egyptian oil refineries at Port Suez are afire.

Nov. 6. Reports out of Washington indicate that the United States has agreed to sell 58 Phantom jets to Israel.

Nov. 19. Israel declares it will allow the return of 7,000 Arabs who fled during the June 1967 war.

Dec. 2. Jordanian and Israeli troops clash in heavy battle. The next day Israeli planes counter a pre-dawn artillery attack along the Jordan border. On Dec. 4, Israeli bombers strike back against Iraqi shelling along the Israeli-Jordan border.

Dec. 5. Jordan's King Hussein sends messages to the U.A.R., Saudi Arabia, Iran, Kuwait and Lebanon calling for unified action to liberate Arab lands.

Dec. 9. President-elect Nixon's special envoy to the Middle East, former Pennsylvania Governor William Scranton, tells newsmen that he believes American policy in the area should be more "even-handed."

Dec. 26. Two Arab terrorists attack an Israeli jet at the Athens airport, setting it afire. In retaliation, an Israeli task force Dec. 28 attacks the Beirut International Airport, destroying several airplanes.

1969

Feb. 2. *Newsweek* magazine publishes an exclusive interview with U.A.R. President Nasser who suggests a five-point peace plan for the Middle East: "a declaration of nonbelligerence; the recognition of the right of each country to live in peace; the territorial integrity of all countries in the Middle East, including Israel, within recognized and secure borders; freedom of navigation on international waterways; a just solution to the Palestinian refugee problem." On Feb. 4, Israel rejects

Nasser's plan as "a plan for liquidating Israel in two stages."

Feb. 18. An Israeli airliner is attacked by four Arab terrorists at the Zurich, Switzerland, airport.

Feb. 26. Israeli Premier Levi Eshkol dies following a heart attack.

March 7. Foreign Minister Golda Meir accepts election as leader of the Labor Party and thereby becomes premier of Israel, succeeding Eshkol.

March 14. Israeli Foreign Minister Abba Eban, in Washington for talks with President Nixon, addresses the National Press Club and denounces attempts by the four major powers to reach a settlement in the Mideast.

March 19. The Shah of Iran says he is opposed to continued use by the United States of the Bahrain Island naval base—used by the U.S. since 1949—after British troops withdraw from the Persian Gulf in 1971.

April 10. In Washington for talks with President Nixon, Jordan's King Hussein addresses the National Press Club and sets forth a six-point peace plan which, he says, has U.A.R. President Nasser's approval. Similar to the U.N. proposal of November, 1967, the plan is contingent upon Israeli withdrawal from occupied lands. Israel rejects the plan the following day as propaganda.

April 19. It is reported that Soviet missiles have been installed along the Suez Canal.

April 22. U.N. Secretary General U Thant says that Israel and Egypt are engaged in "a virtual state of active war," and declares that the U.N. cease-fire has become "totally ineffective in the Suez Canal sector." The U.A.R. April 23 repudiates the U.N. cease-fire, contending that Israeli forces had not advanced to the eastern bank of the Canal when the cease-fire was adopted in 1967.

May 5. Israel's Prime Minister Meir says "signed peace treaties" are the only acceptable follow-up to the U.N. cease-fire of 1967.

May 11. Palestinian guerrilla leaders meet with Jordanian leaders in an attempt to reverse Jordan's new policy of forbidding Jordan-based raids on Israel.

May 25. The government of the Sudan is overthrown by a military coup. Abubakr Awadallah becomes premier and pledges to work more closely with the U.A.R. and other "progressive" Arab states.

June 3. Israel asks the United States to provide protection against Arab sabotage for the American-owned pipeline from Saudi Arabia to Lebanon. Until protection is provided, the line will be closed.

June 18. Jordan reports that Palestinian guerrillas are withdrawing from the country.

July 3. Turkey and the United States sign a new mutual defense treaty under which Turkey controls U.S. military installations within its borders.

July 7. U.N. Secretary General U Thant announces the resumption of open warfare along the Suez Canal.

July 20. After two weeks of sporadic fighting along the Suez Canal, Israeli jets attack U.A.R. ground installations for the first time since the June 1967 war.

July 31. Staging an offensive for the first time since the 1967 war, Syria launches an attack, supported by jets and heavy artillery, against the main Israeli post on Mount Hermon and on the Israeli-Lebanon border.

Aug. 3. Israel announces it will retain the Golan Heights, the Gaza Strip and part of the Sinai Peninsula in order to protect its security.

Aug. 10. Iraq announces a major aid agreement with the Soviet Union. Iraq will pay for the aid with crude oil.

Aug. 23. U.A.R. President Nasser calls for an all-out war with Israel, charging Israel with responsibility for the fire at the Al Aksa Mosque in Jerusalem Aug. 22.

Aug. 31. Arab hijackers blow up a TWA airliner after diverting it to Damascus following take-off from Rome. The hijackers demand the imprisonment of all the Israeli passengers, but Syria released all but six Israelis Aug. 30. Those six are being held hostage for the release of Syrian prisoners of war in Israel.

Sept. 1. Libya's King Idris is overthrown by a revolutionary council. The council, on Sept. 2, says it will honor existing agreements with oil companies. Muammar el-Qaddafi, head of the Revolutionary Command Council, emerges as leader of the new regime.

Sept. 18. President Nixon addresses the U.N. General Assembly, suggesting an arms curb in the Middle East by the big powers. The Soviet Union rebuffs the suggestion Sept. 19.

Oct. 7. An Australian sheepherder pleads guilty at his trial in Israel to setting fire to the Al Aksa Mosque in Jerusalem Aug. 22.

Oct. 13. Israel proposes home rule for the West Bank of occupied Jordan.

Oct. 22. The nine-nation Federation of Persian Gulf Emirates is established with Sheikh al-Nahayan of Abu Dhabi as president.

Oct. 28. The new military regime in Libya Sept. 1 notifies the United States that Wheelus Air Base, near Tripoli, must be evacuated by Dec. 24, 1970.

Oct. 28. The Sudan's Premier Awadallah is deposed by the Revolutionary Command Council and the chairman of the council, Gaafar al-Nimeiry, assumes the premiership.

Dec. 9. Secretary of State Rogers discloses a previously private U.S. proposal for peace in the Mideast, including a provision for Israel's withdrawal from occupied lands in exchange for a binding peace treaty signed by the Arabs. Israeli Premier Golda Meir says Dec. 12 that the plan is an attempt by the United States to "moralize."

Dec. 13. Britain announces its agreement to withdraw its forces from Libya by March 31, 1970.

1970

Jan. 16. Muammar el-Qaddafi, leader of the Revolutionary Command Council, becomes premier and defense minister of Libya, succeeding Mahmoud Soliman al-Maghreby.

Jan. 21. Israel, launching what it terms its largest ground operation since June 1967, captures the Egyptian island of Shadwan at the entrance of the Gulf of Suez.

Feb. 2. The heaviest fighting since the June 1967, war breaks out between Israeli and Syrian troops in the Golan Heights.

Feb. 4. It is reported that President Nixon has sent a note to the Soviet Union urging cooperation in resolving the Middle East problem.

Feb. 21. A bomb enclosed in a letter addressed to Israel explodes in mid-air in a Swiss aircraft bound for Israel and kills all 47 passengers aboard.

March 19. A large number of Soviet troops and antiaircraft missiles are reported by diplomatic observers to have arrived in Cairo.

March 31. Libya stages nationwide celebrations as the last British troops withdraw after a 30-year presence there.

April 14. The civil war in Yemen between republican and royalist forces ends. Saudi Arabia signs an agreement with the republican regime, pledging to discontinue the arms and funds to royalist rebels that had been supplied since the outbreak of hostilities in 1962.

May 9. Israel warns that the installation of Soviet SAM-3 missiles along the Suez Canal will not be permitted and threatens to attack Soviet planes if they interfere with Israeli attacks on Egyptian bases.

June 11. Jordanian King Hussein takes control of the army and removes the commander in chief, in response to guerrilla demands.

June 11. The United States formally turns over Wheelus Air Force Base to Libya, ending 16 years of operation.

June 24. Foreign intelligence reports received in Washington indicate that Soviet pilots have taken over the air defense of Egypt against Israel and are flying combat missions south of the Suez Canal.

June 25. Secretary of State Rogers tells a news conference in Washington of a broad-based diplomatic effort to encourage Arab and Israeli representatives "to stop shooting and start talking" under U.N. supervision. The heart of the proposal is a 90-day cease-fire tied to withdrawal of Israeli forces from territory occupied during the June 1967 war. Israeli Prime Minister Meir rejects the plan June 29.

July 5. Libya's Revolutionary Command Council announces nationalization of that country's four oil distributing companies.

July 17. At the conclusion of U.A.R. President Nasser's visit to Moscow, a joint Soviet-U.A.R. communique is issued calling for a political settlement of the Middle East crisis.

July 23. The U.A.R. accepts a U.S. proposal of June 19 calling for a 90-day cease-fire in the Middle East.

July 26. Jordan accepts the U.S. cease-fire proposal. One of the terms of the cease-fire requires Jordan to control guerrilla activities organized within its borders.

July 31. Yasir Arafat, chairman of the Palestine Liberation Organization, rejects the U.S. cease-fire proposal and all other compromise solutions to the conflict with Israel.

Aug. 4. Israel formally accepts the Middle East cease-fire. Israeli Prime Minister Golda Meir tells the Israeli parliament that she overcame her reluctance to accept the proposal after assurances of military and political support from President Nixon.

Aug. 7. A Middle East cease-fire goes into effect.

Aug. 18. Iraq's 12,000 troops in Jordan are placed at the disposal of the Palestinian commandos.

Aug. 23. The U.A.R. and Iran agree to renew diplomatic relations.

Sept. 6. The 14 nations of the Arab League call for an end to fighting between the Jordanian army and Arab commandos which has continued since the Sept. 1 aborted attempt to assassinate King Hussein.

Sept. 6. Members of the Popular Front for the Liberation of Palestine, an Arab commando group, are successful in three of four attempts to hijack commercial jets. A Pan Am 747 is forced to land in Cairo, passengers are disembarked, and the plane is blown up. A Swissair and a TWA plane are forced to land at a desert air strip in Jordan controlled by the commandos. The next day, the commandos release nearly half of the passengers from the planes brought down in the desert, and demand the release of Arab guerrillas held in Israel and Western Europe in exchange for the remaining hostages.

Sept. 9. Members of the Popular Front seize a fifth plane, a British BOAC jet, and hijack it to Jordan to join the two other planes in the desert. Hostages total nearly 300.

Sept. 12. Arab commandos release all but 54 of their hostages and blow up the three empty airplanes. Britain announces it will release the Arab commando seized in an aborted hijack effort Sept. 6.

Sept. 16. Jordanian King Hussein proclaims martial law and installs a military government as the civil unrest continues in his country.

Sept. 18. Israeli Prime Minister Meir meets with President Nixon in Washington and says Israel will not participate in the U.N. peace talks until new Egyptian missile installations along the Suez Canal are removed.

Sept. 26. President Nixon says he has ordered $5-million in relief for Jordan, which has been battered by a civil war.

Sept. 27. A 14-point pact is signed in Cairo by Arab heads of state—including Jordan's King Hussein and the leader of the Arab commandos—to end hostilities in Jordan. The agreement calls for King Hussein to remain on the throne, but for a three-member committee, headed by Tunisian Premier Ladgham, to supervise the government until conditions are normalized.

Sept. 28. U.A.R. President Gamal Abdel Nasser, 52, dies suddenly of a heart attack.

Sept. 29. Arab commandos release the last hostages held since four planes were hijacked earlier in the month. Forty-eight others had been released Sept. 25. Switzerland announces that a total of 19 Arabs will be released by Britain, West Germany, Switzerland and Israel.

Oct. 17. Anwar Sadat is sworn in as president of the U.A.R. following an Oct. 15 election in which he received 90 per cent of the vote.

Oct. 23. It is disclosed that the United States will send 180 tanks to Israel as part of $500-million in aid.

Nov. 4. The U.N. General Assembly votes for a 90-day extension of the Middle East cease-fire and for unconditional resumption of the peace talks between Arab states and Israel.

Nov. 13. Syrian President and Premier al-Attassi is reported to have been placed under house arrest. "Provisional leadership" will guide the government until a national congress can elect permanent leaders.

Nov. 27. Syria joins an alliance of the U.A.R., Libya and the Sudan to pool resources "for the battle with Israel."

Dec. 13. Jordanian King Hussein, via American television, urges a joint effort by the United States and Soviet Union to assume a peacekeeping role in the Middle East.

Dec. 22. Libya nationalizes all foreign banks.

1971

Jan. 15. U.A.R. President Sadat and Soviet President Podgorny dedicate the Aswan Dam.

Feb. 14. Representatives of six oil-producing countries (Iran, Iraq, Saudi Arabia, Kuwait, Abu Dhabi and Qatar) reach agreement with Western oil companies. The accord has a five-year tenure and increases payments by more than $1.2-billion for 1971. Agreements have yet to be reached with four other oil-producing countries.

March 12. Golda Meir, stating Israel's position on a Middle East settlement, calls for Israeli retention of Sharm el Sheik, Israel's sole land link with East Africa and Asia, demilitarization of the Sinai, and Israeli possession of Jerusalem.

March 13. Premier Hafez al-Assad is proclaimed president of Syria.

March 19. Israeli Foreign Minister Abba Eban declares that Israel will not withdraw to boundaries that existed before the June 1967 war.

April 2. Libya signs an agreement with 25 Western oil companies raising the price of Libyan oil from $2.55 to $3.45 a barrel.

April 3. Amid continued Palestinian guerrilla activity, Jordanian King Hussein says the guerrillas must remove their weapons from Amman within two days. The commandos have said they will stay in Amman and continue their fight to overthrow Hussein and to use Jordan as a base for operations against Israel.

April 7. The United States agrees to increase military aid to Jordan.

April 17. Egypt, Syria and Libya sign an agreement to form the Federation of Arab Republics. Plebiscites will be held Sept. 1 in the three countries to gain popular approval for the union.

May 1. Secretary of State Rogers arrives in the Middle East to confer with Saudi Arabian King Faisal, King Hussein of Jordan, Egyptian President Sadat, Lebanese officials and Israeli Premier Golda Meir on proposals for reopening the Suez Canal.

May 27. Saudi Arabian King Faisal arrives in Washington on an official visit to discuss the Middle East with President Nixon.

May 27. U.A.R. President Sadat and Soviet President Podgorny sign a 15-year treaty of friendship and cooperation.

June 7. By agreement, Iraq raises the price of oil to foreign oil companies by 80 cents a barrel.

July 4. The U.A.R. and the Soviet Union issue a joint communique, declaring that the Suez Canal will be opened only after Israel withdraws all of its forces from Arab territory.

July 6. Syria announces an agreement with Western-owned Iraq Petroleum Company under which Syria will receive 50 per cent more in payments for permitting pipelines across the country.

July 22. Sudanese Premier Nimeiry is returned to power after his ouster two days before by a faction of the military.

July 26. U.A.R. President Sadat is granted "full powers" by the national congress of the Arab Socialist Union to take whatever action necessary to recover Arab lands from Israel.

Aug. 2. Soviet officials are ordered out of the Sudan following charges that they influenced the coup that temporarily ousted Premier Nimeiry.

Aug. 12. Syria breaks off diplomatic relations with Jordan following clashes on their common border.

Aug. 14. Jordan demands the end of economic pressures exerted by other Arab states as a condition for Jordan's efforts to resolve hostilities between the army and Palestinian commandos.

Aug. 28. It is reported that Lebanon will buy arms from the Soviet Union.

Sept. 2. Citizens of Egypt, Libya and Syria vote almost unanimously for the Federation of Arab Republics aimed at providing a solid front against Israel.

Oct. 4. Egyptian President Sadat is selected first president of the Federation of Arab Republics.

Oct. 4. Secretary of State Rogers presents a detailed account of the U.S. position on the Middle East. He calls on Israel and Egypt to agree to open the Suez Canal as a first step towards peace in the area. Egypt rejects the proposal Oct. 6, lacking assurances of Israeli withdrawal from Arab lands.

Nov. 1. Israel says it will not agree to the U.S. proposal for indirect talks with Egypt without U.S. guarantees of a continuing supply of Phantom jets.

Nov. 28. Jordanian Premier Wasfi Tal is assassinated while visiting Cairo. Ahmed al-Lawzi succeeds him as Premier Nov. 29. The Jordanian government Dec. 17 formally charges Al Fatah, the Palestinian guerrilla group, with responsibility for the slaying.

Nov. 30. Iranian troops occupy the Iraqi territory of Abu Musa, Greater Tumb and Lesser Tumb. Iraq severs relations with Iran and Britain as a result.

Dec. 2. Israeli Premier Meir confers with President Nixon in Washington.

Dec. 2. The United Arab Emirates proclaims its independence. Zaid ben Sultan al-Nahayan of Abu Dhabi is named president of the union, which consists of six Persian Gulf sheikdoms.

Dec. 7. Libya nationalizes British oil interests and withdraws all deposits from British banks in protest of what it regards as British collusion in the Iranian seizure of Iraqi lands.

1972

Jan. 5. The United States announces an agreement with Bahrain for the establishment of a U.S. naval base in the Persian Gulf.

Jan. 20. An agreement to adjust oil prices to account for devaluation of the dollar is signed in Geneva between six oil-producing Persian Gulf nations (Abu Dhabi, Iran, Iraq, Kuwait, Qatar and Saudi Arabia) and Western oil companies. It raises the posted price of oil by 8.49 per cent.

Feb. 11. Ras al Khaimah, a small sheikdom, becomes the seventh member of the United Arab Emirates.

Feb. 26. Sixteen years of civil war in the Sudan are ended by an agreement between the government and the South Sudan Liberation Front.

March 12. The Organization of Petroleum Exporting Countries votes to accept an Arabian-American Oil Company (Aramco) offer to give a 20 per cent share of the company to the six countries of Iraq, Iran, Kuwait, Saudi Arabia, Abu Dhabi and Qatar.

March 15. Jordanian King Hussein unveils his plan to make Jordan a federated state comprised of two autonomous regions on the East and West Bank of the Jordan River. Israel currently holds the West Bank region. Hussein proposes Jerusalem as the capital of the West Bank, or Palestine, region. Israel, the same day, denounces the plan. The Federation of Arab Republics denounces the plan March 18 and calls on all Arab governments to similarly reject it.

March 28. King Hussein of Jordan meets with President Nixon in Washington.

April 6. Egypt severs diplomatic relations with Jordan, criticizing King Hussein's proposal for a federation of Jordan and the West Bank.

May 30. President Nixon receives a warm welcome in Iran on a stopover visit en route to Poland and then Washington after the U.S.-Soviet summit in Moscow.

June 1. Iraq nationalizes the Iraq Petroleum Company, owned jointly by American, British, French and Dutch oil companies. The company produces 10 per cent of Middle East oil.

July 18. Egyptian President Sadat orders all Soviet military advisers and experts out of his country and places all Soviet bases and equipment under Egyptian control. Sadat says July 24 during a four-hour speech that the Soviet Union's "excessive caution" as an ally led him to his decision.

Aug. 2. Libyan leader Qaddafi and Egyptian President Sadat issue a joint declaration to establish "unified political leadership."

Sept. 5. Arab commandos of the Black September organization seize a building housing 26 Israeli athletes at the Olympic Games in Munich, West Germany. Two Israelis are killed; nine are held hostage. When day-long negotiations fail, the nine hostages are killed. Israel launches reprisal raids Sept. 8 on Arab guerrilla bases in Syria and Lebanon, the most extensive raids since the June 1967 war.

Sept. 13. Syria and the Soviet Union agree to security arrangements. The Soviet Union will improve naval facilities in two Syrian ports for Soviet use and Syria will receive jet fighters and air defense missiles.

Sept. 18. Egyptian President Sadat and Libyan leader Qaddafi agree to make Cairo the capital of their projected unified state, to popularly elect one president, and to allow one political party. This action marks the first step toward gradual unification since the announcement Aug. 2 of the intent to unite.

Sept. 19. A letter bomb, believed to have been sent by the Black September organization, explodes in the Israeli embassy in London, killing the Israeli agricultural counselor. Similar terrorist activities in the next two days are blamed on the Black September group.

Oct. 15. Israel, launching its first unprovoked attack on Palestinian guerrilla bases in Syria and Lebanon, says "we are no longer waiting for them to hit first."

Oct. 15. A New York City postal clerk's hands are maimed as a letter bomb, addressed to an undisclosed official of the Women's Zionist Organization, explodes. The incident follows a flurry of such letter bombs in New York.

Oct. 28. Ending several weeks of heavy fighting, Yemen and South Yemen sign an accord in Cairo calling for their merger.

Oct. 29. Two Arab guerrillas of the Black September group hijack a West German airliner, forcing the release of three commandos held in the Sept. 5 murder of 11 Israeli athletes at the Olympic Games. Israel protested the German action on Oct. 30, calling it "capitulation to terrorists."

Nov. 1. It is reported that the Soviet Union will restore missiles to Egypt's air defense system that were removed when the Soviets were ousted by the government in July.

Nov. 14. Western diplomatic sources report that the attack on Israeli athletes at the Olympic Games was aimed at obstructing secret Egyptian-Israeli negotiations.

Nov. 27. Jordanian King Hussein confirms reports of an aborted coup to overthrow him, planned by Libyan leader Qaddafi, Yasir Arafat, leader of the Palestinian guerrillas, and other Palestinians.

Dec. 16. Tunisian President Bourguiba rejects a proposal for the union of his country with Libya.

1973

Jan. 8. An agreement between Kuwait and two Western oil companies grants Kuwait a 25 per cent share of oil concessions in the country. Over 10 years, Kuwait will assume 51 per cent ownership.

Feb. 7. Jordanian King Hussein visits the United States.

Feb. 21. A Libyan passenger airliner, reportedly failing to heed Israeli instructions to land after straying over Israeli-occupied Sinai, is fired upon and crashes, killing 106 persons. Israel assumes no responsibility for the crash and instead blames the airline pilot for not landing and the Cairo air control for misguidance.

Feb. 26. Israeli Premier Meir arrives in the United States for 10-day state visit.

Feb. 28. Iraq announces that Western oil companies have accepted the nationalization of Iraq Petroleum Company in exchange for compensation.

March 1. The U.S. ambassador to the Sudan, Cleo A. Noel, Jr., and U.S. charge d'affaires, George C. Moore, are seized and later killed by Black September terrorists in Khartoum who demand the release of several hundred Arab prisoners, including the convicted slayer of Sen. Robert F. Kennedy. A Belgian diplomat also is killed.

March 7. Sudanese President Nimeiry bans all guerrilla activity, charging that Al Fatah, a Palestinian commando groups, planned the embassy siege that left two Americans dead.

March 14. Golda Meir offers Jordan guardianship of the Islamic shrines in the Old City of Jerusalem.

March 16. The Shah of Iran announces that Western oil companies have turned over "full control" of that country's oil industry.

March 28. Egyptian President Sadat proclaims martial law.

May 7. Martial law is proclaimed in Lebanon as renewed fighting between the army and Palestinian guerrillas breaks out.

May 7. Israel celebrates its 25th national anniversary.

May 15. In a symbolic protest against Israel, Iraq, Libya, Kuwait and Algeria temporarily suspend oil shipments to the West.

June 11. Libyan leader Qaddafi nationalizes an American oil company in protest of the U.S. policy on Israel.

July 1. An Israeli military attache in the Israeli embassy in Washington, D.C., is slain, apparently by Arab terrorists.

July 20. Arab and Japanese hijackers seize a Japan Air Lines jet and demand the release of a man serving a life sentence for taking part in the May 1972 massacre of 26 persons at the Tel Aviv airport. The hijackers blow up the plane July 24 at Libya's Benghazi airport after the passengers and crew have been evacuated. The hijackers are arrested by Libyan officials.

July 25. The Shah of Iran pays a state visit to the United States.

Aug. 5. Two Arab Black September terrorists kill three persons and wound another 55 after firing machine guns and hurling grenades in the Athens airport.

Aug. 11. Israel forces a Middle East Airlines jet, flying over Lebanon, to land in Israel. Israel announces it diverted the wrong plane in its search for the leader of the Popular Front for the Liberation of Palestine, the group held responsible by Israel for the slayings in the Athens airport.

Aug. 29. Libyan leader Qaddafi and Egyptian President Sadat announce the "birth of a new unified Arab state" and the gradual approach to unification of their countries. Egypt had insisted on gradual unification instead of completion of the union by Sept. 1, 1973, as originally agreed.

Sept. 1. Libya nationalizes 51 per cent of the assets of all foreign oil companies.

Sept. 29. The Austrian government closes the Schonau facility, a key transit point for Jews leaving the Soviet Union for Israel. The action is taken to meet the demands of Arabs who kidnaped and later released three Soviet Jews and an Austrian customs official.

Oct. 6. War breaks out in the Middle East on the Jewish holy day of Yom Kippur. Egyptian forces cross the Suez Canal and Syria attacks the Golan Heights. Israeli forces counter on Oct. 7, striking back in the Sinai and on the Golan Heights.

Oct. 7. Iraq nationalizes the American-owned Mobil Oil Corporation and Exxon Corporation.

Oct. 8. Tunisia, the Sudan, and Iraq pledge support of Egyptian and Syrian forces battling Israel.

Oct. 10. Israel announces it has abandoned the Bar-Lev line along the Suez Canal but has pushed back Syrian forces from the Golan Heights. Egyptian forces cross the Suez and advance nearly 10 miles onto the East bank. The Syrian army is pushed back to the 1967 cease-fire line.

Oct. 12. Israeli forces advance to within 18 miles of Damascus, the capital of Syria.

Oct. 13. Jordan announces it will join Egypt and Syria in the war against Israel. The same day, Israel claims to have nearly eliminated an Iraqi division in Syria.

Oct. 13. Saudi Arabian troops join the war against Israel after urging by Egyptian President Sadat.

Oct. 15. The United States announces it is resupplying Israel with military equipment to counterbalance a "massive airlift" to Egypt by the Soviet Union.

Oct. 17. Arab oil-producing states announce a 5 per cent reduction in the flow of oil to the United States and other countries supporting Israel.

Oct. 17. Egyptian President Sadat, in an open letter to President Nixon, proposes an immediate cease-fire on the condition that Israel withdraws to pre-1967 boundaries. The same day, foreign ministers of four Arab states meet in Washington with President Nixon and Secretary of State Henry Kissinger to present a similar peace proposal.

Oct. 18. Libya cuts off all shipments of crude oil and petroleum products to the United States.

Oct. 18. Saudi Arabia announces a 10 per cent cut in oil production and pledges to cut off all U.S. oil shipments if American support of Israel continues.

Oct. 19. President Nixon asks Congress to appropriate $2.2-billion for emergency military aid for Israel.

Oct. 19. Libya cuts off all exports to the United States and raises the price of oil from $4.90 to $8.92 per barrel.

Oct. 20. Saudi Arabia halts oil exports to the United States.

Oct. 20. Secretary of State Kissinger arrives in Moscow for talks with Soviet Communist Party chief Leonid I. Brezhnev on restoring peace to the Middle East.

Oct. 21. Iraq nationalizes the holdings of Royal Dutch Shell Corporation.

Oct. 21. Kuwait, Qatar, Bahrain and Dubai announce suspension of all oil exports to the United States, theoretically marking the total cut-off of all oil from Arab states to the United States.

Oct. 21. The United States and the Soviet Union present a joint resolution to the U.N. Security Council calling for a cease-fire in place in the Middle East and for implementation of a Security Council resolution calling for Israeli withdrawal from lands occupied since the 1967 war. The proposal, formulated during Kissinger's trip to Moscow, is adopted by the Security Council early Oct. 22.

Oct. 22. A cease-fire takes effect on the Egyptian-Israeli front, but fighting continues nonetheless.

Oct. 22. Kissinger confers with Israeli Premier Golda Meir in Israel on his way back to Washington from Moscow. Meanwhile, Jordan accepts the U.S.-U.S.S.R. cease-fire proposal. Iraq and the Palestinian Liberation Organization reject it.

Oct. 23. The U.N. Security Council votes to reaffirm the Middle East cease-fire, asks Egypt and Israel to return to the cease-fire line established the day before, and asks that U.N. observers be stationed along the Israeli-Egyptian cease-fire line. The U.N. secretary general announces Syria will accept the cease-fire if Israel withdraws from lands occupied during the 1967 war. Egypt and Israel accuse each other of cease-fire violations as heavy fighting resumes on the canal front. Israeli forces on the West Bank of the canal push south to cut off completely both the city of Suez and the 20,000-man Egyptian III Corps on the East Bank.

Oct. 24. Egypt's Sadat appeals for the United States and the Soviet Union to send troops to supervise the cease-fire. The White House announces it will not send forces. Israel claims it rebuffs the III Corps' attempt to break out of the trap, after which Israel says calm returns to the Suez front. Egyptians say Israelis reached Adabiya on the Red Sea coast.

Oct. 25. President Nixon orders a world-wide U.S. military alert as tension mounts over whether the Soviet Union may intervene in the Middle East crisis. Kissinger says there are "ambiguous" indications of

that action. Speculation is that the Soviets might try to rescue the trapped Egyptian army.

Oct. 25. To avert a U.S.-U.S.S.R. confrontation in the Middle East, the U.N. Security Council votes to establish an emergency supervisory force to observe the cease-fire. The force would exclude troops from the permanent Security Council members, particularly the United States and the Soviet Union.

Oct. 27. The United States announces that Egypt and Israel have agreed to negotiate directly on implementing the cease-fire.

Oct. 28. The trapped Egyptian III Corps receives food, water and medical supplies after Israel agrees to allow a supply convoy to pass through Israeli lines. It is reported that Israel yielded following U.S. warnings that the Soviet Union threatened to rescue the troops. Israeli sources concede that on Oct. 23 their units drove to the port of Adabiya to isolate the III Corps.

Oct. 29. In a flurry of diplomatic activity, Egyptian Foreign Minister Fahmy meets with Kissinger in Washington.

Oct. 29. Syrian President Assad says Syria accepted the cease-fire after U.S.S.R. guarantees of Israeli withdrawal from all occupied territory and recognition of Palestinian rights.

Oct. 31. Israeli Prime Minister Golda Meir arrives in Washington for talks with President Nixon on her country's concern over U.S. pressure to make concessions. The same day, Egyptian President Sadat warns that his country will take up the fight again if Israel does not withdraw to the cease-fire lines of Oct. 22, 1973.

Nov. 1. Israeli Prime Minister Meir, meeting in Washington with President Nixon, says she has been assured of continued U.S. support.

Nov. 2. Secretary of State Kissinger meets separately in Washington with Meir and Egyptian Foreign Minister Fahmi.

Nov. 4. The Organization of Arab Petroleum Exporting Countries (OAPEC) reports that exports are running 25 per cent below the September export level, plans an additional 5 per cent production cut for later in the year and sends Saudi Arabian and Algerian oil ministers on a tour of western nations to explain the embargo.

Nov. 6. Israel lists 1,854 casualties from the war.

Nov. 7. After talks between Kissinger and Sadat, it is announced that Egypt and the United States will resume diplomatic relations. Ties are resumed Feb. 28, 1974.

Nov. 8. Kissinger flies to Jordan and Saudi Arabia to meet with leaders there.

Nov. 11. Israel and Egypt sign a cease-fire accord, drawn up by Kissinger and Sadat during recent talks. The six-point plan calls for (1) both sides to observe the cease-fire, (2) immediate discussions on the return to the Oct. 22 cease-fire lines, (3) immediate food and medical supplies for Suez City, (4) access for non-military supplies to the stranded Egyptian III Corps on the East Bank of the Suez Canal, (5) replacement of Israeli troops along the Suez by U.N. forces and (6) exchange of all prisoners of war. The signing is the first by the two parties on an important joint document since the 1949 armistice ending the first Arab-Israeli war. The ceremonies are in a tent at the kilometer 101 marker, signifying the distance to Cairo, on the Cairo-Suez road. High officers of the two countries immediately begin direct discussions to implement the cease-fire.

Nov. 14. Kilometer 101 negotiators agree to exchange POWs and to turn over check points on the Cairo-Suez road to a U.N. truce force.

Nov. 15. The first planeloads of Egyptian and Israeli POWs are exchanged.

Nov. 18. OAPEC cancels its 5 per cent output cut slated for December in a conciliatory gesture to most West European nations. The Netherlands and the United States are exempted because of their pro-Israeli stance.

Nov. 22. Saudi Arabia threatens to cut oil production by 80 per cent if the United States retaliates for Arab oil cuts or embargoes.

Nov. 26. The conference of Arab heads of state opens in Algeria to discuss the recent war. On Nov. 28, 15 Arab leaders declare Middle East peace is conditional on Israeli withdrawal from "all occupied Arab territories."

Dec. 9. Nine Arab oil ministers, meeting in Kuwait, order a new oil cutback of 750,000 barrels a day, a 5 per cent reduction, effective Jan. 1, 1974, to be lifted only after Israel begins withdrawal from lands occupied during the 1967 war.

Dec. 17. Arab guerrillas attack an American airliner at Rome airport, killing 31 persons. Then they hijack a West German aircraft to Athens with hostages aboard. At Athens, Arab guerrillas kill one Italian hostage but are unsuccessful in their demands for the release of two Palestinian commandos held by Greek authorities. The aircraft flies to Kuwait Dec. 18, where the 12 hostages aboard are freed and five hijackers surrender to police.

Dec. 21. The first Arab-Israeli peace conference opens in Geneva. Israel, Egypt, Jordan, the United States, the Soviet Union and the United Nations are represented. Syria boycotts the conference.

Dec. 23. Six Persian Gulf states raise the price of their oil from $5.11 to $11.65 a barrel, effective Jan. 1, 1974.

Dec. 25. The Saudi Arabian oil minister, speaking for the OAPEC countries, announces the cancellation of the 5 per cent oil production cut and instead discloses a 10 per cent increase. The U.S. oil embargo will continue, however.

Dec. 31. Israel holds general elections, resulting in a loss of parliamentary seats for Prime Minister Meir's Labor alignment and in a governmental crisis extending into spring of 1974 as Meir seeks to form a government. Results for the 120-member Knesset: Labor alignment, 51 seats, a loss of five; right-wing Likud coalition, 39, a gain of seven; National Religious Party (Labor's former coalition partner), 11, a loss of one; minor parties, 19 seats.

1974

Jan. 9. Egypt and Israel suspend the Geneva conference on troop disengagement along the Suez front to await new mediation by Kissinger, who arrives in Egypt two days later.

Jan. 17. Kissinger's "shuttle diplomacy" results in announcement of accords on Suez disengagement; agreements include the "U.S. proposal" for limiting the number of troops and deploying military equipment along the canal front.

Jan. 18. The accords are signed. The chief provisions are: Israel is to abandon its West Bank bridgehead and to withdraw on the East Bank about 20 miles from the canal; Egypt is to keep a limited force on the East Bank; a U.N. truce force is to patrol the buffer zone between the two; the pullback is to be completed in

40 days. Sadat says he will press Syria to open talks with Israel.

Jan. 25. Israeli forces begin the Suez withdrawal.

Jan. 28. The pullback lifts the siege of the city of Suez and ends the isolation of the Egyptian III Corps.

Jan. 30. In Jerusalem, Meir accepts a formal request to form a new cabinet.

Feb. 9. France and Iran sign a $5-billion energy agreement, which includes French construction of five nuclear power plants in Iran.

Feb. 11. Libya announces the complete nationalization of three American oil companies.

Feb. 13. At a Washington meeting dealing with the world energy shortage, 13 oil-consuming nations agree to seek a meeting with the oil-producing nations. France dissents.

Feb. 22. Israeli Defense Minister Dayan's refusal to serve in a new cabinet complicates the Meir bid to form a minority government.

Feb. 27. Kissinger, seeking a Syrian-Israeli disengagement on the Golan Heights front, arrives in Israel from Damascus and turns over to Meir a list of 65 Israeli POWs held in Syria.

Feb. 28. The United States and Egypt renew full diplomatic relations after a seven-year break. President Sadat announces he has invited President Nixon to visit Egypt.

March 4. The nine Common Market countries offer the Arab world a long-term plan for technical, economic and cultural cooperation. The move leads to a U.S. charge that it was not informed of the action by its West European partners. Paris claims Washington was consulted in advance.

March 4. Israel completes its Suez front pullback, restoring to Egypt control of both banks of the canal for the first time since the 1967 war.

March 10. A nine-week crisis ends in Israel with the formation of a new cabinet, including Moshe Dayan again as defense minister. He had wanted the right-wing Likud Party included in the coalition, a move repeatedly rejected by Meir.

March 11. Iraq offers self-rule to its Kurdish minority in the north, but the Kurds reject the proposal and sporadic fighting continues. Also during the month, an undetermined number of casualties results from Iraqi-Iranian border clashes.

March 18. After a joint meeting in Vienna, Saudi Arabia, Algeria, Egypt, Kuwait, Abu Dhabi, Bahrain and Qatar lift a five-month oil embargo against the United States, but Libya and Syria refuse to join in the decision.

March 18. The United States joins in international operation to clear obstructions in the Suez Canal, closed since the 1967 war.

April 6. Reports say Libya's Qaddafi has been relieved of "political, administrative and traditional" duties, but continues as armed forces chief. However, later it is said he has relinquished only some ceremonial duties.

April 10. Meir quits the Israeli premiership in an intraparty squabble over where to put the blame for military shortcomings in the October war.

April 11. Three Arab guerrillas storm an apartment building in an Israeli town near the Lebanese-Syrian border, killing 18 persons, mostly women and children. The terrorists die from their own explosives.

April 12. Israel retaliates by raiding Lebanese villages and blowing up houses said to belong to Palestinian sympathizers.

April 18. President Sadat says Egypt will no longer rely solely on the Soviet Union for arms.

April 19. Kurdish rebels declare all-out war on the Iraqi government as bloody clashes continue.

April 23. Yitzhak Rabin is asked to form a new Israeli government. Labor minister in the last cabinet, he is former ambassador to the United States and commanded the Israeli army in the 1967 war.

April 29. Meeting in Geneva, Kissinger and Gromyko pledge U.S.-Soviet cooperation in seeking a troop separation accord on the Syrian-Israeli front.

April 30. Kissinger in Cairo begins a month-long quest to end the Golan Heights confrontation.

May 7. The Egyptian State Council rules illegal the confiscation of private property that began under Nasser.

May 15. In a schoolhouse battle at the Israeli town of Maalot, 16 teen-agers are killed and 70 are wounded after three Arab terrorists seize the school and demand the release of 23 prisoners held by Israel. The Arabs are slain when Israeli soldiers attack the school.

May 16. Israel initiates a week-long series of raids in replying to the Maalot tragedy. Planes and gunboats hit Palestinian camps and hideouts in Lebanon, killing at least 61 persons; the Israelis kill six Arab guerrilla infiltrators, who, Israel says, were planning a massacre similar to the one at Maalot.

May 28. Premier-designate Rabin forms a new Israeli cabinet.

May 29. Syria and Israel agree on disengagement.

May 31. The accords, achieved by Kissinger in his latest round of "shuttle diplomacy," are signed in Geneva. Israel and Syria accept a separation of forces, a U.N.-policed buffer zone between them and a gradual thinning out of forces.

June 6. Israel returns 382 Arab prisoners to Syria, which hands over 56 Israeli POWs.

June 9. Saudi Arabia announces it will assume 60 per cent ownership of Arabian-American Oil Company (Aramco).

June 12. Nixon starts his Middle East tour in Egypt. Other stops are Saudi Arabia, Syria, Israel and Jordan.

June 14. Sadat and Nixon sign a friendship pledge. The United States promises Egypt nuclear technology for peaceful purposes.

June 16. Syrian President Assad and Nixon establish full U.S.-Syrian diplomatic relations, ruptured in the 1967 war. ,

June 17. At the end of his visit to Israel, Nixon says the United States and Israel will cooperate in nuclear energy, and the United States will supply nuclear fuel "under agreed safeguards."

June 23. Israel evacuates the last portion of Golan Heights territory occupied in the October 1973 war.

July 15. Rabin says there is "no possibility whatsoever" that Israel will hold discussions with Palestinian guerrilla organizations.

Aug. 7. Egyptian President Sadat blames Libyan President Qaddafi for plots against Sadat and for the recall of Libya's Mirage jets loaned to Egypt.

Aug. 18. Qaddafi and Sadat meet in an attempt to settle disputes.

Aug. 27. France ends its embargo on arms sales to Middle East "battlefield" countries.

Sept. 10. Rabin meets in Washington with President Ford (sworn in Aug. 9), who says the United States remains "committed to Israel's survival and security."

Sept. 15. Rabin, after a four-day U.S. visit, says Israel can count on continued U.S. friendship, although the two countries "do not see eye to eye" on all issues. The Israeli premier also proposes troop withdrawals in the Sinai for a state of non-belligerence with Egypt, including the end of Egyptian economic and diplomatic boycotts.

Sept. 18. Addressing the U.N. General Assembly, Ford says the oil-producing nations should define "a global policy on energy to meet the growing need and to do this without imposing unacceptable burdens on the international monetary and trade system."

Sept. 19. The U.N., heeding a request by Arab nations, slates a debate on the Palestine question.

Sept. 21. Meeting in Cairo, the Palestine Liberation Organization (PLO), Egypt and Syria recognize the PLO as the sole representative of the Palestinian people.

Sept. 23. Ford, speaking to the World Energy Conference in Detroit, Mich., says that exorbitant oil prices threaten worldwide depression and the breakdown of international order and safety. ,

Sept. 26. The shah of Iran turns down Ford's bid for lower oil prices.

Oct. 9. Israeli troops prevent at least 5,000 Israelis from establishing new settlements in the Israeli-occupied West Bank of the Jordan.

Oct. 12. About 8,000 Israelis in Jerusalem demonstrate in opposition to the surrender of any West Bank land to Jordan as Kissinger arrives on a new Middle East peace-seeking mission.

Oct. 13. After talks with King Faisal, Kissinger tells reporters he has assurances that Saudi Arabia will take "constructive steps" to lower the world price of oil.

Oct. 14. The U.N. General Assembly overwhelmingly passes a resolution inviting the Palestine Liberation Organization to take part in its debate on the Palestine question.

Oct. 15. Israel denounces the U.N. on the PLO vote.

Oct. 20. Israel says it will seek oil supply guarantees before any withdrawal from occupied Egyptian oil fields at Abu Rudeis in the Sinai.

Oct. 23. The U.N. extends its peacekeeping force in the Sinai for six months.

Oct. 28. The 20 Arab League heads of state in a summit meeting at Rabat, Morocco, recognize unanimously the PLO as the "sole legitimate representative of the Palestinian people on any liberated Palestinian territory." Hussein agrees to honor the PLO's claim to negotiate for the West Bank.

Nov. 4. King Hussein says Jordan will rewrite its constitution to exclude the West Bank from Jordan and that it is "totally inconceivable" that Jordan and a Palestinian state could form a federation.

Nov. 5. An estimated 100,000 persons demonstrate in New York City over the U.N. invitation to Palestine Liberation Organization leader Yasir Arafat.

Nov. 9. The Israeli pound is devalued by 43 per cent and other austerity measures are instituted to cope with economic woes brought on by the 1973 war.

Nov. 12. The United States and Algeria renew diplomatic ties severed during the 1967 war.

Nov. 13. Addressing the U.N. General Assembly, Arafat says the PLO goal is "one democratic [Palestinian] state where Christian, Jew and Moslem live in justice, equality and fraternity." In rebuttal, Israeli delegate Yosef Tekoah asserts the Arafat proposal would mean destruction of Israel and its replacement by an Arab state.

Nov. 20. UNESCO, by a 64-27 vote in Paris, adopts a resolution cutting off annual financial aid to Israel because of its "persistence in altering the historical features of Jerusalem."

Nov. 22. The U.N. General Assembly approves a resolution recognizing the right of the Palestinian people to independence and sovereignty and giving the PLO observer status at the U.N.

Dec. 1. Israel President Ephraim Katzir says Israel has the capacity to produce atomic weapons and will do so if needed.

Dec. 13. OPEC countries, meeting in Vienna, announce an oil price boost of 38 cents a barrel, effective Jan. 1, 1975, and to continue to Oct. 1, 1975.

Dec. 17. Israeli Defense Minister Shimon Peres charges that 3,000 Soviet soldiers are in Syria, manning ground-to-air missiles.

Dec. 30. Soviet leader Brezhnev calls off his January visit to Egypt, Syria and Iraq. No official reason is given. Speculation ranges from poor health to serious diplomatic differences between Cairo and Moscow.

Dec. 31. The *London Times* reports Libya has quietly ended its 14-month-old oil embargo against the United States.

1975

Jan. 1. Some 1,000 Egyptian industrial workers stage Cairo riots in protest against soaring prices and low wages.

Jan. 2. In a *Business Week* interview, Kissinger warns that the United States might use force in the Middle East "to prevent the strangulation of the industrialized world" by Arab oil producers. His remarks arouse angry world reaction.

Jan. 6. At the U.N., Lebanon charges Israel with 423 acts of aggression in the past month. These include border crossings made by Israel to wipe out guerrilla forces in South Lebanon.

Jan. 9. Saudi Arabia agrees to buy 60 American F-5 jets for $750-million.

Jan. 14. King Faisal begins a tour of Syria, Jordan and Egypt, pledging Saudi Arabia's oil wealth to the struggle against Israel.

Jan. 23. The Pentagon announces the Israeli purchase of 200 Lance missiles, to be armed with conventional warheads but capable of carrying nuclear ones. Israel also asks for $2-billion in U.S. military and economic aid.

Feb. 7. At the conclusion of a Paris meeting, the International Energy Agency of oil-consuming nations tentatively agrees on plans to continue the search for new fuel sources, to reduce their dependence on Arab oil and to eventually force down the price of petroleum.

Feb. 18. The shah of Iran says he will send additional oil to Israel if Israel cedes Abu Rudeis oil fields to Egypt in a general peace settlement. His offer comes after a meeting with Kissinger, who visited several Middle East countries seeking "a framework for new negotiations."

Feb. 18. Egypt confirms it is getting Soviet arms, including MIG-23 fighters, from the Soviet Union for the first time since the 1973 war, but Foreign Minister Ismail Fahmy says the weapons do not replace losses of that war and that Egypt will not return to the Geneva conference until they are replaced.

Feb. 21. The U.N. Commission on Human Rights passes resolutions condemning Israel for carrying out the "deliberate destruction" of Quenitra, a Syrian city in the Golan Heights, and for "desecrating" Moslem and Christian shrines.

Feb. 26. A U.S. Senate subcommittee publishes a list of 1,500 U.S. firms and organizations boycotted by Saudi Arabia because of links to Israel. In conjunction, the Anti-Defamation League of B'nai B'rith charges that two U.S. agencies and six private companies had violated civil rights laws by discriminating against Jews in order to do business with Arab states. President Ford calls such alleged discrimination "repugnant to American principles" and promises a probe.

March 5. Eighteen persons, including six non-Israeli tourists, are slain when eight Palestinian guerrillas seize a shorefront hotel in Tel Aviv. Israeli troops kill seven attackers and capture the other.

March 5. Iraq and Iran agree to end their long-standing dispute over frontiers, navigational claims and Iranian supply of the Kurdish rebellion in north Iraq.

March 7. Baghdad launches a major military offensive against the Kurds, who seek total autonomy.

March 8. In a new round of shuttle diplomacy, Kissinger seeks further disengagement in the Sinai.

March 22. Kissinger suspends his efforts to draw Israel and Egypt into new accords, calling the breakdown "a sad day for America." Obstacles include the fate of Israeli-held Abu Rudeis oil fields, Mitla and Gidi passes and an Egyptian pledge of non-belligerency.

March 22. The Kurdish rebellion collapses in Iraq. Rebel leader Mustafa al-Barzani flees into Iran.

March 24. After the breakdown of the Kissinger mission, Ford announces a total Middle East policy reassessment.

March 25. Saudi King Faisal is shot to death by his nephew, Prince Faisal Ibn Musaed. Crown Prince Khalid becomes new king. Prince Fahd is named heir apparent. The royal family says the assassin is deranged and acted alone.

April 13. Six days of fighting breaks out in Beirut between the rightist Christian Phalangist Party militia and Palestinian guerrillas, leaving 120 dead and 200 wounded.

May 5. The United States announces a $100-million sale of Hawk surface-to-air missiles to Jordan.

May 15. Criticized for his handling of the Lebanese riots in April, Premier Rashid al-Solh resigns.

May 17. Nine Lebanese children die from the explosion of a shell left over from an Israeli raid on a town.

May 19. The resumption of new Beirut clashes kills 130 persons.

May 19. Lebanese President Suleiman Franjieh appoints a military cabinet, which quits in three days, in an attempt to restore order in Beirut.

May 28. Rashid Karami is appointed Lebanese premier, promising an end to the bloody Christian-Moslem strife over the Palestinian refugee question.

June 2. At the end of a two-day conference with Egyptian President Sadat in Salzburg, Austria, President Ford says, "The United States will not tolerate stagnation in our efforts for a negotiated settlement."

June 2. During the Ford-Sadat parley, Israel orders partial withdrawal of its limited forces in the Sinai in response to reopening of the Suez Canal. Sadat cautiously hails the Israeli gesture as a step toward peace.

June 3. Syria agrees to release additional water from behind a dam on the Euphrates River, ending a bitter dispute with Iraq, which had claimed a severe water shortage.

June 5. The Suez Canal reopens after an eight-year closure to commercial shipping. President Sadat leads a ceremonial convoy of ships through the waterway to mark the opening.

June 5. Civil strife ends in Beirut with the dismantling of barricades and roadblocks.

June 11. Israeli Premier Rabin begins five days of talks in Washington with Ford and Kissinger. They agree on renewing efforts to negotiate another limited Israeli-Egyptian accord in the Sinai.

June 18. Prince Faisal Ibn Musaed is beheaded in Riyadh, Saudi Arabia, for the March 25 assassination of his uncle, King Faisal.

June 23. New fighting breaks out and continues for 10 days in Beirut between the right-wing Christian Phalangist Party and the left-wing Moslem Progressive Socialist supporters of the Palestinian guerrillas. At least 280 persons are killed and 700 are wounded.

June 29. A U.S. Army officer, Col. Ernest R. Morgan, is kidnaped in Beirut by radical Palestinian terrorists who threaten to kill him unless the United States pays a ransom.

July 1. Another truce is proclaimed in Beirut. Premier Rashid Karami, appointed May 28, forms a "salvation cabinet," which includes all major Moslem and Christian groups except the warring Socialists and Phalangists.

July 4. A Palestinian terrorist bomb explodes in Jerusalem's Zion Square, killing 14 Israelis and wounding 78.

July 7. Israel retaliates for the Jerusalem bombing by launching a sea and ground attack on suspected Palestinian bases in south Lebanon, killing 13 persons and destroying many buildings.

July 7. President Sadat releases 2,000 Egyptian prisoners convicted of trying to overthrow the late President Nasser, as a wave of anti-Nasser commentary runs through the Egyptian press.

July 8. Egypt, Israel and Secretary Kissinger deny world rumors that new Sinai accords are imminent.

July 11. Col. Morgan is released unharmed in Lebanon by his Palestinian abductors, who say he is freed because he is black and that blacks seldom obtain such high rank in the U.S. Army. The State Department says his release is secured without concessions to the kidnapers.

July 15. Egypt avows it will not renew the U.N. forces mandate in the Sinai unless progress toward peace is made, and accuses Israel of exploiting the state of "no war, no peace" to perpetuate its Sinai occupation.

July 20. In Cairo, King Khalid ends his first tour as Saudi Arabia's sovereign by loaning Egypt $600-million.

July 23. A senior Egyptian official denounces Israeli Premier Rabin's call for direct Egyptian-Israeli talks as secret U.S.-led negotiations for a new Sinai accord mount.

July 24. The U.N. Security Council approves a three-month extension of an emergency force in the Sinai after Egypt drops opposition to renewal of the mission.

July 25. Rabin terms Egypt's new disengagement proposal "substantially not acceptable," but better than the one in March, when Kissinger's shuttle diplomacy collapsed. In addressing an Arab-Socialist Union congress, Sadat says it does not matter whether or not a certain step in negotiations succeeds or fails, because "our armed forces are ready."

July 28. The Ford administration informs Congress it is deferring plans to sell Jordan 14 Hawk antiaircraft missile batteries. The action is taken after Congress, which has power to veto the sale, shows signs of balking over the number of Hawks in the arms package. Reacting angrily, King Hussein says Jordan will seek weapons elsewhere unless he can buy all 14 batteries.

Aug. 1. At a summit meeting in Kampala, Uganda, heads of member nations of the Organization of African Unity refuse to adopt an Arab-backed policy proposal calling for Israel's suspension from the United Nations.

Aug. 17. The Israeli cabinet endorses the Rabin stand on new Sinai negotiations, paving the way for new direct negotiations by Kissinger. Cairo also approves of new Kissinger mediation.

Aug. 21. Kissinger arrives in Israel to begin a new round of shuttle diplomacy. He is met by nationwide demonstrations by Israelis who dislike his brand of diplomacy and fear the projected agreement. At Tel Aviv airport, Kissinger says, "the gap in negotiations has been substantially narrowed by concessions on both sides."

Aug. 22. Reports indicate Israel wants written assurance for U.S.-Israeli joint consultations in the event of Soviet intervention in the Middle East.

Aug. 22. King Hussein concludes a 5-day visit to Syria and both countries announce a "supreme command" to co-ordinate foreign policy, information and military affairs.

Aug. 24. An Israeli official says agreement has been reached on setting up early warning installations, to be manned partly by American technicians, in the Sinai, thus clearing away one last major obstacle to new accords.

Aug. 25. Arab nations stop short of calling directly for Israeli expulsion from the U.N. at a ministerial conference of 108 nonaligned nations in Lima, Peru.

Aug. 28. A senior official with the Kissinger party in Jerusalem says implementation of a new Sinai agreement hinges on approval by Congress of the use of American civilian technicians to man Sinai monitoring posts.

Aug. 30. Egypt joins Israel in asking that Congress approve the stationing of American technicians.

Sept. 1. In separate ceremonies in Jerusalem and Alexandria, Israeli and Egyptian leaders initial the new Sinai pact. Israel yields to Egyptian demands that it withdraw from Sinai mountain passes and return Abu Rudeis oil fields to Egypt in return for modest Egyptian political concessions. Kissinger initials provisions for stationing of U.S. technicians in the Sinai. Ford asks that Congress approve the new U.S. Middle East role.

Sept. 4. Egypt and Israel sign the agreement at Geneva.

Sept. 5. Syria calls the Sinai pact "strange and shameful" while Zuhayr Muhsin of the PLO calls Sadat a "traitor and conspirator" for signing the accord.

Sept. 8. The U.S. announces talks with Israel on the sale of F-15s and other arms are resuming.

Sept. 11. Egypt closes the PLO's radio station, "Voice of Palestine," which broadcasts from Cairo.

Sept. 11. Israeli jets raid targets in southern Lebanon.

Sept. 16. Four Palestinians, for which the PLO denies responsibility, seize hostages at the Egyptian Embassy in Madrid threatening to blow up the embassy unless Egypt repudiates the Sinai accord.

Sept. 21. Israeli cabinet approves Israel's initiating the second Sinai agreement but delays formal signing until U.S. Congress approves sending U.S. technicians to Sinai.

Sept. 24. Israeli Foreign Minister Allon and Soviet Foreign Minister Gromyko hold 3-hour discussion at U.N.

Sept. 26. France tells U.N. it is willing to participate in military safeguards for a Middle East peace.

Sept. 26. The White House announces U.S. will now consider Egypt's request for limited types of arms.

Oct. 13. President Ford signs a congressional resolution authorizing U.S. technicians for Sinai.

Oct. 15. An Arab League Conference convenes in Cairo to discuss the fighting in Lebanon. Syria, Libya and the PLO boycott the meeting.

Oct. 22. Two USIA officials are kidnaped in Beirut.

Oct. 23. U.N. Security Council votes to extend the peace force in Sinai for one year by a vote of 16 to 0.

Oct. 26. President Sadat and President Ford meet in Washington with Ford emphasizing the U.S. will not "tolerate stagnation or stalemate."

Oct. 28. Sadat urges the U.S. to open a dialogue with the PLO while Egypt and the U.S. sign four economic and cultural exchange agreements.

Oct. 31. France authorizes the PLO to open an office in Paris while urging the PLO "to take a responsible and moderate course."

Nov. 3. PLO delegate Farouk Kaddoumi opens the U.N. General Assembly debate on the Palestinian issue.

Nov. 5. Sadat addresses a joint session of Congress.

Nov. 7. The U.S. says in the General Assembly that it will work for a settlement taking into account the legitimate rights of the Palestinians.

Nov. 8. Britain agrees to sell Egypt $2-billion in military equipment.

Nov. 10. U.N. General Assembly passes resolution defining Zionism as "a form of racism or racial discrimination" on a 72 to 35 vote with 32 abstentions and 3 absences. U.S. Ambassador Daniel Moynihan says, "The United States...does not acknowledge, it will not abide by, it will never acquiesce in this infamous act." Second resolution recognizes Palestinians' right to self-determination and to attend any U.N. Middle East negotiation.

Nov. 10. Israeli Knesset passes resolution rejecting the U.N. resolution on Zionism and indicating Israel will not participate in the Geneva talks if the PLO is ever invited.

Nov. 11. Kissinger states the U.S. will ignore the U.N. resolution on Zionism.

Nov. 12. State Department official Harold Saunders tells a committee of the Congress that "In many ways...the Palestinian dimension of the Arab-Israeli conflict is the heart of the conflict."

Nov. 13. A large bomb explodes in Jerusalem's Zion Square killing 6 persons and wounding 40.

Nov. 16. Syria's Foreign Minister says Syria will "bring down the Sinai agreement even if we have to shed blood for it."

Nov. 16. The Israeli Cabinet expresses considerable criticism of the U.S. State Department for the Saunders statement on the Palestinians.

Nov. 20. CIA Director Colby asserts to Congress that another Middle East war would probably result in 8,000 Israeli casualities.

Nov. 22. U.N. Secretary-General Waldheim arrives in Damascus to begin a Middle East tour.

Dec. 2. Israeli jets attack Palestinian refugee camps in northern and southern Lebanon killing 74 and wounding at least a hundred others.

Dec. 3. The Egyptian Minister of Petroleum announces Egypt will claim more than $2.1-billion for the oil Israel extracted from Sinai.

Dec. 4. U.N. Security Council votes 9 to 3 with 3 abstentions to invite the PLO to participate in debate about Israeli air attacks in Lebanon. PLO is granted speaking privileges of a member nation.

Dec. 5. U.N. General Assembly by 84 to 17 with 27 abstentions passes a resolution condemning Israel's occupation of Arab territories and calling upon all states to refrain from aiding Israel.

Dec. 17. U.N. General Assembly ends session after appointing a Committee on the Exercise of the Inalienable Rights of the Palestinian People.

Dec. 17. UNESCO votes by 36 to 22 with seven abstentions to insert reference to General Assembly resolution condemning Zionism as a form of racism into a draft policy declaration.

Dec. 22. Pope Paul VI appeals to Israel to "recognize the rights and legitimate aspirations" of the Palestinians.

Dec. 26. OPEC headquarters in Vienna are raided by 6 terrorists killing three and taking hostages including Saudi Petroleum Minister Yamani. PLO denounces the attack.

Dec. 26. Iran and Iraq sign a number of good neighbor agreements.

Dec. 31. Egypt reveals that its nonmilitary debt to foreign countries and international organizations is $7-billion.

1976

Jan. 7. Protesting the name "Arab Gulf" rather than Persian Gulf, the Shah reveals Iran's recall of ambassadors from a number of Arab states after word of plans for an "Arabian Gulf News Agency."

Jan. 12. The U.N. Security Council opens its Middle East debate by voting 11 to 1 with 3 abstentions to allow the PLO to participate with speaking rights of a member.

Jan. 12. The Israeli Council for Israeli-Palestinian Peace calls for negotiations with "a recognized and authoritative body of the Palestinian Arab people" which could lead to "establishment of a Palestinian Arab state" alongside Israel.

Jan. 13. Sadat says Egypt will attend a Geneva conference without the Palestinians but would then "fight for the Palestinians to join."

Jan. 28. Rabin addresses a joint meeting of the U.S. Congress ruling out any negotiations with the PLO.

Jan. 29. Rabin and Ford end talks in Washington reportedly with the understanding the U.S. would try to see if the Geneva conference can be convened without the PLO.

Feb. 13. The U.N. Commission on Human Rights votes 23 to 1 with 8 abstentions for a resolution accusing Israel of having committed "war crimes" in the occupied Arab territories. U.S. casts lone "no" vote.

Feb. 15. The Israeli cabinet approves appointment of Shlomo Avineri, a dovish critic of Rabin's policies toward the Palestinian Arabs, to be Director-General of the Foreign Ministry.

Feb. 18. A Syrian mediation team headed by Foreign Minister Kaddum continues efforts to find a solution to the Lebanese crisis.

Feb. 22. The final step in the previous September's Sinai accord is carried out with U.N. personnel turning over the final 89 square miles to Egyptian forces.

Feb. 25. The two American USIA officials kidnaped in Beirut 4 months earlier are released.

March 2. Ford administration informs key congressional leaders it wants to lift arms embargo to Egypt by selling 6 C-130 military transport planes.

March 7. In Cairo, U.S. Treasury Secretary William Simon praises Sadat for liberalizing Egypt's economy and pledges a total of $1.85-billion in U.S. aid for fiscal 1976 and 1977.

March 10. Demonstrations and strikes break out on the occupied West Bank and in East Jerusalem.

March 12. The 44-nation Islamic Conference at the U.N. adopts statement denouncing Israel's systematic policy "to change the status of Jerusalem and gradually obliterate the Moslem and Christian heritage in the Holy City."

March 13. Lebanese President Franjieh is presented with a petition signed by two-thirds of parliament asking him to resign, but he refuses.

March 14. The Shah of Iran warns the U.S. that Iran "can hurt you as badly if not more so than you can hurt us" if the Congress imposes an arms embargo on the Persian Gulf region.

March 14. Senior CIA officials estimate Israel has 10 to 20 nuclear weapons "ready and available for use."

March 19. Israel announces it will participate in Security Council debate on the West Bank disturbances even though the PLO will be represented.

March 23. U.S. Ambassador to the U.N., William Scranton, tells the Security Council the U.S. considers the presence of Israeli settlements in the occupied territories to be "an obstacle to the success of the negotiations for a just and final peace."

March 25. The Security Council in a 14 to 1 vote, the U.S. vetoing the action, deplores Israel's efforts to change the status of Jerusalem, calls on Israel to refrain from measures harming the inhabitants of the occupied territories, and calls for an end to Israeli settlements in the occupied territories.

March 29. West Bank rioting spreads into Israel itself.

March 30. Israeli Arabs hold general strike protesting government land expropriation scheme in Galilee area. Violent clashes with police take place in more than a dozen villages resulting in 6 Arabs killed and more than 70 persons wounded.

March 30. Former Ambassador L. Dean Brown is designated special envoy to Lebanon by the State Department.

April 4. While endorsing police action against Israeli Arabs in Galilee, Israeli cabinet decides to reexamine policy toward Arab citizens.

April 4. Kissinger pledges the U.S. "will never abandon Israel."

April 5. Israel says it is not a nuclear power and will not be the first to introduce nuclear weapons into the Middle East conflict.

April 12. Syrian army begins to cautiously advance into Lebanon.

April 13. Militants and PLO supporters sweep to victory in the voting on the West Bank for new mayors and municipal councilmen. New mayors are elected in 10 of 24 towns and 148 new councilmen are selected leaving only 43 incumbents.

April 18. About 30,000 Israelis march for 2 days through the West Bank under the leadership of Gush Emunim. Arab counter demonstrations in Nablus and Ramallah are broken up.

April 20. Prime Minister Rabin tours Jordan Valley settlements and assures the settlers in the 16 new villages that they are "here to stay for a long time."

April 21. Units of the Palestine Liberation Army (PLA) begin taking up positions in Beirut.

April 27. Arab League states at a meeting of Finance Ministers in Rabat agree to establish an Arab Monetary Fund.

April 28. The Soviet Union calls for resumption of the Geneva conference in two stages with Palestinian partition in each stage.

May 3. A bomb explodes near Zion Square in Jerusalem injuring 30.

May 3. An Arab march from Ramallah to Jerusalem, planned in response to the Gush Emunim march the month before, is prevented by Israeli authorities.

May 4. Former Secretary of Defense Schlesinger says President Ford is undermining American support for Israel by putting undue pressure on Israel to make concessions to the Arabs.

May 8. Several thousand Israelis participate in a demonstration sponsored by the Mapam Party for the ejection of 125 Gush Emunim settlers from Camp Kadum, an illegal settlement in the West Bank.

May 8. Elias Sarkis is elected President of Lebanon. Backers of Raymond Edde boycott the election protesting interference by Syria.

May 19. Israeli Arab protestors at Hebrew University are attacked by Jewish counter demonstrators led by Rabbi Meir Kahane of the Jewish Defense League.

May 19. The U.N. Committee on the Exercise of the Inalienable Rights of the Palestinian People adopts by consensus a set of recommendations stressing the Palestinians' "right to return" to their homeland.

May 23. The head of the largest Jewish women's organization in the U.S., Hadassah, criticizes American Jews "who have taken it upon themselves to publicly criticize certain policies of Israel at this critical juncture."

May 24. Israeli Prime Minister Rabin refuses a request by Israeli Arab leaders to cancel plans to take over Arab land in Galilee and turns down demands for a special inquiry into the Galilee riots of March.

May 25. A suitcase bomb explodes at Ben-Gurion International Airport outside Tel-Aviv.

May 26. The Security Council presents a majority statement deploring Israeli measures altering the demographic character of the occupied territories at the end of its debate on the Middle East. The U.S. disassociates itself from the statement.

May 30. A rally in Paris in support of Israel draws 100,000.

May 31. Egypt asks the Arab League to admit the PLO to full membership.

May 31. Syrian troops numbering 2,000 advance into Lebanon's Akkar Valley in the north.

June 1. An additional 3,000 Syrian troops advance into Lebanon.

June 3. About 300 students seize the Syrian embassy in Cairo to protest Syria's role in Lebanon.

June 7. Egypt announces the PLO will be allowed to resume broadcasting in Cairo.

June 8. Large numbers of additional Syrian forces enter Lebanon.

June 10. Member nations of the Arab League agree to send forces to Lebanon to "replace" the Syrian forces.

June 16. U.S. Ambassador Francis Meloy and Economic Counselor Robert Waring are shot to death on their way to a meeting with President Sarkis in Beirut.

June 18. King Hussein, while visiting Moscow to inquire about possible arms purchases, strongly backs Syrian intervention in Lebanon.

June 19. The U.S. strongly urges all remaining American citizens to leave Lebanon.

June 20. The U.S. evacuates from Lebanon by sea, with the help of the PLO, 263 American and foreign nationals.

June 21. About a thousand Syrian and Libyan troops, vanguard of the Arab League peacekeeping force, arrive in Lebanon.

The State Department confirms a U.S. message, through indirect channels, to the PLO leadership thanking them for their help in the sea evacuation of Western nationals from Beirut.

June 27. A jetliner on its way from Tel Aviv to Paris with 257 persons is hijacked in Athens and taken to Entebbe airport in Uganda the following day.

June 29. West Bank Arab merchants call for a strike to protest the new Israeli value-added tax and the Israeli Treasury decides to postpone imposition of the tax until August 1.

July 2. The seige of Tel al-Zaatar refugee camp near Beirut begins as Christian forces overrun the outer defenses.

July 4. Israeli commandos raid the hijacked airliner at Entebbe airport freeing the 103 remaining hostages.

July 14. The Security Council ends debate on the Israeli Entebbe raid without approving either a resolution condemning the raid or a resolution condemning the hijacking and terrorism.

July 16. The American embassy in Beirut announces closure of all consular services and urges all Americans to leave Lebanon.

July 27. U.S. evacuates 308 American and foreign nationals from Beirut, again with the PLO helping to provide security.

Aug. 28. The PLO announces a general conscription for all Palestinians between ages of 18 and 30.

Aug. 28. Terrorists in Iran kill 3 American employees of the American firm Rockwell International.

Sept. 6. The PLO is unanimously granted full voting membership in the Arab League.

Sept. 7. A report by the Israeli Interior Ministry's Representative in the Northern District of Israel, Yisrael Koenig, is published in the newspaper *Al Hamishmar*. The report predicts an Arab majority in Galilee by 1978 and recommends measures to minimize Arab influence there.

Sept. 15. Syria and Israel open their security fences in the Jawlan region and allow Druze villagers from Syria to visit with relatives from the Israeli occupied areas.

Sept. 17. Israeli Foreign Minister Allon publishes an article in *Foreign Affairs* advocating Israeli withdrawal from most occupied Arab territory and creation of a demilitarized joint Jordanian-Palestinian entity in the West Bank and Gaza Strip.

Sept. 17. President Sadat of Egypt receives over 99 per cent approval for a second 6-year term as President.

Sept. 18. Fighting in Lebanon intensifies on all fronts.

Sept. 23. Elias Sarkis is inaugurated as President of Lebanon before 67 members of the National Assembly.

Sept. 28. PLO leader Yasir Arafat sends an urgent appeal to all Arab heads of state asking for immediate intervention to prevent Syria from "liquidating the Palestinian resistance."

Oct. 1. A public council to advise the Ministerial Committee on Israeli Arabs is established with 54 Arabs and 46 Jews.

Oct. 6. France and Iran sign a nuclear cooperation agreement under which France will build two nuclear reactors for Iran.

Oct. 11. During the heat of the Presidential campaign President Ford agrees to sell Israel military equipment previously not offered for sale.

Oct. 14. Lebanon's U.N. representative tells the General Assembly that "the Palestinian revolution" and its supporters caused the civil war in Lebanon.

Oct. 16. President Sadat is sworn into office for a second six-year term.

Oct. 18. Arab leaders of Saudi Arabia, Kuwait, Syria, Egypt, Lebanon, and the PLO, meeting in Riyadh, sign a peace plan calling for a cease-fire and a 30,000-man peacekeeping force under the command of Lebanese President Sarkis.

Oct. 25. All members of the Arab League, meeting in Cairo, approve the Riyadh agreement except for Iraq and Libya.

Nov. 1. The Security Council decides, over U.S. opposition, to allow the PLO to participate in the debate on the occupied territories.

Nov. 2. The Israeli government raises prices of most basic staple foods and services by about 20 per cent in an effort to gradually abolish subsidies for essential foods.

Nov. 8. UNESCO's general conference votes by 70 to 0 with 14 abstentions to let each regional group select its own members, thus making it possible again for Israel to be included in the European group.

Nov. 8. An International Symposium on Zionism opens in Baghdad.

Nov. 11. The Security Council, in a consensus statement, deplores the establishment of Israeli settlements in occupied Arab territories and declares "invalid" the annexation of eastern Jerusalem by Israel.

Nov. 11. Sadat announces that the three political groupings that had participated in the election will now be called parties, though they will still come under the overall umbrella of the Arab Socialist Union (ASU).

Nov. 15. Syrian peacekeeping forces take up positions in both Christian and Moslem sections of Beirut.

Nov. 17. OPEC decides to increase aid to non-oil-producing counties by $800-million.

Nov. 18. The PLO formally registers with the Justice Department in a step towards opening an office in Washington.

Nov. 19. Beirut's airport reopens.

Nov. 22. In Israel, former Army Chief of Staff Yigal Yadin announces formation of a new party, the "Democratic Movement."

Nov. 22. UNESCO votes by 61 to 5 with 28 abstentions to condemn Israel's educational and cultural policies in the occupied Arab territories.

Israel is restored to full membership in UNESCO.

Nov. 23. The General Assembly of the U.N. votes 118 to 2 with 2 abstentions for a resolution calling on Israel to halt resettlement of Palestinian refugees in Gaza and to return all refugees to their camps.

Nov. 23. Israeli forces are deployed along the Lebanese border following reported movements of Syrian peacekeeping forces toward the border.

Nov. 24. U.N. General Assembly approves by 90 to 16 with 30 abstentions the report of the Committee on the Inalienable Rights of the Palestinian People proclaiming right of Palestinian Arab refugees to establish their own state and reclaim former properties in Israel.

Nov. 25. Iraq and Syria withdraw most forces from their common frontier.

Dec. 9. U.N. General Assembly votes by 122 to 2 with 8 abstentions for a resolution calling for reconvening the Geneva peace conference by March 1.

Dec. 15. A general strike is held by Arabs in the West Bank and Gaza to protest the value-added tax.

Dec. 15. Arab League special envoy Ghassan Tueni meets with U.S. Under Secretary of State for Political Affairs Philip Habib on U.S. economic aid to Lebanon.

Dec. 15. Beirut's port reopens.

Dec. 17. OPEC announces that 11 members will increase oil prices by 10 per cent on Jan. 1 and a further 5 per cent on July 1, 1977. Saudi Arabia and the UAE announce only a 5 per cent price rise for Jan. 1 thus setting up two prices within OPEC.

Dec. 19. Rabin ousts the National Religious Party from his coalition government 5 days after the NRP abstained on a vote of no-confidence in the Knesset.

Dec. 20. Rabin resigns and new elections are called.

Dec. 21. Egypt and Syria announce formation of a "united political leadership" and agree to study the possibility of future union.

1977

Jan. 2. Egypt permits the Abie Nathan "peace ship" from Israel to proceed through the Suez Canal.

Jan. 2. Israeli Council for Israeli-Palestinian Peace publishes what is said to be a joint statement with the PLO calling for Zionist and Palestinian states to coexist peaceably.

Jan. 3. Press censorship begins in Lebanon.
Rabin forms temporary government until elections.

Jan. 5. Israeli Knesset votes to dissolve and calls election for May.

Jan. 11. French authorities free PLO terrorist Abu Daoud after a judicial hearing rejecting West German and Israeli extradition claims.

Jan. 15. Sadat and Hussein both call for a separate Palestinian delegation at the Geneva peace conference.

Jan. 18. Thousands of Egyptian workers demonstrate against price rises.

Jan. 19. Demonstrations and rioting continue in Egypt and Sadat cancels the price increases. At least 65 persons are reported killed in clashes with police.

Jan. 25. Lebanon lifts press censorship for outgoing dispatches but retains it for domestic publications.

Jan. 26. Egypt bans demonstrations and strikes.

Feb. 7. U.S. blocks sale of Israeli Kfir jets with American jet engines to Ecuador.

Feb. 10. In a referendum on Sadat's decree outlawing demonstrations and strikes, 99 per cent vote to approve, according to the government.

Feb. 12. About 400 students demonstrate in Cairo against the new law banning demonstrations.

Feb. 15. On his first international mission as Secretary of State, Cyrus R. Vance arrives in Israel on his first tour of the Middle East.

Feb. 15. The U.N. Human Rights Commission adopts a resolution accusing Israel of practicing "torture" and "pillaging of archeological and cultural property" in occupied Arab territories.

Feb. 20. Biweekly bus service begins between Haifa and points in southern Lebanon.

Feb. 22. By a vote of 1,445 to 1,404 the Israeli Labor Party selects Yitzhak Rabin over Shimon Peres as its candidate for prime minister.

Feb. 22. A delegation of Israeli Arabs—the first ever to visit an Arab country—returns after a 5-day visit to Amman.

Feb. 24. Jordan and the PLO agree, in their first talks since 1970, on forming some kind of "link."

Feb. 25. In exchange for a real peace agreement, Israeli Labor Party platform calls for return of some West Bank territory to Jordan.

Feb. 27. Israeli army halts an attempt by Gush Emunim to establish another illegal West Bank settlement.

Feb. 28. Carter administration comes out in opposition to secondary and tertiary aspects of the Arab boycott against Israel.

March 6. George Habash tells reporters that the Popular Front for the Liberation of Palestine (PFLP) and 3 other "rejectionist" groups will break from the PLO if the Palestine National Council decides to go to the Geneva conference or to recognize Israel.

March 7. Foreign Ministers from 60 African and Arab countries meet in Cairo for an unprecedented Afro-Arab summit conference. Saudi Arabia immediately pledges $1-billion in aid to black Africa.

March 7. President Carter welcomes Israeli Prime Minister Rabin to Washington and says Israel should have "defensible borders."

March 9. Yasir Arafat and King Hussein meet in Cairo publicly for the first time since "Black September" in 1970.

March 9. President Carter distinguishes between "defensible borders" (temporarily extending beyond Israel's sovereign frontiers) and "secure borders" (the eventual permanent and recognized borders).

March 9. Ambassadors from Egypt, Iran and Pakistan play a major role in negotiating the release of hostages being held by the Hanafi Muslims in the B'nai B'rith and two other buildings in Washington.

March 12. In a report to Congress on human rights conditions in 82 countries receiving U.S. aid, the State Department criticizes Israel's treatment of the Arabs in the occupied territories.

March 12. The Palestine National Council opens in Cairo and President Sadat pledges that Egypt "will not cede a single inch of Arab land."

March 15. The Israeli newspaper *Ha'aretz* reports that Prime Minister Rabin's wife has an illegal bank account in Washington.

March 16. At a Clinton, Massachusetts town meeting President Carter—the first American President ever to do so—endorses the idea of a Palestinian "homeland."

March 16. Leftist leader Kamal Jumblatt is assassinated near Beirut.

March 17. A PLO official shakes President Carter's hand at a reception following Carter's U.N. speech.

May 20. Prime Minister Rabin admits that he maintained an illegal Washington bank account with his wife.

May 20. The Palestine National Council concludes its nine-day 13th session in Cairo by adopting a 15-point political declaration by a vote of 194 to 13.

May 21. Samuel W. Lewis is revealed as President Carter's choice for Ambassador to Israel.

May 27. Arab League approves a six-month extension of the Arab peacekeeping force in Lebanon at the request of Lebanese President Sarkis.

May 30. Israel admits secretly holding two Germans and three Arabs who are accused of attempting to shoot down an El Al plane in Nairobi.

April 3. Kuwait concludes its first arms deal with the USSR.

April 4. President Sadat visits Washington and tells President Carter that the Palestinian question is the "core and crux" of the Arab-Israeli dispute.

April 5. About 15,000 Gush Emunim marchers march on the West Bank.

April 7. Arafat and Communist Party Secretary Brezhnev meet publicly in Moscow for the first time.

April 7. Prime Minister Rabin withdraws from the top spot on the Labor Party ticket with elections only 6 weeks away.

April 8. Sadat says relations with Israel could be normalized within 5 years, according to U.S. officials.

April 10. Shimon Peres is selected to head Labor Party ticket in Israeli election.

April 11. Prime Minister Rabin is fined $1,500 for his role in maintaining an illegal bank account in Washington.

April 13. While the fighting continues in southern Lebanon, the State Department reveals it is deeply involved in the diplomatic effort to stabilize southern Lebanon.

April 14. Cairo bars Libyan citizens from leaving Egypt in apparent retaliation for a similar restriction placed on Egyptians and others in Libya.

April 16. Egypt delivers to the Arab League a note accusing Libya of plotting against Sudan, seizing portions of Chad, and harboring "international criminals."

April 17. Mrs. Leah Rabin, wife of Prime Minister Rabin, pleads guilty to maintaining an illegal bank account and is fined $27,000.

April 17. A Library of Congress report urges the U.S. to seek a more secure airlift route to the Middle East.

April 22. Prime Minister Rabin begins an extended vacation and turns over the day-to-day affairs of the government to Shimon Peres.

April 25. King Hussein visits Washington for talks with President Carter.

April 27. Moscow accuses Egypt of attempting to provoke armed clashes between Egypt and Libya. Libya is reported planning to expel some of the 200,000 Egyptians working in Libya.

May 1. Egypt sends pilots to Zaire.

May 3. The White House announces a compromise between Jewish groups and business groups regarding anti-boycott legislation pending in the Congress.

May 5. For the first time, Syrian President Assad endorses the idea of demilitarized zones between Israel and the Arab states.

May 8. The U.S. State Department accuses Libya, Iraq, South Yemen, and Somalia of actively supporting terrorism.

May 9. President Carter and Syrian President Assad meet in Geneva to discuss Middle East peace prospects.

May 9. Saudi Crown Prince Fahd says the PLO would be likely to recognize Israel in the context of an overall peace settlement.

May 12. President Carter pledges "special treatment" for Israel in regard to arms request and co-production of advanced U.S. weaponry. Carter again calls for a Palestinian homeland and says "there's a chance that the Palestinians might make moves to recognize the right of Israel to exist."

May 12. Bahrain announces that after June 30 the U.S. base there will be downgraded to a "facility."

May 13. A serious fire in a major Saudi oil field is finally extinguished.

May 15. Israel reveals a new 56-ton tank with armor impenetrable to existing Arab shells.

May 17. Menachem Begin's right-wing Likud Party unexpectedly wins a plurality in the Israeli election.

May 18. Secretary of State Vance and Soviet Foreign Minister Gromyko begin several days of talks in Geneva about the Middle East and about nuclear arms limitations.

May 19. The leaders of Saudi Arabia, Syria and Egypt hold talks in Riyadh to "create a cohesive Arab position" in light of Begin's victory in Israel.

May 19. Begin calls for many new Jewish settlements in Israeli-occupied territories.

May 21. Talks in Baghdad between U.S. and Iraqi officials lead to speculation of resumed relations.

May 24. Saudi Arabian Crown Prince Fahd begins talks with Carter in Washington.

May 24. Sudan's President Nimeri asks for U.S. aid after expelling Soviet military personnel.

May 25. Moshe Dayan agrees to serve in a Begin government as Foreign Minister.

May 26. At a news conference, President Carter says the Palestinians should be compensated for their losses.

May 27. Lebanese rightist leaders declare the 1969 Cairo agreement invalid and call the Palestinian presence in Lebanon illegal.

May 27. Moshe Dayan resigns from the Labor Party due to the furor over his acceptance of the role of Foreign Minister in the government being formed by Menachem Begin.

May 30. Saudi Arabia declares that within one year all banks will be under majority control of Saudi nationals.

June 5. Businesses close in 3 West Bank towns to protest 10 years of Israeli occupation.

June 5. Acting Prime Minister Rabin tells the cabinet that Israel is strong enough to resist U.S. pressures to force Israel "to accept views inimical to our security."

June 7. President Katzair formally asks Menachem Begin to form Israel's next government.

June 10. The anti-boycott bill passes both Houses of Congress.

June 10. Menachem Begin's representative, Samuel Katz, meets with Carter's national security adviser, Zbigniew Brzezinski, preparing the way for Begin's expected visit in July.

June 10. The PLO signs an addition to the Geneva war convention that prohibits terrorism against civilians.

June 11. Egyptian Foreign Minister Fahmy and Soviet Foreign Minister Gromyko complete two days of talks in Moscow aimed at improving Egyptian-Soviet relations.

June 16. The U.S. delegation and others walk out of an African-sponsored U.N. gathering which excluded Israel.

June 17. Vice-President Walter Mondale delivers a major speech on the Middle East comprehensively outlining the Carter administration's views and emphasizing a three-point peace plan: return to approximately the 1967 borders, creation of a Palestinian homeland probably linked to Jordan, and establishment of complete peace and normal relations between the countries in the area.

June 19. The London *Sunday Times* in a major report charges that "Israeli interrogators routinely ill-treat and often torture Arab prisoners."

June 19. Two religious parties agree to join Begin's Likud Party in forming the next Israeli government.

June 21. The Labor Party wins a decisive victory in the Histadrut elections in Israel.

June 21. Menachem Begin officially becomes Prime Minister of Israel after winning a 63 to 53 vote of confidence in the new Knesset.

June 22. President Carter signs the bill aimed at limiting participation of American firms in the Arab boycott of Israel.

June 23. In his first major speech as Prime Minister, Begin announces that Israel will not "under any circumstances" relinquish the West Bank or allow the creation of a Palestinian state west of the Jordan River.

June 25. President Carter recommends the sale of an additional $115-million in arms to Israel.

June 26. Sixty-six Vietnamese refugees arrive in Israel and are granted asylum.

June 27. The State Department issues a statement on the Middle East warning that "no territories, including the West Bank, are automatically excluded from the items to be negotiated." Israel's government is infuriated by the timing as well as the substance of this statement, coming just weeks before Prime Minister Begin's scheduled visit to Washington.

June 29. The nine members of the European Economic Community issue a Middle East statement endorsing the idea of a Palestinian "homeland."

June 29. Nine top Democratic senators release a letter to President Carter giving him "strong support in the Senate for your efforts to help Israel and the Arab nations secure a genuine and lasting peace."

July 3. An extremist Moslem group in Cairo kidnaps a former cabinet minister who three days later is found murdered. The demand had been for the release of 30 imprisoned colleagues of the terrorists.

July 3. Saudi Arabia and the UAE raise their price for oil 5 per cent bringing them back in line with the other OPEC countries.

July 3. Israel "emphatically denies" with a detailed rebuttal the London *Sunday Times* torture story.

July 6. Carter holds an hour-long White House meeting with 53 prominent American Jewish leaders to reassure them of his commitment to Israel.

July 6. Carter again refuses to allow Israel to sell Ecuador 24 Kfir fighters.

July 10. King Hussein and President Sadat agree in Cairo to an "explicit link" between Jordan and the Palestinians.

July 12. The United States' 1977 contribution to the U.N. Relief and Works Agency's program of Palestinian refugee aid totals $48.7-million, after an additional pledge of $22-million.

July 12. Iran's and Saudi Arabia's leading oil officials, attending OPEC's first ministerial meeting this year, advocate, in view of the world economy, a freeze on crude oil prices during 1978.

July 12. President Carter notes his personal preference "that the Palestinian entity...should be tied in with Jordan and not independent."

July 13. It is reported that the PLO is seriously considering forming a government-in-exile.

July 13. A spokesman for the Palestinian "rejection front" threatens any Arab leader who signs a peace agreement with Israel with assassination.

July 13. President Sadat, speaking to American congressmen, expresses Egypt's willingness to establish diplomatic and trade relations with Israel within five years of signing a peace agreement.

July 15. U.S. congressmen report that PLO leader Yasir Arafat told them the PLO is prepared to settle for a West Bank-Gaza Strip state and to coexist with Israel.

July 16. Speaking live over Cairo radio, Sadat announces he is willing to accept Israel as a Middle East nation after a peace treaty is signed.

July 16. President Sadat reveals that Saudi Arabia has agreed to finance Egypt's military development for the next five years.

July 17. The new Israeli government announces a major austerity program reducing food subsidies and trimming the defense budget.

July 19. Egypt returns to Israel with full military honors 19 bodies of Israeli soldiers killed during the 1973 war.

July 20. Israeli Prime Minister Begin visits Washington and confers with President Carter, who after their meeting states, "I believe that we've laid the groundwork now...that will lead to the Geneva Conference in October."

July 20. At a news conference telecast live to Israel from Washington Begin reveals his "peace plan" which is loudly criticized by all Arab parties.

July 20. A Beirut newspaper reveals that William Scranton met in London in June with a high-ranking PLO official. Speculation is that Scranton was acting on behalf of the Carter administration.

July 21. Egypt and Libya have a major military clash on their common border.

July 22. Egyptian planes continue bombing Libya and Sadat vows to teach Qaddafi "a lesson he will never forget."

July 22. The PLO becomes the first non-state to have full membership in any U.N. body when it is accepted as a member of the Economic Commission for Western Asia of ECOSOC.

July 22. The Carter Administration announces approval of a $250-million arms package for Israel.

July 25. The home of the Executive Director of the American Israel Public Affairs Committee (AIPAC—Israel's most important lobbying body in Washington) is bombed. Morris Amitay and his family are not injured but the home is greatly damaged.

July 27. The Israeli government legalizes three formerly unapproved settlements in heavily-populated areas of the West Bank.

July 27. Secretary of State Vance and President Carter indicate their disapproval of the Israeli government's legalization of the West Bank settlements.

July 28. President Carter states at a press conference that "The major stumbling block" to reconvening the Geneva Conference "is the participation...by the Palestinian representative." He offers to discuss this matter with the PLO and to possibly advocate a Palestinian role at Geneva if the PLO will agree to recognize Israel and to negotiate on the basis of U.N. Resolutions 242 and 338.

July 31. Secretary of State Vance leaves for nearly a two-week trip to the Middle East in an attempt to narrow the differences between Israel and the Arabs and to find a way to proceed with diplomacy either at Geneva or through some other mechanism.

Aug. 1. Secretary of State Vance confers with President Sadat in Cairo to push resumption of the Geneva Peace Conference on the Middle East. Sadat proposes a pre-Geneva meeting of Egyptian and Israeli foreign ministers.

Aug. 2. The Carter administration announces the suspension of the proposed sale to Iran of seven Airborne Warning and Control Systems planes (AWACS), because of congressional opposition to the deal.

Aug. 3. Prime Minister Begin gives his support to the proposed meeting of Arab and Israeli foreign ministers and calls President Sadat's position "a very positive development in the Egyptian attitude."

Aug. 4. Syrian President Assad tells a news conference he opposes President Sadat's plan for a preliminary conference and sees no chance of reconvening the Geneva talks in 1977.

Aug. 4. Israeli troops attack a Palestinian guerrilla group that infiltrates the Jordan Valley and kill three of the terrorists. Israeli officials accuse the PLO of attempting to disrupt Secretary Vance's visit to the Middle East.

Aug. 5-6. Secretary Vance continues his Middle East shuttle holding meetings in Amman with Jordan's King Hussein.

Aug. 7. PLO spokesman Mahmoud Labady suggests the PLO might shift its stand and agree to recognize Israel if U.N. Resolution 242 is modified to include discussion of "the legitimate rights of the Palestinians."

Aug. 9. Secretary Vance arrives in Jerusalem and encounters strong opposition to the PLO's suggestion that it may accept U.N. Resolution 242 and become a partner in the Geneva peace talks.

Aug. 10. Secretary Vance officially ends his peace mission with a round of talks with Israeli officials. Leaving Tel Aviv, Vance says both sides remain far apart on the basic issues that have to be resolved before the Geneva talks can resume.

Aug. 14. The Israeli government announces it will extend "equal rights, the same as those enjoyed by residents of Israel" to Arabs in the occupied West Bank and Gaza Strip. Israeli Prime Minister Begin denies the move is the beginning of "annexation" of the territories.

Aug. 14. Secretary Vance briefs President Carter on his two-week peace mission to the Middle East. Carter announces he will confer with the foreign ministers of Israel and the Arab nations when they attend the opening meeting of the U.N. General Assembly in New York in September.

Aug. 17. The Israeli government approves plans for three new settlements in the West Bank. U.S. and Palestinian leaders call the action illegal, citing a Geneva convention ruling barring civilian settlements on occupied land.

Aug. 23. In a news conference President Carter reiterates the administration's position that Israel's plan for new settlements in the West Bank are "illegal" and "an unnecessary obstacle to peace."

Aug. 24. Major fighting between Christian forces and Palestinian guerrillas continues in southern Lebanon. *Time* magazine reports heavy Israeli military involvement in support of the Christians.

Aug. 25. Violence hits Beirut when a bomb explodes in a marketplace, killing three persons and wounding 12.

Aug. 25-26. The Central Council of the Palestine Liberation Organization meets in Damascus, Syria and denounces U.S. efforts toward peace in the Middle East. The PLO underscores its objection to Resolution 242 as the basis for a settlement in the Middle East, calling for an agreement that recognizes the Palestinian people's right to independence and sovereignty.

Aug. 26. Syrian President Assad declares he would sign a peace treaty with Israel, but would oppose normalizing relations until Israel changes its "expansionist policies."

Aug. 30. PLO leader Yasir Arafat hits U.S peace efforts while meeting with Soviet Foreign Minister Andrei Gromyko in Moscow, saying resolution of the Palestinian problem is the "cornerstone of any Middle East settlement."

Aug. 31. Israel agrees to permit UNESCO to investigate the "cultural freedom" of Arabs living in Israeli-occupied lands.

Sept. 2. Israel discloses plans to resettle two million citizens along a strip of occupied land stretching from the Golan Heights to the Sinai Peninsula.

Sept. 3-6. Foreign ministers of the Arab League meet in Cairo and condemn Israel's settlement policies.

Sept. 12. The U.S. State Department unveils a new policy emphasizing that "the Palestinians must be involved in the peace-making process."

Sept. 13. Palestinians and Egyptians praise the U.S statement. Cairo calls the action "a new chance for the PLO to put their trust in the U.S. peace effort."

Sept. 13. The twin sister of the Shah of Iran, Princess Ashraf Pahlevi, escapes an assassination attempt by gunmen while traveling to a resort on the French Riviera.

Sept. 16. Israeli forces provide air and artillery support to Christian militia forces battling Palestinian guerrillas during renewed fighting in southern Lebanon.

Sept. 18. The American Palestine Committee in the U.S. releases CIA documents suggesting Israel deliberately attacked the U.S. Navy ship *Liberty* during the 1967 Arab-Israeli war. Thirty-four Americans died in the attack. A CIA spokesmen calls the documents "unevaluated information."

Sept. 19. U.S voices concern over intensified fighting in southern Lebanon and presses efforts to establish a cease-fire in that region.

Sept. 19. Israeli Foreign Minister Moshe Dayan submits his country's proposal for a Middle East peace agreement during White House talks with President Carter and U.S. officials. The proposal contains provisions for internal autonomy and self-government for Arabs in the occupied West Bank.

Sept. 21. President Carter and Secretary of State Vance meet with Egyptian Foreign Minister Ismail Fahmy as part of the pre-Geneva peace talks. Fahmy reports Arab countries are prepared "for the first time to accept Israel as a Middle East country to live in peace...in secure borders."

Sept. 25. Israel accepts U.S plan for reconvening the Geneva peace conference. The plan calls for a unified Arab delegation, including Palestinians, at the talks. Egypt, Syria and Jordan also approve the plan but reject Israel's conditions regarding Palestinian participation. A PLO spokesman in Beirut emphasizes the organization's position as the "sole legitimate representative of the Palestinian people" at any peace negotiations.

Sept. 26. Heavy fighting ends in southern Lebanon as a U.S.-arranged cease-fire goes into effect. Key elements of the truce include withdrawal of Palestinian guerrillas six miles from the Israeli border and their replacement with Lebanese troops.

Sept. 26. President Carter tells a news conference he favors PLO involvement in a Middle East settlement, but does not consider the organization "the exclusive representative of the Palestinians."

Sept. 28. The Israeli government stops attempts by an ultra-religious Jewish sect to establish unauthorized settlements in the West Bank.

Oct. 1. The U.S and the Soviet Union issue a joint declaration on the Geneva peace conference suggesting that talks guarantee "the legitimate rights of the Palestinian people."

Oct. 2. Israel rejects the joint U.S.-Soviet statement as "unacceptable."

Oct. 5. U.S and Israel announce agreement on procedures for reconvening the Geneva conference following talks between President Carter and Foreign Minister Moshe Dayan in New York.

Oct. 5. U.S.-arranged cease-fire in southern Lebanon breaks down as serious fighting between Christian and Palestinian forces resumes in that region.

Oct. 11. Israel's cabinet unanimously approves plan for reconvening the Geneva talks.

Oct. 16. PLO leaders in Beirut reject U.S.-Israeli plan for Geneva talks.

Oct. 19. Egypt asks that the U.S.-Israeli plan for reconvening the Geneva talks specifically include PLO participation. Israel opposes any PLO presence at Geneva.

Oct. 21. U.N. Security Council approves a one-year extension for U.N. troops stationed in the Sinai Desert as a peacekeeping force.

Oct. 25. Black June Palestinian terrorists claim responsibility for the unsuccessful assassination attempt on Syrian Foreign Minister Abdul Halim Khaddam at Abu Dhabi airport.

Oct. 26. Egypt announces it will suspend payment on its $4 billion military debt to the Soviet Union because of Moscow's refusal to continue arms sales to Egypt.

Oct. 28. U.N. General Assembly approves an Egyptian-sponsored resolution stating that it "strongly deplores" Israel's occupation and establishment of settlements on Arab lands captured in the 1967 war.

Nov. 6. PLO leader Yasir Arafat declares leftist guerrilla forces will not pull out of southern Lebanon according to the U.S.-arranged truce agreement.

Nov. 8. U.S. turns down an Israeli request to coproduce American-designed F-16 fighter jets in Israeli plants.

Nov. 9. Israeli jets bomb Palestinian guerrilla enclaves in southern Lebanon. The Lebanese government reports more than 100 people are killed.

Nov. 9. Egyptian President Sadat addresses Parliament and urges an all-out effort to reconvene the peace talks in Geneva. Sadat says "I am ready to go to the Israeli parliament itself to discuss [peace]."

Nov. 11. Israeli forces continue to raid Palestinian bases in southern Lebanon in retaliation for Lebanese shelling of northern Israeli villages.

Nov. 15. Prime Minister Begin extends a formal invitation to President Sadat to address the Israeli Knesset (parliament), at the same time offering an informal invitation to other Arab leaders to come to Israel for diplomatic discussions.

Nov. 15. President Carter applauds Sadat's action, calling it a "very courageous, unprecedented step." Moscow charges Begin with attempting "to make greater inroads into the Arab front." Radical Arabs and Palestinian groups criticize the move.

Nov. 17. Egyptian Foreign Minister Ismail Fahmy resigns in apparent disagreement over Sadat's decision to go to Israel.

Nov. 17. Arab leaders react sharply to Sadat's plans to visit Israel, fearing Sadat will negotiate a separate settlement with Israel and abandon his support of the Palestinians.

Nov. 19. President Sadat arrives in Israel, the first Arab leader to visit that nation since it was established in 1948.

Nov. 20. President Sadat, in an historic address to the Israeli Knesset in Jerusalem, tells Jewish leaders that "we welcome you among us with all security and safety."

Nov. 21. Sadat and Begin hold a joint press conference and express their desire for peace and the hope that the Geneva peace conference will reconvene in the near future. At Sadat's departure Begin calls his visit "a great moral achievement."

Nov. 21. Sadat is welcomed as a hero in Cairo upon his return from Israel.

Nov. 22. The Egyptian delegate to the U.N. walks out on a speech by the Syrian delegate after the Syrian called Sadat's visit to Israel "a stab in the back of the Arab people."

Nov. 22. The European Community adopts a resolution praising Sadat's visit and "his courageous initiative."

Nov. 25. The U.N. General Assembly votes to condemn the Israeli occupation of Arab lands seized in the 1967 war and to reopen the Geneva talks with the inclusion of PLO representatives.

Nov. 26. Sadat invites all parties in the Middle East conflict to a pre-Geneva preparatory meeting in Cairo to resolve procedural differences.

Nov. 26. Israel announces it will accept a formal invitation to the Cairo conference, but Syria, Lebanon and Jordan reject Sadat's offer.

Nov. 29. President Carter appoints former Assistant Secretary of State Alfred L. Atherton Jr. to be the U.S. representative at the Cairo talks.

Nov. 29. The Soviet Union announces it will not participate in the Cairo summit.

Dec. 2. U.N. General Assembly approves an Arab-initiated proposal to establish a special unit to publicize what it calls "Palestinian rights."

Dec. 5. Egypt severs diplomatic relations with Syria, Iraq, Libya, Algeria and South Yemen, citing attempts by the hardline Arab states to disrupt Sadat's recent peace efforts. The action follows conclusion of a Dec. 2 meeting in Tripoli, Libya where the Arab states declared a new "front for resistance and opposition" to thwart Egypt's peace initiatives. Egypt also closes several Soviet and Soviet-bloc cultural centers and consulates in Cairo because of the U.S.S.R.'s endorsement of the Tripoli Declaration.

Dec. 8. Syrian President Assad meets with officials of Saudi Arabia, Kuwait, Bahrain, Qatar and the United Arab Emirates to enlist their support in his stand against Sadat's peace moves.

Dec. 9-14. Secretary of State Vance visits six Middle East nations to persuade Arab leaders to attend the upcoming Cairo conference.

Dec. 14. The Cairo conference to discuss procedures for reconvening the Geneva peace talks opens. Egypt, Israel, U.S. and a U.N. representative participate.

Dec. 15. President Carter declares that the PLO has removed itself from "serious consideration" as a participant in the Middle East peace talks because of its refusal to recognize Israel.

Dec. 21. The Organization of Petroleum Exporting Countries (OPEC) decides against raising crude oil prices at a meeting in Caracas, Venezuela.

Dec. 25. Begin and Sadat hold a summit in Ismailia, Egypt to draft guidelines for establishing peace in the Middle East. Talks conclude with no substantive agreement on any major issue.

Dec. 25. Five thousand Palestinians participate at a rally in Beirut to denounce Sadat's meeting with Begin in Ismailia.

Dec. 28. Begin presents to the Israeli Knesset the 26-point peace plan he submitted to Sadat at the Ismailia summit. Legislators approve the plan after 11 hours of debate.

1978

Jan. 3. Fierce fighting erupts again between Israeli-supported Christians and Palestinian and Lebanese leftists in southern Lebanon.

Jan. 4. Said Hammani, chief representative of the PLO in Britain, is killed in London by an unknown assassin. Hammani had been in ill favor with other PLO representatives because of his moderate stance on coexistence with Israel and his opposition to terrorism.

Jan. 6. President Carter unveils a plan for joint Israeli-Arab administration of the occupied West Bank and Gaza Strip.

Jan. 8. The Israeli Cabinet bars establishment of new settlements in the Sinai, but approves expansion of existing ones.

Jan. 9. In a meeting with President Sadat in Aswan, Egypt, the Shah of Iran endorses Egypt's peace initiatives.

Jan. 11. An Israeli-Egyptian Military Committee convenes in Cairo to discuss Israel's withdrawal from the Sinai as part of a peace agreement.

Jan. 11. Syria and the Soviet Union sign an arms deal under which Damascus will begin receiving shipments of Soviet planes, tanks and advanced air-defense missiles.

Jan. 18. Talks in Jerusalem between the Israeli-Egyptian Political Committee end abruptly following Egypt's recall of its delegation. President Sadat blames the breakdown on Israel's "aim at deadlocking the situation and submitting partial solutions."

Jan. 18. President Carter urges President Sadat to continue the negotiations with Israel despite the recall of Egypt's delegation from Jerusalem.

Jan. 26. Egypt and Israel conduct private talks in a move to reopen peace negotiations in Jerusalem. Meetings between the two countries broke down when President Sadat recalled his delegation because of an apparent impasse.

Jan. 31. The Egyptian-Israeli Military Committee resumes talks in Cairo on arranging a technical agreement for Israel's return of the Sinai Peninsula to Egypt.

Feb. 1. Assistant Secretary of State Alfred L. Atherton Jr. returns from the Middle East after failing to prompt Egypt and Israel to agree to a set of principles for an overall peace agreement in the Middle East.

Feb. 1. A shipment of Israeli oranges to the Netherlands and West Germany is poisoned with mercury. A radical Palestinian group claims responsibility for the incident, claiming its aim was to "sabotage the Israeli economy."

Feb. 3. President Sadat visits the U.S. to press his plans for peace in the Middle East and to seek American arms assistance.

Feb. 7. Syrian peacekeeping troops clash with Lebanese army units in the outskirts of Beirut.

Feb. 9. President Sadat leaves the U.S. for Europe to continue his campaign to gain support for his Middle East peace initiatives.

Feb. 11. Syria and Lebanon agree on terms to prevent a recurrence of fighting between their forces in Beirut.

Feb. 14. U.S. announces it will sell $4.8 billion worth of jet warplanes to Egypt, Saudi Arabia and Israel.

Feb. 14. Two Israelis are killed and 35 are wounded when a terrorist bomb explodes aboard a crowded bus in Jerusalem.

Feb. 18. Two Palestinian gunmen assassinate Youssef el-Sebai, an Egyptian newspaper editor and confidant of Anwar Sadat, in a hotel lobby in Nicosia, Cyprus. After killing Sebai, the terrorists seize 30 hostages and demand safe conduct to the Larnaca airport.

Feb. 18. Six persons are killed and 125 injured in anti-government riots in the northern Iranian city of Tabriz.

Feb. 19. Seventy-four Egyptian commandos land at Larnaca airport in Cyprus in an attempt to free hostages being held aboard a Cypriot jet by two Palestinian terrorists. The terrorists are accused of assassinating an Egyptian newspaper editor the day before. Cypriot national guard troops intercept the commando attack and 15 persons are killed in an exchange of gunfire. Following the attack the Palestinians release their hostages and surrender.

Feb. 22. Egypt cuts diplomatic ties with Cyprus in anger over the attack by Cypriot troops on Egytian commandos at Larnaca airport.

Feb. 24. Sale of American warplanes to Israel, Egypt and Saudi Arabia must be a "package deal" according to Secretary of State Vance. The administration plans to withdraw from the deal if Congress tries to veto any part of the sale.

Feb. 27. Egypt announces it is revoking special privileges granted to the 30,000 Palestinians living in Egypt following the assassination of an Arab editor by two Palestinians in Cyprus.

March 4. Prime Minister Begin informs President Carter that his government does not interpret U.N. Resolution 242 to say that Israel is specifically obligated to withdraw from the occupied West Bank and Gaza Strip. Carter reiterates the U.S. position that the resolution means Israeli withdrawal "from all three fronts."

March 14. Israel launches an all-out attack on Palestinian bases in Lebanon in retaliation for a terrorist raid March 11 that killed 30 Israeli civilians. Israeli troops occupy a six-mile deep "security belt" on Lebanese territory along the Israeli border.

March 15. Egyptian, Syrian and Lebanese leaders denounce Israel's actions in southern Lebanon and call on world opinion to pressure Israel to withdraw from Lebanese territory.

March 21. Israel declares a unilateral truce in southern Lebanon and U.N. troops move into the region to enforce the cease-fire.

March 23. President Carter and Prime Minister Begin conclude two days of talks in Washington after failing to reach agreement on any of the major points blocking progress in the Middle East peace negotiations. Carter tells U.S. senators the diplomatic process has been brought "to a halt."

March 30. Israeli Defense Minister Ezer Weizman goes to Cairo to meet with President Sadat in an attempt to revive the faltering peace talks.

April 1. An estimated 25,000 Israelis rally in Tel Aviv, calling on Prime Minister Begin to soften his stance on relinquishing Israeli-occupied territory in the West Bank and Gaza Strip.

April 9. Fighting breaks out in Beirut between Lebanese Moslems and Christian militiamen; 102 persons are reported killed in the hostilities.

April 11. Israel begins a two-phase withdrawal of its forces from positions in southern Lebanon.

April 17. U.N. Secretary-General Kurt Waldheim visits Lebanon and Israel to inspect U.N. peacekeeping forces there.

April 26. Israeli Foreign Minister Moshe Dayan meets with Secretary of State Vance in Washington to continue the search for a solution to break the impasse in the Middle East peace negotiations.

April 26. Four thousand Israelis stage a rally protesting Prime Minister Begin's West Bank policies.

May 2. Three French soldiers of the U.N. peacekeeping force in Lebanon are killed in a clash with Lebanese left-wing guerrillas.

May 8. Anti-government riots continue in Iran as part of a campaign mounted by Moslem leaders to disrupt the modernization plans of the Shah.

May 15. The U.S. Senate votes to support the Carter administration's plan to sell warplanes to Israel, Egypt and Saudi Arabia.

May 20. Three Arab gunmen at Paris' Orly airport open fire on a crowd of tourists about to board an El Al Airlines flight to Israel. A Lebanese terrorist group claims responsibility for the attack.

May 21. Israel announces it will withdraw all of its remaining military forces in southern Lebanon by June 13.

May 24. PLO leader Yasir Arafat pledges to the Lebanese government to keep his guerrilla forces out of southern Lebanon.

May 25. The Israeli Supreme Court issues a temporary restraining order to halt work on a new settlement in the West Bank. Arab landowners claim the land had been illegally confiscated by the Israeli army.

June 6. In a speech to Egyptian troops President Sadat warns that if Israel "continues not to understand" what is behind his peace initiative, Egypt's armed forces would have "no alternative but to complete the battle of liberation."

June 9. An Israeli commando unit attacks a PLO military base on the Lebanese coast.

June 13. Israeli troops complete their withdrawal from southern Lebanon.

June 13. Forty-five persons die in a clash between two Lebanese Christian factions north of Beirut.

June 15. Ali Yasin, the PLO's chief representative in Kuwait, is shot to death in his home by an unidentified gunman. Al Fatah accuses Iraqi extremists of the murder.

June 18. The Israeli Cabinet adopts a policy backing Prime Minister Begin's hard-line stand on the future of the occupied West Bank and Gaza Strip.

June 19. Israeli gunboats seize a ship in Lebanese coastal waters loaded with arms and military equipment and bound for Palestinian guerrilla camps in southern Lebanon.

June 24. North Yemen President Ahmed Hussein al-Ghashni is slain in Sana, the capital.

June 26. South Yemen President Salem Rubaya Ali is deposed and executed in Aden.

July 1. Syrian troops of the Arab League peacekeeping force in Lebanon attack Christian militiamen in Beirut. At least 200 people are killed in the worst fighting since the 1975-76 civil war.

July 2. South Yemen accuses North Yemen of invading its northwestern province.

July 5. Egypt formally announces its plan for peace in the Middle East. Under the proposal Israel will withdraw from occupied territories over a five-year period and the Arab residents of the West Bank and Gaza Strip "will be able to determine their own future."

July 9. The Israeli Cabinet rejects the Egyptian peace plan that calls for Israel to relinquish the occupied West Bank and Gaza Strip.

July 9. Former Iraqi Prime Minister Abdul Razak al-Naif is shot and killed in London.

July 13. Israeli Defense Minister Ezer Weizman meets unexpectedly with President Sadat in Austria and receives a new Egyptian peace plan.

July 13. Iraqi authorities seize an Al Fatah arms plant and naval facility in a dispute over the Fatah's position on negotiation with Israel.

July 18. U.S. sponsors a conference in England for Israeli and Egyptian foreign ministers to discuss peace proposals for the disputed West Bank and Gaza Strip.

July 20. Leaders of Israel's opposition Labor Party question Prime Minister Begin's physical and mental fitness to stay in office. The party cited what it called "irresponsible and unchecked expressions" by the premier. Begin suffers from a heart ailment and diabetes.

July 22. President Sadat calls Prime Minister Begin an "obstacle" to peace in a speech at a political rally.

July 27. The U.S. cuts its embassy staff in Beirut and advises other Americans in Lebanon to leave because of the hostilities there.

July 30. President Sadat opposes the resumption of direct peace talks with Israel because of what he calls "negative and backward" moves from the Israelis.

July 31. A newly organized attack by Lebanese army troops in southern Lebanon is repelled by Christian militiamen.

July 31. Four persons are killed in Paris following clashes between Arab terrorists and Iraqi officials there. The violence is part of a rash of incidents in a growing dispute between hardline Iraqis and more moderate factions of the PLO.

Aug. 3. Israeli jets bomb a Palestinian guerrilla base in Lebanon in retaliation for a terrorist bomb explosion that killed one person and injured 50 in Tel Aviv.

Aug. 5. Fighting erupts again in Beirut between Syrian troops and Christian militiamen after the breakdown of a cease-fire agreement.

Aug. 8. U.S. announces that President Sadat and Prime Minister Begin will meet with President Carter in September at Camp David, Md., to explore ways to resolve the Middle East deadlock.

Aug. 13. Two hundred people die in an explosion that levels a nine-story building in Beirut. The building housed the headquarters of the pro-Iraqi Palestine Liberation Front and the rival Al Fatah faction of the PLO.

Aug. 14. Israel halts consideration of five new settlements planned in the West Bank pending the outcome of the forthcoming Camp David summit.

Aug. 20. Four Palestinian terrorists attack an El Al Israel Airlines bus in London, killing a stewardess and wounding nine others.

Aug. 20. Four hundred people die in a fire that sweeps through a movie theater in Abadan, Iran. Government officials suspect the blaze was set by Moslem extremists opposed to the government's liberalization policies.

Aug. 22. Anti-government riots break out in Abadan, Iran during mourning ceremonies for the 430 persons who died in a movie theater fire there two days earlier.

Sept. 5-17. President Carter, Prime Minister Begin and President Sadat hold peace talks at Camp David, and on Sept. 17 sign two documents: "A Framework for Peace in the Middle East" and a "Framework for the Conclusion of a Peace Treaty Between Israel and Egypt."

Sept. 8. Hundreds of Iranian demonstrators are killed when government troops open fire on them during an anti-government march in Teheran.

Sept. 10. In a White House statement President Carter assures the Shah of Iran of continued U.S. support for his regime.

Sept. 19. The Egyptian Cabinet unanimously approves the Camp David agreements.

Sept. 23. King Hussein of Jordan says he will not take part in peace negotiations unless Israel agrees to withdraw from the West Bank and East Jerusalem.

Sept. 24. Syria, Algeria, South Yemen, Libya and the PLO break off all political and economic relations with Egypt because of the Camp David accords.

Sept. 24. Secretary of State Vance meets in Damascus with Syrian President Assad. The Israeli Cabinet approves Camp David accords.

Sept. 28. The Knesset votes 84-19 to approve the Camp David agreements and dismantle Jewish settlements in the Sinai Peninsula.

Sept. 28. President Carter calls for an international conference to end the hostilities between Moslems and Christians in Lebanon. Fighting between Syrian troops and Christian militiamen is the fiercest since 1975 civil war.

Oct. 7. Syria declares a unilateral cease-fire in Beirut after a week of heavy fighting with Christian militia forces.

Oct. 12-21. Negotiations on a U.S. draft treaty between representatives of Egypt and Israel are held in Washington. President Carter intervenes to head off a breakdown in the talks after Israel announces its delegation will be called home for consultations. As a result, Israeli and Egyptian negotiators reach agreement on main elements of a peace treaty.

Oct. 15. Syrian troops withdraw from key positions in Beirut under terms of an emergency agreement worked out at a meeting of seven Arab nations.

Oct. 25. The Israeli Cabinet approves the draft treaty "in principle," but adds amendments drafted by Prime Minister Begin dealing with linkage between the treaty and the future of the West Bank and the Gaza Strip. Cabinet submits the treaty to the Knesset for approval.

Oct. 26. President Carter sends a message to Prime Minister Begin expressing concern over Israel's decision to enlarge West Bank settlements. Egypt says its negotiators may be recalled in protest.

Oct. 27. Norwegian Nobel Prize Committee announces that the 1978 Peace Prize will be awarded to President Sadat and Prime Minister Begin for their contributions to peace in the Middle East.

Oct. 28. President Sadat reverses his decision to call his chief negotiators home after a personal plea from President Carter.

Oct. 31. Forty thousand Iranian petroleum workers go on strike in the largest single anti-government move to date. The strike drastically reduces Iranian oil production and exports.

Nov. 1. The U.S.S.R. and the PLO issue a joint communique assailing the Camp David pact between Israel and Egypt.

Nov. 2-5. Arab nations, minus Egypt and six other moderate nations, meet in Baghdad, and vow to impose an economic and political boycott on Egypt if President Sadat signs a separate treaty with Israel.

Nov. 3. Secretary of State Vance says "we have now resolved almost all the substantive issues," and that the West Bank can be dealt with separately.

Nov. 4. President Sadat refuses to meet with the Arab delegation from the Baghdad summit.

Nov. 6. The Israeli Cabinet rejects Secretary of State Vance's views on the West Bank and insists on elimination of treaty linkage to the Palestinian question.

Nov. 6. The Shah of Iran imposes martial law in his country in an effort to quell the violent anti-government riots that have shaken the country since January.

Nov. 10. Egypt asks Israel to agree in advance to a detailed timetable for relinquishing rule in the West Bank and the Gaza Strip and transferring power to the Palestinians.

Nov. 11. National Front leader Karim Sanjabi is arrested in Teheran while attempting to hold a news conference. Sanjabi had just returned from two weeks in Paris where he had been consulting with exiled religious leader Ayatollah Khomeini.

Nov. 12. Secretary of State Vance and Israeli Foreign Minister Moshe Dayan reach a tentative agreement on a new linkage formula. Vance presents the latest U.S. compromise plan to Prime Minister Begin. Administration officials say President Carter gave no secret guarantees or commitments to Sadat on the West Bank, Gaza or Jerusalem. The Israeli Cabinet, meeting without Begin, Dayan or Defense Minister Ezer Weizman, rejects Egypt's demands for linking treaty to a timetable for transferring power to the Palestinians.

Nov. 13. Most oil workers in Iran return to their jobs under pressure from the military government.

Nov. 16. President Carter says the U.S. would demand that Egypt and Israel live up to the Camp David accords even if they don't agree to sign a treaty.

Nov. 19. The Iranian government frees 210 political prisoners in a move to ease opposition to the Shah's regime.

Nov. 21. The Israeli Cabinet votes 15-2 to accept a U.S.-proposed draft of a peace treaty that contains a generalized commitment to move forward on the West Bank and the Gaza Strip. But the Cabinet rejects Egypt's demands that a treaty be linked to a timetable for Palestinian autonomy. Egypt announces the recall of its chief negotiator from Washington in an apparent expression of displeasure.

Dec. 1. Carter meets with Egyptian Prime Minister Mustafa Khalil, who presents President Sadat's latest proposals. They agree that peace talks should be renewed.

Dec. 4. Prime Minister Begin tells President Sadat that Israel does not want to change the draft treaty text, but would be willing to discuss wording of side letters.

Dec. 4. Thousands more anti-government workers go on strike in Iran, reducing oil output by 30 percent.

Dec. 6. Hundreds of American dependents flee Iran in the wake of the turmoil there.

Dec. 7. President Carter pressures Israel and Egypt to meet the original Dec. 17 deadline for completing a peace treaty. He says failure to meet that date would "cast doubt on whether the Egyptians and Israelis would carry out the difficult terms" of the treaty. He also says establishment of new Israeli settlements in the West Bank would violate the Camp David accords.

Dec. 10. President Sadat and Prime Minister Begin receive the Nobel Peace Prize. Secretary of State Vance meets with Sadat in Cairo in first session of expected shuttle diplomacy.

Dec. 11. Secretary of State Vance says he and President Sadat have made "good progress" in the talks. Prime Minister Begin hints Israel may abandon plans for more settlements in the West Bank.

Dec. 11. Fifty Iranians die and 500 are wounded in an anti-government riot in Isfahan, Iran's second largest city. The U.S. begins evacuation of American dependents.

Dec. 12. Seventy percent of Iran's petroleum workers stay off the job in response to exiled Moslem leader Ayatollah Khomeini's call for continuance of the strike. Oil production there drops to near record lows.

Dec. 12. President Sadat accepts the latest U.S. proposal, which would resolve the outstanding issues in side letters to the peace treaty.

Dec. 13. Secretary of State Vance gives the latest proposals to Prime Minister Begin, who raises strong objections to proposed side letters to the treaty: one explaining Egypt's legal commitment to other Arab nations, and a second letter setting a "target" date, rather than a timetable, for talks on Palestinian self-rule.

Dec. 14-21. Widespread anti-government demonstrations in Iran result in hundreds of deaths and injuries. Oil output there drops to a record low.

Dec. 15. The Israeli Cabinet backs Begin's rejection of the latest draft. Begin says Egypt bears "total responsibility" for the failure of negotiators to settle on a treaty by the Dec. 17 deadline. President Carter says the decision on future negotiations "is primarily in the hands now of the Israeli Cabinet."

Dec. 17. The deadline for signing of a treaty passes. Secretary of State Vance says Egypt's last proposals were "reasonable" and that Israel should reconsider them.

Dec. 17. OPEC ends an 18-month price freeze by adopting a phased-in increase plan that would raise crude oil prices 14.5 percent by Oct. 1, 1979.

Dec. 18. Foreign Minister Moshe Dayan says Israel will not initiate new negotiations until Egypt drops its latest proposals.

Dec. 29. The Shah of Iran appoints Shahpur Bakhtiar, a member of the opposition National Front, to head a new civilian government. The Shah had earlier established a military government to bring the uprising against the monarchy under control.

Dec. 31. The U.S. urges all American dependents to leave Iran.

Dec. 31. Prime Minister Begin says Israel is willing to discuss Egypt's proposals for the exchange of letters on the status of the West Bank and Gaza.

1979

Jan. 2. Two hundred Iranian students stage a violent demonstration in front of the Beverly Hills, Calif. home of Princess Chams, a sister of the Shah.

Jan. 3. Premier-designate Shahpur Bakhtiar receives preliminary approval from the Iranian parliament to form a new civilian government.

Jan. 4. The U.S. says it is prepared to cooperate with the new Baktiar government.

Jan. 6. The Shah of Iran officially installs a new civilian government headed by Shahpur Baktiar. A crowd of 100,000 Iranians demonstrates in a rally denouncing the new government. The Shah announces he will leave the country soon for a vacation.

Jan. 13. A nine-member regency council is formed in Iran to carry out the duties of the Shah after he leaves.

Jan. 13. The U.S. announces the start of a two-stage effort to revive the Middle East peace talks. Special Ambassador for the Middle East Alfred L. Atherton Jr. is to go to Egypt and Israel to try to resolve some relatively minor issues. The second stage talks would involve Secretary of State Vance and top Egyptian and Israeli officials.

Jan. 16. Shah Mohammed Reza Pahlevi leaves Iran for a "vacation" abroad. Foreign observers agree the monarch will probably remain in permanent exile, ending his 37-year rule.

Jan. 16. Exiled religious leader Ayatollah Khomeini, from his home near Paris, hails the Shah's departure, calling it "the first step" toward ending the reign of the Pahlevi dynasty.

Jan. 16-27. Alfred Atherton meets with Israeli officials in Jerusalem, and then with Egyptian officials in Cairo, but fails to make substantial progress toward a treaty.

Jan. 18. A CIA-monitoring post in Iran is closed because of the political turmoil there.

Jan. 19. Israeli ground troops strike inside Lebanon in retaliation for a terrorist bomb explosion in Jerusalem.

Jan. 23. The Shah of Iran cancels plans to visit the U.S. as part of his "extended vacation."

Jan. 24. A subcommittee of the House Select Intelligence Committee issues a report blaming the Carter administration and U.S. intelligence for misjudging the severity of the Iranian crisis.

Jan. 26. Ayatollah Khomeini plans to return to Iran from Paris, then postpones trip after Iranian officials close the nation's airports.

Jan. 26. Iranian army troops open fire on a crowd of demonstrators in Teheran killing more than 60 people.

Jan. 30. The U.S. orders evacuation of all dependents and nonessential American officials from Iran.

Feb. 1. Ayatollah Khomeini returns to Iran after 15 years in exile and threatens to arrest Premier Shahpur Bakhtiar if he does not resign. Speaking to a crowd of his followers, Khomeini says, "The parliament and the government are illegal...I will appoint a government with the support of the Iranian people."

Feb. 4. Iran cancels a $7 billion arms deal with the U.S.

Feb. 5. In the first step of a plan to establish an Islamic Republic in Iran, Ayatollah Khomeini appoints Mehdi Bazargan to head a proposed "provisional government."

Feb. 11. Armed revolutionaries and army sympathizers overthrow the government of Premier Shahpur Bakhtiar in Iran. A provisional government formed by religious leader Ayatollah Khomeini takes power.

Feb. 12. President Carter says the U.S. hopes for "very productive and peaceful cooperation with the new government of Iran."

Feb. 12. President Carter says he will consider "favorably" the idea of a summit meeting between himself, Begin and Sadat if ministerial-level talks fail to break the peace treaty deadlock.

Feb. 14. Leftist guerrillas storm the U.S. Embassy in Teheran and hold more than 100 employees hostage. The embassy personnel are later freed by armed supporters of the Ayatollah Khomeini.

Feb. 15. Three OPEC nations—Abu Dhabi, Qatar and Libya—announce they are raising oil prices above the levels agreed to by OPEC in December 1978.

Feb. 15. Leftist groups in Iran seek to undermine the new Khomeini regime, charging that the ayatollah is surrounded by reactionary religious leaders.

Feb. 18. In Teheran, PLO leader Yasir Arafat meets with Khomeini and Prime Minister Bazargan. Arafat says the Iranian revolution "turned upside down" the balance of forces in the Middle East. The former head of SAVAK, the Iranian secret police, and three former army generals are executed in Iran.

Feb. 21. Egyptian, Israeli and U.S. officials arrive at Camp David to resume peace negotiations.

Feb. 23. Saudi Arabian Crown Prince Fahd cancels a scheduled visit to the U.S. Sources say he did not want his visit to be linked to an impending Israeli-Egyptian peace agreement.

Feb. 24. Fighting breaks out along the border of North and South Yemen; both sides accuse the other of starting the attack.

Feb. 27. Iran's revolutionary government announces it will resume exports of crude oil, at a price 30 percent higher than the level set by OPEC in December 1978.

Feb. 28. U.S. Air Force personnel flee from two top-secret intelligence gathering stations in Iran after leftist guerrillas take over the posts.

March 1-4. Prime Minister Begin arrives in Washington for new talks with President Carter. In a strongly worded statement, Begin says the Egyptian-Israeli talks are "in a state of deep crisis." Carter and Begin fail to make progress toward resolving remaining issues. Carter gives Begin new proposals.

March 4. President Carter announces he will fly to Egypt and Israel in the hope of breaking the impasse blocking a peace treaty between the two nations.

March 5. The U.S. sends a naval task force to the Arabian Sea as the fighting continues between North and South Yemen.

March 5. After more than five hours of closed-door debate, the Israeli Cabinet approves Carter's latest Middle East treaty proposals.

March 8. President Carter arrives in Cairo for talks with President Sadat. Sadat says Egypt and Israel are "on the verge of an agreement."

March 8. Syrian President Assad warns that despite a peace treaty between Egypt and Israel, "the state of war will prevail" in the Middle East.

March 8. Thousands of Iranian women march through the streets of Teheran protesting alleged government imposition of Islamic rules that would restrict their rights.

March 10. President Carter arrives in Jerusalem for talks with Prime Minister Begin. Among the issues still unresolved at the conclusion of Carter's talks with Sadat are: a date for achieving autonomy for Palestinians in the West Bank and Gaza Strip; Israeli access to Egyptian oil; the timing of full diplomatic relations; and the relationship between Egypt's treaty obligations to Israel and its mutual defense commitments to other Arab nations.

March 12. President Carter appears to have failed to resolve the outstanding issues. White House officials announce the president will return to Washington without the accord and with no agreed procedure for continuing the talks. Carter schedules a final meeting with Begin.

March 12. The U.S. announces plans to send military advisers to North Yemen.

March 13. In a dramatic announcement at the Cairo airport upon returning from Israel, Carter says Sadat has approved all outstanding points of a proposed treaty. Carter says Begin has agreed to submit to his Cabinet "the few remaining issues" that Israel has yet to endorse. In Jerusalem, Begin says that if the Knesset rejects the compromise his "government will have to resign."

March 14. The Israeli Cabinet votes for the compromise proposals, paving the way for endorsement by the Knesset. Carter tells congressional leaders the United States will provide an additional $4 billion in aid to Egypt and Israel over three years. U.S. readiness to pledge additional aid is said to have made both sides agree to the peace treaty.

March 15. The Egyptian Cabinet votes unanimously to approve the draft peace treaty.

March 15. Arab residents in the West Bank stage violent demonstrations in protest against President Carter's Middle East peace mission.

March 17. National Security Adviser Zbigniew Brzezinski travels to Saudi Arabia and Jordan to enlist their support for the Egyptian-Israeli peace treaty.

March 17. A cease-fire goes into effect in the border war between North and South Yemen.

March 18. Brzezinski's mission ends with failure to obtain Saudi Arabia's or Jordan's endorsement of the peace treaty.

March 19. The Israeli Cabinet approves the treaty by a 15-2 vote. In Washington, officials disclose pledges of support for Israel and Egypt: $2 billion in planes, tanks and anti-aircraft weapons for Egypt; $3 billion to help Israel pay the cost of withdrawing from the Sinai.

March 21. The Israeli Knesset approves the peace treaty by a vote of 95-16 after two days of debate.

March 26. Prime Minister Begin and President Sadat sign a peace treaty, formally ending the state of war between their two countries, in a White House ceremony witnessed by President Carter.

March 27. OPEC oil ministers vote to raise the base price of oil by nine percent at a meeting in Geneva.

March 29. North and South Yemen agree to attempt to unite under one government.

March 30-31. Iranian voters approve the formation of an Islamic republic in a national referendum. Ayatollah Khomeini proclaims the establishment of the regime April 1, calling it "the first day of a government of God."

March 31. Eighteen Arab League countries and the PLO sever diplomatic relations with Cairo and vote to impose an economic boycott against Egypt because it signed a separate peace treaty with Israel.

April 1. The Israeli Cabinet approves the Egyptian-Israeli peace treaty.

April 7. The Iranian government executes 35 former officials who had served under the Shah.

April 8. The PLO warns that it will step up its terrorist attacks to block the autonomy plan for the West Bank and Gaza Strip contained in the Egyptian-Israeli peace treaty.

April 9. Saudi Arabia's deputy petroleum minister says that his country will cut back crude oil production by one million barrels a day.

April 10. The Egyptian People's Assembly (parliament) ratifies the Egyptian-Israeli pact.

April 15. Iran announces it will raise oil prices by 13 percent over the basic level set by OPEC in March.

April 18. Leaders of the Christian militia in southern Lebanon declare a six-mile wide strip of land there "independent" from Beirut's control. Militiamen say the "independent area" will return to Lebanese control only after all Palestinian and Syrian troops have left Lebanon.

April 19. The Egyptian-Israeli treaty is overwhelmingly approved in a nationwide Egyptian referendum.

April 19. It is reported that a private emissary of the Carter administration in a March meeting in Morocco told the Shah of Iran he would not be able to live in the U.S. at the present time because of the unstable relations between the U.S. and Iran.

April 22. The Israeli Cabinet gives approval for two new settlements in the West Bank.

April 22-23. Kuwait and Saudi Arabia sever diplomatic relations with Egypt.

April 23. The former military chief of staff for the Khomeini regime is assassinated by gunmen near his home in Teheran.

April 24. President Carter names Robert S. Strauss as the new ambassador-at-large for negotiations on Palestinian autonomy in the West Bank and Gaza Strip. Strauss replaces Alfred L. Atherton Jr. who is slated to become the U.S. ambassador to Egypt.

April 24. Premier Mehdi Bazargan of Iran lashes out against the komitehs (committees) of the Islamic Revolutionary Council that control civil functions. Bazargan says they are conducting a "rule of revenge" and interfering with his government.

April 25. The Egyptian-Israeli peace treaty formally goes into effect as the two nations exchange ratification documents.

April 26. A U.N.-arranged cease-fire halts the fighting between Israeli troops and PLO guerrillas in southern Lebanon.

April 27. Morocco and Tunisia sever diplomatic relations with Egypt, making a total of 15 Arab states that have cut ties with Cairo.

April 29. Israeli and Egyptian military officers begin talks detailing Israel's withdrawal from the Sinai.

April 30. An Israeli freighter, the first since Israel became a state in 1948, transits the Suez Canal.

April 30. In Iran, Ayatollah Khomeini severs diplomatic relations with Egypt.

May 1. President Sadat at May Day rally accuses Saudi Arabia of pressuring other Arab countries to break diplomatic ties with Egypt.

May 1. High official of Iran's Islamic Revolutionary Council is assassinated in Teheran by the same guerrilla group which claimed credit for the April 23 killing of a former military chief of staff.

May 7. Lebanon rejects peace treaty with Israel proposed by Prime Minister Begin in speech to Knesset.

May 7-9. In Iran executions of officials connected with the former Shah, including two private businessmen, continue as toll is reported to have reached 200.

May 9. Egypt is suspended from the 43-member Conference of Islamic States during a five-day meeting in Fez, Morocco, because of its peace treaty with Israel.

May 9. Israeli ground troops follow up air and naval strikes by invading southern Lebanon in retaliatory raid against Palestinian guerrillas. This represents a new Israeli policy of sustained raids rather than strikes against particular terrorist attacks.

May 10. The Arab People's Congress meeting in Aden, South Yemen, proposes boycott against U.S. because of its sponsorship of the Egyptian-Israeli peace treaty.

May 12. Iran's leading independent newspaper ceases publication under the Ayatollah Khomeini's reported restrictive press policies.

May 13. In Iran the Ayatollah Khomeini issues decree limiting death sentences to those found guilty of killing others. The former Shah and family members in exile are condemned to death.

May 14. Saudi Arabia announces the closing of a consortium that operates Egyptian arms factories, as it continues economic sanctions against Cairo.

May 16. Lebanese President Sarkis accepts resignation of Premier al-Hoss and his ministers in an effort to resolve disunity between warring Christian and Moslem factions.

May 18. U.S. negotiator Robert S. Strauss agrees to assume duties as special mediator in the Middle East earlier than planned, in June rather than September.

May 19. King Hussein of Jordan rejects Prime Minister Begin's offer of a peace treaty with Israel, citing Israel's refusal to withdraw from the West Bank which was controlled by Jordan from 1948 until the 1967 Arab-Israeli war.

May 20. Iran asks U.S. delay sending new ambassador, Walter Cutler, to Teheran in response to U.S. Senate resolution May 17 condemning the executions in Iran.

May 25. Israel begins withdrawal from the Sinai Peninsula and returns to Egypt El Arish, capital of the Sinai, in accordance with terms of the peace treaty. Both countries open talks in Beersheba on granting Palestinian autonomy in the West Bank. Secretary of State Vance, also in attendance, said "Today marks a milestone on the road to a comprehensive peace."

May 27. Egypt and Israel announce the opening of borders between the two countries, agreeing not to wait until January 1980 as originally planned.

May 29. Three Israeli warships sail through the Suez Canal in first peacetime transit of the waterway by Israel's armed forces.

May 30-31. Government troops in Iran's Khuzistan province on the Persian Gulf fight Iranian Arabs demanding full recognition of rights.

May 31. Iran announces another oil price increase in the continuing round of oil price hikes since OPEC set the $14.55 per barrel base price in March.

May 31. U.N. truce ends fighting in southern Lebanon between Israeli-Lebanese Christian forces and Palestinian guerrillas.

June 1. Moslem leader and supporter of Sadat's peace efforts, Sheik Hussendair, is slain in Gaza. The Popular Front for the Liberation of Palestine claims credit.

June 3. The Israeli Cabinet approves new settlement near Nablus in West Bank.

June 4. U.S. State Department expresses regret over the Israeli move to establish a new West Bank settlement, calling such settlements illegal under international law.

June 4. Iran has reversed its decision and refused to accept new American ambassador, Walter Cutler, U.S. officials disclose.

June 5. President Sadat announces an Egyptian agreement to buy arms from China.

June 6. The Palestine Liberation Organization and its leader, Yasir Arafat, promise to withdraw forces from southern Lebanon and to close its headquarters in Tyre.

June 6. The foreign ministers of Egypt and Israel conclude a pact allowing their citizens to travel freely between both countries by air and sea, but not overland through the Sinai Peninsula.

June 10. The former Shah of Iran is granted a six-month tourist visa and takes up residence in Mexico after his 60-day visa for the Bahamas expires.

June 11. Prime Minister Begin defends Israel's right to establish settlements in the West Bank and Gaza and pledges to implement the autonomy plan for residents of occupied Arab territories, as agreed to in the September 1978 Camp David accord. Work was begun on the settlement of Elon Moreh near Nablus June 7.

June 12-13. North Yemen reportedly is increasing efforts to obtain additional U.S. military aid as South Yemen reinforces its border defenses.

June 14. The U.N. Interim Force in Lebanon (UNIFIL) is granted a six-month extension by the U.N. Security Council.

June 18. Army troops in Lebanon restore order after three weeks of fighting in Beirut suburbs between rival Christian factions.

June 19. Syria and Iraq, after talks in Baghdad, announce formation of a joint political command to coordinate the foreign, defense and economic policies of the two countries.

June 20. The Israeli Supreme Court, in response to a suit by Arab landowners, halts work on the controversial West Bank settlement of Elon Moreh. Arabs in Nablus continue riots and demonstrations protesting the settlement.

June 21. Prime Minister Mustafa Khalil and his cabinet are sworn in after President Sadat's National Democratic Party won a large majority in parliamentary elections held June 7 and 14, the first multiparty elections since the 1952 revolution in Egypt.

June 22. The Syrian government reports that members of the Moslem Brotherhood killed 50 military cadets in a recurrence of violence between rival Moslem sects. The killings were considered the most serious incident of the religious rivalry since President Assad came to power in 1970.

June 24. Israeli Defense Minister Ezer Weizman is removed from team negotiating with Egypt and the U.S. on Arab self-rule in the West Bank and Gaza. Weizman had earlier opposed establishment of the Israeli settlement near Nablus.

June 27. Syrian fighter planes challenge Israeli air strikes on guerrilla bases in southern Lebanon and engage in air battles, the first in five years.

June 28. OPEC, at the end of a three-day meeting in Geneva, agrees to raise the average price of oil 16 percent, making the price rise for the first six months of 1979 above 50 percent.

Text of Camp David Framework for Peace In the Middle East

Muhammad Anwar al-Sadat, President of the Arab Republic of Egypt, and Menachem Begin, Prime Minister of Israel, met with Jimmy Carter, President of the United States of America, at Camp David from September 5 to September 17, 1978, and have agreed on the following framework for peace in the Middle East. They invite other parties to the Arab-Israeli conflict to adhere to it.

Preamble

The search for peace in the Middle East must be guided by the following:

• The agreed basis for a peaceful settlement of the conflict between Israel and its neighbors is United Nations Security Council Resolution 242, in all its parts. *(See text, box, p. 221)*

• After four wars during 30 years, despite intensive human efforts, the Middle East, which is the cradle of civilization and the birthplace of three great religions, does not yet enjoy the blessings of peace. The people of the Middle East yearn for peace so that the vast human and natural resources of the region can be turned to the pursuits of peace and so that this area can become a model for coexistence and cooperation among nations.

• The historic initiative of President Sadat in visiting Jerusalem and the reception accorded to him by the Parliament, government and people of Israel, and the reciprocal visit of Prime Minister Begin to Ismailia, the peace proposals made by both leaders, as well as the warm reception of these missions by the peoples of both countries, have created an unprecedented opportunity for peace which must not be lost if this generation and future generations are to be spared the tragedies of war.

• The provisions of the Charter of the United Nations and the other accepted norms of international law and legitimacy now provide accepted standards for the conduct of relations among all states.

• To achieve a relationship of peace, in the spirit of Article 2 of the United Nations Charter, future negotiations between Israel and any neighbor prepared to negotiate peace and security with it, are necessary for the purpose of carrying out all the provisions and principles of Resolutions 242 and 338.

• Peace requires respect for the sovereignty, territorial integrity and political independence of every state in the area and their right to live in peace within secure and recognized boundaries free from threats or acts of force. Progress toward that goal can accelerate movement toward a new era of reconciliation in the Middle East marked by cooperation in promoting economic development, in maintaining stability, and in assuring security.

• Security is enhanced by a relationship of peace and by cooperation between nations which enjoy normal relations. In addition, under the terms of peace treaties, the parties can, on the basis of reciprocity, agree to special security arrangements such as demilitarized zones, limited armaments areas, early warning stations, the presence of international forces, liaison, agreed measures for monitoring, and other arrangements that they agree are useful.

Framework

Taking these factors into account, the parties are determined to reach a just, comprehensive, and durable settlement of the Middle East conflict through the conclusion of peace treaties based on Security Council Resolutions 242 and 338 in all their parts. Their purpose is to achieve peace

Carter after Address to Congress

and good neighborly relations. They recognize that, for peace to endure, it must involve all those who have been most deeply affected by the conflict. They therefore agree that this framework as appropriate is intended by them to constitute a basis for peace not only between Egypt and Israel, but also between Israel and each of its other neighbors which is prepared to negotiate peace with Israel on this basis. With that objective in mind, they have agreed to proceed as follows:

A. West Bank and Gaza

1. Egypt, Israel, Jordan and the representatives of the Palestinian people should participate in negotiations on the resolution of the Palestinian problem in all its aspects. To achieve that objective, negotiations relating to the West Bank and Gaza should proceed in three stages:

(a) Egypt and Israel agree that, in order to ensure a peaceful and orderly transfer of authority, and taking into account the security concerns of all the parties, there should be transitional arrangements for the West Bank and Gaza for a period not exceeding five years. In order to provide full autonomy to the inhabitants, un-

der these arrangements the Israeli military government and its civilian administration will be withdrawn as soon as a self-governing authority has been freely elected by the inhabitants of these areas to replace the existing military government. To negotiate the details of a transitional arrangement, the Government of Jordan will be invited to join the negotiations on the basis of this framework. These new arrangements should give due consideration both to the principle of self-government by the inhabitants of these territories and to the legitimate security concerns of the parties involved.

(b) Egypt, Israel, and Jordan will agree on the modalities for establishing the elected self-governing authority in the West Bank and Gaza. The delegations of Egypt and Jordan may include Palestinians from the West Bank and Gaza or other Palestinians as mutually agreed. The parties will negotiate an agreement which will define the powers and responsibilities of the self-governing authority to be exercised in the West Bank and Gaza. A withdrawal of Israeli armed forces will take place and there will be a redeployment of the remaining Israeli forces into specified security locations. The agreement will also include arrangements for assuring internal and external security and public order. A strong local police force will be established, which may include Jordanian citizens. In addition, Israeli and Jordanian forces will participate in joint patrols and in the manning of control posts to assure the security of the borders.

(c) When the self-governing authority (administrative council) in the West Bank and Gaza is established and inaugurated, the transitional period of five years will begin. As soon as possible, but not later than the third year after the beginning of the transitional period, negotiations will take place to determine the final status of the West Bank and Gaza and its relationship with its neighbors, and to conclude a peace treaty between Israel and Jordan by the end of the transitional period. These negotiations will be conducted among Egypt, Israel, Jordan, and the elected representatives of the inhabitants of the West Bank and Gaza. Two separate but related committees will be convened, one committee, consisting of representatives of the four parties which will negotiate and agree on the final status of the West Bank and Gaza, and its relationship with its neighbors, and the second committee, consisting of representatives of Israel and representatives of Jordan to be joined by the elected representatives of the inhabitants of the West Bank and Gaza, to negotiate the peace treaty between Israel and Jordan, taking into account the agreement reached on the final status of the West Bank and Gaza. The negotiations shall be based on all the provisions and principles of UN Security Council Resolution 242. The negotiations will resolve, among other matters, the location of the boundaries and the nature of the security arrangements.

The solution from the negotiations must also recognize the legitimate rights of the Palestinian people and their just requirements. In this way, the Palestinians will participate in the determination of their own future through:

1) The negotiations among Egypt, Israel, Jordan and the representatives of the inhabitants of the West Bank and Gaza to agree on the final status of the West Bank and Gaza and other outstanding issues by the end of the transitional period.

2) Submitting their agreement to a vote by the elected representatives of the inhabitants of the West Bank and Gaza.

3) Providing for the elected representatives of the inhabitants of the West Bank and Gaza to decide how they shall govern themselves consistent with the provisions of their agreement.

4) Participating as stated above in the work of the committee negotiating the peace treaty between Israel and Jordan.

2. All necessary measures will be taken and provisions made to assure the security of Israel and its neighbors during the transitional period and beyond. To assist in providing such security, a strong local police force will be constituted by the self-governing authority. It will be composed of inhabitants of the West Bank and Gaza. The police will maintain continuing liaison on internal security matters with the designated Israeli, Jordanian, and Egyptian officers.

3. During the transitional period, representatives of Egypt, Israel, Jordan, and the self-governing authority will constitute a continuing committee to decide by agreement on the modalities of admission of persons displaced from the West Bank and Gaza in 1967, together with necessary measures to prevent disruption and disorder. Other matters of common concern may also be dealt with by this committee.

4. Egypt and Israel will work with each other and with other interested parties to establish agreed procedures for a prompt, just and permanent implementation of the resolution of the refugee problem.

Texts of United Nations Resolutions

Security Council Resolution 242

Adopted unanimously at the 1382nd meeting, Nov. 22, 1967

The Security Council,

Expressing its continuing concern with the grave situation in the Middle East,

Emphasizing the inadmissibility of the acquisition of territory by war and the need to work for a just and lasting peace in which every State in the area can live in security,

Emphasizing further that all Member States in their acceptance of the Charter of the United Nations have undertaken a commitment to act in accordance with Article 2 of the Charter,

1. Affirms that the fulfilment of Charter principles requires the establishment of a just and lasting peace in the Middle East which should include the application of both the following principles:

(i) Withdrawal of Israeli armed forces from territories occupied in the recent conflict;

(ii) Termination of all claims or states of belligerency and respect for and acknowledgement of the sovereignty, territorial integrity and political independence of every State in the area and their right to live in peace within secure and recognized boundaries free from threats or acts of force;

2. Affirms further the necessity

(a) For guaranteeing freedom of navigation through international waterways in the area;

(b) For achieving a just settlement of the refugee problem;

(c) For guaranteeing the territorial inviolability and political independence of every State in the area, through measures including the establishment of demilitarized zones;

3. Requests the Secretary-General to designate a Special Representative to proceed to the Middle East to establish and maintain contacts with the States concerned in order to promote agreement and assist efforts to achieve a peaceful and accepted settlement in accordance with the provisions and principles of this resolution.

4. Requests the Secretary-General to report to the Security Council on the progress of the efforts of the Special Representative as soon as possible.

Security Council Resolution 338

Adopted by the Security Council at its 1747th meeting, Oct. 21-22, 1973

The Security Council

1. Calls upon all parties to the present fighting to cease all firing and terminate all military activity immediately, no later than 12 hours after the moment of the adoption of this decision, in the positions they now occupy;

2. Calls upon the parties concerned to start immediately after the cease-fire the implementation of Security Council Resolution 242 (1967) in all of its parts;

3. Decides that, immediately and concurrently with the cease-fire, negotiations start between the parties concerned under appropriate auspices aimed at establishing a just and durable peace in the Middle East.

B. Egypt-Israel

1. Egypt and Israel undertake not to resort to the threat or the use of force to settle disputes. Any disputes shall be settled by peaceful means in accordance with the provisions of Article 33 of the Charter of the United Nations.

2. In order to achieve peace between them, the parties agree to negotiate in good faith with a goal of concluding within three months from the signing of this Framework a peace treaty between them, while inviting the other parties to the conflict to proceed simultaneously to negotiate and conclude similar peace treaties with a view to achieving a comprehensive peace in the area. The Framework for the Conclusion of a Peace Treaty between Egypt and Israel will govern the peace negotiations between

them. The parties will agree on the modalities and the timetable for the implementation of their obligations under the treaty.

C. Associated Principles

1. Egypt and Israel state that the principles and provisions described below should apply to peace treaties between Israel and each of its neighbors — Egypt, Jordan, Syria and Lebanon.

2. Signatories shall establish among themselves relations normal to states at peace with one another. To this end, they should undertake to abide by all the provisions of the Charter of the United Nations. Steps to be taken in this respect include:

(a) full recognition;

(b) abolishing economic boycotts;

(c) guaranteeing that under their jurisdiction the citizens of the other parties shall enjoy the protection of the due process of law.

3. Signatories should explore possibilities for economic development in the context of final peace treaties, with the objective of contributing to the atmosphere of peace, cooperation and friendship which is their common goal.

4. Claims Commissions may be established for the mutual settlement of all financial claims.

5. The United States shall be invited to participate in the talks on matters related to the modalities of the implementation of the agreements and working out the timetable for the carrying out of the obligations of the parties.

6. The United Nations Security Council shall be requested to endorse the peace treaties and ensure that their provisions shall not be violated. The permanent members of the Security Council shall be requested to underwrite the peace treaties and ensure respect for their provisions. They shall also be requested to conform their policies and actions with the undertakings contained in this Framework.

For the Government of the
Arab Republic of Egypt:

For the Government of Israel:

Witnessed by:
Jimmy Carter, President of the
United States of America

Text of Framework For Conclusion of A Peace Treaty Between Egypt And Israel

In order to achieve peace between them, Israel and Egypt agree to negotiate in good faith with a goal of concluding within three months of the signing of this framework a peace treaty between them.

It is agreed that:

The site of the negotiations will be under a United Nations flag at a location or locations to be mutually agreed.

All of the principles of U.N. Resolution 242 will apply in this resolution of the dispute between Israel and Egypt.

Unless otherwise mutually agreed, terms of the peace treaty will be implemented between two and three years after the peace treaty is signed.

The following matters are agreed between the parties:

(a) the full exercise of Egyptian sovereignty up to the internationally recognized border between Egypt and mandated Palestine;

(b) the withdrawal of Israeli armed forces from the Sinai;

(c) the use of airfields left by the Israelis near El Arish, Rafah, Ras en Naqb, and Sharm el Sheikh for civilian purposes only, including possible commercial use by all nations;

(d) the right of free passage of ships of Israel through the Gulf of Suez and the Suez Canal on the basis of the Constantinople Convention of 1888 applying to all nations; the Strait of Tiran and the Gulf of Aqaba are international waterways to be open to all nations for unimpeded and nonsuspendable freedom of navigation and overflight;

(e) the construction of a highway between the Sinai and Jordan near Elat with guaranteed free and peaceful passage by Egypt and Jordan; and

(f) the stationing of military forces listed below.

Stationing of Forces

A. No more than one division (mechanized or infantry) of Egyptian armed forces will be stationed within an area lying approximately 50 kilometers (km) east of the Gulf of Suez and the Suez Canal.

B. Only United Nations forces and civil police equipped with light weapons to perform normal police functions will be stationed within an area lying west of the international border and the Gulf of Aqaba, varying in width from 20 km to 40 km.

C. In the area within 3 km east of the international border there will be Israeli limited military forces not to exceed four infantry battalions and United Nations observers.

D. Border patrol units, not to exceed three battalions, will supplement the civil police in maintaining order in the area not included above.

The exact demarcation of the above areas will be as decided during the peace negotiations.

Early warning stations may exist to insure compliance with the terms of the agreement.

United Nations forces will be stationed: (a) in part of the area in the Sinai lying within about 20 km of the Mediterranean Sea and adjacent to the international border, and (b) in the Sharm el Sheikh area to ensure freedom of passage through the Strait of Tiran; and these forces will not be removed unless such removal is approved by the Security Council of the United Nations with a unanimous vote of the five permanent members.

After a peace treaty is signed, and after the interim withdrawal is complete, normal relations will be established between Egypt and Israel, including: full recognition, including diplomatic, economic and cultural relations; termination of economic boycotts and barriers to the free movement of goods and people; and mutual protection of citizens by the due process of law.

Interim Withdrawal

Between three months and nine months after the signing of the peace treaty, all Israeli forces will withdraw east of a line extending from a point east of El Arish to Ras Muhammad, the exact location of this line to be determined by mutual agreement.

For the Government of the
Arab Republic of Egypt:

For the Government of Israel:

Witnessed by:
Jimmy Carter, President of the
United States of America

Text of Egyptian-Israeli Treaty and Annexes

The Egyptian-Israeli Treaty

The Government of the Arab Republic of Egypt and the Government of the State of Israel:

Preamble

CONVINCED of the urgent necessity of the establishment of a just, comprehensive and lasting peace in the Middle East in accordance with Security Council Resolutions 242 and 338;

REAFFIRMING their adherence to the "Framework for Peace in the Middle East Agreed at Camp David," dated Sept. 17, 1978;

NOTING that the aforementioned framework as appropriate is intended to constitute a basis for peace not only between Egypt and Israel but also between Israel and each of its other Arab neighbors which is prepared to negotiate peace with it on this basis;

DESIRING to bring to an end the state of war between them and to establish a peace in which every state in the area can live in security;

CONVINCED that the conclusion of a treaty of peace between Egypt and Israel is an important step in the search for comprehensive peace in the area and for the attainment of the settlement of the Arab-Israeli conflict in all its aspects;

INVITING the other Arab parties to this dispute to join the peace process with Israel guided by and based on the principles of the aforementioned framework;

DESIRING as well to develop friendly relations and cooperation between themselves in accordance with the United Nations Charter and the principles of international law governing international relations in times of peace;

AGREE to the following provisions in the free exercise of their sovereignty, in order to implement the framework for the conclusion of a peace treaty between Egypt and Israel.

Article I

1. The state of war between the parties will be terminated and peace will be established between them upon the exchange of instruments of ratification of this treaty.

2. Israel will withdraw all its armed forces and civilians from the Sinai behind the international boundary between Egypt and mandated Palestine, as provided in the annexed protocol (Annex I), and Egypt will resume the exercise of its full sovereignty over the Sinai.

3. Upon completion of the interim withdrawal provided for in Annex I, the parties will establish normal and friendly relations, in accordance with article III (3).

Article II

The permanent boundary between Egypt and Israel is the recognized international boundary between Egypt and the former mandated territory of Palestine, as shown on the map at Annex II, without prejudice to the issue of the status of the Gaza Strip. The parties recognize this boundary as inviolable. Each will respect the territorial integrity of the other, including their territorial waters and airspace.

Article III

1. The parties will apply between them the provisions of the Charter of the United Nations and the principles of international law governing relations among states in times of peace. In particular:

A. They recognize and will respect each other's sovereignty, territorial integrity and political independence.

B. They recognize and will respect each other's right to live in peace within their secure and recognized boundaries.

C. They will refrain from the threat or use of force, directly or indirectly, against each other and will settle all disputes between them by peaceful means.

2. Each party undertakes to ensure that acts or threats of belligerency, hostility or violence do not originate from and are not committed from within its territory, or by any forces subject to its control or by any other forces stationed on its territory, against the population, citizens or property of the other party. Each party also undertakes to refrain from organizing, instigating, inciting, assisting or participating in acts or threats of belligerency, hostility, subversion or violence against the other party, anywhere, and undertakes to ensure that perpetrators of such acts are brought to justice.

3. The parties agree that the normal relationship established between them will include full recognition, diplomatic, economic and cultural relations, termination of economic boycotts and discriminatory barriers to the free movement of people and goods, and will guarantee the mutual enjoyment by citizens of the due process of law. The process by which they undertake to achieve such a relationship parallel to the implementation of other provisions of this treaty is set out in the annexed protocol (Annex III).

Article IV

1. In order to provide maximum security for both parties on the basis of reciprocity, agreed security arrangements will be established including limited force zones in Egyptian and Israeli territory, and United Nations forces and observers, described in detail as to nature and timing in Annex I, and other security arrangements the parties may agree upon.

2. The parties agree to the stationing of United Nations personnel in areas described in Annex I, the parties agree not to request withdrawal of the United Nations personnel and that these personnel will not be removed unless such removal is approved by the Security Council of the United Nations, with the affirmative vote of the five permanent members, unless the parties otherwise agree.

3. A joint commission will be established to facilitate the implementation of the treaty, as provided for in Annex I.

4. The security arrangements provided for in paragraphs 1 and 2 of this article may at the request of either party be reviewed and amended by mutual agreement of the parties.

Article V

1. Ships of Israel, and cargoes destined for or coming from Israel, shall enjoy the right of free passage through the Suez Canal and its approaches through the Gulf of Suez and the Mediterranean Sea on the basis of the Constantinople Convention of 1888, applying to all nations. Israeli nationals, vessels and cargoes destined for or coming from Israel, shall be accorded nondiscriminatory treatment in all matters connected with usage of the canal.

2. The parties consider the Strait of Tiran and the Gulf of Aqaba to be international waterways open to all nations for unimpeded and nonsuspendable freedom of navigation and overflight. The parties will respect each other's right to navigation and overflight for access to either country through the Strait of Tiran and the Gulf of Aqaba.

Article VI

1. This treaty does not affect and shall not be interpreted as affecting in any way

the rights and obligations of the parties under the Charter of the United Nations.

2. The parties undertake to fulfill in good faith their obligations under this treaty, without regard to action or inaction of any other party and independently of any instrument external to this treaty.

3. They further undertake to take all the necessary measures for the application in their relations of the provisions of the multilateral conventions to which they are parties, including the submission of appropriate notification to the Secretary General of the United Nations and other depositories of such conventions.

4. The parties undertake not to enter into any obligation in conflict with this treaty.

5. Subject to Article 103 of the United Nations Charter, in the event of a conflict between the obligations of the parties under the present treaty and any of their other obligations, the obligations under this treaty will be binding and implemented.

Article VII

1. Disputes arising out of the application or interpretation of this treaty shall be resolved by negotiations.

2. Any such disputes which cannot be settled by negotiations shall be resolved by conciliation or submitted to arbitration.

Article VIII

The parties agree to establish a claims commission for the mutual settlement of all financial claims.

Article IX

1. This treaty shall enter into force upon exchange of instruments of ratification.

2. This treaty supersedes the agreement between Egypt and Israel of September, 1975.

3. All protocols, annexes and maps attached to this treaty shall be regarded as an integral part hereof.

4. The treaty shall be communicated to the Secretary General of the United Nations for registration in accordance with the provisions of Article 102 of the Charter of the United Nations. Done at Washington this 26th day of March 1979, in duplicate in the Arabic, English and Hebrew languages, each text being equally authentic. In case of any divergence of interpretation, the English text shall prevail. ∎

Annexes to the Treaty
Military Annex I
Protocol Concerning Israeli Withdrawal
and Security Arrangements

Article I
Concept of Withdrawal

1. Israel will complete withdrawal of all its armed forces and civilians from the Sinai not later than three years from the date of exchange of instruments of ratification of this treaty.

2. To ensure the mutual security of the parties, the implementation of phased withdrawal will be accompanied by the military measures and establishment of zones set out to this annex and in map 1, hereinafter referred to as "the zones."

3. The withdrawal from the Sinai will be accomplished in two phases:

A) The interim withdrawal behind the lines from east of El Arish to Ras Muhammed as delineated on map 2 within nine months from the date of exchange of instruments of ratification of this treaty.

B) The final withdrawal from the Sinai behind the international boundary not later than three years from the date of exchange of instruments of ratification of this treaty.

4. A joint commission will be formed immediately after the exchange of instruments of ratification of the treaty in order to supervise and coordinate movements and schedules during the withdrawal, and to adjust plans and timetables as necessary within the limits established by paragraph 3, above. Details relating to the joint commission are set out in Article IV of the attached appendix. The joint commission will be dissolved upon completion of final Israeli withdrawal from the Sinai.

Article II
Determination of Final
Lines and Zones

[I]

In order to provide maximum security for both parties after the final withdrawal, the lines and the zones delineated on map I are to be established and organized as follows:

A. ZONE A

(1) Zone A is bounded on the east by line A (red line) and on the west by the Suez Canal and the east coast of the Gulf of Suez, as shown on map I.

(2) An Egyptian armed force of one mechanized infantry division and its military installations, and field fortifications, will be in this zone.

(3) The main elements of that division will consist of:

(a) three mechanized infantry brigades

(b) one armored brigade

(c) seven field artillery battalions including up to 126 artillery pieces

(d) seven antiaircraft artillery battalions including individual surface-to-air missiles and up to 126 antiaircraft guns of 37mm. and above

(e) up to 230 tanks

(f) up to 480 armored personnel vehicles of all types

(g) up to a total of 22,000 personnel

B. ZONE B

(1) Zone B is bounded by line B (green line) on the east and by line A (red line) on the west, as shown on map I.

(2) Egyptian border units of four battalions equipped with light weapons and wheeled vehicles will provide security and supplement the civil police in maintaining order in Zone B. The main elements of the four border battalions will consist of up to a total of 4,000 personnel.

(3) Land-based, short-range, low power coastal warning points of the border patrol units may be established on the coast of this zone.

(4) There will be in Zone B field fortifications and military installations for the four border battalions.

C. ZONE C

(1) Zone C is bounded by line B (green line) on the west and the international boundary and the gulf of Aqaba on the east, as shown on map I.

(2) Only United Nations forces and Egyptian civil police will be stationed in Zone C.

(3) The Egyptian civil police armed with light weapons will perform normal police functions within this zone.

(4) The United Nations force will be deployed within Zone C and perform its functions as defined in Article VI of this annex.

(5) The United Nations force will be stationed mainly in camps located within the following stationing areas shown on map I, and will establish its precise locations after consultations with Egypt:

(a) In that part of the area in the Sinai lying within about 20 km. of the Mediterranean Sea and adjacent to the international boundary

(b) in the Sharm el Sheikh area.

D. ZONE D

(1) Zone D is bounded by line D (blue line) on the east and the international boundary on the west, as shown on map I.

(2) In this zone there will be an Israeli limited force of four infantry battalions, their military installations and field fortifications, and United Nations observers.

(3) The Israeli forces in Zone D will not include tanks, artillery and antiaircraft missiles except individual surface-to-air missiles.

(4) The main elements of the four Israeli infantry battalions will consist of up to 180 armored personnel vehicles of all types and up to a total of 4,000 personnel.

[2]

Access across the international boundary shall only be permitted through entry checkpoints designated by each party and under its control. Such access shall be in accordance with laws and regulations of each country.

[3]

Only those field fortifications, military installations, forces and weapons specifically permitted by this annex shall be in the zones.

Article III
Aerial Military Regime

1. Flights of combat aircraft and reconnaissance flights of Egypt and Israel shall take place only over Zones A and D, respectively.

2. Only unarmed, noncombat aircraft of Egypt and Israel will be stationed in Zones A and D, respectively.

3. Only Egyptian unarmed transport aircraft will take off and land in Zone B and up to eight such aircraft may be maintained in Zone B. The Egyptian border units may be equipped with unarmed helicopters to perform their functions in Zone B.

4. The Egyptian civil police may be equipped with unarmed police helicopters to perform normal police functions in Zone C.

5. Only civilian airfields may be built in the zones.

6. Without prejudice to the provisions of this treaty, only those military aerial activities specifically permitted by this annex shall be allowed in the zones and the airspace above their territorial waters.

Article IV
Naval Regime

1. Egypt and Israel may base and operate naval vessels along the coasts of Zones A and D, respectively.

2. Egyptian Coast Guard boats, lightly armed, may be stationed and operate in the territorial waters of Zone B to assist the border units in performing their functions in this zone.

3. Egyptian civil police equipped with light boats, lightly armed, shall perform normal police functions within the territorial waters of Zone C.

4. Nothing in this annex shall be considered as derogating from the right of the innocent passage of the naval vessels of either party.

5. Only civilian maritime ports and installations may be built in the zones.

6. Without prejudice to the provisions of this treaty, only those naval activities specifically permitted by this annex shall be allowed in the zones and in their territorial waters.

Article V
Early Warning Systems

Egypt and Israel may establish and operate early warning systems only in Zones A and D respectively.

Article VI
United Nations Operations

1. The parties will request the United Nations to provide forces and observers to supervise the implementation of this annex and employ their best efforts to prevent any violation of its terms.

2. With respect to these United Nations forces and observers, as appropriate, the parties agree to request the following arrangements:

a. Operation of checkpoints, reconnaissance patrols and observation posts along the international boundary and line B, and within Zone C.

b. Periodic verification of the implementation of the provisions of this annex will be carried out not less than twice a month unless otherwise agreed by the parties.

c. Additional verifications within 48 hours after the receipt of a request from either party.

d. Ensuring the freedom of navigation through the Strait of Tiran in accordance with Article V of the treaty of peace.

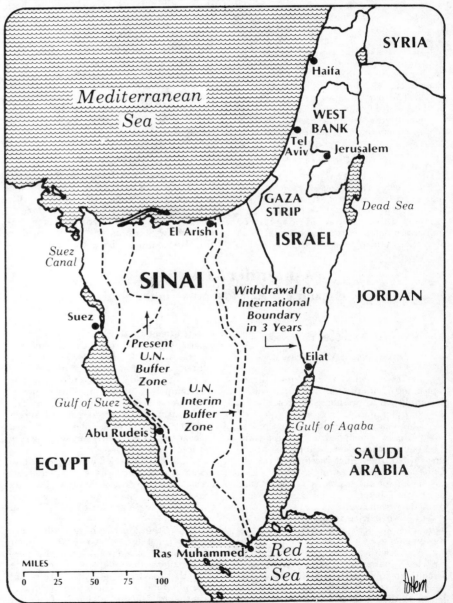

Israel will withdraw east of the interim U.N. buffer zone within nine months and will completely pull out of the Sinai and the Gaza Strip by April 1982. Three maps referred to in the treaty documents are not reproduced. They show agreed upon phases for troop withdrawl and permissible troop strengths.

3. The arrangements described in this article for each zone will be implemented in Zones A, B and C by the United Nations force and in Zone D by the United Nations observers.

4. United Nations verification teams shall be accompanied by liaison officers of the respective party.

5. The United Nations force and observers will report their findings to both parties.

6. The United Nations force and observers operating in the zones will enjoy freedom of movement and other facilities necessary for the performance of their tasks.

7. The United Nations force and observers are not empowered to authorize the crossing of the international boundary.

8. The parties shall agree on the nations from which the United Nations force and observers will be drawn. They will be drawn from nations other than those which are permanent members of the United Nations Security Council.

9. The parties agree that the United Nations should make those command arrangements that will best assure the effective implementation of its responsibilities.

Article VII
Liaison System

1. Upon termination of the joint commission, a liaison system between the parties will be established. This liaison system is intended to provide an effective method to assess progress in the implementation of obligations under the present annex and to resolve any problem that may arise in the course of implementation, and refer other unresolved matters to the higher military authorities of the two countries respectively for consideration. It is also intended to prevent situations resulting from errors or misinterpretation on the part of either party.

2. An Egyptian liaison office will be established in the city of El Arish and an Israeli liaison office will be established in the city of Beersheba. Each office will be headed by an officer of the respective country and assisted by a number of officers.

3. A direct telephone link between the two offices will be set up and also direct telephone lines with the United Nations Command will be maintained by both offices.

Article VIII
Respect for War Memorials

Each party undertakes to preserve in good condition the war memorials erected in the memory of soldiers of the other party, namely those erected by Israel in the Sinai and those to be erected by Egypt in Israel, and shall permit access to such monuments.

Article IX
Interim Arrangements

The withdrawal of Israeli armed forces and civilians behind the interim withdrawal line, and the conduct of the forces of the parties and the United Nations prior to the final withdrawal, will be governed by the attached appendix and map 2. ∎

Appendix to Annex I
Organization of Movements in the Sinai

Article I
Principles of Withdrawal

1. The withdrawal of armed Israeli forces and civilians from the Sinai will be accomplished in two phases as described in Article I of Annex I.

The description and timing of the withdrawal are included in this appendix. The joint commission will develop and present to the chief coordinator of the United Nations forces in the Middle East the details of these phases not later than one month before the initiation of each phase of withdrawal.

2. Both parties agree on the following principles for the sequence of military movements:

A. Notwithstanding the provisions of Article IX, paragraph 2, of this treaty, until Israeli armed forces complete withdrawal from the current "J" and "M" lines established by the Egyptian-Israeli agreement of September 1975, hereinafter referred to as the 1975 agreement, up to the interim withdrawal line, all military arrangements existing under that agreement will remain in effect, except those military arrangements otherwise provided for in this appendix.

B. As Israeli armed forces withdraw, United Nations forces will immediately enter the evacuated areas to establish interim and temporary buffer zones as shown on maps 2 and 3, respectively, for the purpose of maintaining a separation of forces. United Nations forces' deployment will precede the movement of any other personnel into these areas.

C. Within a period of seven days after Israeli armed forces have evacuated any area located in Zone A, units of Egyptian armed forces shall deploy in accordance with the provisions of Article II of this appendix.

D. Within a period of seven days after Israeli armed forces have evacuated any area located in Zones A or B, Egyptian border units shall deploy in accordance with the provisions of Article II of this appendix, and will function in accordance with the provisions of Article II of Annex I.

E. Egyptian civil police will enter evacuated areas immediately after the United Nations forces to perform normal police functions.

F. Egyptian naval units shall deploy in the Gulf of Suez in accordance with the provisions of Article II of this appendix.

G. Except those movements mentioned above, deployments of Egyptian armed forces and the activities covered in Annex I will be effected in the evacuated areas when Israeli military forces have completed their withdrawal behind the interim withdrawal line.

Article II
Subphases of the Withdrawal to the Interim Withdrawal Line

1. The withdrawal to the interim withdrawal line will be accomplished in subphases as described in this article and as shown on map 3. Each subphase will be completed within the indicated number of months from the date of the exchange of instruments of ratification of this treaty.

A. First subphase: Within two months, Israeli armed forces will withdraw from the area of El Arish, including the town of El Arish and its airfield, shown as area I on map 3.

B. Second subphase: Within three months, Israeli armed forces will withdraw from the area between line "M" of the 1975 agreement and line "A," shown as area II on map 3.

C. Third subphase: Within five months, Israeli armed forces will withdraw from the areas east and south of area II, shown as area III on map 3.

D. Fourth subphase: Within seven months, Israeli armed forces will withdraw from the area of El Tor — Ras el Kenisa, shown as Area IV on map 3.

E. Fifth subphase: Within nine months, Israeli armed forces will withdraw from the remaining areas west of the interim withdrawal line, including the areas of Santa Katrina and the areas east of the Gidi and Mitla Passes, shown as Area V on map 3, thereby completing Israeli withdrawal behind the interim withdrawal line.

2. Egyptian forces will deploy in the areas evacuated by Israeli armed forces as follows:

A. Up to one-third of the Egyptian armed forces in the Sinai in accordance with the 1975 agreement will deploy in the portions of Zone A lying within area I, until the completion of interim withdrawal. Thereafter, Egyptian armed forces as described in Article II of Annex I will be deployed in Zone A up to the limits of the interim buffer zone.

B. The Egyptian naval activity in accordance with Article IV of Annex I will commence along the coasts of areas II, III and IV upon completion of the second, third and fourth subphases, respectively.

C. Of the Egyptian border units described in Article II of Annex I, upon completion of the first subphase one battalion will be deployed in area I. A second battalion will be deployed in area II upon completion of the second subphase. A third battalion will be deployed in area III upon completion of the third subphase. The second and third battalions mentioned above may also be deployed in any of the subsequently evacuated areas of the southern Sinai.

3. United Nations forces in Buffer Zone I of the 1975 Agreement will redeploy to enable the deployment of Egyptian forces described above upon the completion of the first subphase, but will otherwise continue to function in accordance with the provisions of that agreement in the remainder of that zone until the completion of interim withdrawal, as indicated in Article I of this appendix.

4. Israeli convoys may use the roads south and east of the main road junction east of El Arish to evacuate Israeli forces and equipment up to the completion of interim withdrawal. These convoys will proceed in daylight upon four hours' notice to the Egyptian liaison group and United Nations forces, will be escorted by United Nations forces, and will be in accordance with schedules coordinated by the joint commission. An Egyptian liaison officer will accompany convoys to assure uninterrupted movement. The joint commission may approve other arrangements for convoys.

Article III
United Nations Forces

1. The parties shall request that United Nations forces be deployed as necessary to perform the functions described in this appendix up to the time of completion of final Israeli withdrawal. For that purpose, the parties agree to the redeployment of the United Nations Emergency Force.

2. United Nations forces will supervise the implementation of this appendix and will employ their best efforts to prevent any violation of its terms.

3. When United Nations forces deploy in accordance with the provisions of Article I and II of this appendix, they will perform the functions of verification in limited force zones in accordance with article VI of Annex I, and will establish checkpoints, reconnaissance patrols and observation posts in the temporary buffer zones described in Article II above. Other functions of the United Nations forces which concern the interim buffer zones are described in Article V of this appendix.

Article IV
Joint Commission and Liaison

1. The joint commission referred to in Article IV of this treaty will function from the date of exchange of instruments of ratification of this treaty up to the date of completion of final Israeli withdrawal from the Sinai.

2. The joint commission will be composed of representatives of each party headed by senior officers. This commission shall invite a representative of the United Nations when discussing subjects concerning the United Nations, or when either party requests United Nations presence. Decisions of the joint commission will be reached by agreement of Egypt and Israel.

3. The joint commission will supervise the implementation of the arrangements described in Annex I and this appendix. To this end, and by agreement of both parties, it will:

A. Coordinate military movements described in this appendix and supervise their implementation.

B. Address and seek to resolve any problem arising out of the implementation of Annex I and this appendix, and discuss any violation reported by the United Nations force and observers and refer to the Governments of Egypt and Israel any unresolved problems.

C. Assist the United Nations force and observers in the execution of their mandates, and deal with the timetables of the periodic verifications when referred to it by the parties as provided for in Annex I and in this appendix.

D. Organize the demarcation of the international boundary and all lines and zones described in Annex I and this appendix.

E. Supervise the handing over of the main installations in the Sinai from Israel to Egypt.

F. Agree on necessary arrangements for finding and returning missing bodies of Egyptian and Israeli soldiers.

G. Organize the setting up and operation of entry checkpoints along the El Arish-Ras Muhammed line in accordance with the provisions of Article IV of Annex III.

H. Conduct its operations through the use of joint liaison teams consisting of one Israeli representative and one Egyptian representative provided from a standing liaison group, which will conduct activities as directed by the joint commission.

I. Provide liaison and coordination to the United Nations Command implementing provision of the treaty, and, through the joint liaison teams, maintain local coordination and cooperation with the United Nations forces stationed in specific areas or United Nations observers monitoring specific areas for any assistance as needed.

J. Discuss any other matters which the parties by agreement may place before it.

4. Meetings of the joint commission shall be held at least once a month. In the event that either party or the command of the United Nations force requests a special meeting, it will be convened within 24 hours.

5. The joint commission will meet in the buffer zone until the completion of the interim withdrawal and in El Arish and Beersheba alternately afterwards. The first meeting will be held not later than two weeks after the entry into force of this treaty.

Article V
Definition of the Interim Buffer Zone and Its Activities

1. An interim buffer zone, by which the United Nations force will effect a separation of Egyptian and Israeli elements, will be established west of, and adjacent to, the interim withdrawal line as shown on map 2 after implementation of Israeli withdrawal and deployment behind the interim withdrawal line. Egyptian civil police, equipped with light weapons, will perform normal police functions within this zone.

2. The United Nations force will operate checkpoints, reconnaissance patrols and observation posts within the interim buffer zone in order to insure compliance with the terms of this article.

3. In accordance with arrangements agreed upon by both parties and to be coordinated by the joint commission, relief personnel will operate military technical installations at four specific locations shown on map 2 and designated as t1 (map central coordinate 57163940), t2 (map central coordinate 59351541), t3 (map central coordinate 59331527) and t4 (map central coordinate 61130979) under the following principles:

A. The technical installations shall be manned by technical and administrative personnel equipped with small arms required for their protection (revolvers, rifles, submachine guns, light machine guns, hand grenades and ammunition), as follows:

t1 — up to 150 personnel
t2 and t3 — up to 350 personnel
t4 — up to 200 personnel

B. Israeli personnel will not carry weapons outside the sites, except officers who may carry personal weapons.

C. Only a third party agreed to by Egypt and Israel will enter and conduct inspections within the perimeters of technical installations in the buffer zone. The third party will conduct inspections in a random manner at least once a month. The inspections will verify the nature of the operation of the installations and the weapons and personnel therein. The third party will immediately report to the parties any divergence from an installation's visual and electronic surveillance or communications role.

D. Supply of the installations, visits for technical and administrative purposes, and replacement of personnel and equipment situated in the sites, may occur uninterruptedly from the United Nations check points to the perimeter of the technical installations, after checking and being escorted by only the United Nations forces.

E. Israel will be permitted to introduce into its technical installations items required for the proper functioning of the installations and personnel.

F. As determined by the joint commission, Israel will be permitted to:

(1) Maintain in its installations firefighting and general maintenance equip-

ment as well as wheeled administrative vehicles and mobile engineering equipment necessary for the maintenance of the sites. All vehicles shall be unarmed.

(2) Within the sites and in the buffer zone, maintain roads, water lines and communication cables which serve the sites. At each of the three installation locations (t1, t2 and t3 and t4), this maintenance may be performed with up to two unarmed wheeled vehicles and by up to 12 unarmed personnel with only necessary equipment, including heavy engineering equipment if needed. This maintenance may be performed three times a week, except for special problems, and only after giving the United Nations four hours' notice. The teams will be escorted by the United Nations.

G. Movement to and from the technical installations will take place only during daylight hours. Access to and exit from the technical installations shall be as follows:

(1) t1: through a United Nations checkpoint, and via the road between Abu Aweigila and the crossroad at km 161 as shown on map 2

(2) t2 and t3: through a United Nations checkpoint and via the road constructed across the buffer zone to Gebel Katrina, as shown on map 2.

(3) t2, t3 and t4: via helicopters flying within a corridor at the times, and according to a flight profile, agreed to by the joint commission. The helicopters will be checked by the United Nations force at landing sites outside the perimeter of the installations.

H. Israel will inform the United Nations force at least one hour in advance of each intended movement to and from the installations.

I. Israel shall be entitled to evacuate sick and wounded and summon medical experts and medical teams at any time after giving immediate notice to the United Nations force.

(4) The details of the above principles and all other matters in this article requiring coordination by the parties will be handled by the joint commission.

(5) These technical installations will be withdrawn when Israeli forces withdraw from the interim withdrawal line, or at a time agreed upon by the parties.

Article VI
Disposition of Installations And Military Barriers

Disposition of installations and military barriers will be determined by the parties in accordance with the following guidelines:

1. Up to three weeks before Israeli withdrawal from any area, the joint commission will arrange for Israeli and Egyptian liaison and technical teams to conduct a joint inspection of all appropriate installations to agree upon condition, structures and articles which will be transferred to Egyptian control and to arrange for such transfer. Israel will declare, at that time, its

plans for disposition of installations and articles within the installations.

2. Israel undertakes to transfer to Egypt all agreed infrastructure, utilities and installations intact, inter alia, airfields, roads, pumping stations and ports. Israel will present to Egypt the information necessary for the maintenance and operation of these facilities. Egyptian technical teams will be permitted to observe and familiarize themselves with the operation of these facilities for a period of up to two weeks prior to transfer.

3. When Israel relinquishes Israeli military water points near El Arish and El Tor, Egyptian technical teams will assume control of those installations and ancillary equipment in accordance with an orderly transfer process arranged beforehand by the joint commission. Egypt undertakes to continue to make available at all water supply points the normal quantity of currently available water up to the time Israel withdraws behind the international boundary unless otherwise agreed to in the joint commission.

4. Israel will make its best effort to remove or destroy all military barriers, including obstacles and minefields, in the areas and adjacent waters from which it withdraws, according to the following concept:

a. Military barriers will be cleared first from areas near populations, roads and major installations and utilities.

b. For those obstacles and minefields which cannot be removed or destroyed prior to Israeli withdrawal, Israel will provide detailed maps to Egypt and the United Nations through the joint commission not later than 15 days before entry of United Nations forces into the affected areas.

c. Egyptian military engineers will enter those areas after United Nations forces enter to conduct barrier clearance operations in accordance with Egyptian plans to be submitted prior to implementation.

Article VII
Surveillance Activities

1. Aerial surveillance activities during the withdrawal will be carried out as follows:

a. Both parties request the United States to continue airborne surveillance flights in accordance with previous agreements until the completion of final Israeli withdrawal.

b. Flight profiles will cover the limited forces zones to monitor the limitations on forces and armaments, and to determine that Israeli armed forces have withdrawn from the areas described in Article II of Annex I, Article II of this appendix and maps 2 and 3, and that these forces thereafter remain behind their lines. Special inspection flights may be flown at the request of either party or of the United Nations.

c. Only the main elements in the military organizations of each party, as described in Annex I and in this appendix, will be reported.

2. Both parties request the United States-operated Sinai field mission to continue its operations in accordance with previous agreements until completion of the Israeli withdrawal from the area east of the Gidi and Mitla passes. Thereafter the mission will be terminated.

Article VIII
Exercise of Egyptian Sovereignty

Egypt will resume the exercise of its full sovereignty over evacuated parts of the Sinai upon Israeli withdrawal as provided for in Article I of this treaty.

Annex III
Protocol Concerning Relations of the Parties

Article 1
Diplomatic and Consular Relations

The parties agree to establish diplomatic and consular relations and to exchange ambassadors upon completion of the interim withdrawal.

Article 2
Economic and Trade Relations

1. The parties agree to remove all discriminatory barriers to normal economic relations and to terminate economic boycotts of each other upon completion of the interim withdrawal.

2. As soon as possible, and not later than six months after the completion of the interim withdrawal, the parties will enter negotiations with a view to concluding an agreement on trade and commerce for the purpose of promoting beneficial economic relations.

Article 3
Cultural Relations

1. The parties agree to establish normal cultural relations following completion of the interim withdrawal.

2. They agree on the desirability of cultural exchanges in all fields, and shall, as soon as possible and not later than six months after completion of the interim withdrawal, enter into negotiations with a view to concluding a cultural agreement for this purpose.

Article 4

Freedom of Movement

1. Upon completion of the interim withdrawal, each party will permit the free movement of the nationals and vehicles of the other into and within its territory according to the general rules applicable to nationals and vehicles of other states. Neither party will impose discriminatory restrictions on the free movement of persons and vehicles from its territory to the territory of the other.

2. Mutual unimpeded access to places of religious and historical significance will be provided on a nondiscriminatory basis.

Article 5

Cooperation for Development and Good Neighborly Relations

1. The parties recognize a mutuality of interest in good neighborly relations and agree to consider means to promote such relations.

2. The parties will cooperate in promoting peace, stability and development in their region. Each agrees to consider proposals the other may wish to make to this end.

3. The parties shall seek to foster mutual understanding and tolerance and will, accordingly, abstain from hostile propaganda against each other.

Article 6

Transportation and Telecommunications

1. The parties recognize as applicable to each other the rights, privileges and obligations provided for by the aviation agreements to which they are both party, particularly by the Convention on International Civil Aviation, 1944 ("the Chicago Convention") and the International Air Services Transit Agreement, 1944.

2. Upon completion of the interim withdrawal any declaration of national emergency by a party under Article 89 of the Chicago Convention will not be applied to the other party on a discriminatory basis.

3. Egypt agrees that the use of airfields left by Israel near El Arish, Rafah, Ras el Nagb and Sharm el Sheikh shall be for civilian purposes only, including possible commercial use by all nations.

4. As soon as possible and not later than six months after the completion of the interim withdrawal, the parties shall enter into negotiations for the purpose of concluding a civil aviation agreement.

5. The parties will reopen and maintain roads and railways between their countries and will consider further road and rail links. The parties further agree that a highway will be constructed and maintained between Egypt, Israel and Jordan near Eilat with guaranteed free and peaceful passage of persons, vehicles and goods between Egypt and Jordan, without prejudice to their sovereignty over that part of the highway which falls within their respective territory.

6. Upon completion of the interim withdrawal, normal postal, telephone, telex, data facsimile, wireless and cable communications and television relay services by cable, radio and satellite shall be established between the two parties in accordance with all relevant international conventions and regulations.

7. Upon completion of the interim withdrawal, each party shall grant normal access to its ports for vessels and cargoes of the other, as well as vessels and cargoes destined for or coming from the other. Such access shall be granted on the same conditions generally applicable to vessels and cargoes of other nations. Article V of the treaty of peace will be implemented upon the exchange of instruments of ratification of the aforementioned treaty.

Article 7

Enjoyment of Human Rights

The parties affirm their commitment to respect and observe human rights and fundamental freedoms for all, and they will promote these rights and freedoms in accordance with the United Nations Charter.

Article 8

Territorial Seas

Without prejudice to the provisions of Article V of the treaty of peace each party recognizes the right of the vessels of the other party to innocent passage through its territorial sea in accordance with the rules of international law.

Agreed Minutes

*To Articles I, IV, V and VI
and Annexes I and III
of Treaty of Peace*

Article I — Egypt's resumption of the exercise of full sovereignty over the Sinai provided for in paragraph 2 of Article I shall occur with regard to each area upon Israel's withdrawal from that area.

Article IV — It is agreed between the parties that the review provided for in Article IV (4) will be undertaken when requested by either party, commencing within three months of such a request, but that any amendment can be made only with the mutual agreement of both parties.

Article V — The second sentence of paragraph 2 of Article V shall not be construed as limiting the first sentence of that paragraph. The foregoing is not to be construed as contravening the second sentence of paragraph 2 of Article V, which reads as follows: "The parties will respect each other's right to navigation and overflight for access to either country through the Strait of Tiran and the Gulf of Aqaba."

Article VI (2) — The provisions of Article VI shall not be construed in contradiction to the provisions of the framework for peace in the Middle East agreed at Camp David. The foregoing is not to be construed as contravening the provisions of Article VI (2) of the treaty, which reads as follows:

"The parties undertake to fulfill in good faith their obligations under this treaty, without regard to action or inaction of any other party and independently of any instrument external to this treaty."

Article VI (5) — It is agreed by the parties that there is no assertion that this treaty prevails over other treaties or agreements or that other treaties or agreements prevail over this treaty. The foregoing is not to be construed as contravening the provisions of Article VI (5) of the treaty, which reads as follows:

"Subject to Article 103 of the United Nations Charter, in the event of a conflict between the obligations of the parties under the present treaty and any of their other obligations, the obligations under this treaty will be binding and implemented."

Annex I — Article VI, paragraph 8 of Annex I provides as follows: "The parties shall agree on the nations from which the United Nations force and observers will be drawn. They will be drawn from nations other than those which are permanent members of the United Nations Security Council."

The parties have agreed as follows: "With respect to the provisions of paragraph 8, Article VI, of Annex I, if no agreement is reached between the parties, they will accept or support a U.S. proposal concerning the composition of the United Nations force and observers."

Annex III — The Treaty of Peace and Annex III thereto provide for establishing normal economic relations between the parties. In accordance therewith, it is agreed that such relations will include normal commercial sales of oil by Egypt to Israel, and that Israel shall be fully entitled to make bids for Egyptian-origin oil not needed for Egyptian domestic oil consumption, and Egypt and its oil concessionaries will entertain bids made by Israel, on the same basis and terms as apply to other bidders for such oil. ∎

Selected Bibliography on the Middle East

Books

Abdullah, Mohammad Morse. *The United Arab Emirates: A Modern History.* New York: Barnes & Noble, 1978.

Abir, Mordechai. *Oil, Power and Politics.* London: Frank Cass, 1974.

Alroy, Gil C. *Behind the Middle East Conflict: The Real Impasse Between Arab and Jew.* New York: Capricorn, 1975.

Amirsadeghi, Hossein, ed. *Twentieth Century Iran.* New York: Holmes & Meier, 1977.

Amos, John W. *Arabs-Israeli Military Political Relations: Arab Perceptions and the Politics of Escalation.* New York: Pergamon, 1979.

Amuzegar, Jahangir. *Iran: An Economic Profile.* Washington, D.C.: Middle East Institute, 1977.

Anthony, John D., ed. *The Middle East: Oil, Politics and Development.* Washington, D.C.: American Enterprise Institute for Public Policy Research, 1975.

Archer, Jules. *Legacy of the Desert: Understanding the Arabs.* Boston: Little, Brown, 1976.

Astor, David and Yorke, Valerie. *Peace in the Middle East.* London: Transworld, 1978.

Azzi, Robert. *Saudi Arabia.* Danbury, N.H.: Addison House, 1979.

Becker, Abraham S. and Kerr, Malcolm H. *The Economics and Politics of the Middle East.* New York: American Elsevier, 1975.

Bill, James A. and Leiden, Carl. *The Middle East: Politics and Power.* Boston: Allyn and Bacon, 1974.

Brecher, Michael. *Decisions in Israel's Foreign Policy.* New Haven: Yale University Press, 1975.

Brookings Institution. *Toward Peace in the Middle East: Report of a Study Group.* Washington, D.C.: 1975.

Bryson, Thomas A. *American Diplomatic Relations with the Middle East, 1784-1975: A Survey.* Metuchen, N.J.: Scarecrow Press, 1977.

Bull, Vivian A. *The West Bank: Is It Viable?* Lexington, Mass.: Lexington Books, 1975.

Carmichael, Joel. *Arabs Today.* Garden City, N.Y.: Doubleday, 1977.

Chubin, Shahram. *The Foreign Relations of Iran: A Developing State in a Zone of Great-Power Conflict.* Berkeley: University of California Press, 1975.

Cohen, Aharon. *Israel and the Arab World.* Boston: Beacon Press, 1976.

Cohen, Michael J. *Palestine: Retreat from the Mandate.* New York: Holmes & Meier, 1978.

Cooley, John K. *Green March, Black September: The Story of the Palestinian Arabs.* London: Frank Cass, 1973.

Cottam, Richard W. *Nationalism in Iran.* Pittsburgh: University of Pittsburgh Press, 1979.

Curtis, Michael, ed. *People and Politics in the Middle East.* New York: E. P. Dutton, 1971.

Elazar, Daniel J. *The Camp David Framework for Peace: A Shift Toward Shared Rule.* Washington, D.C.: American Enterprise Institute for Public Policy Research, 1979.

Evron, Yair. *The Middle East: Nations, Superpowers, and War.* New York: Praeger, 1973.

Faddad, Mohammed I. *The Middle East in Transition: A Study of Jordan's Foreign Policy.* New York: Asia Publishing House, 1974.

First, Ruth. *Libya: The Elusive Revolution.* Baltimore: Penguin Books, 1974.

Gerson, Allan. *Israel, the West Bank and International Law.* London: Frank Cass, 1978.

Goldmann, Nahum. *The Jewish Paradox.* New York: Grosset & Dunlap, 1978.

Graham, Robert. *Iran: Illusion of Power.* New York: St. Martin's Press, 1979.

Haddad, George. *Revolution and Military Rule in the Middle East.* 3 vols. New York: Speller, 1965-1973.

Hammond, Paul Y. and Alexander, Sidney S., eds. *Political Dynamics in the Middle East.* New York: American Elsevier, 1971.

Harkabi, Yehoshafat. *Arab Strategies and Israel's Response.* New York: Free Press, 1977.

Hatem, Abdel-Kader. *Land of the Arabs.* London: Longman, 1977.

Hirst, David. *The Gun and the Olive Branch: The Roots of Violence in the Middle East.* London: Faber, 1977.

Horowitz, Dan and Lissak, Moshe. *Origins of the Israeli Polity: Palestine Under the Mandate.* Chicago: University of Chicago Press, 1978.

Hourani, A. H. *Syria and Lebanon: A Political Essay.* New York: Gordon Press, 1977.

Hudson, Michael C. *Arab Politics: The Search for Legitimacy.* New Haven: Yale University Press, 1977.

Hurewitz, J. C. *The Arab-Israeli Dispute and the Industrial World.* Boulder, Colo.: Westview Press, 1976.

———. *The Struggle for Palestine.* New York: Schocken Books, 1976.

Ismael, Tareq Y. *The Middle East in World Politics: A Study in Contemporary International Relations.* New York: Syracuse University Press, 1974.

Jureidini, Paul A. and Hazen, William E. *The Palestinian Movement in Politics.* Lexington, Mass.: Lexington Books, 1977.

Khadduri, Majid. *Socialist Iraq: A Study in Iraqi Politics Since 1968.* Washington, D.C.: Middle East Institute, 1978.

Kierman, Thomas. *Yasir Arafat.* London: Abacus, 1976.

Kimball, Lorenzo. *The Changing Pattern of Political Power in Iraq, 1958-1971.* New York: Speller, 1978.

Kimche, Jon. *The Second Arab Awakening.* New York: Holt, Rinehart and Winston, 1974.

Klebanoff, Shoshana. *Middle East Oil and U.S. Foreign Policy: With Special Reference to the U.S. Energy Crisis.* New York: Praeger, 1974.

Koury, Fred J. *The Arab-Israeli Dilemma.* New York: Knopf, 1976.

Laqueur, Walter. *Confrontation: The Middle East and World Politics.* New York: Quadrangle Books, 1974.

Lenczowski, George, ed. *Iran Under the Pahlavis.* Stanford, Calif.: Hoover Institution Press, 1978.

———. *Middle East Oil in a Revolutionary Age.* Washington, D.C.: American Enterprise Institute for Public Policy Research, 1976.

Long, David E. *The Persian Gulf.* Boulder, Colo.: Westview Press, 1976.

Mangold, Peter. *Superpower Intervention in the Middle East.* New York: St. Martin's Press, 1978.

McLaurin, R. D. et al. *Foreign Policy Making in the Middle East: Domestic Influences on Policy in Egypt, Iraq, Israel, and Syria.* New York: Praeger, 1977.

Middle East Institute. *The Arabian Peninsula, Iran and the Gulf States: New Wealth, New Power.* Washington, D.C.: 1973.

———. *World Energy Demands and the Middle East.* Washington, D.C.: 1972.

Mishal, Shaul. *West Bank/East Bank: The Palestinians in Jordan, 1949-1967.* New Haven: Yale University Press, 1978.

Nakhleh, Emile A. *The United States and Saudi Arabia.* Washington, D.C.: American Enterprise Institute for Public Policy Research, 1975.

———. *The West Bank and Gaza: Toward the Making of a Palestinian State.* Washington, D.C.: American Enterprise Institute for Public Policy Research, 1979.

O'Neill, Bard E. *Armed Struggle in Palestine: A Political-Military Analysis.* Boulder, Colo.: Westview Press, 1978.

Penrose, Edith and Penrose, E. F. *Iraq: International Relations and National Development.* Boulder, Colo.: Westview Press, 1978.

Perlmutter, Amos. *Politics and the Military in Israel.* London: Frank Cass, 1978.

Politics in the Middle East. Boston: Little, Brown, 1979.

Pranger, Robert J. *American Policy for Peace in the Middle East, 1969-1971.* Washington, D.C.: American Enterprise Institute for Public Policy Research, 1971.

Quandt, William D. *Decade of Decisions: American Policy Toward the Arab-Israeli Conflict, 1967-1976.* Berkeley: University of California Press, 1977.

Reich, Bernard. *Quest for Peace: United States-Israel Relations and the Arab-Israeli Conflict.* New Brunswick, N.J.: Transaction Books, 1977.

Roosevelt, Kermit. *Countercoup: The Bloody Struggle for the Control of Iran.* New York: McGraw-Hill, 1979.

Sadat, Anwar. *In Search of Identity.* New York: Harper & Row, 1977.

Safran, Nadav. *From War to War: The Arab-Israeli Confrontation, 1948-1967.* New York: Pegasus, 1969.

———. *Israel: The Embattled Ally.* Cambridge, Mass.: Harvard University Press, 1978.

Sayigh, Yusif A. *The Determinants of Arab Economic Development.* New York: St. Martin's Press, 1978.

———. *The Economies of the Arab World.* New York: St. Martin's Press, 1978.

Schurr, Sam H. et al. *Middle Eastern Oil and the Western World: Prospects and Problems.* New York: American Elsevier, 1971.

Senniger, Donald C. *The Fraud at Camp David and the Middle East Crisis.* Albuquerque, N.M.: Institute for Economic and Political World Strategic Studies, 1979.

Sherbiny, Naiem A. *Arab Oil: Impact on the Arab Countries and Global Implications.* New York: Praeger, 1976.

Sid-Ahmed, Mohamed. *After the Guns Fall Silent: Peace or Armageddon in the Middle-East.* New York: St. Martin's Press, 1976.

Szyliwicz, Joseph S. and O'Neill, Bard E., eds. *The Energy Crisis and U.S. Foreign Policy.* New York: Praeger, 1975.

Udovitch, A. L. *The Middle East: Oil, Conflict and Hope.* Lexington, Mass.: Lexington Books, 1976.

Van Arkadie, Brian. *Benefits and Burdens: A Report on the West Bank and Gaza Strip Economics Since 1967.* New York: Carnegie Endowment for International Peace, 1977.

Waterbury, John. *Egypt: Burdens of the Past, Options for the Future.* Bloomington: Indiana University Press, 1978.

Wells, Donald A. *Saudi Arabian Development Strategy.* Washington, D.C.: American Enterprise Institute for Public Policy Research, 1976.

Zeine, Zeine N. *The Struggle for Arab Independence.* Delmar, N.Y.: Caravan Books, 1977.

Articles

Ajami, Fouad. "The End of Pan-Arabism." *Foreign Affairs,* Winter 1978/79, pp. 355-373.

———. "Stress in the Arab Triangle." *Foreign Policy,* Winter 1977/78, pp. 90-108.

Allon, Yigal. "Israel: The Case for Defensible Borders." *Foreign Affairs,* October 1976, pp. 38-53.

Arieli, Yehoshua. "For a Jordanian Solution." *New Outlook,* May/June 1978, pp. 29-34.

Avineri, Shlomo. "Peacemaking: The Arab-Israeli Conflict." *Foreign Affairs,* Fall 1978, pp. 51-69.

Apple, R. W. Jr. "Iran: Heart of the Matter." *New York Times Magazine,* March 11, 1979, pp. 19; 101-106.

Bailey, Clinton. "Changing Attitudes Toward Jordan in the West Bank." *Middle East Journal,* Spring 1978, pp. 155-166.

Ball, George W. "America's Interests in the Middle East." *Harper's Magazine,* October 1978, pp. 18-21.

Barnes, John. "Israel: Yesterday, Today and Tomorrow." *Asian Affairs,* October 1978, pp. 271-279.

Belfiglio, Valentine J. "The Role of the United States in the Middle East." *International Problems,* Spring 1978, pp. 18-35.

Bill, James A. "Iran and the Crisis of '78." *Foreign Affairs,* Winter 1978/79, pp. 323-342.

Binder, Leonard. "Revolution in Iran: Red, White, Blue or Black." *Bulletin of the Atomic Scientists,* January 1979, pp. 48-54.

Bruzonsky, Mark A. "The U.S. and Israel: In the Eye of the Storm." *Worldview,* July/August 1978, pp. 4-9.

Campbell, John C. "Middle East: The Burdens of Empire." *Foreign Affairs,* Spring 1979, pp. 613-632.

———. "Oil Power in the Middle East." *Foreign Affairs,* October 1977, pp. 89-110.

Carus, W. Seth. "The Military Balance of Power in the Middle East." *Current History,* January 1978, pp. 29-32.

Corrigan, Richard. "The Impact Abroad of Iran's Problems at Home." *National Journal,* Dec. 2, 1978, pp. 1939-1941.

Costello, Mary. "Arab Disunity." *Editorial Research Reports,* Oct. 29, 1976, pp. 787-806.

———. "Middle East Transition." *Editorial Research Reports,* Dec. 1, 1978, pp. 883-904.

Cottam, Richard; Schoenbaum, David; Chubin, Shahram; Moran, Theodore H.; Falk, Richard A. "The United States and Iran's Revolution." *Foreign Policy,* Spring 1979, pp. 3-34.

Crecelius, Daniel. "Saudi-Egyptian Relations." *International Studies,* October/December 1975, pp. 563-585.

Darin-Drabkin, Haim. "From Settlemen to Colonization," *New Outlook,* February/March 1978, pp. 42-46.

Eban, Abba. "Camp David: The Unfinished Business." *Foreign Affairs,* Winter 1978/79, pp. 343-354.

Falk, Richard A. "Khomeini's Promise." *Foreign Policy,* Spring 1979, pp. 29-34.

Farmer, Richard N. "Long Term Future of the Arab Oil States." *Business Horizons,* February 1977, pp. 74-80.

Feoktistov, A. "Saudi Arabia and the Arab World." *International Affairs,* July 1977, pp. 101-107.

Gerstenfeld, Manfred. "Israel After Peace." *Midstream,* December 1978, pp. 15-19.

Goldstein, Michael. "Israeli Security Measures in the Occupied Territories: Administrative Detention." *Middle East Journal,* Winter 1978, pp. 35-44.

Greene, Preston L., Jr. "The Arab Economic Boycott of Israel: The International Law Perspective." *Vanderbilt Journal of Transnational Law,* Winter 1978, pp. 77-94.

Heikal, Mohamed Hassanein. "Egyptian Foreign Policy." *Foreign Affairs,* July 1978, pp. 714-727.

Hoyt, Robert G. "Israel and the Territories: Realism vs. Survival." *Christianity and Crisis,* Feb. 20, 1978, pp. 18-20.

Jiryis, Sabri. "The Arab World at the Crossroads: An Analysis of the Arab Opposition to the Sadat Initiative." *Journal of Palestine Studies,* Winter 1978, pp. 26-61.

———. "On Political Settlement in the Middle East: The Palestinian Dimension." *Journal of Palestine Studies,* Autumn 1977, pp. 3-25.

Kanovsky, Eliahu. "Economic Aspects of Peace Between Israel and the Arab Countries." *New Outlook,* October 1978, pp. 27-36.

Kapeliuk, Amnon. "To Whom Does the West Bank Belong?" *New Outlook,* December 1977/January 1978, pp. 45-47.

Khalidi, Walid. "Thinking the Unthinkable: A Sovereign Palestinian State." *Foreign Affairs,* July 1978, pp. 695-713.

Kimche, Jon. "The Saudi Connection." *Midstream,* October 1977, pp. 3-8.

Knoll, Erwin. "O Promised Land!" *Progressive,* April 1979, pp. 14-19.

Kyle, Keith. "The Palestinian Arab States: Collision Course or Solution?" *World Today,* September 1977, pp. 343-352.

Lanouette, William J. "Carter Moves to Center Stage as Middle East Peacemaker." *National Journal,* Dec. 9, 1978, pp. 1968-1972.

Laqueur, Walter. "Why the Shah Fell." *Commentary,* March 1979, pp. 47-55.

Lens, Sidney. "Decline and Fall: Iran's Revolution Marks a Turning Point for the American Empire." *Progressive,* April 1979, pp. 30-32.

Lesch, Ann M., comp. "Israeli Settlements in the Occupied Territories." *Journal of Palestine Studies,* Autumn 1978, pp. 100-119.

"Middle East, 1979." *Current History,* January 1979.

Miller, Aaron D. "The Influence of Middle East Oil on American Foreign Policy: 1941-1948." *Middle East Review,* Spring 1977, pp. 19-24.

Mishlawi, Tewfik. "Saudis Tip the Balance: A New Direction." *The Middle East,* May 1979, pp. 25-31.

Monroe, Elizabeth. "The West Bank: Palestinian or Israeli?" *Middle East Journal,* Autumn 1977, pp. 397-412.

"1967-1977: A Ten Year Perspective of the Arab-Israel Conflict." *Middle East Review,* Summer 1977, pp. 3-62.

Ovinnikov, R. "The Middle East: The Shifting Sands of Separate Agreements." *International Affairs,* December 1978, pp. 31-39.

Oweiss, Ibrahim M. "Strategies for Arab Economic Development." *Journal of Energy and Development,* Autumn 1977, pp. 103-114.

"Palestinian Dilemma." *Atlas,* December 1978, pp. 29-35.

Perlmutter, Amos. "Begin's Strategy and Dayan's Tactics: The Conduct of Israeli Foreign Policy." *Foreign Affairs,* January 1978, pp. 357-373.

———. "Dateline Israel: A New Rejectionism." *Foreign Policy,* Spring 1979, pp. 165-181.

Plascov, Avi. "The Palestinian Predicament After Camp David." *World Today,* December 1978, pp. 467-471.

Ramazani, R. K. "Iran and the Arab-Israeli Conflict." *Middle East Journal,* Autumn 1978, pp. 413-428.

Rustow, Dankwart A. "U.S.-Saudi Relations and the Oil Crises of the 1980s." *Foreign Affairs,* April 1977, pp. 494-516.

Salpeter, Eliahu. "Lessons of the Mideast Peace Process." *New Leader,* April 9, 1979, pp. 5-7.

———. "What Separates Israel and Egypt." *New Leader,* Jan. 5, 1979, pp. 5-7.

Singer, S. Fred. "Limits to Arab Oil Power." *Foreign Policy,* Spring 1978, pp. 53-67.

Spiegel, S. L. "Toward a Middle East Alternative." *Commentary,* January 1979, pp. 30-33.

"Stalemate and Stagnation: United States Policy in the Near East; An Interview with Richard Falk." *Journal of Palestine Studies,* Autumn 1978, pp. 85-99.

Stone, I. F. "The Lesson of Iran: Enormous Military Power Can Be Meaningless." *Progressive,* April 1979, pp. 28-29.

Taher, Abdulhady H. "The Middle East Oil and Gas Policy." *Journal of Energy and Development,* Spring 1978, pp. 260-269.

Tannenbaum, Michael. "Politics and the Sword in Syria." *New Leader,* Oct. 9, 1978, pp. 10-12.

———. "Voices of the West Bank and Gaza." *New Leader,* March 26, 1979, pp. 7-9.

Teter, D. Park. "Iran Between East and West." *Editorial Research Reports,* Jan. 26, 1979, pp. 67-84.

Tal, Israel. "Israel's Defense Doctrine: Background and Dynamics." *Military Review,* March 1978, pp. 22-37.

Turner, Louis and Bedore, James. "Saudi Arabia: The Power of the Purse-Strings," *International Affairs,* July 1978, pp. 405-420.

"West Bank and Gaza: Ten Years Occupied." *Economist,* April 23, 1977, pp. 78-79.

Whetten, Lawrence L. "Changing Perceptions About the Arab-Israeli Conflict and Settlement." *World Today,* July 1978, pp. 252-259.

Government Publications

U.S. Congress. House. Committee on International Relations [Foreign Affairs]. *Peace in the Mideast: A Delicate Balance; Report of a Study Commission to the Mideast and Ireland, January 2-20, 1978.* 95th Cong., 2nd sess. Washington, D.C.: Government Printing Office, 1978.

———. *Proposed Aircraft Sales to Israel, Egypt, and Saudi Arabia: Hearings, May 8-10, 16, 1978.* 95th Cong., 2nd sess. Washington, D.C.: Government Printing Office, 1978.

———. Subcommittee on Europe and the Middle East. *Assessment of the 1978 Middle East Camp David Agreements: Hearings September 28, 1978.* 95th Cong., 2nd sess. Washington, D.C.: Government Printing Office, 1979.

———. Subcommittee on Europe and the Middle East. *Foreign Assistance Legislation for FY78; Part 5: Economic and Military Aid Programs in Europe and the Middle East: Hearings February 22, 23; March 3, 7, 9, 14, 16, 21; April 21, 27, 1977.* 95th Cong., 1st sess. Washington, D.C.: Government Printing Office, 1977.

———. Subcommittee on Europe and the Middle East. *Foreign Assistance Legislation for FY79. Part 5: Economic and Military Aid Programs in Europe and the Middle East: Hearings February 6, 8, 15, 28; March 1, 6, 13, 16, 1978.* 95th Cong., 2nd sess. Washington, D.C.: Government Printing Office, 1978.

———. Subcommittee on Europe and the Middle East. *Israeli Settlements in the Occupied Territories: Hearings September 12-October 19, 1977.* 95th Cong., 1st sess. Washington, D.C.: Government Printing Office, 1978.

———. Subcommittee on Europe and the Middle East. *Review of Developments in the Middle East, 1978: Hearings June 12, 1978.* 95th Cong., 2nd sess. Washington, D.C.: Government Printing Office, 1978.

———. Subcommittee on Europe and the Middle East. *U.S. Arms Sale Policy and Recent Sales to Europe and the Middle East: Hearings October 5, 1978.* 95th Cong., 2nd sess. Washington, D.C.: Government Printing Office, 1979.

———. Subcommittee on International Organizations. *Human Rights in Iran: Hearings October 26, 1977.* 95th Cong., 1st sess. Washington, D.C.: Government Printing Office, 1978.

U.S. Congress. House. Permanent Select Committee on Intelligence. Subcommittee on Evaluation. *Iran: Evaluation of U.S. Intelligence Performance Prior to November 1978.* 95th Cong., 2nd sess. Staff report. Washington, D.C.: Government Printing Office, 1979.

U.S. Congress. Senate. Committee on Energy and Natural Resources. *Access to Oil: The United States Relationships with Saudi Arabia and Iran.* 95th Cong., 1st sess., Committee print no. 95-70. Washington, D.C.: Government Printing Office, 1977.

U.S. Congress. Senate. Committee on Foreign Relations. *United Nations Relief and Works Agency for Palestine Refugees in the Near East: A Staff Report.* 95th Cong., 2nd sess. Washington, D.C.: Government Printing Office, 1978.

———. *West Bank: A Key Element in the Search for Peace in the Middle East; Report of August 1977 Study Mission to Israel, the Occupied West Bank, and Jordan.* 95th Cong., 1st sess. Washington, D.C.: Government Printing Office, 1977.

U.S. Congress. Senate. Committee on the Judiciary. Subcommittee on Immigration and Naturalization. *The Colonization of the West Bank Territories by Israel: Hearings on the Question of West Bank Settlements and the Treatment of Arabs in the Israeli-Occupied Territories, October 17-18, 1977.* 95th Cong., 1st sess. Washington, D.C.: Government Printing Office, 1978.

U.S. Congress. Senate. Select Committee on Intelligence. Subcommittee on Collection, Production, and Quality. *U.S. Intelligence Analysis and the Oil Issue, 1973-1974.* 95th Cong., 1st sess. Washington, D.C.: Government Printing Office, 1978.

Index